Windows NT TCP/IP Network Administration

Windows NT TCP/IP Network Administration

Craig Hunt and Robert Bruce Thompson

O'REILLY™

Beijing · Cambridge · Köln · Paris · Sebastopol · Taipei · Tokyo

Windows NT TCP/IP Network Administration
by Craig Hunt and Robert Bruce Thompson

Published by O'Reilly and Associates, Inc., 101 Morris Street, Sebastopol, CA 95472.

Editor: Robert Denn

Production Editor: Paula Carroll

Production Service: *TIPS* Technical Publishing

Printing History:

October 1998: First Edition.

This book is printed on acid-free paper with 85% recycled content, 15% post-consumer waste. O'Reilly & Associates is committed to using paper with the highest recycled content available consistent with high quality.

ISBN: 1-56592-377-4

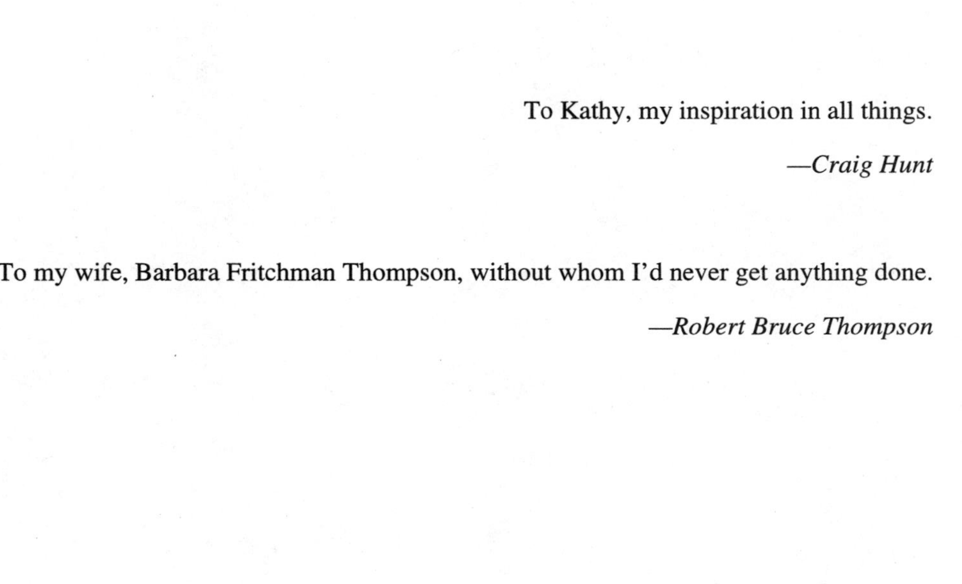

To Kathy, my inspiration in all things.

—Craig Hunt

To my wife, Barbara Fritchman Thompson, without whom I'd never get anything done.

—Robert Bruce Thompson

Table of Contents

Preface

The protocol wars are over and TCP/IP won. TCP/IP is now universally recognized as the preeminent communications protocol for linking diverse computer systems. The importance of interoperable data communications and global computer networks are no longer debated. But that was not always the case. A few years ago things were different. IPX was far and away the leading PC communications protocol. Microsoft did not bundle communications protocols in their operating systems. Corporate networks were so dependent on SNA that many corporate network administrators had not even heard of TCP/IP. Back then it was necessary to tout the importance of TCP/IP by pointing out that it was used on thousands of networks and hundreds of thousands of computers. How times have changed! Today we count the hosts and users connected to the Internet in the tens of millions. And the Internet is only the tip of the TCP/IP iceberg. The largest market for TCP/IP is in the corporate *intranet*. An intranet is a private TCP/IP network used to disseminate information within the enterprise. Today, the competing network technologies have shrunk to niche markets where they fill special needs, while TCP/IP has grown to be the communications software that links the world.

Windows NT and TCP/IP have a close association. Windows NT was the first Microsoft operating system that included TCP/IP as part of the basic system. And TCP/IP has been a part of NT from the very first release of the operating system. The availability of TCP/IP for Windows NT has helped to make NT a popular choice as a network server.

The acceptance of TCP/IP as a worldwide standard and the size of its global user base have created an explosion of books about TCP/IP and the Internet. Today, NT administrators can choose from a large number of books that have TCP/IP and the Internet as a theme. However, there are still too few books that concentrate on what an NT system administrator really needs to know about TCP/IP administration and too many books that try to tell you how to surf the Web. In this book we strive to keep focused on TCP/IP and NT, and not to be distracted by the phenomenon of the Internet.

This book is the combined effort of Craig Hunt and Robert Bruce Thompson. Craig is an expert on TCP/IP and is the author of the best-seller *TCP/IP Network Administration*. Robert is an expert on Windows NT. He is the author of several books, three of which are books on Windows NT including the recently released *Windows NT Server 4.0 for NetWare Administrators*.

This new book is the Windows NT version of *TCP/IP Network Administration*: the book that Byte magazine called "the definitive volume on the subject" of creating your own TCP/IP network. If you're familiar with that book you will see the similarities, particularly in the background material about the TCP/IP protocols. However, all of the examples are Windows NT–specific.

On the other hand, this new book is much more than an NT version of an existing book. Extensive amounts of Windows NT–specific material have been added. Coverage of NetBIOS, Windows Internet Name Service (WINS), Routing and Remote Access Service (RRAS), Internet Information Server (IIS), and Microsoft's implementations of Domain Name Service (DNS) and Dynamic Host Configuration Protocol (DHCP) all combine to make this a unique book in its own right.

The combination of Windows NT and TCP/IP expertise provides the perfect blend for a book about TCP/IP for Windows NT. This book covers the issues that are most important to the Windows NT system administrator who is building a TCP/IP network.

The use of Windows NT systems to provide TCP/IP network services is growing rapidly. This book provides practical, detailed TCP/IP network information for the NT system administrator. It is a book about building your own network based on TCP/IP and NT servers. It is both a tutorial covering the why and how of TCP/IP networking and a reference providing the details about specific network programs.

Audience

This book is intended for everyone who has an NT computer connected to a TCP/IP network. This obviously includes the network managers and the system administrators who are responsible for setting up and running computers and networks, but the audience also includes any user who wants to understand how a computer communicates with other systems. The distinction between a system administrator and an end-user is a fuzzy one. You may think of yourself as an end-user, but if you have an NT workstation on your desk, you're probably also involved in system administration tasks.

We assume that you have a good understanding of computers and their operation, and that you're generally familiar with NT system administration. In recent years there has been a rash of books for "dummies" and "idiots." If you really think of yourself as an "idiot" when it comes to NT, this book is not for you. Likewise, if you are a network administration genius, this book is probably not suitable. However, if you fall anywhere in between these two extremes, this book has something to offer you.

Organization

This book is divided into three parts: fundamental concepts, tutorial, and reference. The first three chapters are a basic discussion of the TCP/IP protocols and services. This discussion provides the fundamental concepts necessary to understand the rest of the book. The remaining chapters provide a how-to tutorial. Chapters 4 and 5 discuss how to plan a network installation and configure the basic software necessary to get a network running. Chapters 6 through 10 discuss how to set up various important network services. The final chapters, 11 through 13, cover how to perform the ongoing tasks that are essential for a reliable network: troubleshooting, security, and keeping up with changing network information. The book concludes with four appendixes that are technical references for important configuration files.

This book contains the following chapters:

Chapter 1, *Overview of TCP/IP*, gives the history of TCP/IP, a description of the structure of the protocol architecture, and a basic explanation of how the protocols function.

Chapter 2, *Delivering the Data*, describes addressing, and how data passes through a network to reach the proper destination.

Chapter 3, *Network Services*, discusses the relationship between clients and server systems, and the various services that are central to the function of a modern internet.

Chapter 4, *Getting Started*, begins the discussion of network setup and configuration. This chapter discusses the preliminary configuration planning needed before you configure the systems on your network.

Chapter 5, *Installing TCP/IP*, provides details of how NT TCP/IP is installed and configured. This chapter describes the various dialogues used to configure TCP/IP, and the meaning and use of all of the configuration choices available in those dialogues.

Chapter 6, *Using Dynamic Host Configuration Protocol*, describes how to install and configure the Windows NT DHCP server.

Chapter 7, *Using Windows Internet Name Service*, describes how to administer the WINS name server program that converts NetBIOS computer names to Internet addresses.

Chapter 8, *Using Domain Name System*, describes how to configure the Microsoft DNS name server program that converts TCP/IP host names to IP addresses.

Chapter 9, *Microsoft Routing and Remote Access Service*, describes how to install and configure the RRAS software that permits a Windows NT server to run a wide variety of TCP/IP routing protocols. In addition to providing advanced routing support, RRAS is used to turn an NT server into a PPP server for remote dial-up Internet access. RRAS also provides the security protocols needed to create encrypted connections.

Chapter 10, *Internet Information Server*, describes how to install and configure the IIS software. IIS is the heart of any Internet server built on a Windows NT system. The Internet Information Server software provides Web services, an FTP server, an SMTP email server, and more.

Chapter 11, *Troubleshooting TCP/IP*, tells you what to do when something goes wrong. It describes the techniques and tools used to monitor the system and troubleshoot it when problems develop.

Chapter 12, *Network Security*, discusses how to live on the Internet without excessive risk. This chapter covers the security threats brought by the network, and the plans and preparations you can make to meet those threats.

Chapter 13, *Information Resources*, describes the information resources available on the Internet and how you can make use of them.

Appendix A, *PPP Scripting Languages*, is a reference guide to the scripting language used on a Windows NT system to create dial-up serial connections for PPP.

Appendix B, *DNS Resource Records*, is a reference for the records used to build a Domain Name Service database.

Appendix C, *DHCP Options*, is a reference for the configuration parameters that a Dynamic Host Configuration Protocol (DHCP) server can provide to configure a client.

Appendix D, *Routing Protocols*, provides a detailed description of the interior routing protocols most commonly used on enterprise networks.

Conventions

This book uses the following typographical conventions:

Italic

is used for the names of files, directories, host names, domain names, URLs, and to emphasize new terms when they are first introduced.

bold

is used for command names.

`constant-width`

is used to show the contents of files or the output from commands.

`constant-bold`

is used in examples to show commands or text that would be typed literally by you.

`constant-italic`

is used in examples to show variables for which a context-specific substitution should be made. (The variable ***`filename`***, for example, would be replaced by some actual filename.)

[option]

When showing command syntax, we place optional parts of the command within brackets. For example, **ls** [**-l**] means that the **-l** option is not required.

Acknowledgments

In addition to thanking the O'Reilly production folks, who are listed individually in the Colophon, we want to thank Mark Friedman, who reviewed most of the manuscript and made numerous helpful corrections and suggestions. We would also like to thank Cricket Liu for his help in improving the DNS material. No one knows DNS better than Cricket! Their efforts allowed us to catch and fix outright errors and ambiguous statements that would otherwise have appeared in print. Any errors that remain are ours alone.

We also want to single out one of our technical reviewers for special thanks. AEleen Frisch, the author of several O'Reilly Unix and Windows NT books, went far above and beyond the call of duty. In addition to devoting a great deal of time and effort to doing a detailed technical review, AEleen made many valuable suggestions about the overall content and structure of the book. This is a better book because she took the time to help us make it so.

Finally, we want to thank our editor, Robert Denn. Robert initiated the project, drove it through the rough patches, and co-ordinated the work of two authors who had not worked together previously. Robert is the best editor that any author could hope for. Without his efforts, you would not be reading this book.

We'd Like to Hear From You

We have tested and verified the information in this book to the best of our ability, but you may find that features have changed (which may in fact resemble bugs). Please let us know about any errors you find, as well as your suggestions for future editions, by writing to:

O'Reilly & Associates, Inc.
101 Morris Street
Sebastopol, CA 95472
1-800-998-9938 (in U.S. or Canada)
1-707-829-0515 (international/local)
1-707-829-0104 (fax)

You can also send us messages electronically. To be put on our mailing list or request a catalog, send email to:

info@oreilly.com

To ask technical questions or comments on the book, send email to:

bookquestions@oreilly.com

If you want to contact one of us directly, we can be reached at:

craigh@oreilly.com
thompson@oreilly.com

We also have a web site for the book, where we'll list errata and plans for future editions:

http://www.ttgnet.com/nttcp.html

1

Overview of TCP/IP

All of us—engineers, educators, scientists, and business people—who use Windows NT or any other advanced desktop operating system have second careers managing that system. Networking increases the complexity of this new task.

Administration tasks such as adding users and local tape backups are isolated to one independent computer system. Not so with network administration. Once you place your computer on a network, it interacts with many other systems. The way you do network administration tasks has effects, good and bad, not only on your system, but also on other systems on the network. A sound understanding of basic network administration benefits everyone.

Networking computers dramatically enhances their ability to communicate—and most computers are used more for communication than computation. Many mainframes and supercomputers are busy crunching the numbers for business and science, but the number of such systems pales in comparison to the millions of systems busily moving mail to a remote colleague or retrieving information from a remote repository. Further, when you think of the hundreds of millions of desktop systems that are used primarily for preparing documents to communicate ideas from one person to another, it is easy to see why most computers can be viewed as communications devices.

The positive impact of computer communications increases with the number and type of computers that participate in the network. One of the great benefits of TCP/IP is that it provides interoperable communications between all types of hardware and all kinds of operating systems.

With the advent of Windows NT, Microsoft acknowledged the importance of interoperable networking. NT was designed from the ground up to include a variety of networking software. The most important of these is TCP/IP, which provides NT systems with truly interoperable data communications.

This book is a practical, step-by-step guide to configuring and managing TCP/IP networking software on Windows NT computer systems. TCP/IP is the software package that dominates data communications. It is the leading communications software for enterprise intranets, and it is the foundation of the worldwide Internet.

The name TCP/IP refers to an entire suite of data communications protocols. The suite gets its name from two of the protocols that belong to it: the Transmission Control Protocol and the Internet Protocol. Although there are many other protocols in the suite, TCP and IP are certainly two of the most important.

The first part of this book discusses the basics of TCP/IP and how it moves data across a network. Let's start with a little history.

TCP/IP and the Internet

In 1969 the Advanced Research Projects Agency (ARPA) funded a research and development project to create an experimental packet-switching network. This network, called the *ARPANET*, became the foundation for the Internet. Today it is larger than ever and encompasses more than 95,000 networks worldwide. The Internet has grown exponentially since 1983—roughly doubling in size every year. Through all of this incredible change one thing has remained constant: the Internet is built on the TCP/IP protocol suite.

Because TCP/IP is required for Internet connection, the growth of the Internet has spurred interest in TCP/IP. As more organizations become familiar with TCP/IP, they see that its power can be applied in other network applications. The Internet protocols are often used for local area networking, even when the local network is not connected to the Internet. TCP/IP is also widely used to build enterprise networks. TCP/IP-based enterprise networks that use Internet techniques and World Wide Web tools to disseminate internal corporate information are called *intranets*. TCP/IP is the foundation of all of these varied networks.

Microsoft recognized the importance of TCP/IP for server systems and included TCP/IP support in Windows NT from the beginning. The role of Windows NT as a TCP/IP server, both inside the enterprise and in the global Internet, grows every year.

TCP/IP Features

The popularity of the TCP/IP protocols did not grow rapidly just because the protocols were there, or because connecting to the Internet mandated their use. They met an important need (worldwide data communication) at the right time, and they had several important features that allowed them to meet this need. These features are:

- Open protocol standards, freely available and developed independently from any specific computer hardware or operating system. Because it is so widely supported, TCP/IP is ideal for uniting different hardware and software, even if you don't communicate over the Internet.
- Independence from specific physical network hardware. This allows TCP/IP to integrate many different kinds of networks. TCP/IP can be run over an Ethernet, a token ring, a dial-up line, an FDDI net, and virtually any other kind of physical transmission medium.
- A common addressing scheme that allows any TCP/IP device to uniquely address any other device in the entire network, even if the network is as large as the worldwide Internet.
- Standardized high-level protocols for consistent, widely available user services.

Protocol Standards

Protocols are formal rules of behavior. In international relations, protocols minimize the problems caused by cultural differences when various nations work together. By agreeing to a common set of rules that are widely known and independent of any one nation's customs, diplomatic protocols minimize misunderstandings; everyone knows how to act and how to interpret the actions of others. Similarly, when computers communicate, it is necessary to define a set of rules to govern their communications.

In data communications these sets of rules are also called *protocols*. In homogeneous networks, a single computer vendor specifies a set of communications rules designed to use the strengths of the vendor's operating system and hardware architecture. But homogeneous networks are like the culture of a single country—only the natives are truly at home in it. TCP/IP attempts to create a heterogeneous network with open protocols that are independent of operating system and architectural differences. TCP/IP protocols are available to everyone, and are developed and changed by consensus—not by the fiat of one manufacturer. Everyone is free to develop products to meet these open protocol specifications.

The open nature of TCP/IP protocols requires publicly available standards documents. All protocols in the TCP/IP protocol suite are defined in one of three Internet standards publications. A number of the protocols have been adopted as *Military Standards (MIL STD)*. Others were published as *Internet Engineering Notes (IEN)*—though the IEN form of publication has now been abandoned. But most information about TCP/IP protocols is published as *Requests for Comments (RFC)*.

RFCs contain the latest versions of the specifications of all standard TCP/IP protocols.*

As the title *Request for Comments* implies, the style and content of these documents is much less rigid than most standards documents. RFCs contain a wide range of interesting and useful information, and are not limited to the formal specification of data communications protocols. As a network system administrator, you probably will read some of the RFCs yourself.

A Data Communications Model

To discuss computer networking, it is necessary to use terms that have special meaning. Even other computer professionals may not be familiar with all the terms in the networking alphabet soup. As is always the case, English and computer-speak are not equivalent (or even necessarily compatible) languages. Although descriptions and examples should make the meaning of the networking jargon more apparent, sometimes terms are ambiguous. A common frame of reference is necessary for understanding data communications terminology.

An architectural model developed by the International Standards Organization (ISO) is frequently used to describe the structure and function of data communications protocols. This architectural model, called the *Open Systems Interconnect (OSI) Reference Model*, provides a common reference for discussing communications. The terms defined by this model are well understood and widely used in the data communications community—so widely used, in fact, that it is difficult to discuss data communications without using OSI's terminology.

The OSI Reference Model contains seven *layers* that define the functions of data communications protocols. Each layer of the OSI model represents a function performed when data is transferred between cooperating applications across an intervening network. Figure 1-1 identifies each layer by name and provides a short functional description for it. Looking at this figure, the protocols are like a pile of building blocks stacked one upon another. Because of this appearance, the structure is often called a *stack* or *protocol stack*.

A layer does not define a single protocol—it defines a data communications function that may be performed by any number of protocols. Therefore, each layer may contain multiple protocols, each providing a service suitable to the function of that layer. For example, a file transfer protocol and an electronic mail protocol both provide user services, and both are part of the Application Layer.

* Interested in finding out how Internet standards are created? Read *The Internet Standards Process*, RFC 1310.

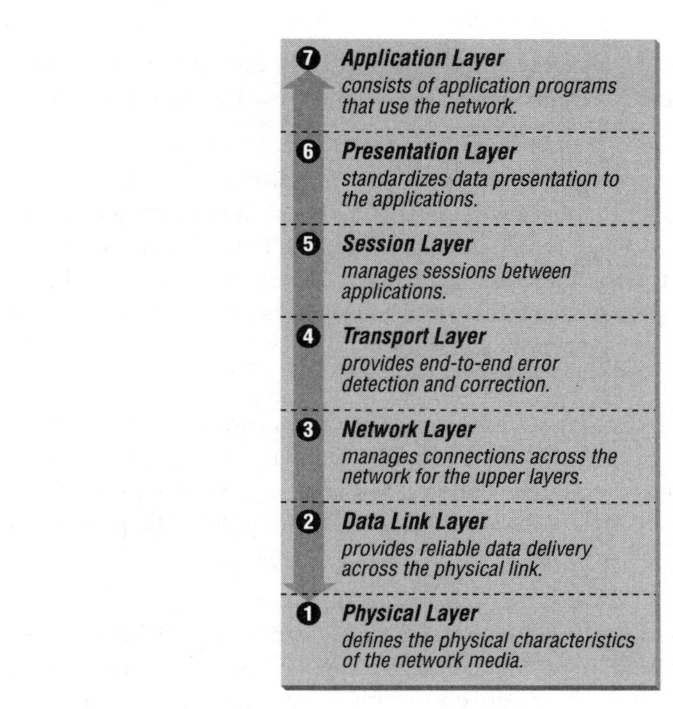

Figure 1-1. The OSI reference model

Every protocol communicates with its peer. A *peer* is an implementation of the same protocol in the equivalent layer on a remote system; for example, the local file transfer protocol is the peer of a remote file transfer protocol. Peer level communications must be standardized for successful communications to take place. In the abstract, each protocol is concerned only with communicating to its peer; it does not care about the layer above or below it.

However, there must also be agreement on how to pass data between the layers on a single computer, because every layer is involved in sending data from a local application to an equivalent remote application. The upper layers rely on the lower layers to transfer the data over the underlying network. Data is passed down the stack from one layer to the next, until it is transmitted over the network by the Physical Layer protocols. At the remote end, the data is passed up the stack to the receiving application. The individual layers do not need to know how the layers above and below them function; they only need to know how to pass data to them. Isolating network communications functions in different layers minimizes the impact of technological change on the entire protocol suite. New applications can be added without changing the physical network, and new network hardware can be installed without rewriting the application software.

Although the OSI model is useful, the TCP/IP protocols don't match its structure exactly. Therefore, in our discussions of TCP/IP we use the layers of the OSI model in the following way:

Application Layer
: The Application Layer is the level of the protocol hierarchy where user-accessed network processes reside. In this context, a TCP/IP application is any network process that occurs above the Transport Layer. This includes all of the processes that users directly interact with, as well as other processes at this level that users are not necessarily aware of.

Presentation Layer
: For cooperating applications to exchange data, they must agree about how data is represented. In OSI, this layer provides standard data presentation routines. This function is frequently handled within the applications in TCP/IP, though increasingly TCP/IP protocols such as XDR and MIME perform this function.

Session Layer
: As with the Presentation Layer, the Session Layer is not identifiable as a separate layer in the TCP/IP protocol hierarchy. The OSI Session Layer manages the sessions (connection) between cooperating applications. In TCP/IP, this function largely occurs in the Transport Layer, and the term *session* is not used. For TCP/IP, the terms *socket* and *port* are used to describe the path over which cooperating applications communicate.

Transport Layer
: Much of our discussion of TCP/IP is directed to the protocols that occur in the Transport Layer. The Transport Layer in the OSI reference model guarantees that the receiver gets the data exactly as it was sent. In TCP/IP this function is performed by the Transmission Control Protocol (TCP). However, not all applications require reliable delivery service. TCP/IP offers a second Transport Layer service, User Datagram Protocol (UDP), that does not perform the end-to-end reliability checks.*

Network Layer
: The Network Layer manages connections across the network and isolates the upper layer protocols from the details of the underlying network. The Internet Protocol (IP), which isolates the upper layers from the underlying network

* The OSI model originally defined only reliable service, but an unreliable protocol, Connectionless Network Protocol (CLNP), was later added.

and handles the addressing and delivery of data, is usually described as TCP/IP's Network Layer.

Data Link Layer
The reliable delivery of data across the underlying physical network is handled by the Data Link Layer. TCP/IP rarely creates protocols in the Data Link Layer. Most RFCs that relate to the Data Link Layer discuss how IP can make use of existing data link protocols.

Physical Layer
The Physical Layer defines the characteristics of the hardware needed to carry the data transmission signal. Features such as voltage levels and the number and location of interface pins are defined in this layer. Examples of standards at the Physical Layer are interface connectors such as RS232C and V.35 and standards for local area network wiring such as IEEE 802.3. TCP/IP does not define physical standards—it makes use of existing standards.

The terminology of the OSI reference model helps us describe TCP/IP, but to fully understand it, we must use an architectural model that more closely matches the structure of TCP/IP. The next section introduces the protocol model we'll use to describe TCP/IP.

TCP/IP Protocol Architecture

While there is no universal agreement about how to describe TCP/IP with a layered model, it is generally viewed as being composed of fewer layers than the seven used in the OSI model. Most descriptions of TCP/IP define three to five functional levels in the protocol architecture. The four-level model illustrated in Figure 1-2 is based on the three layers (Application, Host-to-Host, and Network Access) shown in the DOD Protocol Model in the *DDN Protocol Handbook—Volume 1*, with the addition of a separate Internet layer. This model provides a reasonable pictorial representation of the layers in the TCP/IP protocol hierarchy.

As in the OSI model, data is passed down the stack when it is being sent to the network, and up the stack when it is being received from the network. The four-layered structure of TCP/IP is seen in the way data is handled as it passes down the protocol stack from the Application Layer to the underlying physical network. Each layer in the stack adds control information to ensure proper delivery. This control information is called a *header* because it is placed in front of the data to be transmitted. Each layer treats all of the information it receives from the layer above as data and places its own header in front of that information. The addition of delivery information at every layer is called *encapsulation*. (Figure 1-3 illustrates this.) When data is received, the opposite happens. Each layer strips off its header before passing the data on to the layer above. As information flows back up the

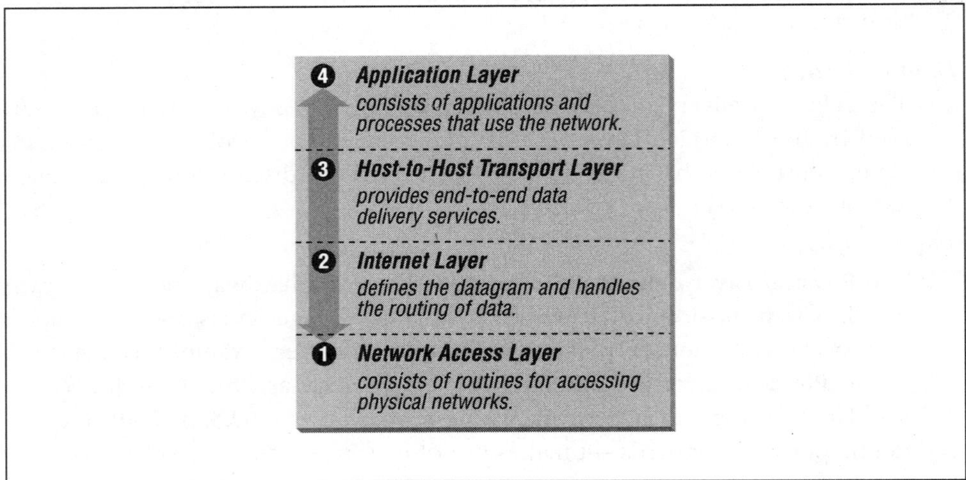

Figure 1-2. Layers in the TCP/IP protocol architecture

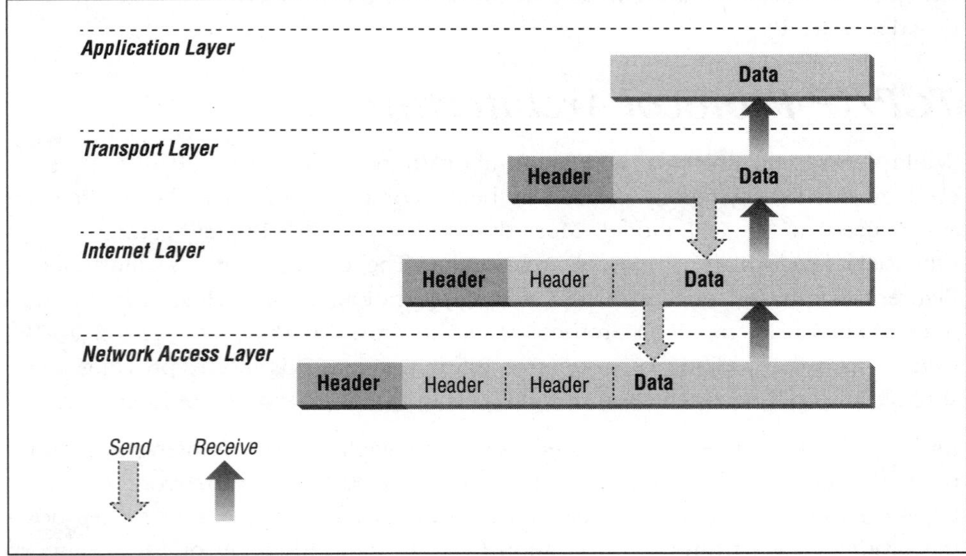

Figure 1-3. Data encapsulation

stack, information received from a lower layer is interpreted as both a header and data.

Each layer has its own independent data structures. Conceptually a layer is unaware of the data structures used by the layers above and below it. In reality, the data structures of a layer are designed to be compatible with the structures used by the surrounding layers for the sake of more efficient data transmission. Still, each layer has its own data structure and its own terminology to describe that structure.

Figure 1-4 shows the terms used by different layers of TCP/IP to refer to the data being transmitted. Applications using TCP refer to data as a *stream*, while applications using the User Datagram Protocol (UDP) refer to data as a *message*. TCP calls data a *segment*, and UDP calls its data structure a *packet*. The Internet layer views all data as blocks called *datagrams*. TCP/IP uses many different types of underlying networks, each of which may have a different terminology for the data it transmits. Most networks refer to transmitted data as *packets* or *frames*. In Figure 1-4 we show a network that transmits pieces of data it calls *frames*. Both of these terms refer to the same thing; the terms vary as the view of the data varies from layer to layer.

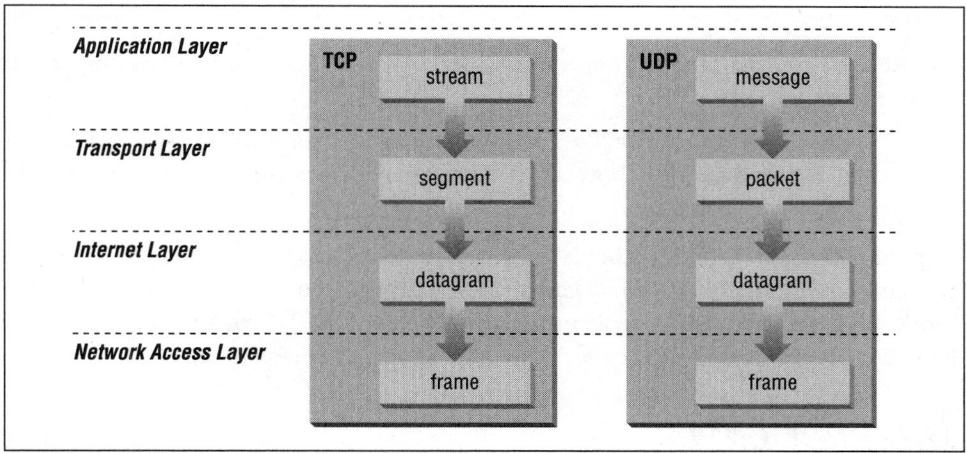

Figure 1-4. Data structures

Let's look more closely at the function of each layer, working our way up from the Network Access Layer to the Application Layer.

Network Access Layer

The *Network Access Layer* is the lowest layer of the TCP/IP protocol hierarchy. The protocols in this layer provide the means for the system to deliver data to the other devices on a directly attached network. It defines how to use the network to transmit an IP datagram. Unlike higher-level protocols, Network Access Layer protocols must know the details of the underlying network (its packet structure, addressing, etc.) to correctly format the data being transmitted to comply with the network constraints. The TCP/IP Network Access Layer can encompass the functions of all three lower layers of the OSI reference Model (Network, Data Link, and Physical).

The Network Access Layer is often ignored by users. The design of TCP/IP hides the function of the lower layers, and the better known protocols (IP, TCP, UDP, etc.) are all higher-level protocols. As new hardware technologies appear, new Network Access protocols must be developed so that TCP/IP networks can use the new hardware. Consequently, there are many access protocols—one for each physical network standard.

Functions performed at this level include encapsulation of IP datagrams into the frames transmitted by the network, and mapping of IP addresses to the physical addresses used by the network. One of TCP/IP's strengths is its universal addressing scheme. The IP address must be converted into an address that is appropriate for the physical network over which the datagram is transmitted.

Two examples of RFCs that define network access layer protocols are:

- RFC 826, *Address Resolution Protocol (ARP)*, which maps IP addresses to Ethernet addresses
- RFC 894, *A Standard for the Transmission of IP Datagrams over Ethernet Networks*, which specifies how IP datagrams are encapsulated for transmission over Ethernet networks

Implementations of the protocols in this layer often appear as a combination of device drivers and related programs. The modules that are identified with network device names usually encapsulate and deliver the data to the network, while separate programs perform related functions such as address mapping.

Internet Layer

The layer above the Network Access Layer in the protocol hierarchy is the *Internet Layer*. The Internet Protocol, RFC 791, is the heart of TCP/IP and the most important protocol in the Internet Layer. IP provides the basic packet delivery service on which TCP/IP networks are built. All protocols, in the layers above and below IP, use the Internet Protocol to deliver data. All TCP/IP data flows through IP, incoming and outgoing, regardless of its final destination.

Internet Protocol

The Internet Protocol is the building block of the Internet. Its functions include:

- Defining the datagram, which is the basic unit of transmission in the Internet
- Defining the Internet addressing scheme

- Moving data between the Network Access Layer and the Host-to-Host Transport Layer
- Routing datagrams to remote hosts
- Performing fragmentation and re-assembly of datagrams

Before describing these functions in more detail, let's look at some of IP's characteristics. First, IP is a *connectionless protocol*. This means that IP does not exchange control information (called a *handshake*) to establish an end-to-end connection before transmitting data. In contrast, a *connection-oriented protocol* exchanges control information with the remote system to verify that it is ready to receive data before any data is sent. When the handshaking is successful, the systems are said to have established a *connection*. Internet Protocol relies on protocols in other layers to establish the connection if they require connection-oriented service.

IP also relies on protocols in the other layers to provide error detection and error recovery. The Internet Protocol is sometimes called an *unreliable protocol* because it contains no error detection and recovery code. This is not to say that the protocol cannot be relied on—quite the contrary. IP can be relied upon to accurately deliver your data to the connected network, but it doesn't check whether that data was correctly received. Protocols in other layers of the TCP/IP architecture provide this checking when it is required.

The datagram

The TCP/IP protocols were built to transmit data over the ARPANET, which was a *packet switching network*. A *packet* is a block of data that carries with it the information necessary to deliver it—in a manner similar to a postal letter, which has an address written on its envelope. A packet switching network uses the addressing information in the packets to switch packets from one physical network to another, moving them toward their final destination. Each packet travels the network independently of any other packet.

The *datagram* is the packet format defined by Internet Protocol. Figure 1-5 is a pictorial representation of an IP datagram. The first five or six 32-bit words of the datagram are control information called the *header*. By default, the header is five words long; the sixth word is optional. Because the header's length is variable, it includes a field called *Internet Header Length (IHL)* that indicates the header's length in words. The header contains all the information necessary to deliver the packet.

The Internet Protocol delivers the datagram by checking the *Destination Address* in word 5 of the header. The Destination Address is a standard 32-bit IP address that identifies the destination network and the specific host on that network. (The

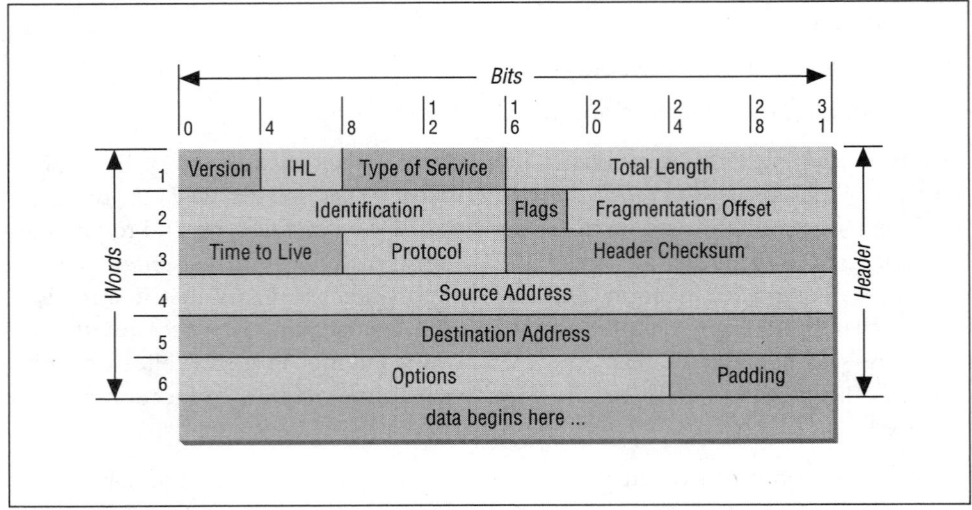

Figure 1-5. IP datagram format

format of IP addresses is explained in Chapter 2, *Delivering the Data.*) If the Destination Address is the address of a host on the local network, the packet is delivered directly to the destination. If the Destination Address is not on the local network, the packet is passed to a gateway for delivery. *Gateways* are devices that switch packets between the different physical networks. Deciding which gateway to use is called *routing*. IP makes the routing decision for each individual packet.

Routing datagrams

Internet gateways are commonly (and perhaps more accurately) referred to as *IP routers* because they use Internet Protocol to route packets between networks. In traditional TCP/IP jargon, there are only two types of network devices—*gateways* and *hosts*. Gateways forward packets between networks, and hosts don't. However, if a host is connected to more than one network (called a *multi-homed host*), it can forward packets between the networks. When a multi-homed host forwards packets, it acts just like any other gateway and is considered to be a gateway. Current data communications terminology makes a distinction between gateways and routers,* but we'll use the terms *gateway* and *IP router* interchangeably.

Figure 1-6 shows the use of gateways to forward packets. The hosts (or *end systems*) process packets through all four protocol layers, while the gateways (or

* In current terminology, a gateway moves data between different protocols and a router moves data between different networks. So, a system that moves mail between SMTP and X.400 is a gateway, but a traditional IP gateway is a router.

intermediate systems) process the packets only up to the Internet Layer where the routing decisions are made.

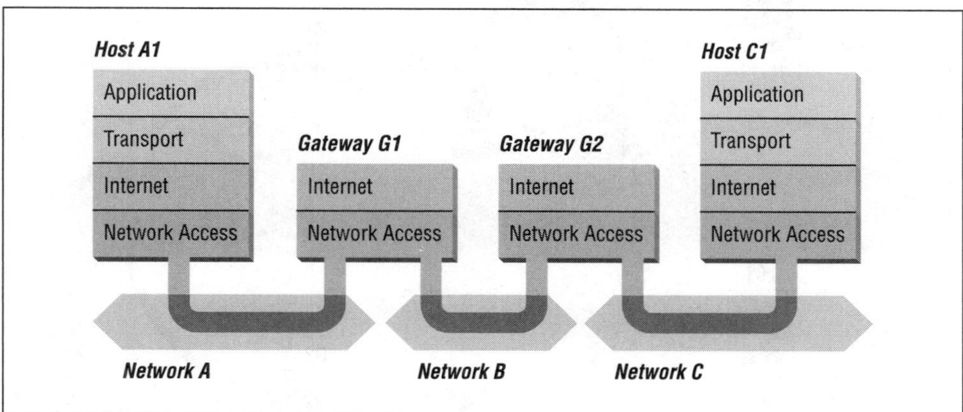

Figure 1-6. Routing through gateways

Systems can only deliver packets to other devices attached to the same physical network. Packets from *A1* destined for host *C1* are forwarded through gateways *G1* and *G2*. Host *A1* first delivers the packet to gateway *G1*, with which it shares network *A*. Gateway *G1* delivers the packet to *G2* over network *B*. Gateway *G2* then delivers the packet directly to host *C1*, because they are both attached to network *C*. Host *A1* has no knowledge of any gateways beyond gateway *G1*. It sends packets destined for both networks *C* and *B* to that local gateway, and then relies on that gateway to properly forward the packets along the path to their destinations. Likewise, host *C1* would send its packets to *G2*, in order to reach a host on network *A*, as well as any host on network *B*.

Figure 1-7 shows another view of routing. This figure emphasizes that the underlying physical networks that a datagram travels through may be different and even incompatible. Host *A1* on the token ring network routes the datagram through gateway *G1*, to reach host *C1* on the Ethernet. Gateway *G1* forwards the data through the X.25 network to gateway *G2*, for delivery to *C1*. The datagram traverses three physically different networks, but eventually arrives intact at *C1*.

Fragmenting datagrams

As a datagram is routed through different networks, it may be necessary for the IP module in a gateway to divide the datagram into smaller pieces. A datagram received from one network may be too large to be transmitted in a single packet on a different network. This condition occurs only when a gateway interconnects dissimilar physical networks.

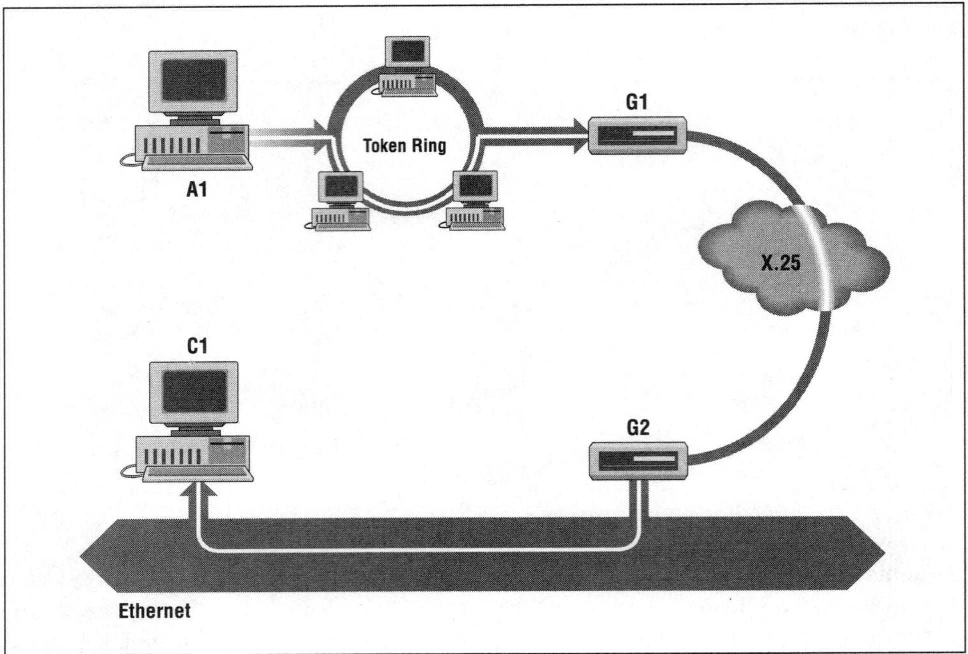

Figure 1-7. Networks, gateways, and hosts

Each type of network has a *maximum transmission unit (MTU)*, which is the largest packet that it can transfer. If the datagram received from one network is longer than the other network's MTU, it is necessary to divide the datagram into smaller *fragments* for transmission. This process is called *fragmentation*. Think of a train delivering a load of steel. Each railway car can carry more steel than the trucks that will take it along the highway; so each railway car is unloaded onto many different trucks. In the same way that a railroad is physically different from a highway, an Ethernet is physically different from an X.25 network; IP must break an Ethernet's relatively large packets into smaller packets before it can transmit them over an X.25 network.

The format of each fragment is the same as the format of any normal datagram. Header word 2 contains information that identifies each datagram fragment and provides information about how to re-assemble the fragments back into the original datagram. The Identification field identifies what datagram the fragment belongs to, and the Fragmentation Offset field tells what piece of the datagram this fragment is. The Flags field has a *More Fragments* bit that tells IP if it has assembled all of the datagram fragments.

Passing datagrams to the transport layer

When IP receives a datagram that is addressed to the local host, it must pass the data portion of the datagram to the correct Transport Layer protocol. This is done by using the *protocol number* from word 3 of the datagram header. Each Transport Layer protocol has a unique protocol number that identifies it to IP. Protocol numbers are discussed in Chapter 2.

You can see from this short overview that IP performs many important functions. Don't expect to fully understand datagrams, gateways, routing, IP addresses, and all the other things that IP does from this short description. Each chapter adds more details about these topics. So let's continue on with the other protocol in the TCP/IP Internet Layer.

Internet Control Message Protocol

An integral part of IP is the *Internet Control Message Protocol (ICMP)* defined in RFC 792. This protocol is part of the Internet Layer and uses the IP datagram delivery facility to send its messages. ICMP sends messages that perform the following control, error reporting, and informational functions for TCP/IP:

Flow control
: When datagrams arrive too fast for processing, the destination host or an intermediate gateway sends an ICMP Source Quench Message back to the sender. This tells the source to temporarily stop sending datagrams.

Detecting unreachable destinations
: When a destination is unreachable, the system detecting the problem sends a Destination Unreachable Message to the datagram's source. If the unreachable destination is a network or host, the message is sent by an intermediate gateway. But if the destination is an unreachable port, the destination host sends the message. (We discuss ports in Chapter 2.)

Redirecting routes
: A gateway sends the ICMP Redirect Message to tell a host to use another gateway, presumably because the other gateway is a better choice. This message can be used only when the source host is on the same network as both gateways. To better understand this, refer to Figure 1-7. If a host on the X.25 network sent a datagram to *G1*, it would be possible for *G1* to redirect that host to *G2* because the host, *G1*, and *G2* are all attached to the same network. On the other hand, if a host on the token ring network sent a datagram to *G1*, the host could not be redirected to use *G2*. This is because *G2* is not attached to the token ring.

Checking remote hosts

A host can send the ICMP Echo Message to see if a remote system's Internet Protocol is up and operational. When a system receives an echo message, it replies and sends the data from the packet back to the source host. The **ping** command, which we discuss later, uses this message.

Transport Layer

The protocol layer just above the Internet Layer is the *Host-to-Host Transport Layer*. This name is usually shortened to *Transport Layer*. The two most important protocols in the Transport Layer are *Transmission Control Protocol (TCP)* and *User Datagram Protocol (UDP)*. TCP provides reliable data delivery service with end-to-end error detection and correction. UDP provides low-overhead, connectionless datagram delivery service. Both protocols deliver data between the Application Layer and the Internet Layer. Applications programmers can choose whichever service is more appropriate for their specific applications.

User Datagram Protocol

The User Datagram Protocol gives application programs direct access to a datagram delivery service, like the delivery service that IP provides. This allows applications to exchange messages over the network with a minimum of protocol overhead.

UDP is an unreliable, connectionless datagram protocol. As noted previously, unreliable merely means that there are no techniques in the protocol for verifying that the data reached the other end of the network correctly. Within your computer, UDP will deliver data correctly. UDP uses 16-bit *Source Port* and *Destination Port* numbers in word 1 of the message header, to deliver data to the correct applications process. Figure 1-8 shows the UDP message format.

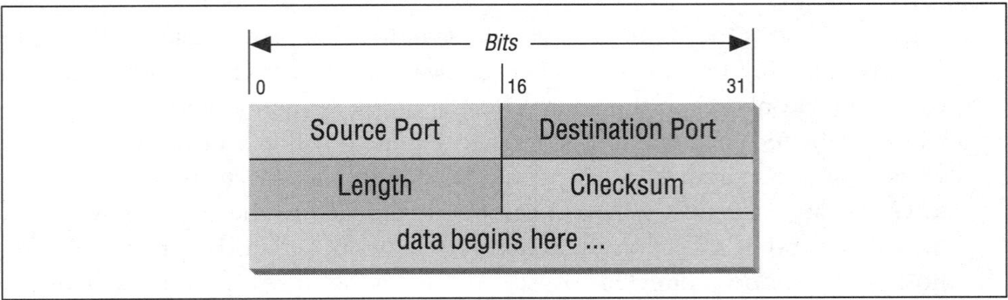

Figure 1-8. UDP message format

Why do applications programmers choose UDP as a data transport service? There are a number of good reasons. If the amount of data being transmitted is small, the overhead of creating connections and ensuring reliable delivery may be greater than the work of re-transmitting the entire data set. In this case, UDP is the most efficient choice for a Transport Layer protocol. Applications that fit a *query-response* model are also excellent candidates for using UDP. The response can be used as a positive acknowledgment to the query. If a response isn't received within a certain time period, the application just sends another query. Still other applications provide their own techniques for reliable data delivery, and don't require that service from the transport layer protocol. Imposing another layer of acknowledgment on any of these types of applications is inefficient.

Many important Windows NT services rely on UDP. A prime example is the Microsoft DHCP Server. The client queries the Dynamic Host Configuration Protocol (DHCP) server for configuration information. The server responds with the requested information. This vital query/response protocol runs efficiently over UDP.

Transmission Control Protocol

Applications that require the transport protocol to provide reliable data delivery use TCP because it verifies that data is delivered across the network accurately and in the proper sequence. TCP is a *reliable*, *connection-oriented*, *byte-stream* protocol. Let's look at each of the terms—reliable, connection-oriented, and byte-stream—in more detail.

TCP provides reliability with a mechanism called *Positive Acknowledgment with Re-transmission (PAR)*. Simply stated, a system using PAR sends the data again, unless it hears from the remote system that the data arrived successfully. The unit of data exchanged between cooperating TCP modules is called a *segment* (see Figure 1-9). Each segment contains a checksum that the recipient uses to verify that the data is undamaged. If the data segment is received undamaged, the receiver sends a *positive acknowledgment* back to the sender. If the data segment is damaged, the receiver discards it. After an appropriate time-out period, the sending TCP module re-transmits any segment for which no positive acknowledgment has been received.

TCP is connection-oriented. It establishes a logical end-to-end connection between the two communicating hosts. Control information, called a *handshake*, is exchanged between the two endpoints to establish a dialogue before data is transmitted. TCP indicates the control function of a segment by setting the appropriate bit in the Flags field in word 4 of the *segment header*.

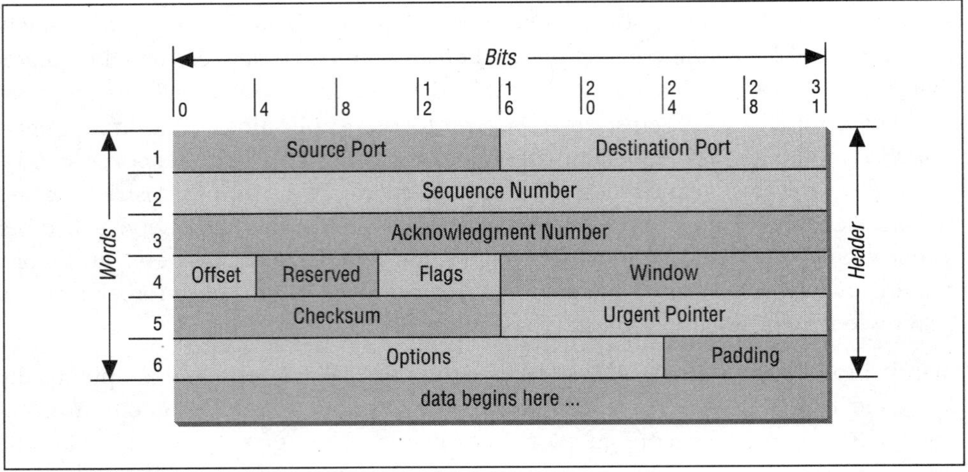

Figure 1-9. TCP segment format

The type of handshake used by TCP is called a *three-way handshake* because three segments are exchanged. Figure 1-10 show the simplest form of the three-way handshake. Host *A* begins the connection by sending host *B* a segment with the Synchronize sequence numbers (SYN) bit set. This segment tells host *B* that *A* wishes to set up a connection, and it tells *B* what sequence number host *A* will use as a starting number for its segments. (Sequence numbers are used to keep data in the proper order.) Host *B* responds to *A* with a segment that has the Acknowledgment (ACK) and SYN bits set. *B*'s segment acknowledges the receipt of *A*'s segment, and informs *A* which Sequence Number host *B* will start with. Finally, host *A* sends a segment that acknowledges receipt of *B*'s segment, and transfers the first actual data.

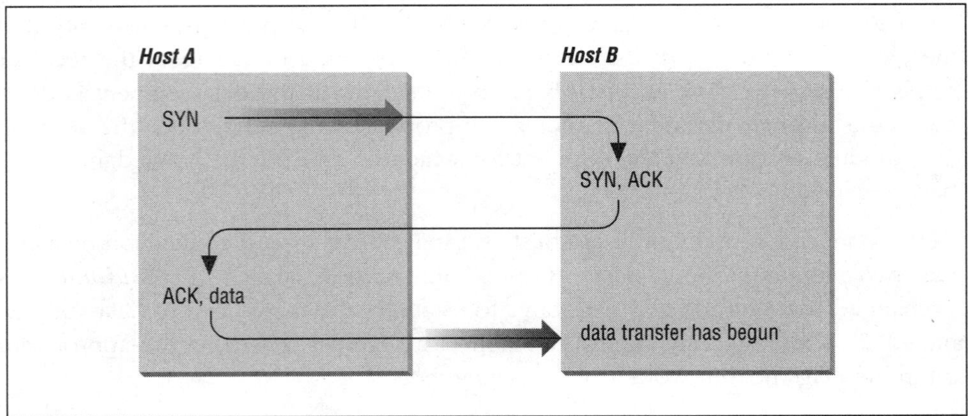

Figure 1-10. Three-way handshake

After this exchange, host *A*'s TCP has positive evidence that the remote TCP is alive and ready to receive data. As soon as the connection is established, data can be transferred. When the cooperating modules have concluded the data transfers, they will exchange a three-way handshake with segments containing the *No more data from sender* bit (called the *FIN* bit) to close the connection. It is the end-to-end exchange of data that provides the logical connection between the two systems.

TCP views the data it sends as a continuous stream of bytes, not as independent packets. Therefore, TCP takes care to maintain the sequence in which bytes are sent and received. The Sequence Number and Acknowledgment Number fields in the TCP segment header keep track of the bytes.

The TCP standard does not require that each system start numbering bytes with any specific number; each system chooses the number it will use as a starting point. To keep track of the data stream correctly, each end of the connection must know the other end's initial number. The two ends of the connection synchronize byte-numbering systems by exchanging SYN segments during the handshake. The Sequence Number field in the SYN segment contains the *Initial Sequence Number* (ISN), which is the starting point for the byte-numbering system. For security reasons the ISN should be a random number, though it is often 0.

Each byte of data is numbered sequentially from the ISN, so the first real byte of data sent has a sequence number of ISN+1. The Sequence Number in the header of a data segment identifies the sequential position in the data stream of the first data byte in the segment. For example, if the first byte in the data stream was sequence number 1 (ISN=0) and 4000 bytes of data have already been transferred, then the first byte of data in the current segment is byte 4001, and the Sequence Number would be 4001.

The Acknowledgment Segment (ACK) performs two functions—*positive acknowledgment* and *flow control*. The acknowledgment tells the sender how much data has been received, and how much more the receiver can accept. The Acknowledgment Number is the sequence number of the next byte the receiver expects to receive. The standard does not require an individual acknowledgment for every packet. The acknowledgment number is a positive acknowledgment of all bytes up to that number. For example, if the first byte sent was numbered 1 and 2000 bytes have been successfully received, the Acknowledgment Number would be 2001.

The Window field contains the *window*, or the number of bytes the remote end is able to accept. If the receiver is capable of accepting 6000 more bytes, the window would be 6000. The window indicates to the sender that it can continue sending segments as long as the total number of bytes that it sends is smaller than the window of bytes that the receiver can accept. The receiver controls the flow of bytes from the sender by changing the size of the window. A zero window tells the sender to cease transmission until it receives a non-zero window value.

Figure 1-11 shows a TCP data stream that starts with an Initial Sequence Number of 0. The receiving system has received and acknowledged 2000 bytes, so the current Acknowledgment Number is 2001. The receiver also has enough buffer space for another 6000 bytes, so it has advertised a window of 6000. The sender is currently sending a segment of 1000 bytes starting with Sequence Number 4001. The sender has received no acknowledgment for the bytes from 2001 on, but continues sending data as long as it is within the window. If the sender fills the window and receives no acknowledgment of the data previously sent, it will, after an appropriate time-out, send the data again starting from the first unacknowledged byte. In Figure 1-11, re-transmission would start from byte 2001 if no further acknowledgments are received. This procedure ensures that data is reliably received at the far end of the network.

TCP is also responsible for delivering data received from IP to the correct application. The application that the data is bound for is identified by a 16-bit number called the *port number*. The *Source Port* and *Destination Port* are contained in the first word of the segment header. Correctly passing data to and from the Application Layer is an important part of what the Transport Layer services do.

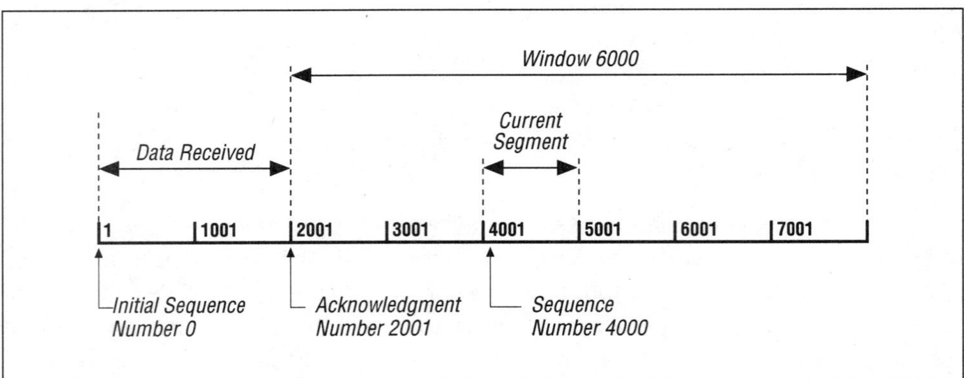

Figure 1-11. TCP data stream

Application Layer

At the top of the TCP/IP protocol architecture is the *Application Layer*. This layer includes all processes that use the Transport Layer protocols to deliver data. There are many applications protocols. Most provide user services, and new services are always being added to this layer. Some widely known and implemented applications protocols are:*

FTP
: the File Transfer Protocol, is used for interactive file transfer.

SMTP
: the Simple Mail Transfer Protocol, delivers electronic mail.

HTTP
: the Hypertext Transfer Protocol, delivers Web pages over the network.

While HTTP, FTP, and SMTP are important TCP/IP applications, you will work with many others as both a user and a system administrator. Some other commonly used TCP/IP applications are:

Domain Name System (DNS)
: Also called *name service*, this application maps IP addresses to the names assigned to network devices. DNS is discussed in detail in Chapter 8, *Configuring DNS Name System*.

Open Shortest Path First (OSPF)
: Routing is central to the way TCP/IP works. OSPF, which is described in Appendix D, *Routing Protocols*, is used by network devices to exchange routing information. Routing is discussed in Chapter 2, *Delivering the Data*, and Chapter 9, *Microsoft Routing & Remote Access Service*.

Dynamic Host Configuration Protocol (DHCP)
: This protocol allows networked computers to be automatically configured from a central server. The DHCP server is covered in Chapter 6, *Using Dynamic Host Configuration Protocol*.

Some protocols, such as FTP, can only be used if the user has some knowledge of the network. Other protocols, like OSPF, run without the user even knowing that they exist. As system administrator, you are aware of all these applications and all the protocols in the other TCP/IP layers. And you're responsible for configuring them!

Summary

In this chapter we discussed the structure of TCP/IP, the protocol suite upon which the Internet is built. We have seen that TCP/IP is a hierarchy of four layers: Applications, Host-to-Host Transport, Internet, and Network Access. We have

* These applications are all part of the Internet Information Server (IIS) software covered in Chapter 10, *Internet Information Server (IIS)*.

examined the function of each of these layers. In the next chapter we look at how the IP packet, the datagram, moves through a network when data is delivered between hosts.

2

In this chapter:

- *Addressing, Routing, and Multiplexing*
- *The IP Address*
- *Subnets*
- *The Routing Table*
- *Address Resolution*
- *Protocols, Ports, and Sockets*
- *Summary*

Delivering the Data

In Chapter 1, *Overview of TCP/IP*, we touched on the basic architecture and design of the TCP/IP protocols. From that discussion, we know that TCP/IP is a hierarchy of four layers. In this chapter, we explore in finer detail how data moves between the protocol layers and the systems on the network. We examine the structure of Internet addresses, including how addresses route data to its final destination, and how addressing rules are locally redefined to create subnets. We also look at the protocol and port numbers used to deliver data to the correct applications. These additional details move us from an overview of TCP/IP to the specific implementation details that affect your system's configuration.

Addressing, Routing, and Multiplexing

To deliver data between two Internet hosts, it is necessary to move the data across the network to the correct host, and within that host to the correct user or process. TCP/IP uses three schemes to accomplish these tasks:

Addressing
: IP addresses, which uniquely identify every host on the network, deliver data to the correct host.

Routing
: Gateways deliver data to the correct network.

Multiplexing
: Protocol and port numbers deliver data to the correct software module within the host.

Each of these functions—addressing between hosts, routing between networks, and multiplexing between layers—is necessary to send data between two cooperating applications across the Internet. Let's examine each of these functions in detail.

To illustrate these concepts and provide consistent examples, we use an imaginary corporate network inspired by the network at Robert's company. Our imaginary network is made up of several networks at different offices, as well as a connection to the Internet. We are responsible for managing the Ethernet in the computing center. This network's structure, or *topology*, is shown in Figure 2-1.

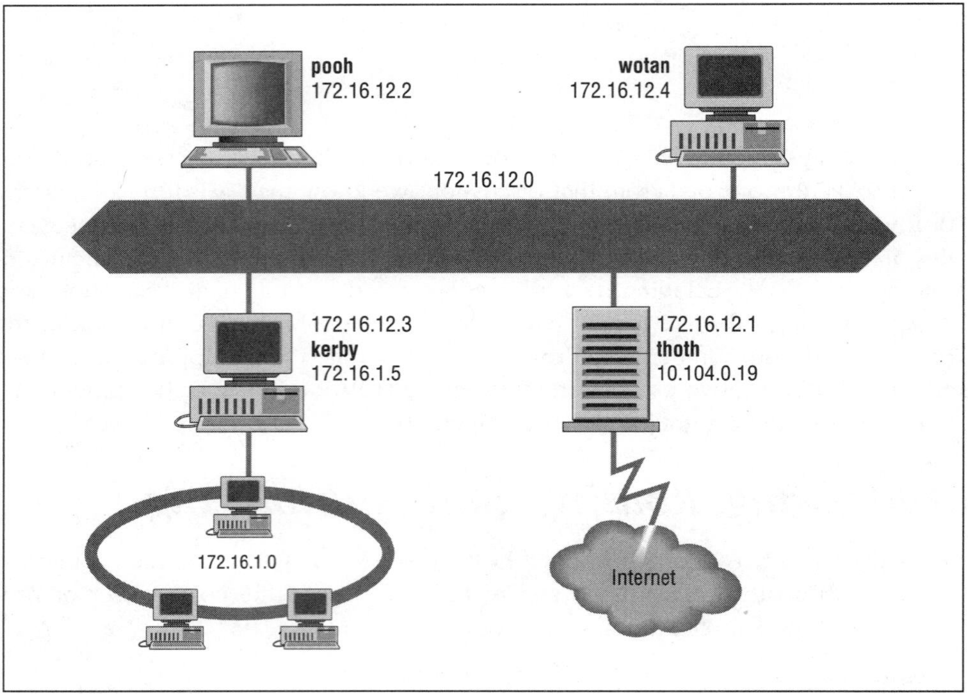

Figure 2-1. Sample network

The icons in the figure represent computer systems. There are, of course, several other imaginary systems on our imaginary network. You'll just have to use your imagination! But we'll use the hosts *pooh* (an NT workstation) and *thoth* (a Windows NT server that also functions as a gateway) for most of our examples. The thick line is our computer center Ethernet, and the circle is the local network that connects our various corporate networks. The cloud is the Internet. What the numbers are, how they're used, and how datagrams are delivered are the topics of this chapter.

The IP Address

The Internet Protocol moves data between hosts in the form of datagrams. Each datagram is delivered to the address contained in the Destination Address (word 5) of the datagram's header. The Destination Address is a standard 32-bit IP address that contains sufficient information to uniquely identify a network and a specific host on that network.

An IP address contains a *network part* and a *host part*, but the format of these parts is not the same in every IP address. The number of address bits used to identify the network, and the number used to identify the host, vary according to the prefix length of the address. There are two ways the prefix length is determined: by address class or by a *Classless Interdomain Routing* (CIDR) address mask. We begin with a discussion of traditional IP address classes.

Address Classes

Originally the IP address space was divided into a few fixed-length structures called *address classes*. The three main address classes are *class A*, *class B*, and *class C*. By examining the first few bits of an address, IP software can quickly determine the class, and therefore the structure, of an address. IP follows these rules to determine the address class:

- If the first bit of an IP address is 0, it is the address of a *class A network*. The first bit of a class A address identifies the address class. The next 7 bits identify the network, and the last 24 bits identify the host. There are fewer than 128 class A network numbers, but each class A network can be composed of millions of hosts.
- If the first 2 bits of the address are 1 0, it is a *class B network* address. The first 2 bits identify class; the next 14 bits identify the network, and the last 16 bits identify the host. There are thousands of class B network numbers and each class B network can contain thousands of hosts.
- If the first 3 bits of the address are 1 1 0, it is a *class C network* address. In a class C address, the first 3 bits are class identifiers; the next 21 bits are the network address, and the last 8 bits identify the host. There are millions of class C network numbers, but each class C network is composed of fewer than 254 hosts.
- If the first 4 bits of the address are 1 1 1 0, it is a multicast address. These addresses are sometimes called *class D* addresses, but they don't really refer to specific networks. Multicast addresses are used to address groups of computers all at one time. Multicast addresses identify a group of computers that

share a common application, such as a video conference, as opposed to a group of computers that share a common network.

- If the first four bits of the address are 1 1 1 1, it is a special reserved address. These addresses are sometimes called *class E* addresses, but they don't really refer to specific networks. No numbers are currently assigned in this range.

Luckily, this is not as complicated as it sounds. IP addresses are usually written as four decimal numbers separated by dots (periods).*

Each of the four numbers is in the range from 0 to 255 (the decimal values possible for a single byte). Because the bits that identify class are contiguous with the network bits of the address, we can lump them together and look at the address as composed of full bytes of network address and full bytes of host address. If the value of the first byte is:

- Less than 128, the address is class A; the first byte is the network number, and the next three bytes are the host address.
- From 128 to 191, the address is class B; the first two bytes identify the network, and the last two bytes identify the host.
- From 192 to 223, the address is class C; the first three bytes are the network address, and the last byte is the host number.
- From 224 to 239, the address is multicast. There is no network part. The entire address identifies a specific multicast group.
- Greater than 239, the address is reserved. We can ignore reserved addresses.

Figure 2-2 illustrates how the address structure varies with address class. The class A address is 10.104.0.19. The first bit of this address is 0, so the address is interpreted as host 104.0.19 on network 10. One byte specifies the network and three bytes specify the host. In the address 172.16.12.1, the two high-order bits are 1 0 so the address refers to host 12.1 on network 172.16. Two bytes identify the network and two identify the host. Finally, in the class C example, 192.168.16.1, the three high-order bits are 1 1 0, so this is the address of host 1 on network 192.168.16—three network bytes and one host byte.

The IP address, which provides universal addressing across all of the networks of the Internet, is one of the great strengths of the TCP/IP protocol suite. However, the original class structure of the IP address has weaknesses. The TCP/IP designers did not envision the enormous scale of today's network. When TCP/IP was being designed, networking was limited to large organizations that could afford substantial computer systems. The idea of a powerful workstation on every

* Addresses are occasionally written in other formats, for example, as hexadecimal numbers. However, the dot notation form is the most widely used. Whatever the notation, the structure of the address is the same.

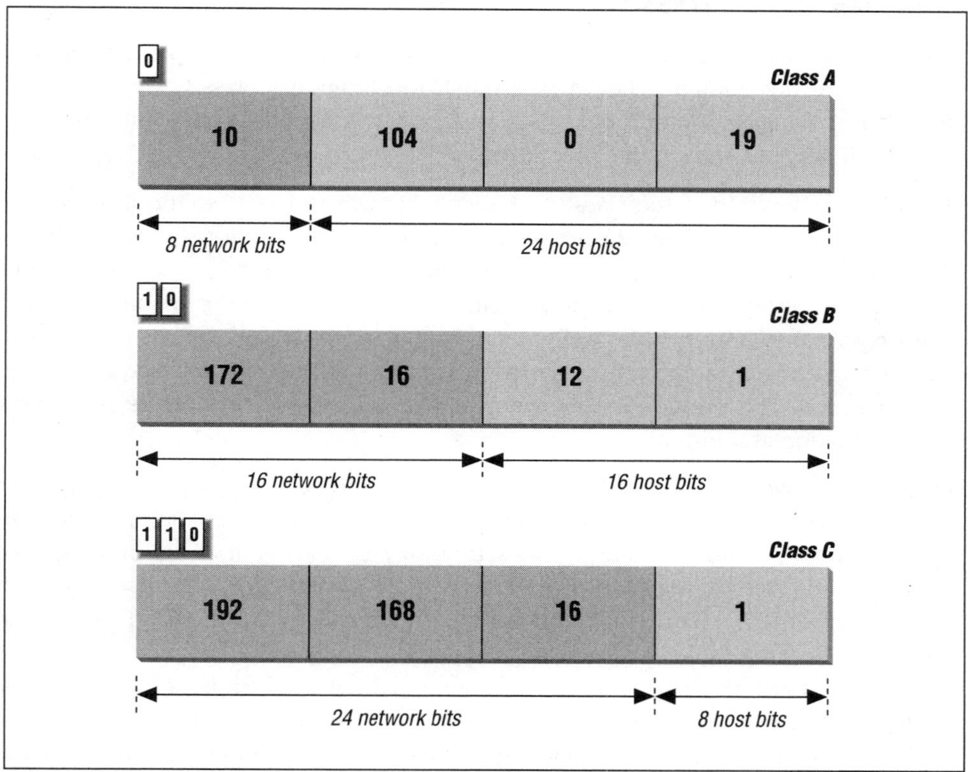

Figure 2-2. IP address structure

desktop did not exist. At that time, a 32-bit address seemed so large that it was divided into classes to reduce the processing load on routers, even though dividing the address into classes sharply reduced the number of host addresses actually available for use. For example, assigning a large network a single class B address, instead of six class C addresses, reduced the load on the router because the router needed to keep only one route for that entire organization. However, an organization that was given the class B address probably did not have 64,000 computers, so most of the host addresses available to the organization were never assigned.

The class-structured address design was critically strained by the rapid growth of the Internet. At one point it appeared that all class B addresses might be rapidly exhausted.*

To prevent this, a new way of looking at IP addresses without a class structure was developed.

* The source for this prediction is the draft of *Supernetting: an Address Assignment and Aggregation Strategy*, by V. Fuller, T. Li, J. Yu, and K. Varadhan, March 1992.

Classless IP Addresses

The rapid depletion of the class B addresses showed that three primary address classes were not enough: class A was much too large and class C was much too small. Even a class B address was too large for many networks but was used because it was better than the alternatives.

The obvious solution to the class B address crisis was to force organizations to use multiple class C addresses. There were millions of these addresses available and they were in no immediate danger of depletion. As is often the case, the obvious solution is not as simple as it may seem. Each class C address requires its own entry within the routing table. Assigning thousands or millions of class C addresses would cause the routing table to grow so rapidly that the routers would soon be overwhelmed. The solution required a new way of assigning addresses and a new way of looking at addresses.

Originally network addresses were assigned in more or less sequential order as they were requested. This worked fine when the network was small and centralized. However, it did not take network topology into account. Thus only random chance would determine if the same intermediate routers would be used to reach network 195.4.12.0 and network 195.4.13.0, which makes it difficult to reduce the size of the routing table. Addresses can only be aggregated if they are contiguous numbers and are reachable through the same route. For example, if addresses are contiguous for one service provider, a single route can be created for that aggregation because that service provider will have a limited number of routes to the Internet. But if one network address is in France and the next contiguous address is in Australia, creating a consolidated route for these addresses does not work.

Today, large, contiguous blocks of addresses are assigned to large network service providers in a manner that better reflects the topology of the network. The service providers then allocate chunks of these address blocks to the organizations to which they provide network services. This temporarily alleviates the shortage of class B addresses and, because the assignment of addresses reflects the topology of the network, it permits route aggregation. Under this new scheme we know that network 195.4.12.0 and network 195.4.13.0 are reachable through the same intermediate routers. In fact both of these addresses are in the range of the addresses assigned to Europe, 194.0.0.0 to 195.255.255.255. Assigning addresses that reflect the topology of the network enables route aggregation but it does not implement it. As long as network 195.4.12.0 and network 195.4.13.0 are interpreted as separate class C addresses they will require separate entries in the routing table. A new, flexible way of defining addresses is needed.

Evaluating addresses according to the class rules discussed above limits the length of network numbers to 8, 16, or 24 bits—1, 2, or 3 bytes. The IP address, however, is not really byte-oriented. It is 32 contiguous bits. A more flexible way to interpret the network and host portions of an address is with a *bit mask*. An address bit mask works in this way: if a bit is on in the mask, that equivalent bit in the address is interpreted as a network bit; if a bit in the mask is off, the bit belongs to the host part of the address. For example, if address 195.4.12.0 is interpreted as a class C address, the first 24 bits are the network number and the last 8 bits are the host address. The network mask that represents this is 255.255.255.0, 24 bits on and 8 bits off. The bit mask that is derived from the traditional class structure is called the *default mask* or the *natural mask*. However, with bit masks we are no longer limited by the address class structure. A mask of 255.255.0.0 can be applied to network address 195.4.0.0. This mask includes all addresses from 195.4.0.0 to 195.4.255.255 in a single network number. In effect, it creates a network number as large as a class B network in the class C address space. Using bit masks to create networks larger than the natural mask is called *supernetting*, and the use of a mask instead of the address class to determine the destination network is called *Classless Inter-Domain Routing* (CIDR).*

CIDR requires modifications to the routers and routing protocols. The protocols need to distribute, along with the destination addresses, address masks that define how the addresses are interpreted. The routers and hosts need to know how to interpret these addresses as classless addresses and how to apply the bit mask that accompanies the address. Older routing protocols, such as *Routing Information Protocol* (RIP), and older operating systems do not support CIDR address masks. As the incorporation of the mask information in the routing table shows, new operating systems like Windows NT 4.0 do support CIDR.

```
C:\>route print
Active Routes:
Network Address   Netmask Gateway        Address        Interface  Metric
        0.0.0.0           0.0.0.0   172.16.26.62     172.16.26.36       1
      127.0.0.0         255.0.0.0      127.0.0.1        127.0.0.1       1
   172.16.26.32   255.255.255.224   172.16.26.36     172.16.26.36       1
   172.16.26.36   255.255.255.255      127.0.0.1        127.0.0.1       1
 172.16.255.255   255.255.255.255   172.16.26.36     172.16.26.36       1
      224.0.0.0         224.0.0.0   172.16.26.36     172.16.26.36       1
255.255.255.255   255.255.255.255   172.16.26.36     172.16.26.36       1
```

There will be much more about the **route** command and the routing table later. For now, it is sufficient to notice that the address mask, listed here under the heading *Netmask*, is included in the routing table. NT is capable of understanding CIDR addresses.

Specifying both the address and the mask is cumbersome when writing out addresses. A shorthand notation has been developed for writing CIDR addresses.

* CIDR is pronounced "cider."

Instead of writing network 172.16.26.32 with a mask of 255.255.255.224, we can write 172.16.26.32/27 because the mask 255.255.255.224 is 27 bits long. The format of this notation is *address/prefix-length*, where *prefix-length* is the number of bits in the network portion of the address. Without this notation, the address 172.16.26.32 could easily be interpreted as a host address. RFC 1878 lists all 32 possible prefix values. But little documentation is needed because the CIDR prefix is much easier to understand and remember than are address classes. You know that 10.104.0.19 is a class A address, but writing it as 10.104.0.19/8 shows you that this address has 8 bits for the network number and therefore 24 bits for the host number. You don't have to remember anything about the class A address structure.

CIDR is an interim solution, though it is capable of providing address and routing relief for many more years. The long-term solution is to replace the current addressing scheme with a new one. In the TCP/IP protocol suite addressing is defined by the IP protocol. Therefore, to define a new address structure, the Internet Engineering Task Force (IETF) created a new version of IP called IPv6.*

IPv6 has a very large 128-bit address, so address depletion is not an issue. The large address also makes it possible to use a hierarchical address structure to reduce the burden on routers while still maintaining more than enough addresses for future network growth. Other benefits of IPv6 are:

- Improved security built into the protocol
- Simplified, fixed-length, word-aligned headers to speed header processing and reduce overhead
- Improved techniques for handling header options

IPv6 has several good features but it is still a few years from widespread availability. In the meantime, the current generation of TCP/IP should be more than adequate for your network needs. On your network you will use IP and standard IP addressing.

Final notes on IP addresses

Not all network addresses or host addresses are available for use. We have already said that the addresses with a first byte greater than 223 cannot be used as host addresses. There are also two large pieces of the address space, 0.0.0.0/8 and 127.0.0.0/8, that are reserved for special uses. Network 0 designates the *default route* and network 127 is the *loopback address*. The default route is used to simplify the routing information that IP must handle. The loopback address simplifies

* The current release of IP is IP version 4 (IPv4). IP version 5 is an experimental Stream Transport (ST) protocol used for real-time data delivery.

network applications by allowing the local host to be addressed in the same manner as a remote host. We use these special network addresses when configuring a host.

There are also some host addresses reserved for special uses. In all network classes, host numbers 0 and 255 are reserved. An IP address with all host bits set to 0 identifies the network itself. For example, 10.0.0.0 refers to network 10, and 172.16.0.0 refers to network 172.16. Addresses in this form are used in routing table listings to refer to entire networks. An IP address with all host bits set to 1 is a *broadcast address*. A broadcast address is used to simultaneously address every host on a network. The broadcast address for network 172.16 is 172.16.255.255. A datagram sent to this address is delivered to every individual host on network 172.16.

IP addresses are often called host addresses. While this is common usage, it is slightly misleading. IP addresses are assigned to network interfaces, not to computer systems. A gateway, such as *thoth* (see Figure 2-1), has a different address for each network to which it is connected. The gateway is known to other devices by the address associated with the network that it shares with those devices. For example, *pooh* addresses *thoth* as 172.16.12.1, while external hosts address it as 10.104.0.19.

Systems can be addressed in three different ways. Individual systems are directly addressed by a host address, which is called a *unicast address*. A unicast packet is addressed to one individual host. Groups of systems can be addressed using a *multicast address*, for example, 224.0.0.9. Routers along the path from the source to the destination recognize the special address and route copies of the packet to each member of the multicast group.*

All systems on a network are addressed using the broadcast address, for example, 172.16.255.255. The broadcast address depends on the broadcast capabilities of the underlying physical network.

Subnets

The structure of an IP address can be locally modified by using host address bits as additional network address bits. Essentially, the dividing line between network address bits and host address bits is moved, creating additional networks, but reducing the maximum number of hosts that can belong to each network. These newly designated network bits define a network within the larger network, called a *subnet*.

---

* This is only partially true. Multicasting is not supported by every router. Sometimes it is necessary to tunnel through routers and networks by encapsulating the multicast packet inside a unicast packet.

Organizations usually decide to subnet in order to overcome topological or organizational problems. Subnetting allows decentralized management of host addressing. With the standard addressing scheme, a central administrator is responsible for managing host addresses for the entire network. By subnetting, the administrator can delegate address assignment to smaller organizations within the overall organization—which may be a political expedient, if not a technical requirement. If you don't want to deal with the data processing department, assign them their own subnet and let them manage it themselves.

Subnetting can also be used to overcome hardware differences and distance limitations. IP routers can link dissimilar physical networks together, but only if each physical network has its own unique network address. Subnetting divides a single network address into many unique subnet addresses, so that each physical network can have its own unique address.

A subnet is defined by changing the bit mask of the IP address. A *subnet mask* functions in the same way as a normal address mask: an *on* bit is interpreted as a network bit; an *off* bit belongs to the host part of the address. The difference is that a subnet mask is only used locally. In the outside world the address is still interpreted as a standard IP address.

Assume we have been assigned network address 172.16.0.0/16. The subnet mask associated with that address is 255.255.0.0. The subnet mask we use in most of our examples extends the network portion of the address by an additional byte, for example, 172.16.0.0/24. The subnet mask that does this is 255.255.255.0; all bits on in the first three bytes, and all bits off in the last byte. The first two bytes define the original network; the third byte defines the subnet address; the fourth byte defines the host on that subnet.

Many network administrators prefer byte-oriented masks because they are easy to read and understand when addresses are written in dotted decimal notation. However, limiting subnet masks to byte boundaries does not take advantage of their true power. The subnet mask is bit-oriented. We could subdivide 172.16.0.0/16 into 16 subnets with the mask 255.255.240.0; in other words, 172.16.0.0/20. Applying this mask defines the four high-order bits of the third byte as the subnet part of the address and the remaining 12 bits, 4 bits of the third byte and all of the fourth byte, as the host portion of the address. This creates 16 subnets that each contain more than four thousand host addresses, which may well be better suited to our network and organization. For example, we may have a small number of large subdivisions. Table 2-1 shows the subnets and host addresses produced by applying this subnet mask to network address 172.16.0.0/16.

Unless you're taking an exam, you shouldn't have to manually calculate a table like Table 2-1 to know what subnets and host addresses are produced by a subnet

Table 2-1. Effect of a Subnet Mask

Network Number	First Address	Last Address
172.16.0.0	172.16.0.1	172.16.15.254
172.16.16.0	172.16.16.1	172.16.31.254
172.16.32.0	172.16.32.1	172.16.47.254
172.16.48.0	172.16.48.1	172.16.63.254
172.16.64.0	172.16.64.1	172.16.79.254
172.16.80.0	172.16.80.1	172.16.95.254
172.16.96.0	172.16.96.1	172.16.111.254
172.16.112.0	172.16.112.1	172.16.127.254
172.16.128.0	172.16.128.1	172.16.143.254
172.16.144.0	172.16.144.1	172.16.159.254
172.16.160.0	172.16.160.1	172.16.175.254
172.16.176.0	172.16.176.1	172.16.191.254
172.16.192.0	172.16.192.1	172.16.207.254
172.16.208.0	172.16.208.1	172.16.223.254
172.16.224.0	172.16.224.1	172.16.239.254
172.16.240.0	172.16.240.1	172.16.254.254

mask. The calculations have already been done for you. RFC 1878 lists all possible subnet masks and the valid addresses they produce.

Organizations have been discouraged from subnetting class C addresses because of the fear that subnetting reduces the number of host addresses to increase the number of network addresses. A class C network is limited to fewer than 255 host addresses. Further limiting the number of hosts would reduce the utility of a class C address. The mask 255.255.255.192 divides a class C address into four subnets of 64 host addresses. The fear is that the subnet address of all 0s and the subnet address of all 1s will not be usable. This leaves only two subnets; and because host addresses of all 1s and all 0s are also unusable, the remaining two subnets can only address 62 hosts. Therefore the address space of this class C network number is reduced from 254 hosts to 124 hosts. The fear of subnetting class C addresses is no longer justified.

Originally the RFCs implied that you should not use subnet numbers of all 0s or all 1s. However, RFC 1812, *Requirements for IP Version 4 Routers*, makes it clear that subnets of all 0s and all 1s are legal and should be supported by all routers. Some older routers do not allow the use of these addresses despite the newer RFCs. Updating router software or hardware should make it possible for you to reliably subnet class C addresses.

Class C subnets are used when very small networks are needed for specialized network equipment, such as terminal servers, cluster controllers, or routers. In some configurations an entire subnet may be consumed for the link between two routers. In this case only two host addresses are needed, one for the router at each end of the link. A subnet mask of 255.255.255.252 applied to a class C address creates 64 subnets each containing four host addresses. In a special case this might be just what is needed.

Whether the address is divided in network and host parts by address class rules, a classless address mask, or a subnet mask, the constituent parts of the address are both used to deliver the data. IP uses the network portion of the address to route the datagram between networks. The full address, including the host information, is used to make final delivery when the datagram reaches the destination network. In the next two sections we look at both of these delivery processes. First we look at how network addresses are used in the routing table, and then we discuss how IP addresses are mapped to physical addresses for final delivery.

The Routing Table

Gateways route data between networks; but all network devices, hosts as well as gateways, must make routing decisions. For most hosts, the routing decisions are simple:

- If the destination host is on the local network, the data is delivered to the destination host.
- If the destination host is on a remote network, the data is forwarded to a local gateway.

Because routing is network-oriented, IP makes routing decisions based on the network portion of the address. The IP module determines the network part of the destination's IP address by applying the network mask to the address. If the destination network is the local network, the mask that is applied may be the local subnet mask. If no mask is provided with the address, the address class determines the network portion of the address.

After determining the destination network, the IP module looks up the network in the local *routing table*.*

Packets are routed toward their destination as directed by the routing table. The routing table may be built by the system administrator or by routing protocols, but the end result is the same; IP routing decisions are simple table look-ups.

* This table is also called the *forwarding table*.

You can display the routing table's contents with the **netstat -nr** command or the **route print** command. The **-r** option tells **netstat** to display the routing table, and the **-n** option tells **netstat** to display the table in numeric form. It's useful to display the routing table in numeric form because the destination of most routes is a network, and networks are usually referred to by network numbers. The **route print** command displays the routing table in numeric format by default. Both commands display the routing table in exactly the same way. We use **route print** in this example and in some others we use **netstat**. Both of these commands are entered at the Windows NT command prompt (Start → Programs → Command Prompt).

The **route print** command displays the routing table with the following fields:

Network Address
: The destination network (or host) for this route.

Netmask
: The address mask used to determine the network portion of an address being matched against this route.

Gateway Address
: The address of the gateway used to reach the specified destination.

Interface
: The address of the network interface used by this route. The network interface is the network access hardware, such as an Ethernet card, installed in the NT computer. This is the address assigned to that card.

Metric
: The routing cost of transmitting packets via this route. As discussed in the section on the RIP routing protocol, the metric is used to select the best route to a destination. The metric has no real purpose for static routing.

The following is a sample routing table:

```
C:\>route print
Active Routes:
Network Address          Netmask  Gateway Address       Interface  Metric
        0.0.0.0          0.0.0.0      172.16.12.1     172.16.12.2       1
      127.0.0.0        255.0.0.0        127.0.0.1       127.0.0.1       1
    172.16.12.0    255.255.255.0      172.16.12.2     172.16.12.2       1
    172.16.12.2  255.255.255.255        127.0.0.1       127.0.0.1       1
 172.16.255.255  255.255.255.255      172.16.12.2     172.16.12.2       1
      224.0.0.0        224.0.0.0      172.16.12.2     172.16.12.2       1
255.255.255.255  255.255.255.255      172.16.12.2     172.16.12.2       1
     172.16.1.0    255.255.255.0      172.16.12.3     172.16.12.2       1
     172.16.3.0    255.255.255.0      172.16.12.3     172.16.12.2       1
     172.16.4.0    255.255.255.0      172.16.12.3     172.16.12.2       1
```

The first table entry is the *default route*. The default route is one of the reserved network numbers mentioned earlier: 0.0.0.0. The gateway specified in this entry is the *default gateway*. The default gateway is used whenever there is no specific route in the table for a destination network address. For example, this routing table has no entry for network 172.16.16.0. If IP receives any datagrams addressed to this network, it will send the datagram via the default gateway 172.16.12.1.

Another unique entry in the routing table is the *loopback route* for the local host. This is the loopback address mentioned earlier as another reserved network number. Because every system uses the loopback route to send datagrams to itself, this entry is in every host's routing table.

You can tell from the sample routing table display that this host (*pooh*) is directly connected to network 172.16.12.0. The routing table entry for that network does not specify an external gateway; i.e., the routing table entry for 172.16.12.0 specifies *pooh* (172.16.12.2) as the route to that network.

All of the gateways that appear in a routing table are on networks directly connected to the local system. In the sample just shown this means that, regardless of the destination address, the gateway addresses all begin with 172.16.12.*

This is the only network to which *pooh* is directly attached, and therefore it is the only network to which *pooh* can directly deliver data. The gateways that *pooh* uses to reach the rest of the Internet must be on *pooh's* subnet.

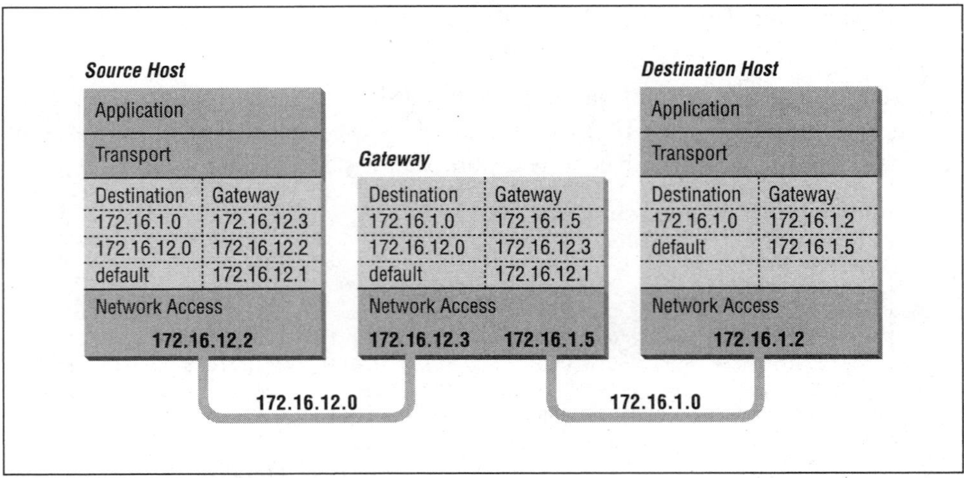

Figure 2-3. Table-based routing

* The loopback address appears to be an exception to this, but the loopback network is not a real network. It is a software construct.

In Figure 2-3, the IP layer of each host and gateway on our imaginary network is replaced by a small piece of a routing table, showing destination networks and the gateways used to reach those destinations. When the source host (172.16.12.2) sends data to the destination host (172.16.1.2), it first determines that 172.16.1.2 is the local network's official address and applies the subnet mask. (Network 172.16.0.0 is subnetted using the mask 255.255.255.0.) After applying the subnet mask, IP knows that the destination's network address is 172.16.1.0. The routing table in the source host shows that data bound for 172.16.1.0 should be sent to gateway 172.16.12.3. Gateway 172.16.12.3 makes direct delivery through its 172.16.1.5 interface. Examining the routing tables shows that all systems list only gateways on networks they are directly connected to. Note that 172.16.12.1 is the default gateway for both 172.16.12.2 and 172.16.12.3. But because 172.16.1.2 cannot reach network 172.16.12.0 directly, it has a different default route.

A workstation's routing table does not contain end-to-end routes. A route points only to the next gateway, called the *next hop*, along the path to the destination network. The workstation relies on the local gateway to deliver the data, and the gateway relies on other gateways. As a datagram moves from one gateway to another, it should eventually reach one that is directly connected to its destination network. It is this last gateway that finally delivers the data to the destination host.

Address Resolution

The IP address and the routing table direct a datagram to a specific physical network, but when data travels across a network, it must obey the physical layer protocols used by that network. The physical networks that underlay the TCP/IP network do not understand IP addressing. Physical networks have their own addressing schemes, and there are as many different addressing schemes as there are different types of physical networks. One task of the network access protocols is to map IP addresses to physical network addresses.

The most common example of this network access layer function is the translation of IP addresses to Ethernet addresses. The protocol that performs this function is *Address Resolution Protocol* (ARP), which is defined in RFC 826.

The ARP software maintains a table of translations between IP addresses and Ethernet addresses. This table is built dynamically. When ARP receives a request to translate an IP address, it checks for the address in its table. If the address is found, it returns the Ethernet address to the requesting software. If the address is not found in the table, ARP broadcasts a packet to every host on the Ethernet. The packet contains the IP address for which an Ethernet address is sought. If a receiving host identifies the IP address as its own, it responds by sending its Ethernet address back to the requesting host. The response is then cached in the ARP table.

The **arp** command displays the contents of the ARP table. The **arp** command is run from the Windows NT command prompt (Start → Programs → Command Prompt). To display the entire ARP table, use the **arp -a** command. Individual entries can be displayed by specifying a host name or address after the **-a** option on the **arp** command line. For example, to check the entire ARP table on a Windows NT system, enter:

```
C:\>arp -a
Interface: 172.16.12.1 on Interface 1
 Internet Address      Physical Address      Type
 172.16.12.11          00-00-c0-e5-07-c7     dynamic
 172.16.12.2           00-40-9a-00-04-eb     dynamic
 172.16.12.95          00-20-af-0f-9c-77     dynamic
 172.16.12.97          08-00-20-10-71-80     dynamic
 172.16.12.102         08-00-69-07-99-20     dynamic
 172.16.12.110         08-00-5a-09-c3-46     dynamic
 172.16.12.126         08-00-20-0c-7b-95     dynamic
 172.16.12.138         00-a0-24-ea-06-8d     dynamic
 172.16.12.145         08-00-69-0a-47-2e     dynamic
 172.16.12.147         08-00-20-8d-26-3e     dynamic
 172.16.12.152         00-a0-24-8d-e9-27     dynamic
 172.16.12.172         08-00-69-0a-40-db     dynamic
 172.16.12.173         00-e0-29-00-be-44     dynamic
 172.16.12.181         00-20-af-16-95-b0     dynamic
 172.16.12.182         00-60-97-5b-69-62     dynamic
 172.16.12.191         00-60-b0-70-9b-8f     dynamic
```

This table tells you that when *thoth* forwards datagrams addressed to *pooh*, it puts those datagrams into Ethernet frames and sends them to Ethernet address 00-40-9a-00-04-eb. The entry in the sample table was added dynamically as a result of a query. The keyword *dynamic* in the *Type* field tells us that. It is also possible to have static entries added manually by the system administrator. Chapter 11, *Troubleshooting TCP/IP*, tells you how to add static entries and why you might want to.

ARP tables normally don't require any attention because they are built automatically by the ARP protocol, which is very stable. However, if things go wrong, the ARP table can be manually adjusted. See the section in Chapter 12, *Network Security*, called "Troubleshooting with the **arp** Command."

Protocols, Ports, and Sockets

Once data is routed through the network and delivered to a specific host, it must be delivered to the correct user or process. As the data moves up or down the layers of TCP/IP, a mechanism is needed to deliver data to the correct protocols in each layer. The system must be able to combine data from many applications into a few transport protocols, and from the transport protocols into the Internet Protocol. Combining many sources of data into a single data stream is called *multiplexing*. Data arriving from the network must be *demultiplexed*: divided for delivery to multiple processes. To accomplish this, IP uses *protocol numbers* to identify transport protocols, and the transport protocols use *port numbers* to identify applications.

Some protocol and port numbers are reserved to identify *well-known services.* Well-known services are standard network protocols, such as FTP and TELNET, that are commonly used throughout the network. The protocol numbers and port numbers allocated to well-known services are documented in the *Assigned Numbers* RFC. Windows NT systems define protocol and port numbers in two simple text files.

Protocol Numbers

The protocol number is a single byte in the third word of the datagram header. The value identifies the protocol in the layer above IP to which the data should be passed.

On an NT system, the protocol numbers are defined in the *protocol* file.* This file is a simple table containing the protocol name and the protocol number associated with that name. The format of the table is a single entry per line, consisting of the official protocol name, separated by white space from the protocol number. The protocol number is separated by white space from the *alias* for the protocol name. Comments in the table begin with #.

```
C:\>type %SystemRoot%\system32\drivers\etc\protocol
# Copyright (c) 1993-1995 Microsoft Corp.
#
# This file contains the Internet protocols as defined by RFC 1060
# (Assigned Numbers).
#
# Format:
#
# <protocol name> <assigned number> [aliases...] [#<comment>]

ip       0   IP       # Internet protocol
icmp     1   ICMP     # Internet control message protocol
ggp      3   GGP      # Gateway-gateway protocol
tcp      6   TCP      # Transmission control protocol
egp      8   EGP      # Exterior gateway protocol
pup      12  PUP      # PARC universal packet protocol
udp      17  UDP      # User datagram protocol
hmp      20  HMP      # Host monitoring protocol
xns-idp  22  XNS-IDP  # Xerox NS IDP
rdp      27  RDP      # "reliable datagram" protocol
rvd      66  RVD      # MIT remote virtual disk
```

* This and many other TCP/IP configuration files are found in the *%SystemRoot%\system32\drivers\etc* directory. *%SystemRoot%* is an environment variable that contains the name of the top level Windows NT directory. For example, *C:\WINNT.*

The listing shown here is the contents of the *protocol* file that comes with an NT 4.0 workstation. This list of numbers is by no means complete. If you refer to the Protocol Numbers section of the *Assigned Numbers* RFC, you'll see many more protocol numbers. However, a system only needs to include the numbers of the protocols that it actually uses. Even the list shown here is more than this specific workstation needed, but the additional entries do no harm.

What exactly does this table mean? When a datagram arrives and its destination address matches the local IP address, the IP layer knows that the datagram has to be delivered to one of the transport protocols above it. To decide which protocol should receive the datagram, IP looks at the datagram's protocol number. Using this table you can see that, if the datagram's protocol number is 6, IP delivers the datagram to TCP. If the protocol number is 17, IP delivers the datagram to UDP. TCP and UDP are the two transport layer services we are concerned with, but all of the protocols listed in the table use IP datagram delivery service directly. Some, such as ICMP, EGP, and GGP, have already been mentioned. You don't need to be concerned with the minor protocols.

Port Numbers

After IP passes incoming data to the transport protocol, the transport protocol passes the data to the correct application process. Application processes (also called *network services*) are identified by port numbers, which are 16-bit values. The source port number, which identifies the process that sent the data, and the destination port number, which identifies the process that is to receive the data, are contained in the first header word of each TCP segment and UDP packet.

Port numbers are not unique between transport layer protocols; the numbers are only unique within a specific transport protocol. In other words, TCP and UDP can, and do, both assign the same port numbers. It is the combination of protocol and port numbers that uniquely identifies the specific process to which the data should be delivered.

On Windows NT systems, port numbers are defined in the *services* file.* There are many more network applications than there are transport layer protocols, as the size of the table shows. Part of the *services* file from a Windows NT 4.0 workstation is shown here. The format of this file is very similar to the *protocol* file. Each single-line entry starts with the official name of the service, separated by white space from the port number/protocol pairing associated with that service. The port numbers are paired with transport protocol names, because different transport protocols may use the same port number. An optional list of aliases for the official service name may be provided after the port number/protocol pair.

---

* This file is in the *%SystemRoot%\system32\drivers\etc* directory.

```
# Copyright (c) 1993-1995 Microsoft Corp.
#
# This file contains port numbers for well-known services as defined by
# RFC 1060 (Assigned Numbers).
#
# Format:
#
# <service name> <port number>/<protocol> [aliases...] [#<comment>]
#
echo             7/tcp
echo             7/udp
discard          9/tcp     sink null
discard          9/udp     sink null
systat           11/tcp
systat           11/tcp    users
daytime          13/tcp
daytime          13/udp
netstat          15/tcp
qotd             17/tcp    quote
qotd             17/udp    quote
chargen          19/tcp    ttytst source
chargen          19/udp    ttytst source
ftp-data         20/tcp
ftp              21/tcp
telnet           23/tcp
smtp             25/tcp    mail
```

This table, combined with the *protocol* table, provides all of the information necessary to deliver data to the correct application. A datagram arrives at its destination based on the destination address in the fifth word of the datagram header. Using the protocol number in the third word of the datagram header, IP delivers the data from the datagram to the proper transport layer protocol. The first word of the data delivered to the transport protocol contains the destination port number that tells the transport protocol to pass the data up to a specific application. Figure 2-4 shows this delivery process.

Despite its size, the *services* file does not contain the port number of every well-known application. *Remote Procedure Call* (RPC) services use a different technique for reserving ports that doesn't involve registering well-known port numbers. When an RPC service starts, it picks any unused port number and registers that number with the *portmapper*. The *portmapper* is a program that keeps track of the port numbers being used by RPC services. When a client wants to use an RPC service, it queries the *portmapper* running on the server to discover the port assigned to the service. The client can find *portmapper* because it is assigned well-known port 111. *portmapper* makes it possible to install well-known services without formally obtaining a well-known port. Windows NT supports the portmapper and RPC service.

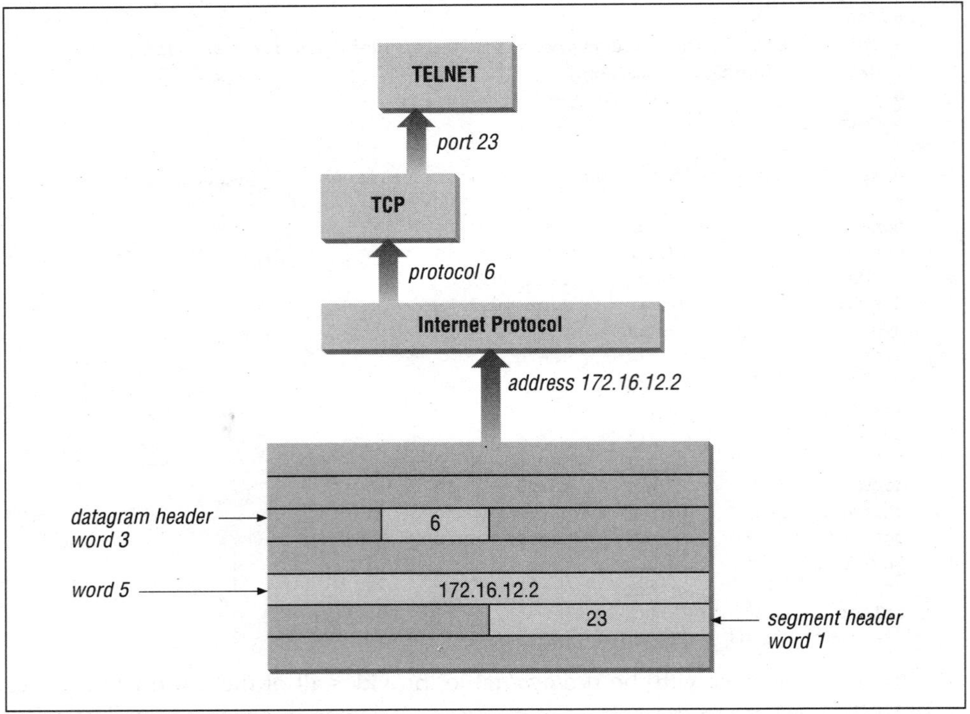

Figure 2-4. Protocol and port numbers

Sockets

Well-known ports are standardized port numbers that enable remote computers to know which port to connect to for a particular network service. This simplifies the connection process because both the sender and receiver know in advance that data bound for a specific process will use a specific port. For example, all systems that offer TELNET do so on port 23.

There is a second type of port number called a *dynamically allocated port*. As the name implies, dynamically allocated ports are not pre-assigned. They are assigned to processes when needed. The system ensures that it does not assign the same port number to two processes, and that the numbers assigned are above the range of standard port numbers.

Dynamically allocated ports provide the flexibility needed to support multiple users. If a TELNET user is assigned port number 23 for both the source and destination ports, what port numbers are assigned to the second concurrent TELNET user? To uniquely identify every connection, the source port is assigned a dynamically allocated port number, and the well-known port number is used for the destination port.

In the TELNET example, the first user is given a random source port number and a destination port number of 23 (TELNET). The second user is given a different random source port number and the same destination port. It is the pair of port numbers, source and destination, that uniquely identifies each network connection. The destination host knows the source port, because it is provided in both the TCP segment header and the UDP packet header. Both hosts know the destination port because it is a well-known port.

Figure 2-5 shows the exchange of port numbers during the TCP handshake. The source host randomly generates a source port, in this example 3044. It sends out a segment with a source port of 3044 and a destination port of 23. The destination host receives the segment, and responds back using 23 as its source port and 3044 as its destination port.

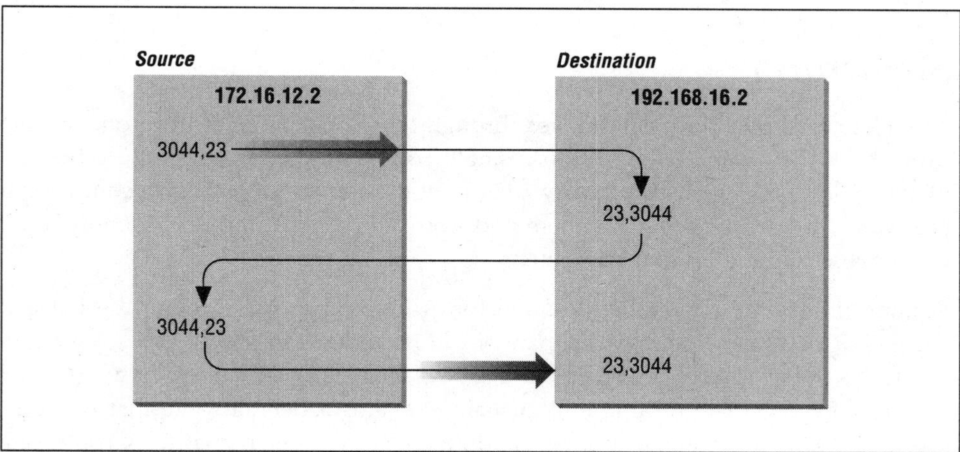

Figure 2-5. Passing port numbers

The combination of an IP address and a port number is called a *socket*. A socket uniquely identifies a single network process within the entire Internet. Sometimes the terms *socket* and *port number* are used interchangeably. In fact, well-known services are frequently referred to as *well-known sockets*. In the context of this discussion, a *socket* is the combination of an IP address and a port number. A pair of sockets, one socket for the receiving host and one for the sending host, define the connection for connection-oriented protocols such as TCP.

Let's build on the example of dynamically assigned ports and well-known ports. Assume a user on host 172.16.12.2 uses TELNET to connect to host 172.16.16.2. Host 172.16.12.2 is the source host. The user is dynamically assigned a unique port number—3382. The connection is made to the TELNET service on the remote host which is, according to the standard, assigned well-known port 23. The socket for the source side of the connection is 172.16.12.2.3382 (IP address 172.16.12.2 plus port number 3382). For the destination side of the connection, the socket is 172.16.16.2.23 (address 172.16.16.2 plus port 23). The port of the destination socket is known by both systems because it is a well-known port. The port of the source socket is known, because the source host informed the destination host of the source socket when the connection request was made. The socket pair is therefore known by both the source and destination computers. The combination of the two sockets uniquely identifies this connection; no other connection in the Internet has this socket pair.

Networks, computers, and the applications within a computer can all be identified by special numeric values—IP addresses, protocol numbers, port numbers, and sockets. In the next chapter we discuss a network service that allows us to refer to computer systems by name instead of by number.

Summary

This chapter shows how data moves through the global Internet from one specific process on the source computer to a single cooperating process on the other side of the world. TCP/IP uses globally unique addresses to identify any computer in the world. It uses protocol numbers and port numbers to uniquely identify a single process running on that computer.

Routing directs the datagrams destined for a remote process through the maze of the global network. Routing uses part of the IP address to identify the destination network. Every system maintains a routing table that describes how to reach remote networks. The routing table usually contains a default route that is used if the table does not contain a specific route to the remote network. A route only identifies the next computer along the path to the destination. TCP/IP uses hop-by-hop routing to move datagrams one step closer to the destination until the datagram finally reaches the destination network.

Routes are disseminated through the network by routing protocols. Routing protocols collect routing information, select the best route to a destination, and use that information to build the routing table. Interior routing protocols provide routing information to gateways within an autonomous system. Exterior routing protocols pass routing information between autonomous systems. Windows NT systems generally do not run routing protocols. But when they do, they run interior routing protocols. The two most popular interior routing protocols are *Open Shortest Route First* (OSPF) and *Routing Information Protocol* (RIP).

At the destination network, final delivery is made by using the full IP address (including the host part) and converting that address to a physical layer address. An example of the type of protocol used to convert IP addresses to physical layer addresses is *Address Resolution Protocol* (ARP). It converts IP addresses to Ethernet addresses for final delivery.

The first two chapters described the structure of the TCP/IP protocol stack and the way in which it moves data across a network. In the next chapter we move up the protocol stack to look at the type of services the network provides to simplify configuration and use.

3

Network Services

In this chapter:
- *Names and Addresses*
- *The Host Table*
- *LMHOSTS*
- *Domain Name System*
- *Windows Internet Name Service*
- *Mail Services*
- *Dynamic Host Configuration Protocol*
- *Summary*

Some network servers provide essential computer-to-computer services. These differ from application services in that they are not directly accessed by end users. Instead these services are used by networked computers to simplify the installation, configuration, and operation of the network.

The functions performed by the servers covered in this chapter are varied:

- Name service for converting IP addresses to host names.
- Configuration servers that simplify the installation of networked hosts by handling part or all of the TCP/IP configuration.
- Electronic mail services for moving mail through the network from the sender to the recipient.

Servers on a TCP/IP network differ from traditional PC LAN servers. Every host on a TCP/IP network can be both a server and a client. The hosts on a TCP/IP network are peers. All systems are equal. The network is not dependent on any one server. All of the services discussed in this chapter can be installed on one or several systems on a network.

We begin with a discussion of name service. It is an essential service that you will certainly use on your network.

Names and Addresses

The Internet Protocol document* defines names, addresses, and routes as follows:

> A name indicates what we seek. An address indicates where it is. A route indicates how to get there.

Names, addresses, and routes all require the network administrator's attention. Routes and addresses are covered in the previous chapter. This section discusses names and how they are disseminated throughout the network. Every network interface attached to a TCP/IP network is identified by a unique 32-bit IP address. A name (called a *host name*) can be assigned to any device that has an IP address. Names are assigned to devices because, compared to numeric Internet addresses, names are easier to remember and type correctly. The network software doesn't require names, but they do make it easier for humans to use the network.

In most cases, host names and numeric addresses can be used interchangeably. A user wishing to **telnet** to the workstation at IP address 172.16.12.2 can enter:

```
C:\>telnet 172.16.12.2
```

or use the host name associated with that address and enter the equivalent command:

```
C:\>telnet pooh.ttgnet.com
```

Whether a command is entered with an address or a host name, the network connection always takes place based on the IP address. The system converts the host name to an address before the network connection is made. The network administrator is responsible for assigning names and addresses and storing them in the database used for the conversion.

There are two common methods used to organize computer system names:

- Flat name space. Uses a simple one-part name to identify each host. Using a flat name space, each host name must be unique within the network. For example, once the name *pooh* has been assigned to a host, no other host on that network can be assigned that name.
- Hierarchical name space. Subdivides the network into multiple named parts called domains. Each host name must be unique within a domain, but may be duplicated in other domains on the same network. For example, a host named *pooh.ttgnet.com* and another host named *pooh.oreilly.com* may exist within the same network—in this case, the Internet.

---

* RFC 791, *Internet Protocol*, Jon Postel, ISI, 1981, page 7.

Originally, both NetBIOS and TCP/IP used a flat name space. This was a workable solution in the early days of networking, when few networks existed and those that did were seldom interconnected. In today's environment, however, using a flat name space is inadequate, for the following reasons:

- Limited name availability. A good computer name is short, easily remembered, and meaningful. In a flat name space, all the good computer names are taken quickly, and you find yourself assigning essentially random names to your hosts.
- Centralized administration requirements. In a flat name space, a centralized naming authority is needed to ensure unique host names. The central authority assigns every host name. You probably can't get the name you want, and you have to wait to get it. Our editor tells us that an engineering net he once worked on had a flat namespace. One consequence was that it took about 3 weeks to get a name for a new machine. As workstations replaced terminals, the flood of name requests brought that whole naming system to its knees.

Clearly, something better than a flat name space is needed. That something is a hierarchical name space. Just as the Windows NT directory structure allows you to have duplicate file names in different directories, a hierarchical naming structure allows you to have duplicate computer names in different domains.

Using a hierarchical name space also minimizes or eliminates the need for a central administrative authority. In a hierarchical name space, administration devolves to the local level. If, for example, you're the administrator responsible for the domain *ttgnet.com*, you can name your hosts anything you'd like.

A central naming authority is still needed, but the degree to which it is involved in the naming process is determined by the extent to which the networks in question are interconnected. Internet names are centralized at the first and second levels. You cannot, for example, just decide on your own that your Internet domain will be *widget.com* or *gadget.org*. InterNIC is responsible for guaranteeing uniqueness at levels one and two. On the other hand, private networks running Microsoft Networking use any Windows NT domain name they please. In fact, given the Windows NT installation default, it's a safe bet that a significant number of Windows NT domains are named simply *DOMAIN*. This doesn't cause any problems because, although many of these identically named networks are internetworked with TCP/IP, they do not communicate across the internetwork using Microsoft protocols.

Because both TCP/IP and NetBIOS started with a flat name space, the original method of name resolution was to simply look up the host name in a flat file called a *host table*. The file that contains TCP/IP host names is *HOSTS* and the file that contains NetBIOS host names is *LMHOSTS*.* Now, however, both TCP/IP and NetBIOS use a hierarchical name space. The hierarchical system is built on a distributed database system. The database system used to translate TCP/IP host names to addresses is called *Domain Name System* (DNS). The database system used for NetBIOS names is called *Windows Internet Name Service* (WINS). We discuss all of these files and database systems in this book. We'll examine the host tables first.

The Host Table

The *host table* is a simple text file that associates IP addresses with host names. On NT systems, the table is in the file *%SystemRoot%\System32\Drivers\etc\hosts*. Each table entry in the *hosts* file contains an IP address separated by white space from a list of host names associated with that address. Comments begin with #.

The host table on the workstation *pooh* might contain the following entries:

```
#
# Table of IP addresses and host names
#
172.16.12.2     pooh.ttgnet.com pooh
127.0.0.1       localhost
172.16.12.1     thoth.ttgnet.com thoth www
172.16.12.4     wotan.ttgnet.com wotan
172.16.12.3     kerby.ttgnet.com kerby
172.16.1.2      kiwi.ttgnet.com kiwi
172.16.6.10     thor.sales.ttgnet.com thor.sales thor
```

The first entry in the sample table is for *pooh* itself. The IP address 172.16.12.2 is associated with the host name *pooh.ttgnet.com* and the alternate host name (or alias) *pooh*. The host name and all of its aliases resolve to the same IP address, in this case 172.16.12.2.

Aliases provide for name changes, alternate spellings, and shorter host names. They also allow for generic host names. Look at the entry for 172.16.12.1. One of the aliases associated with that address is *www*. *www* is the generic name most users expect to find when searching for information via the Web. Other commonly used generic host names are *ns* for name servers, *mailhost* for mail servers, and *news* for network news servers.

The second entry in the sample file assigns the address 127.0.0.1 to the host name *localhost*. As we have discussed, the network address 127.0.0.0 is reserved for the loopback network. The host address 127.0.0.1 is a special address used to designate the loopback address of the local host—hence the host name *localhost*. This

* Both of these files are found in the *%SystemRoot%\System32\Drivers\etc* directory.

special addressing convention allows the host to address itself the same way it addresses a remote host. The loopback address simplifies software by allowing common code to be used for communicating with local or remote processes. This addressing convention also reduces network traffic because the *localhost* address is associated with a loopback device that loops data back to the host before it is written out to the network.

Although the host table system has been superseded by DNS, it is still widely used for the following reasons:

- Most systems have a small host table containing name and address information about the important hosts on the local network. This small table is used when DNS is not running, such as during the initial system startup. Even if you use DNS, you should create a small *hosts* file containing entries for your host, for *localhost*, and for the gateways and servers on your local net.
- Very small sites that are not connected to the Internet sometimes use the host table. If there are few local hosts and the information about these hosts rarely changes, and there is no need to communicate via TCP/IP with remote sites, then there is little advantage to using DNS.

The old host table system is inadequate for the global Internet for two reasons: inability to scale and lack of an automated update process. We have already addressed the problems with scaling a flat name space. A flat space simply lacks sufficient unique names and requires too much central administration. There is no way that a flat file system could provide adequate service for the enormous number of hosts in today's Internet.

Another problem with the host table system is that it lacks a technique for automatically distributing information about newly registered hosts. Newly registered hosts can be referenced by name as soon as a site receives the new version of the host table. However, there is no way to guarantee that the host table is distributed to a site. The lack of guaranteed uniform distribution is a major weakness of the host table system. Today, of course, the host table has been superseded by DNS for all but the smallest applications. All hosts connected to the Internet necessarily use DNS.

Translating names into addresses isn't simply a local issue. The command **telnet pooh.ttgnet.com** is expected to work correctly on every host that's connected to the network. If *pooh.ttgnet.com* is connected to the Internet, hosts all over the world should be able to translate the name *pooh.ttgnet.com* into the proper address. Therefore, some facility must exist for disseminating the host name information to all hosts on the network. The host table lacks this facility.

TCP/IP host names are not the only computer names used by Windows NT. Microsoft networking is based on NetBIOS and most NT systems also have a

NetBIOS computer name. These names must be converted to IP addresses when NetBIOS connections are made over a TCP/IP network. NT can use a flat file for NetBIOS to IP address resolution. It is the *LMHOSTS* file.

LMHOSTS

The *LMHOSTS* file looks exactly like a *hosts* file and functions in a similar way. The difference is that the *LMHOSTS* file maps NetBIOS names to IP addresses, and the *hosts* file maps TCP/IP host names to IP addresses. A sample *LMHOSTS* file shows how similar these two files look:

```
172.16.6.16         anubis
172.16.6.10         thor
172.16.6.7          theodore
```

Each entry in an *LMHOSTS* file contains an IP address that is separated by whitespace from the NetBIOS name associated with that address. An entry must not exceed a single line and comments begin with the pound sign (#). The *LMHOSTS* file is stored in the *%SystemRoot%\system32\drivers\etc* directory.

The *LMHOSTS* file does have some features that are not supported by the *host* file. These special commands begin with pound signs (#) so that older Microsoft operating systems will treat them as comments, allowing the same file to be used on both NT systems and older operating systems. The NT commands are:

`#PRE`
: Causes the entry to be pre-loaded into the cache and permanently retained there. Normally entries are only cached when they are used for name resolution and are only retained in the cache for a few minutes. Use `#PRE` to speed up address resolution for frequently used host names.

`#DOM:`***`domain`***
: Identifies NT domain controllers. The ***`domain`*** variable is the name of the NT domain for which this system is a controller. Every domain controller in the *LMHOSTS* file should be identified by a `#DOM` command. If you don't use NT domains, this command is not needed.

`#INCLUDE` *`<UNC path and filename>`*
: Specifies a remote file that should be incorporated in the local *LMHOSTS* file. This allows a centrally maintained *LMHOSTS* file to be automatically loaded. To provide redundant sources for *LMHOSTS*, enclose a group of `#INCLUDE` commands inside a pair of `#BEGIN_ALTERNATE` and `#END_ALTERNATE` statements. The system tries the various sources in order and stops as soon as it successfully downloads one copy of the *LMHOSTS* file.

The following *LMHOSTS* file contains examples of all of these commands. The first line of the file assigns the IP address 172.16.6.16 to the NetBIOS host *anubis*, which is the Windows NT domain controller for the domain *ACCOUNTS*. The **#PRE** command is combined with **#DOM** to pre-load the address of the NT domain controller. The second line simply assigns the IP address 172.16.6.10 to the NetBIOS name *thor*. Next we assign the address 172.16.6.7 to *theodore* and we load that address into the cache with the **#PRE** command. The **#BEGIN_ALTERNATE** and **#END_ALTERNATE** commands enclose the network paths to additional sources of address information. The two **#INCLUDE** statements define the alternate sources of *LMHOSTS* information. Notice that the address of *theodore*, the system specified in the second **#INCLUDE** statement, is defined in this file. If a source of *LMHOSTS* information is not in the local broadcast area, the address of that source must be included in the file.

```
172.16.6.16       anubis    #PRE #DOM:ACCOUNTS
172.16.6.10       thor
172.16.6.7        theodore    #PRE
#BEGIN_ALTERNATE
#INCLUDE \\mandy\admin\lmhosts
#INCLUDE \\theodore\admin\lmhosts
#END_ALTERNATE
```

The cache is pre-loaded during the system boot. Additional information is added to the cache every time the system references the *LMHOSTS* file, but only the entry used to resolve an address is added. When you add new **#PRE** entries to the *LMHOSTS* file they are not cached unless you reboot the system or flush the existing cache and force it to reload with the **nbtstat -R** command. The **nbtstat -cf** command shows the entries that are currently cached.

Even for the small networks normally served by NetBIOS, the flat file system has been superseded by a distributed database system called Windows Internet Name Service (WINS). We cover WINS later in the chapter. We begin our discussion of the distributed database systems that implement the hierarchical name space with a discussion of Domain Name System (DNS)—the distributed database that converts TCP/IP host names to IP addresses.

Domain Name System

The Domain Name System (DNS) overcomes both major weaknesses of the host table:

- DNS scales well. It doesn't rely on a single large table; it is a distributed database system that doesn't bog down as the database grows. DNS currently provides information on approximately 16,000,000 hosts, while fewer than 10,000 were ever listed in the host table.
- DNS guarantees that new host information will be disseminated to the rest of the network as it is needed.

Information is automatically disseminated, and only to those who are interested. Here's how it works. If a DNS server receives a request for information about a host for which it has no information, it passes on the request to an *authoritative server.* An authoritative server is any server responsible for maintaining accurate information about the domain being queried. When the authoritative server answers, the local server saves (*caches*) the answer for future use. The next time the local server receives a request for this information, it answers the request itself. The ability to control host information from an authoritative source and to automatically disseminate accurate information makes DNS superior to the host table, even for networks not connected to the Internet.

The Domain Hierarchy

DNS is a distributed hierarchical system for resolving host names into IP addresses. Under DNS, there is no central database with all of the Internet host information. The information is distributed among thousands of name servers organized into a hierarchy similar to the hierarchy of the filesystem. DNS has a *root domain* at the top of the domain hierarchy that is served by a group of name servers called the *root servers*.

Just as directories in the NT filesystem are found by following a path from the root directory through subordinate directories to the target directory, information about a domain is found by tracing pointers from the root domain through subordinate domains to the target domain.

Directly under the root domain are the *top-level domains*. There are two basic types of top-level domains—geographic and organizational. Geographic domains have been set aside for each country in the world, and are identified by a two-letter code. For example, the United Kingdom is domain UK, Japan is JP and the United States is US. When US is used as the top-level domain, the second-level domain is usually a state's two-letter postal abbreviation (e.g., WY for Wyoming). US geographic domains are usually used by state governments and K through 12 schools and are not widely used for other hosts within the United States.

Within the United States, most systems are registered in organizational top-level domains. Membership in these domains is based on the type of organization (commercial, military, etc.) to which the system belongs.* The top-level domains used in the United States are:

COM
: commercial organizations

* There is no relationship between the organizational and geographic domains in the US. Each system belongs to either an organizational domain *or* a geographical domain, not both.

EDU
: educational institutions

GOV
: government agencies

MIL
: military organizations

NET
: network support organizations, such as network operation centers

INT
: international governmental or quasi-governmental organizations

ORG
: organizations that don't fit in any of the above, such as non-profit organizations

Several proposals have been made to increase the number of top-level domains. The proposed domains are called *generic top level domains* or gTLDs. The proposals call for the creation of additional top-level domains and for the creation of new registrars to manage the domains. One motivation for these efforts is the huge size of the *.com* domain. It is so large some people feel it will be difficult to maintain an efficient *.com* database. But the biggest motivation for creating new gTLDs is money. All of the current domains are handled by a single registrar—the InterNIC. It charges $70 for the first two years and $35 a year thereafter for domain registration. Some people see the InterNIC as a profitable monopoly. They have asked for the opportunity to create their own domain registration businesses. A quick way to respond to that request is to create more official top-level domains and more registrars. The best known gTLDs proposal is the one from the *International Ad Hoc Committee* (IAHC). The initial IAHC proposal suggested the following new generic top-level domains:

FIRM
: businesses or firms

STORE
: businesses selling goods

WEB
: organizations emphasizing the World Wide Web

ARTS
: cultural and entertainment organizations

REC
: recreational and entertainment organizations

INFO
: sites providing information services

NOM
: individuals or organizations that want to define a personal nomenclature

Will the IAHC proposal be adopted? Will it be modified? Will another proposal win out? We don't know. There are several other proposals, and as you would expect when money is involved, plenty of controversy. At this writing the only official organizational domain names are: COM, EDU, GOV, MIL, NET, INT, and ORG.

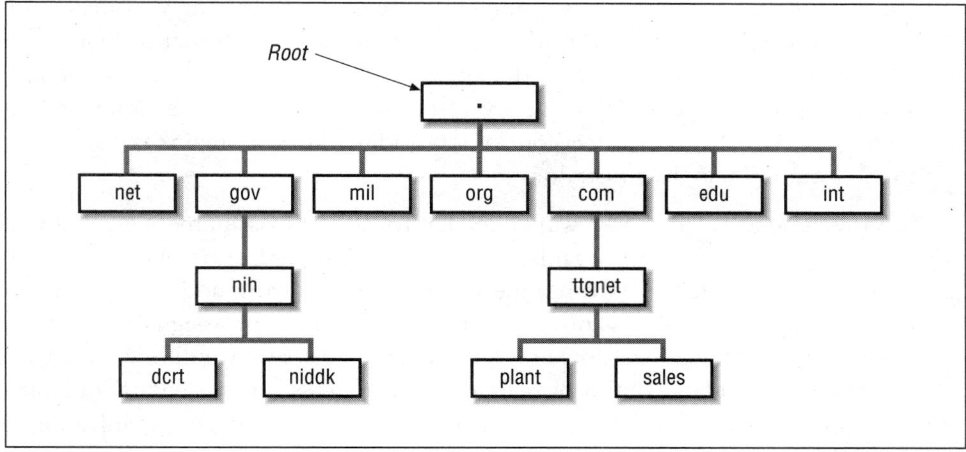

Figure 3-1. Domain hierarchy

Figure 3-1 illustrates the domain hierarchy by using the organizational top-level domains. At the top is the root. Directly below the root domain are the top-level domains. The root servers only have complete information about the top-level domains. No servers, not even the root servers, have complete information about all domains, but the root servers have pointers to the servers for the second-level domains.* So while the root servers may not know the answer to a query, they know who to ask.

Creating Domains and Subdomains

The Network Information Center has the authority to allocate domains. To obtain a domain, you apply to the InterNIC for authority to create a domain under one of the top-level domains. Once the authority to create a domain is granted, you can create additional domains, called *subdomains*, under your domain. Let's look at how this works for our imaginary network.

* Figure 3-1 shows two second-level domains: *nih* under *gov* and *ttgnet* under *com*.

Our company is a commercial profit-making (we hope) enterprise. It clearly falls into the *com* domain. We apply to the registrar for authority to create a domain named *ttgnet* within the *com* domain. The request for the new domain contains the host names and addresses of at least two servers that will provide name service for the new domain. (Chapter 4, *Getting Started*, discusses applying for a domain name.) When the registrar approves the request, it adds pointers in the *com* domain to the new domain's name servers. Now when queries are received by the root servers for the *ttgnet.com* domain, the queries are referred to the new name servers.

The registrar's approval grants us complete authority over our new domain. Any registered domain has authority to divide its domain into subdomains. Our imaginary company can create separate domains for the sales organization (*sales.ttgnet.com*) and for the production facility (*plant.ttgnet.com*). This is done without consulting the InterNIC. The decision to add additional subdomains is completely up to the local domain administrator.

Name assignment is, in some ways, similar to address assignment. A network address is assigned to an organization, and the organization assigns subnet addresses and host addresses within the range of that network address. Similarly, a domain is assigned to an organization, and the organization assigns subdomains and host names within that domain. The central registration authority delegates authority and distributes control over names and addresses to individual organizations. Once that authority has been delegated, the individual organization is responsible for managing the names and addresses it has been assigned.

The parallel between subnet and subdomain assignment can cause confusion. Subnets and subdomains are not linked. A subdomain may contain information about hosts from several different networks. Creating a new subnet does not require creating a new subdomain, and creating a new subdomain does not require creating a new subnet.

A new subdomain becomes accessible when pointers to the servers for the new domain are placed in the domain above it (see Figure 3-1). Remote servers cannot locate the *ttgnet.com* domain until a pointer to its server is placed in the *com* domain. Likewise, the subdomains *sales* and *plant* cannot be accessed until pointers to them are placed in *ttgnet.com*. The DNS database record that points to the name servers for a domain is the NS (*name server*) record. This record contains the name of the domain and the name of the host that is a server for that domain. Chapter 8, *Configuring DNS Name System*, discusses the actual DNS database. For now, let's just think of these records as pointers.

Figure 3-2 illustrates how the NS records are used as pointers. A local server has a request to resolve *thor.sales.ttgnet.com* into an IP address. The server has no

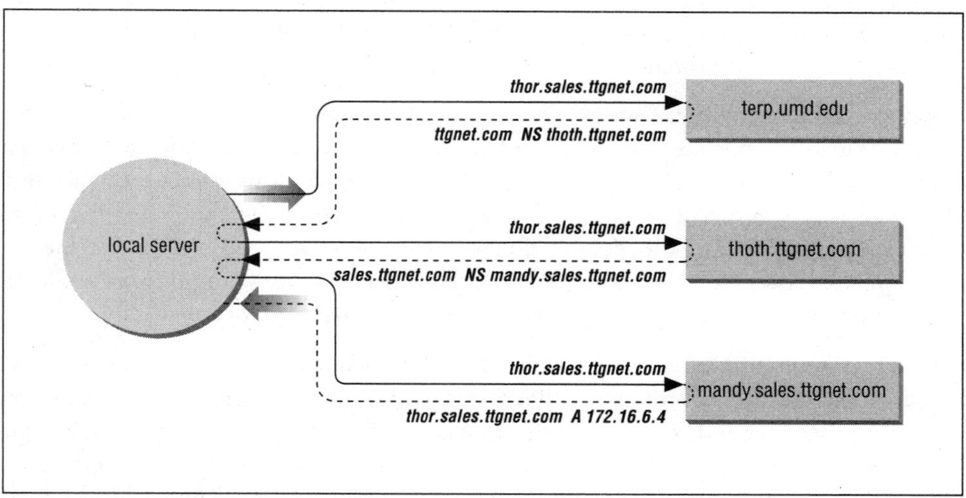

Figure 3-2. Non-recursive query

information on *ttgnet.com* in its cache, so it queries a root server (*terp.umd.edu* in our example) for the address. The root server replies with an NS record that points to *thoth.ttgnet.com* as the source of information on *ttgnet.com*. The local server queries *thoth*, which in turn points to *mandy.sales.ttgnet.com* as the server for *sales.ttgnet.com*. The local server then queries *mandy.sales.ttgnet.com*, and finally receives the desired IP address. The local server caches the A (address) record and each of the NS records. The next time it has a query for *thor.sales.ttgnet.com*, it will answer the query itself. And the next time the server has a query for other information in the *ttgnet.com* domain, it will go directly to *thoth* without involving a root server.

Figure 3-2 is an example of a non-recursive query. In a *non-recursive* query, the remote server tells the local server who to ask next. The local server must follow the pointers itself. In a *recursive* search, the remote server follows the pointers and returns the final answer to the local server. The root servers generally perform only non-recursive searches.

Domain Names

Domain names reflect the domain hierarchy. Domain names are written from most specific (a host name) to least specific (a top-level domain), with each part of the domain name separated by a dot.*

* The root domain is identified by a single dot, i.e., the root name is a null name written simply as "`.`".

A *fully qualified domain name* (FQDN) starts with a specific host and ends with a top-level domain. *pooh.ttgnet.com.* is the FQDN of workstation *pooh*, in the *ttgnet* domain, of the *com* domain.

Domain names are not always written as fully qualified domain names. Sometimes domain names are written relative to a *default domain* in the same way that file names are written relative to the current (default) working directory. DNS adds the default domain to the user input when constructing the query for the name server. For example, if the default domain is *ttgnet.com*, a user can omit the *ttgnet.com* extension for any host names in that domain. *thoth.ttgnet.com* could be addressed simply as *thoth*. DNS adds the default domain *ttgnet.com*.

On NT systems the extension is added to every host name request unless it *ends* with a dot, in other words, is qualified out to the root. For example, assume that there is a host named *thor* in the subdomain *sales* of the *ttgnet.com* domain. Further, assume that the default domain of the local host has been set to *ttgnet.com*. *thor.sales* does not end with a dot, so *ttgnet.com* is added to it giving the domain name *thor.sales.ttgnet.com*. The sample shown below is from a workstation running Windows NT 4.0.

```
C:\>ping thor.sales

Pinging thor.sales.ttgnet.com [172.16.6.10] with 32 bytes of data:

Reply from 172.16.6.10: bytes=32 time=40ms TTL=251
Reply from 172.16.6.10: bytes=32 time=20ms TTL=251
Reply from 172.16.6.10: bytes=32 time=20ms TTL=251
Reply from 172.16.6.10: bytes=32 time=20ms TTL=251
```

How the default domain is used and how queries are constructed varies depending on the operating system. It can even vary by release level. For this reason, you should exercise caution when embedding a host name in a program. Only a fully qualified domain name or an IP address is immune from changes in the name server software.

DNS Resolver and Server

DNS name service software is conceptually divided into two components—a resolver and a name server. The *resolver* is the software that forms the query; it asks the questions. The *name server* is the process that responds to the query; it answers the questions.

All computers resolve host names but not all computers act as a name server. A computer that does not run a local name server process and relies on other systems for all name service answers is called a *resolver-only* system. Resolver-only configurations are common on single user systems. Most NT workstations run resolver-only configurations.

Name servers are classified differently depending on how they are configured. The three main categories of name servers are:

primary
: The *primary server* is the server from which all data about a domain is derived. The primary server loads the domain's information directly from a disk file created by the domain administrator. Primary servers are *authoritative*, meaning they have complete information about their domain and their responses are always accurate. There should be only one primary server for a domain.

secondary
: Secondary servers transfer the entire domain database from the primary server. A particular domain's database file is called a *zone file*; copying this file to a secondary server is called a *zone file transfer*. A secondary server assures that it has current information about a domain by periodically transferring the domain's zone file. Secondary servers are also authoritative for their domain.

caching-only
: Caching-only servers get the answers to all name service queries from other name servers. Once a caching server has received an answer to a query, it caches the information and will use it in the future to answer queries itself. Most name servers cache answers and use them in this way. What makes the caching-only server unique is that this is the only technique it uses to build its domain database. Caching servers are *non-authoritative*, meaning that their information is secondhand and incomplete, though usually accurate.

The relationship between the different types of servers is an advantage that DNS has over the host table for most networks, even very small networks. Under DNS, there should be only one primary name server for each domain. DNS data is entered into the primary server's database by the domain administrator. Therefore, the administrator has central control of the host name information. An automatically distributed, centrally controlled database is an advantage for a network of any size. When you add a new system to the network, you don't need to modify the *hosts* files on every node in the network; you only modify the DNS database on the primary server. The information is automatically disseminated to the other servers by full zone transfers or by caching single answers. Chapter 8 discusses the configuration of all types of DNS servers.

Windows Internet Name Service

Historically, Microsoft Networking meant small, peer networks running NetBIOS. NetBIOS was designed with small networks in mind. It was never intended to function in a large scale network environment, let alone in a TCP/IP internetworking environment. When Microsoft decided to extend their networking to encompass the enterprise, they had to find a way to incorporate NetBIOS into the enterprise network. Their solution is an implementation of NetBIOS-over-TCP/IP as defined in the Internet standards:

- RFC1001 *Protocol standard for a NetBIOS service on a TCP/UDP transport: Concepts and methods*. This RFC provides an overview of NetBIOS over TCP/IP protocols, focusing on underlying concepts rather than on implementation details.
- RFC 1002 *Protocol standard for a NetBIOS service on a TCP/UDP transport: Detailed specifications*. This RFC defines the detailed implementation issues for NetBIOS over TCP/IP, including packet definitions, protocols, and so forth.

NetBIOS names must map to IP addresses to run NetBIOS-over-TCP/IP. The Microsoft Windows Internet Name Service (WINS) is a centralized dynamic database that maps NetBIOS resource names to IP addresses. WINS overcomes the administrative burdens and functional limitations associated with using other methods NetBIOS name resolution like static *LMHOSTS* files and IP broadcasts.

Each host running NetBIOS over TCP/IP is uniquely identified by two names: the Windows Computer Name, which is also called the NetBIOS name, and the DNS host name. The computer name and the DNS host name are assigned by the system administrator. Although nothing requires that the NetBIOS computer name and the DNS host name be identical for a particular machine, most administrators choose to use the same name for both purposes. Doing otherwise is a leading cause of insanity among network administrators.

The process of translating back and forth between people-friendly names and the corresponding computer-friendly IP addresses is called *resolution*. Resolving an unknown address from a known name is called *address resolution*. Resolving an unknown name from a known address is called *name resolution*. The DNS and WINS servers are the tools you will install to perform these tasks.

Name service is not the only service that you will install on your network. Another service that you are sure to use is electronic mail.

Mail Services

Electronic mail is an important network service because it is used for interpersonal communications. Some applications are newer and fancier. Other applications consume more network bandwidth. Others are more important for the continued operation of the network. But email is the application people use to communicate with each other. It isn't very fancy, but it's vital.

TCP/IP provides a reliable, flexible email system built on a few basic protocols. These are: *Simple Mail Transfer Protocol* (SMTP), *Post Office Protocol* (POP), and *Multipurpose Internet Mail Extensions* (MIME). There are other TCP/IP mail protocols. However, these are the basic mail protocols. Our coverage concentrates on the three protocols you are most likely to use building your network: SMTP, POP, and MIME. We start with SMTP, the foundation of all TCP/IP email systems.

Simple Mail Transfer Protocol

SMTP is the TCP/IP mail delivery protocol. It moves mail across the Internet and across your local network. SMTP is defined in RFC 821, *A Simple Mail Transfer Protocol*. It runs over the reliable, connection-oriented service provided by Transmission Control Protocol (TCP), and it uses well-known port number 25.[*]

Table 3-1 lists some of the simple, human-readable commands used by SMTP.

Table 3-1. SMTP Commands

Command	Syntax	Function
Hello	`HELO` <***sending-host***>	Identify sending SMTP
From	`MAIL FROM:`<***from-address***>	Sender address
Recipient	`RCPT TO:`<***to-address***>	Recipient address
Data	`DATA`	Begin a message
Reset	`RSET`	Abort a message
Verify	`VRFY` <***string***>	Verify a username
Expand	`EXPN` <***string***>	Expand a mailing list
Help	`HELP` [***string***]	Request online help
Quit	`QUIT`	End the SMTP session

SMTP is such a simple protocol you can literally do it yourself. Telnet to port 25 on a remote host and type mail directly into the telnet window using the SMTP commands. This technique is sometimes used to test a remote system's SMTP server, but we use it here to illustrate how mail is delivered between systems.

To Telnet to a specific port add the port number to the **telnet** command when it is entered at the Windows NT command prompt. You can use either the numeric value for the port or the name associated with the numeric value in the *services* file. An example of entering the port number at the command prompt is:

```
C:\>telnet thoth.ttgnet.com 25
```

[*] Most standard TCP/IP applications are assigned a well-known port in the *Assigned Numbers RFC*, so that remote systems know how to connect the service.

Once the connect is made, SMTP commands can be entered directly in the telnet window.*

The sample lines here show the commands, and the responses to those commands, that could be input through the telnet window:

```
220 thoth ready at Tue, 19 Nov 97 17:21:26 EST
helo pooh.ttgnet.com
250 thoth Hello pooh.ttgnet.com, pleased to meet you
mail from:<daniel@pooh.ttgnet.com>
250 <daniel@pooh.ttgnet.com>... Sender ok
rcpt to:<tyler@thoth.ttgnet.com>
250 <tyler@thoth.ttgnet.com>... Recipient ok
data
354 Enter mail, end with "." on a line by itself
Hi Tyler!
.
250 Mail accepted
quit
221 thoth delivering mail
Connection closed by foreign host.
```

In the example, mail is manually input from Daniel on *pooh.ttgnet.com* to Tyler on *thoth.ttgnet.com*. The user input is shown in bold type. All of the other lines are output from the system. The example shows how simple it is. A TCP connection is opened. The sending system identifies itself. The *From* address and the *To* address are provided. The message transmission begins with the **data** command and ends with a line that contains only a period (.). The session terminates with a **quit** command. Very simple, and very few commands are used.

SMTP provides direct end-to-end mail delivery. Most other mail systems use *store and forward* protocols like X.400 that move mail toward its destination one hop at a time, storing the complete message at each hop and then forwarding it on to the next system. The message proceeds in this manner until final delivery is made. Figure 3-3 illustrates both store and forward and direct delivery mail systems. The UUCP email address clearly shows the path that the mail takes to its destination, while the SMTP mail address implies direct delivery.†

Direct delivery allows SMTP to deliver mail without relying on intermediate hosts. If the delivery fails, the local system knows it right away. It can inform the user who sent the mail or queue the mail for later delivery without reliance on remote systems. The disadvantage of direct delivery is that it requires both systems to be fully capable of handling mail. Some systems cannot handle mail, particularly small desktop systems or mobile systems such as laptops. These systems are usually shut

* You may need to enable Local Echo through the Terminal Preference box to see the SMTP commands as you type them.

† The address doesn't have anything to do with whether or not a system is store and forward or direct delivery. It just happens that UUCP provides an address that helps to illustrate this point.

down at the end of the day and are frequently offline. Mail directed from a remote host fails with a *cannot connect* error when the local system is turned off or offline. To handle these cases, features in the DNS system are used to route the message to a mail server in lieu of direct delivery. The mail is then moved from the server to the client system when the client is back online. The protocol most TCP/IP networks use for this task is POP.

Post Office Protocol

There are two versions of POP in widespread use: POP2 and POP3. POP2 is defined in RFC 937 and POP3 is defined in RFC 1725. POP2 uses port 109 and POP3 uses port 110. These are incompatible protocols that use different commands, but they perform the same basic functions. The POP protocols verify the user's logon name and password, and move the user's mail from the server to the user's local mail reader. POP3 is the more recent protocol and it is the one provided by Windows NT software.

A sample POP3 session clearly illustrates how a POP protocol works. POP3 is a simple request/response protocol, and just as with SMTP, you can type POP3 commands directly into its well-known port (110) and observe their effect. First telnet to the POP3 port on a mail server:

```
C:\>telnet thoth.ttgnet.com 110
```

Next enter the POP commands directly in the telnet window. Here's an example with the user input shown in bold type:

```
+OK thoth POP3 Server Process 3.3(1) at Mon 15-May-95 4:48PM-EDT
user hunt
+OK User name (hunt) ok. Password, please.
pass Watts?Watt?
+OK 3 messages in folder NEWMAIL (V3.3 Rev B04)
stat
+OK 3 459
retr 1
+OK 146 octets
 The full text of message 1
.
dele 1
+OK message # 1 deleted
retr 2
+OK 155 octets
 The full text of message 2
.
dele 2
+OK message # 2 deleted
retr 3
+OK 158 octets
 The full text of message 3
.
```

```
dele 3
+OK message # 3 deleted
quit
+OK POP3 thoth Server exiting (0 NEWMAIL messages left)
Connection closed by foreign host.
```

The **user** command provides the username and the **pass** command provides the password for the account of the mailbox that is being retrieved. (This is the same username and password used to log onto the mail server.) In response to the logon the server displays the number of messages in the mailbox, three in our example. The **stat** command causes the server to display the number of messages and the total number of bytes contained in those messages. **retr 1** retrieves the full text of message number 1. **dele 1** deletes message 1 from the server. We retrieve and delete messages until there are no more messages to be retrieved and the client ends the session with the **quit** command. Simple! Table 3-2 lists the full set of POP3 commands.

Table 3-2. POP3 Commands

Command	Syntax	Function
User	USER ***username***	The user's account name
Password	PASS ***password***	The user's password
Statistics	STAT	Display the number of unread messages/bytes
Retrieve	RETR ***n***	Retrieve message number ***n***
Delete	DELE ***n***	Delete message number ***n***
Last	LAST	Display the number of the last message accessed
List	LIST [***n***]	Display the size of message ***n*** or of all messages
Reset	RSET	Undelete all messages; reset message number to 1
Top	TOP ***n l***	Print the headers and ***l*** lines of message ***n***
No operation	NOOP	Do nothing
Quit	QUIT	End the POP3 session

Naturally you don't really type these commands in yourself, but experiencing hands-on interaction with SMTP and POP gives you a clearer understanding of what these programs do and why they are needed. Chapter 10, *Internet Information Server (IIS)*, describes how an SMTP server is installed and configured on a Windows NT server.

Multipurpose Internet Mail Extensions

The last email protocol on our quick tour is MIME. As its name implies, *Multipurpose Internet Mail Extensions* is an extension of the existing TCP/IP mail system, not a replacement for it. MIME is more concerned with what the mail system delivers than it is with the mechanics of delivery. It doesn't attempt to replace SMTP or TCP; it extends the definition of what constitutes mail.

The structure of the mail message carried by SMTP is defined in RFC 822, *Standard for the Format of ARPA Internet Text Messages*. RFC 822 defines a set of mail headers that are so widely accepted they are used by many mail systems that do not use SMTP. This is a great benefit to email because it provides a common ground for mail translation and delivery through gateways to different mail networks. MIME extends RFC 822 into two areas not covered by the original RFC:

- Support for various data types. The mail system defined by RFC 821 and RFC 822 only transfers 7-bit ASCII data. This is suitable for carrying text data composed of US ASCII characters, but it does not support several languages that have richer character sets and it does not support binary data transfer.
- Support for complex message bodies. RFC 822 does not provide a detailed description of the body of an electronic message. It concentrates on the mail headers.

MIME addresses these two weaknesses by defining encoding techniques for carrying various forms of data, and by defining a structure for the message body that allows multiple objects to be carried in a single message. The RFC 1521, *MIME (Multipurpose Internet Mail Extensions) Part One: Mechanisms for Specifying and Describing the Format of Internet Message Bodies*, defines two headers that give structure to the mail message body and allow it to carry various forms of data. These are the *Content-Type* header and the *Content-Transfer-Encoding* header.

As the name implies, the Content-Type header defines the type of data being carried in the message. The header has a Subtype field that refines the definition. Many subtypes have been defined since the original RFC was released. A current list of MIME types can be obtained from the Internet.*

The original RFC defines seven initial content types and a few subtypes:

text
: Text data. RFC 1521 defines text subtypes *plain* and *richtext*. Several subtypes have since been added, including *enriched* and *html*.

application
: Binary data. The primary subtype defined in RFC 1521 is *octet-stream*, which indicates the data is a stream of 8-bit binary bytes. One other subtype, *PostScript*, is defined in the standard. Since then more than 90 subtypes have been defined. They specify binary data formatted for a particular application. For example, *msword* is an application subtype.

---

* Go to *ftp://ftp.isi.edu/in-notes/iana/assignments/media-types* and retrieve the file *media-types*.

image
: Still graphic images. Two subtypes are defined in RFC 1521: *jpeg* and *gif*. More than 10 additional subtypes have since been added, including widely used image data standards such as *tiff*, *cgm*, and *g3fax*.

video
: Moving graphic images. The initially defined subtype was *mpeg*, which is a widely used standard for computer video data. A few others have since been added, including *quicktime*.

audio
: Audio data. The only subtype initially defined for audio was *basic*, which means the sounds are encoded using pulse code modulation (PCM).

multipart
: Data composed of multiple independent sections. A multipart message body is made up of several independent parts. RFC 1521 defines four subtypes. The primary subtype is *mixed*, which means that each part of the message can be data of any content type. Other subtypes are: *alternative*, meaning that the same data is repeated in each section in different formats; *parallel*, meaning that the data in the various parts is to be viewed simultaneously; and *digest*, meaning that each section is data of the type *message*. Several subtypes have since been added, including support for voice messages (*voice-message*) and *encrypted* messages.

message
: Data that is an encapsulated mail message. RFC 1521 defines three subtypes. The primary subtype, *rfc822*, indicates that the data is a complete RFC 822 mail message. The other subtypes, *partial* and *External-body*, are both designed to handle large messages. *partial* allows large encapsulated messages to be split among multiple MIME messages. *External-body* points to an external source for the contents of a large message body, so that only the pointer, not the message itself, is contained in the MIME message. Two additional subtypes have been defined: *news* for carrying network news, and *http* for HTTP traffic formatted to comply with MIME content typing.

The Content-Transfer-Encoding header identifies the type of encoding used on the data. Traditional SMTP systems only forward 7-bit ASCII data with a line length of less than 1000 bytes. To ensure that the data from a MIME system is forwarded through gateways that may only support 7-bit ASCII, the data can be encoded. RFC 1521 defines six types of encoding. Some types are used to identify the encoding inherent in the data. Only two types are actual encoding techniques defined in the RFC. The six encoding types are:

7bit
: US ASCII data. No encoding is performed on 7-bit ASCII data.

8bit

Octet data. No encoding is performed. The data is binary, but the lines of data are short enough for SMTP transport; in other words, the lines are less than 1000 bytes long.

binary

Binary data. No encoding is performed. The data is binary and the lines may be longer than 1000 bytes. There is no difference between *binary* and *8bit* data except the line length restriction; both types of data are unencoded byte (octet) streams. MIME does not handle unencoded bitstream data.

quoted-printable

Encoded text data. This encoding technique handles data that is largely composed of printable ASCII text. The ASCII text is sent unencoded, while bytes with a value greater than 127 or less than 33 are sent encoded as strings made up of the equal sign followed by the hexadecimal value of the byte. For example: the ASCII form feed character, which has the hexadecimal value of 0C, is sent as *=0C*. Naturally there's more to it than this—for example, the literal equal sign has to be sent as *=3D*, and the newline at the end of each line is not encoded. But this is the general idea of how *quoted-printable* data is sent.

base64

Encoded binary data. This encoding technique can be used on any bytestream data. Three octets of data are encoded as four 6-bit characters, which increases the size of the file by one-third. The 6-bit characters are a subset of U.S. ASCII, chosen because they can be handled by any type of mail system. The maximum line length for *base64* data is 76 characters. Figure 3-3 illustrates this 3-to-4 encoding technique.

x-token

Specially encoded data. It is possible for software developers to define their own private encoding techniques. If they do so, the name of the encoding technique must begin with *X–*. Doing this is strongly discouraged because it limits interoperability between mail systems.

The number of supported data types and encoding techniques grows as new data formats appear and are used in message transmissions. New RFCs constantly define new data types and encoding. Read the latest RFCs to keep up with MIME developments.

MIME defines data types that SMTP was not designed to carry. To handle these and other future requirements, RFC 1869, *SMTP Service Extensions*, defines a technique for making SMTP *extensible*. The RFC does not define new services for SMTP; in fact, the only service extensions mentioned in the RFC are defined in other RFCs. What this RFC does define is a simple mechanism for systems to negotiate which SMTP extensions are supported. The RFC defines a new *hello*

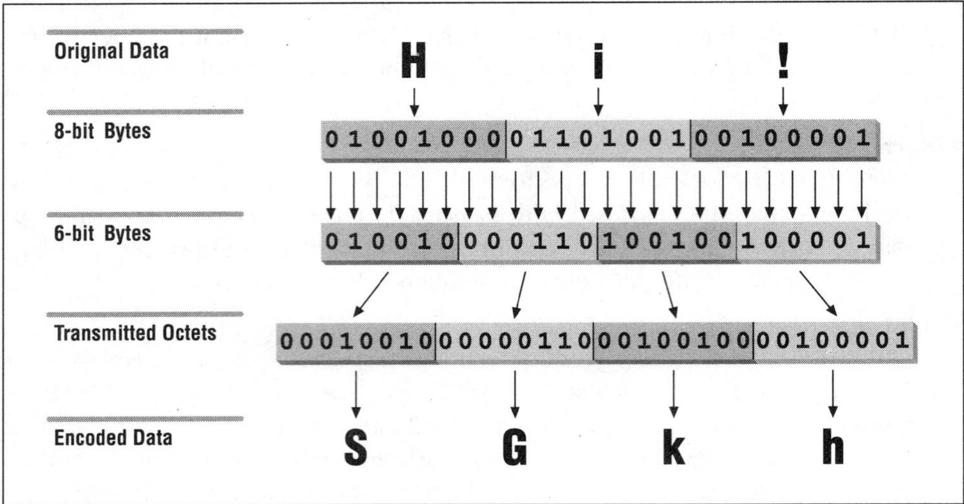

Figure 3-3. BASE64 encoding

command (EHLO) and the legal responses to that command. One response is for the receiving system to return a list of the SMTP extensions it supports. This response allows the sending system to know what extended services can be used, and to avoid those that are not implemented on the remote system. SMTP implementations that support the EHLO command are called Extended SMTP (ESMTP).

Several ESMTP service extensions have been defined for MIME mailers. Table 3-3 lists some of these. The table lists the EHLO keyword associated with each extension, the number of the RFC that defines it, and its purpose. These service extensions are just the beginning. Undoubtedly more will be defined to support MIME and other SMTP enhancements.

Table 3-3. SMTP Service Extensions

Keyword	RFC	Server Extension
8BITMIME	1652	Accept 8-bit binary data.
CHUNKING	1830	Accept messages cut into chunks.
CHECKPOINT	1845	Checkpoint/restart mail transactions.
PIPELINING	1854	Accept multiple commands in a single send.
SIZE	1870	Display maximum acceptable message size.
DSN	1891	Provide delivery status notifications.
ETRN	1985	Accept remote queue processing requests.
ENHANCEDSTATUSCODES	2034	Provide enhanced error codes.

It is easy to check which extensions are supported by your server by using the EHLO command. Telnet to port 25 of your mail server. Enter EHLO in response to the server's greeting. If the server supports Extended SMTP it will display the list of optional SMTP commands it supports. Otherwise it will display an error message. The specific SMTP extensions implemented on each operating system are different. The purpose of EHLO is to identify these differences at the beginning of the SMTP mail exchange.

ESMTP and MIME are important because they provide a standard way to transfer non-ASCII data through email. Users share lots of application-specific data that are not 7-bit ASCII. Many users depend on email as a file transfer mechanism.

SMTP, POP, and MIME are essential parts of the mail system. See Chapter 10 for information on installing the SMTP service that comes with Microsoft Internet Information Server software.

In the next section we look at the various types of TCP/IP configuration servers. The demand for easier installation and improved mobility may make configuration servers part of your network's future.

Dynamic Host Configuration Protocol

The powerful features that add to the utility and flexibility of TCP/IP also add to its complexity. TCP/IP is not as easy to configure as some other networking systems. TCP/IP requires that the configuration provide hardware, addressing, and routing information. It is designed to be independent of any specific underlying network hardware, so configuration information that can be built into the hardware in some network systems cannot be built in for TCP/IP. The information must be provided by the person responsible for the configuration. This assumes that every system is run by people who are knowledgeable enough to provide the proper information to configure the system. Unfortunately, this assumption does not always prove correct.

Dynamic Host Configuration Protocol (DHCP) servers make it possible for the network administrator to control TCP/IP configuration from a central point. This relieves the end user of some of the burden of configuration and improves the quality of the information used to configure systems.

The DCHP client broadcasts a request for TCP/IP configuration information. When a DHCP server receives the request, it returns a packet that contains an IP address and all of the other TCP/IP configuration parameters provided by the server. The exact exchange of packets between the client and the server is covered in Chapter 6, *Using Dynamic Host Configuration Protocol*. The result of the exchange is that the client obtains its configuration from the server.

The configuration parameters provided by a DHCP server can include everything defined in the *Requirements for Internet Hosts* RFC. DHCP provides a client with the complete set of TCP/IP configuration values. DHCP calls the configuration values *options*.

You don't usually need to use the full set of configuration options. Don't get us wrong. The parameters are needed for a complete TCP/IP configuration. It's just that you don't need to define values for them. Default values are provided in most TCP/IP implementations, and the defaults only need to be changed in special circumstances.

The expanded configuration parameters of DHCP make it the most complete TCP/IP configuration protocol, but for most network administrators automatic allocation of IP addresses is a more interesting feature. DHCP allows addresses to be assigned in three ways:

manual allocation
: The network administrator keeps complete control over addresses by specifically assigning them to clients. This is exactly the same way that addresses are handled under BOOTP.

automatic allocation
: The DHCP server permanently assigns an address from a pool of addresses. The administrator is not involved in the details of assigning a client an address.

dynamic allocation
: The server assigns an address to a DHCP client for a limited period of time. The limited life of the address is called a lease. The client can return the address to the server at any time, but must request an extension from the server to retain the address longer than the time permitted. The server automatically reclaims the address after the lease expires if the client has not requested an extension.

Dynamic allocation is useful in a large distributed network where many systems are being added and deleted. Unused addresses are returned to the pool of addresses without relying on users or system administrators to take action to return them. Addresses are only used when and where they're needed. Dynamic allocation allows a network to make the maximum use of a limited set of addresses. It is particularly well-suited to mobile systems that move from subnet to subnet and therefore must be constantly reassigned addresses appropriate for their current network location.

Dynamic address allocation does not work for every system. Name servers, email servers, logon hosts, and other shared systems are always online, and they are not mobile. These systems are accessed by name, so a shared system's domain name must resolve to the correct address. Shared systems are manually allocated permanent, fixed addresses.

Dynamic address assignment has major repercussions for DNS. DNS is required to map host names to IP addresses. It cannot perform this job if IP addresses change and DNS is not informed of the changes. To make dynamic address assignment work for all types of systems, we need a new DNS that can be dynamically updated by the DHCP server. The IETF is currently working on a standard for *Dynamic DNS*, but it is not fully operational.

Microsoft already integrates DHCP on both the client and the server with Microsoft Domain Name Service (DNS) and Windows Internet Name Service (WINS). To get the maximum benefits from this tight integration, you must run Microsoft operating systems on all of your servers and clients. On many networks that's not much of a hardship. NetWare servers, Macintosh clients, and other non-Microsoft DHCP devices on your network can still participate, although with a somewhat reduced level of integration.

Given the nature of dynamic addressing, most sites assign permanent fixed addresses to shared servers. This happens through traditional system administration and is not handled by DHCP. In effect, the administrator of the shared server is given an address and puts that address in the shared server's configuration. Using DHCP for some systems doesn't mean it must be used for all systems. The Windows NT DHCP server makes it easy to set aside some addresses for permanent assignment to systems that can't use DHCP while making all of the other addresses available for dynamic assignment to DHCP clients. The Windows NT DHCP server is covered in detail in Chapter 6, *Using Dynamic Host Configuration Protocol*.

Summary

TCP/IP provides some network services that simplify network installation, configuration, and use. Name service is one such service and it is used on every TCP/IP network.

Name service can be provided by a flat file called a host table, or by a distributed database. The host table for Internet host names is a simple text file named *hosts*. The host table for NetBIOS names is a text file called *LMHOSTS*. Most systems have a small host table, but they cannot be used in all cases because they are not scalable and do not have a standard method for automatic distribution. DNS, which is a TCP/IP standard, does scale. DNS is a hierarchical, distributed database system that provides host name and address information for all of the systems in the Internet. WINS, which is a Microsoft package, is a distributed database system for NetBIOS name resolution.

Simple Mail Transfer Protocol (SMTP), Post Office Protocol (POP), and Multipurpose Internet Mail Extensions (MIME) are the building blocks of a TCP/IP email network. SMTP is a simple request/response protocol that provides end-to-end mail delivery. Sometimes end-to-end mail delivery is not suitable and the mail must be routed to a mail server. TCP/IP mail servers can use POP to move the mail from the server to the end system where it is read by the user. SMTP can only deliver 7-bit ASCII data. MIME extends the TCP/IP mail system so that it can carry a wide variety of data.

Many configuration values are needed to install TCP/IP. These values can be provided by a configuration server. Dynamic Host Configuration Protocol (DHCP) provides the full set of configuration parameters defined in the *Requirements for Internet Hosts* RFC. It also provides for *dynamic address* allocation, which allows a network to make maximum use of a limited set of addresses.

This chapter concludes our introduction to the architecture, protocols, and services of a TCP/IP network. In the next chapter we begin to look at how to install a TCP/IP network by examining the process of planning an installation.

In this chapter:

- *To Connect or Not to Connect*
- *Basic Information*
- *Planning Routing*
- *Planning Naming Service*
- *Other Services*
- *Informing the Users*
- *Summary*

4

Getting Started

In this chapter, our emphasis shifts from how TCP/IP functions to how it is configured. Chapters 1 through 3 describe the TCP/IP protocols and how they work. Now we begin to explore the network configuration process. The first step in this process is planning. Before configuring a host to run TCP/IP, you must have certain information. At the very least, every host must have a unique IP address and host name. You should also decide on the items below before configuring a system:

default gateway address
: If the system communicates with TCP/IP hosts that are not on its local network, a default gateway address may be needed. Alternatively, if a routing protocol is used on the network, each device needs to know what protocol it is.

name server addresses
: To resolve host names into IP addresses, each host needs to know the addresses of the domain name servers.

domain name
: Hosts using the domain name service must know their correct domain name.

subnet mask
: To communicate properly, each system on a network segment must use the same subnet mask.

WINS server address
: If you run a WINS server to resolve NetBIOS host names, every Microsoft system on the network should know the name and address of the WINS server.

The network administrator is responsible for making and communicating decisions about overall network configuration. If you're the network administrator make sure you provide the necessary configuration information to the system administrators on your network. If you're a system administrator, make sure you find out the answers from your network administrator before putting the system online.

If you have an established TCP/IP network, you can skip several sections in this chapter, but you may still want to read about selecting hostnames, planning mail systems, and other topics that affect mature networks as much as they do new networks. If you are creating a new TCP/IP network, you will have to make some basic decisions. Will the new network connect to the Internet? If it will, how is the connection to be made? How should the network number be chosen? How do I register a domain name? How do I choose host names? In the following sections, we cover the information you need to make these decisions.

To Connect or Not to Connect

That is the question! First, you must decide whether or not your new network will be directly connected to the Internet. A distinction is made between networks connected to the Internet and those that are not connected. A *connected network* is directly attached to the Internet and has full access to other networks on the Internet. A *non-connected network* is not directly attached to the Internet, and its access to Internet networks is limited. An example of a non-connected network is a TCP/IP network that attaches to the outside world via a mail gateway at America Online (AOL). Users on the network can send mail to Internet hosts but they cannot directly telnet to one of them.

Many TCP/IP networks are not connected to the Internet. On these networks, TCP/IP is used for communication between the organization's various networks. Private networks that interconnect the various parts of an organization are often called *enterprise networks*. When those private networks use the information service applications that are built on top of TCP/IP, particularly Web servers and browsers, to distribute internal information, those networks are called *intranets*.

There are a few basic reasons why many sites do not connect to the Internet. One reason is security. Connecting to any network gives more people access to your system. Connecting to a global network with millions of users is enough to scare any security expert. There is no doubt about it: connecting to the Internet increases the security risks for your computer. Chapter 12, *Network Security*, covers some techniques for reducing this risk.

Cost versus benefit is another consideration. Many organizations do not see sufficient value in an Internet connection. For some organizations, low use or limited requirements, such as only needing email access, make the cost of an Internet connection exceed the benefit. For others, the primary reason for an Internet connection is to provide information about their products. It is not necessary to connect the entire enterprise network to the Internet to do this. It is often sufficient to connect a single Web server to the local Internet Service Provider (ISP) or to buy Web services from an ISP to provide information to your customers.

Other organizations consider an Internet connection an essential requirement. Educational and research institutions depend on the Internet as a source of information. Many companies use it as a means of delivering service and support to their customers.

You may have both types of networks: a non-connected enterprise network sitting behind a security firewall, and a small connected network that provides services to your external customers and proxy service for your internal users.

Unless you have carefully determined what your needs are and what an Internet connection will cost, you cannot know whether an Internet connection is right for your organization. Your local Internet service provider (ISP) can give you the various cost and performance alternatives. The next section offers ways to locate appropriate ISPs.

Network Contacts

Choosing an ISP for your network can be confusing. Currently more than 5,000 ISPs operate in the United States alone. No attempt is made to list them all here. Instead we provide pointers to where you can obtain information on ISPs via email, newsgroups, the Web, and in print.

Readers who want basic information about the Internet can start by reading a book about the Internet. My favorite is *The Whole Internet Users Guide and Catalog*, by Ed Krol. It provides a user-oriented focus on the Internet and a substantial list of ISPs.

If you can send email to the Internet, request information about the ISPs in your area by sending mail to *zahner@aimnet.com* with the words "MY AREA CODE =" followed by your telephone area code in both the subject line and the body of the message.

Use network news to obtain information about ISPs from the newsgroups *alt.internet.services* and *alt.internet.services.wanted*. Monitor *alt.internet.services* for announcements. Post a query to *alt.internet.services.wanted* asking if anyone knows of a good ISP in your area. Generally people in newsgroups have strong opinions and are willing to share them!

A good source of information about service providers is *The List* from Mecklermedia, which is accessible on the Web at *http://thelist.iworld.com*. The List contains information on thousands of ISPs. The information is sorted into country code and telephone area code lists to make it more useful.

Ask prospective ISPs about services as well as prices. Some ISPs specialize in providing low-cost service to home users. They emphasize price. However, if you are connecting a full network to the Internet, you may want an ISP that can provide network address, name service, Web services, and other features that your network might need.

Basic Information

Regardless of whether or not you decide to connect your network to the Internet, one thing is certain: you should build your enterprise network using the TCP/IP protocols. To do so, you must provide certain basic information to configure the physical TCP/IP network interface. The network interface needs an IP address and may also need a subnet mask. In this section we look at how the network administrator arrives at each of the required values.

Obtaining an IP Address

Every interface on a TCP/IP network must have a unique IP address. If a host is part of the Internet, its IP address must be unique within the entire Internet. If a host's TCP/IP communications are limited to a local network, its IP address only needs to be unique locally. Administrators whose networks will not be connected to the Internet select an address from RFC 1918, *Address Allocation for Private Internets*, which lists network numbers that are reserved for private use.*

The private network numbers are:

- Class A network 10.0.0.0 (10/8 prefix and a 24-bit block of addresses).
- Class B networks 172.16.0.0 to 172.31.0.0 (172.16/12 prefix and a 20-bit block of addresses).
- Class C networks 192.168.0.0 to 192.168.255.0 (192.168/16 prefix and a 16-bit block of addresses).

Networks connecting to the Internet must obtain official network addresses. An official address is needed for every system on your network that *directly* exchanges data with remote Internet hosts.†

Obtain the address from your ISP. Your ISP may have been delegated authority over a group of network addresses, and should be able to assign you a network number. If your local ISP doesn't offer this service, perhaps the ISP's upstream

* The address (172.16.0.0) used in this book is an address set aside for use by non-connected enterprise networks. Feel free to use this address on your network if it will not be connected to the Internet.

† Hosts that communicate with the Internet through a firewall or proxy server may not need official addresses. Check your firewall/proxy server documentation.

provider does. Ask your local ISP who it receives service from and ask that organization for an address. If all else fails you may be forced to go directly to an Internet registry. The box *Internet Registries* provides information about the Internet registry services. The form required for registering an address is available at *ftp://rs.internic.net/templates/internet-number-template.txt*. Use the application as a last resort to obtain an address.

Internet Registries

The original network information center was the SRI NIC, *sri-nic.arpa*. In 1992 the NIC moved to *nic.ddn.mil* and became the DDN NIC. Then in April 1993 the registration, directory, and information services it provided for the Internet moved to the new Internet NIC, *internic.net*. The InterNIC still provides these services but it does not do so alone.

Almost every large network has its own network information center. Most of these NICs provide access to all the RFCs, FYIs, and other TCP/IP documentation. A few provide registration services. For the Internet to work properly, IP addresses and domain names must be unique. To guarantee this, addressing authority is carefully delegated. Authority to delegate domains and addresses has been given to the Internet Resource Registries (IRR). Currently these are: RIPE for Europe, APNIC for Asia and the Pacific, CA*net for Canada, RNP for Brazil, and InterNIC for the rest of us. More registries may be created at any time.[a]

Additionally, large groups of addresses have been delegated to ISPs so that they can assign them to their customers.

The place to start looking for registry services is your ISP. If it does not provide these services, contact the InterNIC. You can contact the InterNIC at the postal address:

Network Solutions InterNIC Registration Services, 505 Huntmar Park Drive, Herndon, VA 22070

You can also reach the InterNIC via telephone at 1-703-742-4777 or via fax at 1-703-742-4811.

All of the forms needed to register an address, domain name, or other essential value can be obtained from the InterNIC using either anonymous FTP[b] or a Web browser. Obtain the forms via anonymous FTP from *rs.internic.net*, where they are stored in the *templates* directory. Via the Web, connect to the Registration Template Guide at *http://rs.internic.net/help/templates.html*. It provides links to all of the forms and descriptions of when they are used and how they are filled in.

[a] See the discussion of generic top-level domains (gTLDs) in Chapter 3, *Network Services*.

[b] How to use anonymous FTP is explained in Chapter 13, *Information Resources*.

The advantage to obtaining your address from an Internet registry is that you will not have to change your address in the future if you do connect to the Internet. However, the InterNIC strongly encourages you to obtain your IP address from an ISP rather than applying directly to InterNIC for your own block of addresses to avoid wasting IP addresses and to slow the growth of routing tables. There is a downside to using addresses provided by your ISP. Addresses provided by your ISP belong to the ISP rather than to you. This means they aren't portable. If you decide to change ISPs, you must change your IP address assignments network-wide to use the addresses provided by your new ISP. In effect, using addresses provided by an ISP locks you into that ISP.

To avoid this problem use DHCP on your network. DHCP allows you to easily change to the address provided by your new ISP when you switch ISPs. Using DHCP you change only the DHCP server configuration and the few static addresses assigned to servers and routers to recast the addresses for an entire network. If you are not running DHCP, you will need to change the IP configurations individually for each machine on your network.

The advantages to choosing a network address from RFC 1918 are that you do not have to apply for an official address and you save address space for those who do need to connect to the Internet.*

If you do choose an address from RFC 1918 it is possible to use DHCP to simplify the renumbering process but it is also possible to connect to the Internet without renumbering all of your systems. It will, of course, take some effort. You'll need a *network address translation* (NAT) box or a proxy server. NAT is available as a separate piece of hardware or as an optional piece of software in some routers and firewalls. It works by converting the source address of datagrams leaving your network from your private address to your official address. Address translation has several advantages.

- It conserves IP addresses. Most network connections are between systems on the same enterprise network. Only a small percentage of systems need to connect to the Internet at any one time. Therefore far fewer official IP addresses are needed than the total number of systems on an enterprise network. NAT makes it possible for you to use a large address space from RFC 1918 for configuring your enterprise network while using only a small official address space for Internet connections.
- It eliminates address spoofing, a security attack in which a remote system pretends to be a local system. The addresses in RFC 1918 cannot be routed over the Internet. Therefore, even if a datagram is routed off of your network

* See "Address Depletion" in Chapter 2, *Delivering the Data*.

toward the remote system, the fact that the datagram contains an RFC 1918 destination address means that the routers in the Internet will discard the datagram as a *martian*.*

- It eliminates the need to renumber your hosts when you connect to the Internet.

Network address translation also has disadvantages:

Cost
: NAT may add cost for new hardware or optional software.

Performance
: Address translation adds overhead to the processing of every datagram. When the address is changed, the checksum must be recalculated. Furthermore, some upper-layer protocols carry a copy of the IP address that also must be converted.

Reliability
: NAT is a new technology and there is very little experience with it in the network. Routers never modify the addresses in a datagram header, but NAT does. This might introduce some instability. Similarly, no one has much experience in determining how many addresses should be kept in a NAT address pool or how long an address should be held by a connection before it is released back to the pool.

Security
: NAT limits the use of encryption and authentication. Authentication schemes that include the header within the calculation do not work because the router changes the addresses in the header. Encryption does not work if the encrypted data includes the source address.

Proxy servers provide many of the same advantages as NAT boxes. In fact, these terms are often used interchangeably. But there are differences. Proxy servers are application gateways originally created as part of firewall systems to improve security. Internal systems connect to the outside world through the proxy server, and external systems respond to the proxy server. Unlike routers, even routers with network address translation, the external systems do not see a network of internal systems. They see only one system—the proxy server. All FTP, Telnet, and other connections appear to come from one IP address: the address of the proxy server. Therefore the difference between NAT boxes and proxy servers is that NAT uses a pool of IP addresses to differentiate the connection between internal and external systems. The true proxy server has only one address and therefore must use protocol numbers and port numbers to differentiate the connections.

---

* A martian is a datagram with an address that is known to be invalid.

Proxy servers often have added security features. Address translation can be done at the IP layer. Proxy services require the server to handle data up to the application layer. Security filters can be put in proxy servers that filter data at all layers of the protocol stack.

Given the differences discussed here, network address translation servers should scale better than proxy servers, and proxy servers should provide better security. Proxy servers are frequently used in place of address translation for small networks. Before you decide to use either NAT or proxy services, make sure they are suitable for your network needs. Often, the best choice for a connected network is to obtain an official address from your ISP and to manage that address with a DHCP server.

Assigning host addresses

So far we have been discussing *network numbers*. Our imaginary company's network was assigned network number 172.16.0.0/16. The network administrator assigns individual host addresses within the range of IP addresses available to the network address; in other words, the administrator assigns the last two bytes of the four-byte address.*

The portion of the address assigned by the administrator cannot have all bits 0 or all bits 1; that is, 172.16.0.0 and 172.16.255.255 are not valid host addresses. Beyond these two restrictions, you're free to assign host addresses in any way that seems reasonable to you.

Network administrators usually assign host addresses in one of two ways:

one address at a time
: Each individual host is assigned an address, perhaps in sequential order, through the address range.

groups of addresses
: Blocks of addresses are delegated to smaller organizations within the overall organization, which then assign the individual host addresses.

The assignment of groups of addresses is most common when the network is subnetted, and the address groups are divided along subnet boundaries. But assigning blocks of addresses does not require subnetting. It can just be an organizational device for delegating authority. Delegating authority for groups of addresses is often very convenient for large networks, while small networks tend to assign host addresses one at a time. No matter how addresses are assigned, someone must retain sufficient central control to prevent duplication and to ensure that the addresses are recorded correctly on the domain name servers.

* The range of addresses is called the *address space*.

Addresses can be assigned statically or dynamically. Static assignment is handled through manually configuring the boot file on the host computer, or through a configuration server. Dynamic address assignments are always handled by a server, such as PPP or DHCP. Before installing a server for dynamic addressing, make sure it is useful for your purposes. Dynamic PPP addressing is useful for servers that handle many remote dial-in clients that connect for a short duration. If the PPP server is used to connect together various parts of the enterprise network and has long-lived connections, dynamic addressing is probably unnecessary. The dynamic address assignment features of DHCP are used for Microsoft clients and other single user systems that have DHCP client software. Servers and other multi-user systems are assigned static addresses. You will use DHCP on your Windows NT network, but not necessarily for every system on that network. See Chapter 9, *Microsoft Routing & Remote Access Service*, for information on PPP, and Chapter 6, *Using Dynamic Host Configuration Protocol*, for details of DHCP.

Clearly, you must make several decisions about obtaining and assigning addresses. In the next section we look at the subnet mask, which changes how the address is interpreted.

Defining the Subnet Mask

Chapter 2 describes the structure of IP addresses and touches upon the reasons for subnetting. Unless you wish to change the interpretation of your assigned network number, you do not have to define a subnet mask. The decision to subnet is commonly driven by topological or organizational considerations.

The topological reasons for subnetting include:

Overcoming distance limitations
: Some network hardware has very strict distance limitations. Ethernet is the most common example. The maximum length of a thick Ethernet cable is 500 meters; the maximum length of a thin cable is 185 meters; the total length of a coax Ethernet, called the maximum diameter, is 2500 meters. If you need to cover a greater distance, you can use IP routers to link a series of Ethernet cables. Individual cable still must not exceed the maximum allowable length, but using this approach, every cable is a separate Ethernet. Therefore the total length of the IP network can exceed the maximum length of an Ethernet.

Interconnecting dissimilar physical networks
: IP routers can be used to link networks that have different and incompatible underlying network technologies. Figure 4-1 shows a central token ring subnet, 172.16.1.0, connecting two Ethernet subnets, 172.16.6.0 and 172.16.12.0.

Filtering traffic between networks
: Local traffic stays on the local subnet. Only traffic intended for other networks is forwarded through the gateway.

Subnetting is not the only way to solve topology problems. Networks are implemented in hardware and can be altered by changing or adding hardware, but subnetting is an effective way to overcome these problems at the TCP/IP software level.

Of course, there are non-technical reasons for creating subnets. Subnets often serve organizational purposes such as:

Simplifying network administration
: Subnets can be used to delegate address management, troubleshooting, and other network administration responsibilities to smaller organizations within the overall organization. This is an effective tool for managing a large network with a limited staff. It places the responsibility for managing the subnet on the people who benefit from its use.

Recognizing organizational structure
: The structure of an organization (or simply office politics) may require independent network management for some divisions. Creating independently managed subnets for these divisions is preferable to having them go directly to an ISP to get their own independent network numbers.

Isolating traffic by organization
: Certain organizations may prefer to have their local traffic isolated to a network that is primarily accessible only to members of that organization. This is particularly appropriate when security is involved. For example, the payroll department might not want their network packets on the engineering network, where some clever person could figure out how to intercept them.

Isolating potential problems
: If a certain segment is less reliable than the remainder of the net, you may want to make that segment a subnet. For example, if the research group puts experimental systems on the network from time to time, or experiments with the network itself, this part of the network will be unstable. You would make it a subnet to prevent experimental hardware or software from interfering with the rest of the network.

The network administrator decides if subnetting is required and defines the subnet mask for the network. The subnet mask has the same form as an IP address mask. As described in Chapter 2, it defines which bits form the network part of the address and which bits form the host part. Bits in the network part are turned *on* (i.e., 1), while bits in the host part are turned *off* (i.e., 0).

The subnet mask used on our network is 255.255.255.0. This mask sets aside 8 bits to identify subnets, which creates 254 subnets. The network administrator has decided that this mask provides enough subnets and that the individual subnets have enough hosts to effectively use the address space of 252 hosts per subnet. Figure 4-1 shows an example of this type of subnetting. Applying this subnet mask to the addresses 172.16.1.0 and 172.16.12.0 causes them to be interpreted as the addresses of two different networks, not as two different hosts on the same network.

Once a mask is defined, it must be disseminated to all hosts on the network. There are two ways this is done: manually, through the configuration of network interfaces; and automatically, through routing protocols. Old routing protocols cannot distribute subnet masks, and old operating systems cannot store the masks in the routing table. In an environment that contains these old systems, every device on the network must use the same subnet mask because every computer believes that the entire network is subnetted in exactly the same way as its local subnet.

New routing protocols distribute address masks for each destination, and new operating systems store those masks in the routing table. This makes it possible to use variable-length subnet masks (VLSM). Using variable-length subnet masks increases the flexibility and power of subnetting. Assume you wanted to divide 172.16.5.0/24 into three networks: one network of 110 hosts, one network of 50 hosts, and one network of 60 hosts. Using traditional subnet masks, a single subnet mask would have to be chosen and applied to the entire address space. At best this would be a compromise. With variable length subnet masks you could use a mask of 255.255.255.128, which creates subnets of 126 hosts, for the large subnet, and a mask of 255.255.255.192 to create subnets of 62 hosts for the smaller subnets. VLSMs, however, require operating systems that know how to store and use the masks and routing protocols that can transmit them. As we saw in Chapter 2, Windows NT stores the masks in its routing table.

Planning Routing

In Chapter 2, we learned that hosts only communicate directly with other computers connected to the same network. Gateways are needed to communicate with systems on other networks. If the hosts on your network need to communicate with computers on other networks, a route through a gateway must be defined. There are two ways to do this:

- Routing can be handled by a *static routing table* built by the system administrator. Static routing tables are most useful when the number of gateways is limited. Static tables do not dynamically adjust to changing network conditions, so each change in the table is made manually by the network administrator. Complex environments require a more flexible approach to routing than a static routing table provides.

- Routing can be handled by a *dynamic routing table* that responds to changing network conditions. Dynamic routing tables are built by routing protocols. Routing protocols exchange routing information that is used to update the routing table. Dynamic routing is used when there are multiple gateways on a network, and it is essential when more than one gateway can reach the same destination.

Many networks use a combination of both static and dynamic routing. Some systems on the network use static routing tables, while others run routing protocols and have dynamic tables. While it is often appropriate for hosts to use static routing tables, gateways usually run routing protocols.

The network administrator is responsible for deciding what type of routing to use and for choosing the default gateway for each host. Make these decisions before you start to configure your system. Here are a few guidelines to help you plan routing. If you have:

A network with no gateways to other TCP/IP networks
: No special routing configuration is required in this case. The gateways referred to in this discussion are IP routers that interconnect TCP/IP networks. If you are not interconnecting TCP/IP networks, you do not need an IP router. Neither a default gateway nor a routing protocol needs to be specified.

A network with a single gateway
: If you have only one gateway, don't run any routing protocols. Specify the single gateway as the default gateway in a static routing table.

A network with internal gateways to other subnets and a single gateway to the world
: Here there is a real choice. You can statically specify each subnet route and make the gateway to the world your default route, or you can run a routing protocol. Decide which you want to do based on the effort involved in maintaining a static table versus the slight overhead of running a routing protocol on your hosts and networks. If you have more than a few hosts, running a routing protocol is probably easiest.

A network with multiple gateways to the world
: If you have multiple gateways that can reach the same destination, use a routing protocol. This allows the gateways to adapt to network changes, giving you redundant access to the remote networks.

Figure 4-1 shows a subnetted network with five gateways identified as *A* through *E*. A central subnet (172.16.1.0) interconnects five other subnets. One of the subnets has a gateway to an external network. The network administrator would probably choose to run a routing protocol on the central subnet (172.16.1.0) and perhaps on subnet 172.16.12.0, which is attached to an external network. Dynamic routing is appropriate on these subnets because they have multiple gateways. Without dynamic routing, the administrator would need to update every one of these gateways manually whenever any change occurred in the network—for example, whenever a new subnet was added. A mistake during the manual update could disrupt network service. Running a routing protocol on these two subnets is simpler and more reliable.

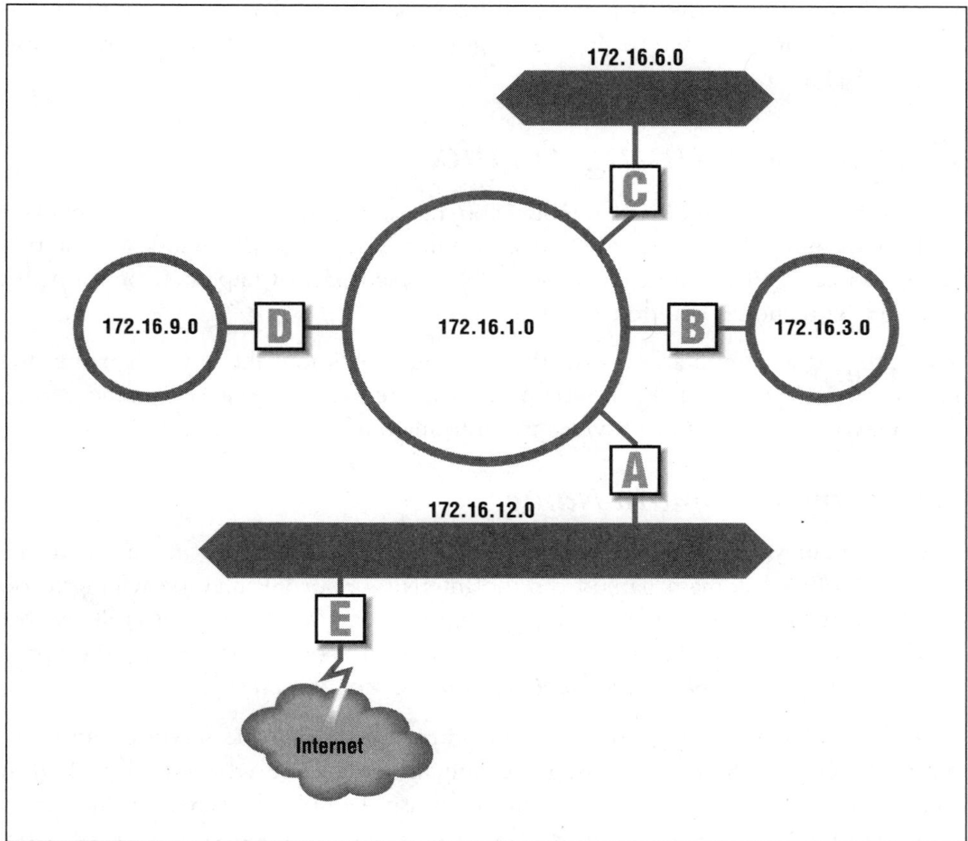

Figure 4-1. Routing and subnets

On the other hand, the administrator would probably choose static routing for the other subnets (172.16.3.0, 172.16.6.0, and 172.16.9.0). These subnets each use only one gateway to reach all destinations. Changes external to the subnets, such as the addition of a new subnet, do not change the fact that these three subnets still have only one routing choice. Newly added networks are still reached through the same gateway. The hosts on these subnets specify the subnet's gateway as their default route. In other words, the hosts on subnet 172.16.3.0 specify *B* as the default gateway, while the hosts on subnet 172.16.9.0 specify *D* as the default, no matter what happens on the external networks.

Some routing decisions are thrust upon you by the external networks to which you connect. In Figure 4-1, the local network connects to an external network. Therefore, gateway *E* has to run the routing protocol used on that network to exchange routes with the other gateways on that network.

All of the items we have discussed so far (addressing, subnetting, and routing) are required to configure the basic physical network on top of which the applications and services run. Now we begin planning the services that make the network useful and usable.

Planning Naming Service

To make your network user-friendly, you need to provide a service to convert hostnames into IP addresses. Domain Name System (DNS), Windows Internet Name Service (WINS), and the host tables, explained in Chapter 3, perform this function. You should plan to use them.

To configure a computer, a network user needs to know the domain name, the system's hostname, and the hostname and address of at least one name server. The network administrator provides this information.

Obtaining a Domain Name

The first item you need for domain name service is a domain name.* You can obtain an official domain name from the InterNIC. Your ISP may be willing to do this for you or to assign you a name within its domain; however, it is likely that you will have to apply for a domain name yourself. You can download the application from *ftp://rs.internic.net/templates/domain-template.txt*.

Pre-select a domain name and have your primary domain name server up and running before you attempt to register the domain name. Use **whois** as described in Chapter 13 to see if the name you want is in use. Double-check with **nslookup** as described in Chapter 8, *Configuring DNS Name System*. When you are reasonably sure the domain name is still available, start your primary name server running. If you don't want to run your own server, ask your ISP if they offer this service. If they don't, you must either find a new ISP that does, or run the service yourself.

Having the primary server up and running doesn't mean that your entire domain must be fully operational, but it does mean that a server must be running to

* Don't confuse this with a Windows NT domain. As described in Chapter 3, a Windows NT domain and a Domain Name System domain name are two different things. Here we are talking about DNS.

respond to basic queries. When asked, the server should answer that it is the name server for your domain. Configure the primary server as described in Chapter 8. Test it with **nslookup**. Once you are sure that it at least answers queries about itself, register the domain name.

Submit the domain name application form via email to *hostmaster@internic.net* with a subject line containing the words "NEW DOMAIN" followed by the name of your domain. In response to your email, you receive a reply that contains a tracking number that you use to monitor the status of your domain registration.

Use the domain name registration form to change or delete your existing domain name registration. Just fill in the form with the corrected information and mail it to *hostmaster@internic.net* with a subject line that contains either "MODIFY DOMAIN" or "REMOVE DOMAIN", as appropriate, followed by your domain name. In the very first field of the application form, item 0, ask for the type of registration action: either New ("N"), Modify ("M"), or Delete ("D"). Make sure the letter in this field matches the action indicated on the subject line when you mail in the application.

You're required to use email to submit the domain name application. The logic behind this is that if you don't have at least email access to the Internet, you don't need an Internet domain name. This helps reduce the number of frivolous domain name requests, and it automates part of the registration, further reducing the burden of handling domain name requests.

Another thing that dramatically reduces the number of frivolous domain name applications is the $100 registration fee. The registration service charges each domain $35 a year to be maintained in the registry. The initial $70 fee covers the first two years. Question 9 asks if the InterNIC should send the bill for the registration fee to you via email or postal mail. Answer with an E or a P. If your bean counters will accept an email bill, go that way. You'll get everything finished more quickly.

The application form is largely self-explanatory, but a few items require some thought. Two things may be confusing—handles and servers. One is the request for a *NIC handle*. You have a NIC handle only if you are registered in the *NIC white pages*. The white pages (discussed in Chapter 13) is a directory of information about users, networks, hosts, and domains. A NIC handle is a record identifier for this directory. A personal NIC handle for a user entry is composed of the user's initials and perhaps a number. For example, Robert's initials are *RT* and his NIC handle is *RT121*. It is unlikely that you will have a handle unless you have contacted the NIC before. If you don't have a handle, just leave it blank. The NIC will assign you one.

You're also asked for the names and addresses of your primary and secondary name servers. The servers listed must be operational and connected to the Internet.*

Provide the full domain name of the primary server in response to question 7a; for example, *thoth.ttgnet.com*. The primary server is usually a name server located at your site, but not always. It isn't necessary to provide your own primary server; and if you aren't directly connected to the Internet, you can't. Even though you are not connected, you may still want to register your domain name with the InterNIC if you have email access to the Internet. This allows you to use an email address that clearly identifies your organization. In order to do this, the online service that receives your email must be able to provide your primary name service. Check with them before you fill out this form.

The secondary server should be on a separate physical network from the primary server. Putting it on a different network guarantees that other sites can look up information about your network, even if access to your network is unavailable for some reason. A large organization may have multiple independent networks, but for many sites this requirement means asking another organization to provide a secondary name server. Whom do you ask?

Again, you should turn to the people who are providing your Internet access. The network that connects you to the Internet should provide secondary name servers as a service to its users. If they do not, they should be able to point you to other organizations that do provide the service. It is even possible for two organizations who are both applying for new domains to provide secondary service for each other. In other words, you provide someone with a secondary server; in return, they provide a secondary server for you.

Read the instructions that come with the domain application. The remainder of the form should be easy to fill out.

Obtaining an IN-ADDR.ARPA domain

When you obtain your Internet domain name, you should also apply for an *in-addr.arpa* domain. This special domain is sometimes called a *reverse domain*. Chapter 8 contains more information about how the *in-addr.arpa* domain is set up and used, but basically the reverse domain maps numeric IP addresses into domain names. This is the reverse of the normal process, which converts domain names to addresses. If your ISP provides your name service or assigned you an address from a block of its own addresses, you may not need to apply for an *in-addr.arpa* domain on your own. Check with your ISP *before* applying. If you do

* Chapter 8 tells you how to get a name server up and running.

need to get a reverse domain, obtain the application from *ftp://rs.internic.net/templates/in-addr-template.txt*.

Choosing a Hostname

Once you have a domain name, you are responsible for assigning host names within that domain. You must ensure that host names are unique within your domain or subdomain, in the same way that host addresses must be unique within a network or subnet. But there is more to choosing a host name than just making sure the name is unique. Choosing a host name is a surprisingly emotional issue. Many people feel very strongly about the name of their computer because they identify their computer with themselves or their work.

RFC 1178 provides excellent guidelines on how to choose a host name. Some key suggestions from these guidelines are:

- Use real words that are short, easy to spell, and easy to remember. The point of using host names instead of IP addresses is that they are easier to use. If host names are difficult to spell and remember, they defeat their own purpose.
- Use theme names. For example, all hosts in a group could be named after human movements: fall, jump, hop, skip, walk, run, stagger, wiggle, stumble, trip, limp, lurch, hobble, etc. Theme names are often easier to choose than unrestricted names, and increase the sense of community among network users. The host names used in our examples are ancient gods and stuffed bears!
- Avoid using project names, personal names, acronyms, numeric names, and technical jargon. Projects and users change over time. If you name a computer after the person who is currently using it or the project it is currently assigned to, you will probably have to rename the computer in the future. Use nicknames to identify the server function of a system, for example, *www*, *ftp*, *ns*, and so on. Nicknames can easily move between systems if the server function moves. See the description of CNAME records in Chapter 8 for information on creating nicknames.

The only requirement for a host name is that it be unique within its domain. But a well-chosen host name can save future work and make the user happier.

Name service is the most basic network service, and it is one service that you will certainly run on your network. There are, however, other services that you should also include in your network planning process.

Other Services

Two services that are used on many Windows NT TCP/IP networks are DHCP configuration servers and mail servers. The purpose of these services and the protocols they are built on is discussed in Chapter 3. In this section we investigate what information must be passed to the users so that the client systems can be successfully configured, and how the network administrator determines that information.

Planning Your Mail System

The TCP/IP protocol suite defines the tools you need to create a reliable, flexible electronic mail system. Servers improve reliability. It is possible to create a peer-to-peer TCP/IP email network in which every end system directly sends and receives its own mail. However, relying on every system to deliver and collect the mail requires that every system be properly administered and consistently up and running. This isn't practical, because many small systems are off-line for large portions of the day. Most networks use servers so that only a few systems need to be properly configured and operational for the mail to go through.

The terminology that describes email servers is confusing because all of the server functions usually occur in one computer, and all of the terms are used interchangeably to refer to that system. In this text we differentiate between these functions, but we expect you will do all of these tasks on one system. We use this term in the following manner:

mail server

The mail server collects incoming mail for other computers on the network. It supports POP so that users can read their mail when they are ready.

A mail relay is a host that forwards mail between internal systems and from internal systems to remote hosts. Mail relays allow internal systems to have simple mail configurations because only the relay host needs to have software to handle special mail addressing schemes and aliases.

A mail gateway is a system that forwards email between dissimilar systems. You don't need a gateway to go from one Internet host to another because both systems use SMTP.

The mail server is the most important component of a reliable system because it eliminates reliance on the user's system. A centrally controlled, professionally operated server collects the mail regardless of whether or not the end system is operational.

The relay host also contributes to the reliability of the email system. If mail cannot be immediately delivered by the relay host, it is queued and processed later. An end system also queues mail, but if it is shut down no attempts can be made to deliver queued mail until the system is back online. The mail server and the mail relay are operated 24 hours a day.

The design of most TCP/IP email networks is based on the following guidelines:

- Use a mail server to collect mail, and POP to deliver the mail.
- Use a mail relay host to forward mail. Implement a simplified email address scheme on the relay host.
- Standardize on TCP/IP and SMTP.
- Standardize on MIME for binary attachments. Avoid proprietary attachment schemes; they just cause confusion when the users of Brand X email cannot read attachments received from Brand Y.

For their client configurations, provide the users with the hostname and IP address of the mail server (i.e., the POP server) and the mail relay. The mail server will also require a username and password for each person.

DHCP Server Planning

If you use a DHCP server you don't need to communicate any configuration information to Windows 95 or Windows NT users. By default, those systems use DHCP and they locate the DHCP server automatically. You still need to do the various planning exercises described in this chapter, but you don't need to communicate the information developed from these plans to the user. Instead you use the information yourself to configure the DHCP server.

However, not all of the systems on your network will run Windows 95 or Windows NT. For those systems on your network that can run DHCP client software but don't run it by default, tell the administrators of those systems to enable DHCP. You will want to use DHCP to the greatest extent possible to simplify the installation and to minimize configuration error. For those systems that cannot run DHCP, you will have to provide the user with the necessary configuration information by some other means.

Informing the Users

All of the configuration information that you gather or develop through the planning process must be given to the users so that they can configure their systems. Configuration servers can play a role in informing the user and in simplifying the configuration process. DHCP offers every parameter needed to configure a TCP/IP system directly to the client. However, the server requires that the client is configured to be a client and some systems do not have the correct client software. Therefore, the network administrator must sometimes directly communicate with the administrator of the end system, usually through written documentation.

Sample Planning Sheets

To communicate this information, the network administrator will often create an *installation planning sheet*—a short list of information for the system administrator. A sample planning sheet for the workstation *pooh*, based on some of the topics we have discussed, provides basic configuration details. The planning sheet lists the name, address, subnet mask, the fact that DNS is used, and the fact that a mail server is used.

Hostname:
: pooh

IP address:
: 172.16.12.2

Subnet mask:
: 255.255.255.0

Default gateway:
: 172.16.12.1 (thoth.ttgnet.com)

Domain name:
: ttgnet.com

Name servers:
: 172.16.12.1 (thoth.ttgnet.com)
: 172.16.2.1 (kiwi.ttgnet.com)

Mail server:
: 172.16.12.1 (thoth.ttgnet.com)

Mail relay:
: 172.16.12.1 (thoth.ttgnet.com)

We use the information from this planning sheet to configure the systems in subsequent chapters.

Summary

Planning is the first step in configuring TCP/IP. We began this chapter by deciding whether or not your network will connect to the Internet and exploring how that decision impacts the rest of your planning. We also looked at the basic information needed to configure a physical network: an IP address and a subnet mask.

We discussed how to plan routing, which is essential for communicating between TCP/IP networks. We outlined the planning for domain name service and email servers. Finally, we looked at the different ways that this planning information is communicated from the network administrator to the system administrators and users.

In the chapters that follow, we put these plans into action, starting with the installation and configuration of the basic network software in Chapter 5, *Installing TCP/IP*.

5

In this chapter:
- *Windows NT Networking*
- *Configuring the TCP/IP Protocol*
- *Summary*

Installing TCP/IP

This chapter covers the installation and configuration of the basic components of Windows NT TCP/IP networking. Installing and configuring other aspects of Windows NT networking—the Remote Access Service, Windows Internet Name Service, Domain Name Service, Dynamic Host Configuration Protocol, and so on—are covered in later chapters. The procedures described in this chapter are initially performed when you install Windows NT, but you can return to them later to make changes to your network configuration.

Windows NT Networking

Windows NT provides a wide variety of networking protocols. All of these protocols, including TCP/IP, are installed and configured from the Network property sheet. Bring up the property sheet from the Control Panel by double-clicking the Network applet. The Network property sheet contains five tabs:

Identification
: Defines the Windows computer name.

Adapters
: Defines the network interface hardware.

Bindings
: Defines the logical connections between services, protocols, and adapters.

Services
: Installs network services.

Protocols
: Installs network protocols.

In the following sections we describe how each of these tabs is used to install networking on a Windows NT system.

The Identification Tab

The Identification page is shown initially when you display Network properties. The Identification page shows the NetBIOS computer name and Windows NT domain name you assigned when Windows NT was installed. This page is normally used only to display this information. Both the Computer Name and the Domain to which it belongs are fundamental characteristics of the computer. Changing either of these items significantly changes the network environment. You ordinarily make such changes only as a part of replacing or relocating a server. Treat changes to the Computer Name or Domain with the same level of caution that you would apply to formatting a disk drive or reinstalling the operating system. Although you will seldom have reason to do so, you can change the Computer Name and the Domain by clicking Change. You may then assign any valid computer name that does not already exist in the specified domain.

When you change the domain name, Windows NT attempts to locate a domain controller for the new domain name. If no domain controller can be located, NT notifies you of that fact and allows you to re-enter a new domain name. If a domain controller for the new domain is located, NT displays a warning message to allow you to verify the change before it is made.

WARNING When you attempt to change the computer name of a server, Windows NT warns you that changing the server name without first having a Domain Administrator change the computer name on the domain will result in domain accounts being unable to log on to the computer. Confirm the change only if you are absolutely certain that you want to make it. Do not change the Computer Name or the Domain unless you know exactly why you want to do so.

A Windows NT server can be a Primary Domain Controller, a Backup Domain Controller, or a standalone server. Only standalone servers can be reassigned to a new domain. Relocating a Domain Controller to a new domain requires reinstalling the Windows NT Server operating system on that server.

The Adapters Tab

Use the Adapters page of the Network property sheet to add and configure a network adapter. Most network adapters do not have to be manually installed in this manner. Most adapters are automatically configured during Windows NT setup. There are, however, occasions when manual configuration is required. You may need to use the Adapters page to add a new adapter to a system that already has Windows NT installed, or to install an upgraded device driver, or to re-install an adapter that has been incorrectly installed by Windows NT.

Windows NT does not support Plug and Play (PnP). PnP requires that the computer BIOS, the adapter card, and the operating system all be PnP compliant. All of these components take an active role in determining what is installed in the system and how best to configure it. A PnP adapter not only tells the system what it is, but also provides information about how it is currently configured and what alternative configurations it might accept. If its settings conflict with those of another installed device, the PnP adapter settings can change on-the-fly, without human intervention.

NOTE Although Windows NT doesn't provide PnP, chances are good that it will correctly identify the adapter. However, autodetection may fail if the network adapter has both a native mode and an emulation mode. For example, when a clone Ethernet adapter is configured to emulate the Novell NE2000 adapter, NT may detect the underlying adapter and incorrectly configure itself on that basis. To use the adapter in emulation mode, you may need to re-install it manually as the emulated adapter, in this case as an NE2000.

The Windows NT autodetection process is essentially passive and static. Windows NT has no way of querying the adapter as to its settings. Neither does the adapter have any mechanism to notify Windows NT that its settings are not the default settings. The result is that Windows NT autodetection fails to properly configure the drivers for any adapter that is set to settings other than its default.

If Windows NT apparently identifies the network adapter correctly, but you can't get the adapter to talk to the network, the most likely cause is that the adapter is currently configured for an IRQ or Base Address other than the default. Correct this problem either by reconfiguring the values used by Windows NT to correspond with the actual settings of the adapter, or by reconfiguring the adapter to correspond with the values expected by Windows NT. For example, assume we are installing a 3Com 3C509 Ethernet adapter. Windows NT presents the default values of 0x300 for the I/O Port Address, 10 for the Interrupt Number, and 10BaseT for the Transceiver Type. Use the drop-down lists in the Adapter Card Setup dialog to change the default values to values that correspond to the actual card settings.

It is also possible that the values used by the adapter conflict with those used by another card. If you think you may have a conflict, run the Windows NT Diagnostics program found in Administrative Tools (Common). Display the Resources page to view the IRQs, DMA channels, I/O ports, and memory addresses that are already in use. Then run the adapter's configuration utility program to determine its current settings. Use the adapter's configuration utility to reconfigure the adapter and the Adapters tab to reconfigure the Windows NT driver to available configuration values.

NOTE Most network adapters are configured under software control rather than by setting physical jumpers. Most of these utility programs are DOS-based and won't run under Windows NT, even in a DOS box. If this is the case, make a DOS-bootable floppy diskette and copy the adapter utility to it. Keep this floppy diskette handy to make changes to the adapter configuration.

Windows NT 4.0 ships drivers for numerous network adapter cards bundled with the operating system. The drivers are of high quality, but things change. Bugs are discovered; new adapters are developed; and drivers are improved. Because of these changes you may want to install updated drivers on your system with the Have Disk option. Many adapter vendors offer drivers through their Web sites. Also, Microsoft frequently posts adapter drivers on their Web site. If you must find an updated driver for your adapter, proceed as follows:

1. Check the adapter card manufacturer's Web site for the latest released version of a production driver. Make sure you don't unintentionally get a beta or unsupported version of the driver. These are commonly posted, but should never be installed on a production server. If you find a release version driver with a relatively recent file date, chances are that this is the best driver to use.
2. If you don't find a suitable driver on the manufacturer's Web site, or if the driver appears to be an old version, check the Microsoft Web site at *http://www.microsoft.com* for the latest version of the Microsoft driver for your adapter. Microsoft drivers are nearly always stable and fast, although they may not implement some special features supported by the manufacturer's driver, in particular management functions.
3. If a driver for your adapter is not available from these sources, you may still be able to use it if the adapter can emulate an adapter for which a driver is provided. Configure the adapter to emulate the other adapter and install the driver for the emulated adapter from the Select Network Adapter pick list reached through the Adapters tab.
4. If none of these solutions is workable, chances are you need to buy a new adapter that is supported by Windows NT.

Like the Identification tab, the Adapters tab is not needed for most TCP/IP installations. Most of the time, Windows NT identifies the adapter and installs a properly configured driver for the adapter. Another tab that is useful when needed, but rarely used for installing TCP/IP, is the Bindings tab.

The Bindings Tab

Microsoft uses the term *bindings* to refer to the logical connections between services, protocols, and adapters that are necessary for those elements to interact. For example, if you install an Ethernet card and the TCP/IP protocol in your server, these elements must be joined by a binding before the Ethernet card can be used by the TCP/IP protocol. Windows NT automatically configures appropriate bindings each time a network adapter, protocol, or service is installed or modified. Most network administrators do not need to modify the bindings created by NT.

You can view the bindings in effect for your system by displaying the Bindings page of the Network property sheet. The Show Bindings drop-down list box determines how the bindings are shown. You may choose to display bindings for all services, all protocols, or all adapters. The bindings are displayed in a hierarchical list like that used by Windows NT Explorer. Use the + or the - icon at the far left to expand or collapse the display for an element. Figure 5-1 shows the Bindings page with the "all services" option selected.

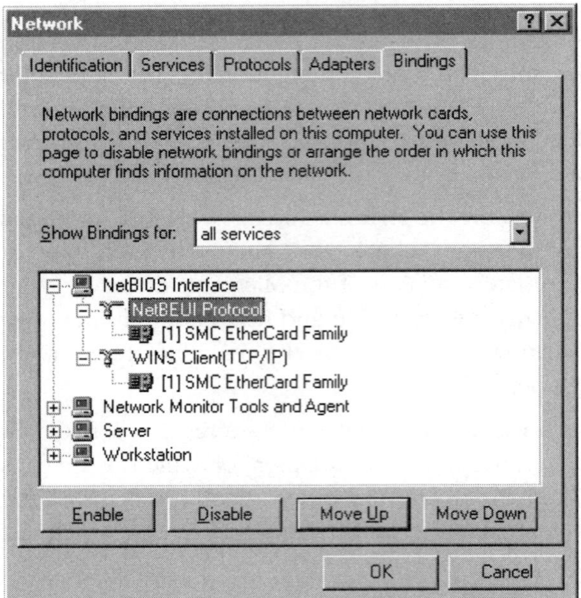

Figure 5-1. The Bindings tab of the Network properties sheet

You may disable an active binding by highlighting it and clicking Disable. Similarly, you may enable an inactive binding by highlighting it and clicking Enable. You may also use Move Up and Move Down to rearrange the order of the bindings. There are only a few reasons to modify the bindings that are automatically built by NT.

Re-order bindings to increase efficiency and performance. Windows NT processes traffic in the order the bindings appear. So, for example, if your primary transport is TCP/IP, but you have installed NWLink for occasional access to a NetWare server, you'd want to make sure that TCP/IP was bound first to the adapter and NWLink second. That way, the TCP/IP stack gets the first chance to process the inbound frame. The example in Figure 5-1 shows that someone has re-ordered the NetBIOS Interface service to use the NetBEUI protocol before it uses TCP/IP. Frankly, the default choice of Windows NT, which is to use TCP/IP in preference to NetBEUI, is a better choice. But the example assumes that the system administrator has some reason to prefer NetBEUI.

A major reason for disabling a service, protocol, or adapter is to prevent a particular type of traffic from flowing over a specific network. For example, assume that you need to use NetBEUI on your Ethernet, that your server is also attached to an ISDN network, and that NetBEUI traffic should not be sent over the ISDN line. Open the Binding page; show bindings for all protocols; expand the NetBEUI item, and disable the ISDN interface under NetBEUI. NetBEUI remains installed in the system, but it is no longer bound to the ISDN interface.

The first three tabs we discussed are used in specialized situations but are not used for the average TCP/IP installation. The last two tabs are essential for installing TCP/IP. The Services tab is used to install many of the essential TCP/IP network services. The Protocols tab is used to install and configure TCP/IP itself.

The Services Tab

Use the Services tab on the Network property sheet to install network services. The Windows NT Server distribution disk includes about two dozen network services. Windows NT Workstation comes with somewhat fewer. Some of these services are installed by default when you install Windows NT. Most are not, but may be added later.

By default, the following services are installed during Windows NT Server installation. Most of these have configuration dialog boxes that are reached through the Services tab. For most systems, however, the standard configuration of these services does not have to be changed. The default services are:

Computer Browser
: Maintains a current list of the resources available on the network for use by applications and system processes. The Browser Configuration dialog allows you to add and remove NetBIOS domains to specify which domains are visible to the browser service.

NetBIOS Interface

Defines a programming interface and naming convention for use by Microsoft Networking. The NetBIOS Configuration dialog allows you to change the mapping of LANA numbers to network drivers, which you will probably never do. A LANA number is an arbitrary number assigned to a network interface. In this case the network interface is the series of protocols and hardware drivers that deliver the NetBIOS data to the network. Changing the LANA number changes the order in which NetBIOS uses the interfaces. Lower number interfaces are used first.

RPC Configuration

Enables Remote Procedure Call (RPC) support. RPC-enabled applications can execute in distributed fashion, using the resources of multiple computers simultaneously. The RPC Configuration dialog allows you to modify the Name Service Provider, the Network Address, and the Security Service Provider. By default, Windows NT Server installs the Windows NT Locator as the name service provider. You may accept the default, or choose the alternative DCE Cell Directory Service. If you select the DCE Cell Directory Service, enter the network address for the provider in the Network Address field. Windows NT Server by default installs the Windows NT Security Service as the only option for the Security Service Provider. If you install the DCE Security Service, you may select it here. DCE is the Distributed Computing Environment standard. It is used most commonly on Unix systems, but is much less popular than RPC.

Server

The Server Message Block (SMB) protocol allows the computer to share its resources with other systems on a Microsoft network, and to function as a server in a NetBIOS client-server application. The Server configuration dialog allows you to choose among four predefined Optimization levels:

Minimize Memory Used

Configures the service to use minimal RAM. This selection is most appropriate for a server used by 10 or fewer clients.

Balance

Configures the service to use the minimum RAM need to provide support for 64 connections. This selection is the default for NetBEUI installations.

Maximize Throughput for File Sharing

This setting is appropriate for a system that provides primary file and printer sharing services on a large network. Choosing this setting devotes additional memory to caching files requested by network clients and otherwise optimizes the server for file and print sharing duties.

Maximize Throughput for Network Applications

This setting is used for an application server on a large network that supports applications, like Microsoft SQL Server, that provide their own caching.

When configuring the SMB server software, mark the "Make Browser Broadcasts to LAN Manager 2.x Clients" checkbox if you have Windows for Workgroups clients on your network and you want resources on the Windows NT system to be "browsable" by those clients.

Workstation

The SMB client software allows the computer to function as a client in a client-server application, and to access resources on the Microsoft network, including logging on to a domain and sharing files and printers. Like the Server service, the Workstation service is implemented as a file system driver. This allows network resources to be accessed as if they were local files. The Workstation service has no user configurable Properties.

In addition to the services that are installed by default, there are a large number of optional services. Some of these, Gateway Service for NetWare, RIP for NwLink IPX/SPX, RPC support for Banyan, SAP Agent, and Services for Macintosh, are not TCP/IP or NetBIOS services, and thus are not listed below. Despite these deletions, the list of available services is substantial. The following TCP/IP and NetBIOS services are supplied with the Windows NT Server distribution:

DHCP Relay Agent

Allows a Windows NT Server to forward Dynamic Host Configuration Protocol (DHCP) broadcasts to a DHCP server on another network. The DHCP Relay Agent service has no user configurable Properties. This service is covered in Chapter 6, *Using Dynamic Host Configuration Protocol.*

Microsoft DHCP Server

Automatically assigns Internet Protocol (IP) addresses to workstations running DHCP client software, and allows you to manage the shared address pool. The Microsoft DHCP Server is not configured through the Services tab. Instead it is configured by the DHCP Manager—a separate process that is covered fully in Chapter 6.

Microsoft DNS Server

The Microsoft Domain Name System (DNS) Server maps Internet Domain Names to IP addresses. The Microsoft DNS Server service is configured with the DNS Manager software covered in Chapter 8, *Configuring DNS Name System*.

Microsoft Internet Information Server 2.0

This is a full-function Web server that provides HTTP, FTP, and gopher services. Clicking the Properties button for this service simply yields a message that tells you to use the Internet Manager to configure the service. Configuration of IIS is covered in Chapter 10, *Internet Information Server (IIS)*.

Microsoft TCP/IP Printing
: Allows the server to print to network printers that use only TCP/IP transport, including those connected to Unix hosts. The Microsoft TCP/IP Printing service has no user configurable Properties.

Network Monitor Agent
: Provides the raw network transaction data needed by monitoring programs like the Performance Monitor and the Network Monitor. The Network Monitor Agent Service has no user configurable Properties. The more complete monitoring package is the one listed below.

Network Monitor Tools and Agent
: Installing this service installs the Network Monitor Agent as well as tools for monitoring and troubleshooting network problems. The Network Monitor Tools and Agent Service has no user configurable Properties. Using the Network Monitor is covered in Chapter 11, *Troubleshooting TCP/IP*.

Remote Access Service
: The Remote Access Service (RAS) supports dial-up network connections to Windows NT Server, allowing RAS clients to connect via modem to the server and to network resources as though they were locally connected. Installing the Remote Access Service invokes the Remote Access Setup procedure, which is covered fully in Chapter 9, *Microsoft Routing & Remote Access Service*.

Remoteboot Service
: This service allows diskless network client computers to boot MS-DOS and Microsoft Windows from the network server. Installing the Remoteboot service requires that the NetBEUI and DLC transport protocols first be installed. During installation, you will be prompted for the name of a directory where the remote boot files are to be stored, by default *C:\WINNT\rpl*. You are also given the opportunity to migrate the remote boot directory from a LAN Manager 2.2 server.

RIP for Internet Protocol
: This service provides the TCP/IP Routing Information Protocol (RIP). The RIP for Internet Protocol service has no user configurable Properties. This service is only one of the possible routing protocols. See Chapter 9 for a detailed treatment of the configuration of the routing software provided by Microsoft. The RIP protocol itself is described in Chapter 2, *Delivering the Data*.

Simple TCP/IP Services
: Provides several TCP/IP programs like Daytime, Echo, and Quote of the Day. None of these are important services and they are rarely installed. As

described in Chapter 12, *Network Security*, these programs can create a security problem because they are often the target of denial of service attacks. The Simple TCP/IP Services service has no user configurable Properties.

SNMP Service
: Provides Simple Network Management Protocol (SNMP) support, allowing the Windows NT computer to be managed remotely using an SNMP manager. Installing this service opens the Microsoft SNMP Properties property sheet, where you provide information about the Agent, Traps, and Security needed to configure the server for SNMP. Chapter 12 provides additional information about SNMP.

Windows Internet Name Service
: The Windows Internet Name Service dynamically maps NetBIOS computer names to IP addresses. This service is configured with the WINS Manager tool that is covered in Chapter 7, *Using Windows Internet Name Service*. The Windows Internet Name Service is not configured through the Services tab.

To install a service, click the Add button on the Services tab of the Network property sheet and then select the service from the Network Service pane. The bundled services are read off of the Windows NT distribution CD-ROM. Use the Have Disk button to install Microsoft and third party services that are not bundled with the Windows NT Server distribution. These other software packages are supplied on a separate diskette or CD-ROM that must be provided by the software vendor.

To remove a service, highlight the name of the service in the Services tab and click Remove. You must reboot after removing a service to completely clear it from the system. There are two common reasons for removing a service: first, because it is no longer needed; second, because some software updates require removing the old version before installing the new one. Take care when removing a service. In order to function, some services require that other services be present. If you attempt to remove a service that is required by another installed service, Windows NT informs you of the dependency and allows you to cancel the removal. If you remove the service anyway, you should also remove the services that depend on it to avoid startup error messages each time you boot.

The Network Access Order button appears on the Services page if your system is connected to multiple networks. It allows you to specify the order in which networks are searched for resources. Once the required server or other resource is located, the search concludes. Ordinarily, you do not need to change the Network Access Order. However if your system is connected to multiple networks that provide the same type of service and you prefer the service from one of these networks, use this button to select that network. Assume, for example, that your server is connected to two networks running RIP and that one of those networks is your preferred source for RIP updates. This feature can be used to take RIP updates from the preferred network. Choose the Network Access Order button to display the Network Access Order dialog. Highlight a network in the Network Providers pane and use the Move Up and Move Down buttons to relocate it as needed.

The Protocols Tab

Use the Protocols tab of the Network property sheet to add, remove, or configure network protocols. Windows NT Server provides six standard protocols. These include:

DLC Protocol

The Data Link Control (DLC) protocol is an IBM mainframe transport protocol. DLC is useful in the Windows NT Server environment in only two specialized situations:

- When the Windows NT Server machine is a part of a network with IBM host connectivity requirements.
- When the network includes remote print servers that use only the DLC transport. DLC print servers allow printers to be connected directly to the network cable instead of requiring that a PC be used to drive the printer.

On most TCP/IP networks there is little reason to install the DLC protocol because most IBM mainframes support TCP/IP and TCP/IP can provide a direct network printer connection. DLC only serves clients that are attached to a single physical network. TCP/IP is preferred because it can provide service across an internet.

NetBEUI Protocol

The NetBIOS Extended User Interface (NetBEUI) protocol provides connectivity for Microsoft network clients. NetBEUI is an extension of NetBIOS. It provides the Transport Driver Interface (TDI) and the NetBIOS Frame (NBF) protocol.

NWLink IPX/SPX Compatible Transport

The NWLink transport protocol is the Microsoft implementation of Novell IPX/SPX protocols. As these protocols have nothing to do with TCP/IP, this is the last time we will mention them.

Point-to-Point Tunneling Protocol

The Point-to-Point Tunneling Protocol (PPTP) provides packet-level encryption for secure end-to-end communications over an insecure path like the Internet. PPTP is supported by RAS, which is covered fully in Chapter 9.

Streams Environment

Streams originated in AT&T Unix System V and provide a standardized method for exchanging messages between protocol layers. Streams are supported in Windows NT primarily for the benefit of programmers who are developing software to integrate Unix and Windows NT.

TCP/IP Protocol

The TCP/IP protocol is the foundation of the Internet and of corporate enterprise networks. The Windows NT implementation of TCP/IP provides full interoperability with Unix systems and the Internet, and is the transport protocol of choice for any large or multi-site Windows NT network. TCP/IP is the world's leading networking protocol, and, of course, the central topic of this book.

Windows NT Server setup always installs the NWLink and TCP/IP protocols by default. Setup installs NetBEUI only if it detects the presence of NetBIOS frames on the wire during installation. The other protocols are never installed automatically by setup; you must add them manually. If you don't need the NWLink or NetBEUI, and they have been installed by the server setup, you may remove them manually.

Adding and removing protocols

To install a protocol, choose the Protocols page of the Network property sheet. Select Add to display the Select Network Protocol dialog. Highlight the protocol in the list and click on OK. Windows NT copies the software from the distribution files.

When all files have been copied, the Network property sheet is redisplayed showing the protocol as available. Click Close to complete the installation. Windows NT configures, stores, and reviews the bindings. After the bindings review process is complete, restart the server so the changes will take effect.

To remove a protocol, highlight the protocol on the Protocols page and click Remove. Reboot the system and the unneeded protocol is removed.

While there are many protocols available on a Windows NT system, this book covers the installation of only two of them. We cover Point-to-Point Tunneling Protocol (PPTP) because it is used to send TCP/IP traffic in a secure manner. And, of course, we cover TCP/IP itself.

Configuring the Point-To-Point Tunneling Protocol

The Point-to-Point Tunneling Protocol (PPTP) provides packet-level encryption, allowing insecure public data networks like the Internet to be used for secure data transport. Because PPTP encrypts the data flowing between the sites, an eavesdropper who intercepts the data is unlikely to be able to read it. PPTP permits private communication over a public network.

A private network is constructed by leasing private lines from a telephone company. The private lines run end-to-end between the sites and can be enormously expensive. In contrast, a Virtual Private Network (VPN) establishes private point-to-point connections over a public network, such as the Internet. Use PPTP to create a VPN to link your sites securely.

Implementing a Virtual Private Network using PPTP may involve more than simply installing PPTP at each of your sites. PPTP can operate in two environments:

- If every client that needs to use secure PPTP connections is running Windows NT 4.0, a secure PPTP link can be established end-to-end directly from the client to the remote PPTP server. This method does not require that the ISPs involved explicitly support PPTP.
- If instead some of your clients are running other operating systems, another method of making a PPTP connection can be used. With this method, the client first establishes a standard (insecure) PPP connection with its local ISP. The ISP, which must explicitly support PPTP on its server, then creates the PPTP connection to the remote server. With this method, the connection is insecure from the local workstation to the local ISP, but secure from the local ISP to the remote PPTP server.

Chances are good that your current ISP supports PPTP or has plans to do so. If you think that PPTP and VPNs might be a useful tool for your environment now or in the future, check with your ISP to find out if they offer PPTP support. If they don't, and PPTP support is essential to you, use the guidance in Chapter 4, *Getting Started*, to locate all of the ISPs in your area and look for one that does support the services you need.

After you install the software, Windows NT displays the PPTP Configuration dialog. Use the Number of Virtual Private Networks drop-down list to specify how many VPN connections you want. Each VPN connection represents one remote network server using PPTP with which your server will be exchanging encrypted data. Specify a number ranging from the default value of 1 to the maximum of 256 connections. Set the number you think you need, but don't worry too much about it. You can return to this dialog and change the value when necessary.

PPTP is implemented as if it were a dial-up networking (DUN) protocol, though the actual connection is via TCP/IP. To use PPTP, first make an ordinary IP network connection to your Internet Service Provider. Once this connection is established, create a PPTP DUN session for each destination host that is also running PPTP. The only difference between an ordinary DUN connection and a PPTP DUN connection is that a telephone number is used for the former and an IP address for the latter. Each PPTP DUN session creates a virtual private network between your server and the remote PPTP host whose IP address was used to establish the session. Each PPTP DUN session represents a VPN connection as defined earlier.

DUN is part of the Remote Access Service (RAS) software. If RAS is not already installed when PPTP is installed, a Setup Message is displayed to inform you that RAS will be automatically installed because it is a prerequisite for PPTP. Information about installing and configuring Remote Access Service and about creating DUN sessions is provided in Chapter 9.

Configuring the TCP/IP Protocol

TCP/IP is installed automatically when Windows NT is installed, or it can be installed manually by using the Protocols tab of the Network properties sheet. Once installed, TCP/IP can be configured automatically by a Dynamic Host Configuration Protocol (DHCP) server or manually through the Microsoft TCP/IP Properties sheet. The Microsoft TCP/IP Properties sheet is accessed by highlighting the TCP/IP Protocol entry in the Network Protocols pane of the Protocols tab and then clicking the Properties button. The remainder of this chapter is about the Microsoft TCP/IP Properties sheet and how it is used to configure TCP/IP.

The Microsoft TCP/IP Properties sheet contains as many as five tabs:

IP Address
: Defines the IP address, subnet mask, and default router.

DNS
: Defines the host name, domain name, and the DNS server addresses.

WINS Address
: Defines the WINS server addresses and options for NetBIOS name resolution.

DHCP Relay
: Configures a DHCP Relay host. This tab does not appear on a Windows NT Workstation, only on a Windows NT Server. This tab is covered in Chapter 6.

Routing
: Controls IP forwarding. This tab is only found on a Windows NT Server system.

The Microsoft TCP/IP Properties sheet has three buttons at the bottom. Two of these buttons (OK and Cancel) are global to the property sheet, and the third (Apply) is local to the tab currently displayed. Do not click on OK until you have completed all tabs. Clicking on OK exits the TCP/IP configuration process, perhaps before you have finished. Similarly, clicking Cancel discards the changes not just to the page currently displayed, but to all pages. As you complete each tab, click the Apply button to save the changes.

Some of the tabs have an Adapter list box. Use the drop-down list to select the adapter to be configured when the server has more than one adapter installed. Enter the configuration values for the adapter and click Apply to set the values for the adapter. Each adapter has its own address and subnet mask. Addresses are not assigned to computers; they are assigned to network adapters.

The IP Address Tab

Figure 5-2 shows the IP Address tab of the Microsoft TCP/IP Properties sheet. This tab is used to manually define the basic configuration or to select automatic configuration from the DHCP server. Every Windows NT client that can use a DHCP configuration server should use one. DHCP is a key component of a manageable, reliable, and efficient network. Every Windows NT workstation and every Windows 95 PC should be configured by selecting the "Obtain an IP address from a DHCP server" option button.

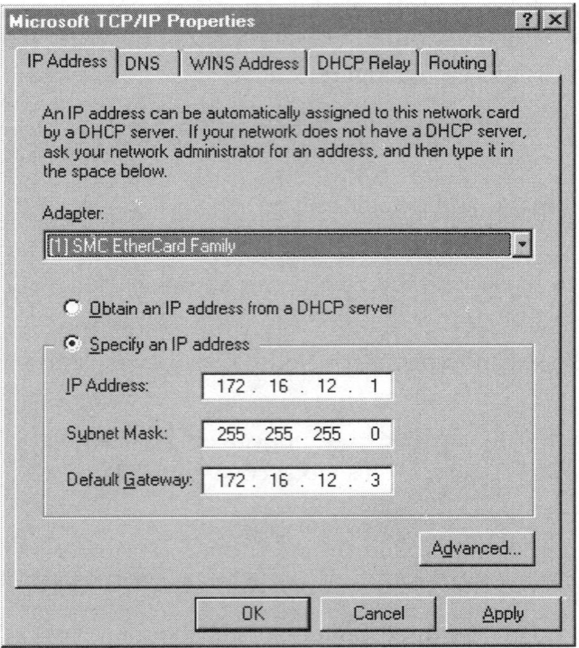

Figure 5-2. The IP Address page of the Microsoft TCP/IP Properties property sheet

Despite the label on this option button, it does much more than just obtain the IP address from a server. The DHCP server provides the complete TCP/IP configuration. Once this option button is selected and the computer is rebooted, the configuration is complete. Nothing remains to be done because everything is provided by the DHCP server. Of course, as the administrator of the network it is your responsibility to set up that server as described in Chapter 6. But your work relieves your users of all configuration responsibilities and reduces the number of user configuration errors that you have to fix. The configuration steps described in this section are not needed for the majority of systems on a network that uses DHCP.

Unfortunately not every Windows NT system can use a DHCP Server for its configuration. Most servers are not configured by DHCP, and no DHCP server can be configured by DHCP. For these systems you must select the "Specify an IP address" option button, and complete the configuration manually. The manual configuration fields on the IP Address tab are:

IP Address:
: Enter a valid IP address for this computer, using dotted decimal format.

Subnet Mask:
: If your TCP/IP network is subnetted, enter the appropriate subnet mask, again using dotted decimal format.

Default Gateway:
: Enter the IP address for the default router in dotted decimal format.

Select the Advanced button on the IP Address tab to display the Advanced IP Addressing dialog, shown in Figure 5-3. The Advanced IP Addressing dialog allows you to enable special security features and to define additional addresses and gateways.

Advanced IP addressing properties

Windows NT allows you to assign multiple IP addresses to a single physical network adapter. This is useful, for example, if you want to run multiple subnets on the same physical network. We'll see a use for this in the discussion of superscopes in Chapter 6.

Add IP addresses to a network adapter by clicking Add in the IP Addresses pane to display the TCP/IP Address dialog. In the dialog enter the IP address and its associated netmask. Windows NT defaults the subnet mask to the natural mask of the IP address you entered, which assumes that your network address is not subnetted. If the IP address is a member of a subnet, the correct value must be entered manually. Always verify that the subnet mask is correct to avoid connectivity problems that can be very difficult to resolve.

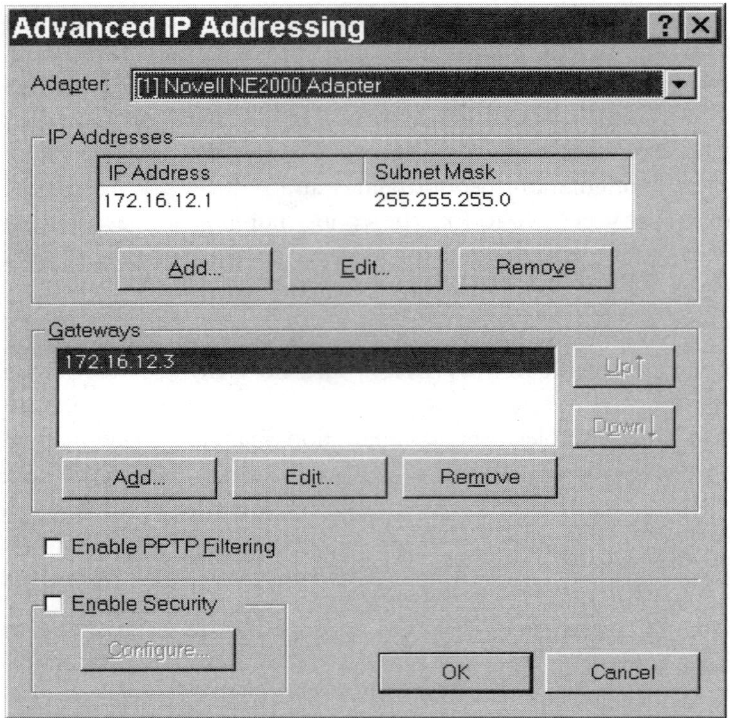

Figure 5-3. The Advanced IP Addressing dialog

Highlight an address in the IP Addresses pane and click Edit to modify an existing IP Address and Subnet Mask. Remove an IP address by highlighting it in the IP Addresses pane and clicking Remove.

Port filtering for security

The two checkboxes in the Advanced IP Addressing dialog provide optional enhancements to TCP/IP security. Mark the Enable PPTP Filtering checkbox if you want the selected adapter to handle only PPTP traffic. Marking this checkbox causes the adapter to discard non-PPTP packets. The most common use for this setting is in a multi-homed server that has one physical network adapter connected to the Internet and another physical network adapter connected to the internal network. Enabling PPTP filtering on the adapter that connects to the Internet allows only secure PPTP sessions to access the server from the Internet. This setting is used in a virtual private network to create a truly private network by limiting all communications to only those systems that are members of the VPN. Be careful with this setting. Marking this checkbox by mistake could cause the server to become unavailable to legitimate users just because they don't run PPTP.

To filter incoming traffic based on ports and protocols, mark the Enable Security checkbox and then click Configure to display the TCP/IP Security dialog shown in Figure 5-4. Through this dialog Windows NT allows you to control which TCP ports, UDP ports, and IP Protocols are available to network users.

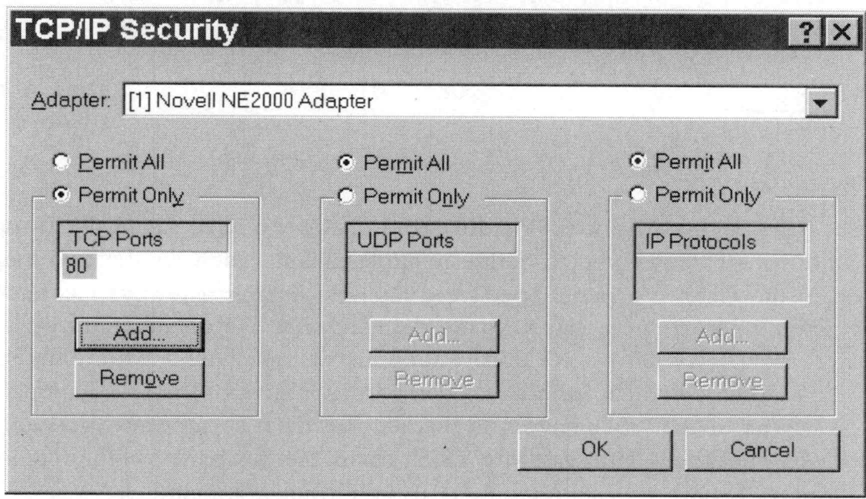

Figure 5-4. The TCP/IP Security dialog

By default, Windows NT sets Permit All for all three categories. This means that any network user can access any TCP/IP service available on the server. In Chapter 2 we saw that each port number represents a network service and that each protocol number identifies a protocol that communicates directly with IP. Control access to a network service or protocol by controlling access to its TCP Port, UDP Port, or IP Protocol. To restrict one of these elements, click the Permit Only option button for that pane, and use the Add and Remove buttons to list only those ports or protocols that users will be permitted to access. Marking the Permit Only option button for a pane and leaving the associated list blank prohibits users from accessing any resources in that category.

The port filtering defined in the TCP/IP Security dialog only affects inbound traffic. For example, a dedicated DNS server might be configured to permit only TCP and UDP port 53 (DNS), and only protocols 0 (IP), 1 (ICMP), 6 (TCP), and 17 (UDP). With these settings DNS would function normally but other inbound connections would be blocked. For example, this would prevent email from coming into the SMTP port but it would not prevent the administrator of this system from sending email out to some remote server's SMTP port. Outbound traffic is not affected by these filters.

NOTE The port filtering ability of Windows NT is very similar to the *inetd.conf* port filtering on Unix systems. It is useful in some security situations, though not all. If you need more capability—for example, the ability to filter port ranges or the ability to deny outbound traffic for a particular port—consider installing the Microsoft Routing and RAS upgrade. RRAS expands the limited IP routing capabilities of Windows NT Server to include most of the features of a dedicated router. RRAS is covered in Chapter 9.

Defining gateways

In our discussion of the Advanced IP Addressing dialog we have saved the least for last. Windows NT allows you to define multiple default gateways through the Add button in the Gateways pane. Specifying multiple default gateways has limited utility. Even when multiple gateways are defined, only one default gateway is active at any one time. Windows NT always uses the first gateway shown. Only if that gateway is down or otherwise not accessible does it attempt to use additional gateways. You can specify as many as five additional default gateways, but you shouldn't. Only enter the default gateway. Don't try to use this pane to build complex static routes. If static routes are required, use the **route** command.

The **route** command is available through the Windows NT command interface. It lets you manually configure the routes in the routing table. The command syntax is:

> **route** [-f] [-p] [*command* [*destination*] [**mask** *netmask*] [*gateway*]]

The options are used as follows:

-f
: Flush all of the routes from the routing tables. If used with one of the commands, the table is flushed before the command is executed.

-p
: Create a permanent route that is reinstalled in the routing table every time the system boots.

command
: The *command* field specifies the action that the **route** command should take. There are four command keywords:

  add Add a route

  delete Delete a route

  change Modify an existing route

  print Display the routing table

destination

This is the network or host that is reached through this route.

mask *netmask*

The *netmask* is applied to the address provided in the destination field to determine the true destination of the route. If a bit in the *netmask* is set to 1, the corresponding bit in the destination field is a significant bit in the destination address. For example, a destination of 172.16.12.1 with a *netmask* of 255.255.0.0 defines the route to network 172.16.0.0, but the same destination with a mask of 255.255.255.255 defines the route to the host 172.16.12.1. If no value is specified for the *netmask*, it defaults to 255.255.255.255.

gateway

This is the IP address of the gateway for this route.

Assume we are configuring an NT workstation that has the IP address 172.16.24.1 and that is located on subnet 172.16.24.0. In the following example we add a route to the host 172.16.12.3 and a route to the subnet 172.16.8. In each case, the netmask determines if the route is interpreted as a network route or a host route. After entering the new routes, we display the routing table with the **route print** command to examine our handiwork.

```
C:\>route -p add 172.16.12.3 mask 255.255.255.255 172.16.24.5
C:\>route -p add 172.16.8.0 mask 255.255.255.0 172.16.24.8
C:\>route print
Active Routes:
  Network Address          Netmask  Gateway Address        Interface  Metric
          0.0.0.0          0.0.0.0    172.16.24.254      172.16.24.1       1
        127.0.0.0        255.0.0.0        127.0.0.1        127.0.0.1       1
       172.16.8.0    255.255.255.0      172.16.24.8      172.16.24.1       1
      172.16.12.3  255.255.255.255      172.16.24.5      172.16.24.1       1
      172.16.24.0    255.255.255.0      172.16.24.1      172.16.24.1       1
      172.16.24.1  255.255.255.255        127.0.0.1        127.0.0.1       1
   172.16.255.255  255.255.255.255      172.16.24.1      172.16.24.1       1
        224.0.0.0        224.0.0.0      172.16.24.1      172.16.24.1       1
  255.255.255.255  255.255.255.255      172.16.24.1      172.16.24.1       1
```

As the display shows, there are several more routes than the two we just entered. The default route (destination 0.0.0.0) is the route we entered in the Default Gateway box in the TCP/IP Properties window. All of the other routes are part of the minimal routing table that is created by installing TCP/IP. By destination, they are:

127.0.0.0

The loopback network route. 127.0.0.1 is the address of the loopback interface.

172.16.24.0

The direct route of the local interface. This is the route this computer uses to reach the network it is directly attached to. The gateway address is the address of this computer's own Ethernet adapter.

172.16.24.1
The localhost route. This is a special route to this localhost. The address 172.16.24.1 is the address of this host. The route to this host is through the loopback interface.

172.16.255.255
The broadcast route. Broadcasts to this network are sent through the local Ethernet interface.

224.0.0.0.
The multicast route. Multicasts are sent through the local Ethernet interface.

255.255.255.255
The limited broadcast route. Limited broadcasts are sent through the local Ethernet interface.

The routes added by the **route add** command will not survive a boot without the **-p** option. Put the **-p** option on every **route add** command to ensure that the routes are reinstalled after a boot.

You only need to use the route command if your system requires complex static routes. Most workstations use a single default route because most local area networks only have one router to the outside world. Most of the time you can do the complete configuration from the TCP/IP Properties window. Let's return to the Microsoft TCP/IP Properties sheet to finish entering configuration data.

The DNS Tab

An important part of a TCP/IP network is the Domain Name System. The client portion of DNS, which is called the resolver, must be configured on every system. To configure the resolver, select the DNS tab, which is shown in Figure 5-5.

The Internet name of the machine is typed in the Host Name field. By default, Windows NT fills in this field with the computer name from the Identification tab of the Network property sheet. Use the default. Although you *can* assign an Internet host name different from the computer name, that way lies madness.

Type the Internet domain name into the Domain field. Windows NT does not enter a default value for this field. Note that this field refers to the Internet domain name, for example, *ttgnet.com*, rather than to the Windows domain, which happens in this case to be *TTGNET*. In many organizations, the Internet domain name and the Windows domain name are very similar. However, don't make the mistake of entering the Windows domain name here. This is the Internet domain name.

The DNS Service Search Order pane has no default entries. Use the Add button to enter the IP address of at least one DNS server. You should also enter the IP

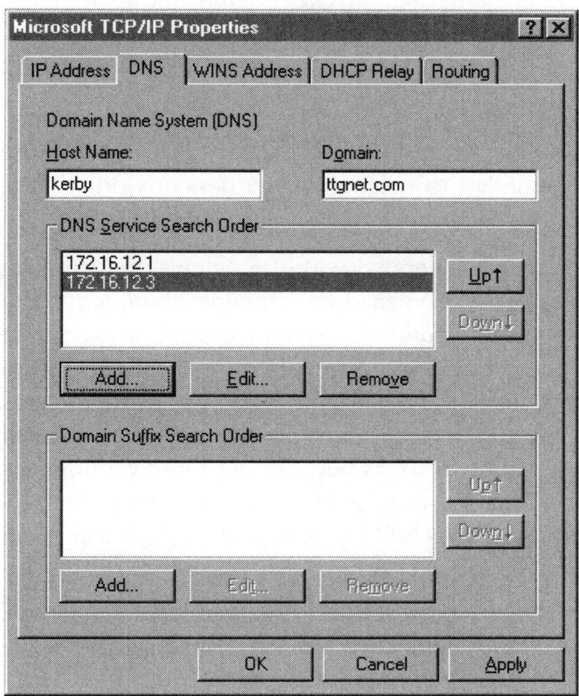

Figure 5-5. The DNS page of the Microsoft TCP/IP Properties sheet

address of an additional DNS server to provide redundancy. If you maintain multiple local servers, enter them here. Small organizations typically provide one local server and depend on a DNS server located at their ISP for a second server. If that is the case for your network, enter the IP address of your local server and the address of the ISP's server. Use the Add, Edit, and Remove buttons as needed to configure the list.

Use the Up and Down buttons to arrange the servers in the order that you want them searched. When Windows NT needs to resolve an IP address, it starts with the first server on the list. If that server is unavailable, it then tries the second server. If that server fails to respond, NT continues to try servers in the order they are listed until it is either able to resolve the address or it runs out of servers to try. Don't enter more than three servers in the list. If you cannot contact any of three different servers, the problem is not with the remote servers; it is with your local system.

The Domain Suffix Search Order box at the bottom of the window is used to define the order in which domains are searched for host information. Normally it is blank. When it is blank, the domain name from the Domain box is used as the default search domain and the parents of that domain are also searched. If domains are specified in the Domain Suffix Search Order pane, those domains, and only those domains, are searched. An example should help make the purpose of the Domain Suffix Search Order clear.

When a query is made for a hostname that does not end with a dot, the hostname is extended to a fully qualified domain name before the query is passed to the name server. The domain name appended to the host name depends on what is entered in the Domain Suffix Search Order pane:

- If nothing is entered, the hostname is extended with the default domain from the Domain box. For example, if the Domain box contains *plant.ttgnet.com* and the hostname to be resolved is *thoth*, the system creates a query for *thoth.plant.ttgnet.com*. If this name cannot be resolved, the system checks the parent domain by generating a query for *thoth.ttgnet.com*. On many systems that is as far as the search goes. These systems do not append a parent domain name that contains less than two fields because the top-level domains do not normally contain host addresses, only pointers to the servers for second-level domains. However, Windows NT 4.0 will search the top level domains. It will generate a query for *thoth.com*
- If the pane contains the domain entries *plant.ttgnet.com* and *sales.ttgnet.com*, a request for the IP address of *mandy* generates a query for *mandy.plant.ttgnet.com* and then one for *mandy.sales.ttgnet.com* (assuming the first query was not successful). The system does not, however, search the parent domain *ttgnet.com*. Even the domain provided in the Domain box is not searched if there are entries in the Domain Suffix Search Order subwindow. When a search list is provided, it must include all of the domains that you want searched.

A query is also issued for the name exactly as it is typed in by the user. If the user asks for the address of *pooh.ttgnet.com*, a query for that domain name is sent regardless of what is entered in this subwindow. The default domains are only used to extend hostnames so that it is possible for a user to enter the names in a shorter form. Default domains do not interfere with the normal processing of a query.

This finishes the DNS client configuration. In most cases, the configuration only requires you to enter the domain name and the IP addresses of two domain name servers.

The WINS Address Tab

The Windows Internet Name Service (WINS) maps NetBIOS names to IP addresses. The WINS client needs to know the address of the WINS server in order to resolve the NetBIOS name. Configure the WINS client through the WINS Address tab shown in Figure 5-6.

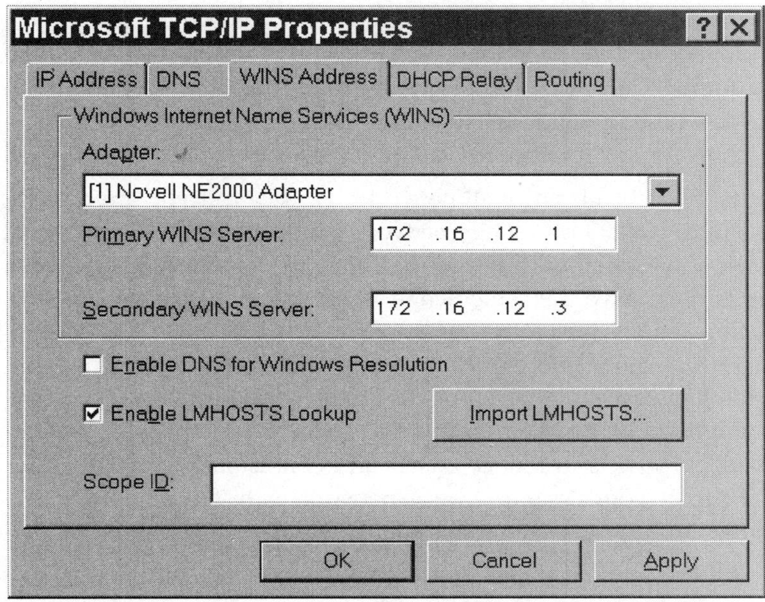

Figure 5-6. The WINS Address page of the Microsoft TCP/IP Properties sheet

The basic configuration of the WINS client is very straightforward. Enter the IP address of the Primary WINS Server and, optionally, of the Secondary WINS Server in the appropriate boxes on this tab. That's all there is to it. Once the client knows the address of the servers, it should be able to use WINS to resolve NetBIOS names. However, there are other optional settings on this tab that provide additional features relating to NetBIOS name resolution. The other items on the WINS Address tab are:

Enable DNS for Windows Resolution

Mark this checkbox to use the DNS server to resolve DNS names that are used as Windows computer names. Marking this box provides *DNS Support in UNC Names*, which allows an Internet domain name or an IP address to be used as part of a Universal Naming Convention (UNC) name. UNC names are used by NetBIOS to identify network resources. A UNC name starts with two backslashes (\\) followed by a computer name, a single backslash (\), and the share name. When this box is marked, the computer name can be a DNS domain name. For example, the names *\\pooh.ttgnet.com\WINNT* and *\\172.16.12.2\WINNT* are both then valid UNC names. If the checkbox is unmarked, neither name is a valid UNC name.

Enable LMHOSTS Lookup

Mark this checkbox to use the *LMHOSTS* file for NetBIOS name resolution. The *LMHOSTS* file is located in the *%SystemRoot%\System32\Drivers\Etc* folder. Use any text editor to create an *LMHOSTS* file based on the sample file Lmhosts.SAM also located in this folder. You can import an existing *LMHOSTS* file by clicking Import LMHOSTS and browsing for the file. See Chapter 3, *Network Services*, for a description of this file.

Scope ID

This field is usually left blank on small networks. However, if you are running NetBIOS over TCP/IP (NBT) on a large network, enter the Scope ID provided by your network administrator. The Scope ID limits communications between NBT hosts. Hosts must have the same Scope ID to communicate successfully. Scope IDs create separate logical NetBIOS networks on a single TCP/IP network. Unlike the domain name, which provides a hierarchical structure but which does not limit access, the Scope ID limits access and prevents the resources being offered by a system from being seen by systems with a different Scope ID. Its purpose is to reduce clutter and confusion, particularly on a large TCP/IP WAN. If your system is on a network with 200 other NetBIOS systems but only 10 of those systems share its Scope ID, you only see 10 systems shared resources. The Scope ID filters out unwanted information.

This is not a security mechanism, but it does limit access. If a user attempts to use a shared directory from a system that has a different Scope ID it fails with an error. It is possible to choose an obscure Scope ID to enhance security but it is not possible to keep it secret. Everyone you want to share data with must know what it is. Therefore few people bother with obscure Scope IDs and most are easily guessed. At best, the Scope ID prevents accidental access. It is not designed to deter a determined effort to breach security.

The network administrator should assign the Scope ID because it is important that the correct systems have the same ID. Resources are visible to systems with the same Scope ID but not to systems with a different Scope ID. The Scope ID is a 15 character name similar to a NetBIOS computer name.

If you do not enter an address for at least one WINS Server, Windows NT will display a warning telling you that you have not specified a WINS Server. If you don't have a WINS server you can safely ignore the warning. Windows NT will resolve NetBIOS names to IP addresses using name query broadcasts in conjunction with the local *LMHOSTS* file. NetBIOS, NetBIOS names, and the techniques used to resolve those names are discussed in Chapter 7. WINS is the NetBIOS name resolution technique recommended for Windows NT network.

The Routing tab

Generally no more than one Windows NT system on a network segment is configured as an IP router, and even that is rare. In most cases, specialized hardware, not a general purpose Windows NT system, is used as a router. To configure an NT system as a basic IP forwarder, click the Routing tab to display the Routing page. Mark the Enable IP Forwarding checkbox to cause a Windows NT system to function as an IP router. If the RIP for Internet Protocol service is installed, NT routes packets using the dynamic routing tables built and maintained by RIP. If it is not installed, Windows NT routes IP packets using the static routes that you enter with the **route -p add** command, as described earlier in this chapter. This is the most basic configuration of a Windows NT Server system as an IP router. More complex configurations require the Routing and Remote Access Service (RRAS). RRAS is covered in Chapter 9.

The Routing tab is rarely used. It is available only on Windows NT Server systems, and only used on those that are configured as routers without RRAS. The Microsoft TCP/IP Properties tabs that are truly important to the TCP/IP configuration process are the IP Address and DNS tabs.

Summary

Windows NT provides a wide variety of networking protocols, including TCP/IP. The basic network software is installed through the Network properties sheet, which contains five tabs:

Identification
: Defines the Windows computer name.

Services
: Installs network services.

Protocols
: Installs network protocols.

Adapters
: Defines and configures the network hardware installed on the computer.

Bindings
: Creates the logical connections between services, protocols and adapters.

The TCP/IP protocol is installed through the Protocols tab. Once installed, TCP/IP is configured through the Microsoft TCP/IP Properties sheet. The tabs on that sheet are used to configure the IP address, subnet mask, default gateway address, Internet host name, domain name, and DNS server address. They provide a complete, basic TCP/IP client configuration.

An alternative to manually defining the TCP/IP configuration is to use the Dynamic Host Configuration protocol to provide all of this information and more. In Chapter 6 we learn how a DHCP server is set up.

In this chapter:

- *Why DHCP Is Needed*
- *How DHCP Works*
- *Planning for DHCP*
- *Installing the DHCP Server Service*
- *Installing and Configuring the DHCP Relay Agent*
- *Managing DHCP with DHCP Manager*
- *Maintaining and Troubleshooting DHCP Server*
- *Summary*

6

Using Dynamic Host Configuration Protocol

The Microsoft Dynamic Host Configuration Protocol (DHCP) Server is a Windows NT Service that automatically assigns IP addresses to clients running DHCP client software. By using DHCP, you can centralize the management of IP addresses, netmasks, and other IP configuration information, greatly reducing the amount of administration needed to maintain a network running TCP/IP transport.

A DHCP client does not have a permanently assigned, hard-coded IP address. Instead, at boot time, the DHCP client requests an IP address from the DHCP Server. The DHCP Server has a pool of IP addresses that are available for assignment. When a DHCP client requests an IP address, the DHCP Server assigns, or *leases,* an available IP address from that pool to the client. The assigned IP address is then owned by that client for a specified period, called the lease duration.

When the lease expires, that IP address is returned to the pool and becomes available for reassignment to another client. When a client reboots, it checks to see if its lease is still valid. If so, it continues using the same IP address. If not, it requests a new IP address from the DHCP server. Servers and other computers that should always have the same IP address may be assigned a permanent IP address using a DHCP *permanent lease*.

Many people believe that DHCP is a proprietary Microsoft protocol. It is not, although Microsoft was instrumental in having DHCP adopted as a formal Internet standard. The Internet community has long recognized that a dynamic means of assigning IP addresses to clients was needed, both to reduce the administrative load of manually managing IP addresses and related information like subnet masks and default routers, and to increase the efficiency with which the limited IP address space is allocated.

DHCP extends an earlier protocol called BOOTP, which provided similar, although more limited, functionality. DHCP added several new configuration options and the ability to allocate reusable network addresses automatically. DHCP and BOOTP clients are largely interoperable, and some network components still depend on BOOTP. BOOTP and DHCP are defined in the following Internet Requests for Comment (RFCs), which you may retrieve with your ftp client at *ds.internic.net/rfc* or with your Web browser at *www.internic.net/ds/dspg2intdoc.html.*

- RFC951 *Bootstrap Protocol.* This RFC, dated September 1, 1985, originally defined the BOOTP protocol and was subsequently updated by RFC1532, RFC1395, and RFC1497.
- RFC1533 *DHCP Options and BOOTP Vendor Extensions.* This RFC, dated October 8, 1993, makes RFC1497 obsolete and specifies the current set of valid DHCP options, which are tagged data items stored in the options field of a DHCP message.
- RFC1534 *Interoperation Between DHCP and BOOTP.* This RFC, also dated October 8, 1993, defines the interactions between DHCP and BOOTP network clients.
- RFC1541 *Dynamic Host Configuration Protocol.* This RFC, dated October 27, 1993, makes RFC1531 obsolete and defines the current implementation of DHCP.
- RFC 1542 *Clarifications and Extensions for the Bootstrap Protocol.* This RFC, also dated October 27, 1993, makes RFC1532 obsolete and defines the functioning of relay agents, a matter of particular concern to those who are running DHCP on a routed network.

DHCP uses a client-server architecture. DHCP servers are available for many operating systems, including Unix, Novell NetWare 4.1x, and, of course, Windows NT Server. Similarly, DHCP clients are available for nearly any client operating system. A workstation running any standards-compliant DHCP client software can communicate with, and be serviced by, any standards-compliant DHCP server. The Microsoft DHCP implementations for both client and server comply fully with the relevant RFC standards.

Microsoft has taken things a step further by integrating DHCP functions on both the client and the server with Microsoft Domain Name System (DNS) and Microsoft Windows Internet Naming Service (WINS) functions. The one downside is that, in order to get the maximum benefits from this tight integration, you must run Microsoft operating systems on all of your servers and clients. Given the realities of today's environment, that's not much of a hardship for many administrators. NetWare servers, Macintosh clients, and other non-Microsoft DHCP devices on your network can still participate, although with a somewhat reduced level of integration.

Why DHCP Is Needed

DHCP has become a practical necessity for large IP networks for two reasons. First, each host in a TCP/IP network must have a unique IP address. This simple fact has caused a tremendous amount of aggravation and extra work for network administrators, and has resulted in more than a few crashed networks. In the early days of TCP/IP networking, there was no automated alternative; you had to assign an IP address manually to each host. Even today, many networks continue to use manual assignment and tracking of IP addresses.

Assigning IP addresses manually is practical only for small networks. As the size and complexity of the network increases, using manual IP address assignment becomes increasingly unworkable. Each time a workstation, server, network printer, router, or other host is added or relocated, someone must determine a valid IP address, ensure that that IP address is not already in use by another host, record the assignment of that address, and then finally configure the host manually for that IP address. This process requires expert staff time and is always prone to error. Accidentally duplicating an IP address will at best cause a communication failure on both affected hosts. At worst—if the duplicated IP address belongs to a server, router, or other critical network component—the duplicate IP address may cause the entire network to crash. Microsoft TCP always checks to see if its address is a duplicate by issuing an ARP before using the address.

The second motivation for using DHCP is that the perceived shortage of IP network addresses has made it necessary to use IP host addresses more efficiently. Only a few years ago, getting a Class C Network Address (256 IP addresses) was a matter of simply asking InterNIC to assign one to you. Requests for as many as 16 contiguous C blocks were routinely honored by InterNIC without much formality. If you said you needed it, they gave it to you. Even getting a Class B Network Address (256 C blocks, or 65,536 IP addresses) required minimal paperwork and justification.

Nowadays, it's a struggle to get InterNIC to assign even a single Class C Network Address. Getting multiple C blocks assigned requires spending hours or days completing detailed justifications, network plans, and so forth. Getting a B block assigned is almost impossible unless you are applying on behalf of a Fortune 500 corporation, and even then it's not a foregone conclusion.

The large granularity of Network Addresses—a C block is the smallest unit that can be assigned—means that many IP addresses are wasted. Consider a small branch office with a router, a server, and seven workstations. If that branch office is assigned a Class C Network Address, only nine of the available 256 IP addresses are in use. The remaining IP addresses cannot be used except at that branch office, and so are wasted. In the past, this didn't much matter, because Network Addresses were free and were easily available from a seemingly inexhaustible supply. Some large companies with many small remote sites wasted 90 percent or more of the many IP addresses assigned to them.

Network addresses are assigned by InterNIC on a first-come, first-served basis, which means that there is absolutely no correlation between Network Address and geographic location. For example, InterNIC assigned to Triad Technology Group, Inc. (Thompson's company, located in Winston-Salem, NC) the Class C Network Address 204.238.30.0. The Network Address immediately preceding that one, 204.238.29.0, is assigned to Warner Brothers Imaging Technologies in Sherman Oaks, CA. The Network Address immediately following that one, 204.238.31.0, is assigned to the Bead Gallery in Juneau, AK.

A side effect of this policy has been the explosive growth of routing tables. Each individually assigned Network Address requires a routing table entry in every router on the backbone. A contiguous block of, say, 16 Class C Network Addresses assigned to the same network requires only a single routing table entry. Those same 16 C blocks, if assigned individually to different companies (and different networks), require 16 individual routing table entries. As of early 1997, the routing tables on the Internet backbone have grown to more than 30 MB.

InterNIC strongly encourages you to use IP addresses assigned to you by your Internet Service Provider (ISP) rather than applying directly to InterNIC for your own block of addresses. They do so both to avoid wastage of IP addresses and to slow the growth of routing tables.

However, there is a downside to using addresses provided by your ISP, and you won't hear either InterNIC or your ISP talking much about it. Addresses provided by your ISP belong to the ISP rather than to you. This means they aren't portable. If you decide to change ISPs, you have no option but to recast your IP address assignments network-wide to use the addresses provided by your new ISP. In effect, using addresses provided by an ISP locks you into that ISP.

At first, InterNIC simply recommended that you use ISP-provided IP addresses, but that didn't accomplish much. Most administrators were concerned about address portability, and so simply continued to apply to InterNIC when they needed additional Network Address blocks. Seeing this, and still determined to slow the growth of routing tables, InterNIC next began warning applicants for Network Address blocks that there was no guarantee that individually assigned blocks would be routable in the future.

Apparently, this hasn't worked either, because InterNIC now proposes to charge for directly assigned IP addresses. Under this proposal, any organization to which InterNIC directly assigns a Network Address must pay a $1,000 annual fee, with additional charges assessed based on the number of IP addresses assigned. If this proposal is implemented, you will see the wholesale abandonment of Class C Network Addresses. Almost everyone will use Network Addresses provided by the ISP.

So, what relationship exists between the source of your IP addresses and using DHCP? Simply this: implementing DHCP on your current network will allow you to recast your IP addressing much more easily when (not if) you find yourself switching to addresses provided by your ISP. If you are using DHCP when the time to recast arrives, you will need to change only the DHCP server configuration and the few static addresses assigned to servers and routers, including the DHCP server. If you are not running DHCP, you will need to change the IP configurations individually for each machine on your network.

How DHCP Works

Now that we know why using DHCP is desirable, if not essential, let's take a look at how it actually works. When you install the Microsoft DHCP Server, a DHCP Server database is created. This database contains two types of information. First, it contains static configuration data supplied by the administrator using DHCP Manager. These static data include the range of IP addresses available to the DHCP Server for assignment to DHCP clients, and various DHCP options set by the administrator. The DHCP Server database also maintains dynamic configuration data that is modified continuously by the interactions between the DHCP Server and its clients, for example, those IP addresses that are currently in use and to which clients they are assigned.

NOTE Although this chapter focuses on the Microsoft DHCP implementations for both server and client, the Microsoft DHCP Server also supports third-party DHCP clients and third-party DHCP servers also support Microsoft DHCP clients. Basic DHCP functionality is provided by any combination of DHCP server and client. The availability of extended DHCP functions is determined by which DHCP options are supported by both the DHCP server and the DHCP client being used.

Windows NT, Windows 95, and LAN Manager 2.2c provide native Microsoft DHCP support. To use Microsoft DHCP on Windows 3.11 for Workgroups clients, install the 32-bit TCP/IP VxD from the file *TCPIP32B.EXE,* which is available free from Microsoft. To use Microsoft DHCP on MS-DOS clients, install the Microsoft Network Client v 3.0 with the real-mode TCP/IP driver.

When a DHCP client boots, the DHCP Server supplies it with the IP configuration information needed by that client to participate in the TCP/IP network. This configuration information includes:

IP Address
: Each client network adapter that is bound to the TCP/IP protocol requires a unique IP address. The DHCP Server supplies this IP address from its available

pool. If a client has more than one network adapter bound to TCP/IP, the DHCP Server supplies one IP address for each such adapter.

Subnet Mask

If IP packets are to be routed correctly to their destinations, the client must know to which subnet it is assigned, which is determined by the subnet mask. The DHCP server assigns a subnet mask to the client based on which subnet (or logical network) that client is a member of.

Default Gateway

Local IP packets—those whose destination IP address is on the same subnet as is the source IP address—are delivered directly. Packets destined for a remote network must be delivered to a local router that connects the local network to remote networks. This router is called the default gateway.

Other IP Configuration Parameters

Other optional IP configuration data, for example, domain name, may be assigned to DHCP clients. If such parameters have been assigned by the administrator, the DHCP Server also delivers them to the DHCP client at boot time.

The TCP/IP configuration parameters that are eventually assigned to the DHCP client are negotiated by messages exchanged between the DHCP Server and the DHCP client in the following sequence:

1. When the DCHP client boots, it broadcasts a *Dhcpdiscover packet* to discover the address of an available DHCP server. In an Ethernet environment, the Dhcpdiscover frame may be either 342 bytes or 590 bytes. New versions of Windows broadcast the smaller frame. Windows NT 3.5, the *TCPIP32B.EXE* Windows 3.11 for Workgroups protocol stack, and earlier versions use the larger frame. The contents of these frames are as follows:
   - The first 14 bytes of the frame comprise the Ethernet header. Because the DCHP client does not yet know the MAC address of a DHCP server, it initiates an Ethernet Type 0800 (IP) frame, with the destination address set to the Ethernet broadcast address of 255.255.255.255.
   - The next 20 bytes comprise the IP header. The source IP address is set to 0.0.0.0 because the DHCP client does not yet have an IP address. The destination IP address is set to the IP broadcast address of 255.255.255.255 because the DHCP client has not yet resolved the IP address of a DHCP server.
   - The next eight bytes are the UDP header. The source port is 68 (BOOTP) and the destination port is 67 (UDP). DHCP is an extension of the BOOTP protocol, and uses the same ports for messaging.

- The remainder of the frame contains Dhcpdiscover packet components, most of which are set to zero or blank because the DHCP client has not yet obtained any configuration parameters. One important non-blank field is the Client Identifier, which contains the client's MAC address. The client includes this value in the packet to identify itself to a DHCP server. If the DHCP server maintains a reserved address for this client, it can use this information to provide the proper specific address that has been reserved.
- If the DHCP client receives no response to the first Dhcpdiscover packet, it again broadcasts a Dhcpdiscover packet. The DHCP client repeats this process four times, at intervals of approximately 2, 4, 8, and 16 seconds. If the DHCP client receives no response to any of these broadcasts, it waits 5 minutes and begins the process again. In Windows 95, the DHCP client displays a message box to inform you that no DHCP server was found, and asks if you want to see DHCP error messages in future. If you elect to suppress such messages, that choice is permanent, which makes troubleshooting more difficult later on.

2. When any DHCP Server receives a Dhcpdiscover packet and is able to fulfill the client request, it returns a *Dhcpoffer packet* that contains an IP address chosen by the DHCP Server from the available IP addresses assigned to its pool, or a reserved lease. In an Ethernet environment, the Dhcpoffer frame is 342 bytes. The contents of these frames are as follows:
   - The first 14 bytes of the frame comprise the Ethernet header. The DCHP server responds to the client with an Ethernet Type 0800 (IP) frame, with the destination address set to the Ethernet broadcast address of 255.255.255.255.
   - The next 20 bytes comprise the IP header. The source IP address is set to that of the DHCP server. The destination IP address is set to the IP broadcast address of 255.255.255.255.
   - The next eight bytes are the UDP header. Again, DHCP uses the BOOTP ports, but this time the source port is 67 and the destination port is 68.
   - The remaining 300 bytes of the frame contain Dhcpoffer packet components, including the IP address of the DHCP server, the "Your IP address" field (the IP address being proposed to the client), and proposed lease duration and lease renewal periods. The Dhcpoffer packet also normally includes other TCP/IP configuration parameters, for example, subnet mask and default gateway.

   More than one DHCP server may respond to the Dhcpdiscover packet. If that occurs, each DHCP Server returns a Dhcpoffer packet, and the DHCP client responds to the first Dhcpoffer packet it receives, whether the responding DHCP Server is located on the client subnet or another subnet.

3. The DHCP client responds to the Dhcpoffer packet by sending a *Dhcprequest packet*. This packet contains the IP address offered by the DHCP Server and notifies the DHCP server that the client wants to use the IP configuration information provided in the Dhcpoffer packet. The Dhcprequest packet is either 342 or 590 bytes long, according to the size of the original Dhcpdiscover frame. The contents of these frames are as follows:

   - The first 14 bytes of the frame comprise the Ethernet header. The DCHP client responds with an Ethernet Type 0800 (IP) frame whose destination address is set to the Ethernet broadcast address of 255.255.255.255. Although the DHCP client now knows the address of the DHCP server, it uses a broadcast to notify other DHCP servers that it has accepted an offer from a DHCP server.
   - The next 20 bytes comprise the IP header. The source IP address is set to 0.0.0.0. This is because, although the client has been offered a proposed IP address from the DHCP server, it has not yet finished initializing TCP/IP. The destination IP address is set to the IP broadcast address of 255.255.255.255, again to notify all DHCP servers that the client has accepted an offer.
   - The next eight bytes are the UDP header. Again, DHCP uses the BOOTP ports, but this time the source port is again toggled to the client-side 68 and the destination port to 67.
   - The remainder of the frame contains Dhcprequest packet components. Most of these values are zero or blank, but two important nonblank fields are "Requested address" (the IP address the client is requesting), and "Server Identifier" (the IP address of the server with which the client is negotiating). The client adds these fields to the frame to notify other DHCP servers that the client has accepted an offer from a specific DHCP server and that other DHCP servers return the addresses they proposed to their available pools.

   If the DHCP client determines that one or more of the TCP/IP parameters provided by the Dhcpoffer packet is invalid, the DHCP client instead returns a *Dhcpdecline packet* to notify the DHCP server of the problem.

4. When the DHCP server receives a Dhcprequest packet, it returns a *Dhcpack packet* to acknowledge the request and to notify the responding DHCP client that the negotiated TCP/IP parameters are reserved for that client. The Dhcpack packet is 342 bytes long, and contains the following:

   - The first 14 bytes of the frame comprise the Ethernet header. The DCHP server responds with an Ethernet Type 0800 (IP) frame whose destination address set to the Ethernet broadcast address of 255.255.255.255.

- The next 20 bytes comprise the IP header. The source IP address is that of the DCHP server, and the destination address is set to 0.0.0.0.
- The next eight bytes are the UDP header. Again, DHCP uses the BOOTP ports, but this time the source port is again toggled to the server-side 67 and the destination port to 68.
- The remaining 300 bytes of the frame contain Dhcpack packet components, including Your IP address (which is set to the IP address of the client), which remains set, as do the lease duration, renewal, and binding times set earlier. This frame may also contain various DHCP option information, for example, Router address, DNS Server address, and so on. This option portion is variable, depending on what options are supported and requested by the client, and what options are supported by the server.

When the client receives the Dhcpack packet, it begins participating in the TCP/IP network using the agreed-upon TCP/IP configuration. If the IP address initially proposed is now in use by another client or has otherwise become invalid, the DHCP Server instead returns a *Dhcpnack packet* to notify the client of that fact. When a client receives a Dhcpnack packet, it restarts the DHCP negotiation process by broadcasting a Dhcpdiscover packet. Microsoft TCP clients must also ARP to make sure the address is unique.

A DHCP client that has no further need to participate on the TCP/IP network can also issue a *Dhcprelease packet* to notify the DHCP server of that fact. When the DCHP Server receives a Dhcprelease packet from a client, it cancels the lease on the IP address allocated to that client. This can be forced by using **ipconfig** or **winipcfg**.

NOTE When a DHCP client has been configured to use a static IP address, or when the client is rebooted after already having been assigned an IP address by the DHCP Server, the DHCP client issues a Dhcprequest packet instead of a Dhcpdiscover packet. The Dhcprequest packet includes the IP address formerly assigned to that client, and notifies the DHCP Server that the client would like, if possible, to be assigned the same IP address that it had been using.

The DHCP Server honors this request—unless the IP address in question has already been assigned to a different client in the interim—by returning a Dhcpack packet. If the requested IP address is not available, the DHCP Server instead returns a Dhcpnack packet to inform the client that it must restart the DCHP negotiation by broadcasting a Dhcpdiscover packet.

Understanding DHCP Scopes

A DCHP *scope* is a collection of IP configuration information that defines the IP parameters that will be used by all DCHP clients on a particular subnet. Each subnet may have exactly one DHCP scope, which comprises a single contiguous range of IP addresses. Each DHCP scope is defined by the administrator using the DHCP Manager application. A DHCP scope defines the following information:

Name
: Identifies the subnet served by this DHCP scope. May be as large as 128 characters, and may use any combination of letters, numbers, and hyphens.

Comment
: Further describes the DHCP scope, if necessary.

IP Address Inclusion Range
: Defines the contiguous range of IP addresses assigned to the IP address pool by specifying the beginning and ending IP addresses in that range. These are the IP addresses available to the DHCP Server for assignment to DHCP clients.

IP Address Exclusion Range
: Specifies one or more IP addresses (or contiguous groups of IP addresses) within the IP Address Inclusion Range that are not available to the DHCP Server for assignment to DHCP clients. Excluding IP addresses allows you to reserve a range of IP addresses that can be manually assigned to DHCP Servers, routers, and other devices that require a static IP address.

Subnet Mask
: Defines the subnet mask that identifies the logical network to which the IP address belongs.

Lease Duration
: Defines the period for which the DHCP Server *lends* or *leases* the IP address to a DHCP client. The lease duration may be unlimited, or may be specified in days, hours, and minutes.

In addition to the DCHP scope characteristics just described, you can use DHCP Manager to modify the following optional DHCP scope items:

Deactivate
: Immediately releases the reserved IP address when a computer is physically removed from the network, and returns that IP address to the pool available for reassignment. This option is particularly useful if you have notebook users who frequently connect to and then disconnect from your TCP/IP network. It is moot if your network comprises only hard-wired desktop systems.

Renewal
: Determines the renewal period for leased IP addresses. By default, the renewal process occurs when half of the lease duration has expired.

Reserve

Allows you to reserve one or more IP addresses and assign them to devices like DHCP Servers and routers that require a static IP address. You needn't use this option. You can simply exclude an IP address range and assign IP addresses from that range to servers and routers as needed. However, using this option maps the assignments of static IP addresses to devices, and allows you to view those assignments in DHCP Manager.

NOTE With the release of Windows NT Server 4.0 Service Pack 2 (SP2), Microsoft added support for a new DHCP feature called *superscopes*. By using superscopes, you can:

- Support DHCP clients in a multinetted environment, in other words, a local network that comprises multiple subnets (or logical networks) on a single physical network. Prior to SP2, Windows NT Server 4.0 did not allow addresses from multiple scopes to be assigned to a single physical network, and the only workaround was to install a separate network adapter to support each IP subnet. The DHCP Server supplied with SP2 allows you to create multiple scopes and then group them together into a superscope.
- Support DHCP clients on a remote multinetted network via a bootp relay agent.

Understanding DHCP Options

In addition to the standard DHCP scope configuration parameters described in the preceding section, you can use DHCP Manager to configure the DHCP options defined by RFC1533 and RFC1541. DHCP options are used to configure advanced TCP/IP settings like WINS and DNS integration.

You can specify DHCP options individually for each DHCP scope, or globally for all DCHP scopes. DHCP option values defined globally are used for all DHCP scopes except under the following circumstances. First, if a global DHCP option is also defined for an individual DHCP scope, the value set for the individual DHCP scope overrides the global setting, and is used for that DHCP scope. Second, DHCP options set for an individual DHCP client override both global and scope DHCP option settings, and are used for that DHCP client.

The Microsoft DHCP Server supports most of the DHCP options defined by RFC1533 and RFC1541. Microsoft DHCP clients, however, understand only a small subset of these DHCP options. Defining DHCP option values in Microsoft DHCP Server that are not supported by Microsoft DHCP clients is useful only to support non-Microsoft DHCP clients that support those options. The client-side and server-side DHCP options supported by Windows NT are detailed in Appendix C, *Microsoft DHCP Option Support*.

A Microsoft DHCP packet can contain up to 312 bytes of DHCP option data, which is more than sufficient for most DHCP configurations. However, this 312-byte limit is fixed. Some third-party DHCP servers and clients allow you to use *option overlays*, which store additional DHCP option data in unused space in the DHCP packet. Neither the Microsoft DHCP Server nor Microsoft DHCP clients support the use of option overlays. If you attempt to specify a complex DHCP option configuration—one that requires more than 312 bytes of storage—option data beyond the 312-byte limit is truncated and ignored. Therefore, if your Microsoft clients obtain their TCP/IP configuration parameters from a non-Microsoft DHCP server, make sure that all DHCP options supplied by that server fit within the allowable length. If that is not possible, make sure that the DHCP options required by the Microsoft clients appear within the first 312 bytes of option data.

Understanding DHCP Databases

The Windows NT Server 4.0 DHCP Server service uses the same database engine as Microsoft Exchange Server 4. Installing DHCP Server automatically creates the following database files in *%SystemRoot%\system32\Dhcp*.

dhcp.mdb
: The main DHCP Server database file.

Dhcp.tmp
: The swap file used when indexing the main DHCP database file. According to Microsoft, this file may remain as an orphan after a crash. However, I found that this file existed in the DHCP directory on a server that had had DHCP Server freshly installed, and had not crashed.

j50.chk
: A checkpoint file, used to maintain and verify database coherency.

j50.log
: Contains a log of DHCP transactions. May be used after a DHCP Server crash to roll back the DHCP database to a coherent state.

j50?????.log
: Another file whose contents are used to recover the DHCP database after a crash. On my server, the actual name of this file is *j50000A2.log*.

res?.log
: Transaction logging data.

The DHCP database is modified dynamically. Each time a DHCP client boots and is assigned TCP/IP configuration parameters by the DHCP Server, these changes are recorded to the DHCP database. Similarly, as DHCP client leases expire, these changes are also recorded.

WARNING The DHCP database remains open at all times while the DHCP Server is operating. Do not attempt to delete or modify any of these database files.

Because the DHCP database files are always open, it is impossible to back them up using traditional means. To ensure that critical DHCP data is not lost, Windows NT Server automatically backs up the DHCP database to the *%SystemRoot%\system32\Dhcp\backup* folder. Once written, these files are then closed, and so can be backed up normally.

NOTE By default, Windows NT Server backs up the DHCP database every 60 minutes, which is usually more than sufficient protection. However, if your network is very large (or very small), you may want to change the default backup frequency. You can do so by modifying the Registry value entry *BackupInterval* in *HKLM\SYSTEM\CurrentControlSet\Services\DHCPServer\Parameters*.

The default value for *BackupInterval* is 0x3C (or 60 minutes). If you have many DHCP clients, particularly ones that connect to and disconnect from the network frequently, setting the *BackupInterval* to a smaller value—perhaps 0x14, or 20 minutes—makes sense. Similarly, if your DHCP environment is small and relatively static, setting *BackupInterval* to a larger value—perhaps 0xF0, or 240 minutes—risks little (but also gains little).

If your primary backup program can be run from a batch file, you can use it to backup the main DHCP database. To do so, create a batch file that shuts down the DHCP Server (closing the database), runs the backup program, and then restarts the DHCP Server. Controlling the DHCP Server from the command line is described at the end of the following section on installing DHCP Server.

Planning for DHCP

Installing the Microsoft DHCP Server is so easy that some administrators install it without much thought, and paint themselves into a corner by doing so. In a typical network, the DHCP Server places such small demands on server resources that you can easily forget that DHCP is even there. That's a mistake. Once it is installed, the DHCP Server becomes a mission-critical component of your network. If the main DHCP Server fails and you do not have a standby DHCP server available, all of your workstations lose TCP/IP connectivity at the end of their lease, or when they reboot.

The size and complexity of your network largely determine how much DHCP planning you need to do. You might be able to plan DHCP for a small network in a few minutes on the back of an envelope. Planning DHCP for a large, complex internetwork may require much more effort. Before you install DHCP, spend some time thinking about how you want DHCP to work for you and how you will cope with a failure.

Planning DHCP for a Simple Network

Planning DHCP for a simple network—one in which all devices are connected to a single logical segment—is pretty straightforward. A simple network may use repeaters to extend the reach of its physical segment. It may also use bridges to connect multiple physical segments into a single logical segment. It does not, however, use routers to link multiple logical networks (or subnets) into a single network—with one exception; a simple network may include a border router that is used to link that network to the public Internet. Take the following steps to plan and implement DHCP:

1. Determine which hosts on the network require static IP addresses and which can use dynamically assigned IP addresses. For those that require static addresses—typically DHCP Servers, WINS Servers, DNS Servers, Web Servers, and the border router—record the IP addresses in use.
2. You may use a single DHCP Server to support all of the clients on a simple network if you are willing to forego DHCP Server redundancy. If you decide that you must have redundancy, as you probably should, determine how to implement it. If you have a second server on the network that can run the Microsoft DHCP Server, you will always have at least the first of the following options, and perhaps the second as well.
   - Configure the second server as a standby DHCP Server, which will be used only if the primary DHCP Server fails. You can use the Windows NT Replicator service to store a nearly real-time copy of the DHCP database on the second server.
   - The Microsoft DHCP Server cannot use shared scopes. That is, IP addresses assigned to the address pool on one DHCP Server cannot also be assigned to a second DHCP Server. However, if you have enough IP addresses available, you can configure both servers to be available simultaneously. During routine network operation, DHCP clients might receive their addresses from either server, depending on which responded first. If one of the DHCP Servers fails, the other would remain available to support clients.

For example, if you are using an Internet Class C address block, and you have fewer than 100 devices that will use dynamic address assignment, you might assign the IP host addresses in the range 1 through 99 to the first DHCP Server and the host addresses in the range 100 through 199 to the second DHCP Server. Devices that require static IP addresses would be assigned host numbers in the range 200 through 254, which would be excluded on both DHCP Servers. Although running two DHCP servers is fine in theory, some administrators have found that attempting to do so causes problems. Instead, they simply keep a good backup of their DHCP database, and are prepared to restore it to another server if necessary.

If you have only one server running Windows NT Server on the network, you can also use a third-party DHCP server, for example, one running on a Unix host, to provide redundancy. You can implement this sort of redundancy using either method described previously—as a standby DHCP server or using independent DHCP scopes.

3. Install the Microsoft DHCP Server and create a scope, excluding the IP addresses used by devices that are assigned static IP addresses. Use DHCP Manager, if necessary, to define DHCP Options for the scope. Start the scope before rebooting the clients.
4. Enable the DHCP client software on each of the clients you want to use dynamic addressing. Reboot the client and verify that it has been assigned a TCP/IP configuration by the DHCP Server and is functioning correctly. For Windows 95 clients, for example, use *Winipcfg.exe* for this task.

Planning DHCP for Large Networks

Planning DHCP for a large, complex network (or internetwork) is considerably more involved than doing so for a simple network. Although there is essentially no theoretical upper limit to the number of clients that a single DHCP server can support, practical limits appear on real-world networks because of issues like IP address classes, subnet topologies, redundancy needs, and server bottlenecks.

If such a thing exists as a typical arrangement for a complex network, it might look something like this:

- The network is arranged in logical subnets that match the physical structure of the internetwork.
- One IP subnet serves as the backbone, with physical subnets branching from this backbone, each of which is defined as a separate IP subnet.
- Each subnet contains a single Windows NT Server computer that is configured as both a DHCP Server and a WINS Server (see Chapter 7, *Using Windows Internet Name Service*). Each of these servers administers a defined range

of IP addresses with a specific subnet mask, and is defined as the default gateway for its subnet. Because this server is also a WINS Server, it can provide NetBIOS name resolution services to all hosts on its subnet.

- These DHCP and WINS Servers can each serve as a backup for the other servers. The administrator partitions the address pool and allocates it among the servers, allowing each server to provide addresses to remote clients.

Beyond this one-size-fits-all generic approach, when you implement DHCP on a routed internetwork, your planning should encompass the issues described in the following sections.

Routing issues

The defining characteristic of a complex network is that it uses routers to connect subnets via LAN or WAN links. Therein lies a difficulty, because DHCP is a broadcast protocol, and some routers simply discard DHCP broadcast packets instead of forwarding them.

Routers that implement the DHCP/BOOTP relay agent (as defined by RFC1542) forward DHCP broadcast packets properly, and are referred to as RFC1542-compliant. Many routers, particularly those that are intended primarily as IPX routers and route IP only as an adjunct, are not RFC1542-compliant. On RFC1542-compliant routers, the relay agent intercepts DHCP broadcast requests from clients on its local subnet and forwards those packets to a DHCP server on a remote subnet. When the DHCP server responds, the router forwards the response to the local client.

Even if your routers are RFC1542-compliant, your goal should be to minimize B-node broadcasts across the routers, particularly on slow WAN links. Accordingly, your existing subnet topology and the types of routers you have installed will have a distinct impact on how many DHCP servers you need and where they must be placed. If all or some of your routers are not RFC1542-compliant and cannot be upgraded to become so, you have two alternatives:

Install additional DHCP servers
: Install one or more DHCP servers on each subnet that connects to your network with a noncompliant router.

Use the Windows NT DHCP Relay Agent
: If your routers can't pass DHCP broadcast packets, and you don't want to place DHCP servers on each subnet, the final alternative is to install the Windows NT DHCP Relay Agent. A *relay agent* is a program used to pass specific types of IP packets between subnets. The DHCP Relay Agent performs this function for DHCP and BOOTP packets according to the RFC1542 specification.

Having the ability to move DHCP broadcast packets across a router—either via compliant router hardware or the DHCP Relay Agent—is probably the single most important component in planning and implementing DHCP in a large-scale environment. Being able to cross routers gives you flexibility. For example, if a DHCP server on one subnet goes down, clients on that subnet will still be able to use a DHCP server on another subnet. If your network is not configured to allow DHCP broadcast packets to cross routers, all of your troubles are amplified. Not only must you provide a DHCP Server for each subnet, but you have to worry about what happens when that DHCP server fails.

Redundancy issues

Once implemented, DHCP becomes a critical part of your network. If no DHCP server is available, clients cannot initialize TCP/IP. The reasons to establish redundancy and the methods for doing so are similar to those in a simple network, but are complicated by the presence of multiple subnets and routers.

If for one reason or another you are unable to provide redundancy on a particular subnet—perhaps one located at a small branch office—consider not using DHCP at all for that subnet. Instead, configure static IP addresses and other TCP/IP parameters for hosts on that subnet, and exclude those addresses elsewhere on your network.

Traffic issues

Although DHCP is a broadcast protocol, DHCP normally has little effect on network traffic. DHCP traffic occurs on the network in the following situations:

IP Address Lease
: The initial discovery and lease process generates only four packets (plus an additional packet for the second and subsequent DCHP servers that respond). The entire exchange totals either 1,368 bytes (4*342) or 1,864 bytes (2*342 + 2*590), and takes only a fraction of a second on a lightly loaded Ethernet. The same process occurs if a client is moved to a different subnet, or if the network adapter in the client is replaced.

Automatic renewal
: This process requires only two packets (Dhcprequest and Dhcpack) and requires even less time than the IP address lease process. If the lease duration remains at the default of three days, the automatic renewal process occurs only once every 18 hours.

Ipconfig
: If a client uses the **ipconfig** utility to manually refresh or release its address, it takes only a fraction of a second to transmit the data over an Ethernet and this process occurs only when invoked by a user.

In the ordinary course of events, therefore, DHCP traffic can usually be safely ignored for planning purposes. At least one exception exists, however. Some networks have many clients that are started almost at the same time—usually at starting time and right after lunch. When this occurs, the network may be very heavily loaded, particularly if clients are configured to download profiles or start applications from a network drive.

We have seen Ethernet utilization climb above 95 percent in situations like this, which means that almost no traffic is getting through due to all the collisions. In such a situation, not only may DHCP be unable to function, it may actually add to the problem because of re-broadcasts by DHCP clients that are unable to obtain a response. In the worst-case scenario on a very heavily loaded network, a DHCP client may require literally minutes to boot (in approximately five minute increments because of the five-minute timeout retry period).

Of course, this is not really a DHCP traffic issue so much as it is a philosophical one. The solutions are either to leave your client computers running all the time (which is probably a good idea anyway), or to subnet the network and install as many additional DHCP servers as are necessary to ensure acceptable response time to DHCP client requests. Using either solution also makes the DHCP boot-time problem go away.

DHCP scope issues

The Microsoft DHCP Server allows you to define DHCP options globally, for a specified scope, or for an individual client. DHCP option values defined specifically for a client override values for the same option defined at the scope level, and values defined at the scope level override those defined at the global level.

Defining DHCP options in a complex network requires some thought. Defining the scope for a DHCP Server on a local subnet defines the required DHCP options—IP address range and subnet mask—for hosts on that subnet. If hosts on that subnet are to be able to communicate outside the subnet, you must also define a default gateway with the *003—Router* DHCP option.

Beyond this, things get a little hazy. If that DHCP Server is supporting only clients on its local subnet using a single scope, it makes little difference whether you define DHCP options at the scope level or the global level. If that DHCP Server is also supporting clients on other subnets—either as the primary or backup DHCP Server—you have to consider which options need to be defined globally and which for the local subnet only.

For example, if your company has only one DNS Domain Name, you might define *015—Domain Name* globally, because clients on all subnets that use this DHCP Server will use the same domain name, so all scopes should inherit it from Global DHCP options. Conversely, if the DHCP Server supports multiple scopes that map to different subnets, you would have to define the value for *003—Router* at the scope level.

In conjunction with this, you must coordinate scopes between the subnets. For example, assume that you have two DHCP Servers, A and B. Each is the primary DHCP Server for its own subnet. DHCP Server A serves subnet 192.168.115 and DHCP Server B serves subnet 192.168.116. However, you would also like DHCP Servers A and B to back each other up. This means that you need to define two scopes on each server, and that you must reserve a portion of the available IP address range on each subnet to be defined as the secondary scope on the server on the other subnet.

For example, on DHCP Server A you might define a primary scope that encompassed 192.168.115.1 through .175, reserving the remaining addresses for DHCP Server B. On DHCP Server B, you might define a primary scope that encompassed 192.168.116.1 through .175, reserving the remaining addresses for DHCP Server A. You would then define the secondary scopes; 192.168.116.176 through .254 on DHCP Server A and 192.168.115.176 through .254 on DHCP Server B.

Installing the DHCP Server Service

To install the DHCP Server service, take the following steps:

1. Right-click the Network Neighborhood icon on your desktop, and then click Properties to display the Network property sheet. Click the Services tab to display the Network Services page, shown in Figure 6-1.

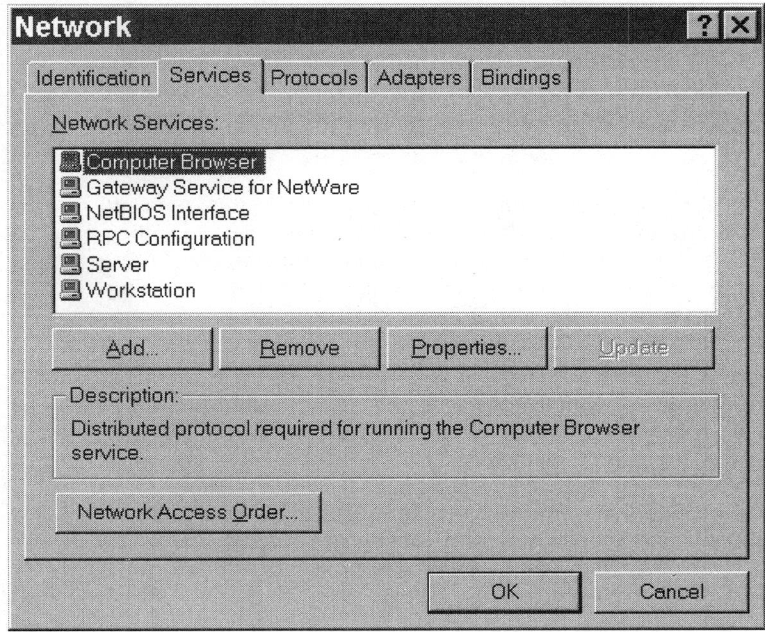

Figure 6-1. The Network Services page

2. Click Add... to display the Select Network Service dialog. Windows NT builds a list of available network services and displays them in the Network Service pane.
3. Highlight Microsoft DHCP Server and click on OK. Windows NT displays the Windows NT Setup dialog to prompt you for the location of the distribution files. Accept the default location, or specify a new location, and then click Continue. Windows NT copies the distribution files and then displays an informational message.

NOTE Any server running the Microsoft DHCP Server service must itself be assigned a static IP address. That is, a DHCP Server cannot obtain its own IP address from another DHCP Server.

---

4. Click on OK to close the informational message box and return to the Network property sheet, which now shows Microsoft DHCP Server as an installed service. Click Close to complete the installation. If this server was configured previously to obtain its IP address from a DHCP Server, the TCP/IP property sheet will be displayed, allowing you to enter a static IP address for the new DHCP Server. Windows NT Server configures, stores, and reviews the bindings, and then displays the Network Settings Change dialog. Click Yes to restart the server immediately, or click No to wait until the next routine server restart to make the DHCP Server service available.

NOTE Windows NT Server configures the DHCP Server service by default to start automatically each time the server is booted. You can use the Services applet in Control Panel to modify the startup settings for the DHCP Server service, or to start, stop, pause, or continue the DHCP Server service.

You can also control the DHCP Server service from the command prompt, using the commands **net start dhcpserver**, **net stop dhcpserver**, **net pause dhcpserver**, and **net continue dhcpserver**. These commands are useful primarily for creating batch files to backup your server, including the DHCP Server database, during off hours. You can stop the DHCP Server service, run the backup, and then restart the DHCP Server service, all from within a batch file.

For more extensive command-line control, use the **dhcpcmd** utility included in the Windows NT Server Resource Kit. This program allows you to perform numerous tasks related to managing your DHCP Server, including: adding additional IP address ranges to an existing scope; adding a reserved IP to an existing scope; listing IP lease information in detailed form, optionally including hardware information; displaying DHCP Server statistics; and displaying and setting DHCP Server parameters.

Installing and Configuring the DHCP Relay Agent

You install the DHCP Relay Agent, like other Windows NT services, from the Services pages of the Control Panel Network dialog. To install it, right-click the Network Neighborhood icon on your desktop to display the context-sensitive menu and choose Properties to display the Network dialog. Display the Services page and choose Add. Windows NT builds a list of available network services and displays the Select Network Service dialog. Highlight DHCP Relay Agent and then choose OK to install it. As usual, you need to restart the server before the changes take effect.

Once the DHCP Relay Agent is installed, you can configure it from the DHCP Relay page of the Microsoft TCP/IP Properties dialog, shown in Figure 6-2. To view this page, display the Network dialog, click the Protocols tab, highlight TCP/IP Protocol, and choose Properties to display the Microsoft TCP/IP Properties dialog.

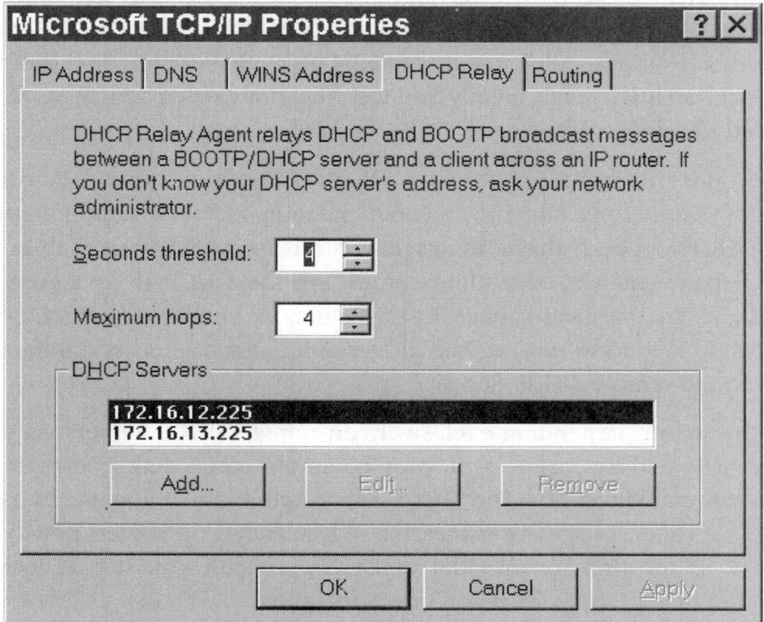

Figure 6-2. The DHCP Relay page of the Microsoft TCP/IP Properties dialog

To enable DHCP Relay, you must enter the IP address of at least one DHCP Server. To do so, choose Add to display the DHCP Relay Agent dialog, enter the IP address, and choose Add. Windows NT copies the address to the DHCP Servers pane. To edit or remove the IP address for a DCHP server, highlight it in the DHCP Servers pane and choose Edit or Remove.

The only remaining configuration steps are to set values for Seconds threshold and Maximum hops. The Maximum hops value controls the maximum number of times a DHCP packet can be relayed, and is analogous to setting the maximum number of router hops in RIP. The Seconds threshold value requires a bit more explanation.

A DHCP client sets the seconds field in the first DHCP packet to zero, and increments this value by one for each subsequent packet it retransmits. The setting of the Seconds threshold field controls whether or not the DHCP Relay agent forwards a received packet to the remote DHCP Server. The DHCP Relay agent compares the value in the seconds field of DHCP packets it receives against the value set for Seconds threshold. If the seconds field in the packet is less than the Seconds threshold value, the DHCP Relay Agent discards the packet. If the seconds field in the packet is greater than or equal to the Seconds threshold value, the DHCP Relay agent forwards it to the DHCP Server on the remote subnet.

Setting a nonzero value for Seconds threshold allows local DHCP Servers time to respond before the DHCP Relay Agent forwards a DHCP request to a DHCP Server located on a remote subnet. Allowing the local DHCP Server the first shot at responding to local DHCP clients greatly reduces the number of DHCP packets that are forwarded to remote subnets.

The value for Seconds threshold is set to 4 by default, which is the value Microsoft recommends. However, implicit in this recommendation is the assumption that there *is* a local DHCP Server. If this is the case, 4 is a reasonable value. If there is no local DHCP Server, you are depending entirely on the DHCP Relay Agent to service DHCP clients on the local subnet. In this situation, you *could* set the Seconds threshold value to zero to ensure that all DHCP request packets will immediately be relayed to the remote DHCP Server.

Needless to say, however, depending exclusively on remote DHCP Servers via the DHCP Relay Agent is a risky business. If your communications link goes down, local clients will be unable to boot. The DHCP Relay Agent is really intended as a means to provide secondary DHCP services for redundancy in a routed network. Rather than use it as the primary provider of DHCP services, you should install DHCP Server and define a DHCP scope on the local subnet.

Managing DHCP with DHCP Manager

After you have installed the DHCP Server Service, you use DHCP Manager to configure and manage it. Before the DHCP Server can support clients, you must complete the initial configuration steps described in the following section. After you have configured the DHCP Server, you can use DHCP Manager to reconfigure the DHCP Server as necessary, and routinely to view the status of the DHCP Server and DHCP clients.

Defining a DHCP Scope

After you have installed the DHCP Server and restarted the server, the next step is to define a DHCP scope. The DHCP scope determines the range of IP addresses that will be available for assignment to DHCP clients, and specifies other IP configuration information. To define a DHCP scope, proceed as follows:

1. From the Start Button, choose Programs → Administrative Tools (Common) → DHCP Manager to start DHCP Manager.
2. In the DHCP Servers pane, highlight the DCHP Server for which you want to create a DHCP scope. From the Scope menu, select Create to display the Create Scope–[machine-name] dialog, shown in Figure 6-3.

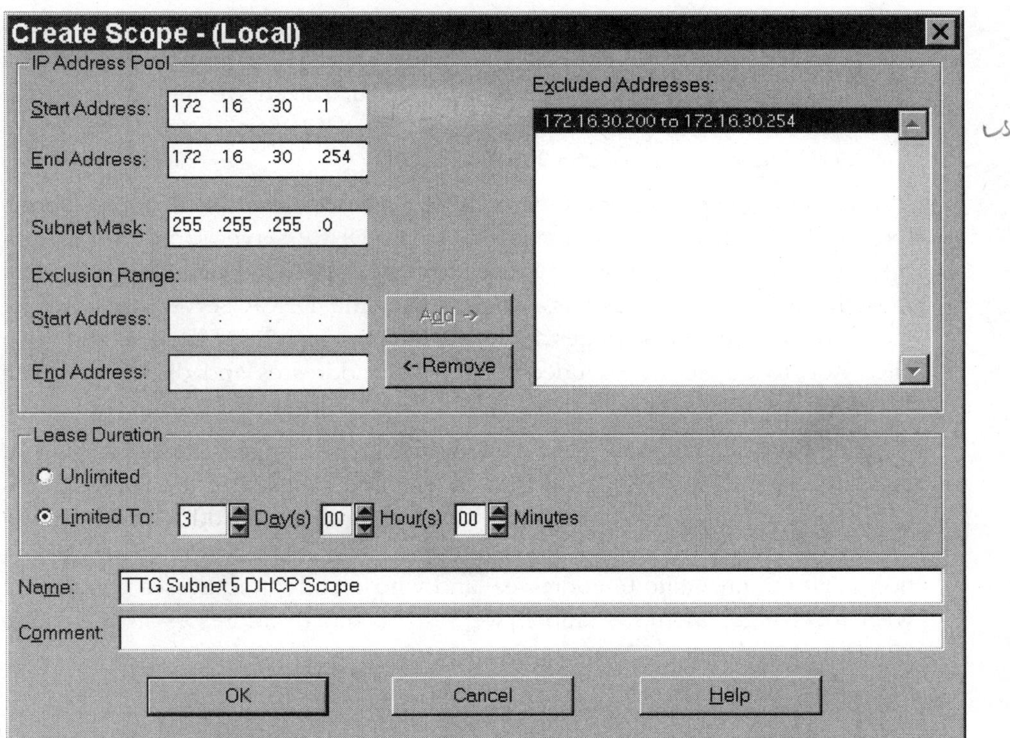

Figure 6-3. The Create Scope dialog

3. Define first the range of IP addresses that will be allocated to the IP Address Pool. These are the IP addresses that the DHCP Server service has available for assignment to DHCP clients. Enter values for the Start Address and End Address to define this range. The example uses the Class B IP address 172.16.0.0. It is subnetted using an 8-bit subnet mask. We have assigned a range of addresses in subnet 30 to the DHCP Server.

WARNING Do not include the first and last host addresses in the range when defining the DHCP scope. For example, to use the entire subnet 172.16.30.0 for the DHCP scope, assign the range 172.16.30.1 through 172.16.30.254 to the scope. Do not use 172.16.30.0 through 172.16.30.255. You don't want DHCP to assign the host address 0 to any device. You really don't want DHCP to assign the host address 255 (broadcast) to a device.

---

4. Enter a valid value for Subnet Mask. The value you enter here must correspond to the range of addresses you entered in the step immediately preceding. For example, we entered the value 255.255.255.0 here because it corresponds to the 8-bit subnet mask in use. If instead we had assigned the entire unsubnetted address 172.16.0.0 to the DHCP Server, we would have specified a subnet mask of 255.255.0.0.
5. Define the range of addresses that will be excluded from the IP address pool. Excluded IP addresses are not available to the DHCP Server service for assignment to clients. You assign addresses from the excluded range to hosts that must have a static IP address, for example, the DHCP Server itself. Under Exclusion Range, enter values for Start Address and End Address and then click Add to define an excluded range of IP addresses and display it in the Excluded Addresses pane.

   You may repeat the process to exclude additional ranges, if necessary. You may also exclude a single IP address by entering its value in the Start Address field, leaving the End Address field blank, and clicking Add. Ordinarily, the only reason to use more than one exclusion range is to accommodate existing hosts that require static IP addresses, and whose current addresses you do not wish to change. In the example, we reserve the IP addresses in the range 172.16.30.200 through 172.16.30.254 inclusive.

TIP Define the DCHP scope to include the entire subnet, and then use exclusions to reduce the size of the available pool. For example, if you want to assign only 10 pooled addresses from the address 172.16.30.0/24, do not specify 172.16.30.1 through 172.16.30.10 as the DHCP scope. Instead, specify 172.16.30.1 through 172.16.30.254 as the DHCP scope, and then exclude 172.16.30.11 through 172.16.30.254.

Either method of restricting the number of addresses assigned to the pool works, at least until you need more pooled addresses. If you defined a small DHCP scope, you must remove the existing scope and create a new one, not something to be undertaken lightly on a production server. If you instead used exclusions to limit the number of pooled addresses, you can simply reduce the size of the excluded range in the existing DHCP scope, which automatically increases the number of available pooled addresses on the fly.

When working with C-block size network addresses, the common convention is to assign the host address 200 to the router for that subnet. Most administrators define the DHCP scope to include the entire C-block, and then exclude host addresses 200 through 254, reserving that range for routers, servers, RAS adapters, and other devices that require static addresses.

---

6. The next step is to specify the period for which IP addresses will be leased. By default, Windows NT Server uses a value of three days, which is appropriate for most environments. If you have relatively few hosts competing for relatively many available IP addresses, you may wish to set a higher value. If IP addresses are in shorter supply relative to the number of hosts contending for them, or if you have many notebook users plugging into and unplugging from your network frequently, you may wish to set a shorter lease duration.

Enter a Name, and optionally a Comment, to identify the DHCP scope. Click on OK to create the new scope. DHCP Manager displays a message to inform you that the new scope has been created but has not yet been activated. Click Yes to activate the new scope.

Defining a DHCP Superscope

To define a DHCP superscope, take the following steps:

1. Use DHCP Manager to create two or more DHCP scopes, as described in the preceding section.
2. Set global or scope properties for each scope individually, and then activate the scope.
3. After you have created, configured, and activated each of the individual scopes that are to be grouped into a superscope, select the DHCP Server in the left pane.

4. Select the Scope menu, and then select Superscopes to display the Superscopes dialog.
5. Click Create Superscope to display the Create Superscope dialog, type a name for the superscope in the Superscope Name: field, and then click on OK to return to the Superscopes dialog, where you will find the name of your new superscope selected and displayed in the Superscope Name drop-down list.
6. Use the Add and Remove buttons to move scopes from the Available Scopes pane to the Child Sub-Scopes pane. Move scopes to the Child Sub-Scopes pane in the reverse order that you want them to be used. That is, scopes are added sequentially, with each newly added scope appearing at the top of the Child Sub-Scopes pane. Scopes are used in the order that they appear, from first at the top to last at the bottom. When all of the scopes that you want to combine into the superscope appear in the Child Sub-Scopes pane in the proper order, click on OK to create the superscope and return to the main DHCP Manager window.

WARNING If the superscope is on a local multi-net—one not connected via a DHCP Relay Agent—and if the Registry value entry *IgnoreBroadcastFlag* is set true, then each logical subnet must be directly accessible to the DHCP Server. In other words, a local route must exist for each subnet. If all of the logical subnets are connected to a single physical network adapter, you can meet this requirement by assigning multiple IP addresses to that single adapter.

Setting DHCP Options

Before the DHCP Server can support clients properly, you must first set various DHCP Options. You can do so by choosing one of the following options from the DHCP Options menu of DHCP Manager:

Scope
: Displays the DHCP Options Scope dialog, which allows you to define the DHCP Options to be used for the currently selected DHCP scope.

Global
: Displays the DHCP Options Global dialog, which allows you to define the DHCP Options to be used for all DHCP scopes on the selected DHCP Server.

Defaults
: Displays the DHCP Options Default Values dialog, which allows you to define the standard DHCP Options to be set whenever a new DHCP scope is defined, and to add, edit, or delete custom DHCP Option types.

Which DHCP Options need to be set depends upon your own environment. At a minimum, you should configure the following DHCP Options:

Option 003—Router
: Defines the default gateway to be used by DHCP clients.

Option 006—DNS Servers
: Defines IP addresses for one or more Domain Name System (DNS) servers to be used by the DHCP clients.

Option 015—Domain Name
: Defines the Internet domain name to which DHCP clients belonging to this scope are assigned.

If you are running Windows Internet Name Service (WINS) servers, you should also define the following two DHCP Options, which are further explained in Chapter 7:

Option 044—WINS/NBNS Servers
: Defines IP addresses for one or more WINS/NBNS (NetBIOS Name Servers) servers to be used by DHCP clients.

Option 046—WINS/NBT Node Type
: Defines the NetBIOS over TCP/IP node type, as defined in RFC1001 and RFC1002, where type 01 equals b-node, type 02 equals p-node, type 04 equals m-node, and type 08 equals h-node. On multi-homed servers (those with more than one adapter), one node type is assigned to the computer and used by all adapters.

To set the DHCP Options required for minimum TCP/IP connectivity, proceed as follows:

1. From DHCP Manager, click DHCP Options, then Scope, to display the DHCP Options Scope dialog.
2. In the Unused Options pane, highlight *003 Router* and then click Add to move it to the Active Options pane.
3. Highlight the Active Option to be modified, in this case *003 Router*, and click Value. The dialog box alters, as shown in Figure 6-4, to display a pane listing currently assigned values for the selected DHCP Option.
4. Click Edit Array to display the IP Address Array Editor. Enter the IP address for your router (default gateway) in the New IP Address field, and click Add to insert it into the IP Addresses pane. If you do not know the IP address of the router, type its fully qualified Internet name (e.g. *kiwi.ttgnet.com*) in the Server Name field and click Resolve. Windows NT resolves the IP address for the host, and inserts it into the New IP Address field. You don't need the domain

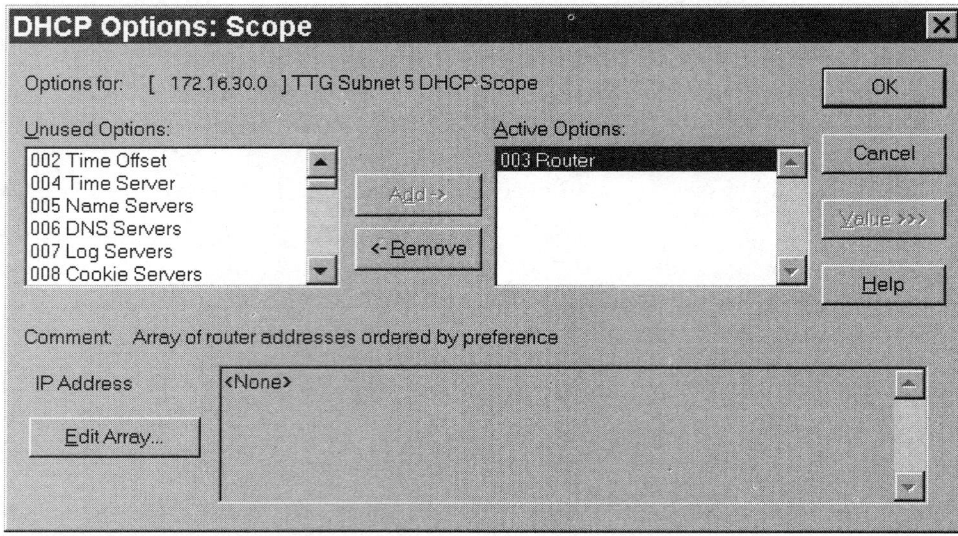

Figure 6-4. The DHCP Options: Scope dialog

name. If it is NT, WINS will find it, but if your DNS is Unix, that has to be configured and working right on the host machine for this to work.

You may repeat this procedure to enter IP address values for additional routers. However, only the first value listed will be used (as the default gateway) unless the server listed as the default gateway fails or is otherwise unavailable. If this occurs, the second address listed will be used as the default gateway, and so on. Use the up and down arrows to rearrange IP addresses so that the host you want to use as your default gateway is shown first. Click on OK to save your changes and return to the DHCP Options: Scope dialog. The Active Options pane now displays *003 Router* with the IP address you assigned showing in the lower pane.

5. In the Unused Options pane, highlight *006 DNS Servers* and then click Add to move it to the Active Options pane. Repeat step 4 to add IP address values for both your Primary and Secondary DNS Servers. Again, use the up and down arrows to ensure that your Primary DNS Server is listed first.
6. In the Unused Options pane, highlight *015 Domain Name* and then click Add to move it to the Active Options pane. The modified DHCP Options: Scope dialog box is displayed. Enter the Internet Domain Name (e.g. *ttgnet.com*) in the String field. Do not enter the Windows NT Domain name here.
7. Click on OK to save your changes and return to the main DHCP Manager screen. The DHCP Options you have set and the values assigned for them are

displayed in the Option Configuration pane. Verify that you have set all necessary DHCP Options to the correct value, and then exit DHCP Manager. The changes you have made to the DHCP configuration take effect immediately. Any DCHP client that now boots will use the currently defined options. Any DHCP client that is already connected to the network will not use the modified DHCP Options until the next time that client is booted and needs to renew its lease.

NOTE The DHCP configuration illustrated in this section prepares the DHCP Server to support basic TCP/IP connectivity. If your network includes WINS Servers, you must also set DHCP Option *044—WINS/NBNS Servers* and DHCP Option *046—WINS/NBT Node Type*. These options are set using a procedure similar to that described above for the required DHCP Options.

Adding Client Reservations

You can use DHCP Manager to configure static TCP/IP configuration information for a specific client, which is called making a *client reservation*. To add a client reservation, take the following steps:

1. Click Add Reservations from the Scope menu to display the Add Reserved Clients dialog, shown in Figure 6-5.
2. Enter the IP address to be reserved for that client in the IP Address field. In the example, the IP address 172.16.6.10 is being reserved.
3. Enter the MAC address of the network adapter in the Unique Identifier field. The MAC address is the hardware address of the network adapter. In the example, the client has an Ethernet network adapter whose MAC address is 00-40-33-23-C0-53.
4. Enter the Internet name of the machine (not including the Internet domain name) in the Client Name field. In the example, the full Internet name of the computer is *thor.ttgnet.com*, so we have specified the client name as *THOR*. The Client Name field is really only a convenience for the administrator. It provides a more meaningful description of the client when viewing the display of active leases. Because the client doesn't register its name with the server, the server cannot provide this information. If the Client Name field is not completed, all you will see in the display of active leases is the IP address and the reservation in use.
5. You may optionally enter a value in the Client Comment field that further describes the client.

6. When you have completed the required fields, click Add to create an entry in the DHCP database for this client reservation and return to the main DHCP Manager screen. Exit DHCP Manager. The changes you have made to the DHCP configuration take effect immediately. Any DCHP client that now boots will use the currently defined options. Any DHCP client that is already connected to the network will not use the modified DHCP Options until the next time that client is booted.

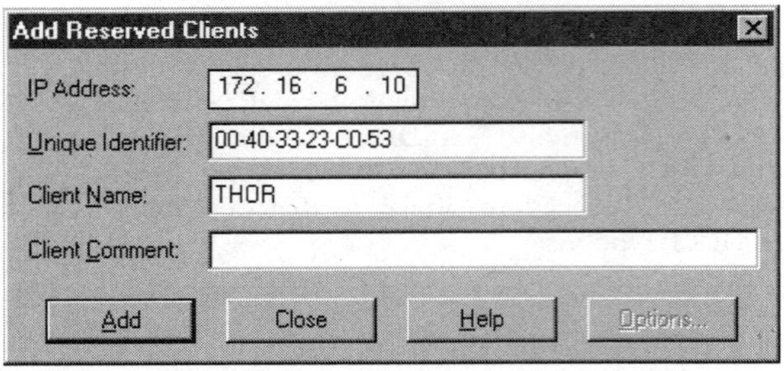

Figure 6-5. The Add Reserved Clients dialog

Viewing, Modifying, and Deleting Active Leases

You can use DHCP Manager to view or delete active leases for ordinary DHCP clients and to view, modify, or delete active leases for Reserved DHCP clients. The options you have available depend on the type of DHCP client that is selected.

Viewing and deleting active leases for ordinary DHCP clients

To work with an ordinary DHCP client—one that is assigned its TCP/IP configuration information dynamically by the DHCP Server—take the following steps:

1. Click Active Leases from the Scope menu to display the Active Leases – [*Scope Name*] dialog, shown in Figure 6-6. You may choose the way in which clients are sorted by marking either the "Sort leases by IP address" option button or the "Sort leases by Name" option button. Reserved DHCP clients are indicated by the word "Reservation" appearing next to the IP address and client name. All other clients shown are ordinary DHCP clients. In this example, only one DHCP client is visible because we have configured only that one client on our test network to use DHCP.
2. Highlight the client that you would like to view or delete, and take one of the following actions:
   - To view the status of the selected DHCP client, click Properties to display the Client Properties property sheet for that DHCP client. The property sheet displays the IP address currently assigned to the selected DHCP

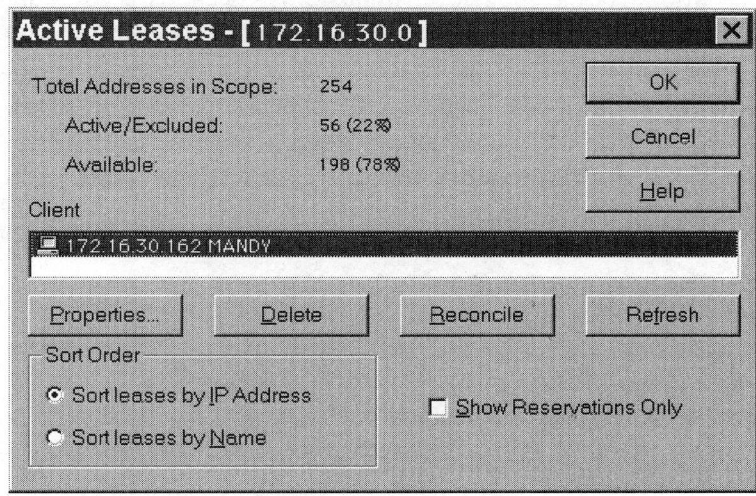

Figure 6-6. The Active Leases dialog

client, the MAC address, the client name, and any comments entered for that client. It also displays the date and time when the currently active lease will expire. If you want to enter a reservation for a client, this is a good place to cut the MAC address from and then paste it.

All of these properties except IP address are grayed out, indicating that they cannot be modified. Although it appears that the IP address field is active and may be changed, attempting to do so simply causes the machine to beep at you.

- Or, to delete a DHCP client, highlight that client and click Delete.

3. Click on OK to save the changes you have made and return to the main DHCP Manager screen. Exit DHCP Manager. The changes you have made to the DHCP configuration take effect immediately. Any DCHP client that now boots will use the currently defined options. Any DHCP client that is already connected to the network will not use the modified DHCP Options until the next time that client is booted. The client can also force a renewal/release by running *Winipcfg.exe*.

Viewing, modifying, and deleting active leases for reserved DHCP clients

To work with a reserved DHCP client—one for which you have created a manual reservation—take the following steps:

1. Click Active Leases from the Scope menu to display the Active Leases – [*Scope Name*] dialog. You may specify client sort order as described in the previous

section. You may also mark the *Show Reservations Only* checkbox if you want to display only DHCP clients for which you have created a client reservation manually.

2. If you want to delete the reserved client, simply highlight its name and click Delete. If instead you want to view properties for the reserved client or to modify it, highlight it and click Properties to display the Client Properties dialog, shown in Figure 6-7.

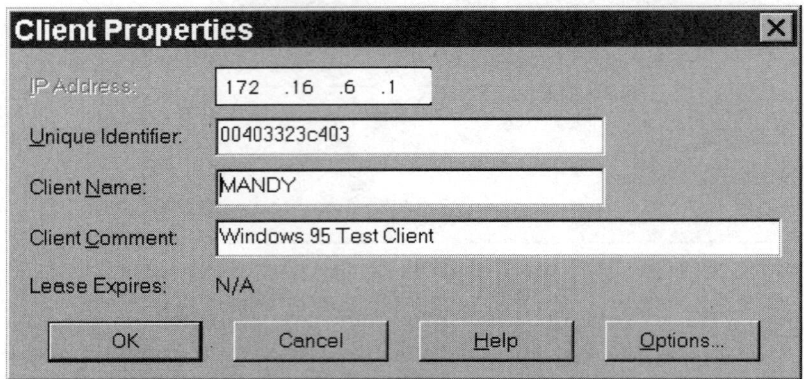

Figure 6-7. The Client Properties dialog

3. Modify the values for Unique Identifier, Client Name, and Client Comment as necessary. The value for Unique Identifier must correspond to the actual MAC address of the network adapter installed in that client. The value for Client Name is informational only; changing it has no effect on the actual computer name of that client. Similarly, the value for Client Comment is free text.

NOTE You cannot directly modify the IP address for a reserved client. Instead, you must first delete that client and then add a new reservation with the new IP address by clicking Add Reservations from the Scope menu.

---

4. The Options button appears on the Client Properties property sheet only for reserved clients. To modify DHCP Options for the selected reserved client, click Options to display the DHCP Options: Reservation dialog. Set DHCP Options for this client as described in the preceding section on setting DHCP Options. Note that the settings you make here apply only to this client. When you have finished setting DHCP Options for this client, click on OK to return to the Client Properties property sheet.

5. When you have finished making changes, click on OK to save your changes and return to the Active Leases – [*Scope Name*] dialog. Click on OK again to save your changes and return to the main DHCP Manager screen. Exit DHCP Manager. The changes you have made to the DHCP configuration take effect immediately. Any DCHP client that now boots will use the currently defined options. Any DHCP client that is already connected to the network will not use the modified DHCP Options until the next time that client is booted or needs to renew its lease. Creating a reservation also allows BootP clients to get an address.

Reconciling leases

Information about active DHCP leases is stored in both the DHCP database and the Registry of the machine running the DHCP Server service. For a variety of reasons, it is possible that the information stored in these two locations will become unsynchronized. The Registry may show one or more IP addresses as leased, or in use, while the DHCP database shows that these same addresses are available for assignment.

If this occurs, you can use the following procedure to run a consistency check between the two databases. Running this procedure lists inconsistent IP address assignments and reconciles the actual state of the DHCP environment—as reflected in the DHCP database—with the incorrect information maintained by the Registry. To reconcile leases, take the following steps:

1. Select Active Leases from the Scope menu to display the Active Leases—[*Scope Name*] dialog.
2. Click Reconcile. If the databases are consistent, DHCP Manager displays a message informing you of that fact. If reconcile finds inconsistencies, it lists the inconsistent addresses.

Run this reconciliation procedure any time the server crashes. You should also run it each time you restore the DHCP databases from backup. Reconcile is nondestructive. You may run it any time to ensure that the DHCP database and the Registry are in sync. Microsoft recommends doing so routinely. Some administrators do so for the warm, fuzzy feeling, but if you have several scopes, reconciling frequently is time-consuming and provides little benefit.

NOTE Reconcile operates on individual scopes. If your DHCP Server supports multiple scopes, you must run reconcile individually for each scope.

Maintaining and Troubleshooting DHCP Server

Once it has been installed and configured correctly, the DHCP Server requires little routine maintenance and is unlikely to have many problems. However, Murphy's Law still applies, so let's look at some of the problems that can occur with DHCP Server and how to go about resolving them. One of the following problems will likely be your first sign that all is not right with the DHCP Server:

- One or more clients receives the warning message "The DHCP Client could not renew the IP address lease". Or, a user will find that he can't access the Web or that a program won't function. Note that if the user turns off the DHCP error notification once, he will never be notified again of what's causing the problem.
- When you attempt to use DHCP Manager, you receive a warning message.
- When you attempt to start the DHCP Server service or the DHCP Client service, you receive a warning message that the service cannot start.

If either of the first two problems occurs, first verify that the DHCP Server service is started. You can do so by running the Services applet from Control Panel. The Status column should report "Started" for both the DHCP Client service and the Microsoft DHCP Server service. If either or both of these services is not running, first attempt to start the service by highlighting its name and clicking Start. If the service starts successfully, verify that the problems you were experiencing have been resolved.

TIP Don't forget to use Event Viewer to check the log for error messages. Although these error messages are sometimes cryptic and of little use—my favorite being "The service did not start because the service could not start"—they sometimes provide enough information to at least get you started in the right place. To run Event Viewer, from the Start Button, choose Programs → Administrative Tools (Common) → Event Viewer. Make sure that you are viewing the correct log file. DHCP error messages are logged to the System log.

If the third problem occurs, or if you are unable to start the service using the procedure described immediately above, more drastic measures are called for. First, notify everyone that the server is going to be shut down. If your communications problems are severe, or if some of your clients are not running Windows NT or *Winpopup.exe*, you may have to do this using some other method than a broadcast to clients. Power down the server and allow it to remain down for at least a minute.

Once your drives have all spun down, turn the power back on, and watch the console for warning messages as the server restarts. Most of the time, you will find that the service has started normally. If not, take a club to it. Get to a command prompt, type **net start dhcpserver**, and then press Enter. The service should start normally. If it doesn't—and I've never had a server *that* recalcitrant—the next step is to restore the DHCP database from backup.

TIP Windows NT includes several command-line utilities that are helpful in diagnosing TCP/IP problems. Although many administrators seldom use them—and some don't even know that they're there—these utilities can provide essential information. Familiarize yourself with at least the following utilities:

- **Ipconfig**—Displays the current Windows NT IP configuration.
- **Netstat**—Displays protocol statistics and current TCP/IP connections.
- **Ping**—Allows you to verify that at least minimum TCP/IP connectivity exists between two hosts.
- **Tracert**—Displays the path, including intermediate hops, that connects two hosts, allowing you to determine at what point TCP/IP connectivity is being lost.

Restoring the DHCP Database

If the procedures described in the preceding section fail, or if they apparently succeed but the problems persist, the only alternative is to restore the DHCP database from a known good copy. To restore the DHCP database, take the following steps:

1. If the DHCP Server service is running, stop it. Use the Services applet from Control Panel or the command **net stop dhcpserver** to do so.
2. For safety's sake, copy all of the files located in the folder *%SystemRoot%\system32\Dhcp* and its subfolders to another location.
3. In the folder *%SystemRoot%\system32\Dhcp*, delete the files *Dhcp.tmp*, *j50.chk*, *j50.log*, and *j50?????.log*.
4. Restore a good backup copy of *dhcp.mdb* to *%SystemRoot%\system32\Dhcp* and restart the DHCP Server service.

Rebuilding the DHCP Database on Another Server

If your DHCP problems arise as a result of hardware problems on the machine running the DHCP Server service, you may have no alternative but to rebuild the

DHCP database on another server. To rebuild the DHCP database, take the following steps:

1. If it is at all possible, attempt to retrieve a copy of the DHCP database from the failed server by stopping the DHCP Server service and making a copy of the database as described above. Otherwise, you must use your most recent good backup of the DHCP database.
2. If it is not already running Windows NT Server 4.0, install the operating system on the new server.

WARNING The DHCP database must reside in the same location on the new server as it did on the old. That is, if the DHCP database was stored in *C:\WINNT\system32\Dhcp* on the original server, it must also reside in the *C:\WINNT\system32\Dhcp* on the replacement server. If Windows NT Server is installed in a different folder on an existing replacement server, you must re-install Windows NT Server to the original *%SystemRoot%* before proceeding.

---

3. Verify that the DHCP Server service is stopped on the replacement server.
4. Use the Registry Editor to restore the DHCP Registry Keys from backup copies made from the original server.
5. Restore the DHCP database files to the DHCP data directory on the replacement server and restart the server.

You can also use this procedure if you simply want to remove the DHCP Server from one server and relocate it to another. If you do so, you will find that DHCP Manager still shows the original scope because Registry entries remain on the original server. Run reconcile, as described earlier in this chapter, to remove DHCP lease information from the Registry of the original server.

Summary

Dynamic Host Configuration Protocol is used to configure the hosts on a TCP/IP network. DHCP is the configuration service used by Windows NT. It allows the administrator to centrally control all TCP/IP configuration parameters including the IP address. With DHCP, addresses can be dynamically assigned.

The range of addresses that are available for dynamic assignment by a Windows NT DHCP server is called a *scope*. The scope is configured by the system administrator using the DHCP Manager software. The administrator defines the range of addresses in the scope, those addresses in the range that should be excluded from dynamic assignment, and the length of the time allowed for an address lease.

The DHCP Manager is also used to define DHCP options. DHCP options are the TCP/IP configuration values passed to the client.

In the next chapter we configure another server that is commonly found on a Windows NT network: the Windows Internet Name Service (WINS).

7

Using Windows Internet Name Service

In this chapter:
- *Why WINS Is Needed*
- *How WINS Works*
- *Installing the WINS Server Service*
- *Managing WINS with WINS Manager*
- *Troubleshooting WINS*
- *Summary*

The Microsoft Windows Internet Name Service (WINS) Server is a Windows NT Service that allows client computers to locate NetBIOS resources in routed TCP/IP networks. By using WINS, you can establish a centralized dynamic database that maps NetBIOS resource names to IP addresses. WINS overcomes the administrative burdens and functional limitations associated with using other methods of NetBIOS name resolution like static *LMHOSTS* files and IP broadcasts. WINS is to NetBIOS and Microsoft Networking what the Domain Name System (DNS) is to TCP/IP and the Internet.

Historically, Microsoft Networking meant small, peer networks running NetBIOS. The NetBIOS environment was really designed with small networks in mind. It was never intended to function in a large scale network environment, let alone in a TCP/IP internetworking environment. Microsoft, however, with its roots in small networks, was committed to supporting NetBIOS. When Microsoft decided to extend their mandate from peer networks to encompass the enterprise, they had little choice but to find a way to incorporate the NetBIOS user base into their enterprise schema. Their solution to this problem is the Windows Internet Name Service.

As is the case with DHCP, many people incorrectly believe that WINS is a purely proprietary Microsoft protocol, although this time they have somewhat more justification. WINS is in fact a proprietary Microsoft implementation of the following generic NetBIOS-over-TCP/IP Internet standards:

- RFC1001 *Protocol standard for a NetBIOS service on a TCP/UDP transport: Concepts and methods*. This RFC, dated March 1, 1987, provides an overview of NetBIOS over TCP/IP protocols, focusing on underlying concepts rather than on implementation details.

- RFC 1002 *Protocol standard for a NetBIOS service on a TCP/UDP transport: Detailed specifications*. This RFC, also dated March 1, 1987, defines the detailed implementation issues for NetBIOS over TCP/IP, including packet definitions, protocols, and so forth.

As you might guess simply by looking at their dates, neither of these RFCs explicitly mentions either Windows or WINS. Because WINS deals with NetBIOS names, which are for all practical terms limited to Microsoft networking, WINS has a much stronger Microsoft cachet than does DHCP. WINS implementations are, however, not limited to running on Windows NT Server. For example, SAMBA running on Unix provides WINS Server functionality, and can support Microsoft WINS clients. For all intents and purposes, if someone tells you he is running WINS, it's almost a certainty that he is doing so on Windows NT Server.

Like DHCP, WINS uses a client/server architecture. The WINS Server is bundled with Windows NT Server. WINS clients are bundled with or available for various Microsoft client operating systems, including MS-DOS, Windows 3.1x, Windows 95, and Windows NT. Microsoft WINS is tightly integrated on both the client side and the server side with Microsoft Dynamic Host Configuration Protocol (DHCP) functions and with Microsoft Domain Name System (DNS) functions. As was noted in the previous chapter, in order to get the maximum benefits from this integration, you must run Microsoft operating systems on all of your servers and clients. NetWare and Macintosh clients and other non-WINS compliant devices on your network can still participate in WINS, although at a reduced level of integration.

Why WINS Is Needed

Windows NT uses TCP/IP as its enterprise transport protocol. However, even when you are using TCP/IP transport, Microsoft Networking still uses NetBIOS at the upper layers for resource naming, file and print sharing, browsing, and other essential network services. To understand the role that WINS plays in a Windows NT network, you must therefore first understand something about NetBIOS.

NetBIOS and Windows Networking

NetBIOS and the associated *NetBIOS Extended User Interface protocol* (NetBEUI) are the foundation of Microsoft Networking. *BIOS*, the *Basic Input Output System*, is the part of DOS that defines the I/O calls that applications use to request DOS I/O services. NetBIOS extends this to include calls that support I/O over a network. Sytek developed NetBIOS for IBM's short-lived PC Network product. It has survived PC Network and gone on to be part of many other network products including Windows for Workgroups, LAN Manager, and Windows NT.

Originally, NetBIOS was implemented in a ROM on the Sytek network interface card. It was a monolithic protocol that took data all the way from the application to the physical network. Today, NetBIOS is an application program interface (API) that defines how an application program requests services from the underlying network.

IBM and Microsoft have added to the basic NetBIOS definition over the years to produce the current version of NetBEUI. Don't confuse NetBEUI and NetBIOS. Although NetBIOS is often used loosely to refer to any NetBIOS-based network, NetBIOS is only one part of NetBEUI, which includes the following components:

NetBIOS API
: Defines the software interface and naming convention used by Microsoft Networking.

Server Message Block (SMB) protocol
: Defines a series of commands used to pass information between networked computers.

NetBIOS Frame (NBF) protocol
: Builds NetBIOS frames for transmission over the network.

NetBEUI requires very little memory and runs on any type of PC equipment, even the oldest PCs. It is a fast, lightweight protocol suitable for small LANs. However, NetBEUI is only suitable for LAN applications. NetBEUI cannot be used by itself for a WAN or an enterprise network because it is a nonroutable protocol, and it depends on an underlying broadcast medium. What do these two limitations mean?

nonroutable
: The protocol cannot be passed through routers. NetBEUI packets can only be passed on a single physical network. It has no routing protocol and no independent address structure. It depends completely on the underlying physical network address, which limits it to a single physical network.

broadcast dependent
: NetBEUI depends on an underlying network that supports physical layer broadcasts. It cannot be used over serial lines, point-to-point networks, or Internets built from dissimilar physical networks.

How a new node inserts itself into a Windows for Workgroups (WfW) network is a good illustration of NetBEUI limitations. When WfW starts, it broadcasts a *name registration request* packet. The packet contains the proposed NetBIOS name that identifies the system. If another computer on the network already uses this name, it responds to the broadcast with a *negative name registration response* packet. If the new node does not receive any negative responses to its broadcast, it uses the name as its identifier.

The name is literally used as the node's "address." The source and destination fields of a NetBIOS frame contain the names of the source and destination computers. Therefore, if a computer named *kerby* sends a frame to a system named *thoth*, the source address is kerby and the destination address is thoth.

This naming scheme has some advantages. For one, it is intuitive. Most people prefer to identify things by names instead of by numbers, and NetBIOS names can be very descriptive, for example, *hpprinter*. Each system is automatically self-registering. The scheme requires no central name authority or name server. However, this scheme does not scale well. Each name must be broadcast to every node on the network, which is difficult in a large network, and each name must be unique throughout the network. With no central name authority and no hierarchical name structure, it is difficult to maintain unique names on large networks. This is clearly an inadequate scheme for a large network—let alone a global internet.

NetBIOS has changed over time from a monolithic protocol to a layered protocol. This change causes confusion in the way the term NetBIOS is used—sometimes it refers to the entire protocol, and sometimes it refers to the application interface. But the real effect of this change is that, in its current form as an applications interface, NetBIOS is not dependent on the underlying NBF protocol. NetBIOS can run over TCP/IP. Installing TCP/IP does not eliminate the availability of NetBIOS-based applications. Rather, it enables the full array of Internet applications *and* it allows NetBIOS applications to run over large networks that include routers. It does this by encapsulating the NetBIOS messages inside TCP/IP datagrams. The protocol that does this is *NetBIOS over TCP/IP* (NetBT).

There are, of course, complications. Encapsulating NetBIOS inside IP datagrams reduces the performance and increases the complexity of the protocol. Both protocols require some level of configuration. Additionally, computers using NetBT must have some method for mapping NetBIOS computer names, which are the addresses of a NetBIOS network, to the IP addresses of a TCP/IP network.

Resolving NetBIOS Computer Names Under Windows NT

In a TCP/IP network, a host is identified by its DNS host name and IP address. In any Windows NT network—including one running TCP/IP—a host is also identified by its *Windows computer name*, also called the *NetBIOS computer name*. In a TCP/IP Windows network, some means is needed to translate Windows computer names to the corresponding IP addresses. Windows NT provides the following methods of resolving computer names to IP addresses:

IP Broadcast
: In the absence of any of the other methods described here, a client can resolve a NetBIOS computer name into an IP address by using IP broadcasts. To do so, the client broadcasts IP packets that contain a message that says something like, "is there a computer on this network whose NetBIOS name is such-and-such? If so, please send me your IP address." If a host hears its own NetBIOS name in such a broadcast, it returns its IP address to the source IP address of the broadcast packet.

Static Mapping Files
: These files maintain a static database that maps computer names to their corresponding IP addresses. The file *Hosts* maps DNS names to IP addresses. The file *Lmhosts* maps NetBIOS computer names to IP addresses. Static mapping files may be installed locally (on the workstation) or centrally (on a server).

: Windows NT Server installs the file *c:\WINNT\system32\drivers\etc\Lmhosts.sam* as an example *Lmhosts* file and the file *c:\WINNT\system32\drivers\etc\Hosts.sam* as an example *Hosts* file. Both of these example files are liberally commented to describe their structure and function.

NetBIOS Name Server (NBNS)
: An NBNS uses a client/server architecture to maintain a centralized, dynamic database that maps NetBIOS computer names to IP addresses. Clients that need to resolve an IP address for a known NetBIOS computer name query the NBNS, which resolves the IP address and returns it to the client. RFC1001 and RFC1002 define a generic NBNS. The Windows NT WINS Server is a standards-compliant superset of that generic NBNS.

Domain Name System (DNS) Server
: A DNS Server uses a hierarchical client-server architecture to maintain a distributed, dynamic database that maps Internet host names to IP addresses. A DNS client (called a resolver) queries the DNS Server to resolve an unknown IP address from a known Internet host name. If the DNS Server can resolve the query locally, it does so and returns the IP address to the client. If the local DNS Server cannot resolve the query using its local database, it queries other DNS Servers to complete the resolution.

Which method or methods are best for you depends on your own environment. For any network, using IP broadcasts is the choice of last resort. First, IP broadcasts generate a large amount of network traffic. Second, IP broadcasts work only within a subnet. That is, they don't cross routers.

You may not need WINS at all. Static mapping files are often a workable choice for small networks, particular those that comprise only a single subnet and are not subject to having computers added and removed frequently. Although using local static mapping files is an administrative nightmare, using global static mapping files stored centrally on a server may be the best way to go on a small, simple network.

For most networks, the two dynamic name resolution methods, WINS and DNS, are the best choices. The Microsoft implementations of WINS and DNS are designed to work together, and to interoperate with the Microsoft DHCP Server. DHCP is covered in the chapter immediately preceding this one; DNS is covered in the chapter immediately following this one.

How WINS Works

NetBIOS over TCP/IP (NetBT) is the session-level network service used to provide NetBIOS naming support in the Windows NT environment, both via broadcast name resolution and via WINS. The two sides of the naming coin are called *name registration* and *name resolution*. Name registration is the process by which each computer is allocated a unique computer name. A computer normally registers its name when it boots. Name resolution is the process described earlier, by which the unknown numeric address is determined from the known computer name. The following sections examine the various NetBT modes used during the naming process first, and then the actual processes of name resolution and name registration.

Understanding NetBT Modes

NetBT defines several modes by which NetBIOS computer resources are identified. These modes differ in terms of which resources they use to resolve addresses, and in which order. They include:

b-node

Stands for broadcast-node and depends entirely on IP broadcasts to resolve names. For example, in a b-node environment, if a computer named *kerby* wants to communicate with a computer named *thoth*, *kerby* broadcasts a message to the entire sub-network that asks *thoth* to respond with its IP address. *kerby* waits a specified time for a response, and, if it receives no response, rebroadcasts the request.

b-node has two significant drawbacks. First, in all but the smallest network, the amount of IP traffic it generates loads the network unnecessarily. Second, as noted earlier, most routers discard these broadcast messages rather than forwarding them, which limits b-node to use on a single subnet.

p-node

Stands for point-to-point-node or peer-to-peer-node. Uses point-to-point communication with a name server to resolve names. p-node attempts to resolve both of the problems listed for b-node. In a p-node environment, computers neither originate IP broadcasts nor reply to them. At boot time, each computer registers itself with the NBNS. Using p-node, if *kerby* wants to communicate with *thoth*, *kerby* directly queries the NBNS, which returns the IP address for *thoth*. *kerby* then communicates directly with *thoth*, without using IP broadcasts.

p-node solves both of the problems of b-node. Bandwidth is used more efficiently because p-node does not use IP broadcasts. Name resolution can occur across a routed internetwork because the queries are directed to name servers with defined IP addresses. p-node introduces a couple of problems of its own, however. First, all clients must know the address of the NBNS. This requirement is typically accommodated by setting options 44 and 46 on the DHCP Server. The second problem is more serious. p-node introduces a single point of failure. If the designated NBNS fails, all clients that depend on it are unable to communicate until the problem is resolved.

m-node

Stands for mixed-node. First uses b-node to resolve the name via IP broadcast. If this fails, then uses p-node to resolve the address from the name server. m-node was created as an attempt to solve the problems associated with b-node and p-node by essentially combining these two earlier methods.

In an m-node environment, a client first uses b-node for name registration and name resolution by IP broadcast. If this fails, presumably because the name to be resolved is on the far side of a router, the client then uses p-node to attempt to use an NBNS for registration and resolution. In theory, m-node offers a couple of advantages. First, because m-node defaults to using IP broadcasts, nodes on the local subnet can be resolved even if an NBNS is unavailable. Second, by using its fallback to p-node, m-node allows names to be resolved across routers. Balanced against these advantages is the continued dependence of m-node on IP broadcasts.

h-node

Stands for hybrid-node. First uses p-node to attempt to resolve the address using the name server. If the name server is unavailable, or if the name in question is not registered in that name server's database, then uses b-node to attempt to resolve the name using IP broadcasts.

Reading through the description of m-node immediately above, it might seem that the designers of m-node got things exactly backwards. After all, p-node is both more efficient than b-node and works across routers. Wouldn't it be better to try the more efficient p-node first and then use b-node only as a fallback if there is no NBNS available? Well, yes it would, and that's exactly what h-node does.

h-node goes further, however. Rather than simply reversing the order in which b-node and p-node are used, h-node makes intelligent choices based on the existing environment. If p-node fails because the NBNS is down, h-node periodically re-polls the NBNS. If the NBNS returns to service, h-node reverts to using p-node. Also, when h-node is operating in b-node and is unable to resolve an address, it will attempt to use the static mapping file *Lmhosts* to resolve the name.

Windows NT supports all of these modes. Which of them NetBT uses by default depends on the configuration of both the server and the clients. If the WINS Server is installed on the server, WINS-enabled clients use h-node and non-WINS clients use b-node. If no WINS Server or other NBNS is available on the network, all clients use b-node by default, unless an *Lmhosts* static mapping file exists. If the local *Lmhosts* static mapping file exists, the client first uses b-node IP broadcasts to resolve the name, and then, if necessary, the client attempts to resolve the name using the *Lmhosts* static mapping file. This method, called *modified b-node*, allows name resolution across routers in a b-node environment and is the default method used by Windows 3.11 for Workgroups clients.

WINS versus IP Broadcast in Mixed Environments

If all of this discussion of NetBT modes and IP broadcasts makes you think that manually managing NetBIOS naming in a complex network is almost impossible, you're right. WINS is Microsoft's solution to the problems of administering NetBIOS naming on a complex network. WINS uses a distributed dynamic database to map NetBIOS computer names to IP addresses. Machines register themselves with the WINS Server when they boot. The WINS server records the NetBIOS name and IP address of each WINS client. Subsequently, WINS clients use p-node to query the WINS Server, which looks up the NetBIOS name provided, resolves the corresponding IP address, and returns this information to the requesting client.

By itself, WINS really does little that you can't accomplish using other methods. WINS simply makes the entire NetBIOS naming process automatic and transparent to both users and administrators. WINS is dynamic in the sense that, rather than depending on static mapping data entered by an administrator, it uses the information provided automatically by the WINS clients to update and maintain its database. WINS is also dynamic in the sense that it interoperates with the Microsoft DHCP Server and the Microsoft DNS Server.

This means, for example, that if a roving user plugs his notebook computer into the network and boots it, several things happen. First, the notebook client is assigned an IP address by the DHCP Server; next, the notebook client registers its own NetBIOS computer name and the IP address provided by the DHCP Server with the WINS Server. If the Microsoft DNS Server is available, the client also registers its DNS name and IP address with the DNS Server.

WINS also makes life much easier in a routed network. Because WINS uses p-node, queries to the WINS Server are directed to the explicit IP address of that WINS Server, allowing it to be either local (on the local subnet) or remote (on the other side of a router). On a Windows NT network running WINS, users can browse network resources whether they are local or remote. If the Windows NT network is not running WINS, local users cannot by default browse remote resources.

The previous statement is not strictly true. You can enable browsing for remote resources on a non-WINS network, but doing so takes a little bit of work. First, at least one machine on each side of the router must be running Windows NT—in either the Server or Workstation flavor—to act as a master browsers for the local subnet. Second, you must manually configure an *Lmhosts* file on each of these Windows NT machines with an entry for the Windows NT domain controller on the other side of the router. All things considered, it's easier just to run WINS.

In a WINS environment that includes some clients that use WINS (h-node) and others that depend on IP broadcasts (b-node), differences exist in how clients resolve, register, release, and renew names. The following sections examine these differences.

WINS versus IP broadcast for name resolution

Name resolution is the process by which a client computer submits the NetBIOS name for another host with which it wishes to communicate and in turn receives the IP address of that destination host. The name resolution process differs between WINS-enabled clients operating in a WINS environment and non-WINS clients only in that the WINS-enabled clients first attempt a WINS lookup. If that lookup fails, the subsequent process is identical for either type of client.

A WINS-enabled client attempts to resolve a name in the following sequence:

1. If the WINS client cannot resolve the name from its local cache, it first uses h-node to send a *name query request* directly to the IP address of its designated WINS Server. The name query request UDP packet includes the NetBIOS name of the computer to be resolved. The WINS Server resolves the IP address that corresponds to the NetBIOS name and returns the IP address to the WINS client. The WINS client then uses that IP address to establish a session directly with the target computer.

   In response to a name query request, the WINS Server examines its database and then returns the IP address that maps to the NetBIOS computer name provided by the WINS client. The WINS Server does not do any checking or verification. That is, simply because the WINS Server returns an IP address does not guarantee that the computer associated with that IP address is not turned off or otherwise inaccessible.

2. If the WINS query fails, and the WINS client is configured as h-node, it then sends a b-node IP broadcast packet containing a name query request. If the target computer is on the same subnet, it returns its IP address to the querying computer and a direct session is established.
3. If the IP broadcast name query request fails to return an IP address, the WINS client next examines its local *Lmhosts* file and, if the local *Lmhosts* contains an #INCLUDE statement pointing to a remote *Lmhosts* file on a server, examines the remote *Lmhosts* file as well.

Any Microsoft Networking client can be configured to use WINS in at least one, and possibly two ways, depending on the network configuration.

- On any network, you can configure a Microsoft Networking client to use WINS by explicitly setting the IP configuration for that client individually to point to the IP addresses for a Primary WINS Server and a Secondary WINS Server. Clients so configured use h-node automatically. This method requires manual configuration of each client.
- On a network that includes a DHCP Server, you can set DHCP Option 044 (WINS/NBNS Servers) and DHCP Option 046 (WINS/NBT Node Type) to configure WINS automatically on all Microsoft clients. Enter the IP addresses for one or more WINS Servers for DHCP Option 044. Set DHCP Option 046 to any of three values: 02 (p-node); 04 (m-node); or 08 (h-node).

A client that is not WINS-enabled attempts to resolve a name in the following sequence:

1. The non-WINS client sends a b-node IP broadcast name query request packet. If the target computer is on the same subnet, it returns its IP address to the querying computer and a direct session is established.
2. If the IP broadcast name query request fails to return an IP address, the non-WINS client next examines its local *Lmhosts* file and, if the local *Lmhosts* contains an #INCLUDE statement pointing to a remote *Lmhosts* file on a server, examines the remote *Lmhosts* file as well.

WINS versus IP broadcast for name registration

Name registration is the process by which a computer reserves a NetBIOS name for itself that is unique within the network. The name registration process differs significantly between WINS-enabled clients operating in a WINS environment and non-WINS clients.

A WINS-enabled client operating on a network that includes a WINS Server registers its NetBIOS computer name using the following procedure:

1. The WINS client sends a *name registration request* packet directly to the IP address of its associated WINS Server. This packet includes the NetBIOS name by which the client wishes to be known.
2. When it receives the name registration request packet, the WINS Server examines its database. If the requested name does not already exist in the database, the WINS Server creates a database entry for that name that includes the NetBIOS computer name, the associated IP address, and a unique incremental version number for the transaction. It then sends a *positive name registration response* packet to the client that generated the name registration request to notify that client that its desired NetBIOS name has been registered successfully.
3. If the requested NetBIOS computer name is already registered in the database to a different IP address, the WINS Server attempts to resolve the conflict. To do so, it first challenges the current entry to determine if the host will actually respond. If the currently registered host does respond, the WINS Server sends a *negative name registration response* packet to the host that submitted the name registration request packet to inform it that the NetBIOS name it wants to use is already in use by another host. This is invisible to the client. The only indication that something is wrong is that you can't connect to the network.

A non-WINS client, or a WINS client operating on a network that has no WINS Server accessible, registers its NetBIOS computer name using the following procedure:

1. The client sends a *name registration request* packet via IP broadcast to the entire local network. This packet includes the NetBIOS computer name by which the client wants to be known, and the IP address of that client. If no challenge is received to this name registration request packet, the client assumes that the NetBIOS computer name is available, and begins using it.
2. If another client on the local network has already claimed that NetBIOS computer name, that client sends a *negative name registration response* packet to the host that is trying to register the duplicate name.

Once a client has successfully claimed a NetBIOS computer name via IP broadcast, it has two responsibilities. First, when it receives a name query packet via IP broadcast that is directed to its own NetBIOS computer name, it must respond to that broadcast by directing a *positive name query response* packet to the IP address of the host that generated the name query. This positive name query response includes the responding host's IP address, which allows a direct session to be established between the querying and responding hosts. Second, the client must defend its turf against any other client on the local subnet that attempts to register the NetBIOS computer name that it is already using. To do so, it generates a negative name registration response packet whenever it receives an IP broadcast name registration request that contains its own NetBIOS computer name.

WINS versus IP broadcast for name release

Name release is the process by which a computer discontinues using a NetBIOS name and makes that name available for use by other clients. The name release process differs significantly between WINS-enabled clients operating in a WINS environment and non-WINS clients.

A WINS-enabled client operating on a network that includes a WINS Server releases its NetBIOS computer name for reassignment to another client. The WINS Server takes several actions, some of which occur in any event, and others of which occur only if another client requests the released name, as follows:

- When a WINS client is shut down normally, it informs the WINS Server that it will no longer be participating on the network. The WINS Server marks the database entry for that client as *released* but takes no further immediate action.
- If the original WINS client subsequently reconnects to the network while the status of the database entry remains as released, the WINS Server issues no challenge, but instead simply honors the client's request for its original NetBIOS computer name and updates the WINS database to reflect the fact that the client is now connected.
- If the original WINS client does not reconnect to the network, and so the released entry remains unused for a certain period (specified in WINS Manager), WINS marks the entry *extinct*. It then assigns a new incremental version number and broadcasts this changed information to the other WINS Servers with which it is partnered on the network.
- If, while the database entry is marked released, a different client (one with an IP address different from that of the original client) requests the released name, the WINS Server immediately grants the request. It need not issue a challenge because the released status of the database entry indicates that the original client has relinquished its claim on the name. This situation commonly occurs when you are upgrading computers or when a roving user first disconnects a portable computer from the network and then reconnects using a different IP address assigned by DHCP. This one is all a matter of timing. If the WINS timeout is longer than the DHCP timeout, you get a new IP address. Otherwise, the address remains the same.
- If the original WINS client was not shut down properly, for example, the power failed or someone simply powered down the computer, the WINS

Server is not aware that the client is no longer participating on the network, and accordingly leaves its associated database entry marked as active. When that WINS client or another client subsequently attempts to register the NetBIOS computer name, the WINS Server believes that the name is already in use, and accordingly issues a challenge to the registered owner of the name. Because that computer is no longer active, the challenge fails and the WINS Server is free to reassign that name to the requesting client.

A non-WINS client, or a WINS client operating on a network that has no WINS Server accessible, releases its NetBIOS computer name as follows:

- If the non-WINS client is shut down normally, it sends an IP broadcast message to release the name reservation. Other computers on the network that have cached this name and its associated IP address clear the entry from their cache. Because the original client is no longer defending its name by issuing negative name registration response packets in response to name registration request packets, any other client on the local network can register the name successfully.
- If the non-WINS client is shut down improperly, it has no opportunity to broadcast a name release packet, and so it continues to appear to the other hosts on the local subnet as an active computer. This situation is resolved in one of two ways. First, because the client is no longer able to generate positive name query response packets in response to name query packets, the other computers on the network will eventually become aware that the client is no longer active on the network. Second, if another client subsequently attempts to register the same name and is not challenged by the original client with a negative name registration response packet, the other computers on the local network recognize immediately that the original client is no longer active. In either event, the other computers on the local network clear the registration information for that client from their caches.

WINS name renewal

Name renewal is the process by which WINS-enabled client computers periodically renew their name registrations with the WINS Server. Non-WINS clients have no analogous function.

When a WINS client initially registers its name with the WINS Server, the WINS Server returns a success message to that client. This message contains a time-to-live (TTL), called the *renewal interval*, that informs the client when it will need to renew the registration. When half the TTL period has expired, the client renews its name for another TTL period. By default, the WINS Server renewal interval is set to 144 hours, or six days, which means that WINS clients renew their names every three days by default.

The renewal interval determines the amount of network traffic that WINS name renewals generate. If you frequently add and remove computers from your network, you may wish to set the renewal period shorter than six days. This is so because when a computer is removed from the network, the computer name remains on browse lists for the remaining duration of the renewal period, and can drive other users crazy. You may also configure an entry as *static*, which means that it is permanent and never need be renewed.

Commonly registered WINS names

In addition to the NetBIOS computer name, WINS registers various other name information for computers, depending on the role they play in the network. Table 7-1 lists names that are commonly registered by Windows clients.

Table 7-1. Commonly Registered WINS Names

Name	Type	Description
Computername	00	Registered by the Workstation service running on the local computer to identify that computer to the network.
Workgroup or Domainname	00	Registers the computer as a member of a domain or workgroup. This name is registered as a Group NetBIOS Name (as opposed to a Unique NetBIOS Name), which means that multiple computers can register under the same name.
Computername	03	Registered by the Messenger service running on the local computer. This allows the computer to receive messages, e.g. **net send computername**
Username	03	Registered by the Messenger service running on the local computer. This allows the current user to receive messages, e.g. **net send username**
Domainname	1B	Registers the computer as the Domain Master Browser for the domain. This is registered as a Unique NetBIOS Name because only one Domain Master Browser may be present in a domain.
Domainname	1C	Registers the computer as a domain controller. This is registered as a Group NetBIOS Name, because multiple domain controllers may exist.
Workgroup or Domainname	1D	Registers the computer as the Master Browser for the workgroup or domain on the local subnet. This is registered as a Unique NetBIOS Name, because only one Master Browser may exist for a domain or workgroup on a subnet.
Workgroup or Domainname	1E	Registers the computer as a participant in browser elections. Registered as a Group NetBIOS Name.
Computername	20	Registered by the Server service running on the local computer to allow that computer to receive connection requests from other computers.

WINS Proxy Agents

As you transition to WINS, you may find yourself thinking that it would be useful to run a hybrid environment, with some hosts using b-node and others using p-node. Although doing this might appear to solve some migration problems, such an environment threatens the stability of your network. The danger is this: p-node hosts ignore IP broadcasts, while b-node hosts use only IP broadcasts. This leaves open the possibility that a b-node host and a p-node host may have identical NetBIOS names, with results that are unpredictable to say the least.

A better solution is to use WINS proxy agents during the transition. A WINS proxy agent is a WINS-enabled computer that uses an NBNS to provide name resolution as a surrogate to one or more non-WINS clients. A non-WINS client uses b-node IP broadcasts as usual to resolve names. When a WINS proxy agent hears an IP broadcast for a computer that is not on the local subnet (or that is running p-node), it intercepts the broadcast, queries the NBNS server on behalf of the non-WINS client, and returns the response to the non-WINS client. This solution is much cleaner—and much safer—than depending on a hybrid b-node/p-node environment.

Windows NT Server, Windows NT Workstation, Windows 95, and the protected-mode TCP/IP-32 for Windows for Workgroups can all function as WINS proxy agents. You should enable one—or at most two—WINS proxy agent computers per subnet. More than this number unnecessarily burdens the network, because all proxy agents respond to each b-node broadcast, query the WINS Server, and then respond to the client that originated the broadcast.

You enable a Windows NT 3.51 computer as a WINS proxy agent by marking the Enable WINS Proxy Agent checkbox in the Advanced TCP/IP Properties dialog. It's harder with Windows NT 4.0. To do so, you must use Registry Editor to change *HKLM\SYSTEM\CurrentControlSet\Services\NetBT\Parameters\EnableProxy* from its default value of 0 to 1. Once you have done so and restarted the computer, it begins functioning as a WINS proxy agent.

Understanding WINS Databases

WINS uses the same database engine as Microsoft Exchange Server 4 and the Microsoft DHCP Server. The WINS database is modified dynamically. Each time a WINS client registers with the WINS Server, releases its name, or renews its name, these changes are recorded in the WINS database.

The WINS database can grow to whatever size is necessary to store the registration data for the WINS clients it supports. The size of the WINS database varies according to the number of clients registered, but not necessarily in direct proportion. Because the WINS database stores both current and historical configuration information, it gradually grows over time. A newly installed WINS database occupies about 2 MB.

Installing WINS automatically creates the following database files in *%SystemRoot%\system32\wins*. The WINS database remains open at all times while WINS is operating. Do not attempt to delete or modify any of these database files.

wins.mdb
: The main WINS database file. This file contains two tables. One table maps IP address to Owner ID, and the other table maps Owner ID to IP address.

winstmp.mdb
: The swap file used when indexing the main WINS database file. According to Microsoft, this file may remain as an orphan after a crash. However, I found that this file existed in the WINS directory on a server that had had WINS freshly installed, and had not crashed.

j50.chk
: A checkpoint file, used to maintain and verify database coherency.

j50.log
: Contains a log of WINS transactions. May be used after a WINS crash to roll back the WINS database to a coherent state.

j50?????.log
: According to Microsoft, another file whose contents are used to recover the WINS database after a crash. On my server, this file did not exist when WINS was initially installed, and was not created when I intentionally crashed WINS.

res1.log and res2.log
: The database engine creates these placeholder log files to ensure that sufficient disk space is always available to the database. During a disk space emergency, the space pre-allocated in these files is available to the database engine.

WINS interval timers

WINS defines four timers, which are used to determine how and when automatic changes are made to the WINS database. These timers are described in more detail in the section on configuring WINS, but for now, consider them as follows:

Renewal Interval.
: Specifies how frequently, in hours, minutes, and seconds, a WINS client must re-register its name with the WINS Server.

Extinction Interval

Specifies, in hours, minutes, and seconds, the minimum duration between the time that a WINS client releases its name and the time that that name will be marked extinct in the WINS database.

Extinction Timeout

Specifies, in hours, minutes, and seconds, the minimum duration between the time that an entry is marked extinct and the time that that name will be deleted from the WINS database by scavenging.

Verify Interval

Specifies, in hours, minutes, and seconds, how often the WINS server must revalidate active names that originated on a remote WINS server and were replicated to the local WINS server.

Scavenging the WINS database

If left to itself, the WINS database would simply continue to grow, with released entries, expired entries, and orphan entries continuing to occupy space. WINS uses a process called *scavenging* to cleanup the database by removing these obsolete entries. WINS automatically scavenges the database periodically. How frequently it does so is determined by the relationship between the Renewal Interval and the Extinction Interval, which are defined when WINS is configured. You may also scavenge manually at any time by selecting the Initiate Scavenging option from the Mappings menu of WINS Manager. Windows recovers space in the WINS database using a process called *compaction*, which reclaims empty but allocated space within the database. Compaction occurs automatically under Windows NT Server 4.0 during idle time after database updates.

Scavenging updates the database in various ways, depending on the current status of each original entry and the status of the timers, as follows:

Owned Name Entries

These are database records that originated on the local WINS server (the one that is being scavenged). Scavenging affects these entries as follows:

- If a name is Active, but the Renewal Interval has not expired, that database entry is left unchanged.
- If a name is Active, and the Renewal Interval has expired, that name is marked Released.
- If a name is Released, but the Extinction Interval has not expired, that database entry is left unchanged.
- If a name is Released, and the Extinction Interval has expired, that database entry is marked Extinct.

- If a name is Extinct, but the Extinction Timeout has not expired, that database entry is left unchanged.
- If a name is Extinct, and the Extinction Timeout has expired, that database entry is deleted.

Replica Name Entries

These are database records that originated on a remote WINS server and were replicated to the WINS server being scavenged. Scavenging affects these entries as follows:

- If a name is Active, but the Verify Interval has not expired, that database entry is left unchanged.
- If a name is Active, and the Verify Interval has expired, that database entry is revalidated.
- If a name is Extinct or Deleted, whether or not the Extinction Interval has expired, that name is deleted.

Backing up the WINS database

Because the WINS database files are always open, it is impossible to back them up using traditional means. Windows NT Server can be configured to back up the WINS database periodically without manual intervention. However, unlike the DHCP databases (which are backed up automatically to a predetermined folder by installation default), you must take explicit action to cause this periodic backup to occur. You do so simply by using the WINS Manager once to do a manual WINS backup to a WINS backup folder that you specify. Backing up the WINS data on a typical server takes only a few seconds. Once you have specified a backup folder in WINS Manager, the system automatically backs up the WINS data every three hours by default.

If your primary backup program can be run from a batch file, you can use it to backup the main WINS database. To do so, create a batch file that shuts down the WINS Server (closing the database), runs the backup program, and then restarts the WINS Server. Controlling the WINS Server from the command line is described at the end of the following section on installing the WINS Server. Even more simply, just backup the backup data files created by WINS Manager.

Installing the WINS Server Service

Install the WINS service from the Network Services page of the Network property sheet (Control Panel → Network → Services tab). Select Add to display the Select Network Service dialog where you can highlight Windows Internet Name Service for installation. Windows NT displays the Windows NT Setup dialog to prompt for the location of the distribution files; accept the default or specify a new location as appropriate. Windows NT copies the distribution files and returns to the Network property sheet, which now shows WINS as an installed service.

When you close the installation dialog, Windows NT configures, stores, and reviews the bindings, and then asks if you want to restart your computer to activate the WINS settings. Windows NT Server configures the WINS Server service by default to start automatically each time the server is booted. You can use the Services applet in Control Panel to modify the startup settings for the WINS Server service, or to start, stop, pause, or continue the WINS Server service.

You can also control the WINS Server service from the command prompt, using the commands **net start wins**, **net stop wins**, **net pause wins**, and **net continue wins**. These commands are useful primarily for creating batch files to backup your server, including the WINS Server database, during off hours. You can stop the WINS service, run the backup, and then restart the WINS service, all from within a batch file. For example, the following batch file stops the WINS Server service (and closes its files so that they may be backed up); uses NT Backup to perform a Normal backup of *C:*, including the registry, with verification on; and then restarts the WINS Server service after the backup completes:

```
@echo off
cls
net stop wins
ntbackup backup c:\ /v /b /t normal
net start wins
```

The Windows NT Server Resource Kit includes several enhanced tools for managing WINS, including the *WINSCL.EXE* command-line administrative tool, the *WINSDMP.EXE* command-line dump utility that exports the WINS database to a *.csv* text file, and the *WINSCHK.EXE* command-line tool that allows you to verify WINS database coherency and to monitor replication activity. If you plan to use WINS, the resource kit is a worthwhile purchase, if only for the bundled utilities.

Managing WINS with WINS Manager

Installing WINS adds the WINS Manager application to the Administrative Tools (Common) program group. You can use WINS Manager to configure and control all aspects of WINS Server operation. At this point, the WINS server is installed and the WINS database has been created, but the WINS Server has not yet been configured. The following sections describe how to use WINS Manager, shown in Figure 7-1, to configure and manage the WINS server.

The WINS Servers pane displays a list of known WINS Servers. By default, WINS Manager displays WINS Servers using their IP addresses. You can use the Address

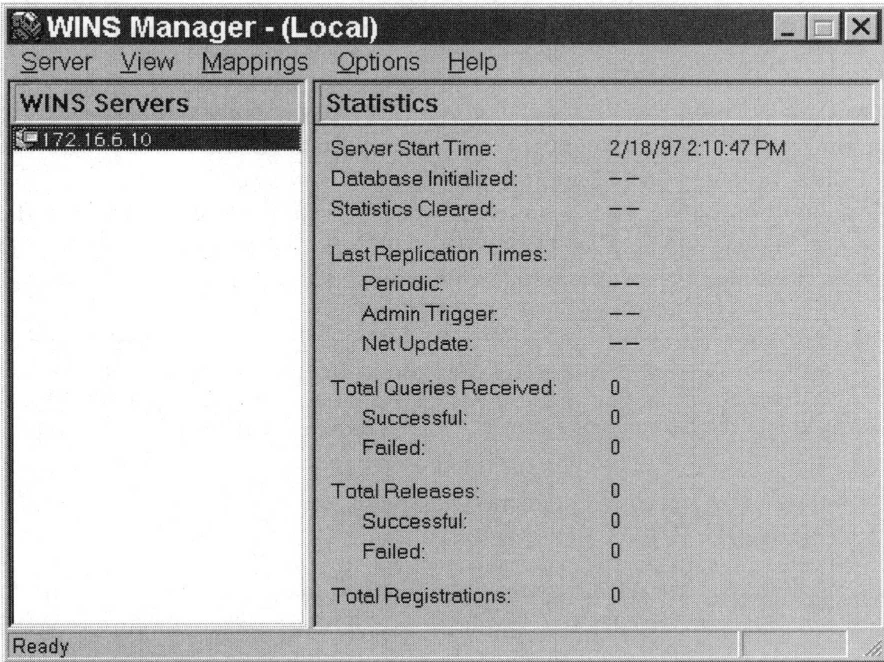

Figure 7-1. WINS Manager

Display pane in Options → Preferences to cause WINS Servers to be displayed by name only, by IP address only, or by both name and IP address. WINS Manager can manage multiple WINS Servers, but only one at a time. Select the WINS Server to be managed or viewed by double-clicking the address or name of that server in the WINS Servers pane. Note that single-clicking the server highlights it, but does not actually select it.

The Statistics pane displays a summary of the most important statistics related to the functioning of the selected WINS Server. You can clear the statistics for the selected WINS Server by selecting Clear Statistics from the View menu. You can update the statistics for the selected WINS Server by selecting Refresh Statistics from the View menu, or by double-clicking the server address or name in the WINS Servers pane.

The topmost block displays the time the WINS Server was started, when the database was initialized, and when the statistics were last cleared. The Last Replication Times section lists the last time replication occurred automatically (Periodic); by a manual replication initiated by the administrator (Admin Trigger); or by Net Update. Total Queries Received and Total Releases are the heart of the Statistics pane. On a normally functioning WINS Server, the values for each of these for

Total and Successful should continue to increment as clients connect to and disconnect from the network routinely. The values for Failed should remain very low. An occasional failure is not cause for alarm.

For more detailed information about the selected WINS Server, choose Detailed Information from the Server menu to display the Detailed Information message box. This lists the name and IP address of the WINS Server; the transport protocol it is using; how long it has been connected; the last time its address changed; the last time scavenging occurred; the number of unique registrations, conflicts, and renewals; and the number of group registrations, conflicts, and renewals.

NOTE The WINS Server Statistics pane displays statistics for only one WINS Server at a time. You can also use the Performance Monitor application to display statistics for all WINS Servers at the same time.

Configuring the WINS Server

To begin configuring the WINS Server, start WINS Manager by choosing Start → Programs → Administrative Tools (Common) → WINS Manager. From the WINS Manager Server menu, choose Configuration to display the WINS Server Configuration—(Local) dialog box. Click Advanced to display the extended dialog shown in Figure 7-2.

In the WINS Server Configuration pane, accept the default values, or set new values for the following WINS timers. The default values are suitable for nearly any WINS environment. None of the WINS administrators we know use anything other than the defaults for these timers.

Renewal Interval
: Specifies how frequently, in hours, minutes, and seconds, a WINS client must re-register its name with the WINS Server. This counter defaults to a value of 144 hours, or six days. WINS clients by default renew their names every two days. Setting this value high reduces network bandwidth demands. Doing so has few drawbacks, particularly if most or all of your clients are desktop systems. If you have many roving users, you can set this value lower to cause the WINS database to be updated more frequently. If possible, leave this value set to at least the default interval to allow for long weekends.

Extinction Interval
: Specifies, in hours, minutes, and seconds, the minimum duration between the time that a WINS client releases its name and the time that that name will be marked extinct in the WINS database. The default value for this counter depends on the renewal interval and on the maximum replication interval

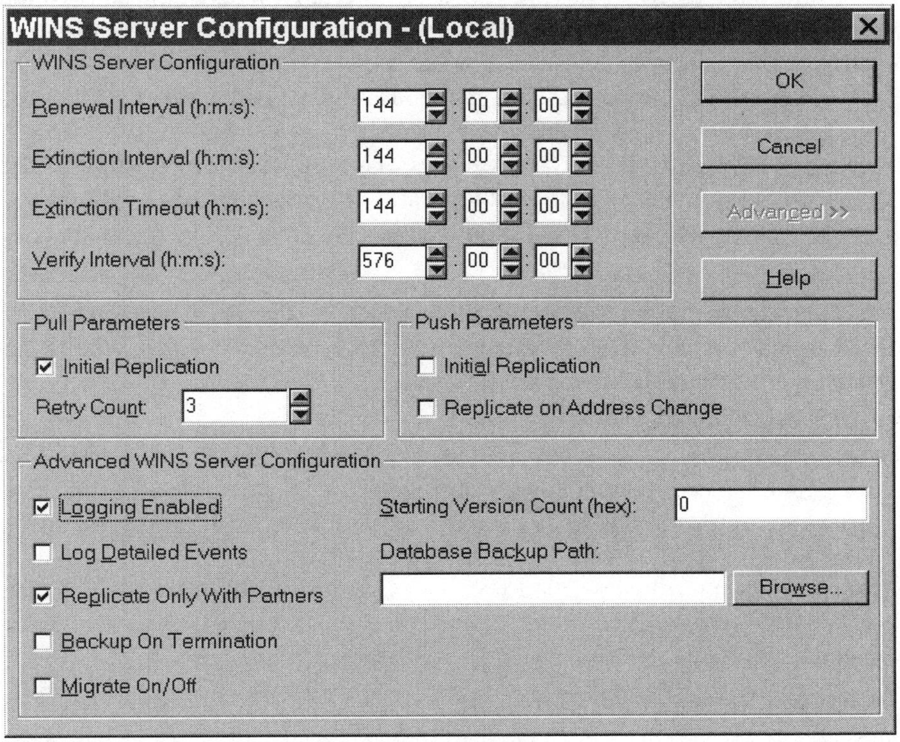

Figure 7-2. The WINS Server Configuration dialog

between WINS partners. Six days is both the maximum allowable value and the default value if you run a single WINS server.

Extinction Timeout
: Specifies, in hours, minutes, and seconds, the minimum duration between the time that an entry is marked extinct and the time that that name will be deleted from the WINS database by scavenging. The default value for this counter depends on the renewal interval and on the maximum replication interval between WINS partners. The default value for a single WINS server is 144 hours, or six days. The maximum allowable value is 9,999 hours, 59 minutes, and 59 seconds.

Verify Interval
: Specifies, in hours, minutes, and seconds, how often the WINS server must revalidate active names that originated on a remote WINS server and were replicated to the local WINS server. The default value for this counter depends on the extinction interval, but if installation defaults are used, this value is set to 576 hours, or 24 days, which is also the maximum allowable value.

If you will run multiple WINS servers you need to enable *replication*. Replication is the process by which a WINS server automatically distributes its database to, and receives WINS databases from, other WINS servers, called *replication partners*. A *pull partner* is a WINS server that initiates replication by asking other WINS servers to send their data to it. A *push partner* is a WINS server that initiates replication by sending its data to other WINS servers. If you plan to run multiple WINS Servers that will be configured as replication partners, set values in the Pull Parameters and Push Parameters panes, as follows:

Pull Parameters
: Initial Replication. Marking this checkbox, which is enabled by default, causes the local WINS Server to pull replicas from its partners whenever the WINS Server is started or replication parameters are changed.

Pull Parameters—Retry Count
: Specifies how many times this WINS Server will immediately retry pull replication if it is unable to connect to a pull partner on its first attempt. The duration between retries is determined by the value for Replication Interval specified in the Options → Preferences dialog described later in this section. If replication fails after the specified number of retries, WINS resets this counter, waits approximately three times the Replication Interval, and then again begins attempting to replicate.

Push Parameters—Initial Replication
: Marking this checkbox, which is cleared by default, causes the local WINS Server to inform its pull partners when the local WINS Server is started.

Push Parameters—Replicate on Address Change
: Marking this checkbox, which is cleared by default, causes the local WINS Server to inform its pull partners that the local WINS database has changed whenever an address mapping changes.

The Advanced WINS Server Configuration pane contains several other configuration parameters:

Logging Enabled
: Marking this checkbox, which is enabled by default, causes WINS to log changes to the WINS database.

Log Detailed Events
: Marking this checkbox, which is cleared by default, causes WINS to generate detailed logging. Enabling this function causes very rapid growth of the log file, and can adversely impact WINS Server performance. Use it only when troubleshooting WINS problems.

Replicate Only With Partners
: Marking this checkbox, which is enabled by default, allows the local WINS Server to replicate only with other WINS Servers that have been configured as partners. If this checkbox is cleared, the administrator can initiate a replication manually with any other WINS Server.

Backup On Termination
: Mark this checkbox to cause the WINS database to be backed up when WINS is terminated normally. Marking this checkbox does not cause the WINS database to be backed up automatically when Windows NT Server is shut down, but only when the WINS Server service itself is manually stopped.

Migrate On/Off
: The setting of this checkbox, which is cleared by default, determines how WINS resolves the collision when a new name entry received from a replication partner is identical to a name assigned a static mapping in the local WINS database. Enabling this checkbox allows the static database record to be dynamically updated. Leave this checkbox cleared unless you are updating to Windows NT Server from another operating system.

Starting Version Count (hex)
: Leave the value in this field alone, unless you experience corruption of your WINS database. If this occurs, specify a value here that is higher than the highest version number counter for this WINS Server database on any replication partner. WINS itself will verify that the value you select is high enough, and will correct the value you supplied to a higher number if necessary. This field may be set to a value as high as 2^{31} - 1.

Database Backup Path
: If you want WINS to backup its database automatically, specify a value for this field. If you do not specify a value here, you can still backup the WINS database, but you must do so manually using the Mappings—Backup Database option, and specifying the destination folder each time. If you specify a folder in this field, WINS Manager will also automatically use that folder as the restore source when you restore the database.

Configuring WINS Server Replication Partners

If your network is very small, you might not need to run WINS at all. If your network serves only one small- or medium-size workgroup, you might decide to run only one WINS Server. If your network serves a medium- to large-size company at a single location, running multiple WINS Servers offers redundancy if one of them fails. On very large, enterprise-level, multi-site networks, running multiple WINS Servers is almost mandatory, both for redundancy and for load sharing. In most

WINS environments, all of the WINS Servers should be configured to be both push and pull partners with the other WINS Servers on the network.

Configuring replication is pretty straightforward. In this section, we start with two newly installed WINS Servers. One of them is running on the Windows NT Server primary domain controller *anubis.ttgnet.com*, whose IP address is 172.16.6.16. The second is running on the Windows NT Server backup domain controller *thor.ttgnet.com*, whose IP address is 172.16.6.10. The initial display in WINS Manager shows only the local WINS Server. In this case, it happens to be *thor*, which we just finished installing.

To configure replication partners, from the WINS Manager Server menu, choose Add WINS Server to display the Add WINS Server dialog. Enter the computer name or the IP address of the remote WINS Server and click on OK to return to the WINS Manager main screen. In the WINS Servers pane of WINS Manager, double-click the IP address of the remote WINS Server (in this case 172.16.6.16) to select it. Note that single-clicking the WINS Server highlights it, but does not select it. After you select the WINS Server, choose Replication Partners from the WINS Manager Server menu to display the Replication Partners—(172.16.6.16) dialog, shown in Figure 7-3.

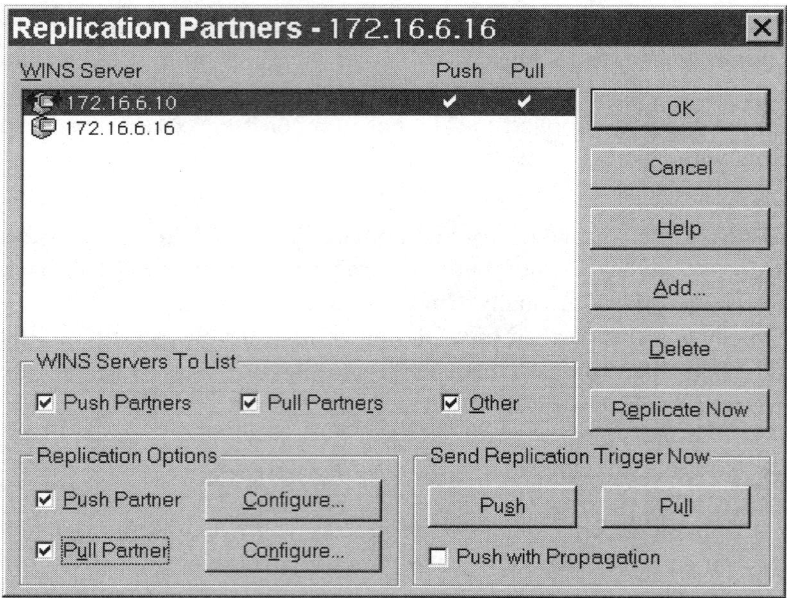

Figure 7-3. The Replication Partner—176.16.6.16 dialog

In the WINS Server pane of the Replication Partners dialog, highlight the IP address of the local WINS Server—in this case, 172.16.6.10. In the Replication

Options pane, mark the Push Partner checkbox to select the server as a push partner. A check mark appears in the Push column of the WINS Server pane next to the IP address of the local WINS Server. Mark the Pull Partner checkbox to select the server as a pull partner. A check mark appears in the Pull column of the WINS Server pane next to the IP address of the local WINS Server. This indicates that the selected WINS Server (172.16.6.16) is now configured as both push and pull partners with 172.16.6.10.

If you need to modify the list of available WINS Servers, click Add to display the Add WINS Server dialog or click Delete to remove the selected WINS Server from the list of replication partners. The Replicate Now button forces an immediate WINS database replication between the replication partners you have already configured.

The process of configuring replication partners is confusing, at least to us. Inevitably, it seems, we end up trying to configure a WINS Server as its own replication partner. Fortunately, WINS Manager recognizes the absurdity of this situation, displays a warning message, and refuses to proceed until you select an appropriate partner. If this happens to you when you are trying to configure two WINS Servers as replication partners, just select the other WINS Server. If you are configuring three or more WINS Servers as replication partners, you simply have to pay close attention to what you are doing.

After you have added all of your WINS Servers and established the replication relationships, next configure the partnership properties for each WINS server. In Replication Options, click Configure to display the Push Partner Properties dialog. Enter a value in the Update Count field. This value determines how many changes must be made to local database records before WINS will push an update to the pull partners of this server. You may also click Set Default Value to revert to the default update count specified in the Options—Preferences dialog, described later in this section. Setting a low value for this field causes replication updates to occur more frequently, which keeps the databases on the replication partners more closely synchronized at the expense of increasing bandwidth consumption

Next, click Configure to display the Pull Partner Properties dialog. Enter a value in the Start Time field to specify when replication should begin. Set the Replication Interval field to specify how often you want pull replication to be initiated. By default, Replication Interval is set to 30 minutes, which is appropriate for most WINS environments. You may also choose Set Default Values to revert to the default values specified in the Options—Preferences dialog, described later in this section.

If you return to the WINS Manager main screen, double-click the local WINS Server (172.16.6.10) to select it, and then display the Replication Partners—

(172.16.6.10) dialog for that WINS Server, shown in Figure 7-4, you will see that the local WINS Server is now also configured as a Push and Pull partner with the remote WINS Server (172.16.6.16).

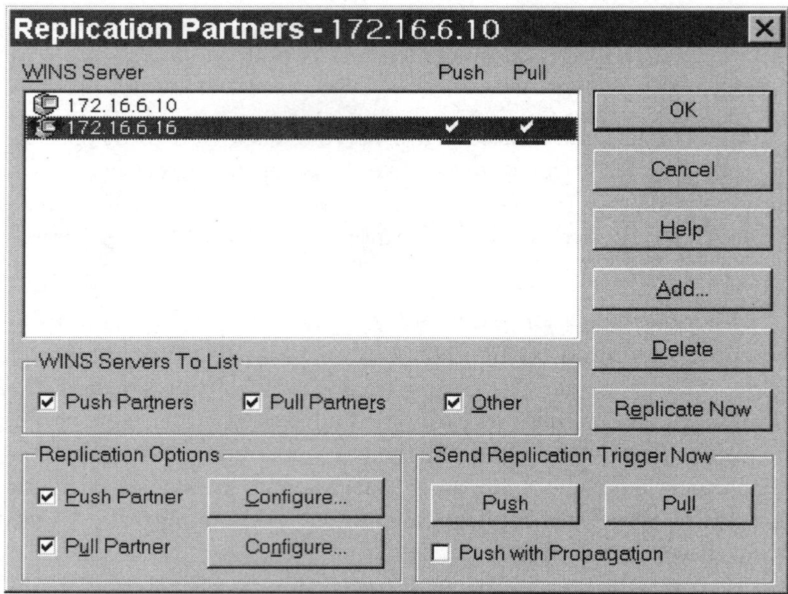

Figure 7-4. The Replication Partners—172.16.6.10 dialog

Setting WINS Server Preferences

Choose the Preferences option from the Options menu of WINS Manager to display the Preferences dialog. Click Partners to display the extended version of the Preferences dialog, shown in Figure 7-5. This dialog allows you to set various parameters that specify how WINS Manager itself functions.

You may set the following preferences:

Address Display pane
: Choose one of the option buttons to specify how you want address information to be displayed throughout WINS Manager. The options are pretty much self-explanatory. You can choose to display only the computer name, only its IP address, or either one followed by the other in parentheses.

Server Statistics pane
: If you want the server statistics to be updated automatically in the Statistics pane of WINS Manager, mark the Auto Refresh checkbox and specify how frequently you want updates to occur by entering a value for Interval (Seconds).

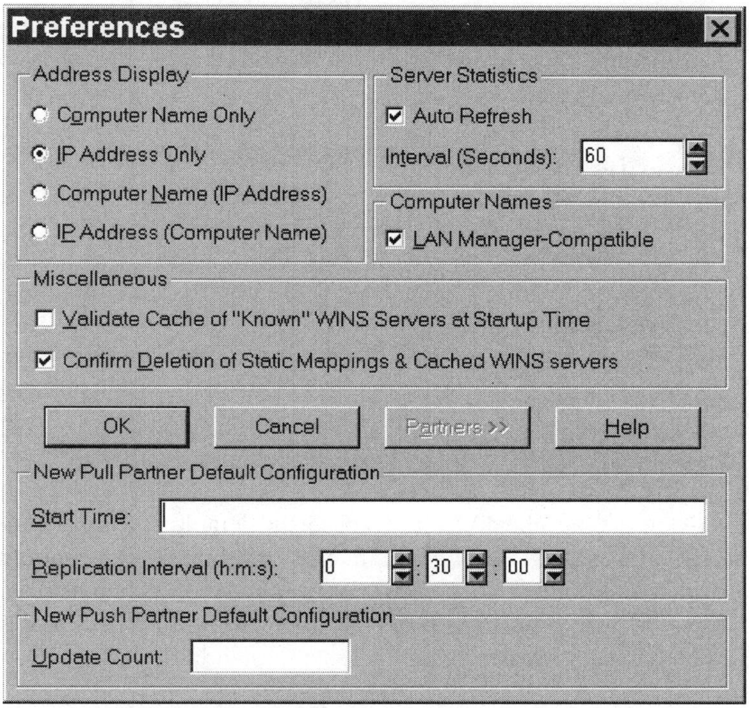

Figure 7-5. The Preferences dialog

If you clear the Auto Refresh checkbox, the display will be updated only when you click View → Refresh Statistics or press F5.

Computer Names pane

Standard NetBIOS computer names can be up to 16 bytes long. Microsoft, originally with LAN Manager and subsequently with all of their networking products, elected to limit NetBIOS computer names to 15 bytes and to use the remaining byte as a special hexadecimal flag character to indicate the type of host or service represented by the name, as follows:

00

A standard NetBIOS computer name, or Workstation Service Name.

03

Used by the Messenger Service. Registered with the WINS Server as the messenger service on the WINS Client, and appended to the computer name and the name of the current user.

06

Owned by the RAS Server service.

1B
Indicates that the name so flagged is owned by the master browser. Identifies the Primary Domain Controller to allow clients and other browsers to contact the domain master browser.

1F
Owned by the NetDDE service.

20
Server service name used for resource shares.

21
Owned by a RAS client.

BE
Owned by the Network Monitor Agent.

BF
Owned by the Network Monitor utility.

The LAN Manager-Compatible checkbox is marked by default. Because Windows NT Server also uses LAN Manager naming conventions, you should leave this checkbox marked unless your network accepts NetBIOS names from non-Microsoft sources. The most common reason for clearing this checkbox is if you are running IBM/Lotus Notes, which uses the standard, 16-byte NetBIOS naming convention.

Miscellaneous pane
The options displayed in this pane allow you to determine how WINS handles validation of other WINS Servers at startup, and how it handles deletions of static mappings and cached data.

Validate Cache of "Known" WINS Servers at Startup Time
Mark this checkbox, which is disabled by default, if you want the WINS Server to query the list of WINS Servers for available servers each time it is started.

Confirm Deletion of Static Mappings & Cached WINS Servers
Mark this checkbox, which is enabled by default, if you want to see a warning message each time a static mapping or a cached WINS Server is deleted.

New Pull Partner Default Configuration pane
Specifies the default values that will be used for Start Time and Replication Interval when you create a new pull partner. Also, clicking Set Default Values in the Pull Partner Properties dialog causes the current values for the selected partner to revert to this default.

New Push Partner Default Configuration pane
: Specifies the default value for Update Count that will be used when you create a new push partner. Also, clicking Set Default Value in the Push Partner Properties dialog causes the current value for the selected partner to revert to this default.

Using Static Mappings

Ideally, you'd prefer that every host on your network be WINS-aware and use h-node name resolution. In the real world, this usually turns out not to be the case. Chances are you'll have at least one device on your network that is limited to using b-node for name resolution. In the normal course of things, this might cause problems, because b-node devices are unaware of h-node devices, and vice versa. WINS, however, makes provision for accommodating b-node devices in an h-node environment. The method it uses to do so is called *static mapping*.

Static mapping allows you manually to create WINS database entries that associate a specific NetBIOS computer name and IP address with a b-node device. To create a static mapping entry, proceed as follows:

1. From WINS Manager, choose Static Mappings from the Mappings menu to display the Static Mappings – <*WINS Server ID*> dialog. By default, this dialog displays all active static mappings. You can use the Set Filter button and Clear Filter button as described in the preceding section to display a subset of the static mappings in the database, filtered by computer name or IP address. Changes you make to the WINS database using the Static Mappings dialog occur in real time. That is, if you mistakenly add an entry, you must delete it manually. Similarly, if you delete an entry accidentally, the only way to recover it is to recreate the entry
2. Click Add Mappings to display the Add Static Mappings dialog. Enter the Name of the host and its IP address in the appropriate fields. Specify the type of host by choosing one of the Type option buttons, as follows:

   Unique
   : An "ordinary" client, i.e. that the host name and IP address have a one-to-one mapping.

   Group
   : Defines the host as a member of a normal group, or one in which individual IP addresses are not stored for each member.

   Domain Name
   : Defines this host as a member of a Domain Name group. See WINS help or the Resource Kit for more details.

Internet group
: Defines this host as a member of a user-defined group that associates multiple IP addresses with multiple computer names in a many-to-many mapping. See WINS help or the Resource Kit for more details.

Multihomed
: A multihomed host has more than one IP address associated with a single unique computer name. Choosing this option button invokes another dialog that allows you to enter additional IP addresses for this entry, to a maximum of 25. See WINS help or the Resource Kit for more details.

3. When you have finished entering information for a static mapping entry, click Close to save that entry and return to the Static Mappings – <*WINS Server ID*> dialog. If you need to create more static mapping entries, instead click Add, which saves the current entry and then displays an empty Add Static Mappings dialog.

You can view and modify existing static mapping entries either by double-clicking the entry or by highlighting the entry and then clicking Edit Mapping to invoke the Edit Static Mapping dialog described previously. Similarly, you can delete a static mapping entry by highlighting it and clicking Delete Mapping.

If you need to create static mapping entries for many hosts—perhaps when you are first installing your WINS Server—there is an alternative to entering them individually as described earlier. Create and save a file in *Lmhosts* format that contains a name and IP address for each host for which you need to create a static mapping entry. Then in the Static Mappings – <*WINS Server ID*> dialog, click Import Mappings and specify the location of the file you just created in the Select Static Mappings File dialog that appears. WINS Manager creates a static mapping entry for each of the records in the file.

Managing the WINS Database

There is little need for an administrator to make routine changes to the WINS database in most WINS environments. WINS clients interact automatically with WINS Servers, and the replication partners exchange information among themselves without manual intervention. Sometimes, however, the WINS administrator will find it necessary to view the WINS database or to make manual changes to it. In particular, if you have b-node clients operating on your network, you will need to create static mappings for them. The following sections describe how to view and modify the WINS database.

Viewing the WINS Database

To view the WINS database, from WINS Manager, choose Show Database from the Mappings menu to display the Show Database – <WINS Server ID> dialog, shown in Figure 7-6. Note that the title bar displays the location of the database you are working with. In this case, it happens to be the WINS database on the local server.

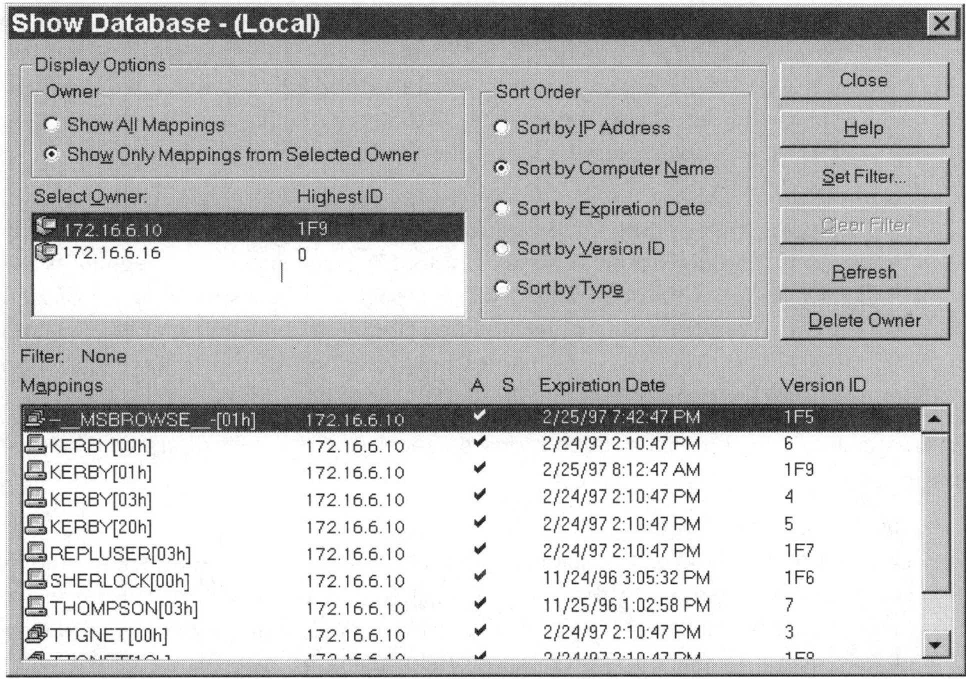

Figure 7-6. The Show Database - <WINS Server ID> dialog

The upper half of the screen displays information and options that allow you to control which data will be displayed, and how it will be displayed, as follows:

Display Options—Owner Section

Choose the Show All Mappings option button to display every mapping in the selected WINS database, regardless of which WINS Server owns it. Choose the Show Only Mappings from the Selected Owner option button and then select one of the WINS Servers in the Select Owner: pane to display only mappings owned by the selected WINS Server. The Highest ID column in the Sort Owner: pane shows the highest WINS version number of records owned by the associated WINS Server in the database of its replication partners.

Display Options—Sort Order

Choose one of the option buttons in this section to specify how the list of mappings will be displayed. The first three choices are self-explanatory. The last two require some explanation:

Sort by Version ID

Choosing this option button causes the list of mappings to be sorted by WINS version ID number, which is ordinarily a pretty useless sort order. However, if a WINS server fails or the database is corrupted, you need to take remedial action, as described in the troubleshooting section that follows. One of the things that you need to do to reconstruct a WINS Server database is determine the highest WINS version ID number that was in use on the problem server. This option button allows you to do so.

Sort by Type

Choosing this option button causes the list of mappings to be sorted by type. In addition to an ordinary computer name used by a regular WINS client (called a unique name), WINS recognizes four special types of NetBIOS computer names, called Group, Domain Name, Internet Group, and Multihomed. These special names are described in the following section on using static mappings.

You can also use the following buttons to specify which mappings will be displayed, and how:

Set Filter.

Use this button to create a filter that limits the range of IP addresses or computer names displayed in the Mappings list. When you click Set Filter, the Set Filter dialog is displayed. You can filter by computer name by entering part or all of a name in the Computer Name: field, using an asterisk as a final wildcard character. You can filter by address by entering part or all of an IP address in the IP address field, using one or more asterisks as wildcards. Mappings are displayed only if they match the filter in effect. For example, if you enter a filter of 172.16.12.*, mappings with any address that begins with 172.16.12 will be displayed, while all others will be suppressed.

If a filter is currently in effect, the name or address of that filter is displayed immediately above the Mappings pane, and the Clear Filter button is activated. Click Clear Filter to remove the filter and display all mappings.

Refresh

Click this button to query the WINS database and display an updated list of mappings.

Delete Owner

Use this button to remove the mappings for one or more WINS Servers from the Mappings list. To do so, highlight a WINS Server in the Select Owner:

pane and then click Delete Owner. Mappings for the selected WINS Server are removed from the Mappings list. Note that on larger networks, it can take literally hours to delete a record.The lower half of the screen displays the Mappings list, each line of which corresponds to a single database record. Note that a single entity has multiple database entries, one for each of its functions. The first column displays three elements:

- An icon that indicates the mapping type. In this example, the icon associated with the first and last entries resembles several computers, indicating that this entry is of the Group, Domain Name, Internet Group, or Multihomed type. The icon associated with the other entries is a single computer, indicating that these entries are of type Unique. Double-clicking an individual entry displays the View Mapping dialog. This dialog shows the Name of the mapping; the Mapping Type, for example, Unique, Group, and so on; and the IP address. You can modify the IP address to specify a new static mapping address for that entry.
- The NetBIOS computer name that is mapped.
- The hexadecimal flag byte, described earlier in this chapter. Recall that Microsoft NetBIOS names use only the first 15 of the 16 available characters, and reserve the final character as a flag byte to indicate type.

The remaining columns provide additional information for each mapping, including the IP address; a check mark to indicate that the mapping is A or active; a check mark to indicate that the mapping is S or static; the expiration date of the record; and the WINS version ID number for the mapping.

Backing up and restoring the WINS database

WINS can backup its databases automatically, although by default it does not do so. To cause WINS to do periodic automatic backups, from the WINS Manager Server menu choose Configuration, click Advanced, and then Browse to display the Select Backup Directory dialog. Select a folder and then click on OK to insert that folder name into the Database Backup Path field. The folder you specify must be located on a local disk drive; WINS will not backup to a network drive.

The Database Backup Path is used as the destination for automatic backups. It is also used as the default source location when you choose Restore Local Database from the Mappings menu. Finally, it is used as the default destination when you initiate a manual backup by choosing Backup Database from the Mappings menu. When you restore or perform a manual backup, WINS Manager gives you the opportunity to specify a different path before proceeding.

Troubleshooting WINS

Once it has been installed and configured correctly, WINS requires little routine maintenance, and is likely to have few problems. When WINS problems do occur, they are usually one of those described in the following sections. To resolve these problems, you must be logged on to the server as a member of the Administrators group.

Resolving Minor WINS Problems

When WINS problems do occur, they are usually minor and affect only one or a few clients. The following list describes four of the most common minor problems that might occur with WINS and how to resolve them:

Clients receive "network path not found" messages
: This problem may occur in environments with a mix of h-node and b-node hosts, and in those with multiple WINS servers configured as replication partners. If this problem occurs, the first step is to look up the name in question in the WINS database. If the name does not exist, check to see if the destination host uses b-node. If so, you must enter a static mapping for the b-node host in the WINS database. If an entry for the destination host does exist in the local WINS database, but that host is connected to a subnet served by a different WINS server, then the most likely cause is that that host's IP address is no longer the same as the value stored in the local WINS database. To resolve the problem, perform a push replication from the remote WINS server to the local WINS server to replicate the changed information to your local database.

WINS returns "duplicate name" messages
: This problem also occurs in environments with multiple WINS servers configured as replication partners. It occurs when a static mapping record exists for a particular name in the local database, and a remote database attempts to replicate that same name to the local database. To resolve the problem, first examine the local WINS database to determine if a static mapping record exists for that name. If so, delete it.

WINS database backup fails
: If you receive an error message during backup of the WINS database, the most likely cause is that the backup folder you specified initially in WINS Manager is located on a network drive. WINS requires that its backup folder be located on a local drive. You will also receive a similar message if the drive containing the backup folder has inadequate space to complete the backup.

WINS replication fails
: If you receive an error message reporting a replication failure, by far the most likely cause is a simple configuration error. A WINS server can be configured

as a push partner, as a pull partner, or as both push and pull. Normally, in an environment with multiple WINS servers configured as replication partners, each WINS server should be configured as both a push partner and a pull partner with each other WINS server. If you receive an error message reporting a replication failure on a newly installed or recently reconfigured WINS server, verify that the partnership settings are configured correctly between the WINS servers. You can do so by using the Registry Editor to examine the values for the Registry subkeys *Pull* and *Push* in the key *HKLM_SYSTEM\CurrentControlSet\Services\Wins\Partners*.

If you haven't made any changes recently to your WINS servers, then an incorrect configuration is unlikely to be the cause of the replication problem. In this case, the most likely cause is a simple network communication problem. The two WINS servers obviously can't replicate if they can't talk to each other. Use the **ping** utility to verify that IP connectivity exists between the two servers.

Resolving Major WINS Problems

The following two problems (or widespread client problems of the sort described above) indicate more severe problems with WINS:

- When you attempt to use WINS Manager to connect to a WINS Server, you are unable to do so and receive a warning message.
- When you attempt to start the Windows Internet Name Service service or the WINS Client service, you receive a warning message that the service cannot start.

If either of these problems occurs, first use Event Viewer to check the log for Error events. To run Event Viewer, from the Start Button, choose Programs → Administrative Tools (Common) → Event Viewer.

If the first problem occurs, first use **ping** to verify that IP connectivity exists between the workstation you are using and the WINS server in question. If you can ping the server successfully, next verify that WINS is running on that server by running the Services applet from Control Panel. The Status column should report "Started" for both the Windows Internet Name Service service and the WINS Client service. If either or both of these services is not running, first attempt to start the service by highlighting its name and clicking Start. If the service starts successfully, verify that the problems you were experiencing have been resolved.

If the second problem occurs and you are unable to start the service using the previously described procedure, the next step is to shut down the server. Before doing so, notify everyone that the server is about to be shut down. If you experiencing severe WINS problems, you may have to notify your users using some method other than a broadcast to clients. Once all clients have disconnected safely, shut down the server, turn the power off, and allow the server to remain down for at least a minute.

Once your drives have all spun down, turn the power back on, and watch the console for warning messages as the server restarts. Most of the time, you will find that WINS starts normally. If WINS still does not start, from the command prompt, type **net start wins**, and press Enter. WINS should start normally. If WINS still refuses to start, or if WINS appears to start properly but you still cannot access the WINS database with WINS Manager, there are two alternatives remaining. Before attempting either, backup your existing WINS database. Make sure that you are not backing up bad data over good, and that you have a copy of your last-known-good WINS database backup stored in a safe location before proceeding.

Restore the WINS database

The penultimate measure to correcting WINS problems is to revert to an earlier version of the WINS database. You can restore the WINS database using WINS Manager or by manually copying files.

- To restore using WINS Manager, select Restore Local Database option from the Mappings menu, enter the location of the backup WINS database files, and click on OK to confirm.
- To restore manually, first stop any running WINS services as described earlier in this section. Next, delete all files in the *\%SystemRoot\system32\wins* folder, and copy a known-good earlier version of *wins.mdb* to this folder. Finally, restart WINS using the command line procedure described earlier.

Reinstall WINS.

If you are running a small network with a simple WINS environment—one without replication partners, numerous static mappings, and so on—the quickest and easiest fix is sometimes simply to reinstall WINS. Even if your WINS environment is more complex, you may have no alternative to reinstalling WINS if you find that all of your existing WINS database copies are corrupt.

To reinstall WINS, from Control Panel → Services, shut down any WINS services that are currently running. Next, from the Services page of the Network property sheet, highlight Windows Internet Name Service and click Remove, but don't restart the server just yet. First, delete the *\%SystemRoot\system32\wins* folder and all of its files and subfolders. Restart the server and install WINS as described earlier in this chapter. Restart the server once more. The WINS database will be rebuilt dynamically as the clients access it. In a small environment, removing and then reinstalling WINS may be quicker and less disruptive than attempting to fix the existing installation.

Rebuilding the WINS Database on Another Server

If your WINS problems arise as a result of hardware problems on the machine running the WINS Server service, you may have no alternative but to rebuild the WINS database on another server. To rebuild the WINS database, take the following steps:

1. Attempt to retrieve a copy of the WINS database from the failed server by stopping the WINS Server service and making a copy of the database as described above. Otherwise, you must use your most recent good backup of the WINS database.
2. If it is not already running Windows NT Server 4.0, install the operating system on the new server. The WINS database must reside in the same location on the new server as it did on the old. That is, if the WINS database was stored in *C:\WINNT\system32\wins* on the original server, it must also reside in the *C:\WINNT\system32\wins* on the replacement server. If Windows NT Server is installed in a different folder on an existing replacement server, you must reinstall Windows NT Server to the original %SystemRoot% before proceeding.
3. Verify that the WINS Server service is stopped on the replacement server.
4. Use the Registry Editor to restore the WINS Registry Keys from backup copies made from the original server.
5. Restore the WINS database files to the WINS data directory on the replacement server and restart the server.

You can also use this procedure if you simply want to remove the WINS Server from one server and relocate it to another.

Summary

NetBIOS is the foundation protocol of Microsoft Networking. Microsoft Networking uses the NetBIOS Extended User Interface (NetBEUI), which combines NetBIOS, Service Message Block (SMB), and NetBIOS Frame (NBF) protocols. Because NetBEUI cannot be routed between networks and relies on the broadcast capabilities of the underlying physical network, it is adequate only for small, local area network application.

NetBIOS over TCP/IP (NetBT) was developed to run NetBIOS applications over a wide area network. A fundamental part of NetBT is the mapping of NetBIOS names to IP addresses. In a NetBIOS network the computer name is its address. To create a connection over a TCP/IP network that name must be converted to an IP address. In Chapter 3, *Network Services*, we discussed various techniques for doing this. The best technique for Windows NT systems is Windows Internet Name Service (WINS).

The WINS server is bundled with Windows NT Server. It is installed in the same manner as most other standard services. WINS is configured by the system administrator using the WINS Manager software. The database that maps NetBIOS names to IP addresses is built automatically. WINS clients register their names and addresses with the WINS server when they connect to the network.

In the next chapter we look at another server that is used to map names to addresses. This server maps Internet domain names to IP addresses. It is called the Domain Name System (DNS).

In this chapter:

8

Configuring DNS Name System

Strictly speaking, name service is not necessary for computers to communicate. It is, as the name implies, a service—specifically, a service intended to make the network more user-friendly. Computers are perfectly happy with IP addresses, but people prefer names. The importance of name service is indicated by the amount of coverage it has in this book. Chapter 3, *Network Services*, discusses *why* name service is needed; Chapter 7, *Using Windows Internet Name Service*, covers *how* the NetBIOS name service (WINS) is configured; this chapter covers *how* Domain Name System (DNS) is configured, and Appendix B, *DNS Resource Records*, is a *reference* for the records used to build a DNS database. This chapter provides sufficient information to show you how to configure DNS software to run under Windows NT. But if you want to know more about why something is done, don't hesitate to refer to Appendix B and Chapter 3.

DNS is a client/server software system. The client side of DNS is called the *resolver*. It generates the queries for domain name information that are sent to the server. The DNS server software, which is called the name server, answers the resolver's queries. Both sides of DNS require configuration.

This book covers three basic DNS configuration tasks:

- Configuring the resolver
- Configuring the name server
- Constructing the name server database files, called the *zone files*

There is a distinction between a DNS domain and a DNS zone. A domain is a logical grouping that encompasses the domain itself, all subdomains of that domain, and all hosts within that domain and its subdomains. A *zone*, on the other hand, is a collection of domain information over which a name server has authority. The zone is an administrative grouping that may encompass parts of domains, entire domains, and groups of domains. A server may have authority over more than one zone.

Rather than being a purely logical grouping, a zone has physical reality, as reflected in the existence of a *zone file*, which contains database records for a zone. A DNS server may manage one or several zone files. The zone may encompass the complete domain, or only a portion of it, as shown in Figure 8-1.

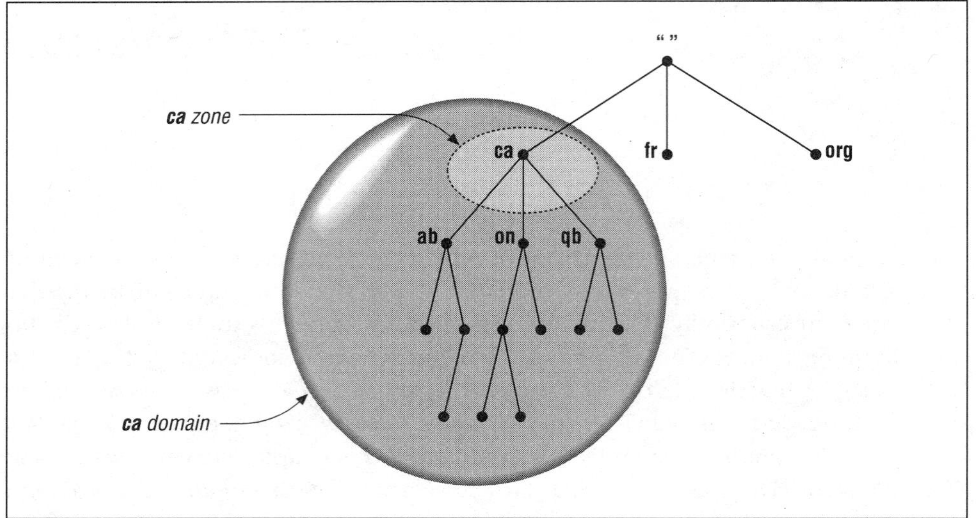

Figure 8-1. A DNS Zone

The term *zone* is often used interchangeably with the word domain, but in this book we use zone to refer to the information in the domain database file, while the term domain is used in more general contexts. In this book, a domain is part of the domain hierarchy identified by a domain name. A zone is a collection of domain information contained in a domain database file. The file that contains the domain information is called a zone file.

RFC 1033, the *Domain Administrators Operations Guide*, defines the basic set of standard records used to construct zone files. Many RFCs propose new DNS records that are not widely implemented. In this chapter and in Appendix B we stick to the basic resource records that you are most likely to use. These records construct the zone files used in this chapter. Whether or not you need to construct zone files for your system is controlled by the type of configuration you decide to use.

DNS configurations are described by the type of service the software provides. The four levels of service are resolver-only clients, caching-only servers, primary servers, and secondary servers. All four of these configurations are described in Chapter 3. The three server configurations require that the local system runs the name server software and has local configuration files. A server may be any one of these configurations or, as is often the case, it may combine elements of more than one type of configuration.

Most systems run as resolver-only systems, because most systems are clients, not servers. The resolver-only configuration does not require that the local system run name server software, just the resolver. On Windows NT systems, the resolver is implemented at the application level, rather than at the operating system level. All systems, clients and servers, run the resolver. Because it is part of every TCP/IP installation, resolver installation and configuration is covered in Chapter 5, *Installing TCP/IP*. (See the discussion of Figure 5-5 in Chapter 5.)

While every system using DNS runs the resolver, only servers run the name server software. For Windows NT servers the name server software is the Microsoft DNS Server service. It is not installed by default. The administrator must install and configure the server.

The Microsoft DNS Server

Microsoft is late to the party with a DNS server for Windows NT. Although they made a DNS server for Windows NT Server 3.51 available, it offered limited functionality and was not well integrated with the other TCP/IP services provided by Windows NT. Most administrators considered this early Microsoft effort to create a DNS server an interesting oddity, but not a product that they would consider using in a production environment. However, the DNS server included with Windows NT Server 4.0 is worth serious consideration. It corrects the problems of the 3.51 DNS server, and adds some bells and whistles all its own.

The Microsoft DNS server is fully compliant with Internet standards, and interoperates well with other DNS servers, so using it doesn't paint you into any corners. It complies with all relevant Internet standards, including RFC1033, RFC1034, RFC1035, RFC1101, RFC1123, RFC1183, and RFC1536. The Microsoft DNS Server is fully compatible with the popular Berkeley Internet Name Domain (BIND) implementation of DNS.* Applications running on any platform can use the Microsoft DNS server for name resolution.

---

* Microsoft themselves state in published material that "The book *DNS and BIND*, published by O'Reilly and Associates, is a valuable resource. The Windows NT DNS essentially conforms to this book." A Windows NT version of the book is *DNS on Windows NT*, by Cricket Liu, Paul Albitz, and Matt Larson.

The Microsoft DNS Server uses the same database files and resource records types used by other DNS servers. It does, however, have some advantages for a Windows networking environment. The advantages are:

Improved Integration
: The Microsoft DNS Server is integrated with Microsoft WINS and with the Microsoft DHCP Server. Using all three of these services on the network allows WINS clients and clients assigned a dynamic IP address by the DHCP Server to participate fully in DNS.

Improved Management
: Traditional implementations of DNS are managed by creating and maintaining ASCII text configuration files. Microsoft DNS Server usually is maintained using the graphical DNS Manager application. If you've ever struggled with maintaining the configuration files used by most DNS servers, you will appreciate just how much easier and faster it is to use DNS Manager.

Planning Your DNS Service

Before installing DNS on your network decide how many servers you'll use, what type they will be, and how they will be placed. These decisions affect all networks but are most significant for enterprise networks connected by wide area links.

The primary server should be located in your central computer facility. This assumes that the facility that holds your key enterprise servers has the best network connectivity, and that it is conveniently located for the domain administrator who needs good access to the server in order to create and maintain the DNS database. The primary DNS server should be located on the same LAN segment as the WINS server because updates from the WINS server are used by the Microsoft DNS Server to build the DNS database.

The number and location of secondary servers depends on the characteristics of the network they are serving. Remember that if you're connected to the Internet, you serve the Internet because some of the queries for DNS information about your domain will come from there. Your primary server should have excellent Internet connectivity and you should have at least one secondary server with a separate path to the Internet. On a large enterprise network you may have a redundant Internet connection that the secondary server could use, but most small networks will need to ask their ISP to host the secondary server.

The location of servers within an enterprise is influenced by the type of physical networks that connect the various parts of the enterprise. If the entire enterprise is connected by a high-speed local area network (LAN), a single secondary server, which is not on the same LAN segment as the primary server, is probably sufficient. However, if the enterprise is connected by wide area network (WAN) links, each piece of the enterprise should have its own server to reduce the amount of traffic sent over the WAN. In most cases a caching server is a good choice for each remote location. Maintaining a local cache reduces the number of queries sent over the WAN. But in the case of pay-per-use networks, such as ISDN, caching-only servers may be a bad idea because each query used to build the cache costs money. A better design for pay-per-use networks is to place a secondary server at each remote location. These servers only provide service to their local networks because they are not advertised as official secondary servers by the primary server. Network costs are controlled by setting a high refresh rate on the primary server to limit the number of times the secondary server loads data from the primary. The procedures for creating caching-only servers, creating secondary servers, defining official secondary servers, and defining the refresh rate are all covered in the following sections of this chapter.

The final thing to plan for is the allocation of subdomains within your domain. Subdomains are created for the same reasons that subnets are created:

For organizational reasons
: A piece of an organization may be assigned a subdomain because it wants or needs local control over naming. An example of an organizational domain name might be *sales.ttgnet.com*.

For topological reasons
: A remote location of an enterprise may be assigned a subdomain that encompasses the systems at that location. This type of domain reduces the number of queries sent over a WAN because on most networks the majority of queries are for local systems. An example of this type of subdomain is *denver.ttgnet.com*.

To distribute control
: Sometimes an organization is so large the only efficient way to handle naming is to break the name space up into smaller, more manageable pieces. The domains that are created for this reason can be either organizational or topological.

Most subdomains are organizational because organizational consideration are generally viewed as more important than network considerations. However, topological subdomains can be more useful for improving performance and reducing the load in a WAN.

Once you have decided what servers are needed and where they should be placed, you can begin the installation.

Installing the DNS Server

Install the Microsoft DNS Server service from the Network Services page of the Network property sheet (Control Panel → Network → Services tab). Select Add to display the Select Network Service dialog and highlight Microsoft DNS Server for installation.

Windows NT displays the Windows NT Setup dialog to prompt for the location of the distribution files; accept the default or specify a new location as appropriate. NT copies the distribution files and returns to the Network property sheet, which now shows the Microsoft DNS Server as an installed service. When you close the installation dialog, the system configures, stores, and reviews the bindings. Restart your computer to activate the DNS server.

Windows NT Server configures the DNS Server service to start each time the system is booted. Use the Services applet in Control Panel to modify the startup settings for the DNS Server service, or to start, stop, pause, or continue the service. You can also control the DNS Server service from the command prompt, using the commands **net start dns**, **net stop dns**, **net pause dns**, and **net continue dns**.

At this point, the DNS server software is installed but it has not yet been configured. Use DNS Manager to configure and manage the DNS server.

The DNS Manager

Installing DNS adds the DNS Manager application to the Administrative Tools (Common) program group. Select the application from that group to open the window shown in Figure 8-2.

Figure 8-2 shows the DNS Manager after servers and zones have been added. The first time you run the DNS Manager the Server List may be empty. This is always true if you are creating the first Microsoft DNS server on your network. To add your server to the Server List, highlight Server List and choose New Server from the DNS menu to display the Add DNS Server dialog. Enter the IP address of your server in the DNS Server box of the dialog. Click OK.

Your server is now listed in the Server List. Highlight it. The statistics associated with the server are displayed in the right half of the DNS Manager Window. All of the DNS files installed on the server are listed under the server's name in the Server List. At first only the cache file is listed. (It is represented by a small globe.)

At this point in the configuration, the server is configured as a caching-only server. If a caching-only server is what you want, you're finished. If you want to create an authoritative server, you have more to do—you must define a zone for the server.

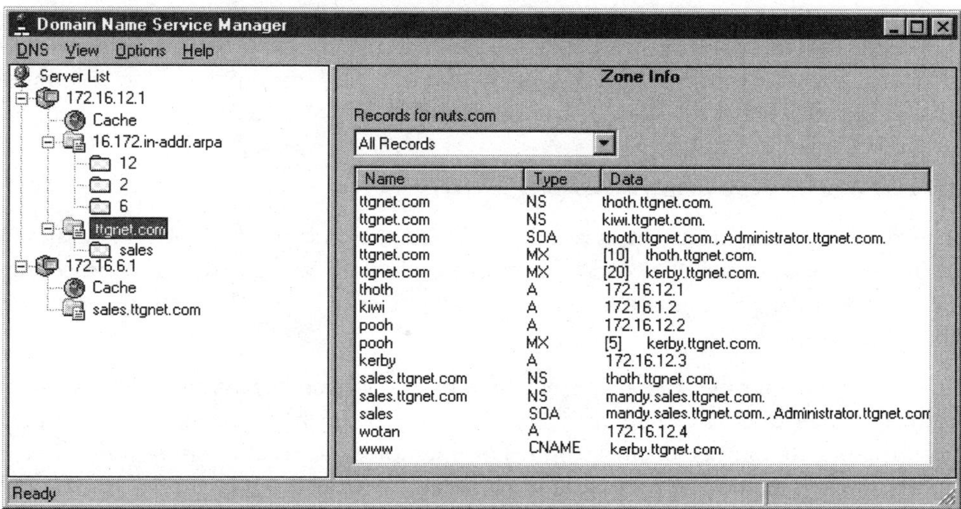

Figure 8-2. The DNS Manager

Creating a New Zone

Before creating a new zone, make sure that the TCP/IP configuration information is set correctly for the computer running Microsoft DNS Server. In particular, verify that IP address, Internet host name, and Internet Domain name are correct. These values are used by DNS Manager when you create a new zone file. Thus an error in the TCP/IP configuration will be propagated through the DNS system if it is not corrected before you create the zone.

To create the new zone, highlight the name of the DNS server in the Server List pane, and from the DNS menu, choose New Zone. The DNS Manager displays the first screen of the *Creating new zone Wizard.*

The first Wizard screen asks you whether the server will be primary or secondary for the zone you're creating. In the Zone Type pane select the Primary option button if this system is the primary DNS server, or the Secondary option button if it is a secondary server. If you select the Secondary option button, the Zone and Server fields activate. In the Zone field enter the name of the domain for which this system will be a secondary server. Enter the IP address of the zone's primary server in the Server field. If, however, you select the Primary option button, there is nothing else to enter on this page. Click Next and the Wizard displays a second screen.

In the second screen, enter the zone name for a primary server or accept the value inserted by the Wizard for a secondary server. This is the domain name, for example, *ttgnet.com*, that is at the root of the DNS name space managed in this zone.

DNS Manager fills in the Zone File name by appending *.dns* to the zone name, as in *ttgnet.com.dns*, for example. Accept the suggested file name, or enter a different name for the zone file. When you click Next, the DNS Manager informs you that all necessary information has been entered, and prompts you to continue. Click Finish and DNS Manager automatically creates the zone file.

Creating a Reverse Lookup Zone

The zone file maps host names to addresses. The reverse lookup zone file maps IP addresses to host names. To create a reverse lookup zone follow the procedure described in the preceding section for creating a new zone. The only difference is the zone name.

When prompted for the zone name, enter the reverse lookup zone name in *in-addr.arpa* format as described in Chapter 3. That is, reverse the numbers in the IP address and append the string *.in-addr.arpa*. For example, the IP address of ttgnet net is 172.16.0.0. To name the reverse lookup zone, reverse the address to 16.172 and append the string *in-addr.arpa* to arrive at the zone name of 16.172.in-addr.arpa.

Always create the reverse lookup zones when you create a primary zone. When you subsequently enter a host name and its address in the primary zone, DNS Manager automatically creates the associated reverse lookup zone entry. If you have not created the reverse lookup zone before entering host information into the primary zone file, you must enter the reverse lookup data manually.

Modifying Zone Properties

The DNS Manager automatically builds the primary and reverse zone files needed for the zones you have created. The various properties of the zones are set to default values. To modify these values, right-click the zone name in the Server List pane and select Properties from the DNS menu to display the Zone Properties sheet shown in Figure 8-3.

The Zone Properties sheet contains four tabs: General, SOA Record, Notify, and WINS Lookup.

The General tab is used to view or change the name of the zone file and to change the server type between primary and secondary. If you change a primary server to a secondary server, specify the master servers from which the zone data should be downloaded, and the order in which they should be tried. A server is only tried if the server before it in the list fails to respond. Use the primary server as the first master in the list.

The SOA Record tab is used to change the settings for the Start of Authority record, which is the standard resource record that defines parameters for the entire

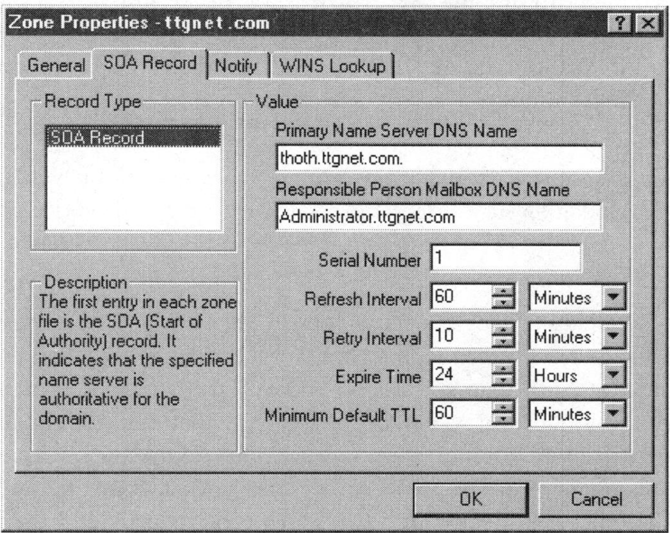

Figure 8-3. Zone Properties

zone file. (More on standard resource records later.) The SOA record stores the name of the primary name server and the email address of the responsible person (RP). The default RP value is the account that was used to install the DNS Server software. You can change these values if you wish.

Values set in the SOA record control the timing of zone transfers. A *zone transfer* is the process by which a primary DNS server distributes data to secondary DNS servers. In essence, it is a simple file copy from the primary by the secondary. The DNS Manager allows you to set the following values that affect zone transfers:

Serial Number
: This value is automatically incremented each time a change is made to DNS zone data, and determines when zone transfers are automatically initiated. A secondary DNS server stores the serial number associated with the zone data it last retrieved from a primary DNS. Periodically, the secondary server downloads the primary server's SOA record and compares the serial number of its data with the current serial number on the primary server. If the serial number on the primary is higher, the secondary server downloads the entire zone file from the primary server. Do not modify this value.

Refresh Interval
: This value, 60 minutes by default, tells the secondary DNS servers how frequently to check the primary server for changes. Setting a low value means that the secondary servers are more likely to be current, but may also result in more frequent zone transfers and increased network traffic. If the data on your

primary DNS server changes frequently, set a low value to ensure that new data is propagated quickly. If the data changes infrequently, set a high value to reduce network traffic without greatly impacting the quality of the zone data. The default value of 60 minutes is a very low refresh value.

Retry Interval
: If the secondary server is unable to contact the primary DNS server, this value, ten minutes by default, specifies how long the secondary server should wait before again trying to contact the primary. Ten minutes is a good retry value.

Expire Time
: This value, 24 hours by default, specifies how long a secondary DNS server continues to respond to queries after it fails to contact its primary DNS server. The assumption is that the zone data on the secondary DNS server becomes more and more dated, the longer the secondary server goes without getting an update from the primary server. After the amount of time defined for Expire Time has passed, the secondary DNS server assumes that its data is invalid and stops responding to queries for the expired zone. The value provided as a default is much too short. If the primary server crashes on Friday night, the secondary server will shutdown the domain on Saturday night. By the time the system administrator discovers the problem on Monday, email and other services would have been interrupted for a day and a half for no other reason than a poorly chosen default value. Use a much longer expire value.

Minimum Default TTL
: This value, 60 minutes by default, defines the default Time to Live (TTL) value used for resource records in this zone. The TTL value specifies how long the recipient is permitted to cache data from this zone. The default value of 60 minutes is a very short time. If your network configuration is relatively stable, you can set this value to several days. If you are about to make significant changes to your network, for example, moving your Web server to a computer with a different IP address, several days before doing so, reset the TTL value to a small number to ensure that the changes you make are propagated in a timely manner. Note that you should not make the TTL lower than the Refresh Interval.

The Notify tab is used to specify the secondary servers for the domain that support the DNS NOTIFY feature. Enter the IP address of each server. When the zone information is updated on the primary server, it notifies the secondary servers that they should update their databases. With the NOTIFY system the primary server can push updates down to the secondary servers as soon as they occur. Originally the only way for a secondary server to get an update was to periodically check the serial number of the zone and pull data down from the primary server when it detected a change. Windows NT DNS Server provides both types of service. On this tab, you may also mark the "Only Allow Access From Secondaries Included on Notify List" checkbox to limit zone transfers to only those servers on the list. Security-conscious sites like to do this to prevent outsiders from listing every entry in the zone.

The WINS Lookup tab determines if WINS provides input to DNS. To enable WINS interoperability, mark the Use WINS Resolution checkbox and enter the IP address of one or more WINS Servers. The "Settings only affect local server" checkbox determines if the data derived from WINS is transferred during a zone transfer. Leave this box unmarked to transfer WINS records during a zone transfer. Mark the box to prevent WINS records from being transferred. Normally you should leave this box unmarked and take advantage of the ability of the Microsoft DNS Server to build DNS records from the information it obtains from WINS.

Building the DNS Database

Compared with other DNS servers, the Microsoft DNS Server does a lot of the work for you. The DNS Manager automatically creates and maintains database entries for any host that is running DHCP or WINS. The DNS server must be in the same Windows NT domain as the WINS server from which it learns the names, and there should be no name conflicts between DNS and WINS. Ensure that there are no name conflicts by using the same host names for WINS and DNS. Use the same name for the Windows NT domain and the DNS subdomain to improve coordination. For example, the primary server for *sales.ttgnet.com* would be in the Windows NT *SALES* domain. Given these few simple considerations, WINS/DNS integration is essentially automatic.

Chances are, however, that at least some of your hosts are not using WINS or DHCP. For these hosts you must enter database records manually. To create a host entry, right-click the zone name in the server list, and then select New Host from the DNS menu to display the New Host dialog. Enter the Host Name specifying only the actual host name; including the domain name portion causes an error message. Enter the IP address associated with the host. To create a reverse lookup record, mark the Create Associated PTR Record checkbox. When you have entered all of the information for the new host, click Add Host to generate the database entries for that host. An empty New Host dialog is displayed. Continue entering data until all of the hosts are entered into the database.

When you have finished adding new hosts, click Done. Highlight the zone name in the Server List pane to display the newly created host entries, or highlight the reverse lookup zone name to display the reverse lookup resource records. Click View → Refresh to ensure that all records are displayed. You can modify the values for an existing host simply by double-clicking the host name in the Zone Info pane to display the Properties sheet for that host.

The DNS Manager creates the Address (A) record and Pointer (PTR) record for each host. You create other resource records manually. To create a database record, right-click the zone name in the server list, and then select New Record from the DNS menu to display the New Resource Record dialog. In the Record Type pane, select the type of resource record to be created. The fields in the Value pane change according to the record type you select.

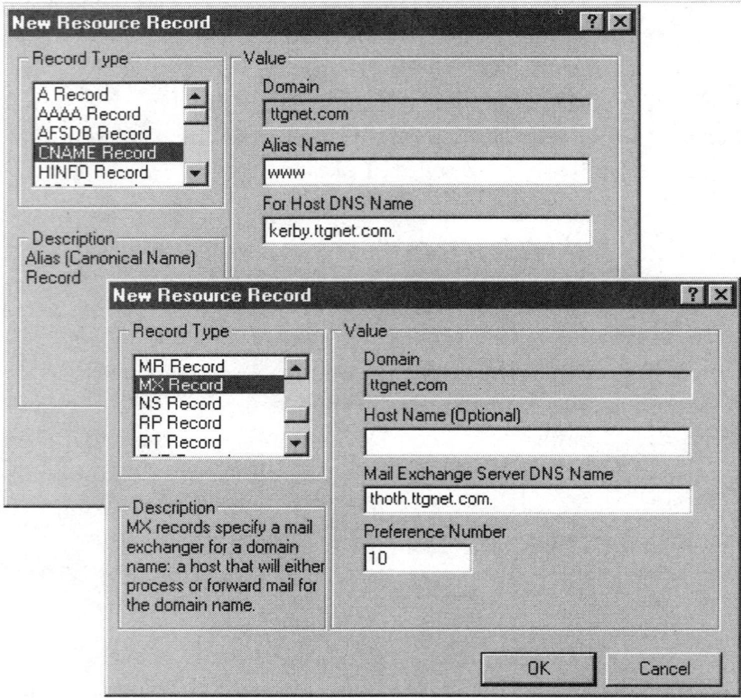

Figure 8-4. Creating resource records

In Figure 8-4 we create a Mail Exchanger (MX) record for the domain and a Canonical Name record for one of the hosts. The MX record defines the Mail Exchanger for the entire domain, which is why the Host Name box is blank. If a host name is provided, the MX record defines the server for that specific host. The CNAME record defines *www.ttgnet.com* as an alias for *kerby.ttgnet.com*.

Delegating a Subdomain

The last thing we will do before leaving the topic of the DNS Manager is delegate a subdomain under the *ttgnet.com* domain to another server on our network. Delegating a subdomain is one of the duties of the domain administrator. No one can create a real subdomain unless a delegation for that domain exists in the domain above. We will create the subdomain *sales.ttgnet.com* and assign it two servers. *mandy.sales.ttgnet.com* will be the primary server for the sales zone and *thoth.ttgnet.com*, which is the primary server for the *ttgnet.com* domain, will be the secondary server for *sales*. All of the work necessary to delegate this new domain will take place on *thoth* because it is the primary server of the domain of which *sales* is a subordinate part.

First, we add *mandy.sales.ttgnet.com* to the server list. Highlight Server List and choose New Server from the DNS menu. The Add DNS Server dialog appears. Enter the server's name, *mandy.sales.ttgnet.com* in this case, and click on OK.

mandy.sales.ttgnet.com now appears in the Server List. Highlight it and select New Zone form the DNS menu. Create the new primary zone, *sales.ttgnet.com*, following the steps for creating a primary zone that were discussed previously. We're finished with *mandy*.

Now highlight *thoth.ttgnet.com*—the primary server for the domain that is above the new domain in the hierarchy. Select New Domain from the DNS menu. In the New Domain dialog box enter the name of the new domain, *sales* in this case, and click on OK.

Now highlight the new *sales.ttgnet.com* domain that appears under *thoth.ttgnet.com* in the Server List. Open the DNS menu and select New Record. In the Record Type scroll list select NS Record and enter *mandy*, the name of the primary server of the *sales* subdomain, in the Name Server DNS Name box. Click on OK.

Again, highlight the new *sales.ttgnet.com* domain that appears under *thoth.ttgnet.com* in the Server List. Open the DNS menu and select New Record. This time, create an address (A) record for *mandy*. This is a special address record called a glue record. You must create a glue record when the server for a domain that is subordinate to the current domain is located in that subordinate domain. The NS record identifies a server by name. An address is needed to communicate with that server, so an address record must also be provided. The address record, combined with the name server record, links the domains together—thus the term glue record. With this, the delegation is complete and the administrator of *mandy* can begin entering the data for the *sales.ttgnet.com* domain.

All of the various resource records we have created in this section become entries in the DNS database files.

The DNS Files

Creating a new server with the DNS Manager automatically creates the *Cache.dns* file needed to locate the Internet root name servers and a dummy boot file. Creating a new zone with the DNS Manager creates the file for that zone. All of these files are located in the *%SystemRoot%\system32\Dns* directory, and all except the dummy boot file are built from standard resource records.

A name server boot file points to sources of DNS information. Some of these sources are local files; others are remote servers. The way in which the boot file is configured controls whether the name server acts as a primary server, a secondary server, or a caching-only server. Its structure and the commands used in the boot file are covered in Appendix B.

The Microsoft DNS server can use the same boot file as a Unix BIND 4 name server. This allows you to copy existing configuration files from a Unix system and run them under Windows NT. However, if you use the DNS Manager to configure the name server, the system does not need or use a boot file. Instead the system boots from registry settings. The boot file contained in the *%SystemRoot%\system32\Dns* folder is just a dummy file that explains that the system is booting from the registry.

If you're interested in finding out more about the boot file, see Appendix B and the sample boot file in *%SystemRoot%\system32\Dns\Samples,* or read the description of the *named.boot* file in *DNS and BIND*, by Liu and Albitz. This is the last we will mention this file. The real database files of the DNS server are built from standard resource records.

Standard Resource Records

All other files in the *%SystemRoot%\system32\Dns* directory store domain database information. These files all have the same basic format and use the same type of database records, which are called standard resource records or RRs. These are defined in RFC 1033, the *Domain Administrators Operations Guide*, and other RFCs. Table 8-1 summarizes all of the commonly used standard resource records. These records are covered in detail in Appendix B.

Table 8-1. Standard Resource Records

Resource Record Text Name	Record Type	Function
Start of Authority	SOA	Marks the beginning of a zone's data, and defines parameters that affect the entire zone.
Name server	NS	Identifies a domain's name server.
Address	A	Converts a host name to an address.
Pointer	PTR	Converts an address to a host name.
Mail Exchanger	MX	Identifies where to deliver mail for a given domain name.
Canonical Name	CNAME	Defines an alias host name.
Text	TXT	Stores arbitrary text strings.

The resource record syntax is described in Appendix B, but a little understanding of the structure of these records is necessary to read the sample configuration files used in this chapter. The format of DNS resource records is:

[*name*] [`ttl`] `IN` *`type data`*

`name`
: This is the name of the domain object the resource record references. It can be an individual host or an entire domain. The string in the *`name`* field is relative to the current domain unless it ends with a dot. If the name field is blank, the record applies to the domain object that was named last. For example, if the A record for *pooh* is followed by an MX record with a blank *name* field, both the A record and the MX record apply to *pooh*.

`ttl`
: Time-to-live (TTL) defines the length of time, in seconds, that the information in this resource record should be kept in a remote system's cache. Usually this field is left blank and the default `ttl`, set for the entire zone in the SOA record, is used.*

`IN`
: Identifies the record as an Internet DNS resource record. There are other classes of records, but they are rarely used. Curious? See Appendix B for the other, non-Internet, classes.

`type`
: Identifies the kind of resource record. Table 8-1 lists the record types under the heading "Record Type." Select one of these values from the Record Type scroll list in the New Resource Record dialog. That dialog lists many more record types than are listed in Table 8-1. The table lists the most commonly used RRs.

`data`
: The information specific to this type of resource record. For example, in an A record this is the field that contains the actual IP address.

In the following sections we look at each database file. As you look at the files, remember that all of the records in these files are standard resource records that follow the format described previously.

The Cache.dns File

The *Cache.dns* file is the cache initialization file. It contains the names and addresses of the root servers. It is used to help the local server locate a root server

* See the section on SOA properties earlier in this chapter.

during startup. Once a root server is found, an authoritative list of root servers is downloaded from that server. The initialization file is not referred to again until the local server is forced to restart. The information in the *Cache.dns* file is not referred to often, but it is critical for booting a DNS server.

The *Cache.dns* file contains NS records that name the root servers, and A records that provide the addresses of the root servers. The *Cache.dns* file is created automatically when the DNS software is installed on a Windows NT 4.0 server is shown below:

```
;
; Cache file:
;
.                       636028672     IN    NS    C.ROOT-SERVERS.NET.
C.ROOT-SERVERS.NET.     2783852032    IN    A     192.33.4.12
.                       636028672     IN    NS    D.ROOT-SERVERS.NET.
D.ROOT-SERVERS.NET.     2783852032    IN    A     128.8.10.90
.                       636028672     IN    NS    E.ROOT-SERVERS.NET.
E.ROOT-SERVERS.NET.     2783852032    IN    A     192.203.230.10
.                       636028672     IN    NS    I.ROOT-SERVERS.NET.
I.ROOT-SERVERS.NET.     2783852032    IN    A     192.36.148.17
.                       636028672     IN    NS    F.ROOT-SERVERS.NET.
F.ROOT-SERVERS.NET.     2783852032    IN    A     192.5.5.241
.                       636028672     IN    NS    G.ROOT-SERVERS.NET.
G.ROOT-SERVERS.NET.     2783852032    IN    A     192.112.36.4
.                       636028672     IN    NS    J.ROOT-SERVERS.NET.
J.ROOT-SERVERS.NET.     2783852032    IN    A     198.41.0.10
.                       636028672     IN    NS    K.ROOT-SERVERS.NET.
K.ROOT-SERVERS.NET.     2783852032    IN    A     193.0.14.129
.                       636028672     IN    NS    L.ROOT-SERVERS.NET.
L.ROOT-SERVERS.NET.     2783852032    IN    A     198.32.64.12
.                       636028672     IN    NS    M.ROOT-SERVERS.NET.
M.ROOT-SERVERS.NET.     2783852032    IN    A     202.12.27.33
.                       636028672     IN    NS    A.ROOT-SERVERS.NET.
A.ROOT-SERVERS.NET.     2783852032    IN    A     198.41.0.4
.                       636028672     IN    NS    H.ROOT-SERVERS.NET.
H.ROOT-SERVERS.NET.     2783852032    IN    A     128.63.2.53
.                       636028672     IN    NS    B.ROOT-SERVERS.NET.
B.ROOT-SERVERS.NET.     2783852032    IN    A     128.9.0.107
```

The file begins with a few comment lines that identify it as the cache file. In all DNS database files lines beginning with a semicolon are comment lines.

This file contains only name server and address records. Each NS record identifies a name server for the root (`.`) domain. The associated A record gives the address of each root server. The ttl value for all of these records is some very large value.

Note that the *Cache.dns* file designates several root name servers, which can be used interchangeably. All of these servers contain the same information, which is replicated between them continually. There are multiple root name servers for two reasons:

Redundancy

The entire DNS resolution process is based on the fact that a root name server is available any time one is needed. If only one root name server existed and it failed, the Internet would be out of business until the root name server was again available. Multiple, widely dispersed root name servers remove this single point of failure, and also guard against network communication failures that temporarily render one or another of the root name servers inaccessible.

Load sharing

Because the root name servers are at the top of the DNS tree, they are accessed frequently by other, subordinate DNS servers. The rapid growth of the Internet has dramatically increased the burden on the root name servers, which now process thousands of queries per second. Recently, DNS resolution failures that occur because a root name server did not respond to a query have become much more common. The use of multiple root name servers allows the burden to be spread across many servers.

The names and addresses of the root name servers are changed more frequently than you might expect. InterNIC periodically posts an updated cache file with the current names and addresses of the root name servers.

Update the *Cache.dns* file by downloading the file *domain/named.root* from *rs.internic.net* via anonymous **ftp**. The file stored at the InterNIC is in the correct format for a Windows NT system. The following example shows the administrator downloading the *named.root* file directly into the local system's *Cache.dns* file. The file doesn't even need to be edited.

```
C:\>ftp rs.internic.net
Connected to rs.internic.net.
Name (rs.internic.net:craig): anonymous
331 Guest login ok, send your email address as password.
Password: craig@ttgnet.com
230 Guest login ok, access restrictions apply.
Using binary mode to transfer files.
ftp> get domain/named.root Cache.dns
200 PORT command successful.
150 Opening data connection for domain/named.root (2119 bytes).
226 Transfer complete.
2119 bytes received in 0.137 secs (15 Kbytes/sec)
ftp> quit
221 Goodbye.
```

Download the *named.root* file every few months to keep accurate root server information in your cache. A bogus root server entry could cause problems with your local server. The data given here is correct as of publication, but could change at any time.

If your system is not connected to the Internet, it won't be able to communicate with the root servers. Initializing your cache file with the servers listed previously would be useless. In this case, initialize your cache with entries that point to name servers on your local network that will act as "root" servers. Those servers must be configured to answer queries for the "root" domain. However, this root domain only contains NS records pointing to the domain servers on your local network. For example: assume that *ttgnet.com* is not connected to the Internet and that *thoth* and *kerby* are going to act as root servers for this isolated domain. Both servers are configured as primary for the root domain. They load the root from a zone file that contains NS records and A records, stating that they are authoritative for the root and delegating the *ttgnet.com* and *16.172.in-addr.arpa* domains to the local name servers that service those domains. Details of this type of configuration are provided in *DNS and BIND*.

Other than the special case noted previously, configuring the cache initialization file requires very little effort from the system administrator. Most of the work in configuring DNS goes into creating the zone file and the reverse lookup file.

The Zone File

The zone file contains most of the domain information. This file converts host names to IP addresses, so A records predominate; but it also contains MX, CNAME, and other records. The zone file is only created on the primary server. All other servers get this information from the primary server.

The zone file created earlier in this chapter is shown here:

```
;
; Database file ttgnet.com.dns for ttgnet.com zone.
;      Zone version: 91
;

@           IN      SOA    thoth.ttgnet.com. Administrator.thoth.ttgnet.com.  (
                     9                ; serial number
                     3600             ; refresh
                     600              ; retry
                     86400            ; expire
                     3600           ) ; minimum TTL

;
; Zone NS records
;

@                    IN       NS       thoth.ttgnet.com.
@                    IN       NS       kiwi
```

```
;
; Zone records
;

@                   IN      MX      10     thoth
@                   IN      MX      20     kerby
thoth               IN      A       172.16.12.1
kiwi                IN      A       172.16.2.1
kerby               IN      A       172.16.12.3
pooh                IN      A       172.16.12.2
                    IN      MX      5      kerby

;
; Delegated sub-zone: sales.ttgnet.com.
;
sales               IN      NS      thoth.ttgnet.com.
sales               IN      NS      mandy.sales
mandy.sales         IN      A       172.16.6.1
; End delegation

wotan               IN      A       172.16.12.4
www                 IN      CNAME   kerby
```

All zone files begin with an SOA record. The `@` in the name field of the SOA record references the current domain. In this case it is the domain name defined in the Zone Name box when a new zone is created with the DNS Manager. This same name field is used on every zone's SOA record; it always references the correct domain defined for that particular zone file in the DNS Manager. You'll see this same SOA format at the beginning of almost every zone file with only the hostname (*thoth.ttgnet.com.*) and the manager's mail address (*Administrator.thoth.ttgnet.com.*) changed.

The NS records that follow the SOA record define the name servers for the domain. The name servers are listed immediately after the SOA, before any other records in the zone. Again, the `@` in the name field means that these records apply to the entire domain. The name servers listed here are the primary server and the official secondary server. Any server can be configured as a secondary but only the servers listed in the zone file are official secondary servers.

The first MX record identifies a mail server for the entire domain. This record says that *thoth* is the mail server for *ttgnet.com,* with a preference of 10. Mail addressed to *user@ttgnet.com* is redirected to *thoth* for delivery. Of course for *thoth* to successfully deliver the mail, it must be properly configured as a mail server. The MX record is only part of the story. We look at configuring an SMTP server in Chapter 10.

The second MX record identifies *kerby* as a mail server for *ttgnet.com,* with a preference of 20. Preference numbers let you define alternate mail servers. The lower the preference number, the more desirable the server. Therefore, our two sample

MX records say "send mail for the *ttgnet.com* domain to *thoth* first; if *thoth* is unavailable, try sending the mail to *kerby*." Rather than relying on a single mail server, preference numbers allow you to create backup servers. If the main mail server is unreachable, the domain's mail is sent to one of the backups instead.

These sample MX records redirect mail addressed to *ttgnet.com*, but mail addressed to *user@wotan.ttgnet.com* will still be sent directly to *wotan.ttgnet.com*—not to *thoth* or *kerby*. This configuration allows simplified mail addressing in the form *user@ttgnet.com* for those who want to take advantage of it, but it continues to allow direct mail delivery to individual hosts for those who wish to take advantage of that.

The A record maps a host name to an IP address. The name field contains the host name and the data field contains the address. The first three A records in this example define the IP address for *thoth*, *kiwi*, and *kerby*.

pooh's A record is followed by an MX record. Note that the records that relate to a single host are grouped together, which is the most common structure used in zone files. *pooh*'s MX record serves a different purpose than the MX record for the entire domain. It directs all mail addressed to *user@pooh.ttgnet.com* to *kerby*. This MX record is required because the MX record at the beginning of the zone file only redirects mail if it is addressed to *user@ttgnet.com*. If you also want to redirect mail addressed to *pooh*, you need a pooh-specific MX record.

As clearly indicated by the comments inserted by the DNS Manager, the next two NS records and the following A record delegate a subdomain. These records define the *sales* subdomain we created earlier in the chapter. The NS records define the two name servers for the subdomain, and the A record is the glue record that provides the address of the subdomain's primary server.

The last record in the file is a CNAME record. The name field of the CNAME record contains an alias for the official host name. The official name, called the canonical name, is provided in the data field of the record. Because of this record, *kerby* can be referred to by the name *www*. The *www* alias is a generic host name used for most Web servers. Host name aliases should *not* be used in other resource records.* For example, don't use an alias as the name of a mail server in an MX record. Use *only* the canonical (official) name that's defined in an A record.

Your zone file will be much larger than the sample file we've discussed, but it will contain essentially the same records. If you know the names and addresses of the hosts in your domain, you have most of the information necessary to create the zone file, and the DNS Manager automatically determines much of that information for you.

---

* See Appendix B for additional information about using CNAME records in the zone file.

The Reverse Lookup File

The reverse lookup file translates IP addresses into host names. It does so with Pointer (PTR) records.

The *16.172.in-addr.arpa.dns* file in our example is the zone file for the reverse domain *16.172.in-addr.arpa*. The domain administrator creates this file on the primary server, and every other host that needs this information gets it from there. We created the sample file earlier in the chapter using the DNS Manager.

```
;
; Database file 16.172.in-addr.arpa.dns for 16.172.in-addr.arpa zone.
;       Zone version: 81
;

@         IN         SOA     thoth.ttgnet.com. Administrator.thoth.ttgnet.com. (
                     8                 ; serial number
                     3600              ; refresh
                     600               ; retry
                     86400             ; expire
                     3600            ) ; minimum TTL

;
; Zone NS records
;

@                    IN       NS       thoth.ttgnet.com.
@                    IN       NS       kiwi.ttgnet.com.

;
; Zone records
;

1.12                 IN       PTR      thoth.ttgnet.com.
2.12                 IN       PTR      pooh.ttgnet.com.
3.12                 IN       PTR      kerby.ttgnet.com.
4.12                 IN       PTR      wotan.ttgnet.com.
1.2                  IN       PTR      kiwi.ttgnet.com.
1.6                  IN       PTR      andy.sales.ttgnet.com.
```

Like the zone file, the reverse file begins with an SOA record and a few NS records that define the domain and its servers, but the zone file contains a wider variety of resource records than a reverse lookup file does. The reverse file is almost entirely composed of Pointer (PTR) records.

PTR records dominate the reverse lookup file because they are used to translate addresses to host names. The PTR records in our example provide address-to-name conversions for hosts 12.1, 12.2, 12.3, 12.4, 2.1, and 6.1 on network 172.16. Because they don't end in dots, the values in the name fields of these PTR records are relative to the current domain. For example, the value 3.12 is interpreted as *3.12.16.172.in-addr.arpa*. The host name in the data field of the PTR record is fully qualified; in other words, it does end in a dot, to prevent it from being relative to the current domain name. Using the information in this PTR record, the server translates *3.12.16.172.in-addr.arpa* into *kerby.ttgnet.com*.

Subdomains in the *in-addr.arpa* domain are not as common or as useful as subdomains in the host namespace. Domain names and IP addresses are not the same thing, and do not have the same structure. When an IP address is turned into an *in-addr.arpa* domain name, the four bytes of the address are treated as four distinct pieces. In reality the IP address is 32 contiguous bits. Subnets divide up the IP address space and subnet masks are bit-oriented, which does not limit them to byte boundaries. *in-addr.arpa* subdomains divide up the domain name space and can only occur at a full byte boundary because each byte of the address is treated as a distinct name. Thus there is not necessarily a direct mapping between a subnet and a subdomain.

The DNS Manager automatically creates entries in the server list that appear to be subdomains in the *in-addr.arpa* domain based on subdividing the name space on byte boundaries. Thus, when we enter the pointer record for 172.16.12.1 into the database that is serving the 172.16.0.0 reverse domain, the DNS Manager appears to create a 12 file under the *16.172.in-addr.arpa* zone file. In fact no file is created. This is simply the way that DNS Manager displays the information in the Servers List. Real subdomains could be created on these byte boundaries, but in most cases they aren't necessary.

Using nslookup

nslookup is a debugging tool provided with Windows NT 4.0. It allows anyone to directly query a name server and retrieve any of the information known to the DNS system. It is helpful for determining if the server is running correctly and is properly configured, or for querying for information provided by remote servers.

nslookup is used in the Windows NT command window to resolve queries either interactively or directly from the command line. Below is a command-line example of using **nslookup** to query for the IP address of a host:

```
C:\>nslookup www.fnc.gov
Server: thoth.ttgnet.com
Address: 172.16.12.1

Non-authoritative answer:
Name: www.fnc.gov
Address: 128.150.6.53
```

Here, a user asks **nslookup** to provide the address of *www.fnc.gov*. **nslookup** displays the name and address of the server used to resolve the query, and then it displays the answer to the query. Notice the "Non-authoritative" message in the response. *thoth.ttgnet.com* is our local server. This messages tells us that the local server retrieved this answer from its cache. As we'll see shortly, when you need to do so, **nslookup** allows you to go directly to the remote authoritative server for an answer.

The real power of **nslookup** is seen in interactive mode. To enter interactive mode, type **nslookup** on the command line without any arguments. Terminate an interactive session by entering Control-C (^C) or the **exit** command at the **nslookup** prompt. Redone in an interactive session, the query shown earlier is:

```
C:\>nslookup
Default Server: thoth.ttgnet.com
Address: 172.16.12.1

> www.fnc.gov
Server: thoth.ttgnet.com
Address: 172.16.12.1

Non-authoritative answer:
Name: www.fnc.gov
Address: 128.150.6.53

> exit
```

By default, **nslookup** queries for A records, but you can use the **set type** command to change the query to another resource record type, or to the special query type ANY. ANY is used to retrieve all available resource records for the specified host.

The following example checks MX records for *ttgnet.com* and *pooh*. Note that once the query type is set to MX, it stays MX. It doesn't revert to the default A-type query. Another **set type** command is required to reset the query type.

```
C:\>nslookup
Default Server: thoth.ttgnet.com
Address: 172.16.12.1

> set type=MX
> ttgnet.com
Server: thoth.ttgnet.com
Address: 172.16.12.1

ttgnet.com preference = 10, mail exchanger = thoth.ttgnet.com
ttgnet.com preference = 20, mail exchanger = kerby.ttgnet.com
thoth.ttgnet.com internet address = 172.16.12.1
kerby.ttgnet.com internet address = 172.16.12.3

> pooh.ttgnet.com
Server: thoth.ttgnet.com
Address: 172.16.12.1

pooh.ttgnet.com preference = 5, mail exchanger = kerby.ttgnet.com
pooh.ttgnet.com internet address = 172.16.12.2
> exit
```

You can use the **server** command to control the server used to resolve queries. This is particularly useful for going directly to an authoritative server to check some information. The following example does just that. In fact, this example contains several interesting commands:

- First we **set type=NS** and get the NS records for the *zoo.edu* domain.
- From the information returned by this query, we select a server and use the **server** command to direct **nslookup** to use that server.
- Next, using the **set domain** command, we set the default domain to *zoo.edu*. **nslookup** uses this default domain name to expand the host names in its queries, in the same way that the resolver uses the default domain name.
- We reset the query type to ANY. If the query type is not reset, **nslookup** would still query for NS records.
- Finally, we query for information about the host *tiger.zoo.edu*. Because the default domain is set to *zoo.edu*, we simply enter *tiger* at the prompt.

```
C:\>nslookup
Default Server: thoth.ttgnet.com
Address: 172.16.12.1

> set type=NS
> zoo.edu
Server: thoth.ttgnet.com
Address: 172.16.12.1

Non-authoritative answer:
zoo.edu nameserver = NOC.ZOO.EDU
zoo.edu nameserver = NS.ZOO.EDU
zoo.edu nameserver = NAMESERVER.AGENCY.GOV

NOC.ZOO.EDU internet address = 172.28.2.200
NS.ZOO.EDU internet address = 172.28.2.240
NAMESERVER.AGENCY.GOV internet address = 172.21.18.31
> server NOC.ZOO.EDU
Default Server: NOC.ZOO.EDU
Address: 172.28.2.200

> set domain=zoo.edu
> set type=any
> tiger
Server: NOC.ZOO.EDU
Address: 172.28.2.200

tiger.zoo.edu inet address = 172.28.172.8
tiger.zoo.edu preference = 10, mail exchanger = tiger.ZOO.EDU
tiger.zoo.edu CPU=ALPHA OS=UNIX
tiger.zoo.edu inet address = 172.28.172.8, protocol = 6
 7 21 23 25 79
tiger.ZOO.EDU inet address = 172.28.172.8
> exit
```

The final example shows how to download an entire domain from an authoritative server and examine it on your local system. The **ls** command requests a zone transfer and displays the contents of the zone it receives.*

If the zone file is more than a few lines long, redirect the output to a file, and use the **view** command to examine the contents of the file. (**view** sorts a file and displays it using the **more** command.) The combination of **ls** and **view** are helpful when tracking down a remote host name. In the example that follows, the **ls** command retrieves the *big.com* zone and stores the information in *temp.file*. Then **view** is used to examine *temp.file*.

```
C:\>nslookup
Default Server: thoth.ttgnet.com
Address: 172.16.12.1

> server minerals.big.com
Default Server: minerals.big.com
Address: 172.30.20.1

> ls big.com > temp.file
[minerals.big.com]
########
Received 406 records.
> view temp.file
 acmite 172.30.20.28
 adamite 172.30.20.29
 adelite 172.30.20.11
 agate 172.30.20.30
 alabaster 172.30.20.31
 albite 172.30.20.32
 allanite 172.30.20.20
 altaite 172.30.20.33
 alum 172.30.20.35
 aluminum 172.30.20.8
 amaranth 172.30.20.85
 amethyst 172.30.20.36
 andorite 172.30.20.37
 apatite 172.30.20.38
 beryl 172.30.20.23
 More  ^C
> exit
```

These examples show that **nslookup** allows you to:

- Query for any specific type of standard resource record.
- Directly query the authoritative servers for a domain.
- Get the entire contents of a domain into a file so you can view it.

* For security reasons, many names servers do not respond to the **ls** command. See the discussion of the Zone Properties sheet Notify tab for information on how to limit access to zone transfers on your NT system.

Use **nslookup**'s **help** command to see its other features. Turn on debugging (with **set debug**) and examine the additional information this provides. As you play with this tool, you'll find many helpful features.

Summary

Domain Name System (DNS) is an important user service that should be used on every system connected to the Internet. DNS is a client/server system.

The DNS client issues name queries and is implemented at the application level. It is called the *resolver*. The resolver is configured during the basic TCP/IP configuration. All systems run the resolver.

The server answers name queries and it runs at the operating system level. It is called the name server. The name server is configured by the DNS Manager, which defines the servers, the zones, and the database information contained in the zones.

DNS servers can be primary, secondary, and caching servers. The original domain database source files are found on the primary server. The domain database file is called a zone file. The zone file is constructed from standard resources records (RR) that are defined in RFCs. The RRs share a common structure and are used to define all DNS database information. All other servers derive the database information from the primary server. Secondary servers make complete copies of the zone information. Caching-only servers cache data one answer at a time.

The DNS server can be tested using **nslookup**. This test tool is included with Windows NT.

In this chapter we have seen how to configure and test domain name service. In the next chapter we look at Routing and Remote Access Service (RRAS).

9

Microsoft Routing and Remote Access Service

The Windows NT 4.0 distribution bundles a competent Remote Access Service (RAS) Server and a primitive IP/IPX multiprotocol routing (MPR) service. In mid-1997, Microsoft released the Routing and Remote Access Services (RRAS) upgrade, which was known during beta testing as Steelhead. The bugs that were present in the beta version are largely eradicated in the shipping version of RRAS. Installing RRAS replaces the RAS and MPR components of Windows NT Server 4.0, and provides significantly enhanced functionality. RRAS includes the following components:

Remote Access Service
: Supports up to 256 concurrent modem, ISDN, or X.25 dial-up networking connections by remote clients.

LAN Routing
: Supports up to 16 interfaces for LAN to LAN routing, and for WAN cards that emulate network adapters.

Demand-Dial Routing
: Supports up to 48 demand-dial interfaces for WAN routing and dial-up interfaces including ISDN and PPTP.

The RRAS upgrade requires Windows NT Server 4.0 with Service Pack 3 or higher. It cannot be used with Windows NT Workstation 4.0, or with earlier versions of Windows NT. RRAS is one of the Windows NT 5.0 components that Microsoft is releasing piecemeal as upgrades to Windows NT 4.0. Microsoft positions RRAS as a solution for small businesses, autonomous departments, and branch offices that require routing, remote access, and virtual private networking capabilities.

On the upside, RRAS is free, tightly integrated with Windows NT Server, moderately fast, and significantly richer in features than the original components. On the downside, however, RRAS can make substantial demands on the processor and memory resources of a server, and is both less stable and less flexible than dedicated RAS or router hardware.

If you're using the original RAS or MPR services to provide remote access or routing services, upgrading to RRAS often makes sense. Most RAS users will perceive the RAS enhancements in RRAS as relatively minor—primarily the addition of server-to-server PPTP and Remote Authentication Dial-In User Service (RADIUS) client support. Routing users will notice a larger difference. MPR supports only static routes and RIPv1 for IP routing, must be managed from the command line, and is suitable only for very simple routing needs. RRAS is a serious router. If you're currently using MPR for IP routing, RRAS is almost a must-have upgrade, although you'd still be better off with a real router.

While a dedicated router may be the best solution from the perspective of performance, a dedicated router is not a realistic solution for every situation. A Small Office/Home Office (SOHO) environment may not need any type of router. (See the box *Do You Really Need a Router?*). A dedicated router is essential for a large network with complex routing, but many networks do not really require advanced routing protocols. A small network with limited technical support may not be able to afford a dedicated router. Sometimes you simply want the server to listen to the routing advertisements that are announced by the routers. RRAS allows an NT server to listen to and understand several different routing protocols. Also, RRAS provides more than just routing. A small office may require remote access or virtual private networks, which may not be provided by a dedicated router.

Although RRAS may never be the best routing solution in an absolute, technical sense, there are times when it may be a useful tool. For budgetary or other reasons, the choice may be RRAS or nothing. RRAS beats nothing every time.

Microsoft Routing and RAS is a major application. Microsoft provides voluminous docs for RRAS, but there's enough missing to make it difficult for a new user to get RRAS installed and running, even at a minimal level. Covering RRAS thoroughly would require an entire book. Accordingly, this chapter covers the essentials of installing, configuring, and managing RRAS at the overview level.

Routing and Remote Access Service Features

The RRAS upgrade includes several incremental improvements to RAS and a complete overhaul of the multi-protocol router (MPR) service. The following sections detail some of the most important improvements included with RRAS relative to the standard Windows NT 4.0 RAS and routing services.

Do you really need a router?

One of the questions we hear most frequently goes something like, "We use Windows NT Server in our small office. Everyone needs web access and Internet mail, so we pay for five separate ISP accounts and five separate phone lines. This is costing us hundreds of dollars a month in phone bills and ISP charges. Is there anything we can do to consolidate this?"

In the past, the only real alternative to individual dial-up accounts was a routed network connection, using a leased line, a demand-dial POTS (Plain Old Telephone Service) or ISDN line, or a nailed up POTS connection.

Dedicated line
: Typically costs $2,000 or more to set up and involves monthly costs of $500 or more, even for a relatively slow connection. For a 1.544 Mbps T1 connection, you can expect total monthly costs for datacomm and Internet service of at least $1,500, and they may exceed $3,000 per month.

Demand dial
: Typically costs $500 to $1,500 to set up, with monthly costs of $100 to $500 or more. Although this method may actually be cheaper overall than maintaining many individual ISP accounts, it is too complex to be managed by most small firms.

Nailed-up POTS connection
: This is the cheapest routed network connection available, assuming that you can find an ISP willing to provide it. One of the authors used to have this type of connection. This method is actually a variation of demand-dial, but with the connection set to never time out. Periodically, the connection may drop for one reason or another, but it's immediately re-established when this occurs. The all-time record for that nailed-up connection lasted from mid-May to the following January—an eight-month long phone call. And they say teenagers stay on the phone forever! Needless to say, using this method makes the phone police unhappy.

Managing a routed network connection requires a higher level of technical knowledge than is usually available in a small office. Most small companies simply can't justify allocating the resources required to set up and maintain a routed network connection, but would nevertheless like to have some level of shared Internet access for their employees.

—Continued—

For a lot of companies, the best answer is to install a proxy server. Over the last year or two, proxy servers have become increasingly popular. Larger companies use them as a firewall to control access by outsiders to their corporate networks, and to control Internet usage by their own employees. For smaller firms, proxy servers are intriguing because they can be used to implement shared Internet access on the cheap.

To use a proxy server for shared Internet access, you provide the computer that runs the proxy server with an Internet connection—which can be as little as an ordinary $20 per month 28.8 v.34 dial-up ISP account. Other computers on the network can then access services on the Internet indirectly, via the proxy server. These proxy clients communicate only with the proxy server. The proxy server communicates with proxy clients and with the Internet, acting as an intermediary. When a proxy client computer accesses the Internet, the proxy server automatically dials the ISP and sends or retrieves data on behalf of the proxy client. While that connection is up, it can be used by any of the proxy clients. After a specified period of inactivity, the proxy server drops the connection.

Many small companies use a proxy server to provide shared Internet access for half a dozen or more employees on a single dial-up ISP account. If you're lucky enough to have cheap, unmetered ISDN in your area, a shared setup like this may be able to support everyone in your company. Because everyone shares the bandwidth, the connection can bog down if many people are simultaneously retrieving web pages, ftp files, or email, particularly if the link runs at only 28.8. Most of the time, however, things even out. One person reads a web page while another is busy downloading his email, and vice versa. To some extent, the shared bandwidth problem is offset by the fact that a proxy server can be configured to cache recently accessed pages, eliminating frequent redundant downloads from the Internet.

There are drawbacks to using a proxy server for Internet access. Two that immediately come to mind are:

No full time connection

Your network is connected to the Internet only when the proxy server is actually dialed in to the ISP. Although your proxy server uses demand-dial to connect to the ISP when it needs to access the Internet, the converse is not true—if traffic arrives at the ISP intended for your network, the ISP doesn't place a call to your proxy server. This means, for example, that you can't run a Web server locally that will be accessible from the Internet (although you can run a local Intranet server). This usually isn't much of a problem. If you want to run a public Web server or ftp server, have your ISP host it on its server. Better yet, use one of the commercial web hosting businesses.

—Continued—

Shared mail

You can use the proxy server connection to retrieve email from any mailbox for which you have the name and password. However, some ISP's provide only one email account per ISP account. Others include anything up to half a dozen email accounts per ISP account. Still others provide only one email account, but allow you to pay a nominal monthly fee for additional email accounts. Even if you can get the email accounts you need, they're going to take the form username@my_isp.net, when what you really want is probably something like username@my_company.com. This isn't much of a problem, either. You (or your ISP) can register your own domain name, which your ISP can host.

In the course of writing this chapter, we decided to find out about some of the alternatives available. We looked first at the Microsoft Proxy Server. It's a pretty impressive product, but it costs almost $1,000, and it's not really intended for small businesses. Fortunately, there are alternatives.

Probably the best known alternative is WinGate, from Deerfield Communications (*sales@deerfield.com, http://www.deerfield.com*). We emailed them late one evening to ask for an evaluation copy of WinGate 2.0 Pro and any other material they thought we might find useful in evaluating the product. The next morning, their response was waiting in the inbox. These folks don't let any grass grow under them.

As pleased as we were by their fast response, we were even happier with the product itself. Within literally five minutes, we had WinGate installed and running on the server. It took only another five minutes or so to configure a client to use the WinGate proxy server to retrieve web pages, files from ftp servers, and email from our POP server. We didn't have occasion to try their technical support, simply because everything worked exactly the way it was supposed to.

WinGate is designed to work with either Windows 95 or Windows NT 4.0 dial-up networking, although we tested it only with Windows NT 4.0. WinGate 2.0 Pro costs $250 for five concurrent users, $450 for ten concurrent users, or $700 for an unlimited user license. You can download a free single user version of WinGate 2.0 Lite from their web site. This free version allows two computers—the WinGate proxy server and any one other computer on your network—to access the Internet concurrently. If you can live with only your server and one other computer at a time having shared Internet access, all you need is the free WinGate 2.0 Lite version. Paying for the Pro version buys you more users, enhanced features (e.g. logging), the Gatekeeper administration utility, and access to tech support.

We looked at some of the alternatives, but didn't find any compelling reason to use anything other than WinGate. This product does what it's supposed to do, and does it perfectly. Recommended.

Protocol Support

The multiprotocol router that ships with Windows NT Server 4.0 allows you to route IP with RIPv1 or static routes. RRAS extends this selection somewhat. Although it does not offer the breadth or depth of protocol support available on dedicated routers, RRAS does provide a useful working set of protocols, including:

RIP for IP
: Routing Information Protocol for IP V1 (RIPv1) was the original distance-vector routing protocol for TCP/IP, and is the most commonly used routing protocol in small and medium TCP/IP networks. RIP is fast and relatively easy to work with, but is not suitable for networks with more than about 20 subnets. RRAS supports both RIPv1 and RIPv2. Both protocols are described in Chapter 2, *Delivering the Data*.

OSPF
: Open Shortest Path First is the most commonly used link-state IP routing protocol. Although it is more processor- and memory-intensive than RIP, and more complex to install and manage, OSPF is better suited to larger networks. The OSPF implementation in RRAS is a based on the Bay Networks OSPF implementation. The OSPF protocol is described in Chapter 2.

DHCP Relay Agent
: Dynamic Host Configuration Protocol eases IP administration burdens by assigning IP addresses and other TCP/IP configuration parameters to clients automatically. The DHCP Relay Agent supports DHCP in a routed LAN or WAN environment, allowing clients to access a DHCP server regardless of their relative locations in the internetwork.

Novell RIP and SAP
: To provide interoperability with Novell NetWare IPX networks, RRAS supports Novell RIP (not to be confused with IP RIP) and Service Advertising Protocol.

Static Routing
: RRAS supports static routes for point-to-point routing.

PPTP
: Microsoft introduced the Point-to-Point Tunneling Protocol with the initial release of Windows NT 4.0. PPTP encrypts and encapsulates IP, IPX, or NetBEUI packets within a standard IP packet, allowing secure point-to-point links to be established while using public data networks—including the Internet—to transport the encrypted data. In its first release, Windows NT 4.0 RAS supported only client-to-server PPTP links. RRAS extends this to support server-to-server PPTP links. By using RRAS server-to-server PPTP, you can establish virtual private networks that secure your data while using an inexpensive (but insecure) Internet connection for transport rather than an expensive leased line.

MPPC

A point-to-point connection that uses Microsoft RAS on both ends and can use Microsoft Point-to-Point Compression to compress the data flow by as much as 4:1 (depending on the type of data), to improve throughput on slow WAN links.

Manageability

The original Windows NT 4.0 distribution provided the graphical RAS Admin tool for managing RAS servers, but required that routing be managed locally from the command line. RRAS provides several manageability improvements, including:

Graphical management utility

RRAS includes Routing and RAS Admin, a comprehensive GUI administration tool that you can use to administer all aspects of your Microsoft routers and RAS servers, including those that run the original Windows NT 4.0 RAS.

Command line management

RRAS includes the *Routemon.exe* line utility to support traditional interactive and scripted command-line administration of RRAS servers.

Remote Management

RRAS provides full remote management support, using either the Routing and RAS Admin GUI tool (via Remote Procedure Calls) or the *Routmon.exe* command line utility (via telnet).

Management APIs

Microsoft designed RRAS management for extensibility. RRAS defines a comprehensive set of user interface and management APIs that are available for use by third parties. It also supports standard SNMP MIB II, which allows you to administer RRAS from an SNMP management console.

Security

RRAS implements several security features that, in conjunction, can provide essentially the same level of TCP/IP security available with traditional dedicated routers. These features include:

Packet filtering

RRAS supports full permit/deny inbound and outbound packet filtering for both IP and IPX. You can filter IP by source address, destination address, TCP port, UDP port, protocol ID, ICMP type, and ICMP code. You can filter IPX by packet type, source address, source node, source socket, destination address, destination node, and destination socket.

RADIUS support
: If you have a Remote Authentication Dial-In User Service (RADIUS) server on your network, RRAS can optionally function as an RFC2058-compliant RADIUS client, and use that server for user authentication and accounting.

Microsoft Proxy Server integration
: RRAS interoperates with the Microsoft Proxy Server, which allows you to improve the security of your network by combining the Application Layer security of Proxy Server with the Network Layer security provided by RRAS packet filtering.

Demand-Dial Routing

RRAS supports Demand-Dial Routing, allowing you to replace a leased line or full-time dial-up connection with a connection that dials the remote site when needed and drops the connection after a specified period of no traffic. If implemented properly, Demand-Dial Routing can greatly reduce communications costs for linking remote sites while still providing the benefits of a routed network connection. Because Demand-Dial Routing can use the Internet and PPTP, it's a natural for connecting small branch offices to the main office.

WARNING RRAS Demand-Dial Routing can be hazardous to your bank account if you use it with a telephone service that charges by the call or by the minute. If you implement demand-dial, be very careful about determining what triggers a connection, and monitor call patterns regularly. A friend of ours who was experimenting with RRAS Demand-Dial Routing was shocked to find that it had placed more than 1,700 ISDN calls in one day. This occurred because Windows NT was doggedly attempting to send packets via a PPTP demand-dial connection to a destination router that was no longer configured to accept them.

Installing Microsoft Routing and RAS

Installing RRAS is a multi-step process. After preparing your server, you install the RRAS distribution file, which creates a setup folder. You then run setup to install the RRAS service and complete the initial configuration. The remainder of this section details each of these steps.

Preparing for Installation

Microsoft Routing and RAS can be installed only on a computer that is running Windows NT Server 4.0 with Service Pack 3 or later. According to Microsoft, RRAS has no special requirements beyond those of Windows NT Server 4.0 itself, other than 40 MB of free disk space on the volume where RRAS is to be installed.

To prepare your server for installing RRAS, take the following steps:

1. If Remote Access Service or any Multiprotocol Routing (MPR) services are installed, remove them. MPR services include RIP for Internet Protocol, RIP for NwLink IPX/SPX compatible transport, and the DHCP Relay Agent. To remove a Windows NT Service, display the Network dialog from Control Panel or by right-clicking the Network Neighborhood icon on the desktop and choosing Properties. From the Network dialog, click the Services tab, select the service to be removed, and click Remove. If you omit this step, RRAS setup will detect the installed services and prompt you to remove them before proceeding.

WARNING Removing the Remote Access Service or an MPR service deletes its current configuration.

---

2. If the SNMP Service is running on the server, pause or stop it. To pause or stop a Windows NT Service, run Services from Control Panel, select the service to be stopped or paused, and click Stop or Pause.
3. If the Remote Winsock client is installed, remove it. You cannot run Remote Winsock on an RRAS server.
4. Install the hardware needed to support routing, including modems, ISDN adapters, and other devices required for remote connectivity, and network adapters required for LAN connectivity. Although best practice is to install LAN and WAN hardware before installing the Remote Access Service, you do not need to reinstall RAS if you later add to or change your hardware configuration.
5. Install the Windows NT drivers for each hardware component you have added. To install a driver for a network adapter, display the Network dialog, click the Adapters tab, and then click Add. Windows NT displays the Select Network Adapter dialog, which lists the network adapters for which Windows NT includes drivers. If the driver for your network adapter does not appear on the list, or if you have obtained an updated driver from the manufacturer, click Have Disk and follow the dialogs.
6. Install the transport protocols needed to support your RRAS configuration. Install the TCP/IP protocol if you want to route IP. Install the NwLink IPX/SPX compatible transport if you want to route IPX. To install a transport protocol, display the Network dialog, click the Protocols tab, and then click Add. Windows NT displays the Select Network Protocol dialog. Select the protocol you

want to install, click on OK, and follow the dialogs to complete the installation. Before installing RRAS for the TCP/IP protocol, verify the setting for IP forwarding in TCP/IP protocol properties. To view this setting, choose Network—Protocols—TCP/IP Protocol to display the Microsoft TCP/IP Properties property sheet. Click the Routing tab to display the Routing page. This page has one checkbox, Enable IP Forwarding. If this checkbox is cleared when RRAS is installed, it need not be marked later to enable RRAS routing. If this checkbox is already enabled on a server that has RRAS installed, *do not clear the checkbox*. Doing so breaks RRAS routing.

7. If you want to use SNMP management, install the SNMP Service. To install a Windows NT Service, display the Network dialog, click the Services tab, and then click Add. Windows NT displays the Select Network Service dialog. Select the service you want to install, click on OK, and follow the dialogs to complete the installation. As noted earlier, make sure that the SNMP service is paused or stopped before you begin installing RRAS. The SNMP *.mib* files for RRAS are written to the *\docs* subfolder of the RRAS setup folder.
8. Install (or re-install) Service Pack 3 or later. Note that you must reinstall the service pack each time you make a change to your server that requires copying files from the original distribution CD-ROM.

Obtaining the Microsoft Routing and Remote Access Service Distribution

After you prepare your server to install Microsoft Routing and RAS, the next step is to obtain the RRAS distribution file and copy it to a folder that is accessible to the server where you will be installing it. To do so, point your web browser to *http://backoffice.microsoft.com/downtrial/moreinfo/rasup.asp*, complete the required license agreement, and begin the download. Choose a download site as close as possible to your location, and be prepared to wait. The distribution file for Intel, *mpri386.exe*, is about 5.5 MB, and the download sites are usually very busy. Save the distribution file to whatever folder you choose as a holding area. If you don't already have Service Pack 3 or later, download and save it as well.

Installing the Distribution File

Although we assume that you're working with the Intel version of RRAS, the process of installing and configuring the RISC versions of RRAS is very similar. The distribution file is a self-extracting archive. Running the distribution executable unpacks the RRAS setup files and stores them in the folder you specify. After extracting the setup files, the Routing and Remote Access Installer gives you the option of actually installing RRAS or of simply leaving the setup files on disk and available for later use.

To install the distribution file, run *mpri386.exe*. The Routing and Remote Access Service Installer displays yet another license agreement. Click Yes to accept the agreement. The Routing and Remote Access Service Installer dialog lists the setup files as they are extracted from the distribution archive and written to a temporary folder. The installer then prompts you for a location to store the setup files. The setup files remain on disk for future use.

By default, the installer copies the setup files to *C:\Program Files\Routing,* regardless of the location from which *mrpi386.exe* is run. You can use this dialog to specify a different destination folder. If the folder you specify does not exist, the installer prompts you for permission to create it.

If Windows NT is installed on a volume other than *C:*, it's a good idea to place the RRAS setup files on that volume. Also, because you must specify a command line argument when you run the main setup program later to add or change RRAS options, it makes things easier if you store the setup files in a folder with a short, DOS 8.3-compliant folder name. For example, we run Windows NT from *D:*, and chose *D:\RRAS* as the destination folder for the RRAS setup files.

When the destination folder is set correctly, click on OK to begin copying the setup files. The RRAS installer displays the Copying Files dialog to indicate progress as the distribution files are copied to the folder you specified. After the setup files have been copied, the RRAS installer displays the Routing and Remote Access Service Installation dialog. At this point, click Yes if you want to install RRAS, or click No to exit the installer. In either case, the RRAS setup files remain in the folder you specified earlier.

Running Microsoft Routing and Remote Access Service Setup

You can set up RRAS as a part of the process of copying the RRAS setup files simply by clicking Yes. If you elect to stop the installation after copying the setup files, you can install RRAS later by running *mprsetup.exe*. If you run *mrpsetup.exe* manually, you must specify the location of the RRAS files as a command line argument, for example, **mprsetup "C:\Program Files\Routing"**. When *mprsetup.exe* runs, the installer first copies the working files to the appropriate folders and displays the Routing and Remote Access Setup dialog, shown in Figure 9-1.

You can use the Routing and Remote Access Setup dialog to install the following options in any combination:

Remote Access Service
: Support for client dial-up networking.

LAN Routing
: Support for LAN-to-LAN routing, and for WAN cards that emulate network adapters.

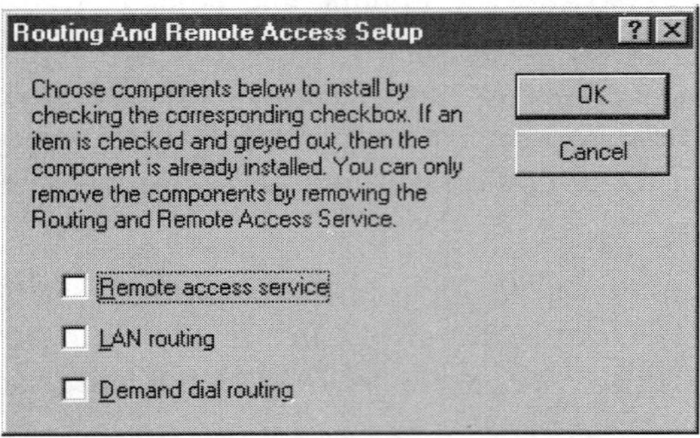

Figure 9-1. The Routing and Remote Access Setup dialog

Demand-Dial Routing
Support for WAN routing and dial-up interfaces including ISDN and PPTP.

When you install RRAS for the first time, none of these checkboxes is marked by default. If you run *mprsetup.exe* later to add options to an existing installation, the checkboxes for installed components are marked and grayed out. To continue the installation, mark the boxes for the components you want to install, and then click on OK. The exact steps required to complete setup depend on the options you choose to install. We assume in the following sections that all options are being installed.

WARNING The only way to remove an installed component is to remove RRAS entirely and then reinstall it without the component.

Once you click on OK in this dialog, you're committed. RRAS setup copies the RRAS version of the file *Oemnsvra.inf* to the *%Systemroot%\system32* folder. If you abort setup, or if you decide later to revert to a previous version of Windows NT 4.0 RAS, you need to retrieve the original version of *Oemnsvra.inf* from your distribution CD-ROM or Service Pack and copy it manually to the *%Systemroot%\system32* folder before the earlier version will install or run.

Running remote access setup

If you marked Remote Access Service, the installer next invokes Remote Access Setup. If no RAS-capable devices are installed—as should be the case if you removed RAS before beginning RRAS setup—the installer notifies you that there are no RAS-capable devices installed and asks if you want to invoke the Modem Installer. Click Yes to display the Install New Modem wizard. When you finish installing the modem, setup displays the Add RAS Device dialog. You can use this dialog to install additional modems and/or X.25 PAD's as RAS capable devices.

After you finish adding RAS devices, click on OK to display the Remote Access Setup dialog shown in Figure 9-2.

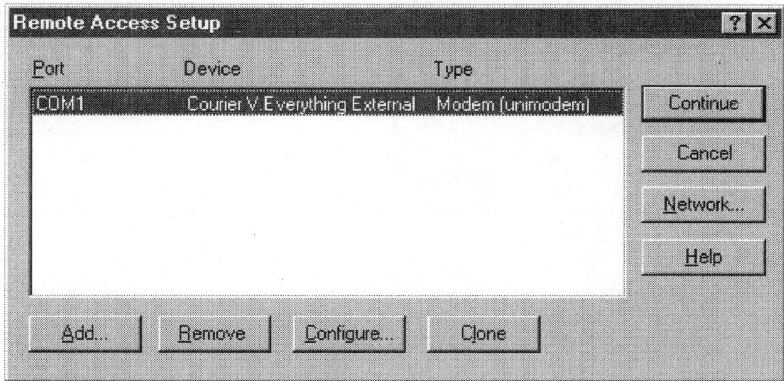

Figure 9-2. Configuring installed RAS devices

Use the Remote Access Setup dialog to perform the following functions:

Add
: To define a new RAS port and install a modem or X.25 PAD for that port, click Add to invoke the Add RAS Device dialog.

Remove
: To remove RAS support for a port that currently supports a RAS-capable device, highlight that port and click Remove.

Configure
: To change the RAS settings for a port, highlight that port and click Configure.

Clone
: To replicate the setup of an existing port to a new port, highlight the current port and click Clone.

Network
: To configure global RAS settings for the RAS server itself (rather than for an individual port), click Network.

Configuring a RAS port

Configure port usage type for each RAS port individually by highlighting that port in the Remote Access Setup dialog and clicking Configure to display the Configure Port Usage dialog, shown in Figure 9-3.

Mark the checkboxes in any combination to define port usage as "Dial out as a RAS client", "Receive calls as a RAS server", and "Dial out and receive calls as a demand dial router". By default, all ports are configured to support inbound calls to the RAS server and outbound/inbound demand dial routing calls.

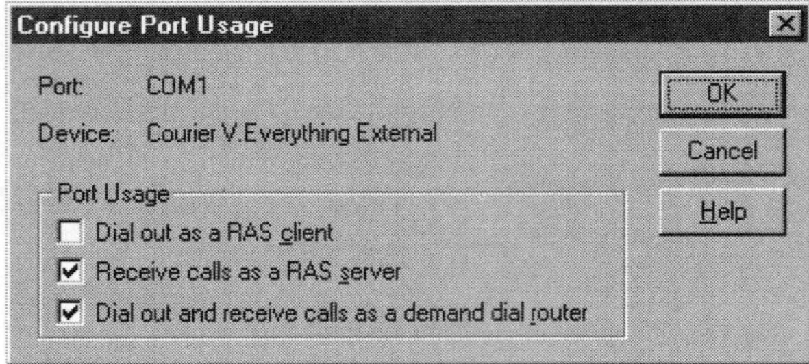

Figure 9-3. The Configure Port Usage dialog.

Configuring RAS network settings

After you've added and configured all of the RAS ports on the server and returned to the Remote Access Setup dialog, click Network to display the Network Configuration dialog shown in Figure 9-4. The computer running RAS can function as a RAS client, a RAS server, or as both at the same time. Use the Network Configuration dialog to configure protocol and authentication settings globally for the RAS computer. The settings you specify in this dialog apply uniformly to all RAS operations on all RAS-enabled ports for this server.

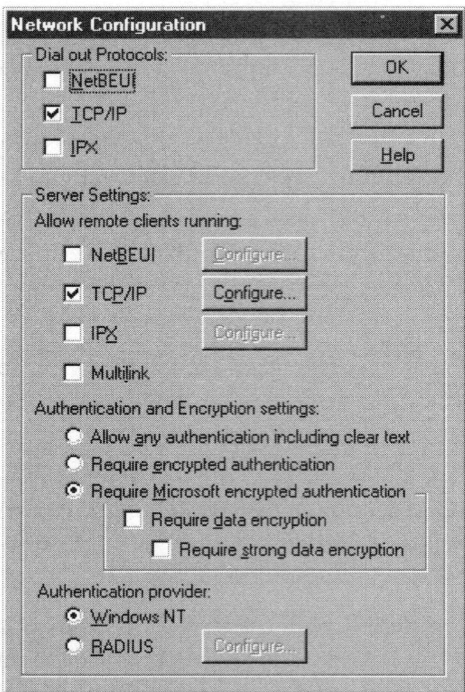

Figure 9-4. Global protocol and authentication settings for the RAS server

The Network Configuration dialog allows you to set the following options:

Dial out Protocols
Mark the checkboxes for the protocols you want to use when placing outbound calls from this computer to a remote RAS server. If a protocol is not marked here, it will not be available when you create phone book entries for remote RAS servers. If no RAS ports are configured for outbound usage, this section is grayed out and unavailable. If at least one RAS port is configured for outbound calls, each installed transport protocol is marked by default.

Server Settings
Use this section to enable and configure transport protocols and authentication and encryption options for the RAS server role. This section does not appear in the Network Configuration dialog if none of the RAS ports is configured to accept inbound calls.

Allow remote clients running
Mark the checkbox associated with each transport protocol that you want RAS clients to be able to use to connect to the RAS server. Marking a checkbox enables the Configure button associated with that protocol. If at least one RAS port is configured for inbound calls, each transport protocol installed on the RAS server is marked by default. Configure each selected protocol before proceeding. TCP/IP configuration is described in the next section.

Multilink
Mark this checkbox if you want to use Multilink channel aggregation. Multilink allows you to increase bandwidth and throughput by combining two or more ISDN or modem connections (in any combination) into a single logical channel. Multilink must be enabled on both the server and client to function.

Authentication and Encryption Settings
Select an option button to set the authentication level required by RAS clients attempting to connect to the RAS server, as follows:

Allow any authentication including clear text
Choose this option to allow clients to connect using their choice of authentication methods, including Password Authentication Protocol (PAP), Shiva Password Authentication Protocol (SPAP), and Microsoft Challenge Handshake Authentication Protocol (MS-CHAP). This is the least secure authentication option, and should be used only if you need to support third party clients that do not support encrypted authentication.

Require encrypted authentication
Choose this option to require encrypted password from all clients. When this option is in effect, clients can authenticate with any support authentication protocol except PAP. This is a moderately secure option in that it

requires encrypted logon authentication, but does not encrypt the data flow during the session.

Require Microsoft encrypted authentication

Choose this option if all of your RAS clients are running Microsoft client software that supports it. With this option in effect, RAS clients can authenticate using MS-CHAP only. If you elect this option, you can choose to encrypt data flow for the entire session, rather than just encrypting the logon sequence. Mark the Require data encryption checkbox to encrypt session data with the moderately secure RSA RC-4 algorithm.

WARNING You can also mark the Require strong data encryption checkbox if you want to use only the most secure encryption available. Marking this checkbox forces use of the strongest encryption available on the server. Right now, that's a moot point. The current release of RRAS supports only 40-bit encryption for demand-dial and RAS. In fact, when you upgrade a 4.0 RAS server that has 128-bit encryption installed to RRAS, you simultaneously downgrade your encryption to 40-bit.

Even when Microsoft gets around to upgrading RRAS to support 128-bit encryption, using this option may be more trouble than it's worth. When this checkbox is marked, it's not a question of negotiating the strongest encryption common to the RAS server and client. Instead, it's all or nothing. For example, installing RRAS 128-bit encryption (once it's available) and marking this checkbox will force all connections to use 128-bit Microsoft encryption. Only RAS clients that are running Windows NT 4.0 with Service Pack 3 or higher and the 128-bit encryption patch will be able to connect to the RAS server. A RAS client that supports no encryption, weak encryption, or strong third-party encryption will simply not be able to connect to the RAS server.

Authentication provider

Select an option button to specify the authentication provider for the RAS server, as follows:

Windows NT

Choose this option, which is the default, if you want RAS clients to be authenticated by the Windows NT security provider.

RADIUS

Choose this option if you have a Remote Authentication Dial-In User Service (RADIUS) server available on your network and want to use it to authenticate RAS clients. Note that marking this option button enables Windows NT as a RADIUS client only. Windows NT does not provide RADIUS server functionality, and requires that a third party

RADIUS server exist on the network. If you choose this option, click Configure to display the RADIUS Configuration dialog and add a RADIUS server. Note that RADIUS authentication and Require Microsoft encrypted authentication are mutually exclusive.

Configuring TCP/IP settings

Before you exit the Network Configuration dialog, configure TCP/IP settings for the RAS server. To do so, click the Configure button next to the TCP/IP checkbox to display the RAS Server TCP/IP Configuration dialog shown in Figure 9-5.

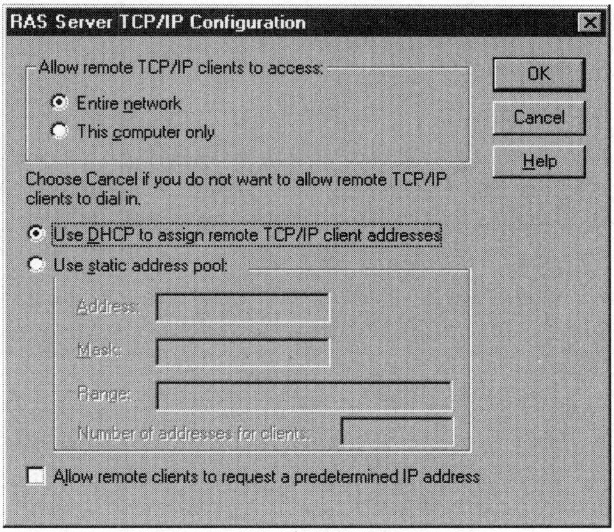

Figure 9-5. TCP/IP options for the RAS server

Use the RAS Server TCP/IP Configuration dialog to set the following options:

Allow remote TCP/IP clients to access
: Choose the Entire Network option button, which is the default, if you want RAS clients to be able to access resources on both the RAS server itself and on other computers on the network. Choose the This Computer Only option button if you want to restrict RAS clients to accessing resources on the RAS server only. Note that specifying one of these options does not authorize users to access resources by itself, but only allows such access to occur if the user otherwise has the necessary permissions.

Use DHCP to assign remote TCP/IP client addresses
: Choose this option button if a DHCP server is available on the network and you want it to assign IP addresses dynamically to RAS clients when they dial in.

WARNING Do not use DHCP to assign IP addresses to RAS clients if the RRAS server is located on a network that includes two or more IP network addresses on a single physical segment. If you do so, some computers may not be able to communicate with other computers on the same subnet. When DHCP assigns addresses from a subnet to RRAS clients, the RRAS server adds a route via the RAS server interface for the entire subnet from which the addresses were assigned. Because DHCP assigns addresses from both subnets to local clients, some clients may find themselves with a bad route (via the RAS interface) and therefore unable to communicate with other clients on the same local subnet. You can avoid this problem either by using a static address pool, as described in the following section, or by adding a static route for each logical subnet on the local segment.

Use static address pool

Choose this option button if there is no DHCP server available on the network, or if you prefer not to use the DHCP server to assign IP addresses to RAS clients. If you choose this option, complete the following items:

Address

Enter the first IP address of the range of addresses to be assigned to RAS clients. This range may be a subset of the subnet assigned to a LAN interface, or it may be a unique subnet defined for this purpose.

Mask

Enter an IP address to define the size of the pool to be assigned to RAS clients. Define this mask using the same concepts as you would to define an IP subnet mask. For example, if the network address 172.16.12.1 is assigned to the LAN interface using the subnet mask 255.255.255.0 and you have reserved the last 16 IP addresses of this address space for RAS clients, you would assign 172.16.12.240 as the Address and 255.255.255.240 as the Mask.

Windows NT uses the values you enter for Address and Mask to calculate and display dynamically the Range (in this case, 172.16.12.242 through 172.16.12.254) and the Number of addresses for clients (in this case, 13).

Allow remote clients to request a predetermined IP address

Mark this checkbox if you want to allow RAS clients to request a specific IP address. About the only good reason for doing this is if you want a non-Windows NT RAS client to be able to establish a routed network connection, which requires a known, static IP address. For example, if a small branch office uses a Unix box to connect to your RAS server, you might use that Unix box to establish a routed network link to your RAS server, which users at the remote office could then use to access the Internet indirectly via the Internet link at your main office.

Completing Routing and Remote Access Service setup

After you finish setting TCP/IP configuration options, click on OK to accept them and return to the Network Configuration dialog. Click on OK again to return to the Remote Access Setup dialog. When you finish configuring RAS ports, click Continue to exit the Remote Access Setup dialog and finish installing RRAS. Setup displays a Setup Message to notify you that RRAS has been installed successfully.

- Click on OK to complete the installation. Setup updates the Registry; configures, stores, and reviews the bindings; and displays the Steelhead Installer dialog. Choose Restart to reboot the server immediately and make RRAS available. Choose Do Not Restart to defer availability of RRAS until the next routine server restart.
- Installing RRAS does not install the RRAS PPTP drivers that are supplied with the RRAS distribution. By default, RRAS uses the Windows NT 4.0 Service Pack 3 drivers (dated May 1, 1997). If you use Multilink PPTP, install the RRAS drivers (dated April 23, 1997) manually. To do so, copy the files *raspptpe.sys, raspptpm.sys,* and *raspptpu.sys* from the RRAS setup folder to the *%Systemroot%\system32\drivers* folder.

Updating Microsoft Routing and Remote Access

If, after installing RRAS, you install an adapter or service that requires Service Pack 3 to be reapplied, you must update RRAS after installing Service Pack 3. To do so, right-click the Network Neighborhood icon on the desktop, and choose Properties from the context-sensitive menu. Click the Services tab to display the Service page, and highlight Routing and Remote Access Service. Click Update to display the Windows NT Setup dialog, enter the folder where the RRAS setup files are stored, and then click Continue. When prompted, restart the server. If you installed the RRAS PPTP drivers, they'll have been overwritten by the Service Pack 3 PPTP drivers, and will need to be reinstalled before you reboot the server.

Administering Microsoft Routing and RAS

Installing Microsoft Routing and Remote Access Service automatically installs the Routing and RAS Admin tool and defines interfaces for all installed network adapters. Before you can use Microsoft Routing, you must use the Routing and RAS Admin tool—or the equivalent command line utilities—to specify the routing protocols to be used and add interfaces for them. This section explains each of the tasks needed to configure and administer Routing and RAS.

You can also use the Routing and RAS Admin tool to configure and administer your RAS servers, including RAS servers running earlier versions of RAS. When you manage a RAS server running Windows NT 4.0 RAS or earlier, Routing and RAS Admin automatically invokes the Windows NT 4.0 RAS Admin tool.

Using the Routing and RAS Admin Tool

The Routing and RAS Admin tool looks and works much like the Windows NT Explorer. The left pane displays a hierarchical view of installed network and routing components of the Routing and Remote Access Service. The right pane lists details for the interface selected in the left pane. Run the Routing and RAS Admin tool from the desktop by choosing Start → Programs → Administrative Tools (Common) → Routing and RAS Admin.

Configuring Routing and RAS components and interfaces

You configure Routing and RAS components by highlighting the component in the left pane and then choosing the Actions menu, shown in Figure 9-6. Alternatively, you can simply right-click an entry in the left pane to display the context-sensitive menu for that component. Changes you make this way apply globally to the component. To configure an individual interface, right-click it in the right pane and choose an action from the context-sensitive menu. Changes you make this way apply only to the selected interface.

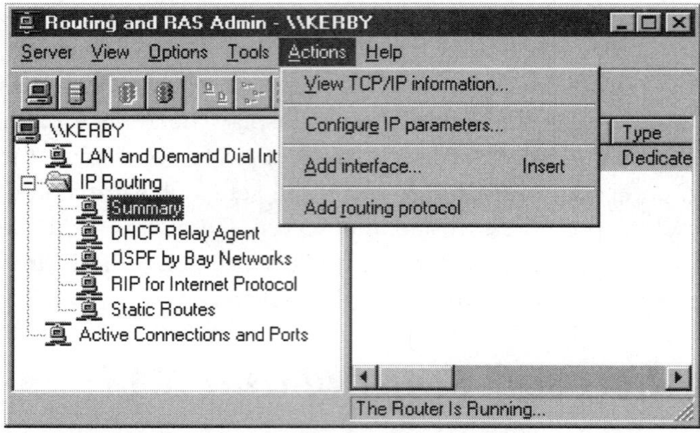

Figure 9-6. Routing protocols and interfaces

Viewing routing tables and router settings

Routing and RAS Admin can display routing tables and other router settings for components or for individual interfaces. To view settings for a component, right-click the component in the left pane of Routing and RAS Admin and choose View.

To view settings for an interface, right-click the interface in the right pane of Routing and RAS Admin and choose the view menu. Depending on the interface you select and its configuration, there may be only one view available. If so, the view command for that interface appears directly on the context-sensitive menu. If more than one view is available, choosing View displays a submenu that lists the available views. Available views include:

IP Routing—Summary
: TCP/IP information, Address translations, IP addresses, IP routing table, TCP connections, UDP listener ports

IP Routing—OSPF
: Areas, Link-state database, Neighbors, Virtual interfaces

IP Routing—RIP for Internet Protocol
: RIP neighbors

IPX Routing—Summary
: IPX global parameters, IPX routing table, IPX service table

Active Connections and Ports
: Status (including port status, device statistics, and network registration information)

Saving and loading configurations

You can use Routing and RAS Admin to save RRAS configurations and to load saved configurations, as follows:

- To save the configuration of the current RRAS server, open the Server menu and choose Save Configuration to display the Save As dialog. By default, Routing and RAS Admin saves these files with a *.mpr* extension in the *%Systemroot%\system32\ras folder*. Type a filename and click on OK to save the configuration. If you are saving the configuration of a remote RRAS server, the folder to which you save the configuration file must exist on both the local computer and the remote computer.
- To load a saved configuration, first stop the RRAS router by opening the Server menu and choosing Stop Router. Once the router is stopped, open the Server menu and choose Load Configuration to display the Open dialog. Highlight one of the configuration files listed, and click Open to load the configuration.

NOTE Saving an RRAS configuration does not save credentials (logon security information) for demand-dial interfaces. When you load a saved configuration, you must reenter the credentials for each demand-dial interface manually.

Managing remote RRAS routers

By default, Routing and RAS Admin manages the service on the machine it's running on. You can also use Routing and RAS Admin to manage other RRAS servers in the same domain or in a domain for which a trust relationship exists. To connect to another RRAS server, display the Server menu and choose Connect to Router. Routing and RAS Admin displays the Connect to Router dialog. Type the name of the remote RRAS router in UNC form, for example, *\\servername\server,* and click on OK. Routing and RAS Admin displays the tree for the remote RRAS server.

The Routing and RAS Admin tool is installed only when you install the RRAS upgrade. Because the RRAS upgrade cannot be installed on Windows NT Workstation, many companies face a conundrum. If all of your servers are locked in closets, using the Routing and RAS Admin tool becomes inconvenient, to say the least. Microsoft addresses this problem by allowing you to install the Routing and RAS Admin tool on a computer that has not had the Routing and RAS Admin upgrade installed, typically a computer running Windows NT Workstation 4.0.

For the purposes of this example, we'll assume that *kerby* is the RRAS server and you want to manage RRAS from *thoth*, a stock Windows NT 4.0 computer that has not been upgraded to RRAS. To install the Routing and RAS Admin tool on *thoth* and use it to manage an RRAS server, take the following steps:

1. Working at the console of *kerby*, open a command prompt window and change to the folder where you installed the RRAS setup files.
2. Run the batch file *copyadmn.cmd,* specifying the source and destination folders on the command line. This batch file copies the files needed to run **mpradmin** to a non-RRAS Windows NT 4.0 computer. For example:

   ```
   copyadmn c:\winnt\system32\ \\kerby\remote
   ```

3. At the console of *thoth*, open a command prompt and make a network connection to the RRAS server. For example:

   ```
   net use \\kerby\ipc$ /u:domain\user
   ```

4. Execute *mpradmin.exe* to run the Routing and RAS Admin tool.
5. From the Server menu, choose Connect to Router. When the Connect to Router dialog appears, type the name of the RRAS server you want to administer, using UNC format, and click on OK.

WARNING Although this workaround does allow you to manage RRAS from a non-RRAS Windows NT 4.0 computer, it is less than completely satisfactory. Running the *copyadmn.cmd* batch file copies the RRAS versions of the files *mpradmin.exe, mpradmin.hlp, mpradmin.cnt, ipadmin.dll, ipxadmin.dll, ddmadmin.dll, ifadmin.dll, mprfiltr.dll, mprapi.dll, rasrpc_c.dll, rasdlg.dll, rasapi32.dll, rasfil32.dll,* and *rasscrpt.dll* to the non-RRAS computer, overwriting the older versions of several important DLLs. As a result, Windows NT 4.0 dial-up networking can no longer be used on that computer.

Viewing RRAS servers in another domain

You can also use Routing and RAS Admin to view and manage RRAS servers in another domain. To view another domain, display the Server menu and choose View Domain. Routing and RAS Admin displays the View Domain dialog. Type the name of the domain and click on OK.

Routing and RAS Admin displays a hierarchical tree for the domain you specified in the left pane. This tree includes a line for each RRAS server in the domain, which may be expanded by clicking on that entry. It also includes a summary entry that displays a single line in the right pane for each Remote Access Server in the domain in the right pane.

Managing Remote Access Service

If you installed the Remote Access Service component of RRAS, you can use Routing and RAS Admin to manage both RRAS RAS and RAS running on older RAS servers. To view and manage RAS, click Active Connections and Ports in the left pane of Routing and RAS Admin. The right pane lists connected RAS clients and inactive lines. You can right-click a user to view the status of that user connection, or expand the user entry and right-click a device to view its status. If you select a RAS server running an earlier version of RAS, the Routing and RAS Admin tool automatically invokes the older Remote Access Admin tool to view and manage that server.

Before an RAS client can connect to the RRAS server, you must grant dial-in permission to the user. This is not a function of RRAS. Instead, use User Manager for Domains to grant dial-in permission to users in your domain. To grant a user dial-in permission, choose Start → Programs → Administrative Tools (Common) → User Manager for Domains. Double-click a username to display the User Properties dialog for that user. Click the Dial-in icon to display the Dial-in Information dialog, and mark the Grant Dial-in Permission to User checkbox.

If many users need dial-in permission, you can grant this permission in a single step rather than user by user. To do so, use the standard Windows Shift-click and

Ctrl-click conventions to select multiple users in the main User Manager for Domains screen. Then, open the User menu and choose Properties to display the modified multi-user User Properties dialog. Click the Dial-in icon to display the Dial-in Information dialog, and mark the Grant dial-in permission to user checkbox as before. Click on OK to save your changes. All selected users now have dial-in permission.

Managing Microsoft Routing

Before you can use RRAS for routing, you must configure it by adding one or more routing protocols, adding interfaces to the installed routing protocols, and adding any demand-dial interfaces required. You can perform these tasks with the Routing and RAS Admin tool. If you are more comfortable working at a command prompt, you can instead configure and manage RRAS routing by using the *Routemon.exe* command line utility. *Routemon.exe* syntax is fully documented in the file *\Doc\appdx_b.doc* in the RRAS setup folder. The remainder of this section focuses on using the Routing and RAS Admin tool to perform the following functions:

- Adding a routing protocol
- Adding an interface to a routing protocol
- Adding demand-dial interfaces
- Removing or disabling an interface
- Managing static routes
- Using packet filters, local host filters, and PPTP filters

Adding a routing protocol

If the NWLink IPX/SPX Compatible Transport protocol is installed when RRAS setup is run, RRAS automatically adds the IPX routing protocols. However, no IP routing protocols are added by default. Before RRAS can route IP packets, you must enter static routes and/or add and configure one or more IP routing protocols to enable dynamic routing. Managing static routes is described later in this section. To add an IP routing protocol, take the following steps:

1. Highlight IP Routing—Summary in the left pane, and right-click it to display the context-sensitive menu shown in Figure 9-7.
2. Choose Add routing protocol to display the Select Routing Protocol dialog. Only routing protocols that have not yet been added are listed in this dialog.
3. Highlight a routing protocol in the Routing protocols pane and click on OK to add it. RRAS raises a configuration dialog specific to the protocol you are adding. In this example, we'll add the RIP Version 2 for Internet Protocol routing protocol. For information about the DHCP Relay Agent see Chapter 6,

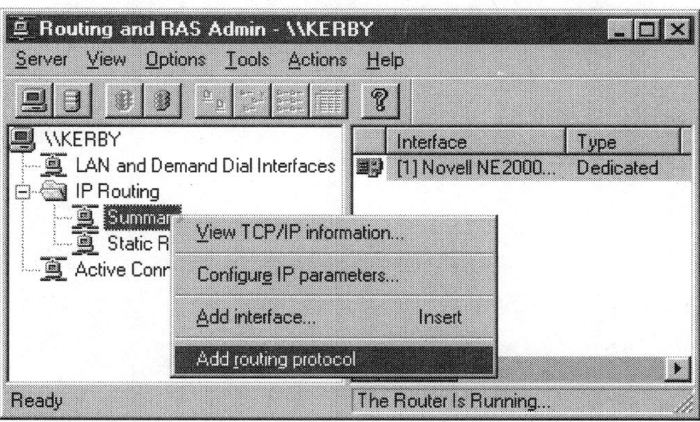

Figure 9-7. Adding a routing protocol

Using Dynamic Host Configuration Protocol, and for the Open Shortest Path First (OSPF) routing protocol see Chapter 2. For additional configuration details, see the Microsoft documentation in the *\doc* subfolder of the folder where you installed the RRAS setup files.

4. Routing and RAS Admin displays the General page of the RIP for Internet Protocol Configuration dialog, shown in Figure 9-8. Accept the default value of 5 seconds for "Minimum seconds between triggered-updates," or use the spinner to modify that value. RIP routers generate triggered updates to notify other routers when a change to the network configuration occurs, for example, when a router or communications link fails. When a RIP router receives such an update, it updates its own routing table and propagates the change to neighboring routers. In the Event logging section, choose an option button to set the logging level you want. The default choice, "Log errors only," is generally appropriate for a properly functioning network. If you have made significant changes to the routing environment, or if you are having routing-related problems, choose the "Log errors and warnings" option button or the "Log the maximum amount of information" option button. The latter choice generates huge log files, and should be used only as a temporary debugging measure. Choose the "Disable event-logging" option button if you believe that ignorance is bliss.
5. Click the Security tab to display the Security page of the RIP for Internet Protocol Configuration dialog. By default, the "Process announcements from all routers" option button is marked, which causes RIP to accept announcements from any router. If you want to configure RIP to accept announcements only from routers you specify, mark the "Process only announcements from the routers listed" option button and enter the IP addresses of those routers in the Routers pane. If you want to configure RIP to accept announcements from all

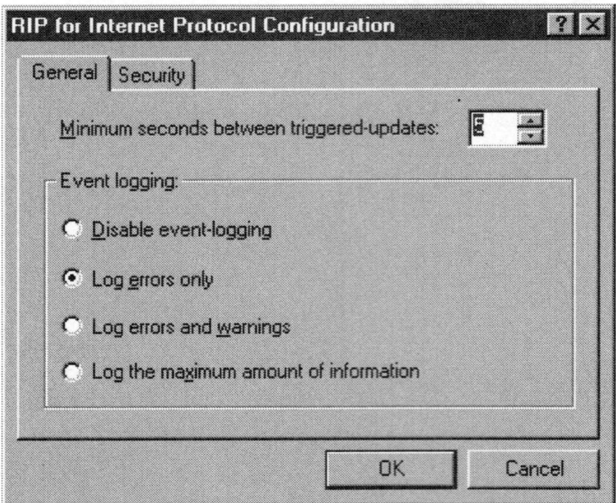

Figure 9-8. The General page of the RIP for Internet Protocol Configuration dialog

routers except those you specify, mark the "Process only announcements from the routers listed" option button and enter the IP addresses of those routers to be excluded in the Routers pane.

6. Click on OK to add the routing protocol with the configuration you've entered.

Adding an interface to a routing protocol

After you've added an IP routing protocol, the next step is to add one or more interfaces to that routing protocol. For IP routing, you can add different interfaces selectively to different IP routing protocols. For IPX routing, adding an interface automatically adds that interface to all IPX routing protocols. To add an interface to an IP routing protocol, take the following steps:

1. Highlight an IP routing protocol in the IP Routing component in the left pane, and right-click it to display the context-sensitive menu.
2. Choose Add interface to display the Select Interface for <protocol name> dialog.
3. Highlight an interface in the Interfaces pane and click on OK to add it. RRAS raises a configuration dialog specific to the interface you are adding and the IP routing protocol it is being added to. In this example, we'll add the RIP Version 2 for Internet Protocol routing protocol to the Novell NE 2000 Adapter interface. For information about the DHCP Relay Agent see Chapter 6, and for the Open Shortest Path First (OSPF) routing protocol see Chapter 2. For further configuration details, see the Microsoft documentation in the *\doc* subfolder of the folder where you installed the RRAS setup files.

4. Routing and RAS Admin displays the General page of the RIP Configuration dialog, shown in Figure 9-9. Configure the following settings:

   Operation Mode

   Use the drop-down list to select Periodic update mode (the default) or Auto-static update mode. In periodic update mode, the router automatically updates, expires, and removes routing table entries according to the timers you set. In auto-static update mode, the router sends requests and stores the responses in a dynamically updated list that is retained if the interface goes down. In other words, the router creates *dynamic static routes*. If you use auto-static mode on a demand-dial interface, you must manually update routes on each end the first time you make a connection by right-clicking the interface and choosing Update routes.

   Protocol for outgoing packets

   Use the drop-down list to select RIP version 1 broadcast (the default), RIP version 2 broadcast, RIP version 2 multicast, or Silent RIP. In Silent RIP mode, the router listens for route announcements from other routers, but does not send route announcements or respond to requests from other routers. If you have a mixed RIPv1 and RIPv2 environment, use RIP version 2 broadcast rather than RIP version 2 multicast. However, keep in mind that RIP may not learn routes on a demand-dial link that uses broadcast rather than multicast, because the end points for the demand dial link may be on different subnets, preventing RIP broadcast requests from being received.

   Protocol for incoming packets

   Use the drop-down list to select RIP version 1 and 2 (the default), RIP version 1 only, RIP version 2 only, or Ignore incoming packets.

   Added cost for routes using this interface

   Accept the default value of 1, or use the spinner to set another value. Use cost to specify how expensive it is to use this interface to send a packet. The router will choose the interface with the lowest cost. For example, if you have both a dedicated line and a backup dial-up line that can be used to link to a remote router, you can assign the dedicated line a lower cost than the dial-up line. That way, the router uses the dedicated line when it is available, and routes packets over the dial-up interface only if the dedicated line interface fails.

   Tag for routes advertised on this interface

   Accept the default value of 0, or use the spinner to set another value.

   Enable authentication

   Mark this checkbox, which is cleared by default, and enter a Password of up to 16 characters if you want to use authentication between routers. If

you enable authentication on an interface, make sure the remote router to which this interface connects has the same password entered.

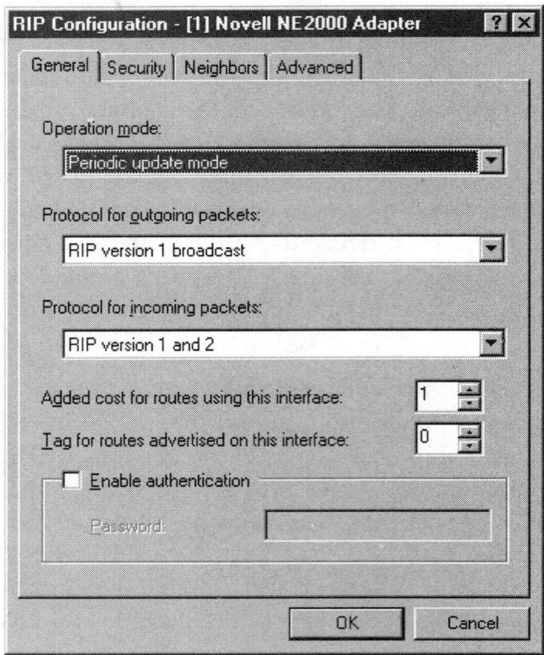

Figure 9-9. Setting general protocol options

5. After you finish configuring General options, click the Security tab to display the Security page. You can use the Security page to restrict the ranges of routes that this router will accept or announce. You may specify separate settings for inbound and outbound routing announcements. Use the drop-down list to select either When accepting routes or When announcing routes and choose one of the following options for each:

Process all routes
: Mark this option button, which is the default, to allow this router to communicate without restricting by range.

Process only routes in the ranges listed
: Mark this option button and add one or more ranges in the Ranges pane to restrict this router to routes within the ranges that you specify.

Discard all routes in the ranges listed
: Mark this option button and add one or more ranges in the Ranges pane to allow this router to process routes from any range except those that you specifically exclude.

6. After you finish configuring Security options, click the Neighbors tab to display the Neighbors page. You can use the Neighbors page to enable or disable use of neighbors-list and to enter the IP addresses for neighbor routers. Ordinarily, RIP announcements are broadcast (sent to all hosts on a specified network) or multicast (sent to all hosts defined as members of a multicast group). However, you can define a neighbor list on a per-interface basis when using non-broadcast media and point-to-point links. Choose one of the following options:

   Disable neighbor-list
   : Mark this option button, which is the default, to use only standard RIP announcements.

   Use neighbor-list in addition to broadcast or multicast
   : Mark this option button and add the IP address of one or more neighboring routers to use both standard RIP announcements and the neighbor list you define.

   Use neighbor-list instead of broadcast or multicast
   : Mark this option button and add the IP address of one or more neighboring routers to disable standard RIP announcements and use only the neighbor list.

7. After you finish configuring Neighbor options, click the Advanced tab to display the Advanced page, shown in Figure 9-10. You can use the Advanced page to configure various RIP settings. Leave these settings at their default values unless you understand exactly why you want to change one.

   Periodic-announcement timer
   : Use the spinner to set the value, 30 seconds by default, that specifies how often the router sends announcements in periodic update mode.

   Route-expiration timer
   : Use the spinner to set the value, 180 seconds by default, that specifies how long a route remains valid before expiring in periodic update mode.

   Route-removal timer
   : Use the spinner to set the value, 120 seconds by default, that specifies how long an expired route is stored before being deleted in periodic update mode.

   Enable split-horizon processing
   : Mark this checkbox, which is marked by default, to enable split-horizon processing. Split-horizon processing is a mechanism used with distance-vector routing protocols to prevent routing loops by not forwarding routing information back to its source. If split-horizon processing is enabled, you can also mark the Enable poison-reverse processing checkbox, which

is marked by default, to enable poison-reverse processing. Poison-reverse processing is an enhancement to split-horizon processing to improve RIP convergence. Poison-reverse processing advertises all network IDs, but *upstream* IDs are advertised with a hop count of 16, effectively advertising that network as unavailable.

Enable triggered-updates

Mark this checkbox, which is marked by default, to enable triggered updates. In a large network that uses RIP in periodic update mode, it may take several minutes for routing changes to propagate through the network. Enabling triggered updates, also called flash updates, minimizes this convergence time by allowing the routers to update their routing tables immediately when a change occurs that significantly affects routing tables, for example, a link failure. In essence, a triggered update is an announcement that is not subject to the periodic update timers set in the timers section.

Send clean-up updates when stopping

Mark this checkbox, which is marked by default, to cause the system to actively remove its routing entries from its neighbors routing tables. If this box is checked, when the system shuts down it sends out routing updates that specify that the cost of reaching any destination through this system is infinitely high. This causes its neighbors to remove it from the routing table.

Override non-RIP routes with RIP-learnt routes

Mark this checkbox, which is cleared by default, to remove non-RIP routes from the routing table when routes to those destinations are learned from RIP. This is used to override static routes when routes to the same destinations are learned from a dynamic routing protocol. With this, an administrator can define static routes to important locations to be used when the routing protocol is not running. The static routes are then overwritten when the routing protocol receives an update.

By default, RIP does not include host routes or default routes from its routing table when it sends routing announcements, nor does it process host routes or default routes if it receives a routing announcement that contains them. If host routes or default routes are not being propagated as you wish, change one or more of the remaining options.

Process host routes in packets received

Mark this checkbox, which is cleared by default, to cause RIP to update its routing table with host routes received in routing announcements from a remote router.

Include host routes in packets sent

Mark this checkbox, which is cleared by default, to cause RIP to include host routes from its routing table when sending routing announcements to remote routers.

Process default routes in packets received

Mark this checkbox, which is cleared by default, to cause RIP to update its routing table with default routes received in routing announcements from a remote router.

Include default routes in packets sent

Mark this checkbox, which is cleared by default, to cause RIP to include default routes from its routing table when sending routing announcements to remote routers.

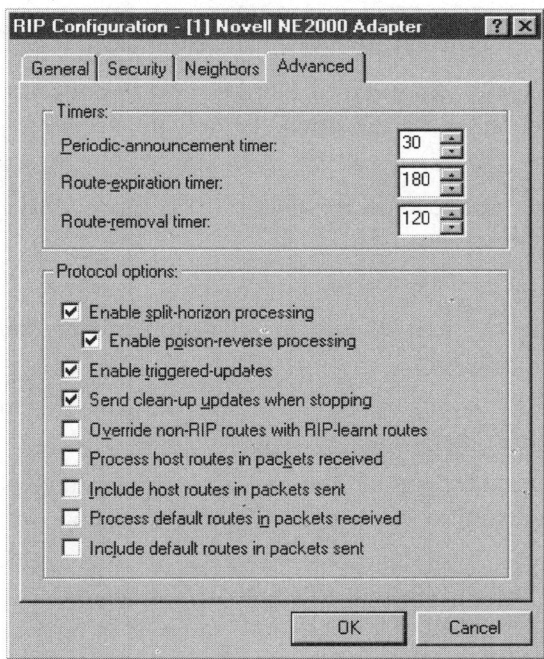

Figure 9-10. The Advanced page of the RIP Configuration dialog

If you need to modify these settings later, click the routing protocol in the left pane to display a list of interfaces in the right pane. Right-click an interface to display the context-sensitive menu, and choose Configure Interface.

Adding a demand-dial interface

A demand-dial interface establishes a link to a remote router when it has data to be transferred to that router, and then drops the link after a specified period of inactivity. You can use RRAS demand-dial routing with a modem or ISDN adapter to establish a low-cost routed connection between sites that do not merit dedicated leased lines.

Enabling demand-dial routing between two points requires that you add a demand-dial interface to each of the two routers, configure transport and routing protocols for the link, and provide the logon security information necessary to authenticate attempted connections. Both ends of the link must be configured properly to recognize each other and communicate before demand-dial routing can occur.

If you use demand-dial interfaces to connect a Windows NT Router to another Windows NT Router, each router acts as a PPP client of the other router, and obtains an IP address for its local demand-dial interface from the remote router. This means that each end of a demand-dial link can be using an IP address from a different subnet. So long as the link is point-to-point, this isn't a problem. However, if you use a routing protocol, configure the interfaces to use multicast rather than broadcast.

Before you add a demand-dial interface, make sure that the RAS port or ports you plan to use are configured to enable demand-dial routing. To do so, take the following steps:

1. Right-click the Network Neighborhood icon on the desktop and choose Properties to display the Network tabbed dialog.
2. Click the Services tab to display the Services page.
3. Highlight Routing and Remote Access Service, and click the Properties button to display the Remote Access Setup dialog.
4. Highlight the RAS port you want to configure and click the Configure button to display the Configure Port Usage dialog.
5. In the Port Usage section, mark the "Dial out and receive calls as a demand dial router" checkbox. Click on OK to return to the Remote Access Setup dialog.
6. Select and configure other RAS ports, if required. When you have configured all of the RAS ports necessary, click Continue from the Remote Access Setup dialog to redisplay the Network dialog. Windows NT configures, stores, and reviews the bindings. Restart the server to place your changes into effect.

After you enable the RAS ports for demand-dial, use Routing and RAS Admin to add and configure the demand-dial interface. Routing and RAS Admin includes the New Demand-dial Interface Wizard to lead you through the process of adding and configuring a demand-dial interface. To do so, take the following steps:

1. In Routing and RAS Admin, right-click the LAN and Demand Dial Interfaces item in the left pane to display the context-sensitive menu. Choose "Add Interface" to continue.

NOTE By default, RRAS uses the New Demand-dial Interface Wizard to add and configure demand-dial interfaces. If you want to add the interface manually, clear the check mark next to Use demand dial wizard before proceeding.

2. Routing and RAS Admin displays the first page of the New Demand-dial Interface Wizard. Enter a descriptive name for the new demand-dial interface and click Next to continue. If you prefer to work directly with the dialogs, mark the "I know all about demand-dial interfaces and would rather edit the properties directly" checkbox before you click Next.

3. Routing and RAS Admin displays the Protocols and Security page, shown in Figure 9-11. Mark the checkboxes as follows:

   Route IP packets on this interface
   Mark this checkbox if you want the demand-dial interface to route IP. This checkbox is marked by default if one or more IP routing protocols is installed in RRAS.

   Route IPX packets on this interface
   Mark this checkbox if you want the demand-dial interface to route IPX. This checkbox is marked by default if IPX routing is installed in RRAS.

   Add a user account so a remote router can dial in
   Mark this checkbox if (a) you are configuring this as an inbound interface (one that will be called by a remote dial-up router), or (b) if you want to use two-way authentication. By default, an RRAS router authenticates calls received from a remote router, but does not authenticate the remote router when placing calls. To enable two-way authentication for improved security, mark both this checkbox and the "Authenticate remote router when dialing out" checkbox when configuring an outbound interface.

   Send a plain-text password if that is the only way to connect
   Mark this checkbox when configuring an outbound interface if the destination router cannot authenticate with any of the authentication handshake protocols supported by RRAS.

   The non-Windows NT router that I am calling expects me to type login information after connecting, or to know TCP/IP addressing before dialing
   Mark this checkbox when configuring an outbound interface if the destination router requires manual or scripted login entries.

   After you finish configuring protocol and security options, click Next to continue.

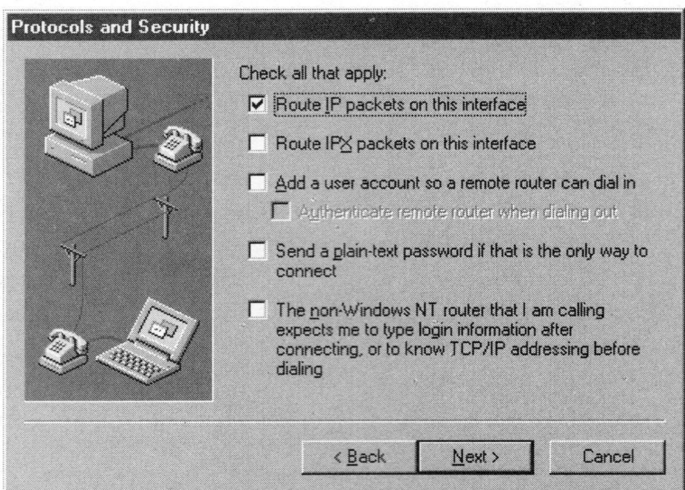

Figure 9-11. The Protocols and Security options

4. Routing and RAS Admin displays the Phone Number page. Enter the phone number for the remote router. If more than one phone number can be used to connect to it, click the Alternates button and provide information about these other phone numbers.
5. Routing and RAS Admin displays the Dial-Out Credentials page. Use this page to define the account information that this interface will use to log on to the remote router. This account information must exist on the remote router before a connection can be established. By default, RRAS fills in the Username field with the computer name. Enter appropriate values for Username and Domain, and complete the Password and Confirm password fields. Click Next to continue.

NOTE If you choose to configure this as an inbound interface by marking the "Add a user account so a remote router can dial in" checkbox earlier, the wizard next displays the Dial-In Credentials page. This page is nearly identical to the Dial-Out Credentials page, differing only in that the Username field is set to the name entered in the first page of the wizard, and cannot be changed. Use the Dial-In Credentials page to enter the information that will be supplied by the remote router when it dials into this interface.

---

6. Routing and RAS Admin displays the New Phonebook Entry Wizard page. If you're used to using Windows NT Wizards, you might reasonably think that you've completed the process, but you'd be wrong. You must select and configure a routing protocol for this interface before the job is complete. Click

Finish to exit the Wizard and invoke some ordinary, non-wizardly Windows NT dialogs.

7. Routing and RAS Admin displays the Select Routing Protocols dialog. Mark one or more of the checkboxes to indicate the routing protocols to be used for that interface, and then click on OK to display the IP Configuration dialog for the interface.
8. Set the IP configuration options and packet filter options as required, and click on OK to continue.
9. Routing and RAS Admin displays configuration dialogs for the routing protocol(s) you selected in the preceding step. Mark one or more of the checkboxes to indicate the routing protocols to be used for that interface, and then click on OK to finish adding the demand-dial interface.

If you use a demand-dial interface to connect a Windows NT Router to a third-party router, you may need to configure the Windows NT Router to request an IP address. To do so, choose Network in Control Panel and display the Services page. Highlight Routing and Remote Access Service, and click Properties to display the Remote Access Setup dialog. Click Network to display the Network Configuration dialog. In the Server Settings section, click TCP/IP Configure to display the RAS Server TCP/IP Configuration dialog. Mark the Allow remote clients to request a predetermined IP address checkbox. As usual, Windows NT configures, stores, and reviews the bindings. Also as usual, you need to reboot the server before the change takes effect.

Removing or disabling interfaces

You can use Routing and RAS Admin to disable an interface, to remove an interface from a routing protocol, or to remove an interface from the router. Which of these actions are available to you depends on the type of interface, as follows:

Disable an interface

Prevents the interface from placing or accepting calls, but does not remove the interface itself from the router or from the routing protocols that you have added it to. You can disable a demand-dial interface, but not a LAN interface. To disable a demand-dial interface, click LAN and Demand Dial Interfaces in the left pane of Routing and RAS Admin to display the available interfaces in the right pane. Right-click the interface to display the context-sensitive menu and choose Disable. To enable a disabled demand-dial interface, repeat this procedure, but choose Enable from the context-sensitive menu.

Remove an interface from a routing protocol

Removes the interface from the selected routing protocol, but allows the interface to continue functioning with other routing protocols. For example, if you had added RIP and the DHCP Relay Agent to an interface, you can remove that interface from the DHCP Relay Agent routing protocol and allow that interface to continue using the RIP routing protocol. You can remove either a demand-dial interface or a LAN interface from a routing protocol. To remove an interface from a routing protocol, click that routing protocol under IP Routing in the left pane of Routing and RAS Admin. The interfaces that have been added to that protocol are displayed in the right pane. Right-click the interface you want to remove to display the context-sensitive menu and choose Remove interface. You cannot remove an interface from a specific IPX routing protocol, but you can disable IPX routing for that interface.

NOTE You cannot remove a routing protocol with Routing and RAS Admin, but you can do so by using the *Routemon.exe* command line utility. To do so, open a command prompt and type one of the following commands:

```
routemon ip delete protocol proto= rip
routemon ip delete protocol proto= ospf
routemon ip delete protocol proto= bootp
```

Remove an interface from the router

Removes the interface from the router and from all routing protocols. The interface is no longer displayed in Routing and RAS Admin. You can remove a demand-dial interface, but not a LAN interface. To remove a demand-dial interface, click LAN and Demand Dial Interfaces in the left pane of Routing and RAS Admin to display the available interfaces in the right pane. Right-click the interface to display the context-sensitive menu and choose Remove Interface.

If you remove a demand-dial interface while the router is running, that interface is removed both from the Registry and from the phone book. If you remove a demand-dial interface while the router is stopped, that interface is removed from the Registry, but the phone book entry remains. If you then attempt to add that same interface, RRAS refuses to do so, informing you that the interface already exists. To resolve this problem, you must remove the phone book entry manually.

To do so, open the file *%systemroot%\system32\ras\Router.Pbk* with Notepad or another ASCII text editor. If you right-click this file and choose Open, Windows NT simply invokes the Dial-up Networking Wizard. Instead, press Shift before right-clicking, choose Open With, and select Notepad from the Open With dialog. Each phone book entry is delimited by the phone book entry name in square brackets, for example, [MyRemoteRouter]. Locate the beginning of the phone book entry for the deleted demand-dial interface, and delete that header and all lines in the file up to the beginning of the header for the next phone book entry, if any. Save the file and exit.

Managing static routes

A static route is a routing entry that is entered manually by an administrator, as opposed to a routing entry that is created and updated dynamically by a routing protocol. Static routes are typically used to enter fixed point-to-point routing information within a network. For example, you might create a static routing entry on a server that points to the border router for your network. RRAS supports static routes for both IP and IPX. You can manage static routes as follows:

View static routes
: In the left pane of Routing and RAS Admin, click IP Routing—Static Routes to display the static routes in the right pane. You can also right-click IP Routing—Static Routes and choose View IP routing table from the context-sensitive menu to display the IP routing table. To view IPX static routes, use the same procedure under IPX Routing.

Add a static route
: In the left pane of Routing and RAS Admin, right-click IP Routing—Static Routes and choose Add static route from the context-sensitive menu to display the Static Route dialog shown in Figure 9-12. Enter appropriate values for Destination, Network mask, and Gateway. Use the spinner to set an appropriate value for Metric. Use the Interface drop-down list to choose an available interface. Click on OK to add the static route.

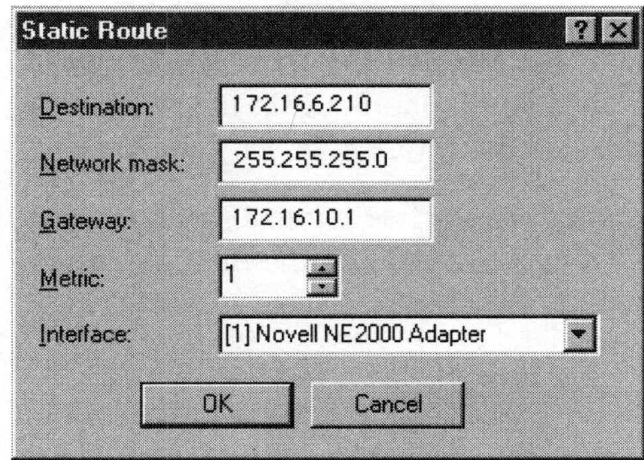

Figure 9-12. The Static Route dialog

Edit a static route
: In the left pane of Routing and RAS Admin, click IP Routing—Static Routes to display the static routes in the right pane. Right-click a static route to display the context-sensitive menu and choose Edit to display the Static Route dialog. Modify the values as necessary and click on OK to save the altered static route.

Remove a static route
: In the left pane of Routing and RAS Admin, click IP Routing—Static Routes to display the static routes in the right pane. Right-click a static route to display the context-sensitive menu and choose Remove.

Using packet filters

By default, RRAS routes IP packets regardless of their type or content. However, to improve security and control the types of traffic that can cross your router, you can configure RRAS to route or discard packets selectively based on their characteristics. This process is called IP packet filtering.

To implement IP packet filtering, you define a series of filters that specify the types of IP packets to *permit* or *deny* for an interface. Packets that match the criteria specified by a permit filter are processed by the router. Packets that match the criteria specified by a deny filter are discarded by the router. You can filter IP packets by source address, destination address, TCP port, UDP port, protocol ID, ICMP type, and ICMP code.

You can define a filter that combines these elements, for example, a filter that permits only specified types of TCP packets that originate from a particular source network. You can also define a filter that includes multiple definitions to permit or deny packets based on multiple criteria. Based on the combination of filter definitions in effect, the router forwards permitted packets and discards denied packets.

Different IP packet filters may be defined for inbound and outbound traffic. Input filters determine which packets arriving at the interface will be accepted and processed by the router and which will be discarded. Output filters determine which packets the router will place on the interface for forwarding to remote routers. Because you can define filters separately for inbound and outbound traffic, it is possible to define a combined set of filters that renders the interface effectively unusable. For example, if you define filters that permit inbound ftp traffic but deny outbound ftp traffic, ftp traffic cannot pass across the router.

If you're used to defining filters on a traditional router, defining RRAS filters may take a little getting used to. On the routers we've used, you define filtering components sequentially, something like:

```
permit a
permit b
permit c
deny all
```

When a packet arrives at the interface, it is compared sequentially against the filter definitions until a match occurs. The router takes the action (permit or deny) defined by the first match. For example, when a type b packet arrives at the router, it is compared against the first definition (permit a), which it fails to match. It is then compared against the second definition (permit b), which it does match. Because type b packets are permitted, the router forwards the packet.

The final definition serves as a catchall for packets that do not match any of the preceding definitions. For example, if a type d packet arrives at the router, it is compared against the first three definitions, none of which it matches. It does match the final definition, because type d is a subset of all, so the router discards the packet.

RRAS filtering works differently. You may define one inbound filter and one outbound filter. Although each of these can include multiple filtering definitions, you must define the filter as a whole globally as a permit filter or a deny filter. In other words, you can only have one inbound filter—permit or deny—and one outbound filter—permit or deny. RRAS matches the packet against all of the definitions that comprise the filter. If the packet matches at least one definition, RRAS takes the action (permit or deny) specified by the filter.

Before you can use IP packet filtering, you must enable it globally. To do so, in the left pane of Routing and RAS Admin, right-click IP Routing—Summary to display the context-sensitive menu. Choose Configure IP parameters to display the General page of IP Configuration dialog. Mark the "Enable packet-filtering" checkbox and click on OK to enable packet filtering globally.

The original Windows NT 4.0 distribution allows you to implement PPTP filtering and limited general TCP/IP packet filtering. To view these settings, choose Network → Protocols → TCP/IP Protocol → Properties → IP Address → Advanced to display the Advanced IP Addressing dialog. Once RRAS is installed, the setting of the Enable PPTP filtering checkbox is immaterial. If the Enable Security checkbox is marked, you can click Configure to view the TCP/IP Security dialog. Any filtering settings that are present in this dialog when RRAS was installed are converted to RRAS packet filters.

NOTE Be careful not to shoot yourself in the foot if you're running the Microsoft Proxy Server and RRAS with packet filtering enabled on the same machine. Configuring RRAS packet filters incorrectly can make it impossible for the Proxy Server to communicate with both clients on the local Intranet and with the public Internet.

If you want to run both RRAS and the Microsoft Proxy server on the same server, be sure to configure local host filters, as described later in this section.

Managing packet filters

Simply enabling packet filtering has no effect on the types of IP packets passed by the router. To route packets selectively, you must first define a filter. You can define a filter using any combination of Source network, Destination network, and

Protocol. If you define multiple settings for the filter, a packet must match all settings to match the filter. To define a packet filter, take the following steps:

1. In the left pane of Routing and RAS Admin, click IP Routing → Summary to list the available interfaces in the right pane. Right-click an interface to display the context-sensitive menu and choose Configure interface to display the IP Configuration dialog, shown in Figure 9-13.

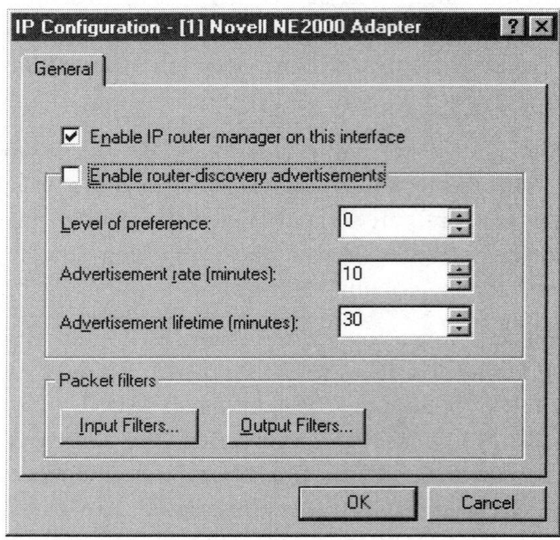

Figure 9-13. Setting packet filters

2. Click Input Filters or Output Filters to display the IP Packet Filters Configuration dialog. You can define separate input and output filters, but the steps and dialogs are identical for both.
3. The IP Packet Filters Configuration dialog displays any existing filters. To add a filter, click Add to display the Add/Edit IP Filter dialog, shown in Figure 9-14. To edit an existing filter, highlight the filter and click Edit. To delete a filter, highlight the filter and click Delete.
4. Set filter options as follows:
   - By default, packets from any source address match the filter. To filter traffic by specific source IP address, mark the Source network checkbox and enter an IP Address and Subnet mask.
   - By default, packets to any destination address match the filter. To filter traffic by specific destination IP address, mark the Destination network check box and enter an IP Address and Subnet mask.

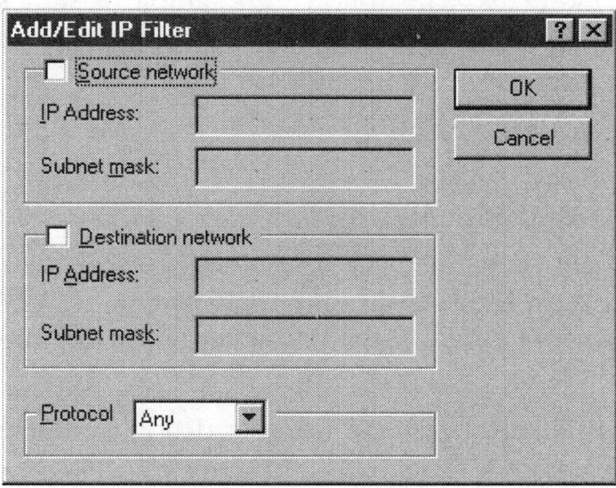

Figure 9-14. The Add/Edit IP Filters dialog

- By default, packets using *Any* protocol match the filter. To filter traffic by specific protocol, use the Protocol drop-down list to choose a protocol type: TCP, UDP, ICMP, or Other.
- If you choose TCP or UDP, enter the Source port and Destination port. Port number 0 is a wildcard. It matches any port number.
- If you choose ICMP, enter the ICMP type and ICMP code.
- If you choose Other, enter the Protocol.

NOTE Changes you make to packet filters take effect immediately, as we found by experience. For the following section on defining local host filters, we wanted to use the Class A private network address 10.0.0.0 for the example, rather than the Class B private network address we use in the other examples. We'd been capturing screens all morning on the computer running RRAS, and saving them to another server on our network, which runs TCP/IP transport. When we finished defining the filter for network 10.0.0.0, we attempted to capture the screen, only to receive an error message that the other server was unavailable. It's embarrassing to admit, but we'd rebooted the RRAS server and spent several minutes trying to figure out the problem before it hit us that we'd just defined a filter that made it impossible for the RRAS machine to communicate with the other server. Duh.

Defining a local host filter

A local host filter permits packets whose destination address is the RRAS computer and broadcast packets to the network of which the RRAS computer is a member to be forwarded, but does not permit packets to be routed through the

RRAS computer to other destination addresses. The following example assumes that your RRAS router is assigned the IP address 10.1.1.1 and the subnet mask 255.255.255.255. To define a local host filter for this configuration, you must define five separate input filters and specify the Drop all except listed below filter action. Do so as follows:

1. In the left pane of Routing and RAS Admin, click IP Routing → Summary to list the available interfaces in the right pane. Right-click an interface to display the context-sensitive menu and choose Configure interface to display the IP Configuration dialog. Click Input Filters to display the IP Packet Filters Configuration dialog.
2. Click Add to display the Add/Edit IP Filter dialog and use that dialog to define the first filter. Mark the Destination network checkbox, and specify 10.1.1.1 for the IP address, 255.255.255.255 for the Subnet mask, and Any for the Protocol. Click on OK to add the filter and redisplay the IP Packet Filters Configuration dialog. This filter permits packets whose destination IP address is that of the RRAS computer to be received.
3. Add a second filter, using 10.1.255.255 for the destination IP address, 255.255.255.255 for the Subnet mask, and Any for the Protocol. This filter permits packets to be broadcast to the local subnet of which the RRAS computer is a member.
4. Add a third filter, using 10.255.255.255 for the destination IP address, 255.255.255.255 for the Subnet mask, and Any for the Protocol. This filter permits packets to be broadcast to other subnets in the network of which the RRAS computer is a member.
5. Add a fourth filter, using 255.255.255.255 for the destination IP address, 255.255.255.255 for the Subnet mask, and Any for the Protocol. This filter permits broadcast packets (255.255.255.255) to reach any host on the network.
6. Add a fifth filter, using 224.0.0.0 for the destination IP address, 255.255.255.0 for the Subnet mask, and Any for the Protocol. This filter permits multicast packets.

Figure 9-15 shows the completed local host filter.

Managing PPTP filters

If you use PPTP to establish a virtual private network over the public Internet, you should take steps to secure the interface that PPTP is running on. Although the PPTP protocol itself is reasonably secure, the interface you run it on may be wide open. You can secure a PPTP link by defining filters for the interface used by that link to deny all traffic except PPTP packets. PPTP uses IP protocol ID 47 for data

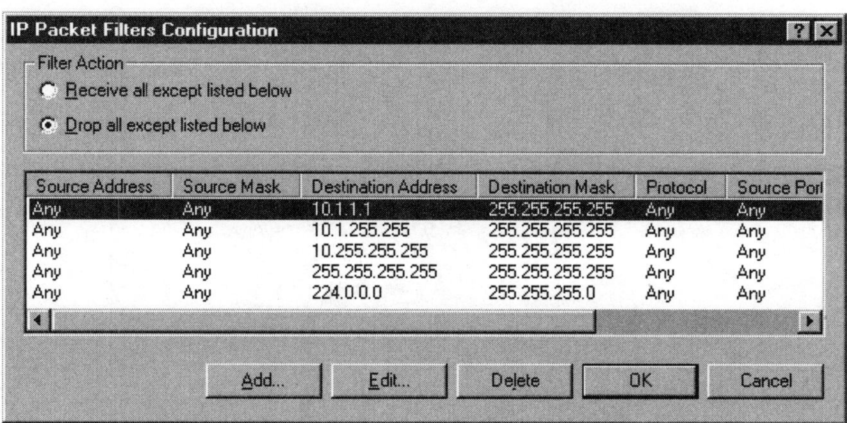
IP Packet Filters Configuration

Filter Action
- Receive all except listed below
- Drop all except listed below

Source Address	Source Mask	Destination Address	Destination Mask	Protocol	Source Port
Any	Any	10.1.1.1	255.255.255.255	Any	Any
Any	Any	10.1.255.255	255.255.255.255	Any	Any
Any	Any	10.255.255.255	255.255.255.255	Any	Any
Any	Any	255.255.255.255	255.255.255.255	Any	Any
Any	Any	224.0.0.0	255.255.255.0	Any	Any

Add... Edit... Delete OK Cancel

Figure 9-15. The completed local host filter for network 10.0.0.0

and TCP port 1723 for control. To do this, you must define three input filters and three output filters for the interface used by PPTP. All six of these filters must be defined correctly if the PPTP link is to be secure. To define a PPTP filter set, take the following steps:

1. In the left pane of Routing and RAS Admin, click IP Routing → Summary to list the available interfaces in the right pane. Right-click the demand-dial interface you are using for PPTP to display the context-sensitive menu. Choose Configure interface to display the IP Configuration dialog for that interface. Click Input Filters to display the IP Packet Filters Configuration dialog.
2. Click Add to display the Add/Edit IP Filter dialog and use that dialog to define the first input filter. Use the Protocol drop-down list to select Other. Enter 47 in the Protocol box and click on OK to save the filter.
3. Click Add to display the Add/Edit IP Filter dialog. Use the Protocol drop-down list to select TCP. Enter 1723 for the Source port and 0 for the Destination port. Click on OK to save the filter.
4. Click Add to display the Add/Edit IP Filter dialog. Use the Protocol drop-down list to select TCP. Enter 0 for the Source port and 1723 for the Destination port. Click on OK to save the filter and redisplay the IP Packet Filters Configuration dialog, shown in Figure 9-16.
5. Choose the Drop all except listed below option button to define the filter to deny all packets except those that meet the criteria you have just entered. Click on OK to redisplay the IP Configuration dialog for the interface.
6. With the three required input filters defined, the next step is to define the corresponding output filters. To begin, click Output Filters to display the IP Packet Filters Configuration dialog.

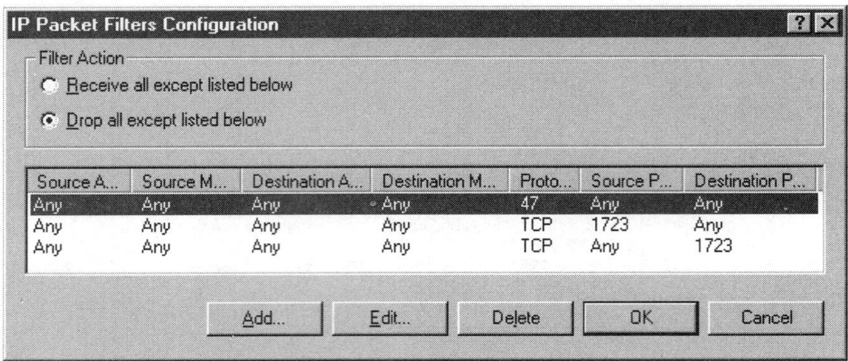

Figure 9-16. The completed PPTP input filter configuration

7. Click Add to display the Add/Edit IP Filter dialog and use that dialog to define the first output filter. Use the Protocol drop-down list to select Other. Enter 47 in the Protocol box and click on OK to save the filter.
8. Click Add to display the Add/Edit IP Filter dialog. Use the Protocol drop-down list to select TCP. Enter 1723 for the Source port and 0 for the Destination port. Click on OK to save the filter.
9. Click Add to display the Add/Edit IP Filter dialog. Use the Protocol drop-down list to select TCP. Enter 0 for the Source port and 1723 for the Destination port. Click on OK to save the filter and redisplay the IP Packet Filters Configuration dialog.
10. Choose the Drop all except listed below option button to define the filter to deny all packets except those that meet the criteria you have just entered. Click on OK to redisplay the IP Configuration dialog for the interface. Click on OK again to exit the IP Configuration dialog for the interface and place the PPTP filter set into effect.

Using Dial-Up Networking (DUN)

Dial-Up Networking (DUN) is the flip side of RAS. The RAS server uses Remote Access Service (a Windows NT service) to handle inbound calls from DUN clients, which may use Microsoft or third-party client software. DUN is a Windows client application that uses the RAS Service to place outbound calls to a remote RAS server, which may be a Windows NT RAS server, a third-party RAS Server, an Internet Service Provider, or a Unix host.

If you have installed and configured Microsoft Routing and RAS on Windows NT Server, DUN is also available on that server. All you need do is configure one or more of your RAS ports to allow outbound calls. If you have not installed RAS or

RRAS, you need to do so before using DUN. This section shows you how to install and configure RAS on a Windows NT Workstation computer (remember that RRAS requires Windows NT Server), create and configure phone book entries, and place DUN calls to a remote RAS server. If you have RRAS installed on Windows NT Server, you can use the same procedures described later in this section to create and configure phone book entries and to place DUN calls.

Installing and Configuring DUN

To install DUN, double-click the My Computer icon to display the My Computer folder. Then double-click Dial-Up Networking to display the Dial-Up Networking installation screen. If, as sometimes happens, someone has already installed DUN while you weren't looking, you'll instead see a phone book entry (or a prompt to create one).

Click the Install button to continue. Windows NT displays an information box to inform you that it is installing dial-up networking, and then copies files from the distribution CD-ROM. If the CD-ROM is not in the drive or it is unable to locate the distribution files for some other reason, it displays the Files Needed dialog to prompt you for the location of the Windows NT distribution files. Type the location of the distribution files in the Copy files from: box, or click the Browse button to search for them. After the RAS distribution files have been copied, Windows NT displays the Remote Access Setup dialog to inform you that no RAS-capable devices are installed.

Click Yes to invoke the Install New Modem Wizard. The opening screen of this Wizard lists the steps needed to prepare your modem for installation, and allows you to specify that you prefer to select the modem from a list, rather than having the Wizard attempt to detect it.

To choose your modem from a list, mark the "Don't detect my modem; I will select it from a list" checkbox. Otherwise, accept the default action, and click Next. The Wizard scans the Com: ports on your computer, attempting to detect installed modems. If the detection fails (which it does surprisingly often), the Wizard gives you another chance to pick your modem from a list.

Once you have detected or manually specified your modem, the Wizard displays the Location Information dialog. Enter your location, area code, and any number you dial to access an outside line. Accept the default Tone dialing, or mark the Pulse dialing option button and click Next to finish installing the modem. When modem installation is complete, RAS Setup displays the Add RAS Device dialog. Unless you want to add additional modems, click on OK to close this dialog and display the Remote Access Setup dialog, shown in Figure 9-17.

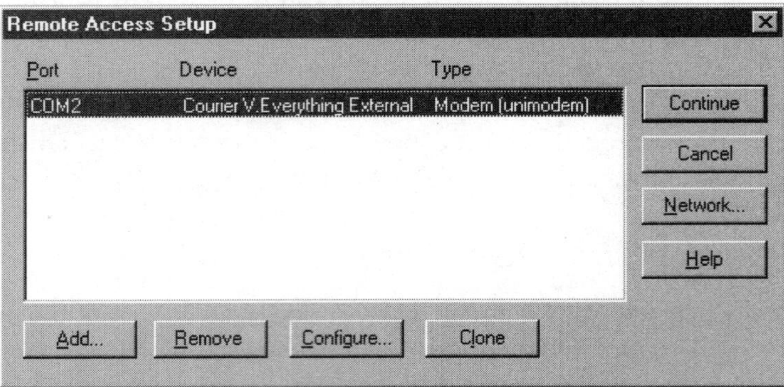

Figure 9-17. Configuring ports and network settings.

Click Configure to display the Configure Port Usage dialog. You can define port usage as Dial out only, Receive calls only, or Dial out and Receive calls. Receive calls only is useful only when you're configuring a RAS server. To use DUN, choose one of the other port usage options, and then click on OK to return to the Remote Access Setup dialog.

Click Network to display the Network Configuration dialog. Mark the checkboxes to specify the dial-out protocols that this port will support, which may be any combination of NetBEUI, TCP/IP, and IPX. After you specify the protocols, click on OK to return to the Remote Access Setup dialog. When you have finished configuring port usage and network settings, click Continue to finish installing DUN.

Remote Access Setup creates the necessary Registry settings. It then configures, stores, and reviews the bindings, and displays a message to inform you that DUN has been installed successfully. As usual, you have to restart the computer for the changes you have just made to take effect. Click the Restart button to reboot immediately, or click the Do Not Restart to defer the reboot.

TIP Because RAS Setup installs components from the original distribution CD-ROM, you should reinstall the latest Service Pack before proceeding to save yourself yet another reboot.

Creating a DUN Phone Book Entry

After DUN is installed, run it by double-clicking the My Computer icon on the desktop to display the My Computer folder and then double-clicking the Dial-Up Networking item. The first time you run DUN, it displays an information box to inform you that you have not yet created any phone book entries. Click on OK to invoke the New Phonebook Entry Wizard and add a phone book entry.

The first screen of the New Phonebook Entry Wizard prompts you for the name of the phone book entry. If you are familiar with the process of adding phone book entries, you can mark the "I know all about phone book entries and would rather edit the properties directly" checkbox to dispense with all the wizardry and do things the old-fashioned way. Real men don't use Wizards if they can help it. Neither do real women.

If you continue with the Wizard, it displays a screen where you can mark checkboxes to specify server settings. By default, none of these checkboxes is marked. Mark the checkboxes as follows:

I am calling the Internet
: Marking this box corresponds to choosing the PPP: Windows NT, Windows 95 Plus, Internet dial-up server type described later in this section. Mark this box if you are dialing an Internet Service Provider, or if you simply want to use PPP and TCP/IP for the connection. Clear this box only if you are unable to connect to the remote server when the box is marked.

Send my plain text password if that's the only way to connect
: Mark this box to allow Password Authentication Protocol (PAP), which sends unencrypted logon information. Leave this box unmarked if you are connecting to a Microsoft RAS server or another RAS server that supports CHAP or another encrypted handshake protocol. Mark this box only if you can't connect to the server when the box is cleared.

The non-Windows NT server I am calling expects me to type login information after connecting, or to know TCP/IP addresses before dialing
: Mark this checkbox if you are connecting to an old, non-Microsoft RAS server (typically, an old Unix box). Leave this box unmarked unless you are unable to connect otherwise.

After you complete the Server screen, click Next to display the Phone number screen. Enter the main phone number of the RAS server you're calling in the Phone number box. If you have more than one access phone number, click the Alternates button to display the Phone Numbers dialog. Enter the additional phone numbers in the New phone number list, and use the Up and Down buttons to arrange the order the numbers should be called in. Marking the "Move successful number to the top of the list on connection" checkbox, which is marked by default, causes the last access number successfully used to be moved automatically to the top of the list.

TIP

Using alternate phone numbers is particularly useful in one common situation. Many ISPs that support 56K modems have one relatively small hunt group of telephone lines equipped with 56K modems, and a much larger hunt group equipped with V.34 33.6K modems. Each of these hunt groups has a different telephone number, and you dial the number for the type of modem you want to connect to.

If you have a 56K modem and find that the number for 56K is often busy, you can define the 56K number as your main number, and the 33.6K number as your alternate. That way, DUN will attempt first to connect to the 56K hunt group. If those lines are busy, it will automatically dial the 33.6K hunt group number. If you clear the "Move successful number to the top of the list on connection" checkbox, DUN will always try the 56K number first, and fall back to the slower modem bank only when the 56K phone lines are all busy.

When you finish entering the phone number information and click Next, the Wizard displays a final screen to tell you that it has added the entry. Click Finish to complete adding the entry and display the Dial-Up Networking dialog, from which you can select a phone book entry, modify settings for it, or use it to connect to the remote server, as described in the following sections.

If you are using DUN on a notebook or other mobile computer, note the Location button. You can use this button to define multiple dialing locations for the same phone book entry. Each dialing location uses the same main telephone number, but allows you to add a prefix and/or suffix string to that main number.

For example, we created a phone book entry to dial our ISP, BellSouth. If we were using DUN on a notebook, we might want to define several locations from which we call BellSouth. At home, we might need to dial just the main number, 724-1160, because it's a local call. At a friend's house, we might always dial 70# to disable call waiting before dialing 724-1160. At the main office, we might need to dial 9 to get an outside line before dialing 724-1160. At a branch office located in another city, we might need to dial 1 and the area code before dialing 724-1160. By defining a dialing location for each of these locations, we can specify for each the exact prefix and/or postfix required to place a call to BellSouth from that location.

Modifying Properties for a Phone Book Entry

To modify the properties for a phone book entry, display the Dial-Up Networking dialog, use the "Phonebook entry to dial" drop-down list to select the entry, and then click More. The Dial-Up Network dialog presents a drop-down menu that offers the following options:

Edit entry and modem properties
: Use this option to configure the phone book entry. It is described in detail in the following section.

Clone entry and modem properties
: Choose this option to replicate the settings for a phone book entry to a new entry with a different name. You may alter these default settings before saving the new entry.

Delete entry
: Remove the selected entry from the phone book.

Create shortcut to entry
: Display an icon for this entry on the desktop, allowing you to dial it directly from the desktop.

Monitor status
: Display the Dial-Up Networking Monitor, which displays various statistics for the device and the connection, and allows you to set preferences for the connection.

Operator assisted or manual dialing
: This option is a toggle. When you select it, a check mark appears next to the menu item to indicate that it is enabled. Use this option if you need to dial the phone number manually, for example, via a manual switchboard.

User Preferences
: Displays a tabbed dialog that allows you to set Dialing, Callback, Appearance, and Phonebook options for DUN calls placed by a user.

Logon preferences
: Displays a similar dialog to User Preferences, but controls calls placed by Windows NT when you elect to log on using Dial-Up Networking at the Ctrl-Alt-Del logon dialog.

Edit Phonebook Entry—Basic page

When you choose the "Edit entry and modem properties" option from the More menu, DUN displays the tabbed Edit Phonebook Entry dialog. The Basic page allows you to specify the following settings:

Entry name and Comment
: Free text boxes you use to describe the entry.

Phone number
: The main telephone number for the phone book entry. Click the Alternates button to enter and configure additional telephone numbers, as described

previously. Mark the "Use Telephony Dialing properties" checkbox to display separate fields for country code, area code, and phone number.

Dial using
: Use this drop-down list to associate a modem or other communications device with the entry. Click the Configure button to display the Modem Configuration dialog for the selected device, where you can change settings for speed, hardware flow control, error control, compression, and so on. You can also use this dialog to turn off the modem speaker. If you have more than one RAS-capable device installed and if you mark the "Use another port if busy" checkbox, DUN will use the other device if the selected device is already in use when you attempt to place a DUN call.

Edit entry and modem properties—Server page

Click the Server tab to display the Server page of the Edit Phonebook Entry dialog, shown in Figure 9-18. You use the Server page to specify what type of dial-up server you will be connecting to and to choose transport protocols for the connection. Use the "Dial-up server type" drop-down list to specify the type of dial-up server you will connect to. What you're really choosing here is the dial-up protocol for the connection—PPP, SLIP, or AsyBEUI. Choose one of the following server types:

PPP: Windows NT, Windows 95 Plus, Internet
: PPP (Point-to-Point Protocol) is the dominant dial-up protocol these days, so this server type is the default choice and the one you'll usually use. It supports any or all of the three transport protocols available in any combination. The "Enable software compression" and "Enable PPP LCP" extensions checkboxes are marked by default. Leave them marked unless you have problems connecting to the dial-up server.

SLIP: Internet
: SLIP (Serial Line Internet Protocol) is a predecessor to PPP, and has been almost completely replaced by it. SLIP is simple and fast, but lacks the features and options of PPP. Choose SLIP only if you're calling a Unix host that doesn't support PPP—an almost unheard of situation nowadays. All protocols except TCP/IP gray out, as do the "Enable software compression" and "Enable PPP LCP extensions" checkboxes.

Windows NT 3.1, Windows for Workgroups 3.11
: These systems use a proprietary Microsoft protocol called AsyBEUI, which is basically NetBEUI hacked to operate on asynchronous dial-up connections. Choose this server type only if you're dialing in to an old Windows NT 3.1 server, or to a Windows 3.11 for Workgroups computer set up to receive calls. All protocol options except NetBEUI gray out. Only the "Enable software compression" checkbox remains active, and it is enabled by default.

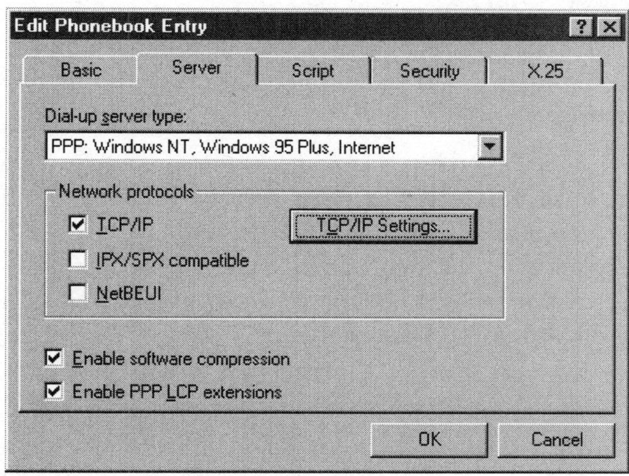

Figure 9-18. Specifying the dial-up server

If you specify SLIP or PPP with TCP/IP enabled, click the TCP/IP Settings button to display the PPP TCP/IP Settings dialog. Set the following options:

IP address
: By default, DUN uses an IP address provided by the remote server. To specify an IP address, mark the "Specify an IP address" option button and enter the IP address.

Name server addresses
: By default, DUN uses DNS and WINS server addresses provided by the remote server. To specify the IP addresses for the name servers yourself, mark the Specify name server addresses option button and enter the IP addresses for each of them.

Use IP header compression
: Marking this checkbox, which is enabled by default, causes DUN to compress the headers of IP packets—a measure intended to improve throughput on slow links. We've never noticed any change in throughput whether this box is marked or not, so we leave it in its default state.

Use default gateway on remote network
: Marking this checkbox, which is marked by default, causes the DUN connection to use the remote server as the default router for the DUN connection. Clearing this checkbox causes DUN to use the default gateway specified in the TCP/IP configuration for Windows NT. For normal dial-up purposes, leave this checkbox marked.

Edit entry and modem properties—Script page

Click the Script tab to display the Script page of the Edit Phonebook Entry dialog. Use the Script page to specify how DUN will handle logging on to the remote server. Choose one of the following:

None
: Choose this option button, which is selected by default, if you do not want to run a script or enter logon information manually. When a Windows DUN client calls a Windows NT RAS server, all logon activity takes place automatically, so this is the proper choice for that environment. Also, nearly all ISPs support automatic logon from Windows DUN clients.

Pop up a terminal window
: Choose this option button if the remote server you are calling does not support automatic logon from a DUN client, and you do not want to write a script to log on automatically. Each time you place a call to this server, DUN will pause during logon and display a terminal screen where you can enter your account name and password manually before completing the logon.

Run this script
: Choose this option button if the remote server you are calling does not support automatic logon from a DUN client, and you prefer to write a script to log on automatically instead of manually entering your logon information each time. Each time you place a call to this server, DUN runs the selected script to log you on. If you mark this option button, use the drop-down list to select an existing script, or click the Edit Script button to invoke Notepad and display *switch.inf*, which details the process of creating a script.

These option buttons control the actions that DUN takes after the call is dialed and the connection to the remote server established. You can also click the Before Dialing button to display the Before Dialing Script dialog, which allows you to configure similar options for actions that occur before the call is dialed.

Edit entry and modem properties—Security page

Click the Security tab to display the Security page of the Edit Phonebook Entry dialog. Use the Security page to specify how DUN will handle authentication and encryption. Choose one of the following:

Accept any authentication including plain text
: Choose this option button, which is selected by default, to use Password Authentication Protocol (PAP), which transmits your login information unencrypted. In practical terms, the security risk of sending your password unencrypted across a dial-up connection is relatively small. If you are concerned, however, choose this option only if the remote server will not authenticate you with one of the other options.

Accept only encrypted authentication

Choose this option to use Challenge Handshake Authentication Protocol (CHAP), a standard protocol that encrypts your login information. This option is useful for connecting to non-Microsoft remote access servers that support CHAP. CHAP encrypts only the login handshake—not the data that subsequently crosses the connection.

Accept only Microsoft encrypted authentication

Choose this option to use Microsoft Challenge Handshake Authentication Protocol (MS-CHAP), a proprietary Microsoft version of the standard CHAP protocol. Use this option to connect to a Microsoft RAS Server. Mark the Require data encryption checkbox to encrypt all data that crosses the connection, rather than just the login handshake. Mark the Use current username and password checkbox to use your current login information rather than be prompted for logon information when DUN connects to the remote server.

The first time you connect to a remote server, DUN raises a dialog to prompt you for your username, password, and domain. Marking a checkbox on that dialog allows you to save your password with the phone book entry, so you won't be prompted to provide it on subsequent calls.

If you choose that option, you can click the Unsave password button in this dialog to remove your password information from the phone book entry so that you will again be prompted for your login information when you next dial that phone book entry.

You might do this, for example, if your password changes on the remote server. When the dialog appears, you can enter the new login information, tell DUN to save your password, and not be bothered again for it until the next time you use this process to change it.

Edit entry and modem properties—X.25 page

The X.25 page of the Edit Phonebook Entry dialog allows you to configure X.25. X.25 is a data communications connection method that is essentially obsolete in the United States and other industrial nations, but is still used in undeveloped countries. For more information about configuring DUN to use an X.25 connection with DUN, contact your X.25 provider.

Dialing a Call with DUN

After you have created and configured a phone book entry, dial it by taking the following steps:

1. Double-click the My Computer icon on your desktop to display the My Computer folder.

2. Double-click the Dial-Up Networking item to display the Dial-Up Networking dialog.
3. Use the Phonebook entry to access the drop-down list to choose the entry you want to dial.
4. Click Dial to place the call.

TIP To place icons for phone book entries that you call frequently on your desktop, take the first three steps above to select a phone book entry, click More to display the menu, and choose the Create shortcut to entry menu item. DUN creates a desktop icon for that entry, which you can dial just by double-clicking the icon.

Although DUN logs you in automatically when you call a remote Microsoft RAS server (and most ISPs) by default, you'll need to provide your logon information initially. The first time you call a particular server, DUN displays the Connect to <phonebook entry name> dialog shown in Figure 9-19. Enter your username, password, and Windows NT domain (if applicable), and click on OK to complete the connection. If you mark the Save password checkbox before you click on OK, DUN saves your account information with the phone book entry, and you will not have to enter login information for this phone book entry again until your password or other information changes.

Figure 9-19. The Connect to <phonebook entry name>

Summary

Microsoft Routing and RAS (RRAS) is an upgrade to the Remote Access Service (RAS) and Multiprotocol Routing service (MPR) bundled with the Windows NT Server 4.0 distribution. RRAS provides minor enhancements to RAS, and a complete overhaul of the primitive routing capabilities provided by MPR. RRAS Routing provides features comparable to a low-end dedicated router, and can be used to provide routing functionality in small branch offices and other situations where installing a dedicated router is not an option.

RRAS includes the Routing and RAS Admin tool to provide unified management of RAS and routing. The Routing and RAS Admin tool replaces the RAS Admin tool used to manage RAS and the command line management used by MPR.

In the next chapter we look at Internet Information Server (IIS), Microsoft's server-side solution to providing HTTP, FTP, SMTP, and other services to Intranet and Internet clients.

10

In this chapter:
- *IIS Components*
- *Installing IIS*
- *Configuring IIS*
- *Managing IIS*
- *Summary*

Internet Information Server (IIS)

Microsoft jumps into anything they do with both feet. When Microsoft belatedly noticed the Internet phenomenon, they were caught with their collective pants down. Without any products to address the needs of this exploding new market segment, they believed themselves to be in danger of losing market share to the new guys on the block—read Netscape. As anyone familiar with Microsoft might guess, they pulled out all the stops to get competitive products to market as soon as possible. On the client side, they bought rights to a third-party web browser, renamed it Internet Explorer, and turned it into a world-class browser in record time. On the server side, they created a multi-purpose product called Internet Information Server, or IIS for short.

IIS has grown in Internet time. Microsoft cobbled together a quick and dirty IIS 1.0 and released it as an update to Windows NT Server 3.51. It wasn't much more than a placeholder, but at least it got the ball rolling. When Windows NT Server 4.0 was released, it bundled IIS 2.0, a significant upgrade that filled most of the gaping holes and killed most of the bugs in IIS 1.0. Still, the major third-party web server vendors like Netscape and O'Reilly weren't too worried—IIS2 couldn't compete with their feature sets.

When Microsoft shipped IIS3, the third party vendors started to sweat. Microsoft was giving away a product that compared favorably in features and performance with their expensive commercial products. Even worse, Microsoft started to ship free supporting components, like Index Server, that made IIS a complete server-side Internet solution.

At this point, the way things are headed is pretty clear. The release of IIS4 as a part of the Windows NT 4.0 Option Pack, which shipped in Q1 1998, may well be the final nail in the coffin of the commercial web server vendors. The majority of

Internet web servers are now running either IIS or the free Apache server. When you consider private Intranet servers, the proportion running IIS is even higher.

The Web, FTP, and email are where the action is on the Internet today. Depending on whose figures you believe, something close to 99 percent of the current traffic on the Internet is web-, ftp-, or email-related. As IP telephony becomes more popular, that may change, but for now at least it is true. IIS4 provides an excellent no-cost server-side solution for all three of these core Internet services.

NOTE To understate the case, IIS4 is a major application, with supporting applications that are major applications in themselves. Covering IIS thoroughly would require an entire book—or several books. Accordingly, this chapter focuses on getting started with IIS—the essentials of installing and configuring the web, FTP, and SMTP components of IIS at the overview level. For a book-length treatment of this topic, see any of the numerous books devoted to it.

IIS Components

The IIS4 distribution, which is contained within the Windows NT 4.0 Option pack, contains the following major functional IIS components:

World Wide Web (WWW) Service
: A standards-compliant HTTP (web) server.

File Transfer Protocol (FTP) Service
: A standards-compliant FTP server.

Simple Mail Transfer Protocol (SMTP) Service
: A standards-compliant SMTP relay server.

Network News Transport Protocol (NNTP) Service
: A standards-compliant NNTP (news) server. The NNTP Service is not installed by default, and we do not cover it in this chapter.

The IIS distribution also includes the following management tools:

Internet Service Manager (ISM)
: The main management tool for IIS and the other applications included in the Windows NT 4.0 Option Pack. You can use ISM to manage IIS on the local IIS server, from another computer on the network, or across the Internet. ISM is a snap-in for the Microsoft Management Console (MMC).

NOTE MMC is a Windows NT 5.0 component that provides an application framework for small dedicated utilities—called snap-ins—that perform management functions for a particular application. For example, you use MMC to manage IIS by loading the ISM snap-in into MMC. Windows NT 5.0 will include snap-ins that replace the patchwork quilt of individual management tools, for example, User Manager for Domains and Server Manager, used by Windows NT 4.0. Like Routing and RAS, MMC is a Windows NT 5.0 technology that Microsoft has released as an upgrade to Windows NT 4.0.

Internet Service Manager (HTML)
: A browser-based management tool that provides most ISM functions. You can use ISM (HTML) to manage IIS on the local IIS server, from another computer on the network, or across the Internet.

In addition, the Windows NT 4.0 Option Pack distribution includes the following components which are not a part of IIS, but provide supporting functionality:

Certificate Server
: Manages the digital certificates used by IIS to provide server and client authentication with the SSL (Secure Sockets Layer) and PCT (Private Communication Technology) protocols.

FrontPage 98 Server Extensions
: Server-based extensions that allow FrontPage clients and IIS to operate as a client-server pair.

Internet Connection Services for RAS
: Supplements and extends basic RAS with tools that provide a customizable dialer, centralized phone book administration, and RADIUS support.

Microsoft Data Access Components 1.5
: Includes ActiveX Data Objects (ADO), Remote Data Service (RDS), the Microsoft OLE DB Provider for ODBC, and Open Database Connectivity (ODBC) components that can be used to provide client/server applications with access to data on remote servers.

Microsoft Index Server
: Indexes documents on an IIS web site, and allows client browsers to search the web site by using an HTML query form.

Microsoft Management Console (MMC)
: Provides the framework for the application-specific management tools for Option Pack components, including IIS4, Index Server, and Transaction Server. MMC is a general-purpose template manager that uses programs called snap-ins to manage specific components. For example, the Internet Service

Manager (ISM) application is actually a snap-in that runs under the MMC framework. Just think of MMC as the socket wrench and the snap-ins as the sockets. In addition to the MMC-based management tools that can be used locally or across the network, IIS4 and Index Server both include HTML-based tools that allow administrators to use a limited subset of management functions from a web browser.

Microsoft Message Queue (MSMQ)
: Allows applications to communicate asynchronously with other applications by sending and receiving messages.

Microsoft Script Debugger
: Debugger for ASP pages that contain VBScript, JScript, or Java scripts. You can also use Microsoft Script Debugger to debug scripts written in other scripting languages, for example, Perl or REXX, that support host-independent debugging.

Microsoft Site Server Express
: A functionally limited version of the commercial Microsoft Site Server product that provides site and usage analysis, the Posting Acceptor, and the Web Publishing Wizard.

Microsoft Transaction Server (MTS)
: A component-based transaction processing system that you can use to develop, deploy, and manage server-based applications. MTS provides a run-time environment and GUI-based administration tool for managing applications.

Windows Scripting Host (WSH)
: Allows you to perform common administrative tasks from the command line. WSH is a language-independent scripting host for 32-bit Windows platforms. Presently, WSH uses only the VBScript and JScript scripting engines supplied by Microsoft. However, it is likely that other companies will soon provide Active-X scripting engines for other scripting languages like Perl and REXX.

Installing IIS

Installing IIS4 is a relatively straightforward (albeit time consuming) multi-step process. After you obtain the IIS4 distribution files and prepare your server, you install Internet Explorer 4.01 or higher and then run IIS4 Setup. Because installing IIS4 may require unloading services that may be needed by users and because it requires at least two system restarts, you may want to schedule the installation outside normal working hours unless you are installing IIS4 on a dedicated server. The remainder of this section details the steps necessary to install IIS4.

Obtaining Distribution Files

Installing IIS4 on a stock Windows NT Server 4.0 computer requires three sets of distribution files. Windows NT 4.0 Service Pack 3 or later and Internet Explorer 4.01 or later must be installed on the computer before you can install the Windows NT 4.0 Option Pack. IE4 requires SP3, and includes numerous dynamic link library files that provide various functions (i.e. the Microsoft Management Console) that are required by IIS4. You can obtain these distribution files by ordering them on CD-ROM from Microsoft, or by downloading them from the Microsoft Web site at the addresses shown.

Windows NT 4.0 Service Pack 3—http://backoffice.microsoft.com/downtrial/moreinfo/nt4sp3.asp

This single 18 MB file typically requires 150 minutes to download at 28.8, or about 30 minutes via ISDN.

Internet Explorer 4.01—http://www.microsoft.com/ie/download/

This single 12 MB file typically requires 100 minutes to download at 28.8, or about 20 minutes via ISDN.

Windows NT 4.0 Option Pack—http://backoffice.microsoft.com/downtrial/optionpack.asp

You may download this as a single file, which the Microsoft Web site assembles on the fly based on the components you specify. If you choose all components, this file is about 77 MB, which requires about 10 hours to download via 28.8, or 2 hours via ISDN. Alternatively, Microsoft provides a mechanism that allows you to download a small executable agent that retrieves the component files individually. If you use this agent and the connection fails during the download, you can simply rerun the agent to retrieve only the files that have not yet been downloaded.

Preparing the Server

In theory, IIS4 has no special hardware requirements beyond those of Windows NT Server 4.0 itself, other than the requisite disk space on the volume where IIS4 is to be installed. In practice, IIS hardware requirements may run the gamut from nothing much to a dedicated high-end multiprocessor server.

The server resources you need to run IIS4 depend entirely on what you will do with it. Unfortunately, there are no hard and fast rules for determining whether a server is adequate to run IIS4 in your own environment. You can use the following rules of thumb:

- Microsoft states that the minimum server required to run IIS4 is a 486/66 with 32 MB RAM and that the recommended server is a Pentium/90 with 64 MB of

RAM. In fact, attempting to run on the minimum server configuration results in delays of literally a minute or more just waiting for administrative screens to update. Consider Microsoft's recommended configuration to be the absolute minimum. A more realistic configuration for a production server is a 200 MHz Pentium or greater with 64 MB of RAM. If that server will also be used for other purposes, consider installing at least 128 MB of RAM.

- If your current server has a reasonable amount of spare capacity and all you plan to do with IIS4 is serve static HTML pages to a relatively small number of users, you may be able to run IIS4 on your current server, as long as it meets or exceeds the recommended minimums for processor and memory.
- If IIS4 will deliver active content, run ISAPI or CGI scripts to access a back-end database, and serve many users, you may need to install it on a dedicated server. Alternatively, you may find that adding a processor and some additional RAM to your current server will allow it shoulder the load IIS puts on it.
- Although it has a minimal memory footprint when running lightly loaded, like most applications, IIS likes memory. Consider installing additional RAM to improve IIS4 caching and minimize disk accesses to retrieve content.
- Although you can use bandwidth throttling to limit the amount of network bandwidth consumed by IIS, consider users' bandwidth requirements when sizing the server. In general, if IIS itself is consuming a T1 (1.544 Mbps) or equivalent, consider running IIS on a dedicated server.

In practical terms, choosing an IIS4 server involves a Catch-22: IIS4 provides tools that you can use to analyze its requirements, but you must install and run IIS4 to use these tools. After you decide—by whatever means—which server you will use to run IIS4, take the following steps to prepare that server to install IIS4:

1. Make sure the Computer Browser and NetLogon services are running on the server, which they are by default. If they are not running, use the Control Panel Services tool to start these services and to reset their startup settings so that they run automatically when you start the server.
2. If an earlier version of IIS4 (IIS4 Alpha, Beta 1, or Beta 2) is installed on the server, remove it before you install the release version of IIS4 from the Option Pack. You can remove the earlier version by running Setup from the earlier distribution CD-ROM. Or, run Start → Programs → Microsoft Internet Information Server (Common) → Internet Information Server Setup. Choose Next and then click Remove All.
3. IIS4 Setup updates ODBC. If any applications or system services that use ODBC are running, stop them before installing IIS4.

4. Install any additional hardware components, drivers, system services, and protocols you plan to use on the IIS4 server.
5. Install Service Pack 3, and restart the computer.
6. Install Internet Explorer 4.01 or higher, and restart the computer.

Installing the Windows NT 4.0 Option Pack

After you finish preparing the server, you are ready to install the Windows NT 4.0 Option Pack. To do so, log on as an administrator on the server where IIS is to be installed, and run *setup.exe* from the Option Pack distribution CD-ROM or from the folder to which you downloaded the Option Pack files. Option Pack Setup first displays an opening screen that lists the components included in the option pack. Click Next to display a license agreement. After you accept the terms, Setup displays a dialog that prompts you to specify the type of installation, as follows:

Minimum
: Installs only the files needed to provide basic web server functionality.

Typical
: Installs all of the components included in the Minimum installation, plus documentation, FTP Service, the HTML version of the Internet Service Manager, the SMTP Service, the Microsoft Script Debugger, and the Windows Scripting Host.

Custom
: Allows you to specify which components will be installed. The components included in the Typical installation are selected by default.

Table 10-1 lists the individual components and subcomponents in the Option Pack. The components installed with each setup type are indicated by a filled square.

Table 10-1. Windows NT 4.0 Option Pack Components

	MB	Min	Typical
Certificate Server			
Certificate Server Certificate Authority	0.5	❏	❏
Certificate Server Documentation	1.2	❏	❏
Certificate Server Web Client	0.7	❏	❏
FrontPage 98 Server Extensions	**2.5**	■	■
Internet Connection Services for RAS			
Connection Manager Administration Kit	4.6	❏	❏
Connection Point Services	5.0	❏	❏
Internet Authenticaion Services	6.1	❏	❏
Product Documentation	1.2	❏	❏

Table 10-1. Windows NT 4.0 Option Pack Components (continued)

	MB	Min	Typical
Internet Information Server (IIS)			
Documentation			
Active Server Pages	5.4	❑	■
Common Documentation Files	0.8	❑	■
IIS Administrator's Documentation	5.1	❑	■
SDK	5.4	❑	❑
Streaming Multimedia	16.8	❑	❑
File Transfer Protocol (FTP) Server	0.1	❑	■
Internet NNTP Service			
NNTP Service	2.8	❑	❑
NNTP Service Documentation	0.6	❑	❑
Internet Service Manager	1.5	■	■
Internet Service Manager (HTML)	0.6	❑	■
SMTP Service			
STMP Documentation	0.7	❑	■
STMP Service	3.2	❑	■
World Wide Web Sample Site	3.5	❑	❑
World Wide Web Server	2.7	■	■
Microsoft Data Access Components 1.5			
Data Sources			
Jet and Access (ODBC)	2.6	■	■
Oracle	0.2	■	■
SQL Server	1.1	■	■
MDAC: ADO, ODBC, and OLE DB			
ADO Documentation	0.8	❑	■
MDAC Core Files: ADO, ODBC, and OLE DB	3.7	■	■
Remote Data Service 1.5 (RDS/ADC)			
RDS Core Files	0.3	■	■
RDS Documents	0.5	❑	■
RDS Samples	0.8	❑	■
RDS v1.1 Files	0.7	❑	❑
Microsoft Index Server			
Index Server System Files	0.0	■	■
Language Resources		❑	❑
Dutch Language	1.3	❑	❑
French Language	1.1	❑	❑
German Language	1.6	❑	❑

Table 10-1. Windows NT 4.0 Option Pack Components (continued)

	MB	Min	Typical
Italian Language	1.1	❑	❑
Japanese Language	0.5	❑	❑
Spanish Modern Language	1.0	❑	❑
Swedish Language	1.2	❑	❑
UK English Language	1.2	❑	❑
US English Language	1.2	■	■
Online Documentation	1.1	■	■
Sample Files	0.3	■	■
Microsoft Management Console	**1.0**	■	■
Microsoft Message Queue			
Administration Tools	0.9	❑	❑
HTML Documentation	2.8	❑	❑
Microsoft Message Queue Core	8.5	❑	❑
Software Development Kit	4.4	❑	❑
Microsoft Script Debugger	**1.7**	❑	■
Microsoft Site Server Express			
Analysis—Content	4.0	❑	❑
Analysis—Usage	15.9	❑	❑
Publishing—Posting Acceptor 1.0	10.0	❑	❑
Publishing—Web Publishing Wizard 1.52	7.0	❑	❑
NT Option Pack Common Files	**3.2**	■	■
Transaction Server			
Transaction Server Core Components	12.1	■	■
Transaction Server Core Documentation	1.9	■	■
Transaction Server Development			
Transaction Server Development	1.5	❑	❑
Transaction Server Development Documentation	1.6	❑	❑
Visual Basic Transaction Server Add-In	0.0	❑	❑
Visual InterDev RAD Remote Deployment Support	**0.1**	❑	❑
Windows Scripting Host	**0.5**	❑	■

WARNING If you are installing the Option Pack to a server that is configured as a Backup Domain Controller (BDC), you must use Custom Setup and deselect Index Server and the World Wide Web Sample Site options. You can add either or both of these options later by using Option Pack Setup to install them manually.

If you select the Custom installation type, you are next given the opportunity to specify the individual components you want to install. If you select the Minimum or Typical installation types, Setup proceeds directly to configuring the locations for system files. Setup first presents a dialog to prompt you for locations for the WWW public root folder, the FTP public root folder, and the folder that will contain the IIS4 program files folder. Accept the defaults, or browse for other locations. By default, Setup creates the folders *\Inetpub\wwwroot* and *\Inetpub\ftproot* on the system drive, in this case *E:*. If a folder does not exist, Setup creates it without prompting for permission to do so.

After you complete this dialog and click Next, Setup displays an SMTP Service dialog to prompt you for the location of the Mailroot directory. (You'd think by this time that Microsoft would have decided whether to call them folders or directories). By default, Setup creates the directory *\Inetpub\Mailroot* on the system drive, and creates mail queue, mailbox, and badmail directories under this directory. Accept the default location or browse for another location, and click Next to continue.

Setup next displays a dialog to notify you of progress as it builds a file list, copies the necessary files, and creates the default web and FTP sites. Microsoft says that this process may take several minutes, depending on the options you choose to install. This appears to be an understatement. When we did a Typical IIS4 install on a test-bed server (a 486/66 with 48 MB), this process required 45 minutes—and the server was doing nothing else at the time. Thinking that perhaps this server was simply too slow, we tried another install—this time with all options selected—to a very lightly loaded 200 MHz Pentium server with 64 MB RAM. Half an hour later, it was still chugging away when we killed the install.

After setup completes and you restart the server, the Content Index, FTP Publishing Service, IIS Admin Service, Microsoft SMTP Service, MSDTC, Protected Storage, and World Wide Web Publishing Service services—and any other services required to support options you selected in Custom setup—are started automatically.

Post-Installation Activities

After you install the Option Pack and restart the server, you may need to take some or all of the following steps to complete the installation:

Reinstall Microsoft Proxy Server
: IIS4 is incompatible with Microsoft Proxy Server 1.0 and with existing Microsoft Proxy Server 2.0 installations. If you want to run Microsoft Proxy Server, install or reinstall version 2.0 after you complete the IIS4 installation.

Verify privileges on the anonymous user account

Installing IIS4 creates a user account for anonymous access. By default, this account is named IUSR_<computer-name>. For example, when we installed IIS on the server *bastet*, Setup created the account IUSR_BASTET. This is a standard Windows NT user account that IIS uses to provide web and FTP clients with access to shared resources. Use User Manager for Domains to verify that this account does not have privileges in excess of those you wish to grant. Note that this account is automatically granted the "Log on locally" user right, which is required. Revoking this user right prevents anonymous web and FTP clients from accessing any resources on the server, and effectively disables the WWW and FTP services.

Verify privileges on the Web Application Manager user account

Installing IIS4 creates a user account for using the web-based administration tools. By default, this account is named IWAM_<computer-name>. For example, when we installed IIS on the server *bastet*, Setup created the account IWAM_BASTET. Use User Manager for Domains to verify that this account does not have privileges in excess of those you wish to grant. Note that this account is automatically granted the "Log on locally" user right, which is required.

Verify permissions on the public directories

Installing IIS4 creates the *\Inetpub* directory and subdirectories for the various installed services on the drive where you install IIS. Verify that permissions on these directories are correct.

Add components to a BDC IIS server

If you used the Custom installation type to install IIS on a BDC, and you want to run Index Server or the Sample Web Site on that server, add these components using the procedure described later in this section. Note that the Sample Web Site application requires SQL Server 6.5.

Create DNS CNAME records

When you install IIS on a computer that has been assigned only one IP address in the Control Panel Network tool, IIS automatically routes HTTP (web) requests directed to that IP address to the WWW Service on that computer, FTP requests to the FTP Service, and SMTP traffic to the SMTP Service. If you want clients to be able to access services by an aliased DNS name (for example, *www.ttgnet.com*) rather than requiring them to use the actual IP address or the actual computer name (for example, *bastet.ttgnet.com*), you must create a DNS CNAME (canonical name) record for each service to map the canonical name, for example, *www.ttgnet.com*, to the actual computer name and IP address.

WARNING Once you have installed the Windows NT 4.0 Option Pack, be very careful if you need to reapply Service Pack 3. SP3 contains older versions of files that are installed by Option Pack Setup. If you must reapply SP3 after installing the Option Pack, do not overwrite the newer Option Pack files with the older files in SP3. If this occurs, you must reinstall the Option Pack to recover.

Viewing option pack documentation

It may seem ridiculous to devote a section to viewing documentation, but some aspects of using IIS documentation are by no means intuitively obvious. Microsoft provides all IIS documentation online. You can access it in any of the following ways:

- By using Help in Internet Service Manager (ISM) and the other administrative tools
- By choosing Start → Programs → Windows NT 4.0 Option Pack → Product Documentation
- By using Internet Explorer 4 to read the hyperlinked HTML-formatted help files. Note that, with this option, you are not simply reading static HTML files—you are actually using a web site provided by the WWW Service to display the documentation actively.

Note the following caveats about using the online documentation:

- Option Pack Setup installs help files selectively, so some help files may not be available on your installation, even though the headers are displayed for them.
- If the WWW Service is not installed and running, you will only be able to access the Release Notes and Troubleshooting files. Attempting to access the other help files results in an error message: "A connection with the server could not be established". You can solve this problem by starting the WWW Service.
- If you are using a proxy server with Internet Explorer 4, and want to use it to view IIS documentation, you must modify the default settings. To do so, start Internet Explorer and Choose View—Internet Options to display the Internet Options tabbed dialog. Display the Connection page. In the Proxy Server section, mark the Bypass proxy server for local (Intranet) addresses checkbox and click on OK to save the change.
- The release notes say that you can view IIS documentation using a browser on a remote computer by entering the URL *http://<iis-servername>/IisHelp/*. It's not quite that easy, and it took us half an hour to figure out the problem.

Believe it or not, access to the online documentation is restricted both by account and by IP address, and to fix the problem you have to modify properties for the Default Web Site. We'll examine how to configure web site properties in much more detail later in the chapter, but for the time being, you can fix this problem with the following procedure:

1. On the computer running IIS, start ISM by choosing Start → Programs → Windows NT 4.0 Option Pack → Microsoft Internet Information Server → Internet Service Manager. In the left pane of ISM, expand the list for the computer to show the IISHELP item in Default Web Site. Right-click IISHELP, choose Properties, and display the Directory Security page.
2. In the Anonymous Access and Authentication Control section, choose Edit to display the Authentication Methods dialog. By default, only the Windows NT Challenge/Response checkbox is marked. This means that you cannot access IISHELP unless you have a valid user account in the directory database of the computer running IIS. Mark the Allow Anonymous Access checkbox to allow any user to access IISHELP and then choose OK to save the change and redisplay the IISHELP Properties dialog. (Alternatively, you can leave this dialog at its default settings and use User Manager for Domains to create an account to use to access the web site.)
3. In the IP Address and Domain Name Restrictions section, choose Edit to display the IP Address and Domain Name Restrictions dialog. By default, all IP addresses are denied access except 127.0.0.1 (*localhost*). To allow any computer to access IISHELP, either highlight the *localhost* entry and choose Remove, or simply mark the Granted Access option button. Choose OK to save the change and OK again to close the IISHELP Properties dialog.

- Once you have completed this procedure, you can view the IIS documentation with your browser by entering the URL *http://<iis-servername>/IisHelp/* (if you have name resolution available via DNS or a hosts file entry) or *http://<iis-server-ipaddress>/IisHelp/*.

Adding and removing Option Pack components

After you've installed the Windows NT 4.0 Option Pack, you use Option Pack Setup to add and remove components for your installation. To do so, from the Start button, choose Programs → Windows NT 4.0 Option Pack → Windows NT 4.0 Option Pack Setup. Setup displays a welcome screen listing the available components. Click Next to display another dialog with two buttons—Add/Remove and Remove All. Click Add/Remove to display the dialog shown in Figure 10-1.

Fully installed components are indicated by a marked checkbox with a white background, for example, FrontPage 98 Server Extensions. Partially installed

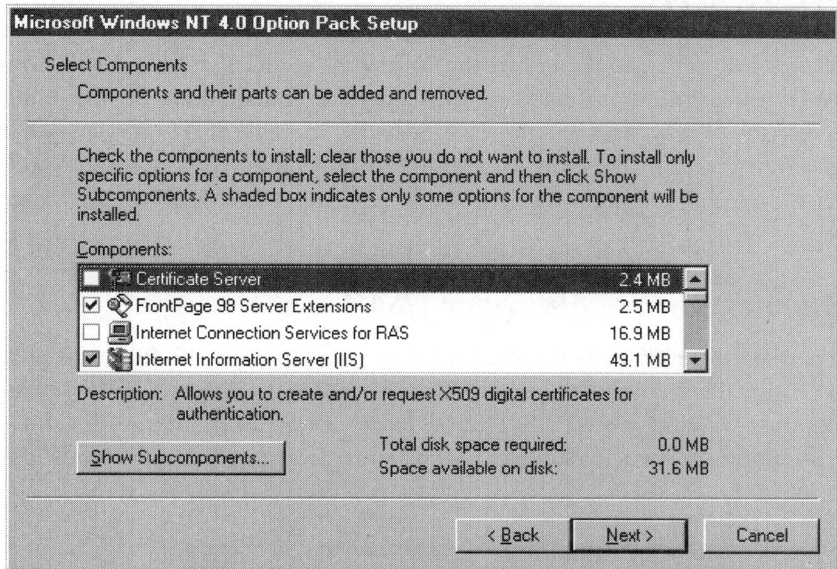

Figure 10-1. The Microsoft Windows NT 4.0 Option Pack Setup dialog

components are indicated by a marked checkbox with a gray background, for example, Internet Information Server (IIS). Components that are not currently installed are indicated by an empty checkbox, for example, Certificate Server. Use this dialog to perform the following actions:

- Some components include subcomponents that can be selected or deselected individually. To view a list of the available subcomponents for a component, highlight that component and click Show Subcomponents. If a component does not contain any individually selectable subcomponents, this button is grayed out. Note that a subcomponent may itself contain individually selectable subcomponents.
- To add a component that is not currently installed, mark the checkbox associated with that component. If that component contains subcomponents, all of them will also be added. You can deselect one or more of them by clicking Show Subcomponents and clearing the checkbox for that item.
- To remove an installed component, clear the checkbox associated with that component. If that component contains subcomponents, all of them will also be removed.

When you finish selecting and deselecting components and subcomponents, click Next to continue. Depending on the components you add or remove, you may or may not need to restart the server for your changes to take effect.

Configuring IIS

The bulk of this chapter is contained in the following sections, which detail how to configure IIS once you've installed it. This material concentrates on the three major services—the WWW Service, the FTP Service, and the SMTP Service—that are installed when you run IIS Setup using the Typical option. Although the NNTP Service is not covered, configuring it is very similar to configuring the other services.

Using Internet Service Manager (ISM)

Internet Service Manager (ISM) is the main management tool for IIS. ISM runs as a snap-in under the Microsoft Management Console (MMC). To start ISM choose Start → Programs → Windows NT 4.0 Option Pack → Microsoft Internet Information Server → Internet Service Manager. MMC runs and automatically loads the ISM snap-in.

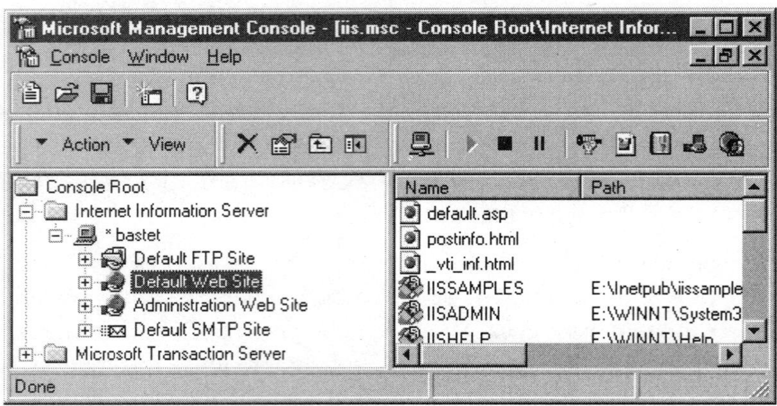

Figure 10-2. The Internet Service Manager

Which toolbar icons and menu choices are available in ISM depend on the object currently selected. For example, Figure 10-2 shows ISM with the Default Web Site object selected. Because we have a web site selected, the toolbar includes three VCR-like icons that you can use to start, stop, or pause the web site. The toolbar also contains icons for Key Manager, Performance Monitor, Event Viewer, Server Manager, and User Manager for Domains, all of which are commonly used when managing a web site. In addition to context-sensitive toolbars, ISM provides the standard context-sensitive menus that you can access by right-clicking an object. We'll use ISM in the following sections to configure settings for the various services installed.

Configuring Computer Properties

Use the Internet Information Server page of the <computer-name> Properties dialog to configure the global IIS properties for the selected computer. To display this dialog, shown in Figure 10-3, log on as an administrator, start Internet Service Manager, right-click the computer name in MMC to display the context-sensitive menu, and choose Properties.

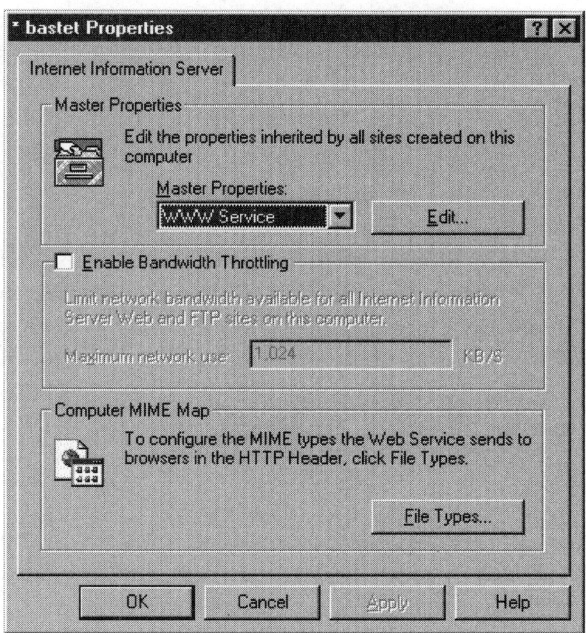

Figure 10-3. Configuring global IIS properties

You use this dialog to set default properties for all Web and FTP sites, control the bandwidth used by all web sites, and set MIME configuration for all sites, as follows:

Master Properties section

Use the Master Properties drop-down list to select a service type—either WWW Service or FTP Service—and click Edit to display the tabbed properties dialog for that service. Using these tabbed properties dialogs is described in the following sections. The settings you make here are the default values that will be used when you create a new Web or FTP site. If these settings are different from those of an existing site, you are given the opportunity to replace the current settings with the new master property settings or to continue to use the existing settings. You can also override these settings later for any particular site. List-formatted properties—for example, access lists, custom error messages, or filters—are treated as single properties. Changes are not merged with existing list data, but are overwritten by the new data.

Enable Bandwidth Throttling section

Use this section to limit the bandwidth available to all WWW sites on the selected computer. To do so, mark the Enable Bandwidth Throttling checkbox and enter a value in the Maximum network use box. You would typically use this option to limit the availability of bandwidth to the WWW Service on a computer that also provides other bandwidth-consuming services, for example, mail or RAS. On such a computer, Microsoft recommends initially allocating 50 percent of the available bandwidth, and adjusting this value up or down as needed. For example, on a T1 (1.544 Mbps) interface, you might initially set throttling to a value of 772 Kbps. Note that bandwidth throttling controls bandwidth use only by static HTML files.

Computer MIME Map section

Use this section to configure MIME (Multipurpose Internet Mail Extensions) mappings, which specify the file types that the WWW Service returns to browsers. To display the registered file types installed with Windows NT, click File Types to display the File Types dialog. Highlight a registered file type in the Registered file types pane to display details about that file type in the File type details section at the bottom of the dialog. You can also take the following actions in the File Types dialog:

Add a MIME mapping

Click New Type to display the File Type dialog, and enter values in the Associated Extension: and Content Type (MIME): boxes. For the latter box, use the syntax *<mime-type>/<file-extension>*, for example, *image/bmp*.

Remove a MIME mapping

Highlight a registered file type and click Remove.

Edit a MIME mapping

Highlight a registered file type, click Edit to display the File Type dialog, and make the necessary changes to the Associated Extension and/or Content Type (MIME): boxes.

Changing MIME mapping in the master property sheet for the computer changes those properties for all sites, and for the computer itself. You can instead modify MIME mappings for a particular site, which displays only the changed mappings. If you subsequently change the MIME mappings in the master property sheet, the custom mappings for individual sites are overwritten by the new master property sheet mappings.

Creating a Web Site

Creating a web site with IIS is a two-step process. You first develop the content—HTML pages, images, and so on—that makes up the web site. Microsoft provides various tools, for example, FrontPage, to help you develop content, but that activity is beyond the scope of this chapter. Once you have developed the content, you configure the properties for the web site that will support it. To create the web site based on the Default Web Site that was installed when you installed IIS, take the following steps:

1. Create a home page for the web site using Microsoft Word, FrontPage, or another HTML authoring tool. Save the home page as *Default.htm*.
2. Copy the home page to the Default Web Site home directory. If you accepted the defaults when installing IIS, this is the *\Inetpub\Wwwroot* directory on the drive where you installed IIS.
3. Create a CNAME DNS entry to alias *www* to the computer name that runs IIS. For example, we installed IIS on the computer *bastet.ttgnet.com*. In order for DNS users to resolve the web site as *www.ttgnet.com*, we added a DNS entry to alias *www.ttgnet.com* to *bastet.ttgnet.com*. When a user enters *www.ttgnet.com* in his browser, DNS resolves the request to the computer *bastet.ttgnet.com*.
4. Modify the Default Web Site Properties dialog as necessary. Configuring Web site properties is done with a tabbed dialog that includes the following pages:

   Web Site
   : Configure identification, connection limits, and logging options for a web site.

   Operators
   : Specify which users and groups can perform routine administrative functions for the web site.

   Performance
   : Configure settings that control the performance of the web site and optimize it for different traffic loads.

   ISAPI Filters
   : Configure ISAPI filters options. An ISAPI filter is a supporting IIS executable that responds to events that occur when an HTTP request is being processed.

   Home Directory
   : Change the location of or modify the properties for the home directory for the web site.

Documents
: Configure the web site to deliver a default document to a requesting browser that does not specify a file name, or to append footer information to each page it delivers.

Directory Security
: Configure security settings for the web site.

HTTP Headers
: Configure the values returned by the web site in the HTML header and set content expiration properties.

Custom Errors
: Configure the type of error message that the WWW Service returns to client browsers when an HTTP error occurs.

Installing IIS4 using Typical installs a Default Web Site and an Administration Web Site. You can use the procedures described in the following sections to modify the properties for either or both of these web sites, as well as for other web sites you create. Changes you make to them affect only the individual web site you are changing. You can also use these same procedures to modify the Master Properties for the WWW Service, described in the preceding section. Changes you make to the Master Properties for the WWW Service are used as default settings when you create a new web site, and may optionally be used to update (and overwrite) the properties for existing web sites.

To change properties for a web site, right-click that web site in MMC to display the context-sensitive menu, and then choose Properties to display the tabbed <web-site-name> Web Site Properties dialog.

Configuring Web Site Properties

Use the Web Site page of the Web Site Properties dialog to configure identification, connection limits, and logging options for a web site, as follows:

- Web Site Identification section

  Description
  : The name of the web server. This is what appears in Internet Service Manager tree view.

  IP Address
  : Use this drop-down list to select an IP address to be associated with this web site. Only IP addresses that have been assigned to this computer (using the Control Panel Network tool) appear in this list. If you accept the default setting for this field, All Unassigned, this web site responds to all IP addresses assigned to this computer that are not assigned to other sites, making this the default web site for the computer.

Advanced
: Click this button to display the Advanced Multiple Web Site Configuration dialog, which you can use to assign multiple identities to this web site.

TCP Port
: Specifies the TCP port upon which the WWW Service responds to queries, by default port 80. You can specify any other TCP port number here, but only clients that explicitly include that port number in the URL will be able to access the server. A TCP Port number is required.

SSL Port
: Specifies the SSL (Secure Sockets Layer) port number that will be used to establish a secure SSL connection. This option is grayed out and unavailable unless you have a server certificate installed. If you do have a server certificate installed, this port number defaults to the standard 443 for the default web site. You can specify any other TCP port number here, but only clients that explicitly include that port number in the URL will be able to access the server. When you create new web sites, you must explicitly assign a value to this field.

- Connections section

Unlimited
: Mark this option button, which is marked by default, to allow an unlimited number of simultaneous connections to the web site.

Limited To
: Mark this option button and enter a value for connections to limit the number of simultaneous connections to the web site.

Connection Timeout
: Specify, in seconds, how long the server waits before disconnecting an inactive user, to ensure that a connection is eventually closed even if the HTTP protocol fails to do so.

- Enable Logging section

Enable Logging
: Mark this checkbox, which is marked by default, to specify that IIS should log user activities, including which users have connected to the site and which pages they accessed.

Active log format
: If you enable logging, use the drop-down list to select one of the following log file formats. Once you have selected a format, click Properties to display a property sheet specific to that format, where you can set various logging options, including log time period, log file location, maximum log file size, items to be logged, and so on.

Microsoft IIS Log File Format
: An ASCII log file format with predefined headings.

NCSA Common Log File Format
: The National Center for Supercomputing Applications log format. (Another fixed ASCII format.)

ODBC Logging
: A fixed format logged to a ODBC-aware database, for example, Access or SQL Server. You must create the database yourself before data can be written to it. Using this format allows you to use the more powerful data analysis and reporting tools available with the database application.

W3C Extended Log File Format
: The default log file format. W3C is a configurable ASCII format. By default, Time, Client IP Address, Method, URI Stem, and HTTP Status are logged. You can select among numerous other data types to be logged.

Clicking Advanced on the Web Site page displays the Advanced Multiple Web Site Configuration dialog. Use this dialog to create, delete, and edit multiple identities for this web site. The dialog contains two panes, the top one for ordinary, insecure web site identities, and the bottom for secure, SSL web site identities. The lower pane is inaccessible unless you have a server certificate installed. Changes are made to either of these panes in similar fashion, as follows:

Add an identity
: Click Add to display the Advanced Web Site Identification dialog, use the drop-down list to select an IP address, enter a value for TCP Port and, optionally, for Host Header Name (described in the following section).

Remove an identity
: Highlight the identity and click Remove.

Edit an identity
: Highlight the identity and click Edit to display the Advanced Web Site Identification dialog, and make the necessary changes to IP Address, TCP Port, and Host Header Name.

Each identity must be uniquely identified by at least one of the three available characteristics—IP Address, TCP Port, or Host Header Name. You can, for example:

- Define two identities with the same IP address by assigning one to TCP Port 80 and the second to TCP Port 81. However, because Port 80 is so completely standardized, using another port number is very unusual. A browser will not be able to access that web site unless the user explicitly includes the port number in the URL. In fact, some administrators use a different TCP Port number as an *ad hoc* security mechanism on the theory that no one looks for something if he doesn't even know there's something hidden.

- Define two identities that both use TCP Port 80 by assigning them different IP addresses. Users that point their browsers to either IP address (or its corresponding DNS name) access the same site under different identities.
- Define two identities that both use TCP Port 80 and the same IP address by assigning them different Host Header Names.

Using Host Header Names allows you to alias multiple domain names to a single IP address. For example, you could use Host Header Names to define the identities *www.ttgnet.com* and *www.oreilly.com* to the same IP address on this web site. For this to work, the client browser must support Host Header Names, which all recent versions of major browsers do. The name the client enters is passed by the browser in the HTTP header as the host name, and IIS routes the client to the correct web site.

If the client browser does not support Host Header Names, and if a default web site is enabled, IIS routes the client to the default web site. If no default web site is enabled, the client receives an error message. If the requested web site is stopped, the client also receives the default web site.

Note also that, because SSL certificates include the domain name, web sites that use certificates cannot share an IP address with another web site.

Configuring Operators properties

Use the Operators page of the Web Site Properties dialog to specify which users and groups have operator privilege for a web site. Users and groups that have been assigned operator status are listed in the Operators pane.

Granting a user operator status allows that user to perform the typical routine day-to-day activities needed to manage the web site, including setting access permissions and logging options; assigning HTTP headers, default documents, and footers; and expiring content and setting ratings. A web site operator cannot perform such administrator-level functions as changing the web site identification properties, changing the anonymous username and password, creating or changing virtual directories and paths, and so forth. Changes to those settings can be made only by a member of the Administrators group.

By default, the Administrators group is assigned operator status. However, you can assign any user or group as an operator. Assign and remove operators as follows:

Add an operator

Click Add to display the Add Users and Groups dialog. Use the List Names From drop-down list to specify the domain from which the account is to be added. The Names pane lists the available users and groups. Double-click a user or group name to add it to the Add Names pane, and then click on OK. Windows NT adds the selected user or group to the Operators pane.

Remove an operator
Highlight the user or group name in the Operators pane and click Remove.

Configuring Performance properties

Use the Performance page of the Web Site Properties dialog, shown in Figure 10-4, to configure various settings that control the performance of the web site.

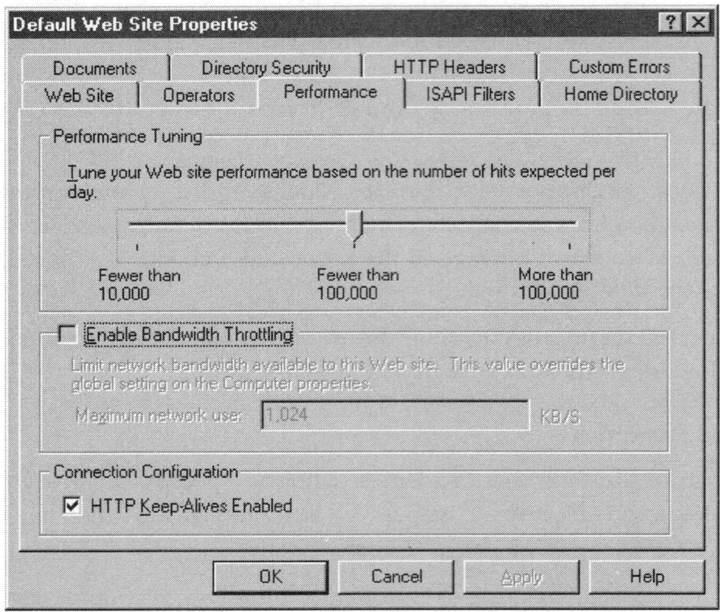

Figure 10-4. The Performance page of the Web Site Properties dialog

Set the following options:

Performance Tuning section
Use the slider to specify the approximate number of daily hits you expect the web site to experience. Although Microsoft implemented this control as a slider, they might just as well have used option buttons, because you cannot set intermediate values—you must choose one of the three values listed. Setting this value too low saves some memory, but greatly reduces the responsiveness of the server. Setting it too high needlessly consumes memory that could otherwise be used to improve overall server performance.

Enable Bandwidth Throttling section

Mark the Enable Bandwidth Throttling checkbox, which is cleared by default, and enter a value to control the amount of bandwidth available to this web site. Note that entering a value here overrides the value specified in the Master Properties for the computer, even if this value is higher.

Connection Configuration section

Mark the HTTP Keep-Alives Enabled checkbox, which is marked by default, to allow clients to maintain an open connection with the server, rather than establishing a new connection for each request. For very simple static HTML pages, clearing this checkbox can improve server performance somewhat. However, for typical web pages—those that contain multiple images and other elements—marking this box reduces overhead by preventing each element from requiring a separate build and tear-down operation.

Configuring ISAPI Filters properties

Use the ISAPI Filters page of the Web Site Properties dialog, shown in Figure 10-5, to configure options for ISAPI filters. An ISAPI filter is a program that is loaded by IIS and responds to events that occur when an HTTP request is being processed.

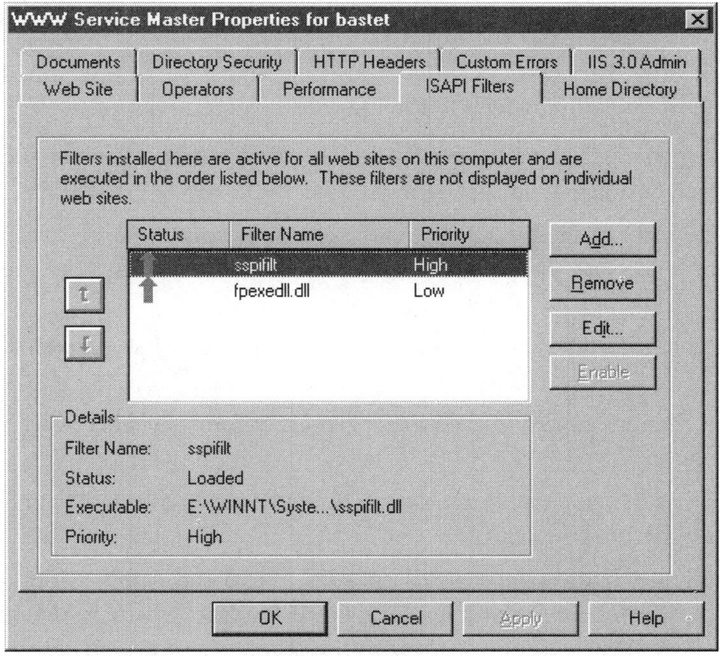

Figure 10-5. The ISAPI Filters page of the Web Site Properties dialog

The pane lists the status of each ISAPI filter (loaded, unloaded or disabled), that filter's name, and the priority assigned to the filter in the DLL. The Details section displays the same information, and adds the name of the executable file that contains the filter. You can modify the ISAPI filter configuration for the web site as follows:

Add an ISAPI filter
: Click Add to display the Filter Properties dialog. Enter the Filter Name and Executable, or browse for the executable that contains the filter.

Remove an ISAPI filter
: Highlight the filter in the pane and click Remove.

Edit an ISAPI filter
: Highlight the filter in the pane and click Edit to display the Filter Properties dialog.

Enable or Disable an ISAPI filter
: Highlight the filter in the pane and click Enable to enable a filter that is currently disabled, or click Disable to disable a filter that is currently enabled.

Change the order in which ISAPI filters are loaded
: ISAPI filters are loaded in the order that they appear in this pane. To change this order, highlight a filter in the pane and use the up arrow or down arrow to rearrange the list.

ISAPI filters are processed according to the following rules:

- All web sites inherit the ISAPI filters configured in Master Properties for the computer, which are not displayed for the individual web sites.
- When you add filters to an individual web site, those filters are merged with the default filters for the site that are configured in Master Properties for the computer.
- If several filters are registered for the same event, they are called sequentially, as follows:
  - A filter with a higher priority is always processed before any filter with a lower priority.
  - If two filters have the same priority, the global filter set in Master Properties is processed before the local filter defined for the individual web site.
  - If two filters at the same level (global or local) have the same priority, they are processed in the order that they were loaded, which is determined by the order in which they appear in the pane.

Configuring Home Directory properties

Use the Home Directory page of the Web Site Properties dialog to change the location of or modify the properties for the home directory for the web site.

Installing IIS creates the web root directory that you specify, ordinarily *\Inetpub\wwwroot*. You can use this dialog to change that location. This is a dynamic dialog, whose contents vary according to the option button you select in the top section, as follows:

A directory located on this computer
: Select this option, which is the default, to use a web root directory on the local computer where you installed IIS. Use this page to specify the location, access permissions, and content control for the local directory, as well as application settings. Uses standard drive/directory syntax, for example *C:\web\htmlfiles*.

A share located on another computer
: Select this option to use a web root directory located on a network share. The options and settings are similar to those available when the web root directory is on the local computer. Uses UNC syntax in the form *\\servername\sharename*, for example, *\\bastet\htmlfiles*.

A redirection to a URL
: When a browser requests the original URL associated with the web site, it is automatically redirected to the URL specified here. You can map requests to another web site by using the fully qualified URL for that web site, for example, *http://www.oreilly.com*. Alternatively, you can map requests to a virtual directory by using a virtual path, for example, */htmlfiles*. You can use redirection variables and wildcards in the target URL to control how the source URL is mapped to the target URL.

These options are described in the following sections.

A directory located on this computer

Use the Home Directory page of the Web Site Properties dialog shown in Figure 10-6 to change the location of or modify the properties for the home directory for the web site, if that home directory is located on the computer where IIS is installed.

Set the following options:

Local Path
: Type the drive and directory for the local path where the home directory resides on the local computer, or browse for the location.

Access Permissions
: Use these checkboxes to specify what type of access is allowed to the home directory. If the home directory is located on an NTFS volume, these settings should match the NTFS permissions for that directory. If the settings do not match, the most restrictive settings are used. For example, if you grant Write

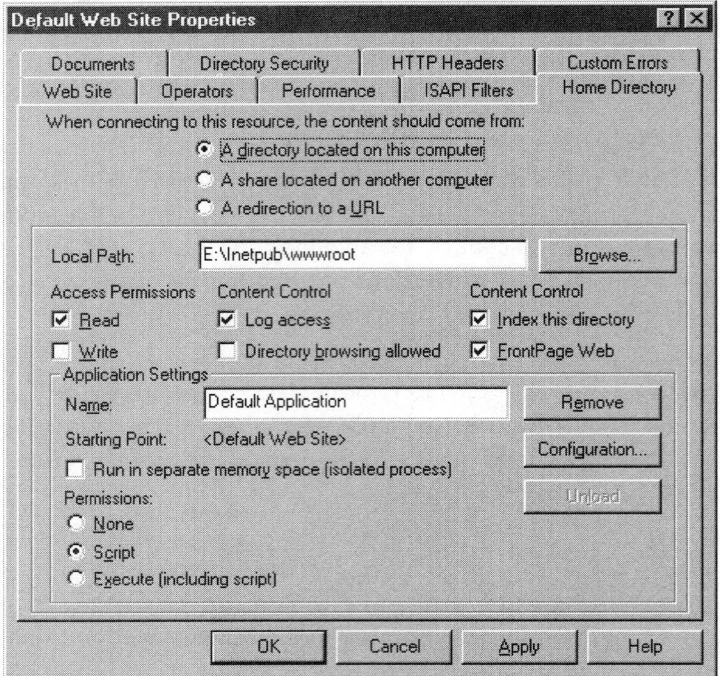

Figure 10-6. The Home Directory page of the Web Site Properties dialog

permission in this dialog, but a particular user has the No Access NTFS permission for the directory, that user will be unable to access the directory.

Read

Mark this checkbox, which is marked by default, to assign Read permission if you want clients to be able to read or download the files contained in the home directory. The WWW Service returns an error if a client attempts to retrieve a file located in a directory for which Read permission has not been granted. Grant Read permission only for directories that contain public information like HTML pages and images. Do not grant Read permission for directories that contain system files, scripts (CGI and ISAPI), and other material that you do not want clients to be able to retrieve.

Write

Mark this checkbox, which is cleared by default, to assign Write permission if you want clients to be able to upload files to the web site, or to change content in files that are write-enabled. Only clients who are using a web browser that supports that HTTP 1.1 put feature can write files.

Content Control

Use these checkboxes to control the behavior of the WWW service for the home directory, as follows:

Log access

Mark this checkbox, which is marked by default, to cause the WWW service to write a log file entry for each visit to this directory. For this setting to be effective, logging must be enabled for the web site in the Web Site properties page, which it is by default

Directory browsing allowed

Mark this checkbox, which is cleared by default, to automatically generate a hypertext directory listing. When this setting is enabled, if a client enters this directory without specifying a file name, and if no default document exists in the directory, the client receives the hypertext directory list, which enables him to navigate the directory tree. Only actual directories are included in the hypertext list. In order to change to a virtual directory, a client must explicitly enter the alias or URL or select a link on another page that points to that virtual directory. This option is disabled by default because enabling it allows a user to navigate the directory structure—a potential security risk.

Index this directory

Mark this checkbox, which is marked by default, to cause Index Server to index the contents of this directory when it does a full-text index of the web site.

FrontPage Web

Mark this checkbox, which is marked by default, to create a FrontPage web for this web site. Clear the checkbox to delete the FrontPage web for this site.

Application Settings

IIS defines an application as all directories and files contained within a directory that is marked as an application starting point, until another application starting point is encountered. If you define the home directory for the web site as an application starting point, all directories (physical and virtual) within that site can participate.

Create/Remove

To define a directory as an application starting point, click Create and name the application. To remove the home directory from the application, click Remove.

Name

Type the name of the application, which appears within the property sheets for any directory contained in the application.

Configuration

Click this button to display the tabbed Application Configuration dialog, which you can use to set ISAPI caching, define application mappings, set application configuration options, and set application debugging options.

Run in separate memory space (isolated process)

Mark this checkbox, which is cleared by default, to run the application as a separate process. Choosing this option protects all other processes—including the WWW Service itself—from being affected if this application crashes and burns. The only downside to marking this checkbox is that it causes the application to consume more memory.

Permissions

Mark one of the following option buttons to specify whether or not applications can run in the directory or to limit the types of applications that can run.

None

Select this option button to prevent any programs or scripts from running in this directory.

Script

Select this option button, which is enabled by default, to allow applications mapped to a script engine to run even though Execute permission is not granted. Set this option button for directories that contain scripts, for example, CGI, IDC, or ASP scripts. Granting Script permission is safer than granting execute permission because it limits the types of programs than can run.

Execute (including script)

Select this option button to allow any application to run in the directory, including applications that are mapped to script engines and Windows NT executables.

A share located on another computer

Use the Home Directory page of the Web Site Properties dialog to change the location of or modify the properties for the home directory for the web site, if that home directory is located on a network share rather than on the computer where IIS is installed. All settings on this page (and the appearance of the page itself) are identical to those described in the preceding section, with the following exceptions:

Network Directory

Enter the location of the home directory on the network share, using UNC format, for example, *servername**sharename*.

Connect As

Click this button to display the Network Directory Security Credentials dialog, and enter the username and password you want to use to connect to this share.

A redirection to a URL

Use the Home Directory page of the Web Site Properties dialog to redirect requests for the source URL to a URL you specify. Set the following options:

Redirect to

Specify a valid URL to which requests will be redirected, as follows:

- To map requests to another web site, enter the fully qualified URL of that web site. For example, if this web site is *www.ttgnet.com* and you want to redirect requests to *www.oreilly.com*, enter *http://www.oreilly.com* here.
- To map requests to a virtual directory, enter the virtual path here. For example, to redirect requests to the virtual directory *wwwtemp*, enter */wwwtemp* here.
- To map requests selectively, you may enter a URL here that uses redirection variables and wildcards, as described in the online IIS documentation.

The client will be sent to

Mark one of the checkboxes below, as follows:

The exact URL entered above

Mark this checkbox, which is cleared by default, to redirect a virtual directory to the target URL without adding any part of the original URL. For example, if you want to redirect requests to the virtual directory */wwwtemp* to the HTML page *index.html*, enter *index.html* in the Redirect to: box and mark this checkbox.

A directory below this one

Mark this checkbox, which is cleared by default, to redirect a parent directory to a child directory. For example, if you want to redirect the home directory (/) to a subdirectory named */wwwtemp*, enter */wwwtemp* in the Redirect to: box and mark this checkbox. If this checkbox is not marked, the WWW Service will always map the parent directory to itself.

A permanent redirection for this resource

Mark this checkbox, which is cleared by default, to permanently redirect one resource to another. Ordinarily, redirects are temporary. When this checkbox is marked, the WWW Service returns a 301 Permanent Redirect message to the requesting browser, which can use that message to permanently alter a stored URL like a bookmark or favorite.

Configuring Documents properties

Use the Documents page of the Web Site Properties dialog to configure default documents and document footers. You can configure Documents properties at the web site, directory, and virtual directory levels, as follows:

Enable Default Document
: Mark this checkbox, which is marked by default, to cause the web site to return a default document to a web browser that does not request a specific file name. The default document may be the home page for the directory, or the index page described earlier that allows the user to navigate the directory structure. You can specify multiple default documents, and the web site will return the first listed document it locates to the requesting browser. Use the Add and Remove buttons to modify the list of documents shown in the pane, and the up and down arrow keys to set the priority for each, with the top-most document having the highest priority.

Enable Document Footer
: Mark this checkbox, which is cleared by default, and enter the full path and file name of an HTML-formatted page fragment in the box if you want the web site to append that HTML fragment as a footer to every page it delivers. This fragment should contain only the HTML tags necessary to format and display the footer content. The most common use of this feature is to append relatively static information, for example, copyright notices, to the bottom of each page delivered by the web site.

Configuring Directory Security properties

Use the Directory Security page of the Web Site Properties dialog, shown in Figure 10-7, to configure security settings for the web site.

Set the following options:

Anonymous Access and Authentication Control section
: To allow anonymous users to access public information on the web site while permitting only designated users to access restricted content, you can configure the web site to authenticate users. To do so, click Edit to display the Authentication Methods dialog, shown in Figure 10-8.

  Configure the following options to control access based on existing Windows NT user accounts and existing NTFS permissions on files and directories:

  Allow Anonymous Access
  : Mark this checkbox, which is marked by default, if you want to allow users to connect to the server anonymously with restricted permissions (the normal state of affairs for a web server). When a user connects anonymously, the web server logs the user on with a valid Windows NT user account, which by default is named IUSR_<computer-name>, in this case

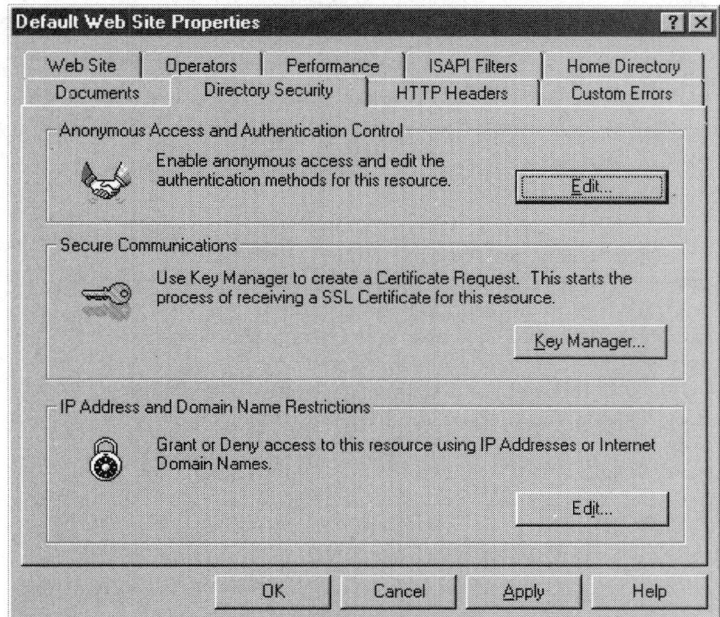

Figure 10-7. The Directory Security page

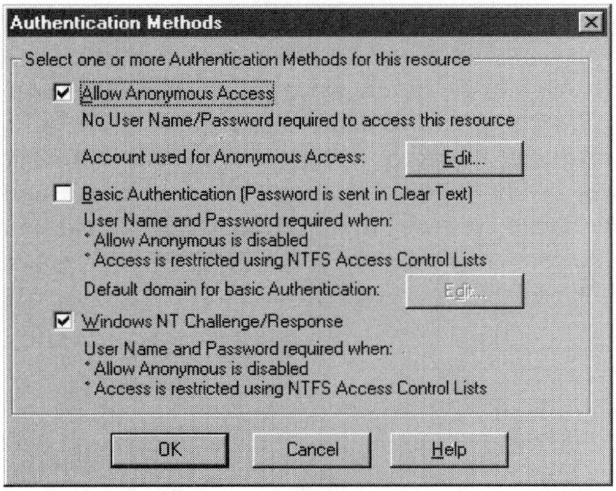

Figure 10-8. The Authentication Methods dialog

IUSR_BASTET. Windows NT creates this user account in User Manager for Domains and Internet Service Manager when IIS is installed, and assigns it the limited permissions needed by anonymous users. To change this anonymous username, click Edit to display the Anonymous User Account dialog, and make the necessary changes. If you create a new anonymous user account, you must make sure that the UMD and ISM password settings are identical. Mark the Enable Automatic Password Synchronization checkbox to ensure that this occurs automatically. If you create a new anonymous account, make sure to grant it the "Log on locally" user right, which is required for anonymous access to the web site.

WARNING You can use ISM to enable password synchronization between ISM and a Windows NT user account located either on the local computer that runs IIS or on a computer elsewhere on the network. However, enabling password synchronization for a non-local user account may result in all anonymous access to the web site or FTP site being denied. If the web or FTP site depends on anonymous users accessing resources located on the network (rather than on the local IIS computer), you cannot use the password synchronization feature. Instead, specify a valid password for the anonymous user.

Basic Authentication (Password is sent in Clear Text)

Mark this checkbox, which is cleared by default, to enable Basic Authentication for the web site as a fallback method. The web site uses Basic Authentication only if anonymous access has been disabled, or with anonymous access enabled, if a user attempts to access content that is forbidden to anonymous users. When either of these conditions obtains, the user's web browser displays a dialog box to prompt the user to enter a valid Windows NT username and password, which is transmitted in unencrypted form, a potential security risk. ISM displays a warning dialog to that effect when you mark this checkbox. Users who log in with Basic Authentication must provide the logon domain in addition to the user name and password. By default, IIS uses the local IIS domain if the user does not enter a logon domain. You can change the default logon domain to other than the local IIS domain by clicking Edit and entering another domain name.

Windows NT Challenge/Response

Mark this checkbox, which is marked by default, to enable Windows NT Challenge/Response authentication, a more secure authentication method than the Basic Authentication described above. The web site uses Windows NT Challenge/Response Authentication only if anonymous access has been disabled, or with anonymous access enabled, if a user attempts to access content that is forbidden to anonymous users. When either of these conditions obtains, the user's web browser (which must be Microsoft Internet Explorer 2.0 or higher) displays a dialog box to prompt the user to enter a valid Windows NT username and password. During this authentication process, the web server encrypts the exchanges required to authenticate the user.

Secure Communications section

You cannot use the secure communications features of the WWW Service until you have applied for, received, and installed a server certificate, and bound that certificate to the server key pair. Until you have taken these actions, the button in this section is labeled Key Manager. Clicking it displays Key Manager, which you use to create an SSL certificate request for this server. Once that certificate is installed and configured, the button in this section is relabeled Edit. Clicking it allows you to configure the SSL and PCT options on the server.

IP Address and Domain Name Restrictions section

You can use this section to deny all but specified IP addresses and/or domain names access to the web site. For example, if you have created a private web site that is intended for use only by your employees, you might use this feature to deny access to all users but those who are members of your own DNS domain. Alternatively, you can elect to grant all but specified IP addresses and/or domain names access to your web site. For example, if for some reason you decide that you don't want any user from the *aol.com* domain to access your web site, you can choose to deny that domain. To configure permit/deny settings, click Edit to display the IP Address and Domain Name Restrictions dialog, shown in Figure 10-9.

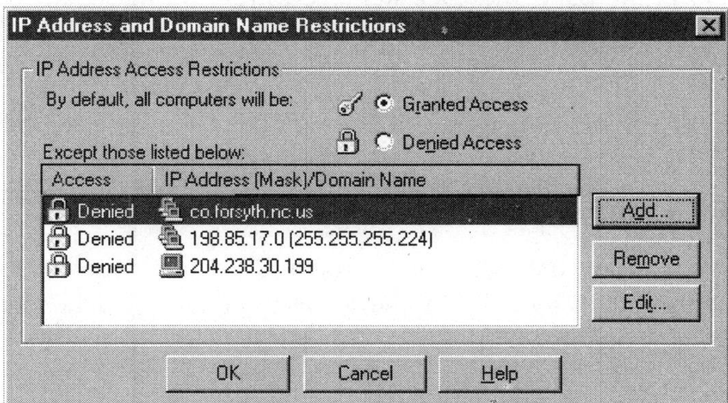

Figure 10-9. The IP Address and Domain Name Restrictions dialog

Begin by marking one of the option buttons at the top of the dialog to specify the default access. Mark the Granted Access option button if you want to grant access to all computers except those you enter in the list. Mark the Denied Access option button if you want to deny access to all computers except those you enter in the list. Once you have specified the default access method, you may take the following actions to modify the list of computers that are granted or denied permission to access the site.

Add
: Click this button to display the Deny Access On dialog (if you marked the Granted Access option button for default access) or Grant Access On dialog (if you marked the Denied Access option button for default access). Under Type, mark one of the following option buttons:

    Single Computer
    : To display an IP address entry field in dotted decimal format. ISM enters a line item in the list that grants (or denies, as appropriate) access to this single computer.

    Group of Computers
    : To display a Network ID entry box and a Subnet Mask entry box, both formatted as dotted decimal. Enter the network ID and subnet mask to grant or deny access to the specified subnet.

    Domain Name
    : To display an entry box for domain name. Note that filtering by domain name is a very resource intensive option, because it requires a reverse DNS lookup for each operation.

Remove
: Highlight the line item in the pane and click Remove to remove that grant or deny filter.

Edit
: Highlight the line item in the pane and click Edit to change the properties for that grant or deny filter.

Configuring HTTP Headers properties

Use the HTTP Headers page of the Web Site Properties dialog, shown in Figure 10-10, to configure the values returned by the web site in the HTML header and to set content expiration properties.

Set the following options:

Enable Content Expiration section
: Mark this checkbox, which is cleared by default, and set expiration options to control the display of time-sensitive content, for example, seasonal material or time-limited offers. The WWW Service embeds content-expiration data in content page HTTP headers. The client browser compares its current date with the expiration date supplied with the content to determine whether to display the

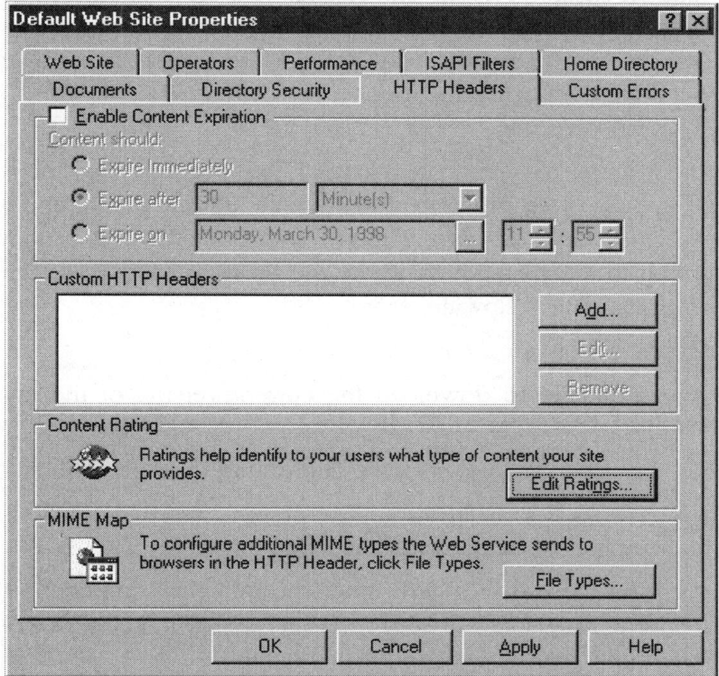

Figure 10-10. The HTTP Headers page

cached page or to request an updated page from the web server. If you enable content expiration, select one of the following option buttons:

Expire Immediately
: Select this option button if you never want the browser to display a cached page. It will instead display the page only once, and then request an updated page on subsequent accesses.

Expire after
: Select this option button, enter a number, and use the drop-down list to select minutes, hours, or days to specify that the browser may display this page from cache for the specified time period before requesting an updated page. The duration defaults to 30 minutes.

Expire on
: Select this option button and enter a date and time to specify that the browser may display this page from cache until the specified date and time. The default value is 10 days since ISM was last started.

Custom HTTP Headers section
: Use this section to enter custom headers that the web server will send to client browsers. To add a custom header, click Add to display the Add/Edit Custom Header dialog, and enter values for Custom Header Name and Custom

Header Value. To edit an existing custom header, highlight the custom header, click Edit to display the Add/Edit Custom Header dialog, and alter the values for Custom Header Name and Custom Header Value as necessary. To remove a custom header, highlight it and click Remove.

Content Rating section

IIS can embed content rating data in content page HTTP headers. This information can be read by some web browsers, for example, Internet Explorer 3.0 or higher, and used to suppress display of pages with potentially objectionable content, according to the preferences set by the browser user. To assign ratings to your content, take the following steps:

1. Click Edit Ratings to display the Content Ratings dialog.
2. Click Ratings Questionnaire to download the current version of the ratings questionnaire from the RSAC web site.
3. After completing the questionnaire, click the Ratings tab to display the Ratings page.
4. Mark the Enable Ratings for this resource checkbox.
5. In the Category pane, expand the RSACi tree, choose each component—Violence, Sex, Nudity, Language—in sequence, and assign it the appropriate rating based on your answers to the questionnaire.
6. In the Optional Information section, enter the email address of the person who rated the content and click Date to enter a date when the rating information expires.

MIME Map section

To change MIME mappings for this web site, click File Types to display the File Types dialog, and use this dialog to add, edit, or remove registered file types as described earlier in the section about configuring Master Properties. The mappings you modify here apply only to this web site. If you set MIME mappings in Master Properties, you can still modify the mappings on a site by site basis. However, when you reapply Master Properties, the individual per-site MIME mappings are overwritten by those contained in Master Properties.

Configuring Custom Errors properties

Use the Custom Errors page of the Web Site Properties dialog to configure the type of error message that the WWW Service returns to the client browser when an HTTP error occurs. For each HTTP 1.1 error, you can select among the following options:

Default

Display the default HTTP 1.1 error message, for example, "404—Object Not Found". If you set an HTTP 1.1 error to use the default message, the contents of that error message are displayed in the Error Message pane. By default, IIS displays default HTTP 1.1 error messages for 403;14 - Forbidden—Directory Listing Denied; 500—Internal Server Error; 501—Not Implemented; and 502—Bad Gateway.

File
: Display the contents of an HTML-formatted file. For most HTTP 1.1 errors, Microsoft supplies a more informative friendly version to replace most default error messages. Each of these messages is contained in an HTML-formatted file that is named with the HTTP 1.1 error number. You can use these replacement error message files as is, modify them to suit you, or replace them with your own versions. If you set an HTTP 1.1 error to use a custom message from a file, the path and filename are displayed in the Error Message pane.

URL
: Display the contents of the specified URL, which must be located on a local server. At first glance, this option appears to duplicate the functionality of the File option. However, it is intended for a different purpose. If you use static HTML files for error messages, always use the File option. Use the URL option only if you are using a custom ASP or ISAPI application to return dynamic error messages. If you do this, the application must set the HTTP header status appropriate for the error. Otherwise, the server will always return HTTP 1.1 status 200—OK. If you set an HTTP 1.1 error to use a custom message from a URL, the URL is displayed in the Error Message pane.

You can configure custom error messages at the web site, directory (physical or virtual), and file level. When you configure custom error messages, all lower entities inherit that list, which replaces the existing list rather than being merged with it.

To configure the error message for an HTTP 1.1 error, highlight the error in the Error Message pane, and click Edit Properties to display the Error Mapping Properties dialog, shown in Figure 10-11. Use the Message Type drop-down list to select Default, File, or URL. If you select Default, there are no further options to choose. If you select File, enter the path and filename of the custom error file in the File box, or click Browse to locate it. If you select URL, type the full URL in the URL box. After you complete your edits, click on OK to save the change and return to the Custom Errors page.

Creating Additional Web Sites

IIS can support multiple web sites on one computer. Each web site must be uniquely identified by a combination of IP address, host header name, and/or TCP port number, as follows:

IP Address
: By far the cleanest method is to assign a unique static IP address to each web site and create a DNS entry for each. For example, we could assign the web

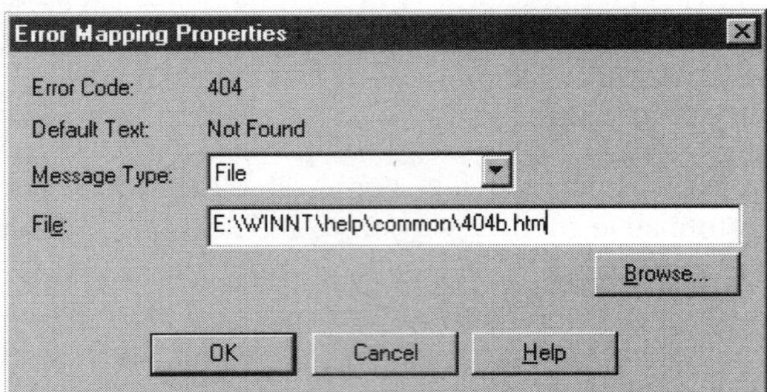

Figure 10-11. Configuring the error messages that will be returned by the server to clients when HTTP errors occur

site *www.ttgnet.com* the IP address 204.238.30.165 and the web site *support.ttgnet.com* the IP address 204.238.30.166, create CNAME records for each, and use the drop-down IP Address list on the Web Site page of the Web Site Properties dialog to associate each IP address with its corresponding web site. There is no ambiguity when a client browser attempts to access one of these sites, because the resolver stub in the browser uses the web site name to resolve a unique IP address for the web site.

Host header name

If you cannot assign a unique IP address to each web site—for example, if your ISP has given you only one static IP address—you can use the same IP address to support multiple web sites by assigning each web site a unique host header name. For example, *www.ttgnet.com* and *support.ttgnet.com* could both use the IP address 204.238.30.165. When a client browser requests either site, the request is directed to the same IP address, but IIS uses the host name requested by the client to determine which web site content to deliver. This method works with modern browsers, but fails with older browsers unless you take the steps described in the IIS documentation under "Supporting Host Header Names in Older Browsers". To configure multiple web sites using host header names, use the Advanced button on the Web Site page of the Web Site Properties dialog to associate each web site with its corresponding host header name.

TCP Port number

As a last resort, you can define multiple unique web sites on an IIS server by assigning each web site the same IP address, but with a unique TCP Port number for each site. We say as a last resort, because every web browser on the planet assumes that a web site will respond to TCP Port 80, the Well-Known Address for HTTP. For a client browser to access a web site that uses a TCP Port number other than 80, the browser must explicitly enter the port number with the URL.

After you have decided how to identify the new site uniquely, take the following steps to create it:

1. Start ISM and highlight the IIS computer in the left pane.
2. Select Action → New → Web Site to invoke the New Web Site Wizard.
3. Enter a name for the new web site in the Web Site Description box and click Next. Note that the name you assign here is only the display name used by ISM. It need not be the same as the DNS name for the web site.
4. Use the Select the IP Address to use for this Web Site drop-down list to choose the IP address for the site, and enter the TCP Port number in the TCP Port this Web Site should use (Default: 80) box. If you have installed a server certificate and want to use SSL, enter the SSL port. Click Next.
5. Enter (or browse for) the home directory path for this web site. By default, the "Allow anonymous access to this web site" checkbox is marked. Clear it if you want to disable anonymous access and require anyone who wants to use the site to provide a valid username and password. Click Next.
6. Set the access permissions for the new web site. By default, only the "Allow Read Access" and "Allow Script Access" checkboxes are marked. The "Allow Execute Access (includes Script Access)", "Allow Write Access", and "Allow Directory Browsing" checkboxes are cleared. Once you have configured the access permissions, click Finish to continue.
7. ISM creates the web site and installs it in the tree for the computer. By default, the new web site is stopped. To start it, right click the new web site name in ISM to display the context sensitive menu and choose Start.
8. Use the Web Site Properties dialog for the new web site to make any configuration changes necessary.
9. Create a DNS CNAME entry for the new web site.

Creating an FTP Site

Like setting up a web site, setting up an FTP site with IIS is a two-step process. You first design your FTP directory structure, create the directory tree, and populate it with the files you want available for download. Once you have done so, you configure the properties for the FTP site that will make those files accessible to users. To create an FTP site based on the Default FTP Site that was installed when you installed IIS, take the following steps:

1. If you accepted the defaults when installing IIS, the Default FTP Site home directory is the *\Inetpub\Ftproot* directory on the drive where you installed IIS. If the FTP site will have only a few files, you can copy them all to this

directory. If you will make many files available for download, create a subdirectory structure under the home directory and use it to organize the files.

2. Create a CNAME DNS entry to alias ftp to the computer name that runs IIS. For example, we installed IIS on the computer *bastet.ttgnet.com*. To allow DNS users to resolve the FTP site as *ftp.ttgnet.com*, we added a DNS entry to alias ftp.ttgnet.com to bastet.ttgnet.com. When a user enters ftp.ttgnet.com in his browser or FTP client, DNS resolves the request to the computer *bastet.ttgnet.com*.
3. Modify the Default FTP Site Properties dialog as necessary. Configuring FTP site properties is done with a tabbed dialog similar to that used to configure web site properties. It includes the following pages:

   FTP Site
   : Configure identification, connection limits, and logging options for the FTP site.

   Security Accounts
   : Configure anonymous connection options and specify which users and groups can perform routine administrative functions for the FTP site.

   Messages
   : Configure the messages that FTP users will see when they connect to and exit the FTP site, and the message that the FTP server returns to clients who attempt to connect to it when the maximum number of concurrent connections has been exceeded.

   Home Directory
   : Configure the location of or modify the properties for the home directory for the FTP site, and specify the type of directory listing—Unix or MS-DOS—that will be returned to FTP clients.

   Directory Security
   : Configure TCP/IP access restrictions for the FTP site, to grant or deny access to particular IP addresses, subnets, or domain names.

Installing IIS4 using Typical installs a Default FTP Site. You can use the procedures described in the following sections to modify the properties for this site, as well as for other FTP sites you create. Changes you make to them affect only the individual FTP site you are changing. You can also these same procedures to modify the Master Properties for the FTP Service, described earlier. Changes you make to the Master Properties for the FTP Service are used as default settings when you create a new FTP site, and may optionally be used to update (and overwrite) the properties for existing FTP sites.

You can designate one FTP site as the default FTP site for IIS 3.0 administration. Any software that creates virtual directories will use the designated default FTP site as the target. To designate a default FTP site, right-click the computer name in MMC to display the context-sensitive menu and choose Properties to display the <computer-name> Properties dialog. In the Master Properties section, use the drop-down list to select FTP Service, and click Edit to display the FTP Service Master Properties for <computer-name> tabbed dialog. Click the IIS 3.0 Admin tab, and use the Default FTP Site drop-down list to select the default FTP site.

To change properties for an FTP site, right-click that web site in MMC to display the context-sensitive menu, and then choose Properties to display the tabbed <FTP-site-name> FTP Site Properties dialog.

Configuring FTP Site properties

Use the FTP Site page of the FTP Site Properties dialog to configure identification, connection limits, and logging options for the FTP site, and to view and manage connected users, as follows:

- FTP Site Identification section

  Description
  : The name of the FTP site. This is what appears in Internet Service Manager tree view.

  IP Address
  : Use the drop-down list to select an IP address to associate with the FTP site. Only IP addresses that have been assigned to this computer (using the Control Panel Network tool) appear in this list. If you accept the default setting for this field, All Unassigned, this web site responds to all IP addresses assigned to this computer that are not assigned to other sites.

  TCP Port
  : Specifies the TCP port upon which the FTP Service responds to queries, by default port 21. You can specify any other TCP port number here, but clients must explicitly use that port number to access the FTP server. TCP Port number is required. If you change the TCP Port, you must restart the server before the change takes effect.

- Connections section

  Unlimited
  : Mark this option button to allow unlimited simultaneous connections to the FTP site.

  Limited To
  : Mark this option button, which is marked by default, and enter a value for connections to limit the number of simultaneous connections to the FTP site. By default, the concurrent connection limit is set to 100,000.

Connection Timeout
Specify, in seconds, how long the FTP server waits before disconnecting an inactive user. The default value is set to 900 seconds.

- Enable Logging section

Enable Logging
Mark this checkbox, which is marked by default, to cause IIS to log FTP user activities.

Active log format
If you enable logging, use the drop-down list to select one of the following log file formats. Once you have selected a format, click Properties to display a property sheet specific to that format, where you can set various logging options, including log time period, log file location, maximum log file size, items to be logged, and so on.

Microsoft IIS Log File Format
An ASCII log file format with predefined headings.

ODBC Logging
A fixed format logged to an ODBC-aware database, for example, Access or SQL Server. You must create the database yourself before data can be written to it. Using this format allows you to use the more powerful data analysis and reporting tools available with the database application.

W3C Extended Log File Format
The default log file format. W3C is a configurable ASCII format. By default, Time, Client IP Address, Method, URI Stem, and HTTP Status are logged. You can select among numerous other data types to be logged.

You can also use this page to view and manage active FTP sessions. To do so, click Current Sessions to display the FTP User Sessions dialog, shown in Figure 10-12. This dialog displays the total number of users currently connected to the FTP server and, for each connected user, the identity of the user (typically, that user's email address), the IP address from which the user is connected, and the elapsed duration of the connection.

This dialog presents a snapshot of the current sessions as of the time you display it rather than updating sessions dynamically. Use this dialog to perform the following activities:

- To update the current sessions list, click Refresh.
- To disconnect one user session, highlight that session and click Disconnect. ISM displays a warning message to notify you that you are about to terminate the session. Click Yes to terminate the session. When you terminate a session, the connected user does not receive any preliminary warning.

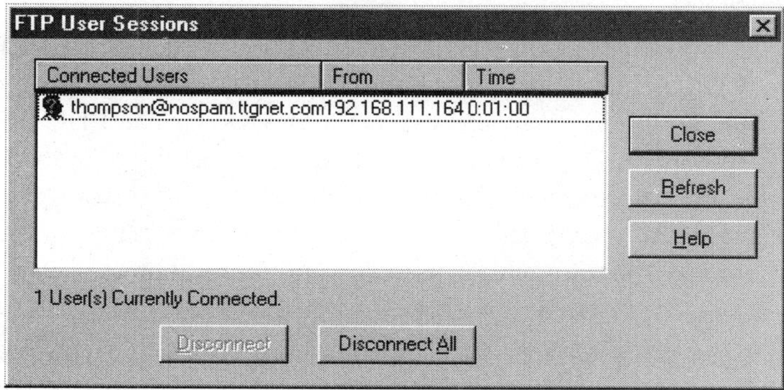

Figure 10-12. The FTP User Sessions dialog.

- To disconnect all user sessions, click Disconnect All. ISM displays a warning message to notify you that you are about to terminate all user sessions. Click Yes to terminate the sessions immediately.

Configuring Security Accounts properties

Use the Security Accounts page of the FTP Site Properties dialog, shown in Figure 10-13, to configure anonymous access options and to specify which users and groups can perform routine administrative functions for the FTP site.

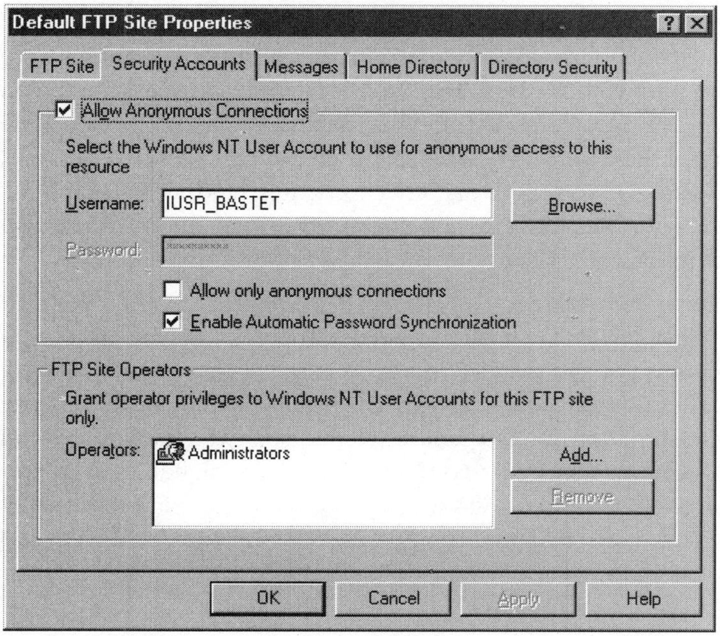

Figure 10-13. The Security Accounts page of the FTP Site Properties dialog

Configure the following settings:

- Allow Anonymous Connections section—Mark this checkbox, which is marked by default, to allow FTP clients to log on to the FTP site by entering anonymous as their username and their email address as the password. The FTP Service then uses the username and password described below as the Windows NT logon account to grant access to resources on the FTP server. Note that this username and password is only used internally by Windows NT to grant access to shared resources. The anonymous user does not enter them.

  Username
  : When you install IIS, Windows NT automatically creates a user account for anonymous logons in User Manager for Domains and in Internet Service Manager, and assigns the same random password to each of them. By default, this account is given the name IUSR_<computer-name>, for example, IUSR_BASTET. When an anonymous user connects to the FTP server, the FTP Service uses this account to access shared Windows NT resources and to determine the permissions available to the anonymous user. To substitute an existing Windows NT user account as the anonymous logon account, click Browse to display the Select Windows NT User Account dialog and select the account you want to use for anonymous logons. This account must have the "Log on locally" user right, which normal user accounts do not have by default.

  Password
  : This field contains the password for the Windows NT user account used to grant access to anonymous users. This field must contain a password. You cannot use a blank password. This field is inactive by default because the Enable Automatic Password Synchronization checkbox described below is enabled by default. If you clear that checkbox, this field activates, allowing you to change the password in ISM. If you do this, you must also change the password in UMD to the same password for this account.

  Allow only anonymous connections
  : Mark this checkbox, which is cleared by default, if you want to allow only anonymous connections to the FTP server. When this checkbox is cleared, users who connect anonymously are granted only the limited permissions associated with the anonymous account, while users who provide a valid Windows NT username and password are granted the higher level of permissions associated with their own user accounts. By marking this checkbox, you limit all users to connecting as user anonymous at the limited privilege level assigned to anonymous logons.

Enable Automatic Password Synchronization

If you configure a different Windows NT user account to be used for anonymous logons, you must ensure that the password for this account is identical in both User Manager for Domains and Internet Service Manager. Mark this checkbox to cause ISM to automatically update the ISM password for the anonymous user account when that password is changed in UMD. This checkbox is marked by default if the account used for anonymous logons exists in ISM but not in UMD when that account is created.

- FTP Site Operators section—By default, the Administrators group is assigned operator status. However, you can assign any user or group as an operator. Assign and remove operators as follows:

  Add an operator

  Click on Add to display the Add Users and Groups dialog. Use the List Names From drop-down list to specify the domain from which the account is to be added. The Names pane lists the available users and groups. Double-click a user or group name to add it to the Add Names pane, and then click on OK. ISM adds the selected user or group to the Operators pane.

  Remove an operator

  Highlight the user or group name in the Operators pane and click Remove.

Granting operator status to a user or group grants privileges only for this FTP site. Note that only members of the Windows NT Administrator group can manage virtual FTP sites. Adding a user or group to the Operators pane does not enable them to manage virtual FTP sites.

Configuring Messages properties

Use the Messages page of the FTP Site Properties dialog to configure the messages that FTP clients will see when they visit your site. You can create or modify the following messages, all of which are blank by default, simply by typing the message into the appropriate box:

Welcome

Enter the message you want FTP clients to see when they first connect to your FTP site. It's a good idea to include the name of the site with the greeting. Nowadays, many sites use this message to display copyright information, legal disclaimers, and a warning that unauthorized access or use of the site is prohibited.

Exit

Enter the message you want FTP clients to see when they log off the server. Traditionally, you thank them for visiting the site and invite them to return soon—kind of like the Beverly Hillbillies.

Maximum Connections
If you restrict concurrent connections, enter the message you want FTP clients to see when they attempt to log on to the server when all available connections are already in use.

Configuring Home Directory properties

Use the Home Directory page of the FTP Site Properties dialog, shown in Figure 10-14, to change the location of or modify the properties for the home directory for the FTP site. Installing IIS creates the FTP root directory that you specify, ordinarily *\Inetpub\ftproot*. You can use this dialog to change that location. This is a dynamic dialog, whose contents vary according to the option button you select in the top section, as follows:

A directory located on this computer
Select this option, which is the default, to use an FTP root directory on the local computer where you installed IIS. Use this page to specify the location, access permissions, and directory listing style for the local directory. Uses standard drive/directory syntax, for example, *C:\web\ftpfiles*.

A share located on another computer
Select this option to use an FTP root directory located on a network share, using UNC syntax in the form \\servername\sharename, for example, *\\bastet\ftpfiles*. When you enter the sharename, click Connect As to provide the username and password that will be used to access that share. The other settings are identical to those available when the FTP root directory is on the local computer.

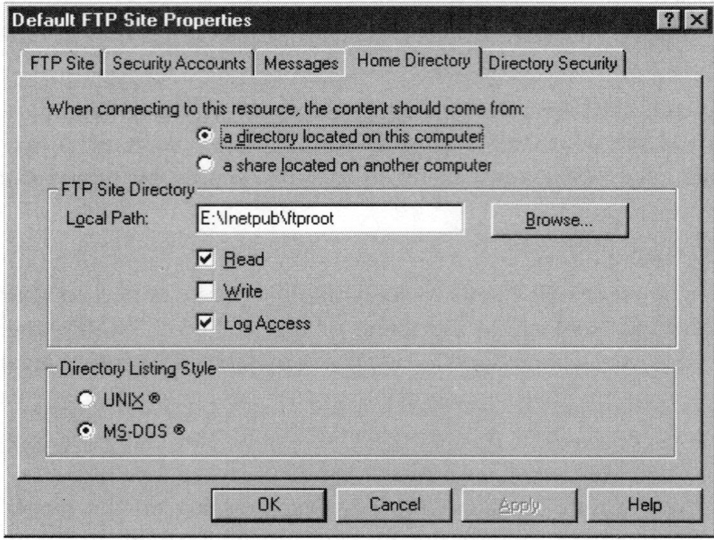

Figure 10-14. The Home Directory page of the FTP Site Properties dialog

Set the following options:

FTP Site Directory section

Local Path / Network Share

Type the drive and directory for the local path where the home directory resides on the local computer, or browse for the location. If you've chosen to locate the FTP root directory on a network share, enter the network share name here in UNC form, and click Connect As to enter the username and password for the account that will be used to access the share.

Read

Mark this checkbox, which is marked by default, to assign Read permission if you want FTP clients to be able to read or download the files contained in the home directory. This checkbox must be marked for FTP to be functional.

Write

Mark this checkbox, which is cleared by default, to assign Write permission if you want FTP clients to be able to upload files to the FTP site. Set this permission only for directories that are intended to receive uploaded files.

Log access

Mark this checkbox, which is marked by default, to cause the FTP Service to write a log file entry for each visit to this directory. For this setting to be effective, logging must be enabled for the FTP site in the FTP Site properties page, which it is by default.

Directory Listing Style section

Specify the directory listing style—Unix or MS-DOS—that the FTP Service will use when returning directory listings to FTP clients. Most modern FTP clients can accept either style, but some clients choke on MS-DOS style listings, so select Unix for maximum compatibility.

Configuring Directory Security properties

Use the Directory Security page of the FTP Site Properties dialog, shown in Figure 10-15, to grant or deny all but specified IP addresses and/or domain names access to the FTP site. For example, if you have created a private FTP site that is intended for use only by your employees, you might use this feature to deny access to all users but those who are members of your own DNS domain. Alternatively, you can elect to grant all but specified IP addresses and/or domain names access to your FTP site. For example, if a particular computer is downloading an excessive number of files from your FTP site, you can deny FTP access to that computer by IP address.

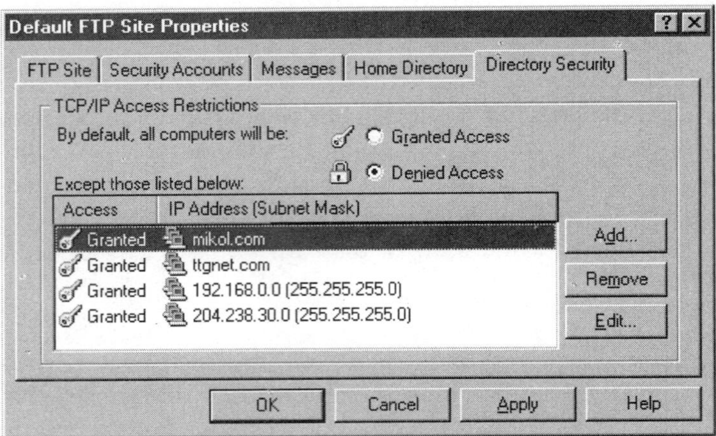

Figure 10-15. The Directory Security page of the FTP Site Properties dialog

Begin by marking one of the option buttons at the top of the dialog to specify the default access. Mark the Granted Access option button if you want to grant access to all computers except those you enter in the list. For a public FTP site, this is the proper choice. Mark the Denied Access option button if you want to deny access to all computers except those you enter in the list. For a private FTP site, this is the usual choice. Once you have specified the default access method, you may take the following actions to modify the list of computers that are granted or denied permission to access the site.

Add

Click this button to display the Deny Access On dialog (if you marked the Granted Access option button for default access) or Grant Access On dialog (if you marked the Denied Access option button for default access). Under Type, mark one of the following option buttons:

Single Computer

To display an IP address entry field in dotted decimal format. ISM enters a line item in the list that grants (or denies, as appropriate) access to this single computer.

Group of Computers

To display a Network ID entry box and a Subnet Mask entry box, both formatted as dotted decimal. Enter the network ID and subnet mask to grant or deny access to the specified subnet.

Domain Name

To display an entry box for domain name. Note that restricting access by domain name is a very resource intensive option, because it requires a reverse DNS lookup for each connection.

Remove
Highlight the line item in the pane and click Remove to remove that grant or deny filter.

Edit
Highlight the line item in the pane and click Edit to change the properties for that grant or deny filter.

Creating Additional FTP Sites

IIS can support multiple FTP sites on one computer. Each FTP site must be uniquely identified by either IP address or TCP port number, as follows:

IP Address
If possible, assign a unique static IP address to each FTP site and create a DNS entry for each. For example, we could assign the FTP site *ftp.ttgnet.com* the IP address 172.16.10.167 and the FTP site *files.ttgnet.com* the IP address 172.16.10.168, create CNAME records for each, and use the drop-down IP Address list on the FTP Site page of the FTP Site Properties dialog to associate each IP address with its corresponding FTP site. There is no ambiguity when an FTP client attempts to access one of these sites, because the resolver stub in the FTP client uses the FTP site name to resolve a unique IP address for the FTP site.

TCP Port number
If you cannot assign a unique IP address to the new FTP site—for example, if your ISP has given you only one IP address—you can define multiple unique FTP sites on an IIS server by assigning each FTP site the same IP address, but with a unique TCP Port number for each site. Use this method only if you must, because FTP clients assume that an FTP server will respond to TCP Port 21, the Well-Known Address for FTP. For an FTP client to access an FTP site using a nonstandard port number, that client must explicitly specify the port number to establish the connection.

After you have decided how to identify the new site uniquely, take the following steps to create it:

1. Start ISM and highlight the IIS computer in the left pane.
2. Choose Action → New → FTP Site to invoke the New FTP Site Wizard.
3. Enter a name for the new FTP site in the FTP Site Description box and click Next. Note that the name you assign here is only the display name used by ISM. It need not be the same as the DNS name for the FTP site.
4. Use the Select the IP Address to use for this FTP Site drop-down list to choose the IP address for the site, and enter the TCP Port number in the TCP Port this FTP Site should use (Default: 21) box. Click Next to continue.

5. Enter (or browse for) the home directory path for this FTP site. Click Next.
6. Set the access permissions for the new FTP site. By default, the Allow Read Access checkbox is marked and the Allow Write Access checkbox is cleared. Accept or modify the default access permissions and click Finish to continue.
7. ISM creates the FTP site and installs it in the tree for the computer. By default, the new FTP site is stopped. To start it, right click the new FTP site name in ISM to display the context sensitive menu and choose Start.
8. Use the FTP Site Properties dialog for the new FTP site to make any configuration changes necessary.
9. Create a DNS CNAME entry for the new FTP site.

Creating an SMTP Site

Installing IIS4 automatically installs the SMTP Site for the Microsoft SMTP Service. You cannot create additional SMTP sites, and you cannot delete the existing SMTP site. There is no SMTP Service selection in Master Properties, because the Default SMTP Site is the one and only SMTP site for the computer. You configure the STMP Site using the SMTP Site Properties tabbed dialog, which includes the following pages:

SMTP Site
: Configure identification, connection options, and logging options for the SMTP site.

Operators
: Specify which users and groups can perform routine administrative functions for the SMTP site.

Messages
: Limit maximum message and session sizes, set the maximum number of outbound messages per connection and the maximum number of recipients per message, and specify what actions the SMTP Service takes when a message cannot be delivered.

Delivery
: Configure message queue options, domain options, smart host settings, and outbound security.

Directory Security
: Configure settings for anonymous access and authentication, secure communications, IP address and domain name restrictions, and SMTP relay restrictions.

To change properties for the SMTP site, right-click the site entry in MMC to display the context-sensitive menu, and then choose Properties to display the tabbed

SMTP Site Properties dialog. Configuring settings for this dialog is described in the following sections.

Configuring SMTP Site properties

Use the SMTP Site page of the SMTP Site Properties dialog, shown in Figure 10-16, to configure identification, connection options, and logging options for the SMTP site.

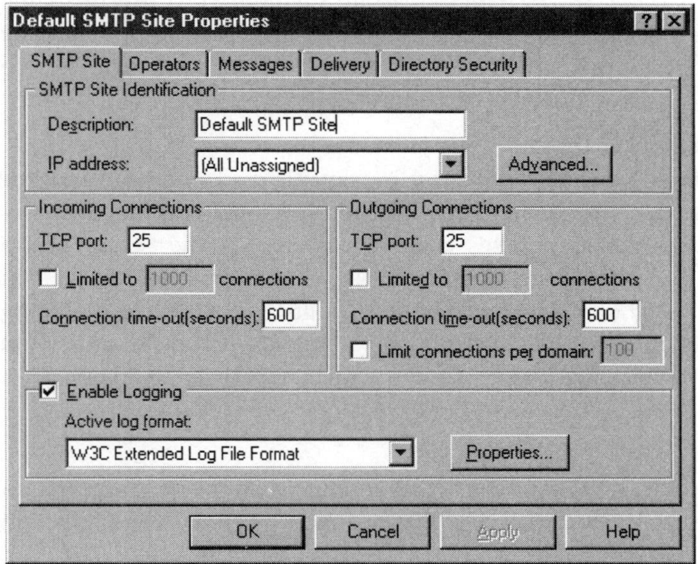

Figure 10-16. The SMTP Site Properties dialog

Use this page to set the following options:

- SMTP Site Identification section

  Description
  : The name of the SMTP site. This is what appears in Internet Service Manager tree view. You can change the name of the Default SMTP Site, but you cannot delete it.

  IP Address
  : Use this drop-down list to select an IP address to be associated with the SMTP site. Only IP addresses that have been assigned to this computer (using the Control Panel Network tool) appear in this list.

  Advanced
  : Click this button to display the Advanced Multiple SMTP Site Configuration dialog, which you can use to assign multiple identities to the SMTP site by mapping additional IP addresses to different TCP port numbers.

Note that any particular TCP port number, for example, the default Port 25, may be mapped to only one IP address.

- Incoming Connections / Outgoing Connections sections

TCP Port

Specifies the TCP port that the SMTP Service uses to connect with other SMTP servers, Port 25 by default. Although you can specify another TCP port number here, doing so restricts the SMTP Service to exchanging messages only with other SMTP Servers that are configured to use the same port. Port 25 is a Well-Known Port, used by all SMTP servers, so changing this port essentially converts your SMTP Service to a private mail service that can interact only with other SMTP servers that you set up yourself.

Limited To x connections

Mark this checkbox, which is cleared by default, and enter a value for connections to limit the number of concurrent inbound or outbound connections for the SMTP site. If this checkbox is cleared, the STMP Service places no limit on simultaneous connections. Microsoft states that if you limit connections, Incoming connections defaults to 1,000 and Outgoing connections defaults to 500, on the theory Outgoing connections should be set to a lower value because the capacity of remote servers is unknown. On our server, at least, both values default to 1,000.

Connection Timeout

Specify, in seconds, how long the STMP Service waits before dropping an inactive connection. The default is 600 seconds for both Incoming and Outgoing connections.

Limit connections per domain

Mark this checkbox, which is cleared by default, and enter a value for connections to limit the number of outgoing to any one remote domain. If you enable this option, it defaults to 100. The value you set here should be less than or equal to the connections limit you set for outgoing connections, if any.

- Enable Logging section

Enable Logging

Mark this checkbox, which is marked by default, to specify that IIS should log individual SMTP transactions on a per-message basis. Because each transaction is logged, enabling this feature may degrade the performance of the SMTP Service.

Active log format

If you enable logging, use the drop-down list to select one of the following log file formats. Once you have selected a format, click Properties to display a property sheet specific to that format, where you can set various logging options, including log time period, log file location, maximum log file size, items to be logged, and so on.

Microsoft IIS Log File Format
: An ASCII log file format with predefined headings.

NCSA Common Log File Format
: The National Center for Supercomputing Applications log format. (Another fixed ASCII format.)

ODBC Logging
: A fixed format logged to an ODBC-aware database, for example, Access or SQL Server. You must create the database yourself before data can be written to it. Using this format allows you to use the more powerful data analysis and reporting tools available with the database application.

W3C Extended Log File Format
: The default log file format. W3C is a configurable ASCII format. By default, Time, Client IP Address, Method, URI Stem, and HTTP Status are logged. You can select among numerous other data types to be logged.

Configuring Operators properties

Use the Operators page of the SMTP Site Properties dialog to specify which users and groups have operator privileges for the SMTP site. Users and groups that have been assigned operator status are listed in the Operators pane. By default, the Administrators group is assigned operator status. However, you can assign any user or group as an operator. Assign and remove operators as follows:

Add an operator
: Click Add to display the Add Users and Groups dialog. Use the List Names From drop-down list to specify the domain from which the account is to be added. The Names pane lists the available users and groups. Double-click a user or group name to add it to the Add Names pane, and then click on OK. Windows NT adds the selected user or group to the Operators pane.

Remove an operator
: Highlight the user or group name in the Operators pane and click Remove.

Configuring Messages properties

Use the Messages page of the SMTP Site Properties dialog, shown in Figure 10-17, to set limits for message and session sizes, the number of messages sent on each outbound connection, the number of recipients for any particular message, and to configure the behavior of the SMTP Service when it is unable to deliver a message.

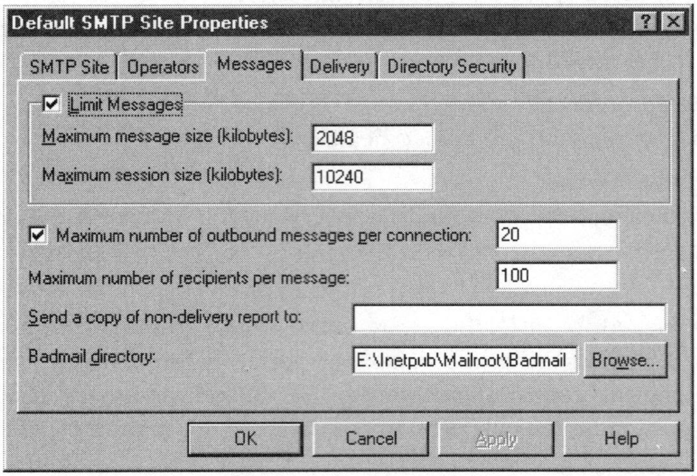

Figure 10-17. The Messages page of the SMTP Site Properties dialog

Configure the following options:

Limit Messages

If you want to limit the maximum size of individual messages or the maximum cumulative size of a session, mark the Limit Messages checkbox, which is marked by default, and enter values for the following fields:

Maximum message size (kilobytes)

Set this value, which defaults to 2,048 KB, to the maximum size that is acceptable for individual messages. This is not a hard limit, but interacts with maximum session size, described below, as follows: if a message exceeds the maximum message size, but is smaller than the maximum session size, it is processed (along with the other queued messages). If the cumulative size of queued messages including this one exceeds the maximum session size, the smaller messages are sent, but this message is not sent during the current session.

Maximum session size (kilobytes)

The maximum cumulative size of all messages acceptable for a single session, by default 10 MB. Once this maximum session size is reached, the connection is automatically closed. This means that if an individual message exceeds the maximum session size, it will never be sent. Set this value carefully, because the message transfer agent may submit large messages repeatedly.

Maximum number of outbound messages per connection

Mark this checkbox, which is marked by default, and enter the number of messages that can be sent on a single outbound connection. With a little bit of experimentation, you can set this value to optimize outbound message throughput for the SMTP Service when it is delivering mail to a remote domain. Each time the limit is reached, the SMTP Service opens an additional connection automatically and immediately, and uses these connections simultaneously to deliver messages in parallel. For example, if this value is set to 20 (the default), and 75 messages are queued for delivery, STMP first opens one connection and begins sending the first 20 messages. When it notices message 21, it opens another connection and begins sending that message. When it notices message 41, it opens a third connection and begins sending that message, and so forth. In this example, SMTP may have 4 connections open and in use simultaneously. By using multiple connections, SMTP can send a large number of messages in parallel, which may be faster than sending all of those messages serially on a single connection.

The dilemma is this: the throughput of any one connection is limited, so you would like to use multiple parallel connections to increase throughput, but opening each additional simultaneous connection imposes additional overhead. You need to strike a balance between the additional throughput added by each connection with the additional overhead required to establish and maintain that connection. To make matters worse, the optimum throughput is also dependent on the response of the remote SMTP server. To determine the best value for this setting, examine the Message Sent/sec performance counter for the SMTP Server object in Performance Monitor, and adjust the setting for this field to a smaller value than Performance Monitor displays.

Maximum number of recipients per message

In theory, sets the maximum number of recipients to which any one message may be sent. The default value is 100, the limit specified in RFC 821. In practice, the Microsoft SMTP Service does not enforce this limit rigidly, as do some SMTP servers. If a sender addresses a single message to more than 100 recipients (or whatever value this field is set to), the SMTP Service simply sends the message to the first 100 recipients, and then sequentially opens however many additional connections are necessary to deliver the message to the remaining recipients. For example, with this limit set to 100, a message addressed to 250 recipients requires three connections. The first connection sends the message to recipients 1 through 100, the second connection, to recipients 101 through 200, and the third, to recipients 201 through 250.

Send a copy of non-delivery report to

When the SMTP Service is unable to deliver an outbound message, it returns that message to the sender with a non-delivery report (NDR). If you want an administrator or other user also to be notified via email of delivery problems by receiving copies of NDRs, enter that person's email address in this box.

Badmail directory

When the SMTP Service generates an NDR in response to an undeliverable outbound message, it can place a copy of that NDR in the location that you specify as the badmail directory. Installing the SMTP Service creates a badmail directory, by default *\Inetpub\Mailroot\Badmail* on the drive where you install IIS. Messages that eventually find their way to this directory because they are improperly addressed or because SMTP cannot deliver them cannot be delivered or returned. The badmail directory is the end of the line. Check it frequently to make sure that delivery problems do not go undetected. Also, allowing many (or large) messages to accumulate in this directory can adversely impact the performance of the SMTP Service.

Configuring Delivery properties

Use the Delivery page of the SMTP Site Properties dialog, shown in Figure 10-18, to set queue, domain, and smart host options for the SMTP Service.

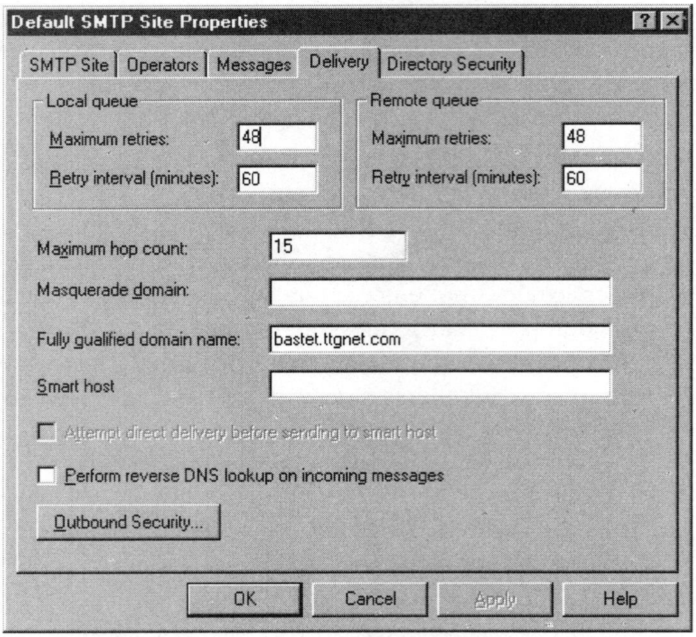

Figure 10-18. The Delivery page of the SMTP Site Properties dialog

Configure the following options:

Local Queue / Remote Queue section

Maximum retries

If SMTP cannot deliver a message on the first attempt, it repeats the attempt either until the message is delivered or until the number of retries specified here is reached. If SMTP cannot deliver the message, it returns an NDR to the sender and copies it to the badmail directory. The value you enter in the Maximum retries box specifies how many attempts SMTP will make before it gives up. The default value for this field for both the local and remote queues is 48.

Retry interval (minutes)

When SMTP cannot deliver a message, it waits for the period specified here before again attempting to deliver the message. The default value for this field for both the local and remote queues is 60 minutes. In conjunction with the default 48 retries value, this means that SMTP will attempt to deliver a message for 48 hours before giving up and returning an NDR to the original sender.

Maximum hop count

Rather than delivering a message directly to the destination server, SMTP may deliver the message to one or more intermediate servers, where it is stored until it can be forwarded to the next server in the chain. The value set for this field, 15 by default, specifies the maximum number of servers through which the message is allowed to pass on its way to the destination. The SMTP server counts the number of hops that the message experiences. When this value exceeds the maximum hop count specified, the SMTP server returns an NDR to the sender.

Masquerade domain

Used to conceal specific host names for improved security. For example, if mail originates from the hosts *kerby.ttgnet.com*, *sherlock.ttgnet.com*, and *thoth.ttgnet.com*, and if *ttgnet.com* is set as the masquerade domain, mail originating from any of those hosts appears to originate instead directly from *ttgnet.com*.

Fully qualified domain name (FQDN)

The domain name used by the DNS MX (mail exchange) record to identify this host. This field defaults to the FQDN specified in the Control Panel Network tool under TCP/IP properties. If you specify an FQDN here, it overrides that FQDN. For example, in this case, the SMTP Service is installed on the computer bastet, whose TCP/IP Properties FQDN is *bastet.ttgnet.com*. By entering another FQDN here, you can alias this computer to respond to that FQDN. For example, most SMTP servers are named mail, so we might enter the FQDN *mail.ttgnet.com* here.

Smart host

Enter the name or IP address of a smart host. If you specify the IP address, enclose it in brackets to increase performance. The SMTP Service parses the contents of this field with the assumption that it is a string rather than an IP address. Using brackets tells SMTP that this is an IP address, and allows it to forgo parsing all but the first character. A smart host is to messages what a router is to IP packets. Rather than simply delivering messages to the designated remote domain, a smart host makes judgements as to the best, fastest, or least costly route by which the message can be delivered to the destination. The smart host is similar to the route domain option for remote domains. It differs in that, once you designate a smart host, all outbound messages are by default delivered to that smart host for processing, whereas when you designate a route domain, only messages destined for that remote domain are delivered to the designated server. If you specify both a smart host and a route domain, the route domain overrides the smart host for messages destined for that domain.

Attempt direct delivery before sending to smart host

Mark this checkbox, which by default is grayed out if no smart host has been specified and cleared if a smart host has been specified, if you want the SMTP Service to attempt to deliver remote messages locally before delivering them to the smart host for processing.

Perform reverse DNS lookup on incoming messages

Mark this checkbox, which is cleared by default, if you want the SMTP Service to verify that the IP address shown for the domain in the From: line matches the originating IP address contained in the header. You do this to verify that the alleged source domain matches the actual IP address. If the reverse DNS lookup succeeds, SMTP inserts the resolved domain name in the Received header. If the reverse DNS lookup fails, SMTP inserts only the IP address. Enabling this option may degrade the performance of the SMTP Service, because it requires a reverse DNS lookup for each inbound message.

Outbound Security

Click this button to display the Outbound Security dialog. Most transactions between SMTP servers are unsecured, which is the default option for this setting. However, if the remote SMTP server requires authentication, you can configure the SMTP Service to provide appropriate credentials to it, as follows:

Clear text authentication

To enable sending authentication credentials to the remote SMTP server in clear text, mark this option button and then click Change to display the SASL/AUTH Account dialog. Enter the Account name, and then enter and confirm the Password. The account information you provide must match an existing account on the remote SMTP server before this SMTP server can connect to the remote server.

Using SMTP Outbound Security

These authentication and encryption options are inappropriate for general use, because most SMTP servers do not support them. Rather than implementing authentication and encryption globally for the SMTP Service by using this dialog, you can define remote route domains for one or more specific SMTP servers, and set authentication/encryption options for the individual route domains.

To define a route domain for SMTP, in the left pane of ISM, take the following steps:

1. In ISM, expand the tree for Default SMTP Site.
2. Right-click the Domains item to display the context-sensitive menu.
3. Choose New and then Domain to invoke the New Domain Wizard.
4. Mark the Remote option button and click Next.
5. Enter the Name to be used for the remote domain and click Finish to define the new remote SMTP domain.
6. Highlight the new remote domain in the right pane of ISM, and right-click to display the context sensitive menu.
7. Choose Properties to display the <remote-domain-name> Properties dialog and click Outbound Security to display the Outbound Security dialog described above. Changes you make in this dialog apply only to the selected remote route domain.

Windows NT Challenge/Response authentication and encryption

To enable sending encrypted Windows NT authentication credentials to the remote Windows NT SMTP server, mark this option button and then click Change to display the Windows NT Account dialog. Enter the User name and Domain, and then enter and confirm the Password. The account information you provide must match an existing Windows NT user account on the remote Windows NT SMTP server before this SMTP server can connect to it.

TLS encryption

Mark this checkbox if you want to use TLS (Transport Layer Security) encryption for outbound messages. The remote SMTP server must understand TLS encryption or it will be unable to process the messages you send it.

Configuring Directory Security properties

Use the Directory Security page of the SMTP Site Properties dialog to configure security settings for the SMTP site. Set the following options:

Anonymous Access and Authentication Control section

Mark one or more of the checkboxes, all of which are marked by default, to allow or deny anonymous access to the SMTP Service and/or allow or deny authenticated access using clear text or Windows NT Challenge/Response authentication. To set anonymous access and authentication options, click Edit to display the Authentication Methods dialog, shown in Figure 10-19.

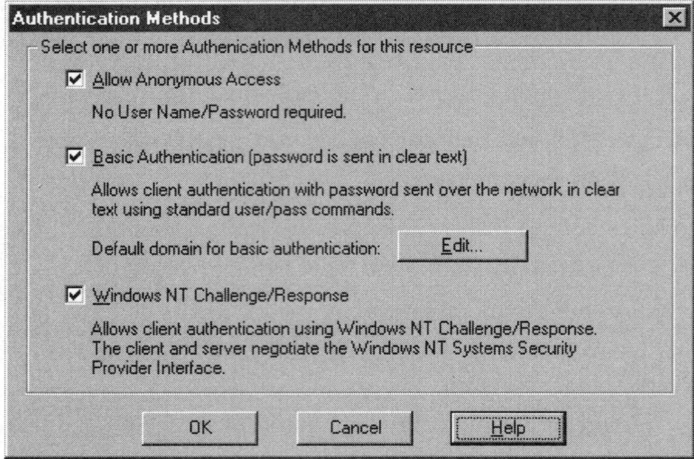

Figure 10-19. The Authentication Methods dialog

Marking a checkbox indicates that that method is an acceptable method for remote SMTP servers to use when connecting to this SMTP site. To require a particular authentication method for the entire SMTP site, mark its checkbox and clear the other two checkboxes. Configure the following options to specify how remote SMTP servers can access this SMTP site:

Allow Anonymous Access
: Mark this checkbox to allow inbound messages to be transferred to the SMTP Service without requiring the remote SMTP server to provide an account name or password. To disable authentication for the SMTP site entirely, leave this checkbox marked and clear the other two checkboxes.

Basic Authentication (password is sent in Clear Text)
: To allow remote SMTP servers to connect to this SMTP site using Basic Authentication, mark this checkbox. By default, authentication is provided by the domain of which the computer running the SMTP Service is a member. To change to another domain, click Edit to display the Basic Authentication Domain dialog, and enter the domain name.

Windows NT Challenge/Response
: Mark this checkbox to enable Windows NT Challenge/Response authentication, a more secure authentication method than the Basic Authentication described above. If the remote SMTP server uses this method to authenticate, it must provide a Windows username, domain name, and password that already exists.

Secure Communications section

You cannot use the secure communications feature of the SMTP Service until you have applied for, received, and installed a server certificate, and bound that certificate to the server key pair. To activate secure channel (TLS) communications, or to manage keys, click Edit to display the Secure Communications dialog. Use this dialog to configure the following items:

Require Secure Channel

To require remote SMTP servers to encrypted message traffic to this SMTP site using TLS encryption, mark this checkbox.

Require 128-bit encryption

Mark this checkbox to require that the remote SMTP server use 128-bit encryption rather than the default 40-bit encryption. 128-bit encryption is available only in the US and Canada.

Key Manager

Click this button to run the Key Manager application, which you can use to apply for, install and manage the keys required to use secure channel communications.

IP Address and Domain Name Restrictions section

Use this section to grant or deny all but specified IP addresses, subnets, and/or domain names access to the SMTP site. To configure grant/deny settings, click Edit to display the IP Address and Domain Name Restrictions dialog shown in Figure 10-20.

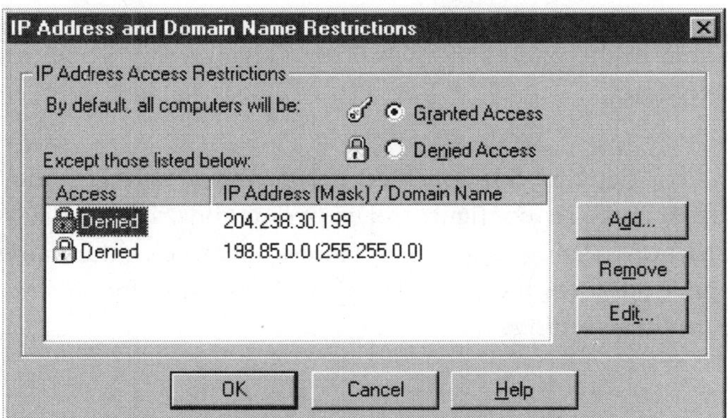

Figure 10-20. The IP Address and Domain Name Restrictions dialog

Begin by marking one of the option buttons at the top of the dialog to specify the default access. Mark the Granted Access option button if you want to grant access to all computers except those you enter in the list. Mark the Denied Access option button if you want to deny access to all computers except those you enter in the list. Once you have specified the default access method, you may take the following actions to modify the list of computers that are granted or denied permission to access the SMTP site.

Add
: Click this button to display the Deny Access On dialog (if you marked the Granted Access option button for default access) or Grant Access On dialog (if you marked the Denied Access option button for default access). Under Type, mark one of the following option buttons:

Single Computer
: To display an IP address entry field in dotted decimal format. ISM enters a line item in the list that grants (or denies, as appropriate) access to this single computer.

Group of Computers
: To display a Network ID entry box and a Subnet Mask entry box, both formatted as dotted decimal. Enter the network ID and subnet mask to grant or deny access to the specified subnet.

Domain Name
: To display an entry box for domain name. Note that filtering by domain name is a very resource intensive option, because it requires a reverse DNS lookup for each operation.

Remove
: Highlight the line item in the pane and click Remove to remove that grant or deny filter.

Edit
: Highlight the line item in the pane and click Edit to change the properties for that grant or deny filter.

Relay Restrictions section
: Use this section to grant or deny all but specified IP addresses, subnets, and/or domain names relay access. To configure relay permissions, click Edit to display the Relay Restrictions dialog, shown in Figure 10-21. Use the same procedures described previously for the IP Address and Domain Name Restrictions section to configure these settings.

Managing IIS

Once you have IIS installed and configured correctly, it normally requires little in the way of routine administration tasks. The following sections provide an overview of some of the administrative tasks you may have occasion to perform. They do not cover monitoring and optimizing IIS performance, which are beyond the

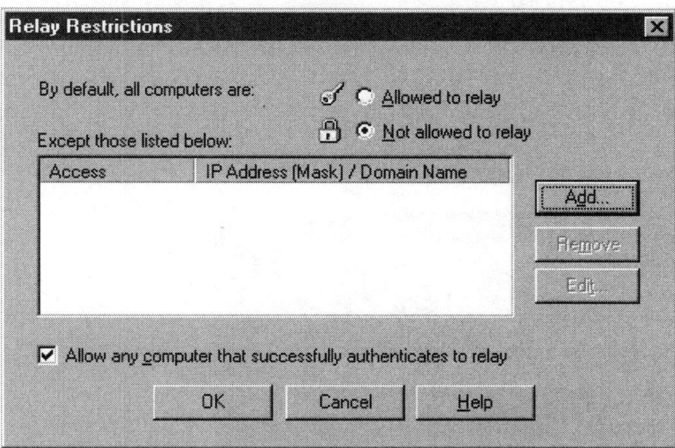

Figure 10-21. The Relay Restrictions dialog

scope of this chapter. For information about how to tune your server, refer to the IIS documentation.

Managing IIS Remotely

In addition to using ISM locally to manage the server running IIS, you can also use ISM to manage the IIS server remotely from another computer on the local network or across the Internet. You can also use the HTML version of ISM to manage the IIS4 server remotely from another computer on the local network or across the Internet.

Managing IIS remotely with ISM

You can install ISM on any computer on your network that runs Windows NT 4.0 (Server or Workstation) and use it to manage IIS servers located anywhere on the network. To install ISM, first make sure that SP3 or higher and Internet Explorer 4.01 or higher is installed on the Windows NT client. Then run Windows NT 4.0 Option Pack Setup and select only the ISM option for installation.

Once you have installed ISM on the client, you can manage remote IIS servers by running ISM and clicking the computer icon on the toolbar to specify the IIS server you want to manage. If you have WINS installed on the network, all IIS servers are displayed. Otherwise, you may see only the IIS servers located on your local subnet. You can use the Connect to Computer dialog to specify an IIS server that is not displayed. Note that if you attempt to use ISM to manage a remote computer over the Internet, you will be unable to do so if the TCP NBT ports have been disabled on the remote network for security reasons.

Managing IIS remotely with ISM (HTML)

You can also use the HTML version of ISM, shown in Figure 10-22, to manage IIS servers located elsewhere on the network or across the Internet. You can run ISM (HTML) either locally on the management workstation, or remotely on the IIS server using only a browser on the management workstation.

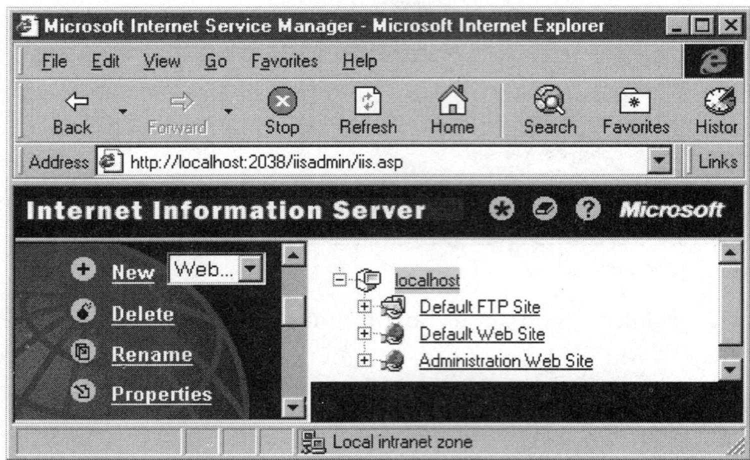

Figure 10-22. The HTML version of Internet Service Manager

To install ISM (HTML) on a client workstation, make sure that SP3 or higher and Internet Explorer 4.01 or higher is installed on the client. Then run Windows NT 4.0 Option Pack Setup and select only the ISM (HTML) option for installation. To use the local copy of ISM (HTML) to manage IIS servers, choose Start → Programs → Windows NT 4.0 Option Pack → Microsoft Internet Information Server—Internet Service Manager (HTML) to load the browser and access the Administration Web Site.

Alternatively, you can use only a browser on the management workstation to run a remote copy of ISM (HTML) on the IIS server and manage that site as an administrator or as an operator, as follows:

- To manage the site as an administrator (with all privileges), start the browser on the management client, and enter both the domain name and the assigned port number for the Administration Web Site. For example, *http://www.ttgnet.com:2042/Iisadmin/*. You can find the administrative port number for the IIS Administrative Web Site by displaying the Web Site page of the Properties dialog for that site.
- To manage the site as an operator (with limited privileges), start the browser on the management workstation, and enter only the domain name for the Administration Web Site. For example, *http://www.ttgnet.com/Iisadmin/*. You

do not need to enter the administrative port number for the IIS Administrative Web Site to manage it as an operator.

Keep the following issues in mind:

- When using ISM (HTML) to manage an IIS4 server, you must set your web browser to refresh each time you visit a page. To set this option in IE4, choose View → Internet Options to display the Internet Options tabbed dialog. In the Temporary Internet Files section of the General page, click Settings to display the Settings dialog and mark the Every visit to the page option button.
- When using ISM (HTML) via a proxy server to manage a remote IIS4 server, you must use the Directory Security page to enable Basic Authentication and disable Windows NT Challenge/Response Authentication, which is not supported on proxy server connections. After you do so, when you attempt to connect to the remote IIS server, you will be prompted to provide credentials before you are granted access.
- With IIS4, you can no longer create a session to *\\iis-server\IPC$* and gain access to the IIS server with another user account. When using ISM (HTML) to administer a remote IIS server, you must log on as an administrator or operator account that is valid on the local IIS server. If you want to use ISM (HTML) on a remote IIS server by logging on with an account other than the account on the local server, you must use the Directory Security page to enable Basic Authentication and disable Windows NT Challenge/Response Authentication. After you do so, when you attempt to connect to the remote IIS server, you will be prompted to provide credentials before you are granted access.
- Some IIS virtual directories appear to ISM (HTML) as nonvirtual directories, which prevents using ISM (HTML) to manage them. Run the script *\WINNT\system32\inetsrv\adminsamples\fixcfg.vbs* to fix this problem.
- If you create a web site with ISM, you must create a virtual directory named *IISADMIN* if you want operators to be able to manage that web site remotely with ISM (HTML). To create the virtual *IISADMIN* directory, take the following steps:
    1. Start ISM and select the web site you want operators to be able to administer remotely with ISM (HTML).
    2. Right-click the web site to display the context-sensitive menu, choose New and then Virtual Directory to invoke the New Virtual Directory Wizard.
    3. Type IISADMIN in the "Alias to be used to access virtual directory" box and then click Next.
    4. Type *C:\WINNT\System32\Inetsrv\Iisadmin* in the "Enter the physical path of the directory containing the content you want to publish" box, replacing *C:* with the local drive that contains the *IISADMIN* directory for

the web site, if different. Click Next to display the access permissions page of the Wizard.

5. By default, only the "Allow Read Access" and "Allow Script Access" checkboxes are marked. Accept these defaults and create the new virtual directory by clicking Finish.
6. ISM redisplays its main screen, with the new virtual directory selected in the left pane. Right-click the new *IISADMIN* directory to display the context-sensitive menu and click Properties to display the Properties dialog for the new virtual directory.
7. Click the Directory Security tab to display the Directory Security page.
8. In the "Anonymous Access and Authentication Control" section, click Edit to display the Authentication Methods dialog.
9. Clear the "Allow Anonymous Access" checkbox, and mark either the "Basic Authentication (Password is sent in Clear Text)" checkbox or the "Windows NT Challenge/Response" checkbox.
10. Click on OK to return to the Properties dialog and click on OK again to save the changes and redisplay ISM.

Note that Administrators do not require this virtual directory to remotely manage the site, because they can use the Administration Web Site to manage any web site on the remote IIS server. Also, you need not perform this procedure if the new web site was created with ISM (HTML). Using ISM (HTML) to create a new web site creates the *IISADMIN* virtual directory automatically, on the assumption that you will want to manage that site remotely.

Managing IIS4 Sites with IIS3 Internet Service Manager

You can use the Internet Service Manager tool supplied with IIS1, IIS2, or IIS3 to manage one web site and one FTP site on an IIS4 server. You must specify the sites in advance. To do so, take the following steps:

1. Start IIS4 ISM and select the computer that runs the web site and/or FTP site you want to manage with the earlier version of ISM.
2. Right click the computer name to display the context-sensitive menu and choose properties to display the <computer-name> Properties dialog.
3. In the Master Properties section, use the drop-down list to select either the WWW Service or the FTP Service.
4. Click Edit to display the WWW Service Master Properties for <computer-name> dialog or the FTP Service Master Properties for <computer-name> dialog.

5. Click the IIS 3.0 Admin tab to display the IIS 3.0 Admin page.
6. Use the Default Web Site drop-down list or the Default FTP Site drop-down list to select the site to be managed by the earlier version of ISM. By default, the Default Web Site and the Default FTP Site are selected in these lists.

Starting, Stopping, and Pausing Sites

By default, sites start automatically when the IIS server starts. To start, stop, or pause a site, start ISM, select the site you want to start, stop, or pause, and:

- Right-click the site to display the context-sensitive menu, and choose Start, Stop, or Pause, or
- Click one of the VCR-like control icons on the toolbar to start, stop, or pause the site.

Keep the following issues in mind:

- Starting, stopping, or pausing a site affects only that site. For example, stopping the Default Web Site prevents users from accessing that site, but allows them to continue to access other web sites on the IIS server.
- If a site hangs for some reason, ISM may still show it as running, which grays out the Start option. To recover when this occurs, stop the site and then restart it.
- You can pause the SMTP Site (as opposed to stopping it) when you need to make configuration changes or maintain the site. Pausing the SMTP Site prevents new inbound or outbound connections from being made, but allows existing connections to continue delivering and receiving messages.

Starting and Stopping Services and Setting Startup Options

By default, installed services—for example, the WWW Service, the FTP Service, and the SMTP Service—start automatically when the IIS server starts. To start or stop a service, or set startup options for that service, use the Control Panel Services tool. To do so, click Start → Settings → Control Panel to display Control Panel. Double click Services to display the Services dialog. Take one of the following actions:

Starting a service
: Highlight the service in the Service pane and click Start to start the service.

Stopping a service
: Highlight the service in the Service pane and click Stop to stop the service.

Configure startup options

Highlight the service in the Service pane and click Startup to display the Service dialog for the service. Mark the Automatic, Manual, or Disabled option button to specify how the service should start.

NOTE In IIS3 and earlier, you can stop the WWW Service or FTP Service by issuing a **net stop** command for the service you want to stop. For example, using the **net stop w3svc** command stops both the web service and the *Inetinfo.exe* process on the IIS3 server.

The multiple site architecture of IIS4 means that this method no longer works. IIS4 uses the IISADMIN Service to manage other services, which means that the IISADMIN service and the *Inetinfo.exe* process continue to run after the WWW Service or the FTP Service is stopped. Using the **net start w3svc** command or the **net start msftpsvc** command also starts the IISADMIN service automatically. To stop the entire IIS service under IIS4, issue the command **net stop iisadmin**.

Backing up and Restoring IIS Configurations

ISM provides the ability to backup your IIS server configuration to a location you designate, and to restore that configuration information when necessary. To back up or restore your IIS configuration, take the following steps:

1. Start ISM and, in the left pane, highlight the IIS computer for which you want to back up the configuration.
2. Right-click the computer to display the context-sensitive menu, and click Backup/Restore Configuration to display the Configuration Backup/Restore dialog.
3. Take one of the following actions:

   To back up the current configuration

   Click Create Backup to display the Configuration Backup dialog, enter a name for the back up set, and click on OK. ISM displays the Configuration Backup dialog to prompt you to enter a name for the backup. This name contain spaces, but may not contain nonprintable characters or any of the following characters: ampersand, asterisk, at sign (@), backslash, backward single quote, caret, dollar sign ($), double quote, equal sign (=), exclamation, forward slash, parenthesis (left or right), percent sign (%), period, pipe (|), plus sign (+), pound sign (#), question mark, or tilde (~).

   To restore a saved configuration

   Highlight the saved configuration in the Backups pane and click Restore.

To remove a saved configuration

Highlight the saved configuration in the Backups pane and click Delete.

Summary

Internet Information Server (IIS) is Microsoft's server-side solution to providing HTTP, FTP, SMTP, and other services to Intranet and Internet clients. IIS 4.0—a component of the downloadable Windows NT 4.0 Option Pack—adds major features to and significantly upgrades the existing capabilities of IIS 2.0, which ships with Windows NT Server 4.0.

IIS 4.0 is managed with Internet Service Manager (ISM), a plug-in for the Microsoft Management Console (MMC), a Windows NT 5.0 component released with the Option Pack. IIS 4.0 also provides ISM/HTML, an administrative tool that allows you to perform most ISM management functions using only a web browser.

In the next chapter we look at troubleshooting.

11

Troubleshooting TCP/IP

In this chapter:

- *Approaching a Problem*
- *Diagnostic Tools*
- *Testing Basic Connectivity*
- *Troubleshooting Network Access*
- *Checking Routing*
- *Checking Name Service*
- *Analyzing Protocol Problems*
- *Protocol Case Study*
- *Simple Network Management Protocol*
- *Summary*

Network administration tasks fall into two very different categories: configuration and troubleshooting. Configuration tasks prepare for the expected; they require detailed knowledge of system configuration but are usually simple and predictable. Once a system is properly configured, there is rarely any reason to change it. The configuration process is repeated each time a new release of Windows NT is installed, but usually with very few changes.

In contrast, network troubleshooting deals with the unexpected. Troubleshooting frequently requires knowledge that is conceptual rather than detailed. Network problems are usually unique and sometimes difficult to resolve. Troubleshooting is an important part of maintaining a stable, reliable network service.

In this chapter we discuss the tools used to ensure that the network is in good running condition. However, good tools are not enough. No troubleshooting tool is effective if applied haphazardly. Effective troubleshooting requires a methodical approach to the problem, and a basic understanding of how the network works. So we'll start our discussion by looking at ways to approach a network problem.

Approaching a Problem

To approach a problem properly, you need a basic understanding of TCP/IP. The first few chapters of this book discuss the basics of TCP/IP, and provide enough background information to troubleshoot most network problems. Knowledge of how TCP/IP routes data through the network, between individual hosts, and between the layers in the protocol stack is important for understanding a network problem, but detailed knowledge of each protocol usually isn't necessary. The fine details of the protocols are rarely needed in debugging, and when they are used, they should be looked up in a definitive reference—not recalled from memory.

Not all TCP/IP problems are alike, and not all problems can be approached in the same manner. But the key to solving any problem is understanding what the problem is. This is not as easy as it may seem. The surface problem is sometimes misleading, and the real problem is frequently obscured by many layers of software. When the true nature of the problem is understood, the solution to the problem is often obvious.

First, gather detailed information about exactly what's happening. When the problem is reported, talk to the user. Find out which application failed. What are the remote host's name and IP address? What are the user's host name and address? What error message was displayed? If possible, verify the problem by having the user run the application while you talk him through it. If possible, duplicate the problem on your own system.

Testing from the user's system, and other systems, find out:

- Does the problem occur in other applications on the user's host, or is only one application having trouble? If only one application is involved, the application may be misconfigured or disabled on the remote host. Because of security concerns, many systems disable some services.
- Does the problem occur with only one remote host, all remote hosts, or only certain groups of remote hosts? If only one remote host is involved, the problem could easily be with that host. If all remote hosts are involved, the problem is probably with the user's system (particularly if no other hosts on your local network are experiencing the same problem). If only hosts on certain subnets or external networks are involved, the problem may be related to routing.
- Does the problem occur on other local systems? Make sure you check other systems on the same subnet. If the problem only occurs on the user's host, concentrate testing on that system. If the problem affects every system on a subnet, concentrate on the router for that subnet.

Once you know the symptoms of the problem, visualize each protocol and device that handles the data. Visualizing the problem will help you avoid oversimplification, and keep you from assuming that you know the cause even before you start testing. Using your TCP/IP knowledge, narrow your attack to the most likely causes of the problem, but keep an open mind.

Troubleshooting Hints

There are several useful troubleshooting hints you should know. These are not a troubleshooting methodology, just good ideas to keep in mind. Here they are, listed in no particular order:

- Approach problems methodically. Allow the information gathered from each test to guide your testing. Don't jump into another test scenario, based on a hunch, without ensuring that you can pick up your original test scenario where you left off.
- Work carefully through the problem, dividing it into manageable pieces. Test each piece before moving on to the next. For example, when testing a network connection, test each part of the network until you find the problem.
- Change only one variable at a time and rerun the test for each variable changed.
- Keep good records of the tests you have completed and their results. Keep a historical record of the problem in case it reappears.
- Keep an open mind. Don't assume too much about the cause of the problem. Don't assume a problem seen at the application level is not caused by a problem at a lower level. Some people assume their network is always at fault, while others assume the remote end is always the problem. Some people are so sure they know the cause of a problem that they ignore the evidence of the tests. Don't fall into these traps. Test each possibility and base your actions on the evidence of the tests.
- Be aware of security barriers. Security firewalls sometimes block **ping, tracert** and even ICMP error messages. If problems seem to cluster around a specific remote site, find out if they have a firewall.
- Pay attention to error messages. Error messages are often vague, but they frequently contain important hints for solving the problem.
- Duplicate the reported problem yourself. Don't rely too heavily on the user's problem report. The user has probably only seen this problem from the application level. If necessary, obtain the user's data files to duplicate the problem. Even if you cannot duplicate the problem, log the details of the reported problem for your records.
- Most problems are caused by human errors. You can prevent some of them by providing information and training on network configuration and usage.
- Keep your users informed. This reduces the number of duplicated trouble reports, and the duplication of effort when several system administrators work on the same problem without knowing others are already working on it. If

you're lucky, someone may have seen the problem before and have a helpful suggestion about how to resolve it.

- Don't speculate about the cause of the problem while talking to the user. Save your speculations for discussions with your networking colleagues. Your speculations may be accepted by the user as gospel, and become rumors. These rumors can cause users to avoid using legitimate network services and may undermine confidence in your network. Users want solutions to their problems; they're not interested in speculative technobabble.
- Stick to a few simple troubleshooting tools. For most TCP/IP software problems, the tools discussed in this chapter are sufficient. You could spend more time learning how to use a new tool than it would take to resolve the problem with an old familiar tool.
- Thoroughly test the problem at your end of the network before locating the owner of the remote system to coordinate testing with him. The greatest complication of network troubleshooting is that you do not always control the systems at both ends of the network. In many cases, you may not even know who does control the remote system. The more information you have about your end, the simpler the job will be when you have to contact the remote administrator.
- Don't neglect the obvious. A loose or damaged cable is always a possible problem. Check plugs, connectors, cables, and switches. Small things can cause big problems.*

Diagnostic Tools

Because most problems have a simple cause, developing a clear idea of the problem often provides the solution. Unfortunately this is not always true, so in this section we begin to discuss the tools that can help you attack the most intractable problems. Most of the tools discussed in this chapter are software tools, but you should also keep some hardware tools handy.

You need enough simple hand tools to maintain the network's equipment and wiring. A pair of needle-nose pliers and a few screw drivers may be sufficient, but you may also need specialized tools to maintain your wiring. For example, attaching RJ45 connectors to Unshielded Twisted Pair (UTP) cable requires special crimping tools. If you buy a network maintenance toolkit from your cable vendor, it will probably contain everything you need.

* Chapter 13, *Information Resources*, explains how to find out who is responsible for a remote network.

A full featured cable tester is also useful. Modern cable testers are small handheld units with a keypad and LCD display that test both thinnet and UTP cable. Tests are selected from the keyboard and results are displayed on the LCD screen. It is not necessary to interpret the results, because the unit does that for you and displays the error condition in a simple text message. For example, a cable test might produce the message "Short at 74 feet." This tells you that the cable is shorted 74 feet away from the tester. What could be simpler? The proper test tools make it easier to locate, and therefore fix, cable problems.

A laptop computer is also a useful piece of test equipment when properly configured. Install TCP/IP software on the laptop. Take it to the location where the user reports a network problem. Disconnect the Ethernet cable from the back of the user's system and attach it to the laptop. Configure the laptop with an appropriate address for the user's subnet and reboot it. Then ping various systems on the network and attach to one of the user's servers. If everything works, the fault is probably in the user's computer. The user trusts this test because it demonstrates something he does every day. Unlike an unidentifiable piece of test equipment displaying the message "No faults found," the user has confidence in the laptop. If the test fails, the fault is probably in the network equipment or wiring. That's the time to bring out the cable tester.

Another advantage of using a laptop as a piece of test equipment is its inherent versatility. It runs a wide variety of test, diagnostic, and management software. Install Windows NT on the laptop and run the software discussed in the rest of this chapter from your desktop or your laptop.

Many diagnostic tools are available, ranging from commercial systems with specialized hardware and software that may cost thousands of dollars, to free software that is available from the Internet. Many software tools are provided with your Windows NT system. This book emphasizes the software diagnostic tools that come with Windows NT. The tools discussed in this book are:

ipconfig
: Provides information about the basic configuration of the interface. It is useful for detecting bad IP addresses, incorrect subnet masks, and improper broadcast addresses.

arp
: Provides information about Ethernet/IP address translation. It can be used to detect systems on the local network that are configured with the wrong IP address. **arp** is covered in this chapter, and is used in an example in Chapter 2, *Delivering the Data*.

netstat

Provides a variety of information. It is used to display interface statistics, network sockets, and the network routing table. **netstat** is used repeatedly in this book.

ping

Indicates whether a remote host can be reached. **ping** also displays information about packet loss and packet delivery time.

nslookup

Provides information about the DNS name service. **nslookup** is covered in detail in Chapter 8, *Configuring DNS Name System*.

tracert

Prints information about each routing hop that packets take going from your system to a remote system.

Network Monitor

Analyzes the individual packets exchanged between hosts on a network. Network Monitor is a TCP/IP protocol analyzer provided with Windows NT Server 4.0. It can examine the contents of packets and is useful for analyzing protocol problems.

Each of these tools, even those covered earlier in the text, are used in this chapter. We start with **ping**, which is used in more troubleshooting situations than any other diagnostic tool.

Testing Basic Connectivity

The **ping** command tests whether a remote host can be reached from your computer. This simple function is extremely useful for testing the network connection, independent of the application in which the original problem was detected. **ping** allows you to determine whether further testing should be directed toward the network connection (the lower layers) or the application (the upper layers). If **ping** shows that packets can travel to the remote system and back, the user's problem is probably in the upper layers. If packets can't make the round-trip, lower protocol layers are probably at fault.

Frequently, a user reports a network problem by stating that he can't Telnet (or FTP, or send email, or whatever) to some remote host. He then immediately qualifies this statement with the announcement that it worked before. In cases like this, where the ability to connect to the remote host is in question, **ping** is a very useful tool.

Using the host name provided by the user, ping the remote host. If your ping is successful, have the user ping the host. If the user's ping is also successful, concentrate your further analysis on the specific application that the user is having trouble with. Perhaps the user is attempting to Telnet to a host that only provides anonymous FTP. Perhaps the host was down when the user tried his application. Have the user try it again, while you watch or listen to every detail of what he or she is doing. If he is doing everything right and the application still fails, detailed analysis of the application with Network Monitor and coordination with the remote system administrator may be needed.

If your **ping** is successful and the user's **ping** fails, concentrate testing on the user's system configuration, and on those things that are different about the user's path to the remote host, when compared to your path to the remote host.

If your ping fails, or the user's ping fails, pay close attention to any error messages. The error messages displayed by **ping** are helpful guides for planning further testing. The details of the messages may vary, but there are only a few basic types of errors:

unknown host
: The remote host's name cannot be resolved by name service into an IP address. The name servers could be at fault (either your local server or the remote system's server), the name could be incorrect, or something could be wrong with the network between your system and the remote server. If you know the remote host's IP address, try to **ping** that. If you can reach the host using its IP address, the problem is with name service. Use **nslookup** to test the local and remote servers, and to check the accuracy of the host name the user gave you.

network unreachable
: The local system does not have a route to the remote system. If the numeric IP address was used on the **ping** command line, re-enter the **ping** command using the host name. This eliminates the possibility that the IP address was entered incorrectly, or that you were given the wrong address. If a routing protocol is being used, make sure it is running and use **netstat** to check the routing table. If a static default route is being used, make sure the default route is in the routing table. If everything seems fine on the host, check its default gateway for routing problems.

no answer
: The remote system did not respond. Most network utilities have some version of this message. Some print the message "100% packet loss"; others print the message "Connection timed out" or the error "cannot connect." All of these errors mean the same thing. The local system has a route to the remote system, but it receives no response from the remote system to any of the packets it sends. There are many possible causes of this problem. The remote host may be down. Either the local or the remote host may be configured

incorrectly. A gateway or circuit between the local host and the remote host may be down. The remote host may have routing problems. Only additional testing can isolate the cause of the problem. Carefully check the local configuration using **ipconfig**. Check the route to the remote system with **tracert**. Contact the administrator of the remote system and report the problem.

All of the tools mentioned here will be discussed later in this chapter. However, before leaving **ping**, let's look more closely at the command.

The ping Command

The basic format of the **ping** command is **ping** *destination*, where *destination* is the host name or IP address of the remote host being tested. Use the host name or address provided by the user in the trouble report. For example, to check that *pooh* can be reached from *thoth*, we use the following command:

```
C:\ping 172.16.12.2

Pinging 172.16.12.2 with 32 bytes of data:

Reply from 172.16.12.2: bytes=32 time<10ms TTL=32
Reply from 172.16.12.2: bytes=32 time<10ms TTL=32
Reply from 172.16.12.2: bytes=32 time<10ms TTL=32
Reply from 172.16.12.2: bytes=32 time<10ms TTL=32
```

By default the Windows NT **ping** command sends out four, 32-byte test packets. The sample test shows an extremely good network link with no packet loss and fast response. The round-trip to *pooh* is taking less than 10 milliseconds. A small packet loss, and the round-trip times an order of magnitude higher, would not be abnormal for a connection made across a wide area network.

If the packet loss is high or the response time is very slow, there could be a network hardware problem. If you see these conditions when communicating great distances on a wide area network, there is nothing to worry about. TCP/IP was designed to deal with unreliable networks, and some wide area networks suffer a lot of packet loss. But if these problems are seen on a local area network, they indicate trouble.

On a local network cable segment the round-trip time should be near zero, there should be little or no packet loss, and the packets should arrive in order. If these things are not true, there is a problem with the network hardware. On an Ethernet the problem could be improper cable termination, a bad cable segment, or a bad piece of active hardware, such as a hub, switch, or transceiver. Check the cable with a cable tester as described earlier. Good hubs and switches often have built in diagnostic software that can be checked. Cheap hubs and transceivers may require the brute force method of disconnecting individual pieces of hardware until the problem goes away.

The results of a simple **ping** test, even if the test is successful, can help you direct further testing toward the most likely causes of the problem. But other diagnostic tools are needed to examine the problem more closely and find the underlying cause.

Troubleshooting Network Access

The "no answer" and "cannot connect" errors indicate a problem in the lower layers of the network protocols. If the preliminary tests point to this type of problem, concentrate your testing on routing and on the network interface. Use the **ipconfig**, **netstat**, and **arp** commands to test the Network Access Layer.

Troubleshooting with the ipconfig Command

ipconfig checks the network interface configuration. Use this command to verify the user's configuration if the user's system has been recently configured, or if the user's system cannot reach the remote host while other systems on the same network can.

When **ipconfig** is entered with the **/all** argument, it displays the current configuration values assigned to the interface. For example:

```
C:\ipconfig /all
Windows NT IP Configuration
        Host Name . . . . . . . . . : pooh
        DNS Servers . . . . . . . . : thoth
        Node Type . . . . . . . . . : Broadcast
        NetBIOS Scope ID. . . . . . :
        IP Routing Enabled. . . . . : No
        WINS Proxy Enabled. . . . . : No
        NetBIOS Resolution Uses DNS : No
Ethernet adapter SMCISA1:
        Description . . . . . . . . : SMC Adapter.
        Physical Address. . . . . . : 00-00-C0-9A-72-CA
        DHCP Enabled. . . . . . . . : No
        IP Address. . . . . . . . . : 172.16.12.2
        Subnet Mask . . . . . . . . : 255.255.255.0
        Default Gateway . . . . . . : thoth
```

The **ipconfig** command displays two types of information. The first type is information about the TCP/IP configuration. The second type is about the network interface and its characteristics. Check the information for configuration errors.

The Windows NT **ipconfig** command clearly labels each piece of information it provides. Every item from Host Name to Default Gateway is explained somewhere in this book. You should know what values are correct for your network, and thus be able to quickly detect a configuration error if one has been made.

Two common interface configuration problems are misconfigured subnet masks and incorrect IP addresses. A bad subnet mask is indicated when the host can reach other hosts on its local subnet and remote hosts on distant networks, but it cannot reach hosts on other local subnets. **ipconfig** quickly reveals if a bad subnet mask is set.

An incorrectly set IP address can be a subtle problem. If the network part of the address is incorrect, every **ping** will fail with the "no answer" error. In this case, using **ipconfig** will reveal the incorrect address. If the host part of the address is wrong, the problem can be more difficult to detect. A small system, such as a PC that only connects out to other systems and never accepts incoming connections, can run for a long time with the wrong address without its user noticing the problem. Additionally, the system that suffers the ill effects may not be the one that is misconfigured. It is possible for someone to accidentally use your IP address on his system, and for the mistake to cause your system intermittent communications problems. An example of this problem is discussed later. This type of configuration error cannot be discovered by **ipconfig**, because the error is on a remote host. The **arp** command is used for this type of problem.

Troubleshooting with the arp Command

The **arp** command is used to analyze problems with IP to Ethernet address translation. The **arp** command has three useful options for troubleshooting:

-a
: Display all ARP entries in the table.

-d *hostname*
: Delete an entry from the ARP table.

-s *hostname ether-address*
: Add a new entry to the table.

With these three options you can view the contents of the ARP table, delete a problem entry, and install a corrected entry. The ability to install a corrected entry is useful in buying time while you look for the permanent fix.

Use **arp** if you suspect that incorrect entries are getting into the address resolution table. One clear indication of problems with the ARP table is a report that the wrong host responded to some command, like **ftp** or **telnet**. Intermittent problems that affect only certain hosts can also indicate that the ARP table has been corrupted. ARP table problems are usually caused by two systems using the same IP address. The problems appear intermittent, because the entry that appears in the table is the address of the host that responded quickest to the last ARP request. Sometimes the correct host responds first, and sometimes the wrong host responds first.

If you suspect that two systems are using the same IP address, display the address resolution table with the **arp -a** command. Here's an example:

```
C:\arp -a
Interface: 172.16.12.1 on Interface 2
  Internet Address      Physical Address      Type
  pooh.ttgnet.com       00-00-c0-dd-d4-da     dynamic
  kerby.ttgnet.com      00:00:0c:e0:80:b1     dynamic
  wotan.ttgnet.com      00:00:c0:22:fd:51     dynamic
```

It is easiest to verify that the IP and Ethernet address pairs are correct if you have a record of each host's correct Ethernet address. For this reason you should record the Ethernet and IP address of each host assigned a static address* when it is added to your network. If you have such a record, you'll quickly see if anything is wrong with the table.

If you don't have this type of record, the first three bytes of the Ethernet address can help you to detect a problem. The first three bytes of the address identify the equipment manufacturer. A list of these identifying prefixes is found in the *Assigned Numbers* RFC, in the section entitled "Ethernet Vendor Address Components." This information is also available at *ftp://ftp.isi.edu/in-notes/iana/assignments/ethernet-numbers*.

From the vendor prefixes we see that two of the ARP entries displayed in our example are PC systems with SMC boards (0:0:c0). If *kerby* is also supposed to be a system with an SMC board, the 0:0:0c Cisco prefix indicates that a Cisco router has been mistakenly configured with *kerby's* IP address.

If neither checking a record of correct assignments nor checking the manufacturer prefix helps you identify the source of the errant ARP, try using Telnet to connect to the IP address shown in the ARP entry. If the device supports Telnet, the logon banner might help you identify the incorrectly configured host.

ARP problem case study

A user called in asking if the server was down, and reported the following problem. The user's workstation, called *theodore*, appeared to lock up for minutes at a time when certain commands were used, while other commands worked with no problems. The network commands that depended on the server all caused the lock-up problem, but some unrelated commands also caused the problem.

The server *thoth* was providing *theodore* with services. The commands that failed on *theodore* were commands that required *thoth's* services, or that were stored in a directory shared from *thoth*. The commands that ran correctly were installed

* We emphasize static addresses because addresses assigned by DHCP do not cause address conflicts, which is one more reason to use DHCP whenever you can.

locally on the user's workstation. No one else reported a problem with the server, and we were able to ping *theodore* from *thoth* and get good responses.

We had the user check the Event Viewer for recent error messages, and she discovered the event shown in Figure 11-1.

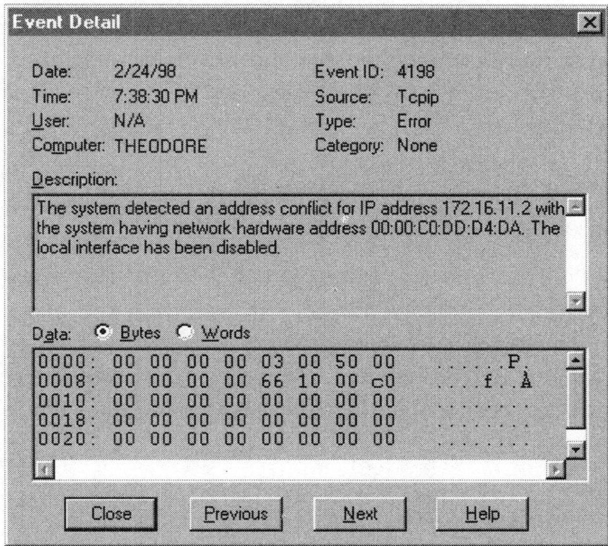

Figure 11-1. Duplicate address warning

The message shown in Figure 11-1 indicates that the workstation detected another host on the Ethernet responding to its IP address. The imposter used the Ethernet address 0:0:c0:dd:d4:da in its ARP response. The correct Ethernet address for *theodore* is 8:0:20:e:12:37.

We checked *thoth's* ARP table and found that it had the incorrect ARP entry for *theodore*. We deleted the bad *theodore* entry with the **arp -d** command, and installed the correct entry with the **-s** option, as shown here:

```
C:\>arp -d theodore
theodore (172.16.6.7) deleted
C:\>arp -s theodore 8:0:20:e:12:37
```

ARP entries received via the ARP protocol are temporary. The values are held in the table for a finite lifetime and are deleted when that lifetime expires. New values are then obtained via the ARP protocol. Therefore, if some remote interfaces change, the local table adjusts and communications continue. Usually this is a good idea, but if someone is using the wrong IP address, that bad address can keep reappearing in the ARP table even if it is deleted. However, manually entered values are permanent; they stay in the table and can only be deleted manually. This allowed us to install a correct entry in the table, without worrying about it being immediately overwritten by a bad address.

This quick fix resolved *theodore's* immediate problem, but we still needed to find the culprit. We checked the DHCP configuration to see if we had an entry for Ethernet address 0:0:c0:dd:d4:da, but we didn't. From the first three bytes of this address, 0:0:c0, we knew that the device was an SMC card. We guessed that the problem address was recently installed because the user had never had the problem before. We sent out an urgent announcement to all users asking if anyone had recently installed a new PC, reconfigured a PC, or installed TCP/IP software on a PC. We got one response. When we checked his system, we found out that he had entered the address 172.16.6.7 when he should have entered 172.16.6.17. The address was corrected and the problem did not recur.

Nothing fancy was needed to solve this problem. Once we checked the error messages, we knew what the problem was and how to solve it. Involving the entire network user community allowed us to quickly locate the problem system and to avoid a room-to-room search for the PC. Reluctance to involve users and make them part of the solution is one of the costliest, and most common, mistakes made by network administrators.

Checking the Interface with netstat

If the preliminary tests lead you to suspect that the connection to the local area network is unreliable, the **netstat -e** command can provide useful information. The example below shows the output from the **netstat –e** command:

```
C:\>netstat -e
Interface Statistics
                            Received          Sent
Bytes                         112088        123876
Unicast packets                  612           613
Non-unicast packets              258           257
Discards                           0             0
Errors                             0             0
Unknown protocols                  2
```

The command displays the total amount of traffic that this system has received from and sent to the Ethernet—in both bytes and packets. It also displays the number of packets in error. *Discards* are packets that were received from the network and then discarded by the local system because they contained errors or could not be processed. *Errors* are damaged packets, including packet sent from this system that were damaged in the local buffer. These errors should be close to zero. Regardless of how much traffic has passed through this interface, 100 errors in either of these fields is high. High output errors could indicate a saturated local network or a bad physical connection between the host and the network. High input errors could indicate that the network is saturated, the local host is overloaded, or there is a physical network problem. Tools, such as the Network Monitor or a cable tester, can help you determine if it is a physical network problem.

The problem may be an overloaded network. To reduce the network load, reduce the amount of traffic on the network segment. A simple way to do this is to create multiple segments out of the single segment. Each new segment has fewer hosts and, therefore, less traffic. We'll see, however, that it's not quite this simple.

The most effective way to subdivide an Ethernet is to install an Ethernet switch. Each port on the switch is essentially a separate Ethernet. Therefore a 16 port switch gives you 16 Ethernets to work with when balancing the load. On most switches the different ports can be used in a variety of different ways (see Figure 11-2). Lightly used systems can be attached to a hub that is then attached to one of the switch ports to allow the systems to share a single segment. Servers and demanding systems can be given dedicated ports so that they don't need to share a segment with anyone. Additionally, some switches provide a few Fast Ethernet 100M bps ports. These are called asymmetric switches because different ports operate at different speeds. Use the Fast Ethernet ports to connect heavily used servers. If you're buying a new switch, buy a 10/100 switch with auto-sensing ports. This allows every port to be used at either 100M bps or at 10M bps, which gives you the maximum configuration flexibility.

Figure 11-2 shows an 8 port 10/100 Ethernet switch. Ports 1 and 2 are wired to Ethernet hubs. A few systems are connected to each hub. When new systems are added they are distributed evenly among the hubs to prevent any one segment from becoming overloaded. Additional hubs can be added to the available switch ports for future expansion. Port 4 attaches a demanding system with its own private segment. Port 6 operates at 100M bps and attaches a heavily used server. Port 7 is reserved for a future 100M bps connection to a second 10/100 Ethernet switch for even more expansion.

Before allocating the ports on your switch evaluate what services are in demand and who talks to whom. Then develop a plan that reduces the amount of traffic flowing over any segment. For example, if the demanding system on Port 6 uses lots of bandwidth because it is constantly talking to one of the systems on Port 1, all of the systems on Port 1 will suffer because of this traffic. The computer that the demanding system communicates with should be moved to one of the vacant ports or to the same port (6) as the demanding system. Use your switch to greatest advantage by balancing the load.

Should you segment an old coaxial cable Ethernet by cutting the cable and joining it back together through a router or a bridge? No. If you have an old network that is finally reaching saturation, it is time to install a new network built on a

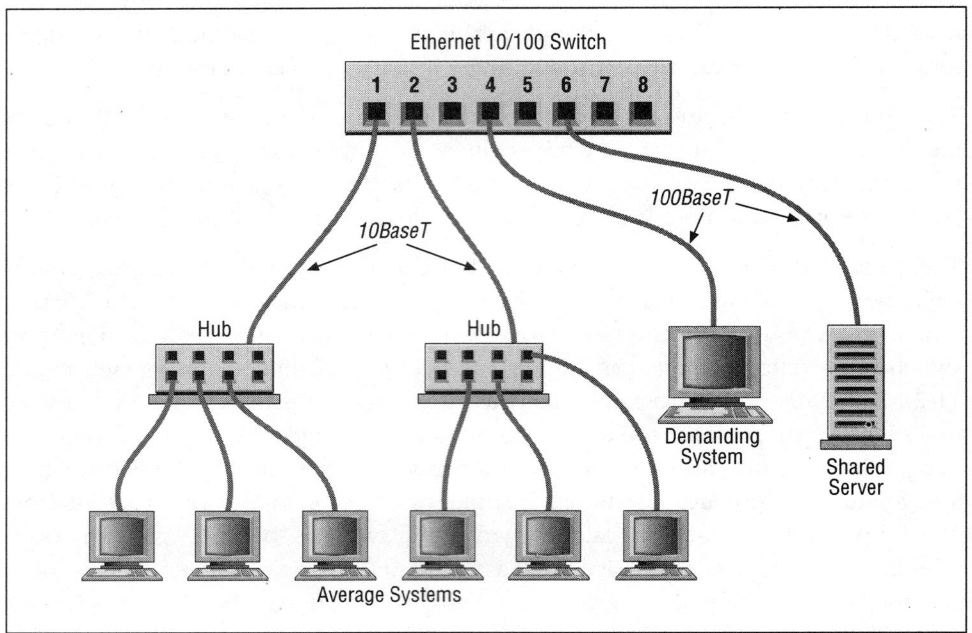

Figure 11-2. Subdividing an Ethernet with Switches

more robust technology. A *shared media* network, which is a network where everyone is on the same cable, as with a coaxial cable Ethernet, is an accident waiting to happen. Design a network that a user cannot bring down by merely disconnecting his system, or even by accidentally cutting a wire in his office. Use the appropriate Unshielded Twisted Pair (UTP) cable to create a 10BaseT Ethernet or 100BaseT Fast Ethernet that wires equipment located in the user's office to a hub securely stored in a wire closet. The network components in the user's office should be sufficiently isolated from the network so that damage to those components does not damage the entire network. The new network will solve your collision problem and reduce the amount of hardware troubleshooting you are call upon to do.

Network hardware problems

Some of the tests discussed in this section can show a network hardware problem. If a hardware problem is indicated, contact the people responsible for the hardware. If the problem appears to be in a leased telephone line, contact the telephone company. If the problem appears to be in a wide area network, contact the management of that network. Don't sit on a problem expecting it to go away. It could easily get worse.

If the problem is in your local area network, you will have to handle it yourself. Some tools, such as the cable tester described above, can help. But frequently the only way to approach a hardware problem is by brute force—disconnecting pieces of hardware until you find the one causing the problem. The switch or hub is a convenient point where this can be done. If you identify a device causing the problem, repair or replace it. Remember the problem can be the cable itself, rather than any particular device.

Checking Routing

The "network unreachable" error message clearly indicates a routing problem. If the problem is in the local host's routing table, it is easy to detect and resolve. First, use **netstat -nr** or **route print** to see whether or not a valid route to your destination is installed in the routing table.

For example, a user reports that the "network is down" because he cannot FTP to *ftp.microsoft.com*, and a **ping** test returns the following results:

```
% ping ftp.microsoft.com
PING ftp.microsoft.com: 32 data bytes
sendto: Network is unreachable
ping: wrote ftp.microsoft.com 32 chars, ret=-1
sendto: Network is unreachable
ping: wrote ftp.microsoft.com 32 chars, ret=-1
```

Based on the "network unreachable" error message, check the user's routing table. In our example, we're looking for a route to *ftp.microsoft.com*. The IP address* of *ftp.microsoft.com* is 205.187.99.57, which is a class C address. Remember that routes are network oriented. So we check for a route to network 205.187.99.0. If a specific route is not found, remember to look for a default route. If **netstat** shows the correct specific route, or a valid default route, the problem is not in the routing table. In that case, use **tracert**, as described in the next section, to trace the route all the way to its destination.

If **netstat** doesn't return the expected route, it's a local routing problem. There are two ways to approach local routing problems, depending on whether the system uses static or dynamic routing. Most systems that use static routing rely on a default route, so the missing route could be the default route. Use the Gateway tab in the TCP/IP Properties window to install the default route as described in Chapter 5. If you use multiple static routes, use **route -p add** to define them, which is also covered in Chapter 5, *Installing TCP/IP*.

* Use **nslookup** to find the IP address if you don't know it. **nslookup** is discussed later in this chapter.

If you're using dynamic routing, make sure that the routing program is running. The various routing protocols for Windows NT are provided by the Routing and Remote Access Service (RRAS). If the correct routing daemon is not running, start it as specified in Chapter 9, *Microsoft Routing and Remote Access Service*.

Tracing Routes

If the local routing table is correct, the problem may be occurring some distance away from the local host. Remote routing problems can cause the "no answer" error message, as well as the "network unreachable" error message. But the "network unreachable" message does not always mean a routing problem. It can literally mean that the remote network cannot be reached because something is down between the local host and the remote destination. **tracert** is the program that can help you locate these problems.

tracert traces the route of UDP packets from the local host to a remote host. It prints the name (if it can be determined) and IP address of each gateway along the route to the remote host.

tracert uses two techniques, small TTL (time-to-live) values and an invalid port number, to trace packets to their destination. **tracert** sends out UDP packets with small TTL values to detect the intermediate gateways. The TTL values start at one and increase in increments of one for each group of three UDP packets sent. When a gateway receives a packet, it decrements the TTL. If the TTL is then zero, the packet is not forwarded and an ICMP "Time Exceeded" message is returned to the source of the packet. **tracert** displays one line of output for each gateway from which it receives a "Time Exceeded" message.

When the destination host receives a packet from **tracert**, it returns an ICMP "Unreachable Port" message. This happens because **tracert** intentionally uses an invalid port number (33434) to force this error. When **tracert** receives the "Unreachable Port" message, it knows that it has reached the destination host, and it terminates the trace. In this way, **tracert** is able to develop a list of the gateways, starting at one hop away and increasing one hop at a time, until the remote host is reached. Figure 11-3 illustrates the flow of packets tracing to a host three hops away.

The following example shows a **tracert** to *ds.internic.net* from a workstation hanging off BBN PlaNET. **tracert** sends out three packets at each TTL value. If no response is received to a packet, **tracert** prints an asterisk (*). If a response is received, **tracert** displays the packet's round-trip time in milliseconds and the address of the gateway that responded.

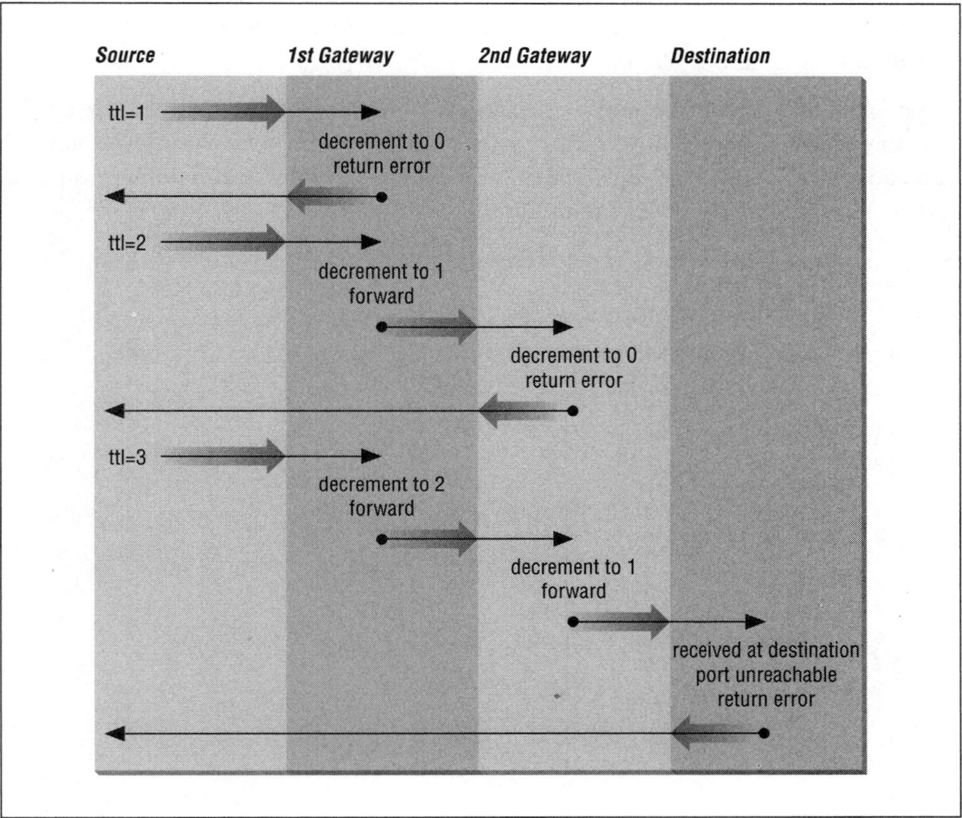

Figure 11-3. Flow of tracert packets

```
C:\>tracert ds.internic.net
Tracing route to ds.internic.net [198.49.45.10]
over a maximum of 30 hops:
  1     10 ms    <10 ms     <10 ms     172.16.55.254
  2    <10 ms               <10 ms     <10 ms 172.16.2.252
  3    <10 ms    <10 ms      10 ms     172.16.13.254
  4    <10 ms     10 ms      10 ms     192.221.253.2
  5    <10 ms     10 ms      10 ms     4.0.1.173
  6    <10 ms     10 ms      10 ms     4.0.1.90
  7     10 ms     10 ms      10 ms     4.0.2.70
  8     10 ms     20 ms      20 ms     4.0.3.126
  9     10 ms     20 ms      20 ms     4.0.2.162
 10     20 ms     10 ms      20 ms     4.0.2.181
 11     20 ms     20 ms      20 ms     4.0.1.122
 12     20 ms     30 ms      20 ms     4.0.3.94
 13     30 ms     40 ms      40 ms     206.34.99.38
 14     130 ms    100 ms     90 ms     198.49.45.10
Trace complete.
```

This trace shows that thirteen intermediate gateways are involved, that packets are making the trip, and that round-trip travel time for packets from this host to *ds.internic.net* is about 107 ms.

Variations and bugs in the implementation of ICMP on different types of gateways and the unpredictable nature of the path a datagram can take through a network can cause some odd displays. For this reason, you shouldn't examine the output of **tracert** too closely. The most important things in the **tracert** output are:

- Did the packet get to its remote destination?
- If not, where did it stop?

Below we show another trace of the path to *ds.internic.net.* This time the trace does not go all the way through to the InterNIC.

```
C:\>tracert -d ds.internic.net
Tracing route to ds.internic.net [198.49.45.10]
over a maximum of 30 hops:
  1      10 ms     <10 ms     <10 ms     172.16.55.254
  2     <10 ms     <10 ms     <10 ms     172.16.2.252
  3     <10 ms     <10 ms      10 ms     172.16.13.254
  4     <10 ms      10 ms      10 ms     192.221.253.2
  5     <10 ms      10 ms      10 ms     4.0.1.173
  6     <10 ms      10 ms      10 ms     4.0.1.90
  7      10 ms      10 ms      10 ms     4.0.2.70
  8      10 ms      20 ms      20 ms     4.0.3.126
  9       *          *          *
 10       *          *          *
 .
 .
 .
 29       *          *          *
 30       *          *          *
```

When **tracert** fails to get packets through to the remote end-system, the trace trails off, displaying a series of three asterisks at each hop count until the count reaches 30. If this happens, contact the administrator of the remote host you're trying to reach, and the administrator of the last gateway displayed in the trace. Describe the problem to them; they may be able to help.*

In our example, the last gateway that responded to our packets was 4.0.3.126. We would contact this system administrator, and the administrator of *ds.internic.net.*

* Chapter 13 explains how to find out who is responsible for a specific computer.

Checking Name Service

Name server problems are indicated when the "unknown host" error message is returned by the user's application. Name server problems can usually be diagnosed with **nslookup**. Three features of **nslookup** are particularly important for troubleshooting remote name server problems. These features have the ability to:

- Locate the authoritative servers for the remote domain using the NS query.
- Obtain all records about the remote host using the ANY query.
- Browse all entries in the remote zone using **nslookup**'s **ls** and **view** commands.

When troubleshooting a remote server problem, directly query the authoritative servers returned by the NS query. Don't rely on information returned by non-authoritative servers. If the problems that have been reported are intermittent, query all of the authoritative servers in turn and compare their answers. Intermittent name server problems are sometimes caused by the remote servers returning different answers to the same query.

The ANY query returns all records about a host, thus giving the broadest range of troubleshooting information. Simply knowing what information is (and isn't) available can solve a lot of problems. For example, if the query returns an MX record but no A record, it is easy to understand why the user couldn't **telnet** to that host! Many hosts are accessible to mail that are not accessible by other network services. In this case, the user is confused and is trying to use the remote host in an inappropriate manner.

If you are unable to locate any information about the host name that the user gave you, perhaps the host name is incorrect. If you have the IP address, use the PTR query to do a reverse lookup. Without a valid host name or address, looking for the correct name is like trying to find a needle in a haystack. However, **nslookup** can help. Use **nslookup**'s **ls** command to dump the remote zone file, and redirect the listing to a file. Then use **nslookup**'s **view** command to browse through the file, looking for names similar to the one the user supplied. Many problems are caused by a mistaken host name.

The **nslookup** features and commands mentioned here are used in Chapter 8. Some examples using these commands to solve real name server problems are shown here. The two examples that follow are based on actual trouble reports.*

* The host and server names are fictitious, but the problems were real.

Some systems work, others don't

A user reported that she could resolve a certain host name from her workstation, but could not resolve the same host name from the central system. However, the central system could resolve other host names. We ran several tests and found that we could resolve the host name on some systems and not on others. There seemed to be no predictable pattern to the failure. So we used **nslookup** to check the remote servers.

```
C:\>nslookup
Default Server: thoth.ttgnet.com
Address: 172.16.12.1

> set type=NS
> foo.edu.
Server: thoth.ttgnet.com
Address: 172.16.12.1

foo.edu nameserver = gerbil.foo.edu
foo.edu nameserver = red.big.com
foo.edu nameserver = shrew.foo.edu
gerbil.foo.edu inet address = 198.97.99.2
red.big.com inet address = 184.6.16.2
shrew.foo.edu inet address = 198.97.99.1
> set type=ANY
> server gerbil.foo.edu
Default Server: gerbil.foo.edu
Address: 198.97.99.2

> hamster.foo.edu
Server: gerbil.foo.edu
Address: 198.97.99.2

hamster.foo.edu inet address = 198.97.99.8
> server red.big.com
Default Server: red.big.com
Address: 184.6.16.2
> hamster.foo.edu
Server: red.big.com
Address: 184.6.16.2

*** red.big.com can t find hamster.foo.edu: Non-existent domain
```

This sample **nslookup** session contains several steps. The first step is to locate the authoritative servers for the host name in question (*hamster.foo.edu*). We set the query type to NS to get the name server records, and queried for the domain (*foo.edu*) in which the host name is found. This returns three names of authoritative servers: *gerbil.foo.edu*, *red.big.com*, and *shrew.foo.edu*.

Next, we set the query type to ANY to look for any records related to the host name in question. Then we set the server to the first server in the list, *gerbil.foo.edu*, and queried for *hamster.foo.edu*. This returns an address record. So server *gerbil.foo.edu* works fine. We repeated the test using *red.big.com* as the server, and it fails. No records are returned.

The next step is to get SOA records from each server and see if they are the same:

```
> set type=SOA
> foo.edu.
Server: red.big.com
Address: 184.6.16.2

foo.edu origin = gerbil.foo.edu
    mail addr = amanda.gerbil.foo.edu
    serial=10164, refresh=43200, retry=3600, expire=3600000,
    min=2592000
> server gerbil.foo.edu
Default Server: gerbil.foo.edu
Address: 198.97.99.2

> foo.edu.
Server: gerbil.foo.edu
Address: 198.97.99.2

foo.edu origin = gerbil.foo.edu
    mail addr = amanda.gerbil.foo.edu
    serial=10164, refresh=43200, retry=3600, expire=3600000,
    min=2592000

> exit
```

If the SOA records have different serial numbers, perhaps the zone file, and therefore the host name, has not yet been downloaded to the secondary server. If the serial numbers are the same and the data is different, as in this case, there is a definite problem. Contact the remote domain administrator and notify her of the problem. The administrator's mailing address is shown in the "mail addr" field of the SOA record. In our example, we would send mail to *amanda@gerbil.foo.edu* reporting the problem.

The data is here and the server can't find it!

This problem was reported by the administrator of a secondary name server. The administrator reported that his server could not resolve a certain host name in a domain for which his server was a secondary server. The primary server was, however, able to resolve the name.

The problem was replicated on several other secondary servers. The primary server would resolve the name; the secondary servers wouldn't. All servers had the same SOA serial number, so why wouldn't they resolve the host name to an address?

Visualizing the difference between the way primary and secondary servers load their data made us suspicious of the zone file transfer. Primary servers load the data directly from local disk files. Secondary servers transfer the data from the primary server via a zone file transfer. Perhaps the zone files were getting corrupted. We displayed the zone file on one of the secondary servers, and it showed the following data:

```
C:\WINNT\System32\Dns>type sales.ttgnet.com.dns
PCpma   IN  A    172.16.64.159
        IN  HINFO"pc" "n3/800salesttgnetcom"
PCrkc   IN  A    172.16.64.155
        IN  HINFO"pc" "n3/800salesttgnetcom"
PCafc   IN  A    172.16.64.189
        IN  HINFO"pc" "n3/800salesttgnetcom"
accu    IN  A    172.16.65.27
cmgds1  IN  A    172.16.130.40
cmg     IN  A    172.16.130.30
PCgns   IN  A    172.16.64.167
        IN  HINFO"pc" "(3/800salesttgnetcom"
gw      IN  A    172.16.65.254
zephyr  IN  A    172.16.64.188
        IN  HINFO"Sun" "sparcstation"
ejw     IN  A    172.16.65.17
PCecp   IN  A    172.16.64.193
        IN  HINFO"pc" "n^Lsparcstationstcom"
```

Notice the odd display in the last field of the HINFO statement for each PC. This data might have been corrupted in the transfer or it might be bad on the primary server. We used **nslookup** to check that.

```
C:\>nslookup
Default Server: thoth.ttgnet.com
Address: 172.16.12.1

> server mandy.sales.ttgnet.com
Default Server: mandy.sales.ttgnet.com
Address: 172.16.6.1

> set query=HINFO
> PCwlg.sales.ttgnet.com
Server: mandy.sales.ttgnet.com
Address: 172.16.6.1

PCwlg.sales.ttgnet.com CPU=pc OS=ov
packet size error (0xf7fff590 != 0xf7fff528)
> exit
```

In this **nslookup** example, we set the server to *mandy.sales.ttgnet.com*, which is the primary server for *sales.ttgnet.com*. Next we queried for the HINFO record for one of the hosts that appeared to have a corrupted record. The "packet size error" message clearly indicates that **nslookup** was even having trouble retrieving the HINFO record directly from the primary server. We contacted the administrator of the primary server and told him about the problem, pointing out the records that appeared to be in error. He discovered that he had forgotten to put an operating system entry on some of the HINFO records. He corrected this, and it fixed the problem.

Analyzing Protocol Problems

Problems caused by bad TCP/IP configurations are much more common than problems caused by bad TCP/IP protocol implementations. Most of the problems you encounter will succumb to analysis using the simple tools we have already discussed. But on occasion, you may need to analyze the protocol interaction between two systems. In the worst case, you may need to analyze the packets in the data stream bit by bit. Protocol analyzers help you do this.

Network Monitor is the tool we'll use. It is provided with Windows NT Server 4.0.* Although we use Network Monitor in our examples, the concepts introduced in this section should be applicable to any analyzer, because most protocol analyzers function in basically the same way. Protocol analyzers display network statistics and allow you to select packets and to examine those packets byte by byte. We'll discuss all of these functions.

Network Monitor

The Network Monitor comes with Windows NT Server 4.0, but it is not installed by default. To install the monitor, go to the Control Panel, open Network, select the Services tab, and click on Add. From the list of services that is displayed, select and install "Network Monitor Tools and Agent". Once the Network Monitor is installed, it is run from the Start menu [Start → Programs → Administrative Tools (Common) → Network Monitor].

When the Network Monitor starts, it just sits there. To see any interesting statistics or data, you must select Start from the Capture menu at the top of the window. Figure 11-4 shows the Network Monitor window while a capture is running. The window displays a graph of the network load. It displays a scroll pane that contains network statistics, statistics about the capture buffer, Ethernet card statistics, and errors. At the bottom of the window, it displays a scroll pane that shows every network address detected, the number of frames and bytes transferred by that address, and whether the frames were unicast, multicast, or broadcast. Clearly, Network Monitor provides much more statistical information than a simple **netstat** command!

---

* The standard Network Monitor can only monitor traffic from or to the Windows NT system on which it is running. A more full-featured version that can monitor all network traffic is available with the optional System Management Server (SMS) software from Microsoft.

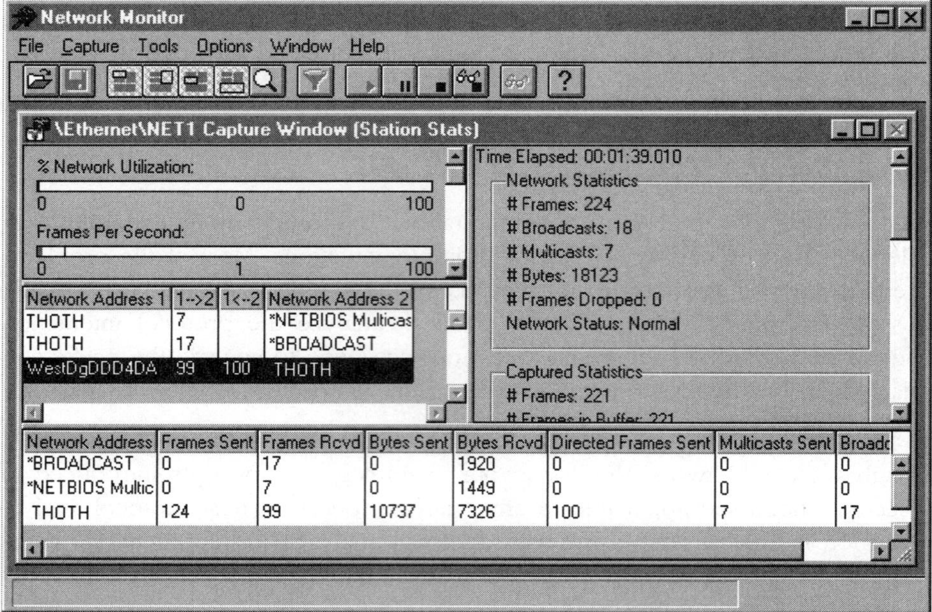

Figure 11-4. Gathering statistics with Network Monitor

Select "Stop and View" from the capture menu to view more details of the packets that have been captured. This stops the packet capture and opens the Capture: Summary pane, which lists summary information about every packet received during the capture. The Network Monitor displays a single line of summary information for each packet received. Each line contains a frame number,* the time the packet was received, the source and destination Ethernet addresses, the protocol being used, and the source and destination IP addresses.

This summary information is sufficient to gain insight into how packets flow between two hosts and into potential problems. Frequently, this is enough to solve the problem. However, troubleshooting protocol problems sometimes requires more detailed information about each packet.

To display the data contained in a packet, double-click on the summary line of the packet in the Capture: Summary window. Figure 11-5 shows how Network Monitor displays the details of a packet. Double-clicking on a frame in the Capture: Summary pane divides the pane into three separate scroll frames. The top scroll is the normal summary information mentioned above. The middle scroll area is a break out of the individual fields in the frame header. The scroll section at the

* The Network Monitor refers to the packets as frames because they contain the Ethernet framing information when they are captured.

bottom of the pane displays the packet data in hex and ASCII. In most cases, you don't need to see the entire packet. Usually, the headers are sufficient to troubleshoot a protocol problem. But the data is there when you need it.

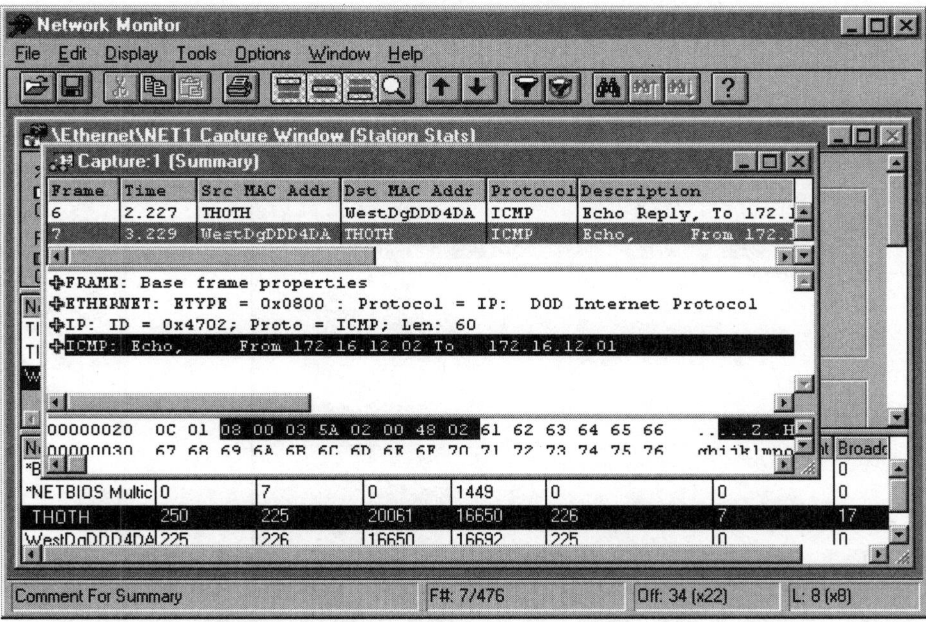

Figure 11-5. Detail packet information

The formatting done by Network Monitor maps the bytes received from the network to the header structure. Look at the description of the various header fields in Chapter 1, *Overview of TCP/IP*, for more information.

By default, Network Monitor captures all of the packets to or from the local host. This can create lots of information, much of which may be of no interest. Filters are used to select a subset of these packets. Filters can be defined to capture packets from, or to, specific hosts or protocols, packets that contain specific data, or combinations of all these.

The Network Monitor supports two types of filters. You can create a capture filter before you start to capture data so that only the data you want is collected in the capture buffer. The advantage of a capture filter is that it saves buffer space. The other type of filter is a display filter. It filters the packets that are already in the buffer so that only those you want are displayed.

To define a capture filter, select Filter from the Capture menu before you start to capture data. The Capture Filter window shown in Figure 11-6 appears. The filter shown in Figure 11-6 is the default filter that Network Monitor uses to capture all data into and out of the NT system. It, and all other Network Monitor filters, can filter on three types of information. First is the physical network frame type (SAP/ETYPE). Second is the source or destination address of the packet. And third is the data contained in the packet. The default filter accepts all frame types going into or out of *thoth* and does not filter out any of them based on the data they contain.

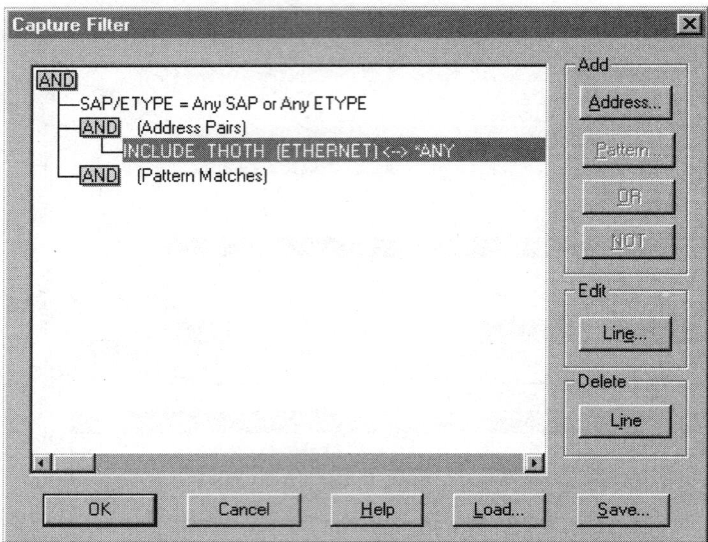

Figure 11-6. Defining a Network Monitor Filter

To change a value in the filter, highlight it and select the Line button that appears in the Edit box. For example, we might highlight the SAP/ETYPE line and edit it to only accept IP-type Ethernet frames. We also might highlight the entry under Address Pairs and change it to only capture packets to a specific host instead of all hosts. All of these changes are made by selecting values from scroll boxes that are displayed when the Edit Line button is selected.

The display filter is defined in a very similar way. The biggest difference is that the filter is defined after the capture. First capture data. Then select "Stop and View" from the capture menu. The Capture: Summary window is displayed. Select Filter from the Display menu. This opens a window that is almost identical to the one shown in Figure 11-6. Modifying values in this filter controls what frames are displayed in the Capture : Summary pane.

In the following section we look at how a protocol analyzer was used to troubleshoot a network problem.

Protocol Case Study

This example is an actual case that was solved by protocol analysis. The problem was reported as an occasional FTP failure with the error message:

```
netout: Option not supported by protocol
421 Service not available, remote server has closed connection
```

Only one user reported the problem, and it occurred only when transferring large files from a workstation to the central computer, via our FDDI backbone network.

We obtained the user's data file and were able to duplicate the problem from other workstations, but only when we transferred the file to the same central system via the backbone network. Figure 11-7 graphically summarizes the tests we ran to duplicate the problem.

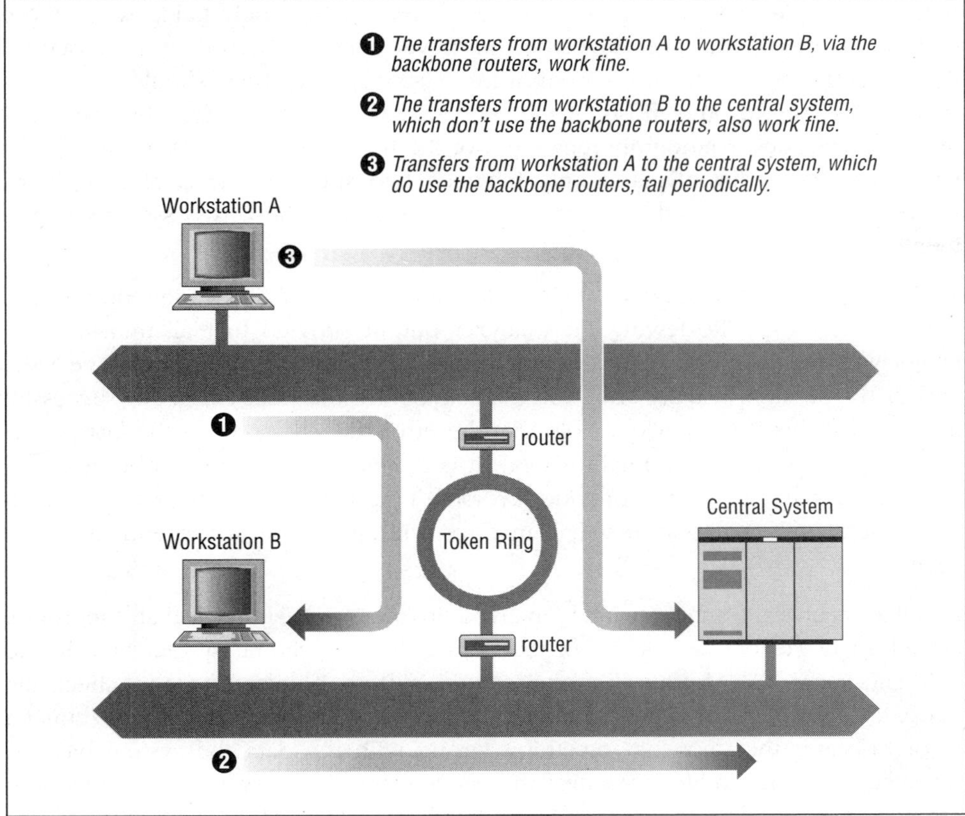

Figure 11-7. FTP test summary

We notified all users of the problem. In response, we received reports that others had also experienced it, but again only when transferring to the central system and only when transferring via the backbone. They had not reported it because they rarely saw it. But the additional reports gave us some evidence that the problem did not relate to any recent network changes.

Because the problem had been duplicated on other systems, it probably was not a configuration problem on the user's system. The FTP failure could also be avoided if the backbone routers and the central system did not interact. So we concentrated our attention on those systems. We checked the routing tables and ARP tables, and ran **ping** tests on the central system and the routers. No problems were observed.

Based on this preliminary analysis, the FTP failure appeared to be a possible protocol interaction problem between a certain brand of routers and a central computer. We made that assessment because the transfer routinely failed when these two brands of systems were involved, but never failed in any other circumstance. If the router or the central system were misconfigured, they should fail when transferring data to other hosts. If the problem was an intermittent physical problem, it should occur randomly regardless of the hosts involved. Instead, this problem occurred predictably, and only between two specific brands of computers. Perhaps there was something incompatible in the way these two systems implemented TCP/IP.

Therefore, we used a protocol analyzer to capture the TCP/IP headers during several FTP test runs. Reviewing the analyzer output showed that all transfers that failed with the *netout* error message had an ICMP Parameter Error packet near the end of the session, usually about 50 packets before the final close. No successful transfer had this ICMP packet. Note that the error did *not* occur in the last packet in the data stream, as you might expect. It is common for an error to be detected, and for the data stream to continue for some time before the connection is actually shut down. Don't assume that an error will always be at the end of a data stream.

Detailed analysis of the packets involved in the error showed that the router issued an IP Header Checksum of 0xffff, and that the central system objected to this checksum. We know that the central system objected to the checksum because it returned an ICMP Parameter Error with a Pointer of 10. The Parameter Error indicates that there is something wrong with the data the system has just received, and the Pointer identifies the specific byte that the system thinks is in error. The tenth byte of the router's IP header is the IP Header Checksum. The data field of the ICMP error message returns the header that it believes is in error. When we displayed that data we noticed that when the central system returned the header, the checksum field was corrected to 0000. Clearly the central system disagreed with the router's checksum calculation.

Occasional checksum errors will occur. They can be caused by transmission problems, and are intended to detect these types of problems. Every protocol suite has a mechanism for recovering from checksum errors. So how should they be handled in TCP/IP?

To determine the correct protocol action in this situation, we turned to the authoritative sources—the RFCs. RFC 791, *Internet Protocol*, provided information about the checksum calculation, but the best source for this particular problem was RFC 1122, *Requirements for Internet Hosts—Communication Layers*, by R. Braden. This RFC provided two specific references that define the action to be taken. These two quotes are taken from page 29 of RFC 1122:

> In the following, the action specified in certain cases is to "silently discard" a received datagram. This means that the datagram will be discarded without further processing and that the host will not send any ICMP error message (see Section 3.2.2) as a result.
>
> ...
>
> A host MUST verify the IP header checksum on every received datagram and silently discard every datagram that has a bad checksum.

Therefore, when a system receives a packet with a bad checksum, it is not supposed to do anything with it. The packet should be discarded, and the system should wait for the next packet to arrive. The system should not respond with an error message. A system cannot respond to a bad IP header checksum, because it cannot really know where the packet came from. If the header checksum is in doubt, how do you know if the addresses in the header are correct? And if you don't know for sure where the packet came from, how can you respond to it?

IP relies on the upper layer protocols to recover from these problems. If TCP is used (as it was in this case), the sending TCP eventually notices that the recipient has never acknowledged the segment, and it sends the segment again. If UDP is used, the sending application is responsible for recovering from the error. In neither case does recovery rely on an error message returned from the recipient.

Therefore, for an incorrect checksum, the central system should have simply discarded the bad packet. The vendor was informed of this problem and, much to their credit, they sent us a fix for the software within two weeks. Not only that, the fix worked perfectly!

Not all problems are resolved so cleanly. But the technique of analysis is the same no matter what the problem.

Simple Network Management Protocol

Troubleshooting is necessary to recover from problems, but the ultimate goal of the network administrator is to avoid problems. That is also the goal of network management software. The network management software used on TCP/IP networks is based on the *Simple Network Management Protocol* (SNMP).

SNMP is a client/server protocol. In SNMP terminology it is described as a *manager/agent protocol*. The *agent* (the server) runs on the device being managed, which is called the *Managed Network Entity*. The agent monitors the status of the device and reports that status to the *manager*.

The *manager* (the client) runs on the *Network Management Station* (NMS). The NMS collects information from all of the different devices that are being managed, consolidates it, and presents it to the network administrator. This design places all of the data manipulation tools and most of the human interaction on the NMS. Concentrating the bulk of the work on the manager means that the agent software is small and easy to implement. Correspondingly, most TCP/IP network equipment comes with an SNMP management agent.

SNMP is a request/response protocol. The request and response messages that SNMP sends in the datagrams are called *Protocol Data Units* (PDU). These message types allow the manager to request management information, and when appropriate, to modify that information. The messages also allow the agent to respond to manager requests and to notify the manager of unusual situations.

The NMS periodically requests the status of each managed device and each agent responds with the status of its device. Making periodic requests is called *polling*. Polling reduces the burden on the agent because the NMS decides when polls are needed, and the agent simply responds. Polling also reduces the burden on the network because the polls originate from a single system at a predictable rate. The shortcoming of polling is that it does not allow for real-time updates. If a problem occurs on a managed device, the manager does not find out until the agent is polled. To handle this, SNMP uses a modified polling system called *trap-directed polling*.

A *trap* is an interrupt signaled by a predefined event. When a trap event occurs, the SNMP agent does not wait for the manager to poll; instead it immediately sends information to the manager. Traps allow the agent to inform the manager of unusual events while allowing the manager to maintain control of polling.

SNMP has a rudimentary security mechanism called *community names*. A community name is a group name known only to the members of the group. Every system in the community must use the same community name. The SNMP agent compares the community name contained in each request it receives against its own community name. If they match, it honors the request. If they don't match, the agent discards the request and generates an *authenticationFailure* trap. The default community name "public" is used when no security is desired.

Every piece of information managed by SNMP has a unique object identifier. These objects are grouped together in a *Management Information Base* (MIB). The MIB refers to all information that is managed by SNMP. However, we usually refer to "a MIB" or "the MIBs" (plural), meaning the individual databases of management information formally defined by an RFC or privately defined by a vendor.

MIBI and MIBII are standards defined by RFCs. MIBII is a superset of MIBI, and is the standard MIB for monitoring TCP/IP. It provides such information as the number of packets transmitted into and out of an interface, and the number of errors that occurred sending and receiving those packets—useful information for spotting usage trends and potential trouble spots. Every agent supports MIBI or MIBII.

Some systems also provide a private MIB in addition to the standard MIBII. Private MIBs add to the monitoring capability by providing system-specific information. Private MIBs are most common on network hardware like routers, hubs, and switches.

A private MIB won't do you any good unless your network monitoring software also supports that MIB. For this reason, most administrators prefer to purchase a monitor from the vendor that supplies the bulk of their network equipment. Another possibility is to select a monitor that includes a *MIB compiler*, which gives you the most flexibility. A MIB compiler reads in the description of a MIB and adds the MIB to the monitor. A MIB compiler makes the monitor *extensible* because if you can get the source from the network equipment vendor, you can add the vendor's private MIB to your monitor.

SNMP has twice as much jargon as the rest of networking—and that's saying something! Managed Network Entity, NMS, PDU, trap, polling, and MIB. Why this bewildering array of acronyms and buzzwords? We think there are two main reasons:

- First, network management covers a wide range of different devices from hubs to computers. A vendor-neutral language is needed to define terms for the manufacturers of all of this different equipment.
- Second, SNMP is based on the *Common Management Information Protocol* (CMIP) that was created by the *International Standards Organization* (ISO). Formal international standards always spend a lot of time defining terms because it is important to make terms clear when they are used by people from many different cultures who speak many different languages.

Don't be put off by the jargon. All of this detail is necessary to formally define a network management scheme that is independent of the managed systems, but you don't need to memorize it. You need to know that a MIB is a collection of management information, that an NMS is the network management station, and that an agent runs in each managed device in order to make intelligent decisions when selecting an SNMP monitor. This information provides that necessary background. The features available in network monitors vary widely; so does the price. Select an SNMP monitor that is suitable for the complexity of your network and the size of your budget!

Windows NT does not provide an SNMP management station, but it does provide an agent. If you install an SNMP manager on your network, enable the SNMP agent on your NT system. To do this, go to the Control Panel, open Network, select the Services tab, and click Add. From the services list that is displayed, select *SNMP Service*. The system will automatically display the SNMP Properties sheet where you configure the agent. The properties sheet contains three tabs:

Agent
: The Agent tab is used to define contact and location information that identifies this system on the management station. The contact is the name of the user of the Windows NT system and the location is the NT system's physical location. For example, the contact might be "Tyler McCafferty" and the location might be "Building 10, room 101."

Traps
: The Traps tab is used to define the IP address of the management station to which traps are sent, and the community name that must be used to communicate with that station.

Security
: The Security tab defines the community names that the Windows NT agent will accept in packets it receives. By default this is set to "public." The Security tab also allows you to define the IP addresses from which your agent will accept SNMP packets.

Define the configuration. Reboot the system, and your NT computer will report its status to the SNMP Network Management Station.

Summary

Inevitably a network breaks. This chapter discusses the tools and techniques that are used to recover from network problems, and the planning and monitoring that can help avoid them. The solution to a problem is sometimes obvious if you can just gain enough information to know exactly what the problem is. Windows NT provides several built-in software tools that can help you gather information about system configuration, addressing, routing, name service, and other vital network components. Gather your tools and learn how to use them before a problem occurs.

In the next chapter we talk about another task that is important to the maintenance of a reliable network. In Chapter 12, *Network Security*, we look at ways to keep your network secure.

12

Network Security

In this chapter:
- *Security Planning*
- *Firewalls*
- *Encryption*
- *User Authentication*
- *Software Security*
- *Security Monitoring*
- *File Security*
- *Words to the Wise*
- *Summary*

A Windows NT system attached to a network, particularly the Internet, is exposed to a wider range of security threats than an unconnected system. Network security reduces the risks of connecting to a network. But by their natures, network access and computer security work at cross purposes. A network is a data highway designed to increase access to computer systems, while security is designed to control access. Providing network security is a balancing act between open access and security.

The highway analogy is very appropriate. Like a highway, the network provides equal access for all—welcome visitors as well as unwelcome intruders. At home, you provide security for your possessions by locking your house, not by blocking the streets. Likewise, network security generally means providing adequate security on individual computers, not providing security directly on the network.

In very small towns, where people know each other, doors are often left unlocked. But in big cities, doors have deadbolts and chains. In the last decade, the Internet has grown from a small town of a few thousand users to a big city of millions of users. Just as the anonymity of a big city turns neighbors into strangers, the growth of the Internet has reduced the level of trust between network neighbors. The ever increasing need for computer security is an unfortunate side effect. Growth, however, is not all bad. In the same way that a big city offers more choices and more services, the expanded network provides increased services. For most of us, security consciousness is a small price to pay for network access.

Network break-ins have increased as the network has grown and become more impersonal, but it is easy to exaggerate the real extent of these break-ins. Overreacting to the threat of break-ins may hinder the way you use the network. Don't make the cure worse than the disease. The best advice about network security is to use common sense. RFC 1244, *Site Security Handbook*, by Holbrook, Reynold, et. al., states this principle very well:

> Common sense is the most appropriate tool that can be used to establish your security policy. Elaborate security schemes and mechanisms are impressive, and they do have their place, yet there is little point in investing money and time on an elaborate implementation scheme if the simple controls are forgotten.

This chapter emphasizes the simple controls that can be used to increase your network's security. A reasonable approach to security, based on the level of security required by your system, is the most cost effective—both in terms of actual expense and in terms of productivity.

Security Planning

One of the most important network security tasks, and probably one of the least enjoyable, is developing a network security policy. Most computer people want a technical solution to every problem. We want to find a program that fixes the network security problem. Few of us want to write a paper on network security policies and procedures. However, a well thought-out security plan will help you decide what needs to be protected, how much you are willing to invest in protecting it, and who will be responsible for carrying out the steps to protect it.

Assessing the Threat

The first step toward developing an effective network security plan is to assess the threat that connection presents to your systems. RFC 1244 identifies three distinct types of security threats usually associated with network connectivity:

Unauthorized access
: A break-in by an unauthorized person.

Disclosure of information
: Any problem that causes the disclosure of sensitive information to people who should not have access to the information.

Denial of service
: Any problem that makes it difficult or impossible for the system to continue to perform productive work.

Assess these threats in relation to the number of users who would be affected, as well as to the sensitivity of the information that might be compromised. For some organizations, break-ins are an embarrassment that can undermine the confidence that others have in the organization, and intruders tend to target organizations that will be the most embarrassed by the break-in. But for most organizations, unauthorized access is not a major problem unless it involves one of the other threats: disclosure of information or denial of service.

Assessing the threat of information disclosure depends on the type of information that could be compromised. No system with highly classified information should ever be directly connected to the Internet, but other types of sensitive information do not prohibit connecting the system to a network. Personnel information, medical information, corporate plans, credit records—all of these things are sensitive and must be protected. In some cases, this information can be adequately protected by NT File System (NTFS) security procedures. In other cases this information should be protected by a firewall. And in some cases, the risk of liability if this information is disclosed may be sufficient to keep the host that stores the information from being connected to the Internet in any manner. Only the organization that controls the information and faces the liability if the data is compromised can decide how much protection is required.

Denial of service attacks are easy to launch and difficult to protect against. Denial of service can be a severe problem if it impacts many users or a major mission of your organization. Some systems can be connected to the network with little concern. The benefit of connecting individual workstations and small servers to the Internet generally outweighs the chance of having service interrupted for the individuals and small groups served by these systems. Other systems may be vital to the survival of your organization. The threat of losing the services of a mission-critical system must be evaluated seriously before connecting such a system to an external network.

In his class on computer security, Brent Chapman describes the three information security threats as threats to the integrity, secrecy, and availability of data. Secrecy is easy to understand. It is the need to prevent the disclosure of sensitive information. Availability means that you want information and information processing resources available when they are needed. A denial of service attack disrupts availability. The need for the integrity of information is equally obvious but its link to computer security is more subtle. Once someone has gained unauthorized access to a system the integrity of the information on that system is in doubt. Furthermore, there are intruders who just want to compromise the integrity of data. We are all familiar with cases where intruders gain access to a web server and change the data on the server in order to embarrass the organization that runs the web site. Thinking about the impact network threats have on your data can make it easier to assess the threat.

Network threats are, of course, not the only threats to computer security, or the only reasons for denial of service. Natural disasters and internal threats (threats from people who have legitimate access to a system) are also serious. Network security has had a lot of publicity, so it's a fashionable thing to worry about; but more computer time has probably been lost because of fires than has ever been lost because of network security problems. Similarly, more data has probably been improperly disclosed by authorized users than by unauthorized break-ins. This book naturally emphasizes network security, but network security is only part of a larger security plan that includes physical security and disaster recovery plans.

Many traditional (non-network) security threats are handled, in part, by physical security. Don't forget to provide an adequate level of physical security for your network equipment and cables. Again, the investment in physical security should be based on your realistic assessment of the threat.

Distributed Control

One approach to network security is to distribute responsibility for, and control over, segments of a large network to smaller groups within the organization. This approach involves a large number of people in security, and runs counter to the school of thought that seeks to increase security by centralizing control. However, the people closest to the data and system being managed are the people most likely to understand what needs protection and what level of protection is required.

Distributing responsibility and control to small groups can create an environment of small networks composed of trusted systems. Using the analogy of small towns and big cities, it is similar to creating a neighborhood watch to reduce risks by giving people connection with their neighbors, mutual responsibility for one another, and control over their own fates. Additionally, distributing security responsibilities formally recognizes one of the realities of network security—most security actions take place on individual systems. The managers of these systems must know that they are responsible for security, and that their contribution to network security is recognized and appreciated. If people are expected to do a job, they must be empowered to do it.

Use subnets to distribute control

Subnets are a possible tool for distributing network control. A subnet administrator should be appointed when a subnet is created. The administrator is then responsible for the security of the network and is empowered to assign IP addresses for the devices connected to the networks. Most administrators use DHCP to assign addresses because of its convenience and flexibility. But some administrators assign addresses manually, because assigning IP addresses gives the subnet administrator more control over who connects to the subnet. It also helps to ensure that the subnet administrator knows each system that is assigned an address and who is responsible for that system. When the subnet administrator assigns a system an IP address, he also assigns certain security responsibilities to the system's administrator. Likewise, when the system administrator grants a user an account, the user is assigned certain security responsibilities.

The hierarchy of responsibility flows from the network administrator, to the subnet administrator, to the system administrator, and finally to the user. At each point in this hierarchy the individuals are given responsibilities and the power to carry them out. To support this structure, it is important for users to know what they are responsible for, and how to carry out that responsibility. The network security policy, described later, provides this information.

Use mailing lists to distribute information

If your site adopts distributed control, you must develop a system for disseminating security information to each group. Mailing lists for each administrative level can be used for this purpose. The network administrator receives security information from outside authorities, filters out irrelevant material, and forwards the relevant material to the subnet administrators. Subnet administrators forward the relevant parts to their system administrators, who in turn forward what they consider important to the individual users. The filtering of information at each level ensures that individuals get the information they need, without receiving too much information. If too much unnecessary material is distributed, users begin to ignore everything they receive.

At the top of this information structure is the information that the network administrator receives from outside authorities. In order to receive this, the network administrator should join the appropriate mailing lists and newsgroups, and browse the appropriate web sites. A few places to start looking for computer security information are the following:

The Microsoft Website
: Microsoft maintains an excellent, if sometimes overwhelming, web site. One spot on the site of particularly interesting for Windows NT security issues is *http://www.microsoft.com/security*. The security page contains important security updates and pointers to some interesting security planning documents.

Security Newsgroups
: The comp.security newsgroups—*comp.security.firewalls*, *comp.security.announce*, and *comp.security.misc*—contain some useful information. Better yet, the *comp.os.ms-windows.nt.security* newsgroup contains security information that is specific to Windows NT. Like most newsgroups, these contain lots of unimportant and uninteresting material. But they also contain an occasional gem.

Computer Security Alerts and Advisories
: Some organizations maintain web sites that list security alerts and advisories. Click the Bulletins button at the *http://ciac.llnl.gov/* web site for a very

complete archive of network security problems. The Computer Emergency Response Team (CERT) also provides advisories that contain information about known security problems, and the fixes to these problems. CERT advisories can be retrieved from *ftp://info.cert.org/pub/cert_advisories*. The CERT web site at *http://www.cert.org* is also worth a visit. Finally, the web site at *http://www.security.mci.net/advisory.htm* is particularly good for finding Windows NT information.

Computer Virus Information
: A good web site for computer virus information is the CIAC site, *http://ciac.llnl.gov/*. CIAC maintains a very complete computer virus database. An equally important document, found at *http://ciac.llnl.gov/ciac/CIACHoaxes.html*, provides information about computer virus hoaxes. False rumors about computer viruses can waste as much time as tracking down real viruses.

Various PC magazines
: *Windows NT Magazine*, *PC Magazine,* and many others occasionally run articles about Windows NT security. Some of these magazines have web sites through which these articles can be retrieved. For example: *http://www.winmag.com* and *http://www.pcmag.com*.

Writing a Security Policy

Security is largely a people problem. People, not computers, are responsible for implementing security procedures, and people are responsible when security is breached. Therefore, network security is ineffective unless people know their responsibilities. It is important to write a security policy that clearly states what is expected, and who it is expected from. A network security policy should define:

The network user's security responsibilities
: The policy may require users to change their passwords at certain intervals, to use passwords that meet certain guidelines, or to perform certain checks to see if their accounts have been accessed by someone else. Whatever is expected from users, it is important that it be clearly defined.

The system administrator's security responsibilities
: The policy may require that specific security measures, welcome messages, and monitoring and accounting procedures be used on every system. It might list applications that should not be run on any computer attached to the network, and require a schedule for installing security updates.

The proper use of network resources
: Define who can use network resources, what things they can do, and what things they should not do. If your organization takes the position that email,

files, and histories of computer activity are subject to security monitoring, tell the users very clearly that this is the policy.

The actions taken when a security problem is detected
: What should be done when a security problem is detected? Who should be notified? It is easy to overlook things during a crisis, so you should have a detailed list of the exact steps that a system administrator, or user, should take when a security breach has been detected. This could be as simple as telling the users to "touch nothing, and call the network security officer." But even these simple actions should be in the policy so that they are readily available.

Connecting to the Internet brings with it certain security responsibilities. RFC 1281, *A Guideline for the Secure Operation of the Internet*, provides guidance for users and network administrators on how to use the Internet in a secure and responsible manner. Reading this RFC will provide insight into the information that should be in your security policy.

A great deal of thought is necessary to produce a complete network security policy. The outline previously shown describes the contents of a network policy document, but if you are personally responsible for writing a policy, you may want more detailed guidance. We recommend that you read RFC 1244. It is a very good guide for developing a security plan.

Security planning (assessing the threat, assigning security responsibilities, and writing a security policy) is a basic building block of network security, but a plan must be implemented before it can have any effect. In the remainder of this chapter, we'll turn our attention to implementing security. There are several different techniques for this. Some secure the entire network; some secure the links within the network; and some secure the individual computers in the network. We begin with a discussion of firewalls, which are a technique for securing entire networks.

Firewalls

A firewall system is a popular way to provide network security. The term *firewall* implies protection from danger, and just as the firewall in your car protects the passengers' compartment from the car's engine, a firewall computer system protects your network from the outside world. A firewall computer provides strict access control between your systems and the outside world.

The concept of a firewall is quite simple. A firewall is a choke point through which all traffic between a secured network and an unsecured network must pass. In practice, it is usually a choke point between an enterprise network and the Internet. Creating a single point through which all traffic must pass allows the traffic to be more easily monitored and controlled, and allows security expertise to be concentrated on that single point.

With a firewall in place, an intruder should not be able to mount a direct attack on any of the systems behind the firewall. The intruder must instead mount an attack directly against the firewall machine. Because the firewall machine can be the target of break-in attacks, it employs very strict security guidelines. But because there is only one firewall versus many machines on the local network, it is easier to enforce strict security at the firewall.

Firewalls are implemented in many ways. In fact there are so many different types of firewalls the term is almost meaningless. When someone tells you they have a firewall you really can't know exactly what they mean. Covering all of the different types of firewall architectures would require an entire book—see *Building Internet Firewalls* by Chapman and Zwicky, O'Reilly & Associates, 1995. Here we cover two common types of firewalls: the screened subnet architecture, and the multihomed host architecture.

The screened subnet firewall contains at least four hardware components: an exterior router, a secure server (called a Bastion Host), an exposed network (called a Perimeter Network), and an interior router. Each hardware component provides part of the complete security scheme. Figure 12-1 illustrates this architecture.

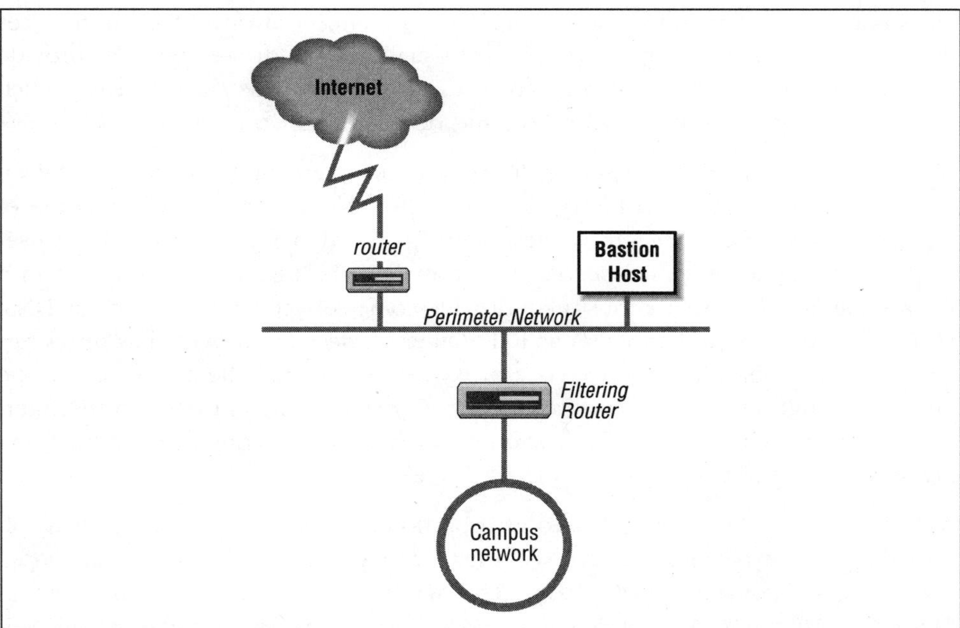

Figure 12-1. Screened subnet firewall

The exterior router is the only connection between the enterprise network and the outside world. This router is configured to do a minimal level of access control. It checks to make sure that no packet coming from the external world has a source address that matches the internal network. Assume our network number is 172.16: the exterior router discards any packets it receives on its exterior interface that contain a source address with the network number 172.16. That source address should only be received by the router on its interior interface. Security people call this type of access control *packet filtering* because packets are filtered out based on IP header information.

The interior router does the bulk of the access control work. It filters packets not only on address but also on protocol and port numbers, to control the services that are accessible to and from the interior network. What services are blocked by this router is up to you. If you plan to use a firewall, the services that will be allowed and those that will be denied should be defined in your security policy document.

Only the minimum number of services truly needed to communicate with external systems should be provided on a firewall system. Almost any service can be a threat. The threat of each must be evaluated in light of your security needs. Services that are only intended for internal users are almost always blocked. Services that allow writing to internal systems are usually blocked. Services that provide information about internal systems are usually blocked. This doesn't leave much running! That is where the bastion host and perimeter network come in.

The bastion host is a secure server. It provides an interconnection point between the enterprise network and the outside world for the restricted services. Some of the services that are restricted by the interior gateway may be essential for a useful network. Those essential services are provided through the bastion host in a secure manner. The bastion host may provide some services directly, such as DNS, SMTP mail services, and anonymous FTP. Other services are provided as *proxy services*. When the bastion host acts as a proxy server, internal clients connect to the outside through the bastion host and external systems respond back to the internal clients through the host. The bastion host can therefore control the traffic flowing into and out of the site to any extent desired.

A Windows NT system can be used as a bastion host and proxy server. Microsoft provides an evaluation copy of their proxy server software at *http://www.microsoft.com/proxy/default.asp*. The WinGate proxy software discussed in Chapter 9, *Microsoft Routing & Remote Access Service*, is another alternative. Neither of these, however, is really designed to be a firewall system. They are primarily intended as simple proxy servers.

All of the bastion host services do not have to be concentrated in a single computer. There can be more than one secure server, and there often is. The perimeter network connects the servers together and connects the exterior router to the interior router. The systems on the perimeter network are much more exposed to security threats than are the systems on the interior network. This is as it must be. After all, the secure servers are needed to provide service to the outside world as well as to the internal network. Isolating the systems that must be exposed on a separate network lessens the chance that a compromise of one of those systems will lead directly to the compromise of an internal system.

The multihomed host architecture attempts to duplicate all of the firewall functions in a single box. It works by replacing an IP router with a multihomed host that does not forward packets at the IP layer.* The multihomed host effectively severs the connection between the interior and exterior networks. To provide the interior network with some level of network connectivity, it performs similar functions to the bastion hosts.

Figure 12-2 shows a comparison between an IP router and a multihomed host firewall. A router handles packets up through the IP layer. The router forwards each packet based on the packet's destination address and the route to that destination indicated in the routing table. A host, on the other hand, does not forward packets. The multihomed host processes packets through the Application Layer, which provides it with complete control over how packets are handled.

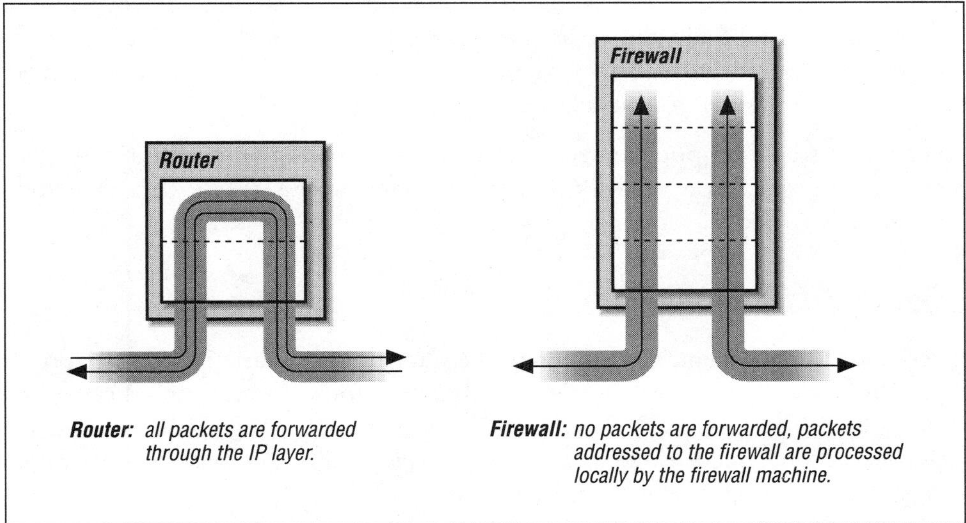

Figure 12-2. Firewalls versus routers

* The role that IP routers play in gluing the Internet together is covered extensively in earlier chapters.

This definition of a firewall, as a device completely distinct from an IP router, is not universally accepted. Some people refer to routers with special security features as firewalls, but this is really just a matter of semantics. Routers with special security features are also called secure routers or secure gateways. Firewalls, while they may include routers, do more than just filter packets.

The security of the entire network depends on the security of the firewall. Most sites that need a firewall use special software or hardware designed for the job. Because a firewall must be constructed with great care to be effective, and because there are many configuration variables for setting up a firewall machine, vendors offer special firewall software. Some vendors sell special-purpose machines designed specifically for use as firewall systems. Before setting up your own firewall, investigate the options available.

The details of setting up a firewall system are beyond the scope of this book. Before proceeding, we recommend that you read *Building Internet Firewalls* and *Firewalls and Internet Security*, both listed in the bibliography at the end of this chapter. Unless you have skilled Windows NT administrators with adequate free time, a do-it-yourself firewall installation is a mistake. Hire a company that specializes in firewall design and installation. If your information is valuable enough to protect with a firewall, it is valuable enough to protect with a professionally installed firewall.

Firewall systems are useful to many sites, but for some others they are not appropriate. The restrictions that they place on individual users are not acceptable to some organizations, and the restrictions can drive independent-minded users to find other ways to handle their communications needs. Think seriously about your real security needs before you select any security technique.

Encryption is another popular security technique. Firewalls limit access to the systems and services on a network. Encryption limits access to the data that flows across the network.

Encryption

Encryption is a technique for limiting access to the data carried on a network or stored in a file. Encryption encodes the data in a form that can only be read by someone who has the key to the encoding scheme. The original text, called the *clear text*, is encrypted using an *encryption device* (hardware or software) and an *encryption key*. This produces encoded text, which is called the *cipher*. To recreate the clear text, the cipher must be decrypted using the same type of encryption device and an appropriate key.

Public-key encryption is the technology that will make encryption an important security technology for data transmissions in an open global network like the Internet. Public-key systems encode the clear text with a key that is widely known and publicly available, but the cipher can only be decoded back to clear text with a secret key. This means that Dan can look up Kristin's public-key in a trusted database and use it to encode a message to her that no one else can read. Even though everyone on the Internet has access to the public-key, only Kristin can decrypt the message using her secret key. Kristin can then look up Dan's public-key to encrypt her reply. This encrypted communication takes place without Dan or Kristin every divulging their secret keys. However, public-key cryptography requires a trusted system for distributing public-keys to ensure that the keys have not been tampered with, and, because the encrypting key is available to everyone, it requires a digital signature system to authenticate that a message is really from the person it purports to be from. Government and industry are working on the standards and infrastructure for public-key cryptography.

The type of encryption that is still most commonly used is *symmetric encryption*. It requires that the same secret key is used for both encrypting and decrypting the message. It does not rely on public-keys, digital signatures, or a widely accepted infrastructure, but its usefulness for transmission across a network is limited because symmetric encryption requires that the same encryption technique and the same key is used at both ends of the data exchange. Unless you control both ends of the network, and can ensure that the key is available to both systems, it is difficult to use symmetric data encryption. For this reason, symmetric encryption is limited to places where the entire system is under the control of a single authority, such as military networks, private networks, or individual systems, or when the individuals at both ends of the communication can reach personal agreement on the encryption technique and key.

It is possible to create a private network running over a public network. This type of private network, called a virtual private network (VPN), has emerged as a popular application of encryption. A VPN creates tunnels through a public network, such as the Internet, over which encrypted data is exchanged. The end-points in the virtual network all agree to cooperate in the encrypted network. Windows NT 4.0 provides the Point to Point Tunneling Protocol (PPTP) for this exact purpose. The installation and configuration of PPTP is covered in the "Adding and Configuring the Point to Point Tunneling Protocol" section of Chapter 5, *Installing TCP/IP*. If you control all ends of the virtual network, you can use this feature for encrypted data communications.

Largely because of spy novels and World War II movies, encryption is one of the first things that people think of when they think of security. However, encryption is not always applicable. Before using encryption, decide why you want to encrypt the data, whether or not the data should be protected with encryption, and whether or not the data should even be stored on a networked computer system or transmitted on a public network. Some information is so sensitive or critical that it should not be stored on a networked computer system or transmitted on a public network, even if it is encrypted.

Encryption is not a substitute for good computer security. Encryption can protect sensitive or personal information from casual snooping, but it should never be the sole means of protecting critical information. Encryption systems can be broken, and encrypted data can be deleted or corrupted just like any other data. So don't let encryption lull you into a false sense of security. Encryption is only a small part of a complete security system.

Firewalls and encryption are useful security techniques. However, we feel that the most important security procedures are those that take place on individual systems. The remainder of this chapter emphasizes the techniques for securing individual Windows NT systems.

User Authentication

Every user that accesses computer or network resources must be authenticated. A secure system must know who is accessing what, and what each user is allowed to access. The Windows NT logon process performs user authentication at the local system level and at the network level. The local system authenticates access to local resources. Authentication for network resources is provided by the Windows NT domain controller.

The Logon dialogue prompts for a username and password. The local systems use this information to authenticate the user and then start the Windows NT *graphical user interface* (GUI). If the user logs on to a Windows NT system that is part of a domain, the user can choose to logon to the domain. In that case, the local system passes the information from the log on process to the domain controller. The domain controller authenticates the user and grants access to all network resources based on the permission granted to the user in the *Security Account Manager* (SAM) database.

The Security Accounts Manager is a vital part of the Windows NT authentication process. It contains the usernames and passwords of every user in the NT domain. The master copy of the accounts database resides on the *Primary Domain Controller* (PDC). Every domain must have one PDC. The critical nature of the accounts database means that is it important to have backup copies of the file. This happens automatically when you create a *Backup Domain Controller* (BDC). Every domain should have at least one backup, and having a few backups is recommended.

A Security Accounts Database contains information for only a single Windows NT domain. To provide resources to other NT domains within your enterprise and to obtain resources from them, you must establish a trust relationship between the domains. There are two types of trust relationships. A *trusted* domain is a domain that is trusted to authenticate users. A *trusting* domain is a domain that accepts users authenticated by a trusted domain. Anyone authenticated by a trusted domain is granted access to the resources of a trusting domain. Using these two basic trust relationships you can centralize all authentication in a single domain to provide tighter management control, by creating a hierarchy where only one domain is trusted and all other domains are trusting, or you can decentralize authentication in order to support a very large enterprise by creating a peer to peer architecture where all domains are both trusted and trusting.

Trust relationships are created through the Policies menu of the User Manager for Domains utility. Select Trust Relationships from that menu. A dialogue will appear that allows you to define both trusted and trusting domains. The administrator of the domain controller for a trusted domain uses this dialog to define the trusting domains that will be using the authentication services of her domain controller. The administrator of the trusting domain controller uses this box to define the domain that will be trusted. Once the trust relationship is established, each Windows NT domain can authenticate its users through its own security database while providing them access to a wider range of network resources.

The Security Accounts Database contains usernames, passwords, and user rights, and is used to determine the permissions granted to each user. User rights define the actions permitted to the user. Permissions define what network resources (file, printers, and so on) a user may access. We will talk more about both rights and permission later in the chapter. For now, we'll concentrate on logon authentication. Only the username and password are used during logon, and of these, only the password is secret. All of the security of the logon resides in picking a good password and then protecting it.

Passwords

Good passwords are one of the simplest parts of good network security. Passwords are used to authenticate users of individual Windows NT systems and of NT Domains. The mythology of the network says that all network security breaches are caused by sophisticated security crackers who discover software security holes to break into computer systems. In reality, many intruders enter systems simply by guessing or stealing passwords, or by exploiting well known security problems in outdated software. Later in this chapter we look at guidelines for keeping software up-to-date, and at ways to prevent a thief from stealing your password. First let's see what we can do to prevent it from being guessed.

A few things that make it easy to guess passwords are:

- Accounts that use trivial passwords
- Guest or other anonymous accounts that require no password, or use a well-publicized password
- Users who tell their passwords to others

Guessing these kinds of passwords requires no skill, just lots of spare time!

A more sophisticated form of password guessing is *dictionary guessing*. Dictionary guessing uses a program that encrypts each word in a dictionary and compares each encrypted word to the encrypted password used by Windows NT. Dictionary guessing is not limited to words from a dictionary. Things known about you (your name, initials, telephone number, and so on) are also run through the guessing program when trying to guess the password for your account.

NTCrack and *l0phtcrack* are password-guessing programs for Windows NT. *NTCrack* is freely available from *ftp://coast.purdue.edu/pub/tools/windows/windowsNT*. l0phtcrack can be found at *http://www.l0pht.com/l0phtcrack*. They can be run by the administrator against the passwords in your Security Account Manager (SAM) to ensure that the passwords stored there cannot be easily guessed.

To reduce the risk of password guessing, help your users pick good passwords. No intruder can take the encrypted password and decrypt it back to its original form, but encrypted passwords can be compared against encrypted dictionaries. If bad passwords are used, they can be easily guessed. Take care to choose good passwords.

Choosing a Password

A good password is an essential part of security. Choosing a good password boils down to this: don't choose a password that can be guessed using the techniques described above. Some guidelines for choosing a good password are:

- Don't use your logon name.
- Don't use the name of anyone or anything.
- Don't use any English or foreign language word or abbreviation.
- Don't use any personal information associated with the owner of the account. For example, don't use initials, phone number, social security number, job title, organizational unit, and so on.
- Don't use keyboard sequences, for example, qwerty.

- Don't use any of the previously mentioned things spelled backwards, or in caps, or otherwise disguised.
- Don't use an all numeric password.
- Don't use a sample password, no matter how good, that you've gotten from a book that discusses computer security.
- *Do* use a mixture of numbers, special characters, and mixed-case letters.
- *Do* use at least six characters. Ten characters is even better, and Windows NT will support passwords up to 14 characters in length.
- *Do* use a seemingly random selection of letters and numbers.

Common suggestions for constructing seemingly random passwords are:

- Use the first letter of each word from a line in a book, song, or poem. For example: "People don't know you and trust is a joke" would produce Pd'ky&tiaj.*
- Use the output from a random password generator. Select a random string that can be pronounced and is easy to remember. For example, the random string "adazac" can be pronounced a-da-zac, and you can remember it by thinking of it as "A-to-Z." Add uppercase letters to create your own emphasis, for example, aDAzac.
- Use two short words connected by punctuation, for example, wRen%Rug.
- Use numbers and letters to create an imaginary vanity license plate password, for example, 2hot4U?.

A common theme of these suggestions is that the password should be easy to remember. Avoid passwords that must be written down to be remembered. If unsavory people gain access to your office and find the password you have written down, the security of your system will be compromised.

However, don't assume that you will not be able to remember a seemingly random password. It may be difficult the first few times you use the password, but any password that is used often enough is easy to remember. If you have an account that you rarely use, you may have trouble remembering a random password. But in that case, the best solution is to get rid of the account. Unused and underutilized accounts are prime targets for intruders. Remove all unused accounts from your systems.

How do you ensure that the guidance for creating new passwords is followed? The most important step is to make sure that every user knows these suggestions and the importance of following them. Cover this topic in your network security plan,

---

* toad the wet sprocket, "walk on the ocean."

and periodically reinforce it through newsletter articles and online system bulletins.

Changing your password is a deterrent to password guessing. However, if you choose good passwords, don't change them so often that it is hard to remember them. Many security experts recommend that passwords should be changed about every three to six months. Windows NT provide features to ensure that your users change their passwords periodically.

Password Aging

Password aging defines a lifetime for each password. When a password reaches the end of its lifetime, the password aging mechanism notifies the user to change the password. If it is not changed, the password is removed from the system and the user is blocked from using the account.

The Windows NT password aging system is configured through the Account Policy sheet. Open the Account Policy sheet by selecting Account from the Policies menu in the User Manager for Domains application. The Account Policy page is shown in Figure 12-3.

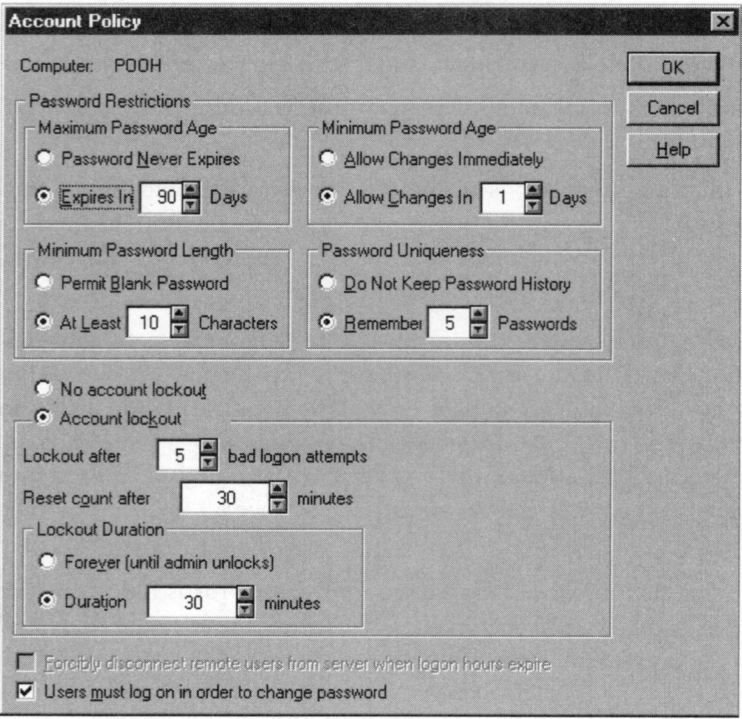

Figure 12-3. Defining Account Policy

Figure 12-3 shows all of the security features that can be set. In the example, we set the password to expire in 90 days. This means that users must change their passwords four times a year. Furthermore, we have set a minimum password age of one day to prevent them from changing to a temporary password and then immediately changing back to a favorite password. The passwords they select must be used for at least one day before they can be changed again. To further discourage users from selecting a temporary password and then jumping back to a preferred password, we set a value in the Password Uniqueness box. The 5 in that box means the system will not accept any of the last five passwords used by a user as that user's new password.

At the bottom of the page the "Users must log on to change password" checkbox is also related to password aging. Normally, when a user's password expires, he is prompted to perform the password change the next time he attempts to log on. He uses her old password to verify her identity and then selects a new password. If this box is checked, the user is not given a chance to select a new password if the password expires. Instead the user must change her password while he is logged on and before it has expired. If it is allowed to expire, it must be reset by the Administrator.

In addition to password aging features, the Account Policy sheet defines other values relating to password security. One of these is the password length. In the example it is set to ten characters. The Account Policy also defines the number of logon failures before the account is locked. In this example, if the user fails to enter the correct password five times in a row, the account is locked. It remains locked for thirty minutes. This setting discourages brute force password guessing. No one wants to make five guesses and then wait half an hour to make five more!

Windows NT provides several nice password features, but a password security system is no better than the passwords used. If a user selects a password that is easily guessed, or allows other people to use his password, the security of the system may be compromised.

Password Security

Sometimes good passwords are not enough. Some applications transmit passwords across the network as clear text. Intruders use protocol analyzer software, such as the Network Monitor, to spy on network traffic and steal passwords. If a thief steals your password, it does not matter how good the password is. The thief can simply read the password and use it to gain access to your computer.

The thief can be on any network that handles your TCP/IP packets. If you log on through your local network you only have to worry about local snoops. But if you log on over the Internet you must worry about unseen listeners from any number of unknown networks.

Windows NT is less vulnerable to password theft than many other operating systems. The standard Windows NT logon sends the password across the network as encrypted text. The encrypted password can be plucked from the network and attacked using *l0phtcrack* or *NTCrack*, but if you have picked a good password, this is not much of a threat.

Unfortunately, some TCP/IP applications require a password that is sent as clear text. Two prime examples are Telnet and FTP. Most Windows NT administrators don't install these services. If you do install the FTP service as described in Chapter 10, *Internet Information Server (IIS)*, it is best to restrict the service to anonymous logons. Otherwise a user may log on to FTP using his account name and password, and thus send a clear text password over the network. If you must send sensitive information like passwords over the Internet, use encryption to secure the network link, if at all possible.

Unwelcome message

Some legal experts say that welcome banners displayed by FTP and Telnet servers should not be so welcoming. Their advice is to spell out in the greeting that the system is intended only for authorized users and that unauthorized users will be prosecuted. The danger posed by FTP makes the FTP server a prime candidate for an unwelcome banner that clearly explains the usage restrictions that apply to your server.

Windows NT IIS makes it very simple to define an appropriate security banner for your FTP server. See Chapter 10 for information on how to define your own FTP welcome banner.

Guest Account Security

Before we leave the subject of user authentication, we should discuss the Guest account and the associated Everyone group. Windows NT systems provide a special account for anonymous logons called the Guest account. For maximum security, you should make sure that this account is disabled.

To disable the Guest account, run the User Manager for Domains and then double-click on the Guest name in the User Manager window. This opens the User Properties sheet. Select Account Disabled.

Related to the Guest account is the group Everyone. Everyone is a hidden group; you won't see it in the Groups pane of the User Manager window. However, the Guest account is a member of the Everyone group, and through that group the anonymous account is granted the right to log on through the network. If you decide to keep the Guest account for local logons, you may still wish to deny remote users access to the Guest account. To do this, remove the Everyone group from the "Access from the network" right. Be aware that doing this prevents all users from logging in over the network because the Everyone group includes all users. Therefore if Everyone is removed, the group User must be given the "Access from the network" right to replace this function. A process to update the Everyone group can be found at *ftp://coast.purdue.edu/pub/tools/windows/windowsNT*. Before you do this, think carefully about why you are doing it. Disabling the Guest account is simpler and more effective than fiddling with the Everyone group.

Software Security

Good passwords and secure communications links are important security measures. However, using good, secure user authentication isn't the only thing that you can do to improve the security of your computer and your network. Many Windows NT security problems occur when well known software bugs are exploited. In this section we'll look at some things you can do to improve software security.

Keep Software Updated

Microsoft frequently releases Windows NT software updates for the express purpose of improving network security. Check for security fixes in the latest version of the Microsoft software as soon as it becomes available. If you aren't keeping up with the latest security updates, rest assured that the crackers are, and are waiting for a chance to exploit any vulnerability in your system.

First and foremost, install the latest service pack for Windows NT. At this writing, it is Windows NT 4.0 with Service Pack 3, though very soon Service Pack 4 will be released. Service packs are very important because they often contain critical security fixes. Always start with the latest service pack before applying any other security fixes.

In addition to the latest Service Pack, check *http://www.microsoft.com/security* for the most recent security patches. Don't wait for the next Service Pack. Install the fixes as soon as they are released. At this writing, there are several hot fixes that have not yet reached a Service Pack. These are:

getadmin

This patch fixes a bug in the kernel that allows a user to gain Administrator rights. A program named **getadmin.exe**, which is freely available on the Internet, allows anyone who is legitimately logged in to a Windows NT 4.0 server to obtain full administrator privileges.

lsa-fix

Windows NT is vulnerable to a network attack that allows a vandal to lock up the logon process and important applications such as the Event Viewer. The problem is in *Lsasrv.dll*, which this patch replaces.

srv-fix

An intentionally misconfigured Server Message Block (SMB) logon request can hang a Windows NT 4.0 system. This fix corrects that problem.

teardrop2-fix

Denial of service attacks are simple to use and very destructive. Several popular attacks—Teardrop, Teardrop2, Land, NewTear, Bonk, Boink, and OOB—are addressed by this patch. The Teardrop attacks use deliberately incorrect packet fragments to cause problems for the target system during packet reassembly.

simptcp-fix

Another denial of service attack used by network vandals is simply to flood the network with UDP packets to the **chargen** TCP/IP service.* Any Windows NT 4.0 system that has the Simple TCP/IP Services installed is vulnerable to this attack unless this fix is installed.

All of the fixes previously shown relate to Service Pack 3 and can be found at *ftp.microsoft.com* in the *bussys/winnt/winnt-public/fixes/usa/nt40/hotfixes-postSP3* directory. By the time you read this there may be other, more recent service packs. When new service packs are released these particular hot fixes will not be needed, but others surely will. Keep up with the latest information!

Failing to keep the software on your system up-to-date opens a big security hole for intruders. Most intruders don't discover new problems; they exploit well known ones. Keep track of the known security problems so you can keep your system up-to-date.

Disable Unnecessary Software

Any software that allows an incoming connection from a remote site has the potential of being exploited by an intruder. Unlike many other operating systems, Windows NT does not install every software option by default. You must make a conscious decision to add individual network services through the Control Panel. Before you do, make sure you actually need the additional services. Some security experts go further; they recommend that you not just limit the services that you add, but that you also remove every network service that you don't absolutely need.

* **chargen** is a rarely used network service intended as an aid to testing.

All of the components of network software—services, protocols, and adapters—can be removed in much the same way that they are added. See the *Network Services* section of Chapter 5 for details. It describes the services that are provided with Windows NT 4.0, and how to add or remove those services. Use those instructions to remove services that you don't need. Not every unused protocol, however, can be removed in this manner. Some protocols are a basic part of the TCP/IP protocol software. To disable these protocols you must block the ports on which they communicate.

Use the port filtering features of Windows NT to disable all inbound ports that are not required by your system. Server systems usually need some ports that accept incoming connections, but most desktop systems need very few, if any. Filtering ports only prevents inbound connections. It does not prevent outbound connections. A user can still initiate an FTP to a remote site even if the FTP port is filtered from his system. A simple approach used by some people is to start by filtering everything and then adding back only those ports that you decide you really need to service.

To block all but a few selected ports, open the TCP/IP Security dialog as described in Chapter 5. (See Figure 5-4 and the text describing it.) Click Permit Only in both the TCP and UDP boxes. Then enter in the port numbers of the specific services you wish to enable. All other TCP/IP services will be disabled. The Adapter drop-down list is useful if you're configuring a Windows NT Server that also acts as a gateway. With the Adapter list you can permit every service to the users on the local area network, while denying many of those same services to the remote users who connect through the other network interface.

A word of caution: before you disable services, make sure you really need this level of security and that you really don't need the service. Many network services have uses beyond the obvious use. Don't cripple your network trying to make it secure.

Security Monitoring

A key element of effective network security is security monitoring. Good security is an ongoing process. Following the security guidelines discussed earlier is just the start. You must also monitor the systems to detect unauthorized user activity and to locate and close security holes. You need to know the system in order to detect and fix these problems as they arise.

Windows NT provides system monitoring through the Event Viewer. Most Windows NT administrators are familiar with the Event Viewer from debugging problems that occur during system startup or from fixing problems with newly installed hardware. An equally important function for the Event Viewer is security monitoring. To perform this important task you must first define the audit policy for your system. Open the User Manager for Domains and select Audit from the Policies menu. This opens the Audit Policy windows shown in Figure 12-4. Use this window to define your security monitoring policy.

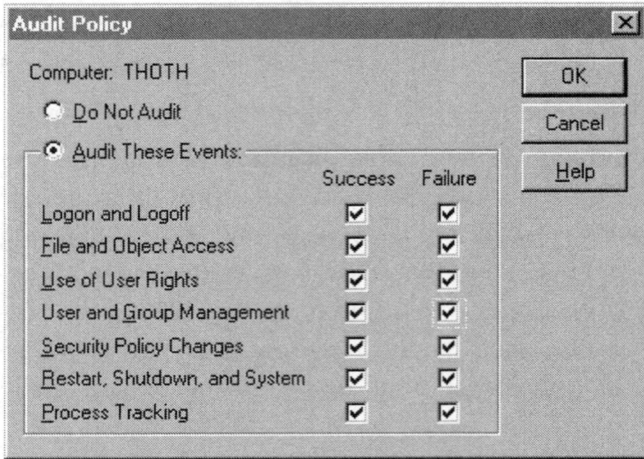

Figure 12-4. Setting an Audit Policy

Network security is monitored by examining the event logs of individual systems on the network. To detect unusual activity on a system, you must know what activity is normal. You need to know this in order to develop a feel for how things should be. Through the Audit Policy window you can enable the following audits that give you insight into the normal activity of your system:

Logon and Logoff
: Tracks the local and network logons to this system, which is important for learning who is usually logged on and who commonly logs on after hours. You need to know this to help you detect when improper logons are taking place.

File and Object Access
: Enables logging of access to files and directories, and the submission of print jobs. This option can create a very large volume of audit data. See the *NTFS Auditing* section of this chapter for information on how to monitor file and directory access.

Use of User Rights
: Audits every time a user uses a right, other than logon, that has been granted to that user. This is useful for checking who uses special rights and can alert you to a problem if a user uses a right that you did not intentionally grant him.

User and Group Management
: Audits all changes to accounts and groups, including password changes. This audit is useful for detecting any changes to the groups to which a user belongs. An intruder who gains access to the administrative account may change groups or even create new accounts in order to exploit your system.

Security Policy Changes
: Logs changes to user rights, to domain trust relationships, and to the audit policy itself. If any of these things have changed, and they have not been changed by you, you have a major problem. This audit should always be selected.

Restart, Shutdown, and System
: Tracks system level events such as reboots. This should always be selected. Even if an intruder does not cause the reboot, you should have a record of when your system unexpectedly restarts.

Process Tracking
: Enables logging of events relating to the executable processes that run on the system. Some applications allow you to specify event logging within the application itself. See the example of Registry monitoring later in this chapter.

If the event logs give you reason to suspect a security problem, examine them in detail for modified security policies, for modified user or group rights, and for unusual logon activity. This close examination is made using the Event Viewer. The next section shows an example of examining logon activity.

Checking logon activity

Strange logon activity, at odd times of the day or from unfamiliar locations, can indicate attempts by intruders to gain access to your system. Use the Event Viewer to check who has logged onto the system in the past.

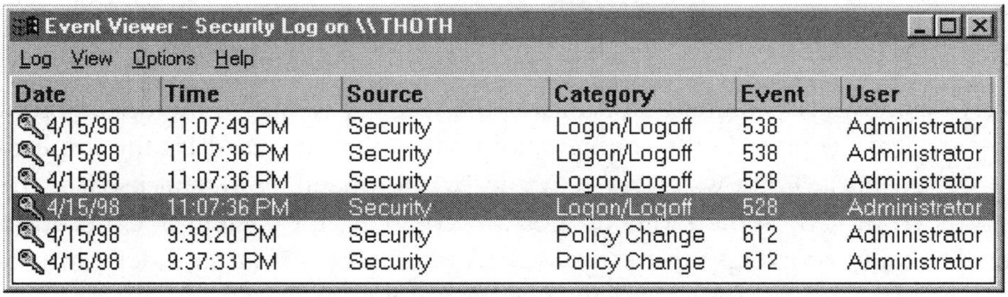

Event Viewer - Security Log on \\THOTH

Log View Options Help

Date	Time	Source	Category	Event	User
4/15/98	11:07:49 PM	Security	Logon/Logoff	538	Administrator
4/15/98	11:07:36 PM	Security	Logon/Logoff	538	Administrator
4/15/98	11:07:36 PM	Security	Logon/Logoff	528	Administrator
4/15/98	11:07:36 PM	Security	Logon/Logoff	528	Administrator
4/15/98	9:39:20 PM	Security	Policy Change	612	Administrator
4/15/98	9:37:33 PM	Security	Policy Change	612	Administrator

Figure 12-5. Event Viewer logon summary

Figure 12-5 shows the summary lines displayed by the Event Viewer for each user logon. Use each day's summary to learn normal logon patterns in order to detect abnormal logon activity. The Event Viewer provides a record of who logged onto the system, when they logged on, and when they logged out.

Figure 12-6 shows the detail of a single logon record from the Event Viewer. To view this level of detail, double-click on an individual summary line in the main Event Viewer window to open the Event Detail box. The Event Detail contains fields that show the user who logged on, the workstation from which the logon originated, the date, the time logged on, and the Windows NT domain.

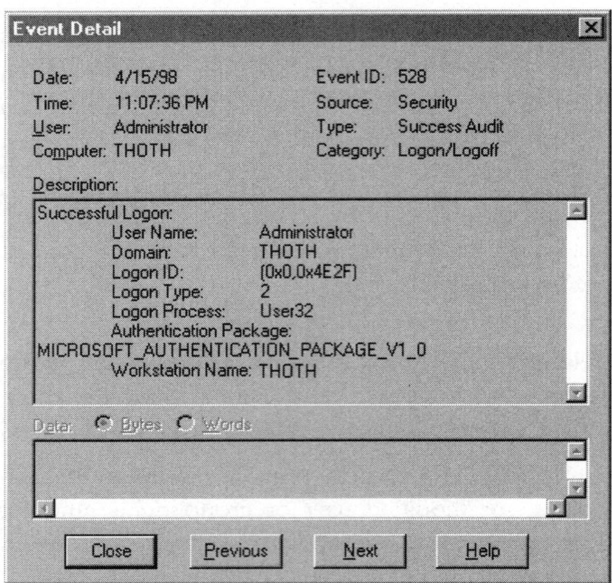

Figure 12-6. Logon Event Detail

If you find any problems, even if you suspect any problems, follow your reporting procedure and let people know about the problem. This is particularly important if you are connected to a local area network. A problem on your system could spread to other systems on the network.

Registry Monitoring

As every Windows NT administrator knows, the Registry is vital to the operation of the system. The Registry holds configuration values that are used by the applications that run on a Windows NT system and by the operating system itself. If the Registry is corrupted, applications do not run correctly, the system is exposed to potential security problems, and it may not boot correctly. If an intruder can corrupt the Registry, he can severely damage your system.

To help prevent this problem, monitor who is accessing and changing the Registry. To do so, use the Audit Policy window discussed in the previous section to enable auditing. Once auditing is enabled, run *regedt32.exe*. From the Security menu in the Registry editor, select Audit. This opens the window shown in Figure 12-7.

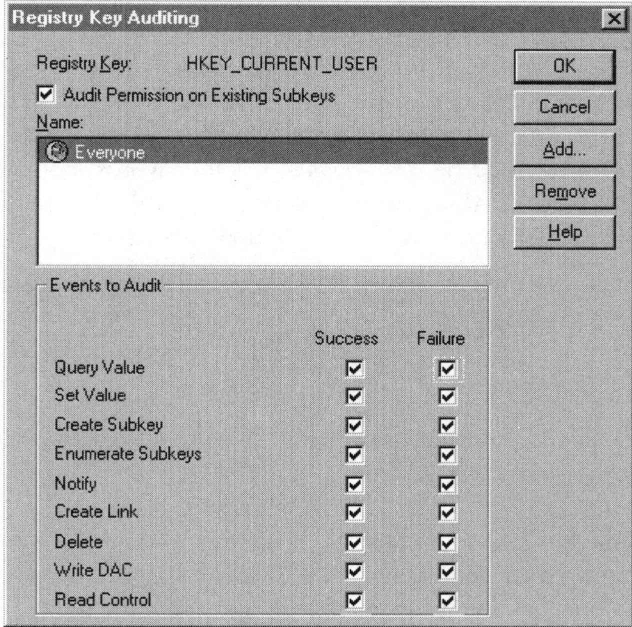

Figure 12-7. Registry Key Auditing

In the Registry Key Auditing window select "Audit Permission on Existing Subkeys". Then select the individual events that you want to audit. At a minimum you should audit when values are set (Set Value), when new keys are created (Create Subkey), and when keys are deleted (Delete). Auditing everything can produce a large amount of data, but you may want to start by monitoring failures on every event to track how often there are failed attempts to access or change keys.

Monitoring, including Registry monitoring, is an important part of keeping your system and network secure. Windows NT provides good system monitoring tools. Learn about them and use them.

File Security

The first line of defense for protecting the data stored on your Windows NT server is adequate file security. File security is the primary defense against *disclosure of information*, one of the three basic security threats. Windows NT has an advanced file system that provides strong security, but to take advantage of this security you must use it.

The first step in securing your file system is to make sure that you use NTFS on your server. For compatibility with other, and older, Microsoft operating systems, Windows NT offers the FAT filesystem. Don't use FAT if you are concerned about security. It provides no real security. To secure your file system use NTFS.

The only disadvantage of NTFS is that it is not compatible with other Microsoft operating systems. *Backward compatibility* was a major marketing issue for Windows NT when it was introduced. Microsoft provided the Windows NT boot manager so that a Windows NT system could be *dual-booted*, in other words, booted under either Windows NT or Windows. At the time Windows meant Windows 3.1, but it later came to mean Windows 95, and now means Windows 98 as well.

Backward compatibility has little use on a Windows NT server supporting a secure network. A real network server runs 24 hours-a-day, 7 days-a-week. It is rarely taken offline so someone can run Windows 95 on it.* For this reason, the disadvantage of NTFS is no real disadvantage for a server. Install your Windows NT server using NTFS.

NTFS Security

NTFS permissions can be applied to individual files, to directories, or to entire volumes (disk drives). File permissions can be granted to individual user accounts or to groups. The access permissions that can be applied to an individual file are:

No Access
: Prevents a user or group from having any type of access to the file.

Read
: Permits the user or group to read or execute the file.

Change
: Permits the user or group to read, execute, change, or delete the file.

Full Control
: Permits the user or group to change the permissions or ownership of the file as well as to read, execute, change, or delete the file.

Special Access
: Allows the user or group to define new permissions to be applied to the file.

The permissions that can be assigned to directories and volumes are very similar to those that can be assigned to a file. Directories have No Access, Read, Change, and Full Control, just as files do. These permissions provide a similar level of

* Some servers have Windows 95 installed on a small FAT partition to help with the installation of Plug and Play hardware. Windows NT 4.0 does not have its own Plug and Play support.

access, though with a directory orientation. In addition to these permission, there are the following permissions that are specific to directories:

List
: Permits the user or group to make a directory listing of the directory and any of its subdirectories.

Add
: Permits the user or group to store files in the directory, though they are not permitted to list the directory or read files from the directory.

Add & Read
: Permits the user or group to store files in the directory, list the contents of the directory, and read files contained in the directory.

Special Directory Access
: Permits the user or group to create special directory permissions.

Special File Access
: Permits the user or group to create special file permissions.

Select the permissions that give the least file and directory access needed to get the job done. Don't provide file permissions that aren't really needed. Unneeded permissions open a hole for your data to be corrupted or improperly disclosed. Only grant permissions to users or groups who really need access to the data. Assess the threat before granting access. Tightening security after information has been disclosed is of no use.

NTFS auditing

The Windows NT auditing capabilities permit you to monitor who is accessing files. To audit files and directories, first open the Audit Policy window as described earlier in the chapter and enable "File and Object Access" auditing. Next select the file or directory that you wish to audit, and open the Properties sheet for the file. Click the Auditing button in the Properties sheet to open the Auditing dialog box.

Like file permissions, auditing is on a per user or per group basis. Click the Add button in the Auditing dialog box to add a user or group whose access will be audited. To audit file or directory access from all users, add the Everyone group.

Use the checkboxes in the Events to Audit pane of the Auditing dialog box to select what type of file access is monitored. The possible events that can be monitored are:

Read
: Logs every time the file or directory is read by the specified user or group.

Write
: Logs each time the specified user or group writes to the file or directory.

Execute
: Records each time the file is executed by the specified user or group.

Delete
: Logs every time a file is deleted by the specified user or group.

Change Permission
: Records every time the file or directory permission is changed by the specified user or group.

Take Ownership
: Records every time the file or directory ownership is changed by the specified user or group.

Use NTFS file monitoring to audit critical files and directories. Do not use it on a large number of directories because it then generates too much data for the Event Viewer. Critical data can be lost in meaningless details when too much data is gathered.

File and directory access monitoring can only be done on NTFS files. The FAT file system does not have this type of capability and does not have a concept of users and permissions. NTFS provides advanced security and monitoring capabilities that are adequate for protecting most data.

Words to the Wise

We believe good security is good system administration and vice versa. Most of this chapter is just common-sense advice. It is probably sufficient for most circumstances, but certainly not for all.

Make sure that you know if there is an existing security policy that applies to your network or system. Find out if your security situation is governed by regulations or laws. If there are policies, regulations, or laws governing your situation, make sure to obey them. Never do anything to undermine the security system established for your site.

No system is completely secure. No matter what you do, you will have problems. Realize this and prepare for it. Prepare a disaster recovery plan and do everything necessary, so that when the worst does happen, you can recover from it with the minimum possible disruption.

A large list of security publications can be found at *http://csrc.nist.gov/secpubs*. If you want to read more about security we recommend the following resources:

- RFC 1244, *Site Security Handbook*, P. Holbrook, J. Reynold, et al., July 1991.
- RFC 1281, *Guidelines for the Secure Operation of the Internet*, R. Pethia, S. Crocker, and B. Fraser, November 1991.

- *Windows NT Server 4 Security Handbook*, Lee Hadfield, Dave Hatter, and Dave Bixler, Que, 1997.
- *Building Internet Firewalls*, Brent Chapman and Elizabeth Zwicky, O'Reilly & Associates, 1995.
- *Firewalls and Internet Security*, William Cheswick and Steven Bellovin, Addison-Wesley, 1994.

Summary

Network access and computer security work at cross purposes. Attaching a computer to a network increases the security risks for that computer. Evaluate your security needs to determine what must be protected and how vigorously it must be protected. Develop a written site security policy that defines your security procedures and documents the security duties and responsibilities of employees at all levels.

Network security is essentially good system security. Good user authentication, up-to-date software, effective system monitoring, and well trained system administrators are the best security. Track the security updates released by Microsoft and use the system monitoring tools available with Windows NT to help with these tasks. The Event Viewer, NTFS file security, encryption, and firewalls are all tools that can help.

Like troubleshooting, network security is a neverending task. It is an ongoing process. In the final chapter we discuss another ongoing process—learning. The network administrator never finishes learning. In the next chapter we look at ways you can keep abreast of the most current information in network administration.

13

Information Resources

In this chapter:

- *The World Wide Web*
- *Anonymous FTP*
- *Retrieving RFCs*
- *Mailing Lists*
- *Newsgroups*
- *The White Pages*
- *Summary*

Now that our network is configured, debugged, and secure, how will we use it? The classic applications Telnet, FTP, and mail, are still popular. But increasingly the network is used not merely as a delivery link between two hosts, but as a path to information resources. Information servers, file repositories, databases, and information directories are available throughout the Internet.

An important application for these information resources is to keep you up-to-date about the latest developments in Windows NT and in TCP/IP network technologies. Computer technology changes very rapidly. The things that you read about in this book will surely change over time.* Online information can help you keep your knowledge current.

This chapter explores various ways to avail yourself of this storehouse of information. We look at how information is retrieved from network servers, and some tools that make it easier to locate that information.

The World Wide Web

The primary method used to retrieve network information is the World Wide Web. The Web is an interlinked network of hypertext servers based on the *Hypertext Transfer Protocol* (HTTP) that runs on top of TCP/IP. The Web is accessed via a *browser*, which is a program that provides a consistent graphical interface to the user. All of the popular browsers, including Microsoft Internet Explorer, are modeled after the original browser developed at the National Center for Supercomputer Applications (NCSA), and therefore share a common look and feel.

* We maintain a web site at *www.ttgnet.com/nttcp.html* that contains online updates for this book and other useful information.

Windows NT systems ship with a built-in browser. The Microsoft Internet Explorer is bundled with the operating system. Other browsers are available on the Internet. The Netscape browser is available at *http://www.netscape.com*. It can be downloaded and quickly installed. Netscape is a popular browser, but Internet Explorer is probably the most popular browser for Windows NT.

You can, of course, also set up your Windows NT Server as a Web server. In this chapter we only look at browsing other services. To see how to set up your own service, refer to Chapter 10, *Internet Information Server (IIS)*.

Obtaining information from hypertext Web pages is a common use for a browser. Use yours to keep up with the most current network information. Figure 13-1 shows a network administrator checking online security information.

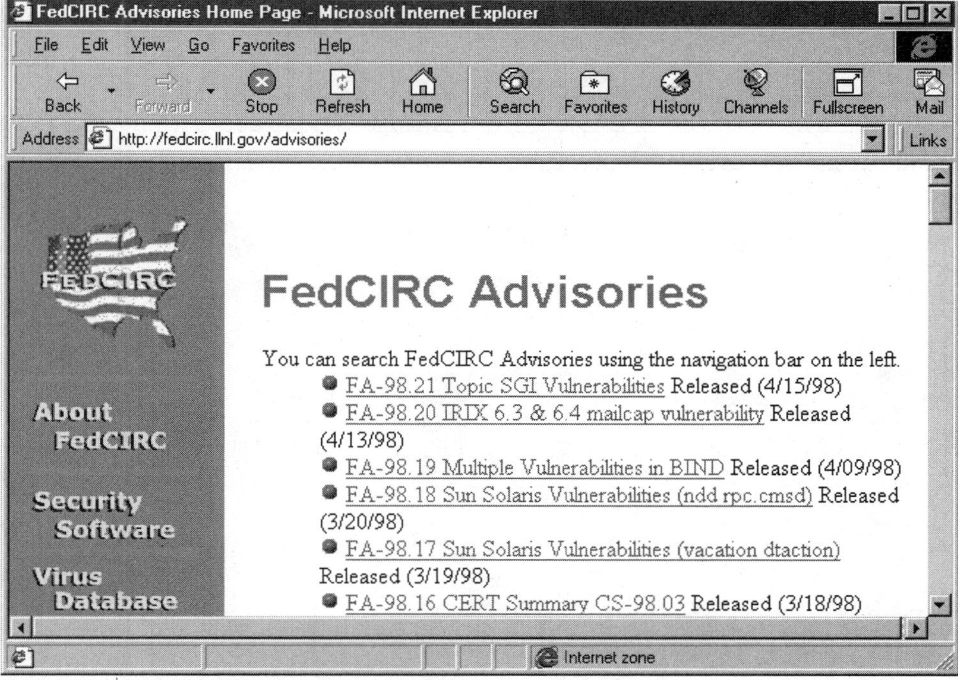

Figure 13-1. Obtaining information with the Web

The Address field near the top of the sample screen is the location of the Web page we are reading. On some other browsers this field is labeled URL, Location, or Netsite, but in all cases it performs the same function: it holds the path to the information resource. In the example the location is *http://fedcirc.llnl.gov/advisories/*. The Address is a *universal resource locator* (URL). It is a standard way of defining a network resource and it has a specific structure:

service://server/path/file

In the sample URL, *http* is the service; *fedcirc.llnl.gov* is the server; and *advisories* is the path to the resource contained on that server. No file name is provided, so the default file, usually *index.html*, is used. This tells the browser to locate a host with the domain name *fedcirc.llnl.gov*, and to ask it for the hypertext information located in the default file in the *advisories* path.

Hypertext is not the only type of information that can be retrieved by a browser. The browser is intended to provide a consistent interface to various types of network resources. HTTP is only one of the services that can be specified in a URL.

A web browser can be used to view local hypertext files. Increasingly this is how documentation is delivered. Figure 13-2 shows an NT administrator reading the mailsrv documentation.

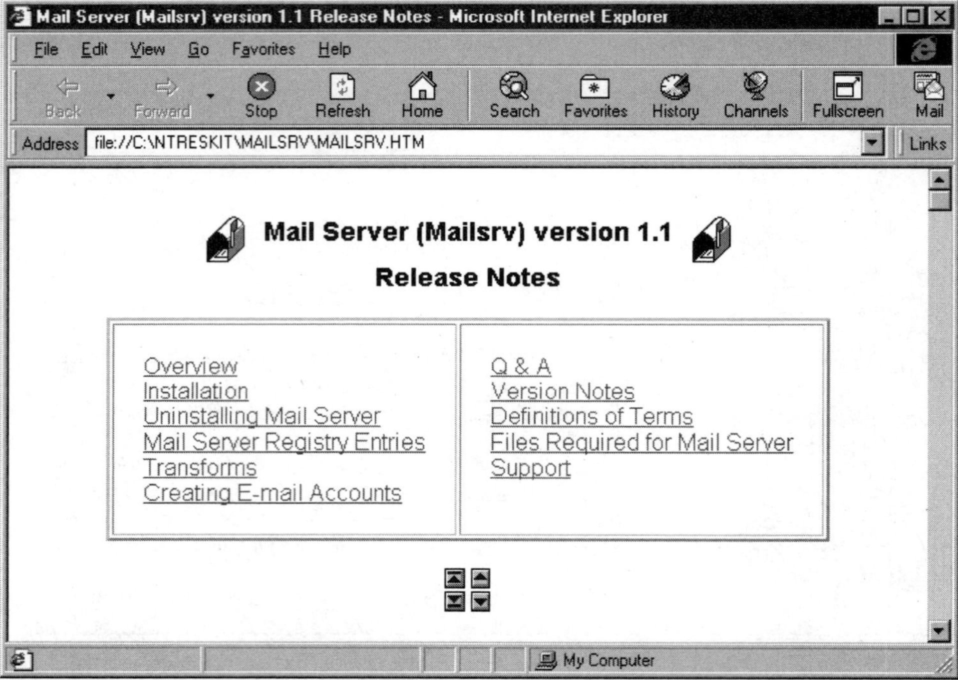

Figure 13-2. Reading documentation with a browser

The URL in Figure 13-2 is *file://c:\ntreskit\mailsrv\mailsrv.htm*. The service is *file*, which means that the resource is to be read via the standard file system. No server name is provided so the Internet Explorer looks for the resource on the local host. The path is *c:\ntreskit\mailsrv*, and the file is *mailsrv.htm*.

The browser is also often used to download files, a role that is similar to FTP. Figure 13-3 shows an NT administrator using a browser to download new Windows NT modem drivers.

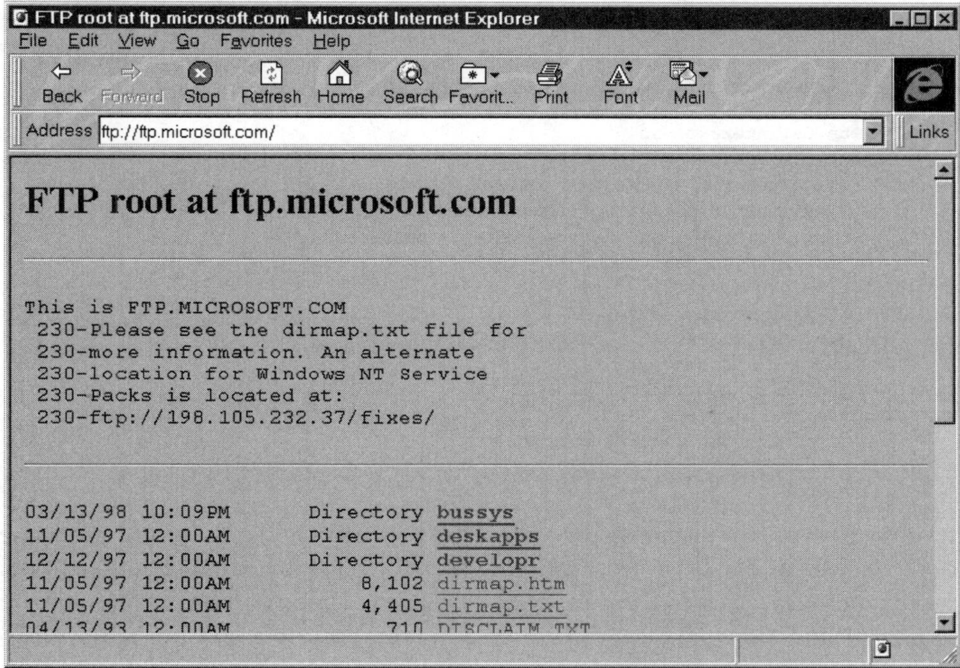

Figure 13-3. Using the Web for file transfer

The URL in Figure 13-3 shows HTTP being used to retrieve a file. FTP can also be the service used to access a resource through the browser. For example, *ftp://ftp.microsoft.com* connects to the anonymous FTP server at Microsoft. Files can be downloaded via HTTP or FTP.

Reading important announcements and documentation and downloading files are probably the most common uses a network administrator has for a Web browser. There are, however, many other things that can be done with a browser and the huge number of resources available on the network. A detailed discussion of browsers and the Web is beyond the scope of this book. See *The Whole Internet User's Guide and Catalog*, by Ed Krol, for a full treatment of these subjects.

The browser provides a consistent interface to a variety of network services. But it is not the only way, or necessarily the best way, to access all of these service. In particular, it may not be the fastest or most efficient way to download a file. An alternative is to invoke **ftp** directly.

Anonymous FTP

Anonymous FTP is a technique for retrieving publicly available files and programs from the many FTP servers around the Internet. Anonymous FTP is simply an **ftp** session in which you log into the remote server using the username *anonymous* and, by convention, your email address as the password.* The anonymous FTP example shown here should make this process clear:

```
C:\>ftp ds.internic.net
Connected to ds.internic.net.
220 FTP server Wed May 21 1997 ready.
Name (ds.internic.net:kathy): anonymous
331 Guest login ok, use email address as password.
Password: kathy@ttgnet.com
ftp> cd rfc
250 CWD command successful.
ftp> get rfc1122.txt
200 PORT command successful.
150 Opening connection for rfc1122.txt.
226 Transfer complete.
local: rfc1122.txt remote: rfc1122.txt
ftp> quit
221 Goodbye.
```

In this example, the user logs into the server *ds.internic.net* using the username *anonymous* and the password *kathy@ttgnet.com*, which is her email address. With anonymous FTP, she can log in even though she doesn't have an account on *ds.internic.net*. Of course what she can do is restricted, but she can retrieve certain files from the system, and that's just what she does. She changes to the *rfc* directory, and gets the file *rfc1122.txt*.

Using the anonymous FTP service offered by a remote server is very simple. However, setting up an anonymous FTP service on your own system is a little more complicated. The Microsoft FTP server is part of the Internet Information Server. See Chapter 10 for information about how it is installed.

Retrieving RFCs

Throughout this book, we have referred to many RFCs. These are the Internet documents used for everything from general information to the definitions of the TCP/IP protocols standards. As a network administrator, there are several important RFCs that you'll want to read. The anonymous FTP example in the previous section shows one method to obtain them.

* Some FTP servers request your real username as a password.

RFCs are stored at *ds.internic.net* in the *rfc* directory. It stores the RFCs with filenames in the form *rfcnnnn.txt* or *rfcnnnn.ps*—where *nnnn* is the RFC number, and *txt* or *ps* indicates whether the RFC is ASCII text or PostScript. Anonymous FTP is generally a very quick way to get an RFC, if you know what you want.

To help you find out which RFC you do want, get the *rfc-index.txt* file. It is a complete index of all RFCs by RFC number, and it's also available from *ds.internic.net* in the *rfc* directory. You'll only need to get a new RFC index occasionally. Most of the time, the RFC you're looking for has been in publication for some time and is already listed in the index. Retrieve the RFC index and store it on your system. Then search it for references to the RFCs you're interested in.

RFCs are also available via the World Wide Web at *http://www.internic.net*. Follow the links from that home page through the directory services to the IETF RFC page. The page allows you to search the RFCs for keywords or to load the RFC index. The index is particularly useful if you know the number of the RFC you want. Figure 13-4 shows a network administrator scrolling through the index looking for RFC 1122.

In another example the network administrator does not know which RFCs contain the information she is looking for, but she knows what she wants. The administrator is trying to find out more about the SMTP service extensions that have been proposed for Extended SMTP. Figure 13-5 shows the four RFCs displayed as a result of her query.

The Web provides the most popular and easiest method for browsing through RFCs. However, if you know what you want, anonymous FTP can be a faster way to retrieve as specific document.

Retrieving RFCs by mail

While anonymous FTP is the fastest way and the Web is the easiest way to get an RFC, they are not the only ways. You can also obtain RFCs through email. Email is available to many users who are denied direct access to Internet services because they are on a nonconnected network or are sitting behind a restrictive firewall. Also, there are times when email provides sufficient service because you don't need the document quickly.

Retrieve RFCs through email by sending mail to *mailserv@ds.internic.net*. Leave the Subject: line blank. Request the RFC in the body of the email text, preceding the pathname of the RFC with the keyword FILE.

The technique works very well. In the time it took to type these paragraphs, the requested RFC was already in my mailbox.

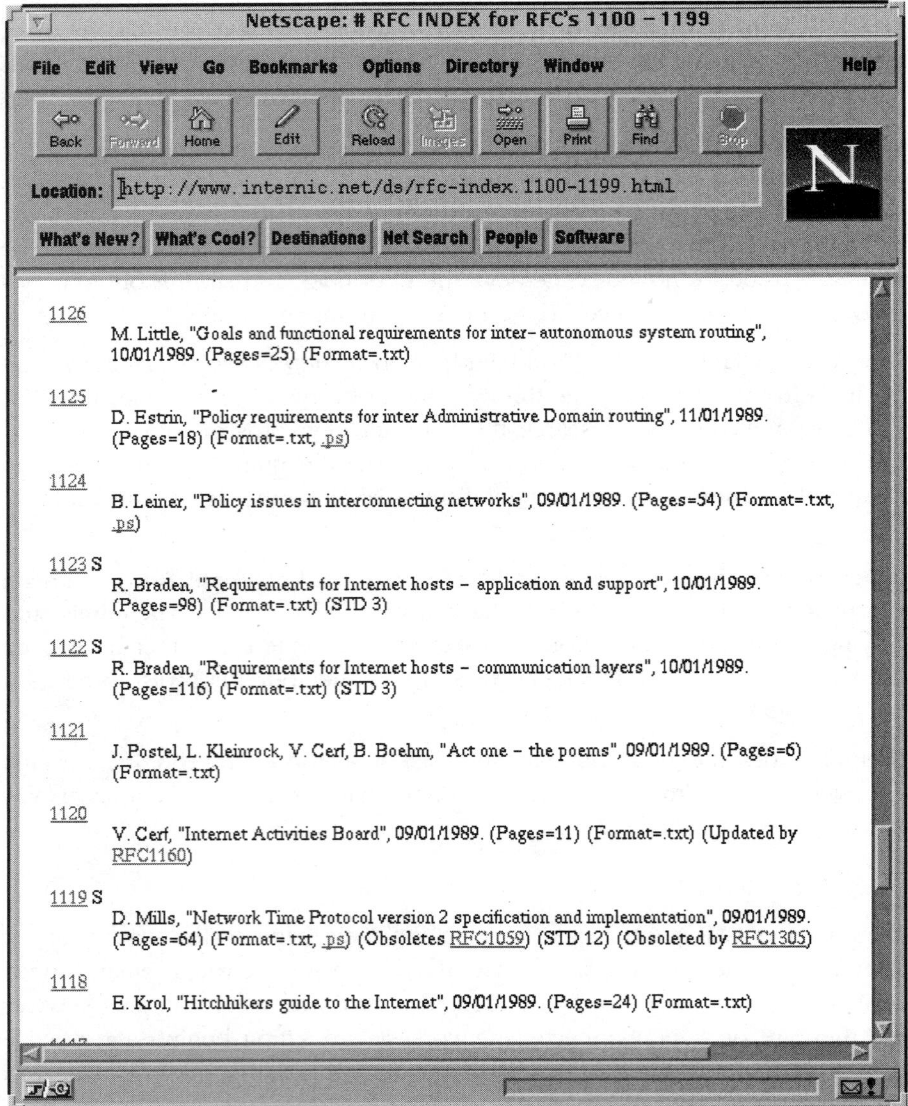

Figure 13-4. The RFC index

Mailing Lists

Mailing lists bring together people with similar interests to exchange information and ideas. Most mailing lists run under usage guidelines that restricted discussion to a specific topic. Mailing lists are often used as places to report problems and get solutions, or to receive announcements. Some mailing lists are digests of newsgroups. (More on newsgroups later in the chapter.)

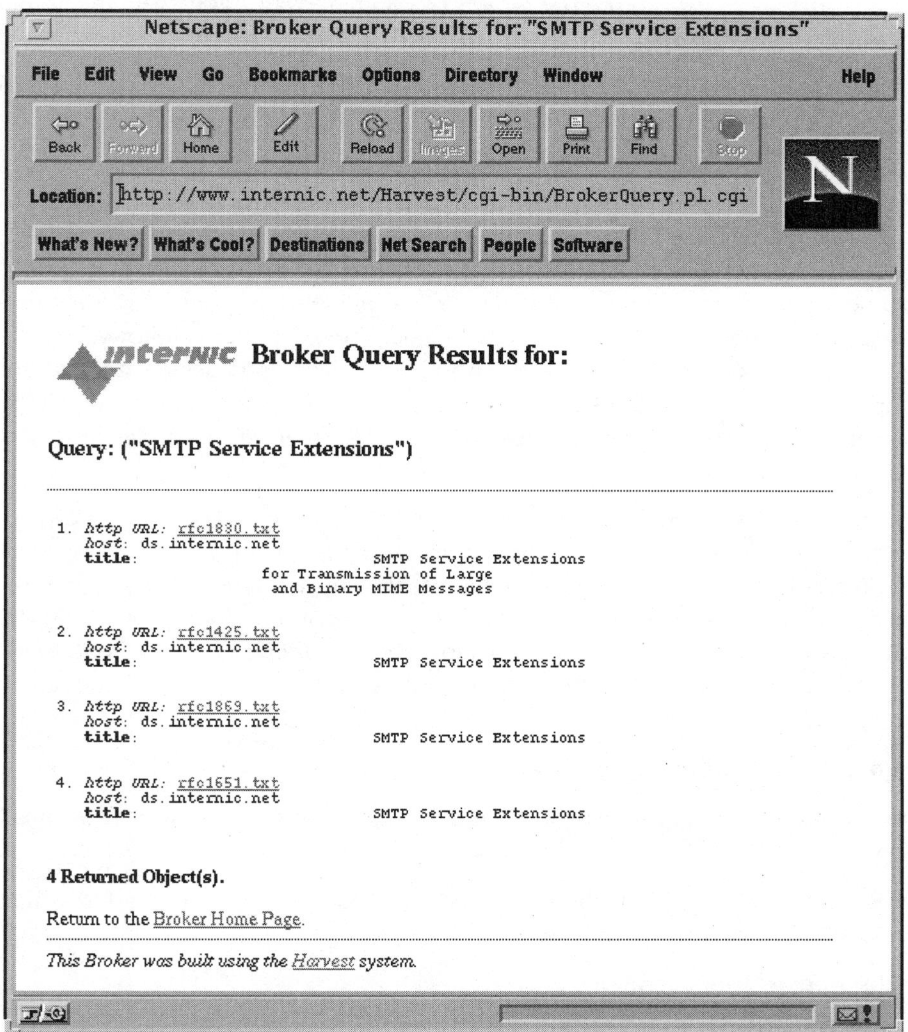

Figure 13-5. An RFC Web search

There are an enormous number of mailing lists. The *list-of-lists* contains information about many of the mailing lists that are of interest to network administrators.*

Use a Web browser to search for mailing lists that interest you at *http://catalog.com/vivian/interest-group-search.html*. If you prefer, the list-of-lists can be downloaded to your system via anonymous FTP from *nisc.sri.com* where it is

* Despite its large size, not every network administration mailing list is contained in the *interest-groups.txt* file. You hear about some lists by word-of-mouth.

stored in the file *netinfo/interest-groups.txt*. Either way, you get the same information.

A list-of-lists entry has five sections: the address of the mailing list, the address to which subscription requests are sent, the address of the owner, the date the entry was last updated, and a description of the mailing list.

When you find a list you wish to join, don't send mail directly to the list asking to be enrolled. Instead, send the enrollment request to the subscription address, which identifies the person or process that maintains the list. If the list is manually maintained, you're asked to send your enrollment request to *list-name*-**request@***host,* where *list-name* is the actual name of the list, and is followed by the literal string **-request**. The **-request** extension is widely used as the address for administrative requests, such as being added to or dropped from a list. Send your enrollment request to the administrative address. All other correspondence is sent directly to the list.

List management is automated for many mailing lists. There are a number of programs to do this. Two of the most popular are *majordomo* and *LISTSERV*. You can tell the type of server being used by looking at the subscription address in the list-of-lists. The user portion of that address will be either *majordomo* or *LISTSERV,* depending on the server being used. To subscribe to a *majordomo* list, send email to the subscription address and put the following in the body of the email message:

> **subscribe** *list-address your-address*

where *list-address* is the address of the email list, and *your-address* is your email address.

To subscribe to a *LISTSERV* mailing list, send email to the subscription address that contains the following in the message body:

> **subscribe** *list your-name*

where *list* is the name of the list, not necessarily its address, as that name appears in the first line of its list-of-lists entry. *your-name* is your first and last name. This is not your email address. *LISTSERV* takes your email address from the email headers.

Newsgroups

A mailing list is one way of distributing announcements and exchanging questions and answers, but it is not the most efficient way. A mail message is sent to every person on the list. It is sent immediately, and it must be stored on the local system until it is read. Thus, if there are 100 people on a list, 100 messages are sent over the network and stored at 100 receiving systems. Network news provides a more efficient method for distributing this kind of information. The information is stored around the network on news servers. Most sites have only one or two news servers. Therefore, instead of moving mail messages to every individual on your network who wants to discuss Windows NT, news articles about NT are stored at one location where they can be read when the user is ready. Not only does this reduce the network load, it reduces the number of redundant copies that are stored on local disk files.

Network news is delivered over TCP/IP networks using the *Network News Transfer Protocol* (NNTP). NNTP is a simple command/response protocol. The NNTP server listens to port 119. NNTP requires no special configuration. The only thing you need to know to configure a news reader is the host name of your network news server. Ask your ISP. Most ISPs provide network news as part of their basic service.

Windows NT 4.0 does not include a news reader. But it doesn't matter. News readers are very easy to obtain. News is supported in the Netscape Web browser. If you use that browser, select Netscape News from the Windows menu in the Netscape browser to open the news reader and you're ready to run. If you use the Internet Explorer browser, you must first install a news reader.

To download a new reader from Microsoft, start the Internet Explorer. From the Help menu select Web, and then select Free Stuff. This connects you to the Microsoft web site. If you are running version 3 of the Internet Explorer you can download a news reader for that version of the browser or you can download the complete Internet Explorer version 4. The full release of Internet Explorer version 4 includes Outlook Express. Outlook Express is an email tool and a news reader.

After you run the setup for the new Internet Explorer, an Outlook Express icon appears on the desktop. Double-click it to start the program. The first time you run it you will be asked where you want to store your messages. The default directory is usually fine.

Outlook Express is both a mail tool and a news reader. When the Outlook Express window opens, click Read News to start the news reader. The first time the news reader starts, it automatically runs the Internet Connection Wizard to gather data to configure the news reader and the mailer. Some of the requested information is obvious: your name, your email address, and the host name of the news server. Other requested information requires an explanation.

You're asked for the username and password used to log on to the server. Many servers do not require a logon. If yours doesn't, ignore this box. You're also given the option of selecting *Secure Password Authentication* (SPA) if that is required by your news server. Only the administrator of the news server can tell you if SPA is required. If you aren't sure, try logging on without it. If the logon fails, ask the news server administrator for help.

The configuration wizard requests a friendly name for the news service. Use an intuitive name such as "News." The label you enter here is used to identify the service in the Outlook Express window.

Finally, you're asked to select the network service that you will use to connect to the news server. Most users select their LAN. Other options are to have Outlook Express demand dial a connection using your modem, or for you to connect via your modem before starting Outlook Express. After entering all of this data, click Finish to complete the configuration.

Now that the news reader is configured, the first thing to do is to decide what newsgroups you want to read. There are many, many newsgroups. Most of the newsgroup that are of interest to a network administrator are found in the *comp* category. *comp.os* contains subgroups for various operating systems. *comp.os.ms-windows.nt* contains groups for various topics concerning Windows NT. *comp.networks* and *comp.internet* provide information about computer networks and the Internet. *comp.security* and *comp.virus* provide security information.

To read a group, you must first subscribe to that group. When you run the news reader the first time it notices that you have not yet subscribed to any groups and asks you if you would like to do so now. Select Yes. This opens the Newsgroups window shown in Figure 13-6.

Highlight the newsgroup name and click Subscribe for each newsgroup you wish to read. When you have selected all that you want, click on OK. Select the *Newsgroups* button in Outlook Express to return to the Newsgroups window at any time to subscribe to new groups or unsubscribe from old groups.

Figure 13-7 shows us reading the *comp.os.ms-windows.nt.security* group that we just subscribed to. Notice the list of Outlook Express services in the pane at the left of the window. "News" is the friendly name we gave the news service. Listed under it are all of the news groups we have subscribed to. Double-clicking on the *comp.os.ms-windows.nt.security* name downloads all unread messages for that group from the news server. Highlighting the message header in the pane on the upper right of the window displays the content of the message in the lower right, where it can be read.

To respond to the message you are reading, select the "Reply to Author" or the "Reply to Group" button, depending on whether or not you want the entire list to read your reply. To post your own message to a list, select the list in the left-hand pane and select the Compose Message button.

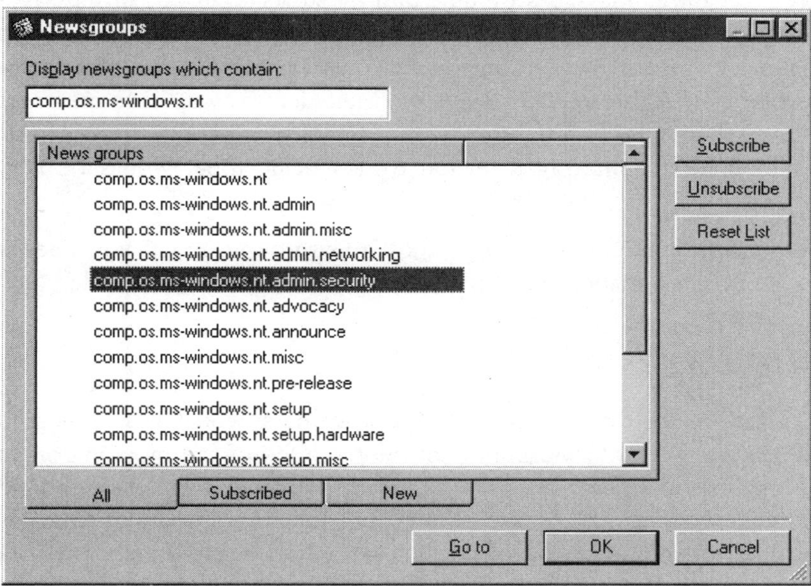

Figure 13-6. Subscribing to newsgroups

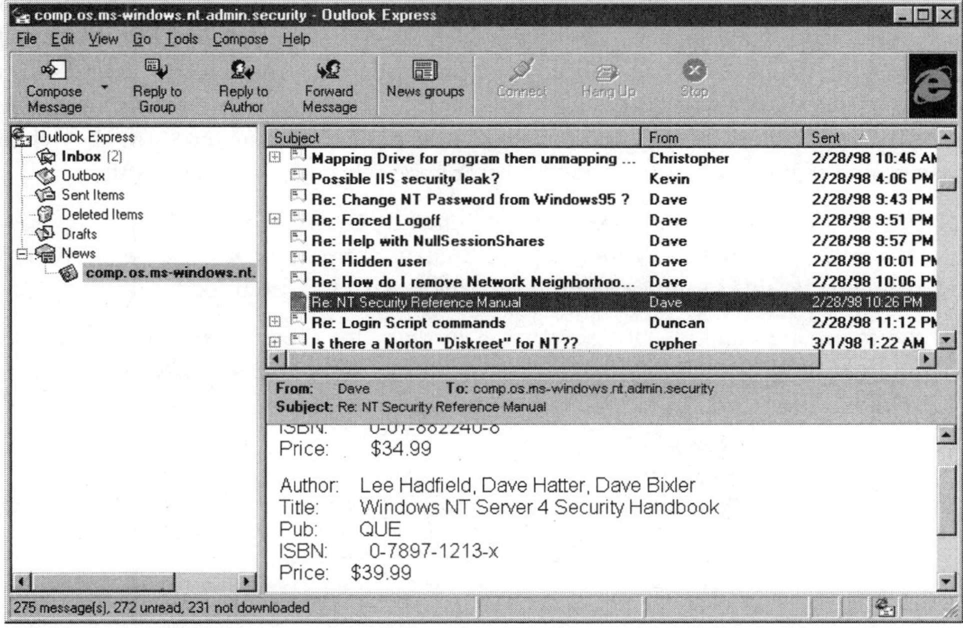

Figure 13-7. Reading News

Outlook Express organizes messages by time and by subject. Groups of messages organized by subject are called *threads*. The first message in a thread appears with a small plus sign (+) next to it. Clicking on the plus sign shows the other messages that are part of that thread. This is a very convenient way to have messages organized because there are often hundreds of messages in a popular news group. Manually searching for the messages related to a specific topic would be very difficult.

There is a tremendous amount of dross in most newsgroups. But if you need a question answered or information on a specific topic, they can be invaluable.

The White Pages

FTP helps you retrieve important programs. The Web helps you locate important documents. **whois** helps you locate important people. One of the most important pieces of information in a network is who is in charge at the other end. In Chapter 11, *Troubleshooting TCP/IP*, we pointed out that it is important to know who is responsible for the other end of the link when troubleshooting a network problem. **whois** is a tool that helps you find this out.

whois obtains the requested information from the Internet white pages. The white pages is a database of information about responsible people that is maintained by the InterNIC. When you request an official network number or domain name, you are asked to provide your *NIC handle*, which is the index of your personal record in the white pages database. If you don't have a handle, the InterNIC assigns you one and automatically registers you in the white pages. Because of this, everyone who is responsible for an official network or domain has an entry in the white pages, and that entry can be retrieved by anyone who needs to contact them.

NT systems do not have a local whois command. To use whois, **telnet** to *rs.internic.net* and enter **whois** at the command-line prompt. You'll then be prompted with *Whois:*. At this prompt enter whatever you wish to search for.

In the following example, we search for an entry for *Craig Hunt*. An individual's name is entered in the white pages as: *last-name, first-name initial*. So we ask to search for *Hunt, Craig*.*

```
[vt100] InterNIC > whois
Whois: Hunt, Craig
Hunt, Craig (CH882) info@BIG.NET +1 (905) 555 7000
Hunt, Craig (CH4851) gadget007@FOO.NET (519) 555-9038
Hunt, Craig W (CWH3) Hunt@ENH.NIST.GOV (301) 555-3600
```

* **whois hunt** would return several matches. Be as specific as possible to reduce the number of matches.

If multiple matches are returned, as in this case, follow with a query for the individual's NIC handle to get the full information display. To query for the NIC handle, which is the field enclosed in parentheses directly following the username, simply enter the handle. For example, to get more details about CWH3, enter:

```
Whois: cwh3
Hunt, Craig W (CWH3) Hunt@ENH.NIST.GOV
 National Institute of Standards and Technology
 Computer Systems and Communications
 Division
 Technology Building, Room A151
 Gaithersburg, MD 20899
 (301) 555-3600

 Record last updated on 12-Oct-97.
 Database last updated on 17-Mar-98 04:21:10 EST.
```

User information is generally of limited use. The white pages database contains several other kinds of records, a few of which are very helpful for locating the people responsible for networks and domains throughout the Internet. These record types are:

Domain
: Provides detailed contact information for the people responsible for the specified DNS domain.

Network
: Provides detailed information for the contacts for the specified network.

These record types can be used in the **whois** query to speed processing and limit the amount of output. The record types listed earlier can be abbreviated to their first two letters.

A sample query for the domain *ora.com* produces the following results:

```
Whois: do ora.com
O Reilly & Associates (ORA-DOM1)
101 Morris Street
Sebastopol, CA 95472

 Domain Name: ORA.COM

 Administrative Contact, Technical Contact, Zone Contact:
 Pearce, Eric (EP86) eap@ORA.COM
 707-829-0515 x221
 Billing Contact:
 Johnston, Rick (RJ724) rick@ORA.COM
 707-829-0515 x331

 Record last updated on 28-Jan-97.
 Record created on 14-Jun-89.
 Database last updated on 17-Mar-98 04:21:10 EST.
```

```
 Domain servers in listed order:

 NS.ORA.COM 207.25.97.8
 NS.SONGLINE.COM 204.148.41.1
```

The query displays the name, address, and telephone number of the contacts for the domain, as well as a list of hosts providing authoritative name service for the domain.

Another interesting query is for the point of contact for a specific network.*

In the previous example the IP address of one of the servers is 207.25.97.8. This is a class C address, so the network number is 207.25.97.0. The **whois** query for the network is shown in the following example:

```
Whois net 207.25.97.0
ANS CO+RE Systems, Inc. (NETBLK-ANS-C-BLOCK4)
100 Clearbrook Rd
Elmsford, NY 10523

 Netname: ANS-C-BLOCK4
 Netblock: 207.24.0.0 - 207.27.255.255
 Maintainer: ANS

 Coordinator:
 Vaidya, Vijay (VV38) vijay@ANS.NET
 914-789-5360
 Alternate Contact:
 ANS Hostmaster (AH-ORG) hostmaster@ANS.NET
 (800)456-6300 fax: (914)789-5310


 Domain System inverse mapping provided by:

 NS.ANS.NET 192.103.63.100
 NIS.ANS.NET 147.225.1.2

 Record last updated on 02-Sep-96.
 Database last updated on 15-Jul-97 04:35:06 EDT.
```

This query could also be done by network name, ANS-C-BLOCK4 in our example, but frequently you won't know the network name until you get the response from your query. In addition to the network name and number, this query tells you who is responsible for this network, and what name servers provide *in-addr.arpa* domain service for this network.

With the information from these queries, we could contact the domain administrator and the network administrator. From these key contacts, we could learn about

* Recently we have had problems running this specific search at the InterNIC. We can only hope they don't drop this important service. The example is from an earlier attempt.

the administrators of individual systems in their domain or on their network. This information could put us directly in touch with the other system administrator we need to talk to when debugging a network problem.

Summary

There is a wealth of information available through the network. Much of the available material provides information about TCP/IP and networking. The RFCs are, of course, a great source of information, but many RFCs are not written for beginners. It can be difficult determining which RFCs to read first. To help you make that decision, some RFCs that provide general information are identified as FYIs (For Your Information). The FYIs can be obtained from *http://www.internic.net* in the same manner as the RFCs.

RFCs and FYIs are not the only sources of information. There are many books and papers published about networking. My favorite reference to Internet information resources is the Nutshell Handbook, *The Whole Internet User's Guide & Catalog*, by Ed Krol. Not only does it explain how to use the information retrieval tools introduced in this chapter, it provides a well organized catalog of many of the information sources available on the network.

As you explore these information sources, you'll see that there is much more to the network than can ever be covered in one book. This book has been your launching pad, helping you connect your system to the network. Now that your system is up and running, use it as a tool to expand your information horizons.

PPP Scripting Languages

PPP installation and configuration are described in the *Using Dial-up Networking (DUN)* section of Chapter 10, *Internet Information Server (IIS)*. A Microsoft DUN client can connect to a RAS server with no additional configuration. But some PPP servers require special logon commands from the client. These commands can be entered manually during each logon or automatically from a logon script. How the DUN client handles the logon process is configured through the Script tab.

If the "Pop up a terminal window" option is selected, a terminal window opens after the local modem has successfully connected to the remote modem. Enter the PPP logon commands required by the remote server through this window. Entering logon procedures through the terminal window allows you to debug the connection before you add the complication of debugging a logon script. The biggest problems with setting up PPP are the modem configuration, which is covered in Chapter 10, and the logon script, which is covered in this appendix. Don't try to debug both at once.

Using the terminal window to make your PPP connection shows you exactly what commands should be programmed into the logon script. This appendix explains the scripting languages used to place those commands into a logon script.

Creating Logon Scripts

The logon sequence of the remote PPP server can be automated with a script. Windows NT provides two scripting languages for that purpose. We cover both. One is a full-featured language that includes commands to control program execution, and the other is a simple expect/send language. We begin our discussion of Windows NT scripting languages with the full-featured language, which is recommended for any situation that demands a complex script.

The first step in building a logon script is to create a script file. The script file is an ASCII file that can be created with any text editor. Notepad is a good choice because it is designed to work on ASCII text files. The script is constructed from the commands shown in Table A-1.

Table A-1. Script Language Commands

Script Command	Function
proc *name*	Begin the script
endproc	End the script
waitfor *"string"*	Wait for *string*
transmit *value*	Send *value*
delay *n*	Pause *n* seconds
goto *label*	Jump to script location *label*
if *cond* **then** *commands* **endif**	If true execute the commands
while *cond* **do** *commands* **endwhile**	Execute commands until false
halt	Stop the script
integer *name* = *n*	Define an integer variable
string *name* = *string*	Define a string variable
boolean *name* = *value*	Define a boolean variable
set port *characteristic*	Modify the port configuration
set ipaddr *string*	Set the local IP address
set screen keyboard on|off	Enable or disable keyboard input to the script

Five of the commands in Table A-1 are used to build most logon scripts. These are the `proc`, `endproc`, `waitfor`, `transmit`, and `delay` commands. A sample script using these basic commands is shown here:

```
; Begin the script
proc main

; Pause two seconds to let the remote system
; initialize.
delay 2

; The remote system requires a carriage-return, so
; send one.
transmit "<cr>"

; Wait for the "Username:" prompt.
waitfor "name:"

; Send the username and a carriage-return.
transmit $USERID
transmit "<cr>"
```

```
; Wait for the "Password:" prompt.
waitfor "word:"

; Send the password and a carriage-return.
transmit $PASSWORD
transmit "<cr>"

; The server s command mode prompt is <.
; Wait for the prompt.
waitfor "\<"

; Send the PPP command required by this server.
transmit "enable ppp<cr>"

; End the script
endproc
```

Every script starts with a `proc main` statement and ends with an `endproc` statement. The `proc/endproc` statement pair is required by the syntax of this script language. The `proc` statement marks the beginning of the script and the `endproc` statement marks its end. Remember to start and end all scripts with these statements.

The `delay` command causes the script to wait the number of seconds specified on the command line. In the example the script waits for two seconds. A `delay` statement is frequently used at the beginning of the script or when the script must send data without receiving a prompt from the remote system. In both cases the delay is used to give the remote server time to complete its processing to ensure that it is ready to receive input. Sometimes delay statements are required to get a script running smoothly.

The bulk of the sample script is composed of `waitfor` and `transmit` statements. These statements are the heart of most scripts. The `transmit` statement sends a value to the remote system and the `waitfor` statement waits until a specific value is received from the remote system. The value on a `waitfor` command line is a string constructed of literal characters and special script language macros. Table A-2 lists the string macros.

Table A-2. String Macros

Macro	Function
<cr>	A carriage return
<lf>	A line feed
\"	A literal quote mark (")
\^	A literal caret (^)
\<	A literal less than (<)
\	A literal backslash (\)
^char	A control character

The value on the `transmit` command line is either a string composed of literal characters and the macros shown in Table A-2, or a keyword. Two keywords are used with the `transmit` command: $USERID and $PASSWORD. $USERID sends the username and $PASSWORD sends the password that were entered in the Connect To window. The keywords allow the logon to be stored in a script without revealing the password in plain text, as would be done if the password was stored in the script as a literal. `transmit` commands in the sample script show examples of using both of these keywords, as well as examples of using the string macros from Table A-2.

The first `transmit` command in the sample script sends a carriage-return (<cr>) to our imaginary PPP server. A carriage-return, which is a control-M on a standard PC keyboard, can also be sent with the following command:

```
transmit "^M"
```

Any control character, the line-feed (control-J), the bell (control-G), the null (control-@), or any other valid ASCII control character, can be sent in this way. Personally we prefer using <cr> for the carriage-return and <lf> for the line-feed, because we think the meaning is clearer to someone reading the script. But if you need to send any other control characters from the 7-bit US ASCII character set, use the ^*char* syntax.

The other entries in Table A-2 are escape sequences. The scripting language uses the backslash as the escape character. A few characters, quote ("), less-than (<), and caret (^), have special meaning when constructing strings for the script. A backslash preceding any one of those characters indicates that the character's literal meaning should be used instead of its special meaning. Therefore, the string "\<" in the last `waitfor` command in the sample script means that the system should wait until it receives a literal < (less-than) character.

The sample script shown previously does not contain any of the commands that control the execution of the script. The `if`, `while`, and `goto` commands add the power to this scripting language that makes it useful for difficult scripting challenges. The following sample script uses all of these commands:

```
; Begin the script
proc main

; Send up to four carriage-returns
integer count = 0
while count < 4 do
    transmit "<cr>"
    waitfor "name:" until 5
    if $SUCCESS then
        goto Logon
    endif
    count = count + 1
endwhile
```

```
; Come here if the server fails to respond
Abort:
    halt

; Come here to complete the logon
Logon:
    transmit $USERID
    transmit "<cr>"
    waitfor "word:" until 2
    if $FAILURE then
        goto Abort
    endif
    transmit $PASSWORD
    transmit "<cr>"
    waitfor "\<" until 2
    if $FAILURE then
        goto Abort
    endif
    transmit "enable ppp<cr>"

; End the script
endproc
```

Assume that we must communicate with a server over a flaky connection. Imagine we may have to send multiple carriage-returns to wake up this server and on occasion it hangs instead of providing the correct response. This script handles these extreme conditions.

The `while` command loops through up to four times sending the server a carriage-return and waiting for a Password prompt. If the server responds we attempt to complete the logon. If the server fails to respond to all four carriage-returns, the script falls through the loop to the section of code we have labeled Abort. The only command in the Abort section is the `halt` command, which terminates the script immediately. (A script normally terminates when it reaches the `endproc` command.) Several interesting features are demonstrated by the code in the while loop.

First, we define a local variable with the `integer` command. You can define three different types of script variables: integers, strings, and booleans. All are defined using a similar syntax. The `while` command tests the value of the integer for each pass and the code inside the while loop increments the integer on each pass.

The `waitfor` command contains the optional keyword `until`. This causes the command to wait for the string for the number of seconds specified. In the example, the script waits for the string "name:" for 5 seconds. If the expected string is received within the specified time, the system variable $SUCCESS is set to true. The `if` command checks if $SUCCESS is true. If it is, the `goto` command causes the script to jump to the section of code we have labeled Logon.

The commands used in the Logon section of the script are a subset of those used in the `while` loop. The only thing new here is the $FAILURE system variable. This variable is set to true if the string expected by the `waitfor` command is not received in the specified time. In the example, if the word: prompt is not received within 2 seconds `waitfor` sets $FAILURE to true. The `if` command detects this condition and executes the `goto` command that jumps to the Abort section of the script. The `while`, `if`, and `goto` commands can help you create a script for the most complex logons.

The remaining commands in Table A-1 are rarely used but they are nice to have when you need them. Most of the remaining commands start with the keyword set and are used to set the characteristics of a specific logon session. The `set port` command takes the largest variety of variables. The port characteristics set by this command are the number of databits, the number of stop bits, and the parity. The command's complete syntax is shown here:

set port databits *value*
: Sets the number of databits for this port to the *value*, for example, `set port databits 7` sets the port for 7 bit data. *value* must be an integer from 5 through 8.

set port stopbits 1 | 2
: Sets the number of stopbits to 1 bit or 2 bits.

set port parity none | even | odd | mark | space
: Sets parity checking for this port to none, even, odd, mark, or space.

You probably recall that Chapter 9 states that databits should be **8** and parity should be **none** for a PPP connection. That's true. So why should we have commands for changing databits and parity if they must always be certain known values? The reason is that it is possible to connect to a multi-purpose terminal server that supports other protocols in addition to PPP and that does not use 8/none as its default setting. You will then need to set the parity and databits to values compatible with the remote server's defaults in order to log on, and then set databits and parity back to 8/none in order to run PPP. A good example of this is provided in the sample file *Cis* located in the *system32\ras* directory.

The other two set commands do not set port characteristics. One sets the IP address and the other enables keyboard input. The `set ipaddr` command can be used to set the IP address locally or to set the IP address from data transmitted from the remote server.

PPP has built into the protocol a standard facility that the server can use to provide the client with an IP address. SLIP has no such facility. To get around this limitation, some servers display the IP address as part of the logon sequence. To capture an address displayed in this manner use the command:

```
set ipaddr getid
```

This assumes that only one IP address is transmitted. Some servers display the server's address and the client's address. If the client's address is the second of two IP addresses in the data stream, add the number **2** to the command as follows:

```
set ipaddr getid 2
```

The `set ipaddr` command can also be used to configure a static IP address as follows:

```
set ipaddr "172.16.12.1"
```

It is unlikely you will ever use the `set ipaddr` command. Static addresses are set through the normal TCP/IP configuration windows. PPP provides the client address through a standard facility that has nothing to do with the `set ipaddr` command. Only in the rare case of connecting to an old SLIP server will this command be of any possible use.

The last set command is `set screen keyboard on`. This allows the user to take over the logon process and provide input from the keyboard. Avoid keyboard input in the script. The reason for creating a script is to automate the logon process and manual input runs counter to that purpose. However, you may find some conditions that require keyboard input. If you do, this command is available for that purpose.

Using the commands from Table A-1, you should be able to build a logon script for any server. Write down every step you take to manually log on to the remote server—every prompt you see and every response you enter. Convert the system prompts into `waitfor` statements and the responses into `transmit` commands. Store these in the script file. Save the script file with a *.scp* extension to make it a little easier to identify the file as a script.

Invoking a logon script

Instructions on how to use the new script are found in the "Modifying Properties for a Phonebook Entry" section of Chapter 9. In particular, the description of the Script tab explains how to invoke a script for a specific connection.

To link the new script to the phone book entry for a connection, click Run this script on the Script tab. Enter the full pathname of your script in the listbox on the Script tab. Then click the OK button. You return to the Dial-Up Networking window. Click the Close button to link the script to the phone book entry or click the Dial button to immediately use the script to make a connection.

The steps we have described so far are pretty straightforward:

1. Use Notepad to create and save an ASCII text script with the scripting language described previously.

2. Go to the Script tab of the Dial-Up Networking configuration. Select "Run this script" and enter the full pathname of the file you created.

Sounds simple enough, but nothing is ever as simple as it sounds. The complication comes from the fact that Windows NT supports two entirely different scripting languages that are created in two entirely different manners. However, the scripts are invoked in an almost identical manner with only a slight difference. Scripts written in the language we have discussed must be identified by a full pathname, for example, */winnt/system32/ras/office.scp*. If the script name entered in the listbox of the Script tab is a simple name, for example, OfficePPP, instead of a full pathname, it refers to a section of the *switch.inf* file and not to a script file. Sections in the *switch.inf* file are written with a different scripting language.

The switch.inf File

Under Windows NT 3.5, all PPP logon scripts were defined in the *switch.inf* file, located in the *C:\winnt\system32\ras directory*.*

This file contained all of the logon scripts. Windows NT 4.0 added the new, more complete scripting language that was discussed in the beginning of the appendix, but it maintained support for the *switch.inf* file to ensure backward compatibility. The *switch.inf* scripting language is adequate for most simple script situations.

To create a new script in the *switch.inf* file, go to the Script tab of the Dial-Up Networking configuration. Click the Edit script button. This opens an editor with the *switch.inf* file. The new script is a new section in the *switch.inf* file.

Each script begins with a section header that provides the name used to invoke the script, which is the simple name entered in the listbox on the Script tab. The section header is the script's name enclosed in square brackets. For example, a script for logging into your office network with PPP might have the header:

```
[OfficePPP]
```

The body of the script follows the header. It defines what you expect to receive from the remote system using the `OK` statement, and what the local system sends in response to the expected values using the `COMMAND` statement. The `OK` and `COMMAND` keywords are always entered in upper case, as the following syntax shows:

```
OK=expect
COMMAND=[send]
```

expect is the value expected from the remote system by the `OK` statement. *send* is the value sent to the remote system by the `COMMAND` statement. The `OK` statement

* This assumes that NT is installed in *C:\winnt*.

requires you to provide a value. If nothing is expected from the remote system, the `NoResponse` statement should be used instead of `OK`. (Additional statements, such as `NoResponse`, are covered later.) The ***send*** value is optional for the `COMMAND` statement. If no value is provided, the script simply waits two seconds and then proceeds to the next line in the script.

expect and ***send*** contain an arbitrary mixture of literals and macros. A literal is a character string. The macros used in a *switch.inf* script are listed in Table A-3.

Table A-3. switch.inf Script Macros

Macro	Usage
`<cr>`	A carriage-return
`<lf>`	A line-feed
`<match> string`	Waits for a match to the literal `string`
`<ignore>`	Ignores the rest of the response
`<?>`	A wildcard character
`<hxx>`	A byte containing the hexadecimal digits `XX`
`<diagnostics>`	Displays a diagnostic message box

A few examples will clarify how the macros and literals are used in *switch.inf* script statements. The following statement sends the command "enable ppp" to the remote system:

```
COMMAND=enable ppp<cr>
```

The literal in this send value is "enable ppp" and the macro is "<cr>". Because the string is followed by a `<cr>` macro, the entire string and the carriage-return are sent immediately to the remote system. This is the most common way commands are sent. If the remote system is so slow that it has trouble processing the characters as fast as the DUN client sends them, you can send the string without the `<cr>` macro.*

When the macro is not used, the string is sent, and there is a slight delay before the script proceeds to the next statement. It is then possible to send small pieces of the string with several `COMMAND` statements, concluding the last statement in the series with the `<cr>` macro. The script expects a response to every command, so if you do use multiple `COMMAND` statements to send a single command, separate the statements with `NoResponse` statements.

* This information is provided for the sake of completeness. It is unlikely that a remote system providing adequate PPP service will not be able to process the string in a timely manner.

In the same way that most COMMAND statements end with a <cr> macro, most OK statements start with a <match> macro. The <match> macro matches its associated string against the data received from the remote system. If the string is found anywhere in that data, the script considers that it has made a successful match and moves on to the next statement. The following example shows how the <match> macro is used:

```
OK=<match>"user"
COMMAND=craig<cr>
```

The OK statement will match any response from the remote system that contains the string user. The match is case sensitive, so Enter username> would match, but Enter Username> would not. If the OK statement detects a match, the script moves to the next statement, which in this case sends the username *craig* to the remote server.

The <ignore> macro is used to ignore data coming from the remote system. Its most common use is to ignore complete lines of data, such as a welcome banner, that do not require a response from the local system. The following statements skip two lines of data received from the PPP server:

```
COMMAND=
OK=<ignore>
COMMAND=
OK=<ignore>
```

The other macros are less frequently used. The <lf> macro is used to send a line-feed or to check for a line-feed in data received from the remote system. The wild-card macro is used to replace an individual character in a string. For example, PORT-<?> will match PORT-1 or PORT-2. The hexadecimal character macro is used when sending or receiving nonprintable characters. For example, <h00> represents the ASCII NULL character. Finally, the <diagnostics> macro is used with the ERROR_DIAGNOSTICS statement to display an error message received by the script.

We have mentioned the NoResponse and ERROR_DIAGNOSTICS statements, but we have not really explained them. There are only two types of statements in a *switch.inf* script: command statements and response statements. All command statements begin with the keyword COMMAND and are used to send a string to the remote system. All response statements handle data sent from the remote system to the local system, but there are multiple response statements and each one begins with a different keyword. The most important one is OK, which we have already discussed. The response statements are listed in Table A-4.

The NoResponse statement is used only when you don't expect the remote host to respond to a command. The CONNECT statement is used only for the last response in the script, and even there it is not required. The script will terminate properly

Table A-4. switch.inf Script Response Statements

Statement	Meaning
`OK=value`	The expected response
`NoResponse`	No response expected
`CONNECT=value`	The response in the script
`ERROR_NO_CARRIER=value`	Checks for loss of carrier
`ERROR_DIAGNOSTICS=value`	Checks for diagnostic messages
`LOOP=value`	Loop waiting for a match

without a closing `CONNECT` statement, but `CONNECT` should be used if the script terminates with a response. For example, assume that the last command in the script sends the command **ppp** to the remote server, and that when it executes on the remote system it returns the message "PPP enabled". The last command/response pair in the script would be:

```
COMMAND=ppp<cr>
CONNECT=<match>"PPP"
```

If the remote server does not return a response to the final command, for example, if the server jumps immediately from terminal mode into SLIP/PPP mode, the script might not end with a `CONNECT` statement. Here is an example of the last two lines in a script that end with a command instead of a response:

```
COMMAND=ppp<cr>
NoResponse
```

Response statements can be clustered together after a single command. It's a stretch, but a cluster of response statements can be thought of as a primitive case statement. The script passes the data received from the remote server through each of the response commands until a match is found. When the data matches, the script takes the action appropriate to that response statement. In the case of an `OK` statement, a match drops the script down to the next command. In the case of both error response statements, the system performs the error processing appropriate to the error condition. An example should help:

```
COMMAND=ppp<cr>
CONNECT=<match>"PPP"
ERROR_NO_CARRIER=<match>"NO CARRIER"
ERROR_DIAGNOSTICS=<cr><diagnostics>
```

This script ends with the same command/response pair we saw earlier. If everything works, we get the response "PPP enabled", which matches the `CONNECT` statement and terminates the script. However, if things go wrong, we have two possible failure modes. In the first case, the remote system drops the line and the modem sends us a "NO CARRIER" message. If that happens, the NT user is informed through a standard error window. In the second case, the remote system does not drop the line but instead sends some error message. All messages from this remote system end with a carriage-return, so we look for that character and use the <diagnostics> macro to display the error message to the NT user.

The LOOP statement is always clustered with at least an OK statement. LOOP is used to walk through several lines of unwanted data until a match is found for the value defined in the OK statement. Because the data is unwanted, the LOOP statement always contains the <ignore> macro. Here's an example:

```
COMMAND=
OK=<match>"user"
LOOP=<ignore>
COMMAND=craig<cr>
```

The remote system sends a banner before the username prompt, and there is no way to tell exactly how many lines are in the banner. The first COMMAND statement delays up to two seconds waiting for data from the remote server. The OK statement checks for the username prompt. If OK finds a match, the script moves to the next COMMAND statement, which sends the username *craig* to the server. If a match is not found, the script drops through to the LOOP=<ignore> statement, which ignores any response from the server until a match is found for the string in the OK statement.

Putting the statements together, let's construct a logon script. The lines that begin with a semicolon (;) are comments:

```
;
; A logon script for the office PPP server
;
[OfficePPP]
;
; Send a carriage-return and wait for the username prompt.
;
COMMAND=<cr>
OK=<match>"username"
;
; Send my username and wait for the password prompt.
;
COMMAND=craig<cr>
OK=<match>"password"
;
; Send my password and look for the command-line prompt,
; which contains the string "PORT".
;
COMMAND=Wats?Watt?<cr>
OK=<match>"PORT"
;
; Send the command that starts PPP. We don t expect any response.
; If we do get a response, it's trouble!
;
COMMAND=set port ppp enabled<cr>
NoResponse
ERROR_NO_CARRIER=<match>"NO CARRIER"
ERROR_DIAGNOSTICS=<cr><diagnostics>
```

A *switch.inf* logon script, such as the one we just wrote, is always invoked after the modems have successfully connected. Therefore, the commands contained in the script are those required by the remote server—not by the modem.

Troubleshooting a switch.inf script

To invoke the new script, go to the Script tab as described in Chapter 9. Enter OfficePPP in the listbox as the name of the new script and click on OK.

Now you are ready to run the script. In the Dial-Up Networking window, click the Dial button. The system displays a series of dialogue boxes tracking the progress of the connection. One of these tells you when the OfficePPP script is being used. If everything works properly, the process ends with a message telling you that the system is successfully connected, and your work is done. If the script fails, turn on logging to debug it. The following steps detail what must be done to enable logging of a *switch.inf* script:

1. Run the registry editor *regedt32.exe*.
2. When the registry editor opens it contains several subwindows. Select the window labeled HKEY_LOCAL_MACHINE.
3. The HKEY_LOCAL_MACHINE window describes a tree-structured database. The branch of the tree that we want to reach is *SYSTEM\CurrentControlSet\Services\RasMan\Parameters*. A double-click on each element in this path—SYSTEM, CurrentControlSet, Services, RasMan, and finally Parameters— walks you down the tree. When you reach Parameters, the values that we are interested in are displayed in a listbox to the right of the window.
4. To change the logging value, double-click Logging:REG_WORD:0x0. In the box that appears enter the value 0x1 and click on OK.

Retest your script. When it fails, take a careful look at the error message displayed by RAS to see if it gives you any clues about the problem. Next, open the *C:\winnt\system32\ras\device.log* file, which contains the log of the interactions between the script and the remote system. The log shows approximately where in the script the logon process failed. A sample log might contain the following:

```
Remote Access Service Device Log 03/06/1998 19:59:34

Port:COM2 Command to Device:AT&F&C1&D2 V1 S0=0 S2=128 S7=55
Port:COM2 Echo from Device :AT&F&C1&D2 V1 S0=0 S2=128 S7=55
Port:COM2 Response from Device:OK
Port:COM2 Command to Device:ATDT5551212
Port:COM2 Echo from Device :ATDT5551212
Port:COM2 Response from Device:CONNECT
Port:COM2 Command to Device:
Port:COM2 Echo from Device :
Port:COM2 Response from Device:Enter Username>
```

The log shows the initialization command sent to the modem, the modem dialing, and the connect message from the modem. After the modem connects, the commands come from our script, and the *device* that the commands are being sent to is the remote server. A command is sent to the remote server that appears to be a blank line. This is the carriage-return at the start of the script.

The last line in this log is a response from the server prompting for the username. The script, however, did not send the username; instead, it timed out with an error. In this case, the script is probably looking for the wrong username prompt. Correct the script and try again. The script may fail several times. Each time correct the problem and move on to the next test. You should note that every time the script runs it appends its log to anything that already exists in the *device.log* file. To keep the log small, delete the old file before running the test.

Once you have a script that works with your server, make a copy of it without your username and password, and distribute it to the other NT systems in your organization that connect through the same server. No one else should have to go through this pain!

Windows NT provides two different languages for developing logon script, but frequently no script is needed. Many servers provide PPP service without requiring any special setup commands from the client. The number of servers providing that level of service is increasing. Before investing effort in creating a logon script, make sure you really need one.

B

DNS Resource Records

This appendix provides detailed information about the DNS *standard resource records* (RR) used to construct domain database files. This is primarily a reference to use in conjunction with the tutorial information in Chapter 8, *Configuring DNS Name System*. This information is useful to any domain administrator.

This appendix covers the most commonly used resource records. It shows the DNS Manager dialog used to enter each record and the syntax of each *standard resource record* (RR) as it appears in the DNS database file.

Standard Resource Records

Standard resource records define the domain data contained in the zone file. The format of standard resource records, sometimes called RRs, is defined in RFC 1033, the *Domain Administrators Operations Guide*. The format is:

[*name*] [*ttl*] *class type data*

The individual fields in the standard resource record are:

name

This is the name of the object affected by this resource record. The named object can be as specific as an individual host, or as general as an entire domain. The string entered for *name* is relative to the current domain unless a fully qualified domain name is used. Certain *name* values have special meaning. These are:*

A blank name field denotes the current named object. The current name stays in force until a new name value is encountered in the name field.

* The FQDN must be specified all the way to the root; in other words, it must end with a dot.

This permits multiple RRs to be applied to a single object without having to repeat the object's name for each record.

..

Two dots in the name field refer to the root domain. However, a single dot (the actual name of the root) also refers to the root domain, and is more commonly used.

@

A single at sign (@) in the name field refers to the current origin. The origin is a domain name derived by the system from the current domain name.

*

An asterisk in the name field is a wildcard character. It stands for a name composed of any string. It can be combined with a domain name or used alone. Used alone, an asterisk in the named field means that the resource record applies to objects with names composed of any string of characters plus the name of the current domain. Used with a domain name, the asterisk is relative to that domain. For example, **.bitnet.* in the name field means any string plus the string *.bitnet.*.

ttl
Time-to-live defines the length of time in seconds that the information in this resource record should be kept in the cache. *ttl* is specified as a numeric value up to eight characters in length. If no value is set for *ttl*, it defaults to the value defined for the entire zone file in the *minimum* field of the SOA record.

class
This field defines the address class of the resource record. The Internet address class is IN. All resource records used by Internet DNS have IN in this field, but it is possible for a zone file to hold non-Internet information. For example, information used by the *Hesiod* server, a name server developed at MIT, is identified by HS in the class field, and *chaosnet* information is identified by a CH in the class field. All resource records used in this book have an address class of IN.

type
This field indicates the type of data this record provides. For example, the A type RR provides the address of the host identified in the name field. The essential standard resource record types are discussed in this appendix.

data
This field contains the information specific to the resource record. The format and content of the data field vary according to the resource record type. The data field is the meat of the RR. For example, in an A record, the data field contains the IP address.

In addition to the special characters that have meaning in the name field, zone file records use these other special characters:

;
: The semicolon is the comment character. Use the semicolon to indicate that the remaining data on the line is a comment.

()
: Parentheses are the continuation characters. Use parentheses to continue data beyond a single line. After an opening parenthesis, all data on subsequent lines is considered part of the current line until a closing parenthesis.

\x
: The backslash is an escape character. A nonnumeric character following a backslash (\) is taken literally and any special meaning that the character may ordinarily have is ignored. For example, \; means a semicolon—not a comment.

\ddd
: The backslash can also be followed by three decimal numbers. When the escape character is used in this manner the decimal numbers are interpreted as an absolute byte value. For example, \255 means the byte value 11111111.

The same general resource record format is used for each of the resource records in a zone file. Windows NT can read and process the same zone files as any other DNS server. Most NT administrators do not edit the zone files directly. Instead they use the DNS Manager to create resource records. We recommend that you do the same and that you never directly edit the zone files.

To create a resource record, first start the DNS Manager (Start → Programs → Administrative Tools (Common) → DNS Manager). In the Servers pane of the DNS Manager window, highlight the name of the zone for which you're creating a resource record. From the DNS menu select New Record. In the New Record dialog, select the type of resource record you're creating from the Type scroll list. The dialog that then appears is different for each record type. In the following sections we examine the different dialog box and the different syntax for each of several key resource record types.

Start of Authority record

The *Start of Authority* (SOA) record marks the beginning of a zone, and is usually the first record in a zone file. All of the records that follow are part of the zone declared by the SOA. Each zone has only one SOA record; the next SOA record encountered marks the beginning of another zone. Because a zone file is normally associated with a single zone, it normally contains only one SOA record.

Unlike the other resource records, the SOA record is not created through the New Resource Record dialog. The SOA is created when a new primary zone is created. However, the values in the SOA record can be modified by double-clicking on the domain in the Server List and then double-clicking on the SOA record in the Zone Info pane. This opens the dialog shown in Figure B-1.

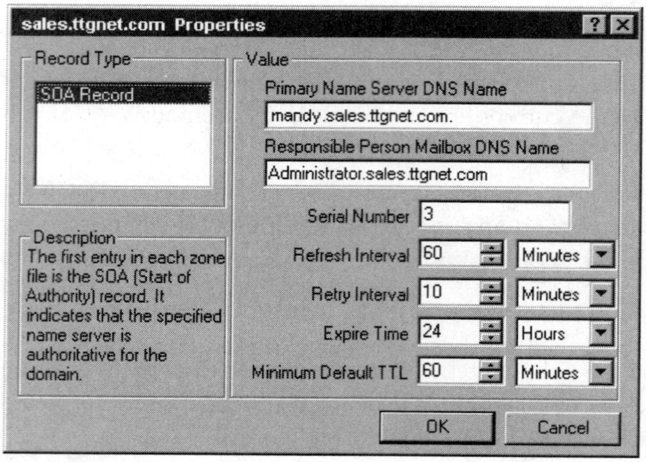

Figure B-1. The SOA dialog box

The format of the SOA record is:

[*zone*] [*ttl*] **IN SOA** *origin contact* (
serial
refresh
retry
expire
minimum
)

The components of the SOA record in the database file are:

zone
This is the name of the zone. Usually the SOA name field contains an at sign (@). When used in an SOA record, the at-sign refers back to the domain name declared in the DNS Manager when the zone was created.

ttl
Time-to-live is left blank on the SOA record.

IN
The address class is IN for all Internet RRs.

SOA

SOA is the resource record type. All the information that follows this is part of the data field and is specific to the SOA record.

origin

This is the host name of the primary master server for this domain. It is normally written as a fully qualified domain name. For example, *mandy* is the master server for *ttgnet.com*, so this field contains *mandy.sales.ttgnet.com.* in the SOA record for *ttgnet.com*. For this field the DNS Manager uses the host name of the system on which the zone file was created.

contact

The email address of the person responsible for this domain is entered in this field. The address is modified slightly. The at sign (@) that usually appears in an Internet email address is replaced by a dot. Therefore, if *Administrator@sales.ttgnet.com* is the mailing address of the administrator of the *ttgnet.com* domain, the *ttgnet.com* SOA record contains *Administrator.sales.ttgnet.com.* in the contact field. The email address of the user who ran DNS Manager to create the zone is used for the contact field.

serial

This is the version number of the zone file. It is an eight-digit numeric field usually entered as a simple number, for example, 9. The number is updated by the DNS Manager every time the data in the zone file is modified. The *serial* field is extremely important. It is used by the secondary master servers to determine if the zone file has been updated. To make this determination, a secondary server requests the SOA record from the primary server and compares the serial number of the data it has stored to the serial number received from the primary server. If the serial number has increased, the secondary server requests a full zone transfer. Otherwise it assumes that it has the most current zone data. The serial number must increase each time you update the zone data. If it doesn't, the new data will not be disseminated to the secondary servers. The DNS Manager automatically increases the serial number each time the zone data changes.

refresh

This specifies the length of time that the secondary server should wait before checking with the primary server to see if the zone has been updated. Every *refresh* second the secondary server checks the SOA serial number to see if the zone file needs to be reloaded. Secondary servers check the serial numbers of their zones whenever they restart. But it is important to keep the secondary server's database current with the primary server, so the *refresh* interval provides a predictable cycle for reloading the zone that is controlled by the domain administrator. The process of retrieving the SOA record, evaluating the serial number and, if necessary, downloading the zone file is called a *zone refresh*. Thus the name *refresh* is used for this value. The value used in *refresh* is a number, up to eight digits long, that is the maximum number of seconds that the primary and secondary servers' databases can be out of synch. A low *refresh* value keeps the data on the servers closely synchronized, but a very low *refresh* value is not usually required. A value set lower than needed places an unnecessary burden on the network and the secondary servers. The value used in *refresh* should reflect the reality of how often your domain database is updated. Most sites' domain databases are very stable. Systems are added periodically, but not generally on an hourly basis. When you are adding a new system, you can assign the host name and address of that system before the system is operational. You can then install this information in the name server database before it is actually needed, ensuring that it is disseminated to the secondary servers long before it has to be used. If extensive changes are planned, the *refresh* time can be temporarily reduced while the changes are underway. Therefore, you can normally set *refresh* time high, reducing load on the network and servers. Two (43200 seconds) to four (21600 seconds) times a day for *refresh* is adequate for many sites. The exception to this is a network with mobile users who frequently connect to or disconnect from the network. In this case, DHCP may be frequently assigning new IP addresses to these hosts. A short refresh period can help the DNS servers stay synchronized in a highly changeable environment. The DNS Manager uses a default value of one hour (3600), which is short enough for highly changeable environments. Don't set refresh any lower than this.

retry

This defines how long secondary servers should wait before trying again if the primary server fails to respond to a request for a zone refresh. *Retry* is specified in seconds and can be up to eight digits long. You should not set the *retry* value too low. If a primary server fails to respond, the server or the network could be down. Quickly retrying a down system gains nothing and costs network resources. A secondary server that backs up a large number of zones can have problems when *retry* values are short. If the secondary server cannot reach the primary servers for several of its zones, it can become stuck in a retry loop. The DNS Manager uses 10 minutes (600) as a default. Don't set retry any lower than this.

expire

This defines how long the zone's data should be retained by the secondary servers without receiving a zone refresh. The value is specified in seconds and is up to eight digits long. If after *expire* seconds the secondary server has been unable to refresh this zone, it should discard all of the data. *expire* is often a very large value. 3600000 seconds (about 42 days) is sometimes used. This says that if there has been no answer from the primary server to refresh requests repeated every *retry* seconds for the last 42 days, discard the data. Forty-two days is extremely long. A week (604800) is adequate. However one day (86400), which is the default provided by the DNS Manager, is much too short.

minimum

This is the value used as the default *ttl* in all resource records where an explicit *ttl* value is not provided. This is a number, up to eight digits long, that specifies how many seconds resource records from this zone should be held in a remote host's cache. Make this a large value if most of the records in your zone remain unchanged for long periods of time. Hosts are added to a zone, but host names (if they are well chosen) and addresses are not frequently changed. Forcing remote servers to query again for data that has not changed, just because it had a short *ttl*, is a waste of resources. If you plan to change a record, put a short *ttl* on that record; don't set the entire zone to a short *ttl* by setting a low *minimum*. Use a short *minimum* only if the entire database is being replaced. Use at least a week (604800) for normal operation. If the addresses in your zone change very frequently because of mobile users, you will need a short *ttl*, perhaps as short as an hour (3600). In that case, you may want to manually set long TTL values on records, such as the DHCP server's address record, that do not change.

A sample SOA record for the *ttgnet.com* domain is:

```
@    IN   SOA     mandy.sales.ttgnet.com. Administrator.sales.ttgent.com. (
                  9                    ; serial
                  43200                ; refresh twice a day
                  1800                 ; retry every half hour
                  604800               ; expire after one week
                  604800               ; default ttl is one week
                  )
```

Notice the serial number in this SOA. The serial number is generated by the DSN Manager when the administrator updates the zone. This SOA record says that *mandy* is the primary server for this zone and that the person responsible for this zone can be reached at the email address *Administrator@sales.ttgnet*. The SOA tells the secondary servers to check the zone for changes twice a day and to retry every half hour if they don't get an answer. If they retry for a week and never get an answer, they should discard the data for this zone. Finally, if an RR in this zone does not have an explicit *ttl*, it will default to one week.

Name server record

Name server (NS) resource records identify the authoritative servers for a zone. These records are the pointers that link the domain hierarchy together. NS records in the top-level domains point to the servers for the second level domains, which in turn contain NS records that point to the servers for their subdomains. Name server records pointing to the servers for subordinate domains are required for these domains to be accessible. Without NS records, the servers for a domain would be unknown.

Figure B-2 shows the dialog box for the NS record.

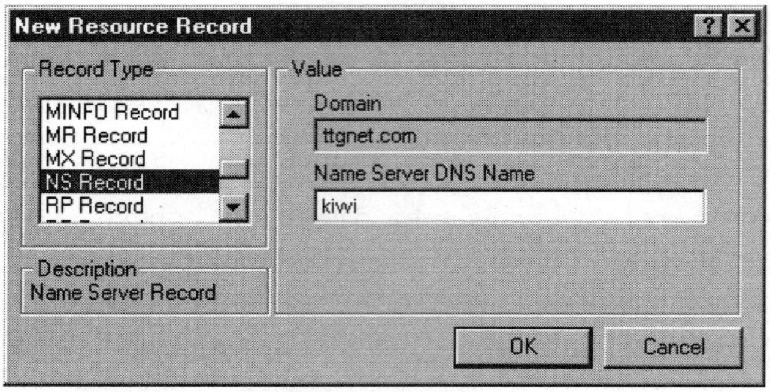

Figure B-2. The NS dialog box

The format of the NS RR in the DNS database is:

[*domain*] [*ttl*] **IN NS** *server*

domain
: The name of the domain for which the host specified in the *server* field is an authoritative name server.

ttl
: Time-to-live is usually blank.

IN
: The address class is IN.

NS
: The Name Server resource record type is NS.

server
: The host name of a computer that provides authoritative name service for this domain. Usually domains have at least one server that is located outside of the local domain. That server name cannot be specified relative to the local domain; it must be specified as a fully qualified domain name. The DNS Manager uses fully qualified names for external servers and for servers within the local domain it uses relative host names.

Address record

The majority of the resource records in a zone file are address records. Address records are used to convert host names to IP addresses, which is the most common use of the DNS database.

Figure B-3 shows the address record dialog box.

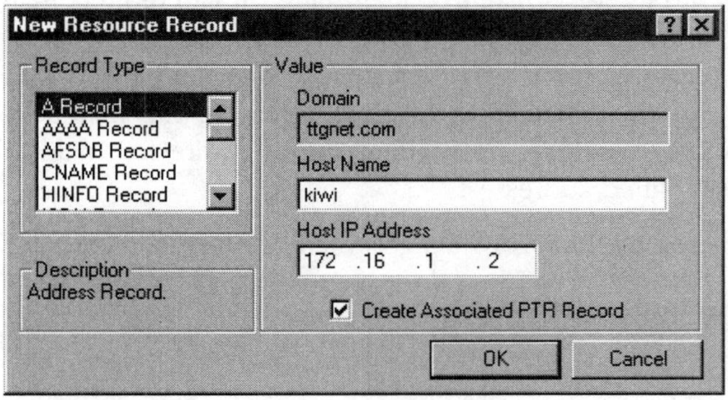

Figure B-3. The Address record dialog

The address RR contains the following:

[*host*] [*ttl*] **IN A** *address*

host
: The name of the host whose address is provided in the data field of this record. In a zone created by the DNS Manager the host name is always written relative to the current domain.

ttl
: Time-to-live is usually blank.

IN
: The address class is IN.

A
: The Address resource record type is A.

address
: The IP address of the host is written here in dotted decimal form, for example, 172.16.12.2.

A *glue record* is a special type of address record. Most address records refer to hosts within the zone, but sometimes an address record needs to refer to a host in another zone. This is done to provide the address of a name server for a subordinate domain. Recall that the NS record for a subdomain server identifies the server by name. An address is needed to communicate with that server, so an A record must also be provided. The address record, combined with the name server record, links the domains together—thus the term glue record. Chapter 8, *Configuring DNS Name System* describes glue records in the discussion of how to delegate a subdomain.

Mail exchanger record

The mail exchanger (MX) record redirects mail to a mail server. It can redirect mail for an individual computer or an entire domain. MX records are extremely useful for domains that contain some systems that don't run mail software. Mail addressed to those systems can be redirected to computers that do run mail software. MX records are also used to simplify mail addressing by redirecting mail to servers that understand the simplified addresses.

Figure B-4 shows the dialog used by the DNS Manager to create the MX record.

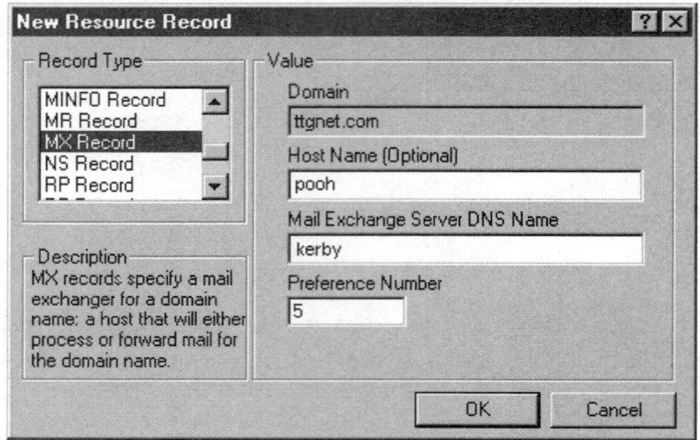

Figure B-4. The MX dialog box

The format of the MX RR is:

[*name*] [*ttl*] **IN MX** *preference server*

name
: The name of a host or domain to which the mail is addressed. Think of this as the value that occurs after the @ in a mailing address. Mail addressed to this name is sent to the mail server specified by the MX record's server field.

ttl
: Time-to-live is usually blank.

IN
: The address class is IN.

MX
: The Mail Exchanger resource record type is MX.

preference
: A host or domain may have more than one MX record associated with it. The *preference* field specifies the order in which the mail servers are tried. Servers with low *preference* numbers are tried first, so the most preferred server has a *preference* of 0. Preference values are usually assigned in increments of 5 or

10, so that new servers can be inserted between existing servers without editing the old MX records.

server
The name of the mail server to which mail is delivered when it is addressed to the host or domain identified in the name field.

Here is how MX records work. If a remote system has mail to send to a host, it requests the host's MX records. DNS returns all of the MX records for the specified host. The remote server chooses the MX with the lowest preference value and attempts to deliver the mail to that server. If it cannot connect to that server, it will try each of the remaining servers in preference order until it can deliver the mail. If no MX records are returned by DNS, the remote server delivers the mail directly to the host to which the mail is addressed. MX records only define how to redirect mail. The remote system and the mail server perform all of the processing that actually delivers the mail.

Here are some MX examples. All of these examples are for the domain *ttgnet.com*. In the first example, mail addressed to *thoth.ttgent.com* is redirected to *mandy.sales.ttgnet* with this MX record:

```
thoth IN MX 10 mandy
```

The second example is an MX record used to simplify mail addressing. People can send mail to any user in this domain without knowing the specific computer on which the user reads mail. Mail addressed to *user@ttgnet.com* is redirected by this MX record to *mandy*, which is a mail server that knows how to deliver mail to every individual user in the domain. The DNS Manager always uses an at sign (@) in the name field for records that apply to the entire domain.

```
@ IN MX 10 mandy
```

The last example is an MX record that redirects mail addressed to any *host* within the domain to a central mail server. Mail addressed to any host, *theodore.ttgnet.com*, *pooh.ttgnet.com*, or *anything.ttgnet.com*, is redirected to *mandy*. This is the most common use of the wildcard character (*).

```
*.ttgnet.com. IN MX 10 mandy.sales.ttgnet.com.
```

There are a couple of things to note about the examples. The *preference* is 10 so that a mail server with a lower preference number can be added to the zone without changing the existing MX record. Also the host names in the examples are relative to the *nuts.com* domain because they do not end in a dot.

Canonical Name record

The *Canonical Name* (CNAME) resource record defines an alias for the official name of a host. The CNAME record provides a facility similar to nicknames in the host table. The facility provides alternate host names for the convenience of users, such as *www* for web servers, *ns* for name servers, and *news* for news servers.

The CNAME record is also used to ease the transition from an old host name to a new host name. While it is best to avoid host name changes by carefully choosing host names in the first place, not all changes can be avoided. When you do make a name change, it can take a long time before it becomes completely effective, particularly if the host name is embedded in a mailing list run at a remote site. To reduce problems for the remote site, use a CNAME record until they can make the change.

Figure B-5 shows the dialog box for the CNAME record.

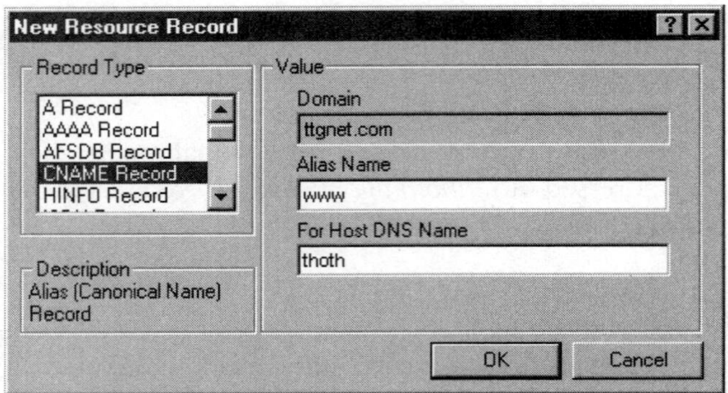

Figure B-5. The CNAME dialog box

The format of the CNAME database record is:

nickname [*ttl*] **IN CNAME** *host*

nickname
: This host name is an alias for the official host name defined in the *host* field. The *nickname* can be any valid host name.

ttl
: Time-to-live is usually blank.

IN
: The address class is IN.

CNAME
: The Canonical Name resource record type is CNAME.

host
: The canonical name of the host is provided here. This host name must be the official host name; it cannot be an alias.

One important thing to remember about the CNAME record is that all other resource records must be associated with the official host name, and not with the nickname. This means that the CNAME record should not be placed between a host and the list of RRs associated with that host. The example below shows a correctly placed CNAME record:

```
thoth  IN   A        172.16.12.2
       IN   MX       5 thoth.ttgnet.com.
tigger IN   CNAME    thoth.ttgnet.com.
```

In this example the host name *thoth* stays in force for the MX record because it has a blank name field. The CNAME record changes the name field value to *tigger*, which is a nickname for *thoth*. Any RRs with blank name fields following this CNAME record would associate themselves with the nickname *tigger*, which is illegal. An improper CNAME placement is shown below:

```
thoth  IN   A        172.16.12.2
tigger IN   CNAME    thoth.ttgnet.com.
       IN   MX       5 thoth.ttgnet.com.
```

Using the DNS Manager ensures that CNAME records are properly placed.

Domain Name Pointer record

The *Domain Name Pointer* (PTR) resource records are used to convert numeric IP addresses to host names. This is the opposite of what is done by the address record that converts host names to addresses. PTR records are used to construct the *in-addr.arpa* reverse domain files.

Many administrators ignore the reverse domains, because things appear to run fine without them. Don't ignore them. Keep these zones up to date. Several programs use the reverse domains to map IP addresses to host names when preparing status displays. Some service providers use the reverse domains to track who is using their service. If they cannot map your IP address back to a host name, they reject your connection. The DNS Manager keeps the reverse domain updated automatically. Notice the "Create Associated PTR Record" checkbox on the address dialog shown in Figure B-3. See Chapter 8 for a description of adding host records to a zone.

Figure B-6 shows the PTR dialog.

The format of the PTR record is:

name [*ttl*] **IN PTR** *host*

name

The *name* specified here is actually a number. The number is defined relative to the current *in-addr.arpa* domain. Names in an *in-addr.arpa* domain are IP addresses specified in reverse order. If the current domain is *16.172.in-addr.arpa*, then the name field for *peanut* (172.16.12.2) is 2.12. These digits

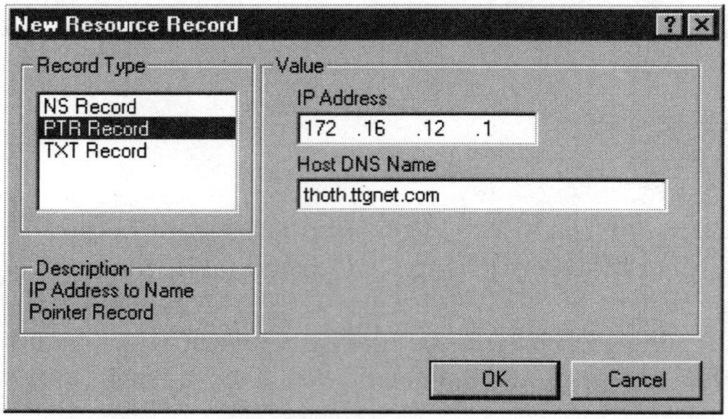

Figure B-6. The PTR dialog box

(2.12) are added to the current domain (*16.172.in-addr.arpa*) to make the name *2.12.16.172.in-addr.arpa*. Chapter 4, *Getting Started*, discusses the unique structure of *in-addr.arpa* domain names.

ttl

Time-to-live is usually blank.

IN

The address class is IN.

PTR

The Domain Name Pointer resource record type is PTR.

host

This is the fully qualified domain name of the computer whose address is specified in the name field. The host must be specified as a fully qualified name because the name cannot be relative to the current *in-addr.arpa* domain.

There are many examples of PTR records in the sample reverse zone file shown in Chapter 8.

This concludes our short tour of the standard resource records. There are many more resource records defined in the RFCs than those shown here. However, the few RRs described in this appendix make up the bulk of most zone files.

The Boot File

There is one DNS configuration file that is not built of standard resource records. The boot file defines the name server configuration and tells the name server where to obtain database information. If the server is configured using the DNS Manager, the boot file is not used. However, the Microsoft DNS server can use a boot file for compatibility with other servers. The boot file contains the following types of records:

primary *domain-name file-name*
: Declares the local name server as the primary master server for the domain specified by *domain-name*. As a primary server, the system loads the name server data base from the local disk file specified by name in the *file-name* field.

secondary *domain-name server-address-list file-name*
: Makes the local server a secondary master server for the domain identified by *domain-name*. The *server-address-list* contains the IP address of at least one other master server for this domain. Multiple addresses can be provided in the list, but at least the primary server's address should be provided. The local server will try each server in the list until it successfully loads the name server database. The local server transfers the entire domain database and stores all of the data it receives in a local file identified by *file-name*. After completing the transfer, the local server answers all queries for information about the domain with complete authority.

cache . *file-name*
: The **cache** command points to the file used to initialize the name server cache with a list of root servers. This command starts with the keyword **cache**, followed by the name of the root domain (.), and ends with the name of the file that contains the root server list. This file is usually named *Cache.dns* on systems running the Microsoft DNS Server.

BindSecondaries | NoBindSecondaries
: This command provides zone transfer compatibility with Unix BIND DNS servers. If any of the secondary servers for the Microsoft DNS Server are BIND servers, use the **BindSecondaries** command for compatibility. If none of the secondary servers are BIND servers, use **NoBindSecondaries** for more efficient zone transfers.

C

Microsoft DHCP Option Support

Although the Microsoft DHCP Server supports most of the DHCP options defined by RFC1533 and RFC1541, Microsoft DHCP clients can use only a few of these options. However, if your network includes non-Microsoft DHCP clients, you can configure the Microsoft DHCP Server to provide values for DHCP options that are not supported by Microsoft DHCP clients. Clients that support these DHCP options will use the values provided by the Microsoft DHCP Server. Microsoft DHCP clients will simply ignore values that the server provides for options that they do not recognize.

Table C-1 lists the DHCP options supported by the Microsoft DHCP Server. DHCP options that are also supported by Microsoft clients are bolded. Also, note that options whose values are listed as "a preference-ordered list of IP addresses" have a minimum length of 4 octets (to contain the IP address). If multiple IP addresses are defined for the option, the length *must be a multiple of 4 octets*. Servers should be listed in the order of preference.

Table C-1. DHCP Options Supported by Microsoft DHCP Server and Microsoft DHCP Clients

#	Name	Description /Value
Basic Options		
0	Pad	Single-octet value used to cause subsequent fields to align on word boundaries.
255	End	Single-octet value used to indicate the end of options in the DHCP packet. Following unused octets should be filled with Pad Options.
1	**Subnet mask**	**Four-octet value that specifies the subnet mask of the client subnet per RFC 950. If both the subnet mask and the router option (3) are specified in a DHCP packet, the Subnet mask option *must* be first. Defined in the Create Scope or Scope Properties dialog. Cannot be set directly in an Option dialog.**

Table C-1. DHCP Options Supported by Microsoft DHCP Server and Microsoft DHCP Clients (continued)

#	Name	Description /Value
2	Time offset	Four-octet value, expressed as a signed 32-bit integer, that specifies the client's offset from Universal Coordinated Time (UCT) in seconds.
3	**Router**	**A preference-ordered list of IP addresses for routers on the client's subnet.**
4	Time server	A preference-ordered list of IP addresses for RFC 868 time servers available to the client.
5	Name servers	A preference-ordered list of IP addresses for IEN 116 name servers available to the client.
6	**DNS servers**	**A preference-ordered list of IP addresses for DNS name servers (STD 13, RFC 1035) available to the client. Multihomed computers can have only one list per computer, not one per adapter card.**
7	Log servers	A preference-ordered list of IP addresses for MIT_LCS User Datagram Protocol (UDP) log servers available to the client.
8	Cookie servers	A preference-ordered list of IP addresses for RFC 865 cookie servers available to the client.
9	LPR servers	A preference-ordered list of IP addresses for RFC 1179 line-printer servers available to the client.
10	Impress servers	A preference-ordered list of IP addresses for Imagen Impress servers available to the client.
11	Resource location servers	A preference-ordered list of RFC 887 Resource Location servers available to the client.
12	Host name	The client host name, which may be up to 63 characters. The name must start with a letter, end with a letter or digit, and may contain only letters, numbers, and hyphens, as defined in RFC 1035. The name may or may not be qualified with the local DNS domain name, although using DHCP Option 15 is the preferred method for retrieving the domain name.
13	Boot file size	The size, in 512-byte blocks, of the default boot image file for the client, expressed as an unsigned 16-bit integer.
14	Merit dump file	The ASCII path name of the file to which the core image of a client should be dumped if the client crashes. Formatted as a character string containing characters from the NVT ASCII character set, and has a minimum length of 1.
15	**Domain name**	**The DNS domain name the client should use when resolving host names via DNS.**
16	Swap server	The IP address of the client's swap server.
17	Root path	The ASCII path name for the client's root disk. Formatted as a string containing characters from the NVT ASCII character set, and has a minimum length of 1.
18	Extensions path	A file, retrievable via TFTP, that contains information interpreted the same as the 64-octet vendor-extension field within the BOOTP response, except the file length is unconstrained and references to Tag 18 (instances of the BOOTP Extensions Path field) in the file are ignored.

Table C-1. DHCP Options Supported by Microsoft DHCP Server and Microsoft DHCP Clients (continued)

#	Name	Description /Value
IP Layer Parameters per Host		
19	IP layer forwarding	A value of 1 specifies that the client should configure its IP layer for packet forwarding. A value of 0 disables packet forwarding.
20	Nonlocal source routing	A value of 1 specifies that the client should configure its IP layer to allow forwarding of datagrams with nonlocal source routes. A value of 0 disables forwarding.
21	Policy filter masks	Specifies policy filters that consist of a list of pairs of IP addresses and masks that specify destination/mask pairs for filtering nonlocal source routes. Any source routed datagram whose next-hop address does not match one of the filters will be discarded by the client. The minimum length for this option is eight octets (one IP address and mask). If multiple policy filter masks are defined with this option, the length *must* be a multiple of eight octets.
22	Max datagram reassembly size	Two-octet value, expressed as an unsigned 16-bit integer, that specifies the largest datagram that the client can reassemble. The minimum value is 576.
23	Default IP time-to-live	Single-octet value that specifies the default time-to-live (TTL) that the client uses on outgoing datagrams.
24	Path MTU aging timeout	Four-octet value, expressed as an unsigned 32-bit integer, that specifies the timeout (in seconds) to use when aging Path MTU values discovered by the mechanism defined in RFC 1191.
25	Path MTU plateau table	Defines a table of MTU sizes to use when performing Path MTU Discovered as defined in RFC 1191. The table is formatted as a list of unsigned 16-bit integers, and is ordered from smallest to largest. The minimum MTU value is 68. The minimum length for this option is two octets, and its length *must* be a multiple of two octets.
IP Parameters per Interface		
26	MTU option	Two-octet value, expressed as an unsigned 16-bit integer, that specifies the MTU to use on this interface. The minimum MTU value is 68.
27	All subnets are local	Specifies whether or not the client may assume that all subnets of the IP network to which the client is connected use the same MTU as the subnet of that network to which the client is directly connected. A value of 1 indicates that all subnets share the same MTU. A value of 0 means that the client should assume that some subnets of the directly connected network may have smaller MTUs.
28	Broadcast address	Four-octet value that specifies the broadcast IP address in use on the client's subnet.
29	Perform mask discovery	Specifies whether or not the client should perform subnet mask discovery using ICMP. A value of 0 indicates that the client should not perform mask discovery. A value of 1 means that the client should perform mask discovery.

Table C-1. DHCP Options Supported by Microsoft DHCP Server and Microsoft DHCP Clients (continued)

#	Name	Description /Value
30	Mask supplier	Specifies whether or not the client should respond to subnet mask requests using ICMP. A value of 0 indicates that the client should not respond. A value of 1 means that the client should respond.
31	Perform router discovery	Specifies whether or not the client should solicit routers using the Router Discovery mechanism defined in RFC 1256. A value of 0 indicates that the client should not perform router discovery. A value of 1 means that the client should perform router discovery.
32	Router solicitation address	Four-octet value that specifies the IP address to which the client should transmit router solicitation requests.
33	Static route	A list of static routes that the client should install in its routing cache. If multiple routes to the same destination are specified, they are listed in descending order of priority. The routes consist of a list of IP address pairs. The first address is the destination address, and the second address is the router for the destination. The default route (0.0.0.0) is an illegal destination for a static route. The minimum length for this option is eight octets (the first IP address pair). If multiple routes are defined with this option, the length *must* be a multiple of eight octets.
Link Layer Parameters per Interface		
34	Trailer encapsulation	Specifies whether or not the client should negotiate the use of RFC 893 trailers when using the ARP protocol. A value of 0 indicates that the client should not attempt to use trailers. A value of 1 means that the client should attempt to use trailers.
35	ARP cache timeout	Four-octet value, expressed as an unsigned 32-bit integer, that specifies the timeout in seconds for ARP cache entries.
36	Ethernet encapsulation	Specifies whether or not the client should use Ethernet Version 2 (RFC 894) or IEEE 802.3 (RFC 1042) encapsulation if the interface is an Ethernet. A value of 0 indicates that the client should use RFC 894 encapsulation. A value of 1 means that the client should use RFC 1042 encapsulation.
TCP Parameters		
37	Default time-to-live	Single-octet value, expressed as an unsigned 8-bit integer, that specifies the default TTL that the client should use when sending TCP segments. The minimum value is 1.
38	Keepalive interval	Four-octet value, expressed as an unsigned 32-bit integer, that specifies the interval (in seconds) that the client TCP should wait before sending a keepalive message on a TCP connection. A value of zero indicates that the client should not generate keepalive messages on connections unless specifically requested by an application.
39	Keepalive garbage	Specifies whether or not the client should send TCP keepalive messages with a octet of garbage for compatibility with older implementations. A value of 0 indicates that a garbage octet should not be sent. A value of 1 indicates that a garbage octet should be sent.

Table C-1. DHCP Options Supported by Microsoft DHCP Server and Microsoft DHCP Clients (continued)

#	Name	Description /Value
Application Layer Parameters		
40	NIS domain name	The name of the client's NIS domain. The NIS domain name is formatted as a character string consisting of characters from the NVT ASCII character set.
41	NIS servers	A preference-ordered list of IP addresses for NIS servers available to the client.
42	NTP servers	A preference-ordered list of IP addresses for Network Time Protocol (NTP) servers available to the client.
Vendor-specific Information		
43	Vendor specific info	This option is used by clients and servers to exchange vendor-specific information. The information is an opaque object of *n* octets, presumably interpreted by vendor-specific code on the clients and servers. The definition of this information is vendor-specific. The vendor is indicated in the class-identifier option. Servers not equipped to interpret vendor-specific information sent by a client *must* ignore it (although they *may* report it). Clients that do not receive desired vendor-specific information *should* attempt to operate without it, although they may do so (and announce that they are doing so) in a degraded mode. If a vendor potentially encodes more than one item of information in this option, then the vendor *should* encode the option using "Encapsulated vendor-specific options". The Encapsulated vendor-specific options field *should* be encoded as a sequence of code/length/value fields of identical syntax to the DHCP options field with the following exceptions: 1. There *should not* be a magic cookie field in the encapsulated vendor-specific extensions field. 2. Codes other than 0 or 255 *may* be redefined by the vendor within the encapsulated vendor-specific extensions field, but *should* conform to the tag-length-value syntax defined elsewhere. 3. Code 255 (END), if present, signifies the end of the encapsulated vendor extensions, not the end of the vendor extensions field. If no code 255 is present, then the end of the enclosing vendor-specific information field is taken as the end of the encapsulated vendor-specific extensions field.
NetBIOS Over TCP/IP		
44	**WINS/NBNS servers**	**A preference-ordered list of IP addresses for NetBIOS name servers (NBNS).**
45	NetBIOS over TCP/IP NBDD	A preference-ordered list of IP addresses for RFC 1001/1002 NetBIOS datagram distribution servers (NBDD).
46	**WINS/NBT node type**	**A single octet stores one base-16 (hexadecimal) value, that allows configurable NetBIOS over TCP/IP clients to be configured as described in RFC 1001/1002, where 0x1=B-node, 0x2=P-node, 0x4=M-node, and 0x8=H-node. On multihomed computers, the node type is assigned to the entire computer, not to individual adapter cards.**

Table C-1. DHCP Options Supported by Microsoft DHCP Server and Microsoft DHCP Clients (continued)

#	Name	Description /Value
47	**NetBIOS scope ID**	**A string that defines the NetBIOS over TCP/IP Scope ID for the client, as specified in RFC 1001/1002. On multihomed computers, the scope ID is assigned to the entire computer, not to individual adapter cards.**
48	X Window system font	A preference-ordered list of IP addresses for X Window System font servers available to the client.
49	X Window system display	A preference-ordered list of IP addresses for X Window System Display Manager servers available to the client.
DHCP Extensions		
51	**Lease time**	**Four-octet value, expressed as an unsigned 32-bit integer, that is used in a client request (DHCPDISCOVER or DHCPREQUEST) to allow the client to request a lease time for the IP address. In a server reply (DHCPOFFER), the DHCP server uses this option to specify the lease time it is willing to offer. This value specifies the time in seconds from address assignment until the client's lease on the address expires. Lease time is specified in the Create Scope or Scope Properties dialog box. It cannot be set directly in a DHCP Options dialog box.**
53	**DHCP message type**	**One-octet value that conveys the type of DHCP message. Legal values are: 1 = DHCPDISCOVER 2 = DHCPOFFER 3 = DHCPREQUEST 4 = DHCPDECLINE 5 = DHCPACK 6 = DHCPNAK 7 = DHCPRELEASE**
58	**Renewal (T1) time value**	**Four-octet value, expressed as an unsigned 32-bit integer, that specifies the time interval in seconds from address assignment until the client transitions to the RENEWING state. Renewal time is a function of the lease time option, which is specified in the Create Scope or Scope Properties dialog box. It cannot be set directly in a DHCP Options dialog box.**
59	**Rebinding (T2) time value**	**Four-octet value, expressed as an unsigned 32-bit integer, that specifies the time interval in seconds from address assignment until the client transitions to the REBINDING state. Rebinding time is a function of the lease time option, which is specified in the Create Scope or Scope Properties dialog box. It cannot be set directly in a DHCP Options dialog box.**
64	NIS+ domain name	The name of the client's Network Information Service+ domain. The name is formatted as a character string consisting of characters from the NVT ASCII character set.
65	NIS + servers	A preference-ordered list of IP addresses for RFC 2132 Network Information Service+ servers.

Table C-1. DHCP Options Supported by Microsoft DHCP Server and Microsoft DHCP Clients (continued)

#	Name	Description /Value
66	TFTP server name	Identifies a TFTP server when the "sname" field in the DHCP header has been used for DHCP options. The minimum length is 1. Microsoft refers to this option as "Boot server host name".
67	Bootfile name	Identifies a bootfile when the "file" field in the DHCP header has been used for DHCP options. The minimum length is 1.
68	Mobile IP home agents	A preference-ordered list of IP addresses for RFC 2132 mobile IP home agents that are available to the client. Minimum length is 0 (indicating no home agents are available) and the length MUST be a multiple of 4. The usual length is the four octets required to contain a single home agent address.

D

Routing Protocols

The distribution of routing information is a fundamental part of the operation of large TCP/IP networks. On most networks, Windows NT systems are not used as routers and do not participate in the routing protocols. Usually this task is handled by dedicated IP router hardware. However, as described in Chapter 9, *Microsoft Routing & Remote Access Service*, it is possible to use a Windows NT system as a router, and it is always important for a TCP/IP network administrator to understand routing. This appendix covers some of the TCP/IP routing protocols, which are a complex technical subject. It is unlikely you will need this information to configure an NT system, but it may come in handy if you are ever called upon to configure your network's router or if you use a Windows NT system for routing.

Routing protocols are divided into two general groups depending on whether the protocol is used to distribute routing information isnside of or between *autonomous systems* (AS). An autonomous system is a collection of networks and gateways with an internal mechanism for collecting routing information and a mechanism for passing it to other independent network systems. Within an autonomous system, routing information is exchanged using an interior routing protocol. The routing information is passed to the other network systems using an exterior routing protocol. If you run a routing protocol on your NT system it will probably be an interior routing protocol.

Interior Routing Protocols

All interior routing protocols perform the same basic functions. They determine the best route to each destination, and they distribute routing information among the systems on a network. How they perform these functions, in particular how they decide which routes are best, is what makes routing protocols different from each other.

There are several interior protocols. We cover the two most widely used:

- The *Routing Information Protocol* (RIP) is the interior protocol most commonly used on private TCP/IP networks. RIP is included as part of the RRAS software available for Windows NT server systems. It is adequate for local area networks and is simple to configure.
- *Open Shortest Path First* (OSPF) is also available as part of the RRAS software package. It is suitable for very large networks and provides some performance advantages over RIP.

We will start the detailed protocol discussion with RIP.

Routing Information Protocol

RIP selects the route with the lowest *hop count* (*metric*) as the best route. The RIP hop count represents the number of gateways through which data must pass to reach its destination. RIP assumes that the best route is the one that uses the fewest gateways. This approach to choosing the best route is called a *distance-vector algorithm*.

When RIP starts, it issues a request for routing updates and then listens for responses to its request. A system configured to supply RIP information responds to the request with an update packet based on the information in its routing table. The update packet contains the destination addresses from the routing table, and the routing metric associated with each destination. In addition to responding to requests, a system configured to supply RIP information periodically issues updates to keep routing information accurate.

RIP uses the information in the update packets to build the routing table. Any route in the update that does not exist in the local routing table is added. A route that is already in the local table is only used if it has a lower cost. The cost of a route is determined by adding the cost of reaching the gateway that sent the update to the metric contained in the RIP update packet. If the total is less than the metric of the current route, the new route is used.

RIP deletes routes in two ways. First, if the gateway to a destination says the cost of the route is greater than 15, the route is deleted. Second, RIP assumes that a gateway that doesn't send updates is dead. All routes through a gateway are deleted if no updates are received from that gateway for 180 seconds.

Although RIP is easy to implement and simple to configure, it has serious shortcomings:

Limited Network Diameter

The longest RIP route is 15 hops. A RIP router cannot maintain a complete routing table for a network that has destinations more than 15 hops away. The hop count cannot be increased because of the second shortcoming.

Slow Convergence

Deleting a bad route sometimes requires the exchange of multiple routing update packets until the route's cost reaches 16. This is called "counting to infinity" because RIP keeps incrementing the route's cost until it becomes greater than the largest valid RIP metric. (In this case, 16 is infinity.) Additionally, RIP may wait 180 seconds before deleting invalid routes. In network-speak we say that these things delay the "convergence of routing", in other words, it takes a long time for the routing table to reflect the current state of the network.

No Support for Classless Routing

RIP interprets all addresses using the class rules described in Chapter 2, *Delivering the Data*. For RIP all addresses are class A, B, or C, which makes RIP incompatible with classless addresses and incapable of supporting variable length subnets.*

Nothing can be done to change the limited network size. A small metric is essential to reduced the impact of counting to infinity. However, the limited network size is the least important of the problems. The real work of improving RIP concentrated on the other two problems.

Features have been added to RIP to address slow convergence. Before discussing them we must understand how the count-to-infinity problem occurs. Figure D-1 illustrates a network where a counting to infinity problem might happen.

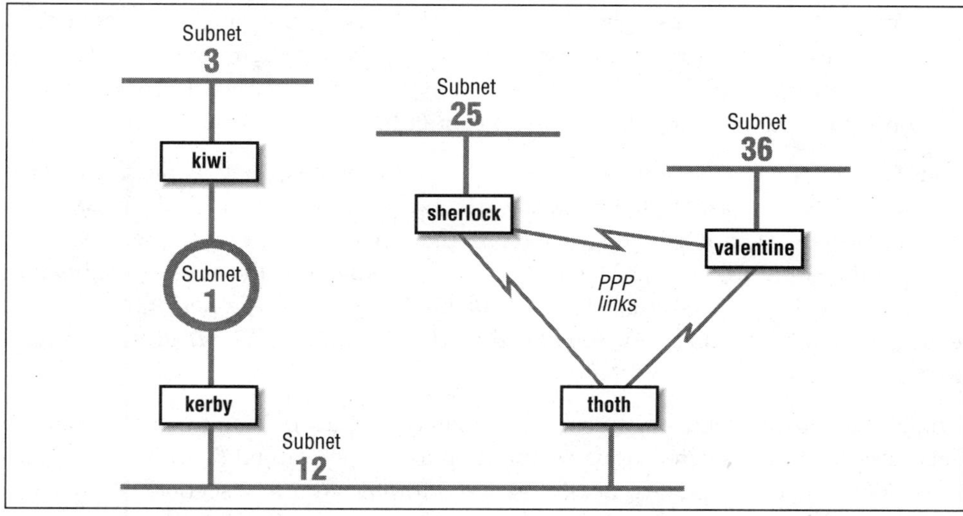

Figure D-1. Routing example

* In network-speak the opposite of classless addressing is classful addressing.

Figure D-1 shows that *thoth* reaches subnet 3 through *kerby* and then through *kiwi*. Subnet 3 is two hops away from *thoth*, and one hop away from *kerby*. Therefore *kerby* advertises a cost of one for subnet 3 and *thoth* advertises a cost of two, and the traffic continues to be routed through *kerby*. That is until something goes wrong. If *kiwi* crashes, *kerby* waits 180 seconds for an update from *kiwi*. While waiting, *kerby* continues to send updates to *thoth* that keep the route to subnet 3 in *thoth's* routing table. When *kerby's* timer finally expires, it removes all routes through *kiwi* from its routing table, including the route to subnet 3. It then receives an update from *thoth* advertising that *thoth* is 2 hops away from subnet 3. *kerby* installs this route and announces that it is 3 hops away from subnet 3. *thoth* receives this update, installs the route, and announces that it is 4 hops away from subnet 3. Things continue on in this manner until the cost of the route to subnet 3 exceeds 15 in both routing tables. If the update interval is 30 seconds, this could take a long time!

Split horizon and *poison reverse* are two features that attempt to avoid counting to infinity. Here's how:

Split horizon
: With this feature a router does not advertise routes on the link from which those routes were obtained. This would solve the count to infinity problem described earlier. Using the split horizon rule, *thoth* would not announce the route to subnet 3 on subnet 12 because it learned that route from subnet 12.

Poison reverse
: This feature enhances split horizon. A router using poison reverse advertises an infinite distance for routes on the link from which the routes were learned. With poison reverse *thoth* advertises subnet 3 with a cost of 16 to all systems on subnet 12, meaning that subnet 3 cannot be reached through *thoth*.

Split horizon and poison reverse solve the problem described earlier. But what happens if *thoth* crashes? Refer back to Figure D-1. With split horizon, *sherlock* and *valentine* do not advertise to *thoth* the route to subnet 12 because they learned the route from *thoth*. They do, however, advertise the route to subnet 12 to each other. When *thoth* goes down, *sherlock* and *valentine* perform their own count to infinity before they remove the route to subnet 12. *Triggered updates* address this problem.

Triggered updates send an update immediately instead of waiting the normal 30 seconds. Without triggered updates counting to infinity can take almost eight minutes! With triggered updates, neighbors are informed in a few seconds. Using triggered updates, a router advertises the routes deleted from its routing table with an infinite cost to force downstream routers to remove them immediately. Triggered updates also use network bandwidth efficiently because the updates only include the routes that have changed.

Split horizon, poison reverse, and triggered updates go a long way to eliminating the shortcomings of RIP. However, the fact that RIP is incompatible with classless addresses was more difficult to fix. To address this problem a new version of RIP was created. The new routing protocol is called RIP-2.

RIP Version 2

RIP Version 2 (RIP-2), defined in RFC 1723, adds a network mask and a next hop address to the destination address and metric found in the original RIP packet. A RIP-2 router applies the network mask to the destination address to determine how the address should be interpreted. Using the mask, RIP-2 routers support variable length subnets and classless addresses.

The next hop address is the IP address of the gateway that handles the route. If the address is 0.0.0.0 the source of the update packet is the gateway for the route. The next hop address permits a RIP-2 supplier to provide routing information about gateways that do not speak RIP-2. Its function is similar to an ICMP Redirect, pointing to the best gateway for a route and eliminating extra routing hops.

RIP-2 adds other new features to RIP. It transmits updates via the multicast address 224.0.0.9 to reduce the load on systems that are not capable of processing RIP-2 packets. RIP-2 also introduces a packet authentication scheme to reduce the possibility of accepting erroneous updates from misconfigured systems.

The original RIP specification allowed for future versions of RIP by including a version number in the packet header and several empty fields for extending the packet. Because of this RIP-2 did not require any change to the structure of the packet. The new values are simply placed in the empty fields that the original protocol reserved for future use. Properly implemented RIP routers can receive RIP-2 packets and extract the data that they need from the packet without becoming confused by the new data.

RIP and RIP-2 are distance vector protocols. They assign a fixed cost to each router and define the best route as the one that passes through the fewest routers. There are other techniques for selecting the best route. *Link-state* routing protocols assign a variable cost to each link and select the route that has the lowest cost links.

Open Shortest Path First

Open Shortest Path First (OSPF), defined by RFC 2178, is the most popular *link-state* protocol. It is very different from RIP. A router running RIP shares information about the entire network with its neighbors. A router running OSPF shares information about its neighbors with the entire network. The entire network means, at most, a single autonomous system. OSPF further refines this task by defining a hierarchy of routing areas within an autonomous system:

Area
: An area is an arbitrary collection of interconnected networks, hosts, and routers. Areas exchange routing information with other areas within the autonomous system through *area border routers*.

Backbone
: A special area that interconnects all of the other areas within an autonomous system. Every area must connect to the backbone, because the backbone is responsible for distributing routing information between the areas.

Stub Area
: A special area that has only one area border router, which means that there is only one route out of the area. In this case, the area border router does not need to advertise external routes to the other routers within the stub area. It can simply advertise itself as the default route.

Only a large autonomous system needs to be subdivided into areas. The sample network shown in Figure D-1 is small and would not need to be divided. We can, however, use it as an example to illustrate the different areas. We could divide this autonomous system into any areas we wish. Assume we divide it into three areas: area 1 contains subnet 3; area 2 contains subnet 1 and subnet 12; and area 3 contains subnet 25, subnet 36, and the PPP links. Furthermore, we could define area 1 as a stub area because *kiwi* is that area's only area border router. We could also define area 2 as the backbone area because it interconnects the other two areas, and all routing information between areas 1 and 3 must be distributed by area 2. Area 2 contains two area border routers, *thoth* and *kiwi*, and one interior router, *kerby*. Area 3 contains three routers: *thoth*, *valentine*, and *sherlock*.

Every OSPF router builds a *directed graph* of the entire network using the Dijkstra *Shortest Path First* (SPF) algorithm. A directed graph is a map of the network from the perspective of the router, in other words, the root of the graph is the router. The graph is built from the link state database, which includes information about every router on the network and all of the neighbors of every router. The link state database for the autonomous system in Figure D-1 contains 5 routers and 10 neighbors: *kiwi* has one neighbor, *kerby*; *kerby* has two neighbors, *kiwi* and *thoth*; *thoth* has three neighbors, *kerby*, *sherlock*, and *valentine*; *sherlock* has two neighbors, *thoth* and *valentine*; and *valentine* has two neighbors, *sherlock* and *thoth*. Figure D-2 shows the graph of this autonomous system from the perspective of *kiwi*.

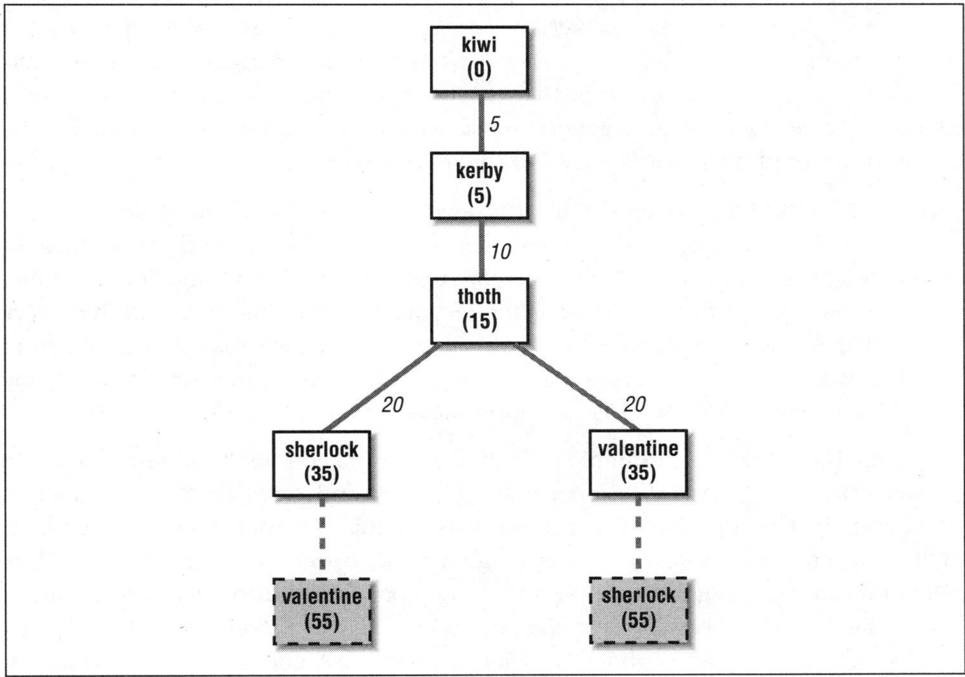

Figure D-2. A network graph

The Dijkstra algorithm builds the map in this manner:

1. Install the local system as the root of the map with a cost of 0.
2. Locate the neighbors of the system just installed and add them to the map. The cost of reaching the neighbors is calculated as the sum of the cost to reach the system just installed plus the cost it advertises for reaching each neighbor. For example: assume that *thoth* advertises a cost of 20 for *sherlock* and that the cost of reaching *thoth* is 15, then the cost for *sherlock* in *kiwi's* map is 35.
3. Walk through the map and select the lowest cost path for each destination. For example: when *sherlock* is added to the map its neighbors include *valentine*. The path to *valentine* through *sherlock* is temporarily added to the map. In this third phase of the algorithm the cost of reaching *valentine* through *thoth* is compared to the cost of reaching it through *sherlock*. The lowest cost path is selected. Figure D-2 shows the deleted paths in dotted lines. Steps 2 and 3 of the algorithm are repeated for every system in the link state database.

The information in the link state database is gathered and distributed in a simple and efficient manner. An OSPF router discovers its neighbors through the use of Hello packets. It sends Hello packets and listens for Hello packets from adjacent routers. The Hello packet identifies the local router and lists the adjacent routers from which it has received packets. When a router receives a Hello packet that lists it as an adjacent router, it knows it has found a neighbor. It knows this because it can hear packets from that neighbor and, because the neighbor lists it as an adjacent router, the neighbor must be able to hear packets from it. The newly discovered neighbor is added to the local system's neighbor list.

The OSPF router then advertises all of it neighbors. It does this by *flooding* a Link State Advertisement (LSA) to the entire network. The LSA contains the address of every neighbor and the cost of reaching that neighbor from the local system. Flooding means that the router sends the LSA out of every interface and that every router that receives the LSA sends it out of every interface except the one from which it was received. To avoid flooding duplicate LSAs, the routers store a copy of the LSAs they receive and discard duplicates.

Figure D-1 provides an example. When OSPF starts on *kerby* it sends a Hello packet on subnet 1 and one on subnet 12. *kiwi* and *thoth* hear the Hello and respond with Hello packets that list *kerby* as an adjacent router. *kerby* hears their Hello packets and adds them to its neighbor list. *kerby* creates an LSA that lists *kiwi* and *thoth* as neighbors with appropriate cost assigned to each. For instance, *kerby* might assign a cost of 5 to *kiwi* and a cost of 10 to *thoth*. *kerby* then floods the LSA on subnet 1 and subnet 12. *kiwi* hears the LSA and floods it on subnet 3. *thoth* receives the LSA and floods it on both of its PPP links. *sherlock* floods the LSA on the link toward *valentine* and *valentine* floods it on the same link to *sherlock*. When *sherlock* and *valentine* received the second copy of the LSA they discard it because it duplicates one that they have already received from *thoth*. In this manner, every router in the entire network receives every other router's link state advertisement.

Following an update, the new LSAs are included into the link state database on every router on the network, and every router recalculates their network map based on this new information. Clearly, limiting the number of routers by limiting the size of the network reduces the burden of recalculating the map. For many networks the entire autonomous system is small enough. For others, dividing the AS into areas improves efficiency.

Another feature of OSPF that improves efficiency is the *designated router*. The designated router is one router on the network that treats all other routers on the network as its neighbors, while all other routers treat only the designated router as their neighbor. This helps reduce the size of the link-state database and thus improves the speed of the shortest path first calculation. For example, five routers each with four neighbors produce a link state database with twenty entries. But if one of those routers is the designated router, that router has four neighbors and all other routers have only one neighbor for a total of ten link state database entries.

OSPF provides the router with an end-to-end view of the route between two systems instead of the limited next-hop view provided by RIP. Flooding quickly disseminates routing information throughout the network. Limiting the size of the link state database through areas and designated routers speeds the SPF calculation. Taken altogether, OSPF is an efficient link state routing protocol.

OSPF has additional features. It provides password authentication to ensure that the update comes from a valid router. Currently OSPF uses an eight character, clear-text password. Work is underway to add a Message Digest 5 (MD5) cryptochecksum for stronger authentication.

OSPF also supports *equal cost multi-path routing*. This mouthful means that OSPF routers can maintain more than one path to a single destination. Given the proper conditions, this feature can be used for load balancing across multiple networks links. However, most systems are not designed to take advantage of this feature. Refer to your router's documentation to see if it supports load balancing across equal cost OSPF routes.

With all of these features, OSPF is the preferred TCP/IP interior routing protocol for dedicated routers. If your network requires the power and flexibility of OSPF, it is unlikely you will use your NT server as a router. Complex networks need dedicated routers.

Exterior Routing Protocols

Exterior routing protocols are used to exchange routing information between autonomous systems. The information passed is called *reachability information*, which is simply information about the networks that can be reached through a specific autonomous system.

Border Gateway Protocol (BGP) is the leading exterior routing protocol of the Internet. BGP exchanges reachability information through UPDATE messages. The UPDATE message lists the destinations that can be reached through a specific path and the attributes of the path. BGP is a *path vector protocol* because it provides the entire end-to-end path of a route in the form of a sequence of autonomous system (AS) numbers. Having the complete (AS) path eliminates the possibility of routing loops and count to infinity problems. A BGP UPDATE contains a single path vector and all of the destinations reachable through that path. Multiple UPDATE packets may be sent to build a routing table.

BGP supports *policy based routing*, which uses nontechnical reasons (for example, political, organizational, or security considerations) to make routing decisions. Thus BGP enhances an autonomous system's ability to choose between the routes it learns from other autonomous systems. This feature is important in an Internet composed of independent service providers. Most ISPs develop private policies based on the bilateral agreements they have with other ISPs. BGP can be used to implement these policies by controlling the routes it announces to others and the routes it accepts from others. Routing policies are not part of the BGP protocol. The network administrator enforces the routing policy through configuring the router. Policies are provided as configuration information.

BGP is implemented on top of TCP, which provides BGP with a reliable delivery service. BGP uses TCP port 179. It acquires its neighbors through the standard TCP 3-way handshake. BGP neighbors are called peers. Once connected, BGP peers exchange OPEN messages to negotiate session parameters, such as the version of BGP that is to be used.

BGP peers send each other complete routing table updates when the connection is first established. After that, only changes are sent. If there are no changes, only a small (19 byte) KEEPALIVE message is sent to indicate that the peer and the link are still operational. BGP is very efficient in its use of network bandwidth and system resources.

By far the most important thing to remember about exterior routing protocols is that most systems never run them. Most routers within an autonomous system only run an interior protocol such as OSPF. Only those gateways that connect one autonomous system to another need to run an exterior routing protocol. Your network is probably not an autonomous system; it is most probably an independent part of the AS run by your Internet Service Provider. It is extremely unlikely that you would ever choose to run an exterior routing protocol on a Windows NT system.

Index

B

C

D

E

F

G

H

I

O

About the Authors

With 25 years of industry experience, **Robert Bruce Thompson** was one of the first Novell Master CNEs, and has been immersed in Windows NT Server 4.0 since it was in alpha. Bob has written or contributed to several computer networking books, including *Windows NT Server 4.0 for NetWare Administrators*, published by O'Reilly, and *Special Edition Using Windows NT Server 4, Special Edition Using Microsoft BackOffice, Windows Magazine Windows NT Workstation 4.0 Internet and Networking Handbook*, and *Upgrading and Repairing Networks*, all published by Que Corporation. Bob is the president of Triad Technology Group, Inc., a Winston-Salem, N.C., network consulting practice.

Craig Hunt has worked with computer systems for the last 25 years. He spent the first few years after receiving his B.A. from American University running an outdoor camp for inner-city kids, but the call of the computer was stronger than the call of the wild. Craig went to work for the federal government as a programmer and then as a systems programmer. He left the government to work for Honeywell on the WWMCCS network in the days before TCP/IP, back when the network used NCP. After Honeywell, Craig went to work for the National Institute of Standards and Technology, where he currently leads the Advanced Network Technologies Division. Craig currently teaches a tutorial on the subject at Networld+Interop. In addition to co-authoring this book, Craig wrote *TCP/IP Network Administration, Networking Personal Computers with TCP/IP,* and Appendix C of *Building Internet Firewalls*.

Craig lives with his wife and children in Gaithersburg, Maryland. He loves the outdoors, splitting vacation time between the mountains and the sea, and he has a passion for rock and roll music.

Colophon

The animal on the cover of *Windows NT TCP/IP Network Administration* is a horseshoe crab, *Limulus polyphemus*. These arthropods aren't true crabs; they are similar to arachnids such as spiders, scorpions, and ticks. Fossils in Canada suggest that the horseshoe crab's relatives lived 520 million years ago; however, *Limulus* itself goes back a mere 20 million years.

Today, horseshoe crabs range from Maine south to the Yucatan. About 30 years ago, scientists from Johns Hopkins Medical School discovered that their blood contains a chemical known as Limulus Amebocyte Lysate (LAL), which causes it to clot when exposed to endotoxins. LAL is now used to test the sterility of injected medicines and such devices as heart valves and kidney dialyzers. Healthy horseshoe crab are bled, loosing 20% of total volume, then returned to the water. Unlike human blood, horseshoe crab blood turns bluish when exposed to air because its oxygen-carrying molecule contains copper.

Horseshoe crabs achieve sexual maturity at 9 to 12 years of their 19-year lifespan. They spawn from late April through mid-August, most intensely on nights with a full or new moon. High tides provide additional protection to the females and eggs. Horseshoe crabs move from deep water to protected bays and inlets. At high tide the animals mate and the female deposits between 2 and 30 thousand eggs. The male fertilizes the eggs, which are covered by sand before ebb tide, when the pair returns to deeper water.

Paula Carroll was the production editor for this book. TIPS Technical Publishing handled production services with Robert Kern as project manager. The illustrations were created in Macromedia Freehand 7.0 by Robert Romano. Edie Freedman designed the cover, using a 19th-century engraving from the Dover Pictorial Archive. The cover layout was produced with QuarkXPress 3.32 using the ITC Garamond font. The inside layout was designed by Edie Freedman and modified by Nancy Priest and implemented in FrameMaker by Mike Sierra. The text and heading fonts are ITC Garamond Light and Garamond Book. Rachel Anderson of Archer Editorial copy edited the book, Karen Brown of Scriptorium Publishing Services, Inc. provided composition and indexing services, and Jill Greeson was the proofreader. This colophon was written by Sheryl Avruch.

Whenever possible, our books use a durable and flexible lay-flat binding, either RepKover™ or Otabind™. If the page count exceeds the maximum bulk possible for this type of binding, perfect binding is used.

More Titles from O'Reilly

Windows NT System Administration

Windows NT in a Nutshell

By Eric Pearce
1st Edition June 1997
364 pages, ISBN 1-56592-251-4

Anyone who installs Windows NT, creates a user, or adds a printer is an NT system administrator (whether they realize it or not). This book features a new tagged callout approach to documenting the 4.0 GUI as well as real-life examples of command usage and strategies for problem solving, with an emphasis on networking. Windows NT in a Nutshell will be as useful to the single-system home user as it will be to the administrator of a 1,000-node corporate network.

Windows NT User Administration

By Ashley J. Meggitt & Timothy D. Ritchey
1st Edition November 1997
218 pages, ISBN 1-56592-301-4

Many Windows NT books introduce you to a range of topics, but seldom do they give you enough information to master any one thing. This book (like other O'Reilly animal books) is different. *Windows NT User Administration* makes you an expert at creating users efficiently, controlling what they can do, limiting the damage they can cause, and monitoring their activities on your system. Don't simply react to problems; use the techniques in this book to anticipate and prevent them.

Windows NT Server 4.0 for NetWare Administrators

By Robert Bruce Thompson
1st Edition November 1997
756 pages, ISBN 1-56592-280-8

This book provides a fast-track means for experienced NetWare administrators to build on their knowledge and master the fundamentals of using the Microsoft Windows NT Server. The broad coverage of many aspects of Windows NT Server is balanced by a tightly focused approach of comparison, contrast, and differentiation between NetWare and NT features and methodologies.

Essential Windows NT System Administration

By Æleen Frisch
1st Edition February 1998
486 pages, ISBN 1-56592-274-3

This book combines practical experience with technical expertise to help you manage Windows NT systems as productively as possible. It covers the standard utilities offered with the Windows NT operating system and from the Resource Kit, as well as important commercial and free third-party tools. By the author of O'Reilly's bestselling book, *Essential System Administration*.

Windows NT Backup & Restore

By Jody Leber
1st Edition May 1998
320 pages, ISBN 1-56592-272-7

Beginning with the need for a workable recovery policy and ways to translate that policy into requirements, *Windows NT Backup & Restore* presents the reader with practical guidelines for setting up an effective backup system in both small and large environments. It covers the native NT utilities as well as major third-party hardware and software.

Windows NT SNMP

By James D. Murray
1st Edition February 1998
464 pages, Includes CD-ROM
ISBN 1-56592-338-3

This book describes the implementation of SNMP (the Simple Network Management Protocol) on Windows NT 3.51 and 4.0 (with a look ahead to NT 5.0) and Windows 95 systems. It covers SNMP and network basics and detailed information on developing SNMP management applications and extension agents. The book comes with a CD-ROM containing a wealth of additional information: standards documents, sample code from the book, and many third-party, SNMP-related software tools, libraries, and demos.

Windows NT System Administration

Windows NT Desktop Reference

By Æleen Frisch
1st Edition January 1998
64 pages, ISBN 1-56592-437-1

A hip-pocket quick reference to Windows NT commands, as well as the most useful commands from the Resource Kits. Commands are arranged ingroups related to their purpose and function. Covers Windows NT 4.0.

MCSE: The Core Exams in a Nutshell

By Michael Moncur
1st Edition May 1998
424 pages, ISBN 1-56592-376-6

MCSE: The Core Exams in a Nutshell is a detailed quick reference for administrators with Windows NT experience or experience administering a different platform, such as UNIX, who want to learn what is necessary to pass the MCSE required exam portion of the MCSE certification. While no book is a substitute for real-world experience, this book will help you codify your knowledge and prepare for the exams.

MCSE: The Electives in a Nutshell

By Michael Moncur
1st Edition September 1998 (est.)
376 pages (est.), ISBN: 1-56592-482-7

A companion volume to *MCSE: The Core Exams in a Nutshell*, *MCSE: The Electives in a Nutshell* is a comprehensive study guide that covers the elective exams for the MCSE as well as the Internet requirements and electives for the MCSE+Internet. This detailed reference is aimed at sophisticated users who need a bridge between real-world experience and the MCSE exam requirements.

Managing the Windows NT Registry

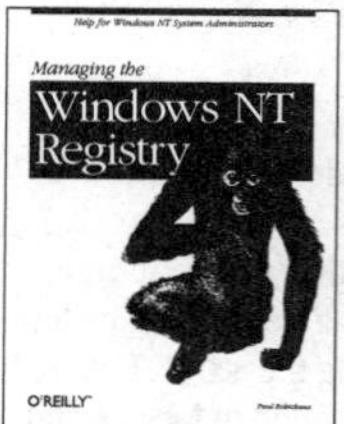

By Paul Robichaux
1st Edition April 1998
470 pages, ISBN 1-56592-378-2

The Windows NT Registry is the repository for all hardware, software, and application configuration settings. This is the system administrator's guide to maintaining, monitoring, and updating the Registry database. A "must-have" for every NT system manager or administrator, it covers what the Registry is and where it lives on disk, available tools, Registry access from programs, and Registry content.

Learning Perl on Win32 Systems

By Randal L. Schwartz, Erik Olson & Tom Christiansen
1st Edition August 1997
306 pages, ISBN 1-56592-324-3

In this carefully paced course, leading Perl trainers and a Windows NT practitioner teach you to program in the language that promises to emerge as the scripting language of choice on NT. Based on the "llama" book, this book features tips for PC users and new, NT-specific examples, along with a foreword by Larry Wall, the creator of Perl, and Dick Hardt, the creator of Perl for Win32.

Windows Programming

Learning VBScript

By Paul Lomax
1st Edition July 1997
616 pages, includes CD-ROM
ISBN 1-56592-247-6

This definitive guide shows web developers how to take full advantage of client-side scripting with the VBScript language. In addition to basic language features, it covers the Internet Explorer object model and discusses techniques for client-side scripting, like adding ActiveX controls to a web page or validating data before sending it to the server. Includes CD-ROM with over 170 code samples.

Windows Programming

Developing Windows Error Messages

By Ben Ezzell
1st Edition March 1998
254 pages, Includes CD-ROM
ISBN 1-56592-356-1

This book teaches C, C++, and Visual Basic programmers how to write effective error messages that notify the user of an error, clearly explain the error, and most important, offer a solution. The book also discusses methods for preventing and trapping errors before they occur and tells how to create flexible input and response routines to keep unnecessary errors from happening.

Win32 Multithreaded Programming

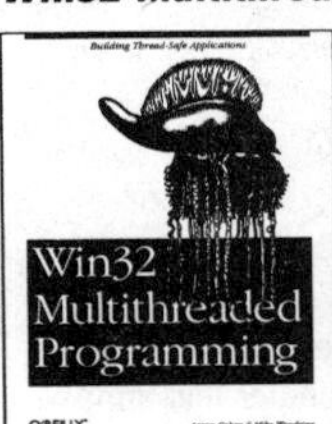

By Aaron Cohen & Mike Woodring
1st Edition December 1997
724 pages, Includes CD-ROM
ISBN 1-56592-296-4

This book clearly explains the concepts of multithreaded programs and shows developers how to construct efficient and complex applications. An important book for any developer, it illustrates all aspects of Win32 multithreaded programming, including what has previously been undocumented or poorly explained.

Windows 95 in a Nutshell

By Tim O'Reilly & Troy Mott
1st Edition June 1998
528 pages, ISBN 1-56592-316-2

This book systematically unveils the Windows 95 operating system and allows the user to modify any aspect of it, using the Command Line from the DOS or Run prompt, the Explorer, the Registry, the Control Panel, or any other tool or application that exists in Windows 95.

Access Database Design & Programming

By Steven Roman
1st Edition June 1997
270 pages, ISBN 1-56592-297-2

This book provides experienced Access users who are novice programers with frequently overlooked concepts and techniques necessary to create effective database applications. It focuses on designing effective tables in a multi-table application; using the Access interface or Access SQL to construct queries; and programming using the Data Access Object (DAO) and Microsoft Access object models.

VB & VBA in a Nutshell: The Languages

By Paul Lomax
1st Edition October 1998 (est.)
656 pages (est.), ISBN 1-56592-358-8

For Visual Basic and VBA programmers, this book boils down the essentials of the VB and VBA languages into a single volume, including undocumented and little documented areas essential to everyday programming. The convenient alphabetical reference to all functions, procedures, statements, and keywords allows VB and VBA programmers to use this book both as a standard reference guide to the language and as a tool for troubleshooting and identifying programming problems.

Windows NT File System Internals

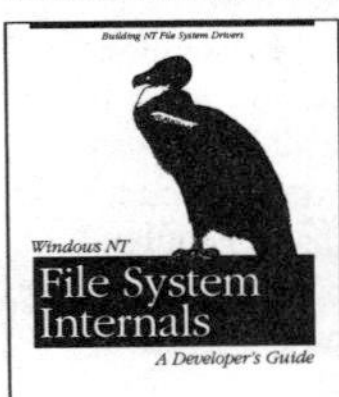

By Rajeev Nagar
1st Edition September 1997
794 pages, Includes diskette
ISBN 1-56592-249-2

Windows NT File System Internals presents the details of the NT I/O Manager, the Cache Manager, and the Memory Manager from the perspective of a software developer writing a file system driver or implementing a kernel-mode filter driver. The book provides numerous code examples included on diskette, as well as the source for a complete, usable filter driver.

Web Server Administration

Stopping SPAM

By Alan Schwartz & Simson Garfinkel
1st Edition October 1998 (est.)
200 pages (est.), ISBN 1-56592-388-X

This book describes spam—unwanted email messages and inappropriate news articles—and explains what you and your Internet service providers and administrators can do to prevent it, trace it,stop it, and even outlaw it. Contains a wealth of advice, technical tools, and additional technical and community resources.

Writing Apache Modules with Perl and C

By Lincoln Stein & Doug MacEachern
1st Edition January 1999 (est.)
400 pages (est.), ISBN 1-56592-567-X

This guide to Web programming teaches you how to extend the capabilities of the Apache Web server. It explains the design of Apache, mod_perl, and the Apache API, then demonstrates how to use them to rewrite CGI scripts, filter HTML documents on the server-side, enhance server log functionality, convert file formats on the fly, and more.

Web Security & Commerce

By Simson Garfinkel
with Gene Spafford
1st Edition June 1997
506 pages, ISBN 1-56592-269-7

Learn how to minimize the risks of the Web with this comprehensive guide. It covers browser vulnerabilities, privacy concerns, issues with Java, JavaScript, ActiveX, and plug-ins, digital certificates, cryptography, web server security, blocking software, censorship technology, and relevant civil and criminal issues.

Apache: The Definitive Guide

By Ben Laurie & Peter Laurie
1st Edition March 1997
274 pages, includes CD-ROM
ISBN 1-56592-250-6

Despite all the media attention to Netscape, Apache is far and away the most widely used web server platform in the world. This book, written and reviewed by key members of the Apache Group, is the only complete guide on the market today that describes how to obtain, set up, and secure the Apache software. Includes CD-ROM with Apache sources and demo sites discussed in the book.

Building Your Own Web Conferences™

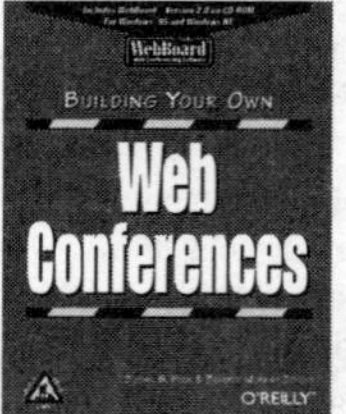

By Susan B. Peck & Beverly Murray Scherf
1st Edition March 1997
270 pages, Includes CD-ROM
ISBN 1-56592-279-4

Building Your Own Web Conferences is a complete guide for Windows® 95 and NT™ users on how to set up and manage dynamic virtual communities that improve workgroup collaboration and keep visitors coming back to your site. The second in O'Reilly's "Build Your Own..." series, this book comes with O'Reilly's state-of-the-art WebBoard™ 2.0 software on CD-ROM.

Building Your Own WebSite™

By Susan B. Peck & Stephen Arrants
1st Edition July 1996
514 pages, Includes CD-ROM,
ISBN 1-56592-232-8

This is a hands-on reference for Windows® 95 and Windows NT™ users who want to host a site on the Web or on a corporate intranet. This step-by-step guide will have you creating live web pages in minutes. You'll also learn how to connect your web to information in other Windows applications, such as word processing documents and databases. The book is packed with examples and tutorials on every aspect of web management, and it includes the highly acclaimed WebSite™ 1.1 server software on CD-ROM.

How to stay in touch with O'Reilly

1. Visit Our Award-Winning Web Site

http://www.oreilly.com/

★"Top 100 Sites on the Web" —*PC Magazine*
★"Top 5% Web sites" —*Point Communications*
★"3-Star site" —*The McKinley Group*

Our web site contains a library of comprehensive product information (including book excerpts and tables of contents), downloadable software, background articles, interviews with technology leaders, links to relevant sites, book cover art, and more. File us in your Bookmarks or Hotlist!

2. Join Our Email Mailing Lists

New Product Releases

To receive automatic email with brief descriptions of all new O'Reilly products as they are released, send email to:
listproc@online.oreilly.com
Put the following information in the first line of your message (*not* in the Subject field):
subscribe oreilly-news

O'Reilly Events

If you'd also like us to send information about trade show events, special promotions, and other O'Reilly events, send email to:
listproc@online.oreilly.com
Put the following information in the first line of your message (*not* in the Subject field):
subscribe oreilly-events

3. Get Examples from Our Books via FTP

There are two ways to access an archive of example files from our books:

Regular FTP

- ftp to:
  ftp.oreilly.com
  (login: anonymous
  password: your email address)
- Point your web browser to:
  ftp://ftp.oreilly.com/

FTPMAIL

- Send an email message to:
  ftpmail@online.oreilly.com
  (Write "help" in the message body)

4. Contact Us via Email

order@oreilly.com
To place a book or software order online. Good for North American and international customers.

subscriptions@oreilly.com
To place an order for any of our newsletters or periodicals.

books@oreilly.com
General questions about any of our books.

software@oreilly.com
For general questions and product information about our software. Check out O'Reilly Software Online at **http://software.oreilly.com/** for software and technical support information. Registered O'Reilly software users send your questions to: **website-support@oreilly.com**

cs@oreilly.com
For answers to problems regarding your order or our products.

booktech@oreilly.com
For book content technical questions or corrections.

proposals@oreilly.com
To submit new book or software proposals to our editors and product managers.

international@oreilly.com
For information about our international distributors or translation queries. For a list of our distributors outside of North America check out:
http://www.oreilly.com/www/order/country.html

O'Reilly & Associates, Inc.
101 Morris Street, Sebastopol, CA 95472 USA
TEL 707-829-0515 or 800-998-9938
(6am to 5pm PST)
FAX 707-829-0104

International Distributors

UK, Europe, Middle East and Northern Africa (except France, Germany, Switzerland, & Austria)

INQUIRIES
International Thomson Publishing Europe
Berkshire House
168-173 High Holborn
London WC1V 7AA
United Kingdom
Telephone: 44-171-497-1422
Fax: 44-171-497-1426
Email: itpint@itps.co.uk

ORDERS
International Thomson Publishing Services, Ltd.
Cheriton House, North Way
Andover, Hampshire SP10 5BE
United Kingdom
Telephone: 44-264-342-832 (UK)
Telephone: 44-264-342-806 (outside UK)
Fax: 44-264-364418 (UK)
Fax: 44-264-342761 (outside UK)
UK & Eire orders: itpuk@itps.co.uk
International orders: itpint@itps.co.uk

France

Editions Eyrolles
61 bd Saint-Germain
75240 Paris Cedex 05
France
Fax: 33-01-44-41-11-44

FRENCH LANGUAGE BOOKS
All countries except Canada
Telephone: 33-01-44-41-46-16
Email: geodif@eyrolles.com
English language books
Telephone: 33-01-44-41-11-87
Email: distribution@eyrolles.com

Germany, Switzerland, and Austria

INQUIRIES
O'Reilly Verlag
Balthasarstr. 81
D-50670 Köln
Germany
Telephone: 49-221-97-31-60-0
Fax: 49-221-97-31-60-8
Email: anfragen@oreilly.de

ORDERS
International Thomson Publishing
Königswinterer Straße 418
53227 Bonn, Germany
Telephone: 49-228-97024 0
Fax: 49-228-441342
Email: order@oreilly.de

Japan

O'Reilly Japan, Inc.
Kiyoshige Building 2F
12-Banchi, Sanei-cho
Shinjuku-ku
Tokyo 160-0008 Japan
Telephone: 81-3-3356-5227
Fax: 81-3-3356-5261
Email: kenji@oreilly.com

India

Computer Bookshop (India) PVT. Ltd.
190 Dr. D.N. Road, Fort
Bombay 400 001 India
Telephone: 91-22-207-0989
Fax: 91-22-262-3551
Email: cbsbom@giasbm01.vsnl.net.in

Hong Kong

City Discount Subscription Service Ltd.
Unit D, 3rd Floor, Yan's Tower
27 Wong Chuk Hang Road
Aberdeen, Hong Kong
Telephone: 852-2580-3539
Fax: 852-2580-6463
Email: citydis@ppn.com.hk

Korea

Hanbit Media, Inc.
Sonyoung Bldg. 202
Yeksam-dong 736-36
Kangnam-ku
Seoul, Korea
Telephone: 822-554-9610
Fax: 822-556-0363
Email: hant93@chollian.dacom.co.kr

Singapore, Malaysia, and Thailand

Addison Wesley Longman Singapore PTE Ltd.
25 First Lok Yang Road
Singapore 629734
Telephone: 65-268-2666
Fax: 65-268-7023
Email: daniel@longman.com.sg

Philippines

Mutual Books, Inc.
429-D Shaw Boulevard
Mandaluyong City, Metro
Manila, Philippines
Telephone: 632-725-7538
Fax: 632-721-3056
Email: mbikikog@mnl.sequel.net

China

Ron's DataCom Co., Ltd.
79 Dongwu Avenue
Dongxihu District
Wuhan 430040
China
Telephone: 86-27-83892568
Fax: 86-27-83222108
Email: hongfeng@public.wh.hb.cn

All Other Asian Countries

O'Reilly & Associates, Inc.
101 Morris Street
Sebastopol, CA 95472 USA
Telephone: 707-829-0515
Fax: 707-829-0104
Email: order@oreilly.com

Australia

WoodsLane Pty. Ltd.
7/5 Vuko Place, Warriewood NSW 2102
P.O. Box 935
Mona Vale NSW 2103
Australia
Telephone: 61-2-9970-5111
Fax: 61-2-9970-5002
Email: info@woodslane.com.au

New Zealand

Woodslane New Zealand Ltd.
21 Cooks Street (P.O. Box 575)
Waganui, New Zealand
Telephone: 64-6-347-6543
Fax: 64-6-345-4840
Email: info@woodslane.com.au

The Americas

McGraw-Hill Interamericana Editores, S.A. de C.V.
Cedro No. 512
Col. Atlampa 06450
Mexico, D.F.
Telephone: 52-5-541-3155
Fax: 52-5-541-4913
Email: mcgraw-hill@infosel.net.mx

South Africa

International Thomson Publishing South Africa
Building 18, Constantia Park
138 Sixteenth Road
P.O. Box 2459
Halfway House, 1685 South Africa
Telephone: 27-11-805-4819
Fax: 27-11-805-3648

O'REILLY™

O'Reilly & Associates, Inc.
101 Morris Street
Sebastopol, CA 95472-9902
1-800-998-9938

Visit us online at:
http://www.ora.com/
orders@ora.com

O'REILLY WOULD LIKE TO HEAR FROM YOU

Which book did this card come from?

____

Where did you buy this book?

- ❑ Bookstore
- ❑ Computer Store
- ❑ Direct from O'Reilly
- ❑ Class/seminar
- ❑ Bundled with hardware/software
- ❑ Other ____________________

What operating system do you use?

- ❑ UNIX
- ❑ Macintosh
- ❑ Windows NT
- ❑ PC(Windows/DOS)
- ❑ Other ____________________

What is your job description?

- ❑ System Administrator
- ❑ Programmer
- ❑ Network Administrator
- ❑ Educator/Teacher
- ❑ Web Developer
- ❑ Other ____________________

❑ Please send me O'Reilly's catalog, containing a complete listing of O'Reilly books and software.

Name ________________ Company/Organization ________________

Address ________________

City ________ State ________ Zip/Postal Code ________ Country ________

Telephone ________________ Internet or other email address (specify network) ________________

Nineteenth century wood engraving of a bear from the O'Reilly & Associates Nutshell Handbook® *Using & Managing UUCP.*

PLACE STAMP HERE

NO POSTAGE NECESSARY IF MAILED IN THE UNITED STATES

BUSINESS REPLY MAIL

FIRST CLASS MAIL PERMIT NO. 80 SEBASTOPOL, CA

Postage will be paid by addressee

O'Reilly & Associates, Inc.
101 Morris Street
Sebastopol, CA 95472-9902